STATISTICAL METHODS
IN
EDUCATION AND PSYCHOLOGY

PRENTICE-HALL SERIES IN
EDUCATIONAL MEASUREMENT, RESEARCH, AND STATISTICS

Gene V Glass, EDITOR

STATISTICAL METHODS
IN
EDUCATION AND PSYCHOLOGY

GENE V GLASS

Laboratory of Educational Research
University of Colorado

JULIAN C. STANLEY

Departments of Education and Psychology
The Johns Hopkins University

PRENTICE-HALL, INC., *Englewood Cliffs, New Jersey*

© 1970 *by PRENTICE-HALL, INC.*
ENGLEWOOD CLIFFS, NEW JERSEY

No part of this book may be reproduced
in any form or by any means without
permission in writing from the publisher.

Current printing (last digit):
10 9 8 7 6 5 4 3

13-844928-7

Library of Congress catalog card number:
79-101579

Printed in the United States of America

Prentice-Hall International, Inc., *London*
Prentice-Hall of Australia, Pty. Ltd., *Sydney*
Prentice-Hall of Canada, Ltd., *Toronto*
Prentice-Hall of India Private Ltd., *New Delhi*
Prentice-Hall of Japan, Inc., *Tokyo*

To Sharon and Julie

To the graduates of the Laboratory of Experimental Design, University of Wisconsin, and the Laboratory of Educational Research, University of Colorado, who teach statistics courses all over North America and elsewhere, for their contributions to our thinking about statistical analysis

PREFACE

This textbook is for use in either a one-semester statistics course or a two-semester sequence of statistics courses in education and the social sciences. Chapters 1 through 8 can be covered thoroughly in a one-semester course meeting three hours weekly, with time left for sampling topics from Chapters 9 and 14. Intensive study of Chapters 10 through 19 in a second course would constitute thorough preparation in the fundamentals of the inferential statistical techniques most useful for research in education, psychology, sociology, and other social sciences.

In writing this text, we sought to produce a more thorough coverage of analysis of variance techniques than now appears in basic statistics texts for social scientists. In addition, an attempt was made to cover correlational techniques comprehensively while emphasizing their interrelationships. We recognize only too clearly the possible shortcomings of this work; but at the same time, we respectfully offer it to the profession with some small measure of pride.

The generosity of publishing companies in allowing the reproduction of scientific material marks them as one of a rapidly dwindling brotherhood of altruistic agents in our society. The publication of this book—and probably any other contemporary statistics textbook—would not have been possible without the cooperation of several publishers. We are indebted to the following: the Literary Executor of the late Sir Ronald A. Fisher, F.R.S., Dr. Frank Yates, F.R.S., and Oliver & Boyd Ltd., Edinburgh, for their permission to reprint tables from their books *Statistical Methods for Research Workers* and *Statistical Tables for Biological, Agricultural and Medical Research; Biometrika* Trustees; Charles Griffin & Company Ltd.; Cambridge University Press; Chandler Publishing Company; *Annals of Mathematical Statistics;* McGraw-Hill Book Company; Prentice-Hall, Inc.; The RAND Corporation; The Free Press; The Psychometric Society; The Psychological Corporation; *Psychological Bulletin;* The National Industrial Conference Board.

During the five years while this text was being written, our colleagues and students contributed in innumerable ways to our efforts. We cannot name them all here, but the following colleagues deserve special thanks for contributing recently to our education in statistical methods: Frank B. Baker, R. Darrell Bock, Raymond O. Collier, Leon J. Gleser, Chester W. Harris, J. Thomas Hastings, John L. Horn, Henry F. Kaiser, William Kruskal, Leonard A. Marascuilo, Leslie D. McLean, Donald L. Meyer, Ellis B. Page, Robert M. Pruzek, Ronald G. Ragsdale, Robert E. Stake, George C. Tiao, and David E. Wiley. Several persons assisted in various ways during their graduate training: Alan Abrams, Donald Bosshart, Glenn Bracht, Russell Chadbourn, James Collins, Ralph Hakstian, Thomas Maguire, Masahito Okada, Perc Peckham, Andrew Porter, Robert Smith, and Peter Taylor. The assistance rendered by four persons merits special mention. Jason Millman and Kenneth D. Hopkins graciously consented to the inclusion of materials which they earlier prepared with the first author for classroom use. Robert Mendro assisted in the preparation of solutions for the problem sets which follow each chapter. Marilyn D. Wang made excellent detailed suggestions for improving much of the book. The task of typing the various drafts of the manuscript was shared by Ann Beadleston, Harriet Clutterbuck, Linda Schmale, and Linda Venter.

GENE V GLASS
JULIAN C. STANLEY

CONTENTS

4
MEASURES OF CENTRAL TENDENCY *57*

5
MEASURES OF VARIABILITY *75*

6
THE NORMAL DISTRIBUTION *95*

7
MEASURES OF RELATIONSHIP *109*

8
PREDICTION AND ESTIMATION *133*

15
THE ONE-FACTOR ANALYSIS OF VARIANCE—FIXED EFFECTS 338

16
MULTIPLE COMPARISON PROCEDURES 381

17
THE TWO-FACTOR ANALYSIS OF VARIANCE—FIXED EFFECTS 400

I

INTRODUCTION

Popular attitudes toward statistics contain a mixture of awe, cynicism, suspicion, and contempt. Statisticians have been uncomplimentarily placed in the company of liars and accused of "statisticulation"—the art of lying with statistics while maintaining an appearance of objectivity and rationality. Someone once remarked that "If all the statisticians in the world were laid end to end—it would be a good thing." A statistican has been scornfully depicted as a man who drowns while wading in a river of average depth 3 feet or who sits with his head in a refrigerator and his feet in an oven and reports that "On the average, I feel fine." In a weekly news magazine, the author of an essay on "The Science and Snares of Statistics" concluded that "... perhaps the time has come for society to be less numerically conscious and therefore less willing to be ruled by statistics."*

Persons beginning the study of statistics will profit from discarding the popular image of statistics and statisticians. They should realize that non-sense can be expressed as readily verbally as it can be expressed quantitatively. However, a knowledge of logic is a good safeguard against an uncritical

* *Time*, September 8, 1967, p. 29.

acceptance of verbal nonsense, and a knowledge of statistics is the best defense against quantitative nonsense. The first step toward replacing popular images of statistics with more realistic ones is the study of the structure of the discipline of "statistical methods" and its historical antecedents.

There were two widely divergent influences on the early development of statistical methods. Statistics had a mother who was dedicated to keeping orderly records of governmental units (*state* and *statistics* come from the same Latin root, *status*) and a gentlemanly gambling father who relied on mathematics to increase his skill at playing the odds in games of chance. From the mother sprang counting, measuring, describing, tabulating, ordering, and the taking of censuses—all of which led to modern *descriptive statistics*. From the adventurous, intellectual father eventually came modern *inferential statistics*, which is based squarely on theories of probability. A recent addition called the *design of experiments* relies heavily on a combination of probability theory and rather elementary but uncommon logic. This text offers an introduction to and a useful explanation of descriptive statistics, inferential statistics, and the design of experiments. Chapters 2 through 9 cover a large portion of descriptive statistics. Beginning with "Probability" in Chapter 10 and extending through Chapter 14, several topics from inferential statistics are covered. Chapters 15 through 19 present the considerations and inferential techniques fundamental to the design and analysis of experiments.

Descriptive statistics involves the tabulating, depicting, and describing of collections of data. These data may be either quantitative, such as measures of height and weight, or qualitative, such as sex and personality type. Large masses of data must generally undergo a process of summarization or reduction before they are interpretable by the human mind. A monkey is unsuccessful in his clumsy attempt to untie a simple knot because the complexity of the problem of untying the knot surpasses the resolving power of the poor creature's intellect. The unsuccessful fumbling attempt of a fisherman to unsnarl a backlash in his fishing reel is analogous to the monkey's plight. For the fisherman, that backlash is a Gordian knot; it presents too great a problem for *his* finite intellect. Similarly, but at a different level, the human mind cannot extract the full import of a mass of data (How do they vary? About how large are they? Is one set useless in reducing uncertainty about the other?) without the aid of special techniques (swords to cut the Gordian knot). Thus descriptive statistics serves as a tool to describe or summarize or reduce to manageable form the properties of a mass of data.

Inferential statistics is a formalized body of techniques for solving another class of problems that present great difficulties for the unaided human mind. This general class of problems characteristically involves attempts to infer the properties of a large collection of data from inspection of a sample of the collection. For example, a school nurse wishes to determine the proportion of children in the fifth grades of a large school system who have never had chicken pox. It would be unnecessary to question each child if the proportion could be reliably estimated from a sample of as few as 100 children. But how does the proportion of children in the sample of 100 who haven't had chicken pox relate to the analogous proportion in the entire fifth-grade population? The answer can be obtained through inferential statistics. Thus the purpose of inferential statistics is to surmise the properties of a population from a knowledge of the properties of only a sample of the population. Inferential statistics builds upon descriptive statistics. The inferences are drawn from particular properties of samples to particular properties of populations; the descriptions of the properties of both the samples and the populations are obtained by methods of descriptive statistics.

The *design and analysis of experiments* is a third important branch of statistical methods. These methods were developed for the discovery and confirmation of causal relationships among variables. Researchers in the social sciences are concerned with causation, a very complex concept in philosophy. Experimental design is so important for the study of causal relationships that in some philosophical systems an experiment constitutes an operational definition of a causal relationship. Adults make causal inferences during all of their waking moments. The frequent use of the word "because" reveals this: "The school bond failed to pass because it was not well publicized," or "He scored poorly on the intelligence test because he was overly anxious about the consequences of the score."

The sentence, "Drug A kills pain faster than Drug B," does not contain the word "because," but it implies that "More of this group of patients than of that group gained fast relief from pain because Drug A was administered to the former, whereas Drug B was administered to the latter." The weakness of the "because" explanation is its potential vagueness. This weakness is betrayed by the favorite remark of many young children when, at the prelogical stages of their thinking, they are confronted with evidence of their misbehavior. If asked, "Why did you do that?" they respond, "Just 'cause." Obviously, the word has many denotations and connotations.

Statistical methods assist researchers in describing data, in drawing inferences to larger bodies of data, and in studying causal relationships. They can be a useful tool in answering such questions as the following: How old is the average man on the day he receives a Bachelor of Arts degree from a certain college? What percentage of these new graduates have blue eyes? What percentage of them are presently married? How many of them already have 0, 1, 2, ... children? Do those who earned good grades as undergraduates attend graduate schools in greater proportions than those who earned mediocre grades? Has the international situation affected attendance at graduate schools? In an experiment, will college students who are received with friendliness by a group conform more to that group's judgments than will college students shunned by a group? Is this differential reaction, if found, contingent on the sex of the student? For instance, are women more or less amenable than men to group influence?

Mastering statistical methods requires some mathematical skill. The subject, statistics, is a branch of applied mathematics. Statistics is inadequately described in the dictionary as "the science of compiling facts." If statistics were only that simple, this text would be short indeed. In its more rigorous form, statistics is usually called mathematical statistics. For social scientists and other nonmathematicians it is termed "applied statistics" and includes much use of intuition, simple arithmetic, and elementary algebra. To study mathematical statistics seriously, one needs a background including at least advanced calculus and matrix theory; however, much of the rationale of applied statistics and many of its techniques can be learned without this mathematical maturity, although of course not as deeply understood. Perhaps this is partly the reason why various social sciences tend to be technique oriented. In large universities, separate courses in "educational and psychological statistics," "sociological statistics," "economic statistics," and the like can usually be found outside the Department of Statistics. Fortunately, however, the most fundamental principles are useful in nearly all disciplines, from agriculture to zoology. A knowledge of statistics is becoming necessary for the pursuit of a career of scholarship in any empirical discipline. Many graduate schools have recently acknowledged its importance by accepting course work in statistics as a replacement for one of the two foreign language courses that are traditionally required for the PhD degree. The substitution is apt: statistics is an increasingly important means of communicating knowledge. The increasing recognition of statistics as a tool of scholarship brings to mind the description of the education of children in B. F. Skinner's utopian community, Walden Two: "We help them in every way short of teaching them. We give them new techniques of acquiring knowledge and thinking . . . . We give them an excellent survey of the methods and techniques of thinking, taken from logic, statistics, scientific method, psychology, and mathematics. That's all the 'college education' they need. They get the rest by themselves in our libraries and laboratories."*

The word statistic is defined by Kendall and Buckland (1957)† as "A summary value calculated from a sample of observations, usually but not necessarily as an estimator of some population parameter; a function of

---

* Skinner, B. F. *Walden Two.* New York: The Macmillan Company (paperback edition), 1962, p. 121.

† For complete information on this and later references, consult the bibliography at the end of this text.

sample values." The contrasting term is "parameter," which we shall define later. Thus, the arithmetic mean of the numbers 1, 4, and 4, which is 3, is a statistic. The fact that a certain man has 2 children is a datum, whereas the average number of children in a town is a statistic. (You can actually see those 2 children, but not the average child.) This distinction between "statistic" and "datum" is not always preserved, however. Some applied statisticians and researchers use "statistic" to cover both, even saying that a person's name or hair color is a statistic.

Individual statistical techniques are unified by an underlying method. We shall attempt to show this unity and the interrelations as clearly as possible by using only the elementary mathematics that those studying this book will normally have learned in secondary school. Some special symbols will be introduced as needed; these will be explained carefully. They must be mastered at the point of introduction because thinking in statistics is facilitated by such symbols.

The approach of this text is from descriptive to inferential, with the statistics and logic of controlled experimentation gradually introduced. Two goals toward which this textbook is directed are (1) ability to read reports of surveys, studies, investigations, and experiments in your substantive field with moderate competence (given that you understand the substantive problems being researched) and (2) appreciable ability to plan your own studies and analyze data resulting from them.

The amount you learn will depend on your quantitative aptitude and diligence, plus the efforts of your instructor. The range of acquistion of statistics during an academic year is usually great for the students in a given class. Some develop considerable expertise, and others build a sound basis for further study in class and out. A few students, especially those traumatized by "symbol shock," find the pace too fast and the explanations too scanty. If they are to avoid a life of stuttering every time they even try to pronounce "statistics," their best hope is a skilled tutor to ease their anxiety, help them develop arithmetic and symbolic competence, and promote over-learning of the basic aspects needed for subsequent sections of the book. The sooner such a tutor is acquired the better.

If you have not studied mathematics, logic, or any other rigorous and deductive body of knowledge for some time, you may find studying statistics uncomfortable for a while. In many disciplines characterized by vague verbal discourse and personalistic use of language, a student can sustain sloppy and erroneous thinking for long periods without being confronted with its inadequacy. It is simply impossible to refute the statement that "We must educate the whole child" or that "Both heredity and environment are important in determining human intelligence." However, the student of statistics is likely to be confronted abruptly and uncomfortably with the results of loose thinking, as when a calculated quantity that cannot possibly be negative resists one's best attempts to make it come out positive. If you are inclined toward critical and precise thought, this restrictive and confining mantle will soon begin to feel comfortable. The satisfying reassurance of knowing that you are mastering a logical and unambiguous language will outweigh the occasional pang of anxiety produced when you are discovered speaking illogically. Being openly and clearly wrong is the price we must pay for knowing when we are correct. Never to know whether you are speaking sense or nonsense is too expensive a luxury to enjoy in an age when sense is precious and nonsense is rampant.

It is easy to succumb to the delusion that you are learning a great deal about statistics from simply reading the text. A statistics text is not a novel; none will ever become a "Book-of-the-Month Club" selection. This statistics text must be studied carefully and thoughtfully. Above all, the exercises and problems that follow each chapter must not be slighted. Working these exercises will put a fine edge on your knowledge of the subject. Skip the exercises and you may never know what you don't know about statistics. In statistics, as in most human endeavors, "A little learning is a dangerous thing; drink deep, or taste not the Pierian Spring. . . ."*

Almost anyone can learn a great deal about statistics. Even many high-school students find it interesting, so do not think it accessible only to the specially appointed. A good textbook helps; in the hands of a gifted teacher it is doubly effective. While writing this book we have held in mind three functions of a textbook: it must be an effective pedagogic instrument; it must serve as a reference work once the material is learned; it must serve to direct the student toward the larger body of knowledge that it only samples. Clearly the first function is primary, for there is no point in referring to what is not known nor should one attempt to read more advanced material until the fundamentals have been mastered. Master the fundamentals now and use them the rest of your life.

* Alexander Pope, *Essay on Criticism* (1711).

2

MEASUREMENT, SCALES, AND STATISTICS

2.1
MEASUREMENT

Everyone chooses to define "measurement" in slightly different terms from slightly different points of view. What is common to all definitions seems to be this: *Measurement* is the assigning of numbers to things according to rules. To measure a person's height is to assign a number to the distance between the top of a person's head and the bottom of his feet with the use of a ruler. Measurement of a child's IQ is the assignment of a number to the pattern of response that he makes to a group of standard problems. Measurement transforms certain attributes of our perceptions into familiar, tractable things called "numbers." What an impossible world it would be if we did not measure! How useful to a physicist would be the knowledge that iron melts at a high temperature, or to a traveler that Chicago is "down the road a piece"? A little reflection will reveal the important role played by measurement in education and almost every other social enterprise.

2.2
MEASUREMENT SCALES

The ideas of "scales of measurement" constitute a useful set of concepts. Behavioral scientists, and very few other scientists, have been concerned with these problems. We shall now discuss briefly the different scales and their implications for statistics.

Nominal Measurement*

Nominal measurement (giving a *name* or *names*) scarcely deserves to be called "measurement." It is the process of grouping objects into classes so that all of those in a single class are equivalent (or nearly so) with respect to some attribute or property. The classes are then given names; that the classes could as well receive, and often do receive, numerals for identification instead of names may account for the title "nominal *measurement*." Classificatory schemes in biology are examples of nominal measurement. Psychologists often code "sex" by assigning 0 to "female" and 1 to "male"; this is nominal measurement, too. We would perform nominal measurement if we assigned 1 to Englishmen, 2 to Germans, and 3 to Frenchmen. Does one Englishman plus one German equal one Frenchman $(1 + 2 = 3)$? Obviously not. The numerals we assign in nominal measurement have all the properties of any other numerals. We can add them, subtract them, divide them, or simply see which is larger than another. But if the process by which we assigned the numerals to objects was nominal measurement, then our playing with the size, order, and other properties of the numerals will imply nothing at all about the objects themselves because we took no cognizance of the size, order, and other properties of the numerals when we assigned them. When measurement is nominal only, one uses only the property of numbers that 1 is distinct from 2 or 4 and that if object A has a 1 and object B a 4, then A and B are different with respect to the attribute measured. It does not necessarily follow that B has any more of the attribute than A. The three remaining scales of measurement we shall encounter make use of three additional properties of numbers: numbers can be ordered with respect to size; they can be added; and they can be divided.

Ordinal Measurement

Ordinal measurement is possible when the measurer can detect differing degrees of an attribute or property in objects. This being possible, he makes

* The names of the scales of measurement used here and many of the concepts are due to S. S. Stevens (1951).

8

use of the "orderedness" property of numbers and assigns numbers to objects so that if the number assigned to object A is larger than the number assigned to B, then A possesses more of the property in question than B.

Suppose we ask a person to rank-order Mary, Jane, Alice, and Betty from least beautiful to most beautiful. We may rank them as follows: Betty, Jane, Mary, Alice. Ordinal measurement occurs when we assign the numbers 1, 2, 3, and 4 to Betty, Jane, Mary, and Alice respectively. Notice that the numbers 0, 23, 49, and 50 would have served just as well since the distance between any two adjacent numbers is of no significance. We may not feel that the measurer was capable of discerning, for example, whether the difference between the amount of beauty possessed by Betty and Jane is greater or less than the difference in beauty between Jane and Mary. Hence, no significance should be attached to the fact that the difference between Betty's and Jane's scores is the same as the distance between Mary's and Alice's scores.

Notice how the numbers take the place of the objects of concern. The numbers are a partial representation of the objects; we agree to treat the numbers as if both the facts that they are distinct and they can be ordered are important. At the ordinal measurement stage, the numbers constitute something of a reduction in effort to convey information. Instead of having to report that "Betty was judged least beautiful, Jane next least, Mary second most beautiful, and Alice most beautiful," we can report simply:

Person	Score
Mary	3
Jane	2
Alice	4
Betty	1

A scale of hardness of minerals is an ordinal scale. If mineral A can scratch mineral B, it is harder; hence, it receives a higher number. Suppose minerals A, B, C, and D have been assigned respectively numbers 12, 10, 8, and 6 in this manner. We know the hardest and the softest mineral. Is the difference between the hardness of A and B the same or different from the difference between the hardness of C and D? We have no way of knowing because the numbers were assigned so that only their uniqueness and ordinal properties were regarded—measurement was ordinal.

Another common ordinal scale is "rank in high school class." Numbers are assigned from 1 for "highest grade-point average" to n for "lowest grade-point average" in a class of n students. (If, for example, the three top students all had perfect averages, each would receive a rank of 2, which is the average of the first three ranks, 1, 2, and 3. This means of resolving ties is conventional, because it keeps the sum of the tied and untied ranks the same: $1 + 2 + 3 = 2 + 2 + 2$.)

There is no law preventing one from adding, subtracting, multiplying, etc. numbers that have been assigned to objects by ordinal measurement. However, the results of these operations may reflect nothing about the amounts of the property in question that the objects corresponding to the numbers possess. For example, the difference between the "beauty scores" of Alice and Betty is 3; the difference between the scores of Mary and Jane is 1. Does this mean that the difference in beauty between Alice and Betty is three times as great as the difference in beauty between Mary and Jane? Of course it doesn't. The results of the arithmetic cannot be interpreted as saying anything about the amounts of the property actually possessed by the objects. You can do what you wish with the numbers you obtain, but you are always faced with the question, "Do the results of these operations have any meaning for me?"

Interval Measurement

Interval measurement is possible when the measurer can distinguish not only between different amounts of the property in objects (the characteristic of ordinal measurement) but can also discern equal differences between objects. For interval measurement a unit of measurement (degree, inch, foot, ounce, etc.) has been defined. A number is assigned to an object that equals the number of units of measurement equivalent to the amount of the property possessed. For example, the temperature of a certain metal bar is 86° centigrade. An important feature which distinguishes interval measurement from ratio measurement (to be studied next) is that an object with a measurement of zero does not necessarily lack the attribute being measured. Hence, water at 0°C is *not* absolutely without temperature. The zero point on an interval scale is an arbitrary one.

The numbers assigned in the process of interval measurement have the properties of distinctness and order, but in addition the difference between the numbers is meaningful. The number assigned to the object is the number of units of measurement it has. Today's temperature is 60°F; yesterday's temperature was 55°F. Today is 5° warmer than yesterday. If tomorrow's temperature is 70°F then we know that yesterday and today are more alike in temperature than are today and tomorrow. The difference between 55 and 60 is half as large as the difference between 60 and 70; furthermore, the sizes of these differences tell us something about the temperature of the air.

The numbering of the years is an interval scale. The year 1 was arbitrarily set originally as the year of the birth of Christ. The unit of measurement is a span of 365¼ days. The year 1931 is more recent than any other year with a smaller number. Finally, the time between 1776 and 1780 equals the length of time between 1920 and 1924. James K. Polk was president for half as long (1845–1849) as Dwight D. Eisenhower (1953–1961).

Interval measurement involves assigning numbers to objects in such a way that equal differences in the numbers correspond to equal differences in the amounts in the objects of the property or attribute measured. The zero point of the interval scale can be placed arbitrarily and does not indicate absence of the property measured.

Ratio Measurement

Ratio measurement differs from interval measurement only in that the zero point is not arbitrary but indicates total absence of the property measured. The measurer can perceive the absence of the property, and he has a unit of measurement with which he records differing amounts of the property. Equal differences between the numbers assigned in measurement reflect equal differences in the amount of the property possessed by the things measured. Furthermore, since the zero point is not arbitrary but absolute, it is meaningful to say that A has two, three, or four times as much of the property as B.

Height and weight are examples of ratio measurement scales. Zero height is no height at all, and a man six-feet tall is twice as tall as a three-foot boy. The ratio scale is so named because the ratios of numbers on a ratio scale are meaningful. These ratios can be interpreted as ratios of amounts of the objects measured. A ratio statement about a strictly interval scale has no meaning in terms of the amounts of the attribute in the objects. For example, if June 3 had a high temperature of 90°F and March 17 had a high of 45°F, it is *not* correct to say that June 3 had twice as much temperature as March 17.

Most measurement in educational research and in the behavioral sciences occurs at the nominal, ordinal, and interval levels. Few important variables in these fields as yet lend themselves to ratio measurement; in fact, one must search diligently to find scales of measurement that will satisfy the conditions of an interval scale. Occasionally, ratio-scale variables such as time (to solve a problem or learn a list of words), height, weight, or distance will be of interest, but such occasions arise infrequently. You must undertake to recognize measurement at the nominal and ordinal levels and prepare for the problems that the analysis and interpretation of such data present.

Table 2.1 summarizes and supplements what has been said thus far about scales of measurement.

TABLE 2.1   SUMMARY OF CHARACTERISTICS AND EXAMPLES OF MEASUREMENT SCALES

Scale	Characteristics	Examples
Nominal	Objects are classified and classes are denoted by numbers. That the number for one class is greater or less than another number reflects nothing about the properties of the objects other than that they are different.	Racial origin, eye color, numbers on football jerseys, sex, clinical diagnoses, automobile license numbers, social security numbers
Ordinal	The relative sizes of the numbers assigned to the objects reflect the amounts of the attribute the objects possess. Equal differences between the numbers do not imply equal differences in the amounts of the attributes.	Hardness of minerals, grades for achievement, ranking on a personality trait, military ranks
Interval	A unit of measurement exists by which the objects not only can be ordered but may also be assigned numbers so that equal differences between the numbers assigned to objects reflect equal differences in the amounts of the attribute measured. The zero point of the interval scale is arbitrary and does not reflect absence of the attribute.	Calendar time, Fahrenheit and centigrade temperature scales
Ratio	The numbers assigned to objects have all the properties of those of the interval scale, and in addition an absolute zero point exists on the scale. A measurement of 0 indicates absence of the property measured. Ratios of the numbers assigned in measurement reflect ratios in amounts of the property measured.	Height, weight, numerosity, time, temperature on the Kelvin (absolute zero) scale

The discussion of measurement scales presented above has been dogmatic. We have attempted to plead the case of a small group of psychologists who have strong opinions about the level at which measurement is performed. We cannot present their arguments as well as they, so we recommend that you go to their own writings before you pass judgment on their position. Read such works as the following in which both pro and con opinions about the validity of the above concepts are presented. Several of these articles will be beyond the grasp of the typical beginning student. However, they ought not to be overlooked at some later stage in one's studies.

Anderson, N. H., "Scales and statistics: parametric and nonparametric," *Psychological Bulletin*, 1961, **58**, No. 4, 305–16.

Kaiser, H. F., "Review of *Measurement and Statistics* by Virginia Senders," *Psychometrika*, 1960, **25**, 411–13. This review of Senders' text is highly critical of the position held by Stevens and Senders.

Lord, F. M., "On the statistical treatment of football numbers," *American Psychologist*, 1953, **8**, 750–51. This satirical article by a noted psychometrician and statistician is a cogent argument against the idea that one's scale of measurement dictates which statistics can be used.

Senders, Virginia L., *Measurement and Statistics* (Oxford University Press, New York, 1958). This textbook is organized around Stevens' concepts; her position is one of the more extreme ones taken by psychologists.

Siegel, S., *Nonparametric Statistics* (McGraw-Hill, New York, 1956). Siegel's position is identical to that of Stevens. Siegel's text emphasizes which statistical techniques are "appropriate" to which scales of measurement. Although a useful text in many respects, its emphasis on "permissible" and "appropriate" statistics is perhaps misplaced.

Stevens, S. S. (Ed.), "Mathematics, measurement and psychophysics," in *Handbook of Experimental Psychology* (Wiley, New York, 1951), pp. 1–49. This early article revived interest in the problem of measurement scales and precipitated debate on the issue.

You are likely to get the impression from the works of Stevens, Senders, Siegel, and others that in some metaphysical way a "scale" underlies certain attributes. A certain set of numbers assigned to a group of objects definitely fits into this one category or that one: the scale is either nominal, ordinal, interval, or ratio; and there is nothing in between. This position can lead to chaos if held to in the face of the less well organized feelings of those who actually perform psychological and educational measurements. Those in the Stevens camp maintain, for example, that IQ scores form an ordinal scale, not an interval scale. Uncritical acceptance of this decree forces one to disregard completely the magnitude of the differences between IQ scores. Suppose Joe has an IQ of 50, Sam an IQ of 110, and Bob an IQ of 112. If IQ is truly an ordinal scale, all that can be said is that Bob is more intelligent than Sam who is more intelligent than Joe. The statement that Bob and Sam are more alike with respect to IQ than are Sam and Joe would not be defensible. To say that this last statement cannot be made because IQ's are only ordinal would be anarchy. Ask the person who administered the IQ test, and he would have told you before he tested the children that Joe is far less intelligent than Sam and Bob, who are much closer together. Try to tell the tester that he must pay no attention to the sizes of the differences between scores, and he will tell you to mind your own business, as he should. Even though an IQ unit is not a completely equivalent unit of measurement at different IQ levels, IQ scores are not on a par with a lowly ordinal scale. The IQ scale defies categorization as strictly ordinal or interval; perhaps it is better to speak of it as "quasi-interval."

It may often be important for a researcher to attempt to categorize his scale of measurement. If the numbers a measurer assigns to n different objects are no more than the n ranks $1, 2, \ldots, n$ (an ordinal scale), some statements with the numbers are meaningless in terms of the amounts of the attribute possessed by the objects. The measurer should be forewarned that this is so. He must also realize that if he has arbitrarily given "males" a 3 and "females" a 2 (nominal measurement), the fact that 3 is greater than 2 means nothing about the attribute measured, namely "sex." In this manner, the distinctions between the various scales can be useful. However, except for a few infrequently used measures (such as time, length, and mass), educational and psychological measurements, especially clinical measurement, defy any easy categorization as "ordinal" or "interval." Surely, the author of a textbook is in no position to pass judgment on the level of measurement at which one is working unless he, too, is intimately involved in the particular problem.

We shall not develop the notions of scales of measurement further. Only a few of the statistical techniques to be discussed in this text were developed with an eye toward the relationship of measures to the things being measured. The nature of this relationship is the concern of the measurement specialist. Statistical methods are means of analyzing numbers as numbers, not as *true* amounts of some attribute. Any statistical technique can be applied to any conglomeration of numbers (with some limitations, of course), but we know of no technique which refuses to be performed because the numbers put into it are not "proper." Statistical methods (with the possible exception of some psychometric scaling methods) do not add to or subtract from the meaningfulness of the numbers on which they are performed. This point was made with humor and insight by Kaplan (1964, pp. 205–6):

> Mathematics can spare us the painful necessity of doing our own thinking, but we must pay for the privilege by taking pains with our thinking both before and after mathematics comes into play.
>
> I recall a childhood puzzle which takes advantage of just this necessity. Three men registered at a hotel, paying ten dollars each for their rooms. The clerk, later realizing that the three rooms constituted a suite, for which the charge was only twenty-five dollars, gave five dollars to the bellhop to refund to the guests. Since five dollars is not evenly divisible by three, as well as for other less subtle reasons, the bellhop kept two dollars for himself and returned only three dollars as a refund. On his way back he calculated as follows. "They each paid ten dollars, making thirty dollars in all. I returned three dollars, or one dollar to each of them, so they each really paid nine. Now three times nine is twenty-seven, and two dollars I kept, making twenty-nine. Where is the thirtieth dollar?" Of course, if his two dollars is subtracted from the twenty-seven, not added, the remainder is twenty-five, the amount paid the hotel. We are quite free to add the numbers if we wish, but not to expect the sum to represent anything in the situation. What is missing in the bellhop's manipulations is not the dollar but good sense; his logic was no better than his morals.

2.3
VARIABLES AND THEIR MEASUREMENT

Variables are characteristic of persons or things, e.g., weight, age, reaction time, ideational fluency, reading speed, number of children, number of students. Intuition and experience tell us that some of these variables are continuous (i.e., measurements of them can take on any value within a certain range), such as weight, age, and reaction time. We know surely that some variables are *discrete* (i.e., measurements of them can take on only separated values), such as number of children. The most familiar discrete variables are those that are measured by counting. "Number of children" can give rise to the numbers 0, 1, 2, 3, ... It is not normally possible for this variable to take on intermediate values such as 1.75.

On the other hand, we feel confident that if we only had the instrumentation, resources, and time, we could measure continuous variables to as fine a degree as we wished. We choose to stop measuring elapsed time in a footrace after we have determined tenths of seconds. Even though it is reported that the hundred-yard dash was won in 10.4 seconds, more precise timing equipment might have revealed the winning time to be 10.416 seconds. But even this time is not exact; it is merely correct to thousandths of a second. The *actual* or *exact* measurement of a variable is something that can never be attained because measurement must always stop short of the *exact value*.* Standing opposite the exact value of a variable is a *reported value*. The *reported value* is the value which the measuring process produced. We do not expect the reported and actual values of a variable to coincide, but the former yields bounds for the latter. For example, if a person's height is 62 in. measured to the nearest inch, then his actual height at that time and under those conditions is between 61.5 and 62.5 in.

The measurement of any continuous variable should always be accompanied by a statement of the accuracy of the measuring process. Races are timed to the nearest tenth of a second; heights may be measured to the nearest inch; ages might be measured to the nearest day. The *sensitivity* of a measuring process is the smallest unit of the number scale which is reported. Thus the sensitivities in the above three examples are tenths of a second, inches, and days, respectively.

We often wish to establish limits around any reported value within which the exact value lies. For example, what are the lowest and highest actual heights that will result in a reported height of 58 in. if measurement of height is to the nearest inch? *The limits for the exact value around any reported value are found by adding and subtracting one-half the sensitivity of the measuring process from the reported value.* Thus a person with a reported height of 58 in. has an actual height between 58 in. $- (1 \text{ in.}/2) = 57.5 \text{ in.}$ and 58 in. $+ (1 \text{ in.}/2) = 58.5 \text{ in.}$ The examples below should clarify this procedure.

---

* An *exact value* or *score* must not be interpreted as a "true" or perfectly stable score, which it is not. The *actual score* may be unstable from one time to the next.

Variable	Sensitivity of measurement	Reported value	Limits of exact value
Weight	Nearest pound	130 lb	129.5–130.5 lb
Age	Nearest year	25	24 yr 6 months–25 yr 6 months
Reaction time	Nearest 1/100 sec	0.53 sec	0.525–0.535 sec
Elapsed time	Nearest 2/10 sec	5.6 sec	5.5–5.7 sec

Scores on educational and psychological tests are often derived by counting the number of correct responses a subject makes. John answered 45 of 90 questions correctly on the verbal section of a scholastic aptitude test. Thus, his number-right score on the variable "verbal scholastic aptitude" is 45. Because we generally conceive of the variables underlying most educational and psychological tests as being continuous, the sensitivity of these measuring devices is one item or one score point (provided the tests are composed of separate items). Thus John's exact score on this test lies between 44.5 and 45.5 items correct. If this strikes you as being odd at first, remember that the continuous variable "verbal scholastic ability" and not the discrete "number of items correct" is being measured.

A practical matter that will occur again later in this text concerns the way reported values are regarded in making calculations. If 10 IQ measurements have the same reported value of 105 and the limits of the exact value are 104.5 to 105.5, the 10 scores are usually regarded as evenly spread over the interval determined by the exact value limits. If for some purpose one needed to know how many scores exceeded 105.2, three of the 10 scores in the interval 104.5 to 105.5 would be counted (see Fig. 2.1). This convenient assumption is made in finding averages and computing scales below which given percentages of persons lie.

FIG. 2.1

It is unfortunate that we are now forced to admit that the concept of limits of the exact value of discrete measurements is one of the statistician's working tools. Even though it is nonsense to talk of the exact number of students taught by a given teacher lying between 33.5 and 34.5—obviously 34 students are being taught—this is sometimes done in making calculations. If we present such instances with little explanation, it is because we are attempting to show the techniques the statistician has found useful instead of attempting to rationalize all of his methods.

2.4
SYMBOLIZING DATA AND OPERATIONS

If we wish to refer to a set of numbers in general without actually writing down any one of them, we refer to any arbitrary value as X_i (read "X sub i"). X takes the place of the number; i, called a *subscript*, indicates that it is the ith number. When the subscript is given a particular value, say 4, then X_4 stands for a particular number: the fourth one of some group. X_1 denotes one number, and X_2 denotes a different one, the 1 and 2 being designators or names only; we cannot tell from the subscript whether X_1 or X_2 is larger. We may denote 4.3, 2.1, 6.7, and 3.5 by X_1, X_2, X_3, and X_4. Of course, we could have denoted 4.3 by X_2 instead of X_1 if we had wished. X_1 is merely the first number in our list of n numbers, and X_n the last.

If we have a group of n numbers (n can be 2, 3, 100 or any other number), we shall denote them by the symbols $X_1, X_2, \ldots, X_n$. In general, the ith number (X) is X_i, where i can be any one of the designator subscripts $1, 2, \ldots, n$.

A datum might be described by its horizontal and vertical distances from the axes. Each datum below can be located if we know the group it is in and its position in the group:

Order within group	Group number		
	1	2	3
First (1)	$X_{11} = 4.0$	$X_{12} = 6.5$	$X_{13} = 4.4$
Second (2)	$X_{21} = 2.3$	$X_{22} = 2.1$	$X_{23} = 5.3$

When we write X_{12}, we mean the *first* number in the *second* group, 6.5. X_{23} stands for the *second* number in the *third* group, 5.3. When we write X_{ij}, we can denote any one of these six numbers by letting i be either 1 or 2, and letting j be either 1, 2, or 3. What is the symbol for the number 4.4? Remember that i is the position of the number in the group and j is the number of the group.

Suppose you were going to run an experiment in which 12 persons would read one pamphlet and 10 persons would read a different pamphlet. Quite likely you would want to talk about the numbers your measuring instrument would yield in this experiment before you had them in hand. Instead of saying, "I think I'll compare the third number in the first group with the second number in the second group," you can say, "I think I'll compare X_{31} with X_{22}." Symbols are meant to be a useful and economical shorthand technique.

Data can be classified with respect to any number of characteristics.

A complicated experiment might produce data which are tabulated in a square with rows and columns; and a symbol X could need three subscripts, i, j, and k, to specify a particular number.   For example, $X_{1.3.6}$ (usually written X_{136}) stands for the *sixth* number in the cell formed by the intersection of row 1 and column 3.

2.5
SIGMA (Σ) NOTATION

You may wish to concentrate only on the first three-quarters of this section the first time through.   You may safely omit the material in this section beyond "Rule 3" below; then you can return to studying the remaining fourth of the section before embarking upon Chapter 15.

The analysis of most data involves adding, subtracting, multiplying, and dividing numbers, among other things.   Since we want to talk about performing these operations on a group of numbers in general, we will perform operations on the symbols for the numbers.

$X_1, X_2, \ldots, X_n$ stands for a group of n numbers, *any one* of which can be referred to as X_i, the ith number. $X_1 + X_2$ stands for the *sum* of the first and second numbers.   The ordering of the subscripts is usually completely arbitrary; $X_2 + X_1$ could be used to designate the sum of the first and second numbers, instead. $X_1 + X_2 + X_{10}$ stands for the *sum* of the *first*, *second*, and *tenth* numbers.

Often we want to add up all of the numbers in a group.   If there are five numbers in the group, $n = 5$ and the sum of all the numbers is $X_1 + X_2 + \ldots + X_5$. $X_1 + X_2 + \ldots + X_n$ stands for the sum of all n numbers in a group when the exact value of n is not specified.

An abbreviation for $X_1 + X_2 + \ldots + X_n$ which is frequently used is $\sum_{i=1}^{n} X_i$.

$$\sum_{i=1}^{n} X_i \quad \text{means} \quad X_1 + X_2 + \ldots + X_n.$$

$$\sum_{i=1}^{3} X_i = X_1 + X_2 + X_3. \qquad \sum_{i=3}^{5} X_i = X_3 + X_4 + X_5.$$

Σ is the Greek capital letter "sigma." $\sum_{i=1}^{5} X_i$ is read "the sum of X_i as i goes from 1 to 5." $\sum_{i=1}^{n} X_i$ is read "the sum of X_i as i goes from 1 to n."

Admittedly, this compact Σ-notation is economical.   Statisticians make great use of it.   You will have to learn how to interpret and use Σ-notation before you learn much about statistics.   The notation takes the place of a set of directions; at first you will have to translate the symbols into a set of verbal directions. As you gain greater facility with Σ-notation, however, you will respond automatically to $\sum_{i=1}^{n} X_i$ without first having to say to yourself, "the sum of X_i as i runs from 1 to n."

Adding up numbers after something has been done to them, such as multiplying each number by 6, or squaring each number (that is, multiplying it by itself), is as common as simply adding the numbers as they are. Suppose one wants to multiply each of n numbers by 2 and add together the resulting n products. The desired sum will be

$$2X_1 + 2X_2 + \ldots + 2X_n.$$

But surely you see that this sum is the same as

$$2(X_1 + X_2 + \ldots + X_n).$$

Using the shorthand Σ-notation discussed above, we can replace $(X_1 + X_2 + \ldots + X_n)$ by $\sum_{i=1}^{n} X_i$. The result can be summarized as follows:

$$2X_1 + 2X_2 + \ldots + 2X_n = \sum_{i=1}^{n} 2X_i = 2\sum_{i=1}^{n} X_i.$$

This result did not come about because of any magic in the number 2; with 4, 60, or 131.4 the result is the same. In fact, if c stands for any constant number (i.e., a number that does not change regardless of what i is), then

$$cX_1 + cX_2 + \ldots + cX_n = \sum_{i=1}^{n} cX_i = c\sum_{i=1}^{n} X_i. \qquad \text{(Rule 1)}$$

If a constant number c is to be added to each of n numbers, one writes $X_1 + c, X_2 + c, \ldots, X_n + c$.

The sum of the above values is

$$(X_1 + c) + (X_2 + c) + \ldots + (X_n + c) = \sum_{i=1}^{n} (X_i + c).$$

Always with addition of numbers we can regroup them in any way before adding.

$$\sum_{i=1}^{n} (X_i + c) = (X_1 + X_2 + \ldots + X_n) + (c + c + \ldots + c).$$

The first sum in parentheses on the right-hand side above is $\sum_{i=1}^{n} X_i$. What about the second sum in parentheses? How many c's are added together? The answer is n. So the second sum equals nc. Consequently,

$$\sum_{i=1}^{n}(X_i + c) = \sum_{i=1}^{n} X_i + \sum_{i=1}^{n} c = \sum_{i=1}^{n} X_i + nc. \qquad \text{(Rule 2)}$$

If c is one constant and d is another, how else can you write $\sum_{i=1}^{n}(cX_i + d)$? (Use Rules 1 and 2.)

Another important expression is the sum of n numbers after each individual number has been squared,

$$(X_1 \cdot X_1) + (X_2 \cdot X_2) + \ldots + (X_n \cdot X_n) = X_1^2 + X_2^2 + \ldots + X_n^2,$$

which is symbolized as

$$\sum_{i=1}^{n} X_i^2.$$

Similarly,

$$X_1^3 + X_2^3 + \ldots + X_n^3 = \sum_{i=1}^{n} X_i^3,$$

although in elementary statistics there will seldom be an occasion to use this expression.

Notice that $\sum_{i=1}^{n} X_i$ stands for a single number: the one that results from the addition of n numbers. $\sum_{i=1}^{n} X_i$ might be 10, 13, or 1300. $c \sum_{i=1}^{n} X_i$ is the product of two numbers, c and $\sum_{i=1}^{n} X_i$. $\left(\sum_{i=1}^{n} X_i\right)\left(\sum_{i=1}^{n} X_i\right)$ is the product of a number (a certain sum) and itself. We also write it as follows:

$$\left(\sum_{i=1}^{n} X_i\right)\left(\sum_{i=1}^{n} X_i\right) = \left(\sum_{i=1}^{n} X_i\right)^2.$$

If $X_1 = 3$, $X_2 = 6$, and $X_3 = 1$, then $\sum_{i=1}^{3} X_i = 10$ and $\left(\sum_{i=1}^{3} X_i\right)^2 = 100$.

Is $\sum_{i=1}^{n} X_i^2$ always the same number as $\left(\sum_{i=1}^{n} X_i\right)^2$? [Hint: When does $a^2 + b^2 = (a + b)^2$?] Calculate each when $X_1 = 2$, $X_2 = 1$, $X_3 = 4$, and $X_4 = 1$.

A common expression in statistical analysis is

$$\sum_{i=1}^{n}(X_i + c)^2 = (X_1 + c)^2 + (X_2 + c)^2 + \ldots + (X_n + c)^2.$$

$(X_i + c)^2$, which is $(X_i + c)(X_i + c)$, can be written in a different way:

$$
\begin{array}{r}
X_i + c \\
X_i + c \\
\hline
cX_i + c^2 \\
X_i^2 + cX_i \\
\hline
X_i^2 + 2cX_i + c^2.
\end{array}
$$

It is true, then, that $\sum\limits_{i=1}^{n} (X_i + c)^2 = \sum\limits_{i=1}^{n} (X_i^2 + 2cX_i + c^2)$. The expression within the parentheses may be written n times, as follows:

$$X_1^2 + 2cX_1 + c^2$$
$$X_2^2 + 2cX_2 + c^2$$

$$\cdot \qquad \cdot \qquad \cdot$$
$$\cdot \qquad \cdot \qquad \cdot$$
$$\cdot \qquad \cdot \qquad \cdot$$

$$X_n^2 + 2cX_n + c^2.$$

What is the sum of the first column above? It is $X_1^2 + X_2^2 + \ldots + X_n^2 = \sum\limits_{i=1}^{n} X_i^2$. What is the sum of the second column above? It is $2cX_1 + 2cX_2 + \ldots + 2cX_n = 2c(X_1 + X_2 + \ldots + X_n)$, which may be written compactly as $2c \sum\limits_{i=1}^{n} X_i$. What is the sum of the third column above? It is $c^2 + c^2 + \ldots + c^2 = nc^2$.

Putting together these three column sums we see that

$$\sum_{i=1}^{n} (X_i + c)^2 = \sum_{i=1}^{n} X_i^2 + 2c \sum_{i=1}^{n} X_i + nc^2. \qquad \text{(Rule 3)}$$

Though it is correct to proceed in this way, by writing each individual expression and summing columns, it is not necessary. Instead, one can "distribute the summation sign" before each term, as follows, and secure the same result more directly:

$$\sum_{i=1}^{n} (X_i + c)^2 = \sum_{i=1}^{n} (X_i^2 + 2cX_i + c^2)$$

$$= \sum_{i=1}^{n} X_i^2 + \sum_{i=1}^{n} 2cX_i + \sum_{i=1}^{n} c^2$$

$$= \sum_{i=1}^{n} X_i^2 + 2c \sum_{i=1}^{n} X_i + nc^2.$$

Note carefully how the summation sign was placed in front of *each* of the three terms *after* the squaring had been done. Also, verbalize to yourself as follows: The sum from 1 to n of the product of a constant (here, $2c$) and a variable (here, X) equals the constant ($2c$) times the sum from 1 to n of the values ($X_1, X_2, \ldots, X_n$) taken by the variable. Similarly, the sum from 1 to n of a constant (here, c^2) is simply n times the constant, this being a fundamental relationship between addition ($c^2 + c^2 + \ldots + c^2$) and multiplication (nc^2).

The data below are symbolized by X written with two subscripts, as X_{ij}, where $i = 1, 2, \ldots, n$ indicates the position of the ith observation or measurement (X) within the jth column $(j = 1, 2, \ldots, J)$

Treatment

1	2	$\ldots$	J
X_{11}	X_{12}	$\ldots$	X_{1J}
X_{21}	X_{22}	$\ldots$	X_{2J}
.	.	$\ldots$	.
.	.	$\ldots$	.
.	.	$\ldots$	.
X_{n1}	X_{n2}	$\ldots$	X_{nJ}

These data could be from an experiment in which n persons were given level 1 of a treatment, a different n persons were given level 2, and so on up to the n persons given level J. There would be nJ different persons in such an experiment. Alternatively, each person might be given all J treatments. The two situations are quite different, as we shall see in later chapters. (For the former, it is not necessary that the number of X's in each column be n, the same for all columns. Instead, the number could be n_j, where $j = 1, 2, \ldots, J$; n_3 would then mean the number of X's in the third column, n_2 the number in the second column, etc. Here we keep the n_j's equal, for simplicity.)

The sum of all the numbers at level 1 (i.e., column 1) is $X_{11} + X_{21} + \ldots + X_{n1}$. Notice that the first number in the subscript tells what *row* the observation is in, and the second number tells the *column* of the observation. To find the sum for column 1, which is $X_{11} + X_{21} + \ldots + X_{n1}$, we sum i from 1 to n while j keeps the value 1. We write this as $\sum_{i=1}^{n} X_{i1}$. The expression $\sum_{i=1}^{n} X_{i2}$ denotes the sum over i from 1 to n while j remains 2, i.e., the sum of the observations in column 2.

$\sum_{j=1}^{J} X_{1j}$ is $X_{11} + X_{12} + \ldots + X_{1J}$ (read "the sum over j from 1 to J for $i = 1$). This expression denotes the sum of the observations in *row* 1 of the layout. $\sum_{i=1}^{n} X_{ij}$ is the sum of the n numbers in column j; $\sum_{j=1}^{J} X_{ij}$ is the sum of the J numbers in row i.

How could we denote the grand sum of all nJ numbers from the experiment? One way would be to add up the numbers in each column individually and then add the J column sums together:

$$\text{Grand Sum} = \sum_{i=1}^{n} X_{i1} + \sum_{i=1}^{n} X_{i2} + \ldots + \sum_{i=1}^{n} X_{iJ}.$$

This sum of J numbers can be denoted more simply:

$$\text{Grand Sum} = \sum_{j=1}^{J}\left(\sum_{i=1}^{n} X_{ij}\right) = \sum_{j=1}^{J}\sum_{i=1}^{n} X_{ij}.$$

The grand sum squared has the form $\left(\sum\limits_{j=1}^{J}\sum\limits_{i=1}^{n} X_{ij}\right)^{2}$. The symbol for the sum of all nJ numbers which result from squaring each original observation and then adding together the squared numbers is $\sum\limits_{j=1}^{J}\sum\limits_{i=1}^{n} X_{ij}^{2}$. This expression is read as follows: "The double summation of X sub ij squared as j runs from 1 to J and i runs from 1 to n." First j is given the value 1 as i runs from 1 to n, then j is given the value 2 as i runs from 1 to n, etc.

The sum, across columns, of the squared values of each column *sum* is denoted by

$$\sum_{j=1}^{J}\left(\sum_{i=1}^{n} X_{ij}\right)^{2}.$$

There will be a time when we want to talk about adding one constant value to every number in column 1 of an array and a different constant to every number in column 2. Since the value of the constant depends only on the column and not on its position in the column, the subscript i is not needed to identify the constant. It is sufficient, then, to speak of c_1 and c_2. We can denote a constant value for the jth column by c_j. Thus, if we wanted to talk about X_{ij} plus a constant which is different for each column but the same for all n observations in one column, we denote this quantity by $X_{ij} + c_j$. The set of such quantities for the jth column is

$$X_{1j} + c_j$$
$$X_{2j} + c_j$$
$$\cdot \quad \cdot \quad \cdot$$
$$\cdot \quad \cdot \quad \cdot$$
$$\cdot \quad \cdot \quad \cdot$$
$$X_{nj} + c_j.$$

Thus

$$\sum_{i=1}^{n}(X_{ij} + c_j) = \sum_{i=1}^{n} X_{ij} + nc_j, \qquad \text{(Rule 4)}$$

because "c_j is a constant with respect to summation over i." For double summation,

$$\sum_{j=1}^{J}\sum_{i=1}^{n}(X_{ij} + c_j) = \sum_{j=1}^{J}\left(\sum_{i=1}^{n} X_{ij} + nc_j\right) = \sum_{j=1}^{J}\sum_{i=1}^{n} X_{ij} + n\sum_{j=1}^{J} c_j.$$

If a constant value d were to be added to all nJ observations, then no subscripts for d would be needed. The value of d is the same regardless of what row and column it is in.   You should be convinced that

$$\sum_{j=1}^{J} \sum_{i=1}^{n} (X_{ij} + d) = \sum_{j=1}^{J} \sum_{i=1}^{n} X_{ij} + nJ \cdot d. \qquad \text{(Rule 5)}$$

Because d is added to observations n times in each of J rows, it figures in the grand sum a total of nJ times.

If you are not yet convinced, list the symbols for every one of the nJ observations or measurements, as below, and sum them all:

$$
\begin{array}{cccc}
1 & 2 & \ldots & J \\
X_{11} + d & X_{12} + d & \ldots & X_{1J} + d \\
\cdot & \cdot & \cdot & \cdot \\
\cdot & \cdot & \cdot & \cdot \\
\cdot & \cdot & \cdot & \cdot \\
X_{n1} + d & X_{n2} + d & \ldots & X_{nJ} + d.
\end{array}
$$

Obviously, there are n d's in each column, and there are J columns, so there are nJ d's in all.

PROBLEMS AND EXERCISES

1. Categorize each of the following as either *nominal*, *ordinal*, *interval*, or *ratio* measurement:

   a. Zip-code numbers
   b. Academic rank (assistant professor, associate professor, professor) as a measure of length of service
   c. Metric system of measuring distance
   d. Telephone numbers

2. A teacher builds a spelling test by selecting a representative sample of 200 words from a particular dictionary.

   a. What scale of measurement is being employed if the teacher scores the test as follows:
      0–the student spelled at least one plural word incorrectly
      1–the student spelled all plurals correctly
   b. The teacher counts the number of correct spellings and calls this number a measure of "general spelling ability."   What scale of measurement is being used (nominal, ordinal, interval, or ratio)?

3. Determine the limits of the exact value corresponding to the reported value in each of the following instances:

Variable	Sensitivity of measurement	Reported value	Limits of exact value
a. Age	Nearest month	6 yr 5 months	
b. Weight	Nearest half ounce	2 lb 13.0 oz	
c. Monetary value	Nearest dollar	$343	

4. Let the symbol X_{ij} denote the ith datum in the jth group of data.

    a. Write the symbol for the 1st datum in the 2nd group.

    b. Write the symbol for the 4th datum in the 1st group.

    c. Write the symbol for the 2nd datum in an arbitrary group.

5. Let $X_1 = 2$, $X_2 = 7$, $X_3 = 1$, $X_4 = 3$, $X_5 = 2$, and $X_6 = 4$. Evaluate each of the following:

    a. $\displaystyle\sum_{i=1}^{6} X_i =$ b. $\displaystyle\sum_{i=1}^{3} X_i =$ c. $\displaystyle\sum_{i=2}^{4} X_i =$ d. $\displaystyle\sum_{i=1}^{6} X_i - \sum_{i=3}^{5} X_i =$

6. Let $X_1 = 0$, $X_2 = 4$, $X_3 = 8$, $X_4 = 2$, and $X_5 = 1$. We see that $\displaystyle\sum_{i=1}^{5} X_i = 15$. Evaluate each of the following *without* operating on the original five numbers.

    a. $\displaystyle\sum_{i=1}^{5} 4X_i =$ (Rule 1)   b. $\displaystyle\sum_{i=1}^{5} (X_i + 3.1) =$ (Rule 2)

    c. $\displaystyle\sum_{i=1}^{5} (X_i - 2) =$ d. $\displaystyle\left(\sum_{i=1}^{5} X_i\right)^2 =$

7. Consider the following data:

$$X_{11} = 4 \qquad X_{12} = 3$$
$$X_{21} = 2 \qquad X_{22} = 2$$
$$X_{31} = 6 \qquad X_{32} = 1$$
$$X_{41} = 3 \qquad X_{42} = 5$$

    a. $\displaystyle\sum_{j=1}^{2}\sum_{i=1}^{4} X_{ij} =$ b. $\displaystyle\sum_{i=1}^{4} X_{i1} =$

    c. $\displaystyle\sum_{j=1}^{2} X_{3j} =$ d. $\displaystyle\sum_{i=1}^{4} X_{i2}^2 =$

8. Write out the following expressions:

    a. $\displaystyle\sum_{i=1}^{4} X_i^2 =$ b. $\displaystyle\sum_{i=4}^{6} X_i =$ c. $\displaystyle\left(\sum_{i=1}^{3} X_i\right)^2 =$

9. Change the following expressions into sigma-notation:

    a. $3X_1 + 3X_2 + 3X_3 =$ b. $(X_1 + \ldots + X_{10})^2 =$

    c. $(X_1 + \ldots + X_n) + 7n =$

    d. $(X_1^2 + X_1) + (X_2^2 + X_2) + \ldots + (X_5^2 + X_5) =$

3

TABULATING
AND
DEPICTING DATA

3.1
TABULATION OF DATA

Before quantitative data can be understood and interpreted, it is usually necessary to summarize them. Table 3.1 shows a class record for a reading readiness test administered at the beginning of the school year. The scores appear in alphabetical order as they are recorded in the teacher's class roll book. However, the scores do not mean very much in this form, and we can tell only with some difficulty whether, for example, the first-listed pupil (David A), with a score of 90 points out of a possible 128, is superior or just average in reading readiness, compared with his classmates.

Rank Order

Ordinarily the first step is to arrange the scores in order of size, usually from highest to lowest. This is called an *ungrouped series*. In a small class, this is often all that is necessary. Table 3.2 shows the same 38 scores as Table

3.1, arranged in order of size from 112 to 44. This table also shows the rank order of the pupils (1st, 2nd, . . . , 38th) and the scores tabulated without further grouping. It is now easy to see that David A's score of 90 gives him a rank of 13 in a class of 38, or about one-third of the way from the top. Similarly, it is easy to interpret each of the other scores in terms of rank. But ties are likely to occur, especially in classes of 20 or more pupils. Notice, for example, that two pupils made a score of 97. Since it is not correct to say that one ranks higher than the other, we must assign them the same rank. Since there are six pupils who rank higher (1, 2, 3, 4, 5, 6), the next two ranks, 7 and 8, are averaged, giving 7.5. In like manner the average of ranks 9 and 10 is 9.5, and so on for the other pupils with tied scores. There are three pupils with scores of 75, and there are 21 pupils who rank above this score; the average of the next three ranks (22, 23, and 24) is 23, which is the rank assigned to each of the scores of 75. In addition to the time and trouble required to determine these ranks, the list is long, unwieldy, and inadequate for making comparisons with other classes that are much larger or much smaller; ranking 19th in a class of 38 pupils is poorer than ranking 19th in an equally capable class of 70 pupils.

TABLE 3.1   A CLASS RECORD FOR A READING READINESS TEST (38 PUPILS)

Pupil	Score	Pupil	Score	Pupil	Score	Pupil	Score
David A.	90	Robert D.	59	Jerome L.	75	Paul S.	81
Barbara B.	66	Dan F.	95	Rosa M.	75	Richard S.	71
Charles B.	106	Larry F.	78	Billy N.	51	Robert S.	68
Robert B.	84	Richard G.	70	Nancy O.	109	William S.	112
Mildred C.	105	Grover H.	47	Carrie P.	89	Jean T.	62
Robbin C.	83	Robert H.	95	Ralph R.	58	Adolfo W.	91
Robert C.	104	Sylvia H.	100	George S.	59	Dolores W.	93
Diney D.	82	Warren H.	69	Gretta S.	72	Richard W.	84
Jim D.	97	Clarence K.	44	Jack S.	74		
John D.	97	David K.	80	Mary S.	75		

The Frequency Distribution

The list of scores can be made shorter by arranging the scores in a frequency distribution, sometimes simply called a *distribution*. The third and fourth columns of Table 3.2 show the simplest form of a distribution. The various scores are arranged in order of size, here from 112 to 44, and to the right of each score is recorded the number of times it occurs. Each entry to the right of a score is called a frequency, abbreviated f, and the total of the frequencies is represented by n.

TABLE 3.2   READING READINESS SCORES FROM TABLE 3.1 ARRANGED IN ORDER OF SIZE, RANKED, AND TABULATED

Order of size	Rank	Score	Frequency (f)
112	1	112	1
109	2	109	1
106	3	106	1
105	4	105	1
104	5	104	1
100	6	100	1
97 }	7.5	97	2
97 }	7.5	95	2
95 }	9.5	93	1
95 }	9.5	91	1
93	11	90	1
91	12	89	1
90	13	84	2
89	14	83	1
84 }	15.5	82	1
84 }	15.5	81	1
83	17		
82	18	80	1
81	19	78	1
80	20	75	3
78	21	74	1
75 }	23	72	1
75 }	23	71	1
75 }	23	70	1
74	25	69	1
72	26	68	1
71	27	66	1
70	28	62	1
69	29	59	2
68	30	58	1
66	31	51	1
62	32	47	1
59 }	33.5	44	1
59 }	33.5		
58	35		
51	36		
47	37		
44	38		

Tabulated without further grouping

Sum = 19

Midpoint of frequencies

Sum = 19

$n = \overline{38} = 19 + 19$

Grouped Frequency Distribution

For a large number of scores—say 100 or more—it may be desirable to carry the summarization of data one step further. As a rule, there is such a wide range of scores that it is economical to group them according to size, such as a group including all scores from 105 to 109, inclusive, from 110 to 114, inclusive, and so on. Each group is called a *score class*. The complete grouping arrangement is usually referred to as a *grouped frequency distribution.* Although there is no fixed rule for the number of score classes, it is usually best to make not fewer than 12 classes nor more than about 15. To have fewer than 12 classes is to run the risk of distorting the results, whereas more than 15 classes produce a table that is inconvenient to handle.

Constructing the Grouped
Frequency Distribution

There are four steps in making the ordinary grouped frequency distribution. These are shown in Table 3.3, using the scores given in Table 3.1.

1. Determine the *inclusive range*, which is 1 plus the difference between the highest score and the lowest. Of these scores, the highest is 112 and the lowest is 44, which gives a range of $(112 - 44) + 1 = 69$. Actually, 112 is considered to cover the one-point score interval 112.5–111.5, and 44 the interval 44.5–43.5. Notice, therefore, that the range is 69 $[(112 - 44) + 1$, or $112.5 - 43.5]$. The real score limits are not always fractional, however. If age is reckoned at the last (most recent) birthday, then persons who report themselves as being 44 years old (that is, not yet 45) lie within the interval 44.00–44.99 . . . (almost, but not quite 45.00), whose midpoint is 44.5. If they report age to nearest birthday, the interval is 43.5–44.5, with a midpoint of 44. Similarly, if they report themselves "going on 44," the interval is 43.00–43.99 . . . , with midpoint 43.5. There will be a difference of almost two years between the youngest possible "going on 44" person, who has just reached the age of 43, and the oldest possible "44 last birthday" respondent, who is almost 45. When we ask merely for "Age_____," without specifying the reckoning system, we will not be able to interpret our results precisely.

2. Select the *score-class grouping interval*, which is the width of the groups into which the scores are to be classified, so that there will be not fewer than 12 score classes nor more than 15. To do this, divide the range by 12 to find the largest group, or score-class interval to be used. Divide the range by 15 to find the smallest class interval to be used. In this case, $69 \div 12 = 5.75$, and $69 \div 15 = 4.60$. Since it is impractical to use any class interval except a whole number, the larger number, 5.75, is "rounded down" to 5 and the 4.60 "rounded up" to 5, even though a class interval of 6 would yield 12 score classes for these 38 scores. Odd-numbered interval widths such as 5, which have whole-number midpoints when the score-class limits are fractional (end in .5), are usually preferred to even-numbered interval widths, which have fractional midpoints when the class limits are fractional. The midpoint of the score class 110–114, which contains the 5 scores 110, 111, 112, 113,

and 114, is 112 (that is, $110 + [(114 - 110) \div 2] = 110 + (4/2) = 110 + 2 = 112$). (Another way to determine the midpoint of an interval is simply to average the reported limits of the interval: $(110 + 114) \div 2 = 112$.) If a class size of 6 were used, with score limits of 108–113, for example, the midpoint of this even-numbered group would be 110.5, which might result in more complex computations. Hence, a class interval of 5 is preferable to 6 when the class limits are fractional.

3. Determine the limits of the classes. There must, of course, be enough classes to include the highest score and the lowest score. To facilitate tabulation, start each class with a multiple of the class interval. If the lowest class starts with 40, which is a multiple of 5, it will accommodate the lowest score, 44, whereas a class beginning with 45 will not. Each succeeding whole-number class lower limit will be 5 points above the one just below it. The next class will start at 45, the next at 50, and so on, until the highest score, 112, is included in the class 110–114.

4. Make the tabulation. A tally is made for each score opposite the class in which it falls. To make the tabulation it is not necessary to have the scores arranged in order, for this process may require more time than the tabulation itself. In the original alphabetical list, the first score is 90. In the tabulation column opposite the class which begins with 90, a tally line is drawn to indicate the score. The next score is 66. This falls in the class which begins at 65, so a tally is made there. In the same way, a tally is placed in the column opposite the appropriate class for each of the other scores.

In the finished table, the steps by which it was made do not appear. Only two columns occur in the simplest form of a frequency distribution. The first shows the various classes, usually arranged in descending order from top to bottom, and the second shows the frequencies—the number of scores in each class.

To be sure that you understand Steps 3 and 4, above, stop at this point and construct a grouped frequency distribution of the 38 scores, using a class (grouping) interval of 6. Does the number of classes that result meet the 12–15 criterion suggested in Step 2, above?

When two or more groups of data are to be compared, it is usually best to include all the data in the same table. In that case there will be a column for the classes into which the scores are grouped and one for each of the schools or grades being compared. Table 3.4 shows a frequency table which combines the record of six schools on a certain text. The number of grouping intervals varies from 9 for School F to 17 for Schools A and D, although some intervals have no tallies.

TABLE 3.3   AN ILLUSTRATION OF THE PROCESS OF MAKING A GROUPED FREQUENCY
                  DISTRIBUTION

Original scores
(from Table 3.1)   *Steps in making the distribution*

Original scores	Steps in making the distribution
90	Step 1. Determining the range.
66	Highest score 112
106	Lowest score 44
84	Range $=$ Difference $+ 1 = 68 + 1 = 69$
105	
83	
104	
82	Step 2. Selecting the class interval.
97	$69 \div 12 = 5.75$, largest class interval desirable.
97	Round *down* to 5.
59	$69 \div 15 = 4.60$, smallest class interval desirable.
95	Round *up* to 5.
78	
70	
47	
95	Steps 3 and 4. Determining the limits of the classes and making
100	the tabulation.
69	
44	
80	

Original scores	*Whole-number limits of the 15 classes*	*Tally*	*Frequency (f)*
75			
75			
51	110–114	/	1
109	105–109	///	3
89	100–104	//	2
58	95–99	////	4
59	90–94	///	3
72	85–89	/	1
74	80–84	### /	6
75	75–79	////	4
81	70–74	////	4
71	65–69	///	3
68	60–64	/	1
112	55–59	///	3
62	50–54	/	1
91	45–49	/	1
93	40–44	/	1
84			$n = \overline{38}$

The Form of the Table

A few words should be said about the pure mechanical makeup of the table
as it often occurs in typed or printed form; Table 3.4 and the other tables
in this book illustrate one format for the printed table. Each table bears an

TABLE 3.4   DISTRIBUTION OF READING READINESS SCORES FOR EACH OF SIX SCHOOLS IN A CERTAIN CITY

Score	School						All six schools
	A	*B*	*C*	*D*	*E*	*F*	
120–124				1			1
115–119							
110–114			1				1
105–109			3		2	2	7
100–104		3	2	2	5	3	15
95–99		6	4	4	4	5	23
90–94	5	2	3	5	6	10	31
85–89	4	4	1	4	4	1	18
80–84	2	3	6	6	4	8	29
75–79	10	5	4	4	1	2	26
70–74	6	2	4	7	6	4	29
65–69	9	4	3		4	1	21
60–64	4	5	1	2	1		13
55–59	1		3		1		5
50–54	1		1				2
45–49	1		1				2
40–44			1	2	2		5
35–39	1	1					2
30–34		2					2
25–29		1					1
20–24							
15–19							
10–14	1						1
N	45	38	38	37	40	36	234

identifying number.   Although either Roman or Arabic numerals may be used, Arabic numerals seem to be increasingly favored.   The table number may be centered above the table title, or it may be given at the beginning of the title.   The table often starts with a single or double horizontal line and usually ends with a single horizontal line.   Another horizontal line separates the column headings from the table body, and other horizontal lines separate any summarizing measures that are given under the table proper.   Vertical lines may be used to separate the columns, but usually no lines are drawn along the margins of the page.   It is considered good form to avoid abbreviations in the table whenever possible, and to make the title and headings complete enough to indicate the contents of the table clearly.

Wallis and Roberts (1965, Chap. 9) present an excellent chapter on the art of reading statistical tables.   They remind the reader of the obvious precautions, e.g., read the title and headnote carefully, and they demonstrate some subtle and sophisticated techniques for extracting hidden information in tables.   Wallis and Roberts have managed to do all this and be entertaining as well.

3.2
QUANTILES

One of the most efficient and useful methods of describing a group of observations is by means of *quantiles*. A quantile is a concept and *percentiles*, *deciles*, and *quartiles* are three examples of it. A *quantile* is a point on a number scale which is assumed to underlie a set of observations; the quantile divides the set of observations into two groups with known proportions in each group. For example, there are three quartiles (Q_1, Q_2, and Q_3); they divide a group of observations into four quarters. Q_1 is that point on the number scale such that one-fourth the observations lie below it; one-half the observations lie below Q_2, and three-fourths of the observations lie below Q_3. Thus the three quartiles divide a set of observations into four portions that are equal in terms of the proportion of observations in each portion. The 99 possible *percentiles* (P_1, . . . , P_{99}) divide a set of observations into 100 portions, each of which contains an equal number of observations. The nine *deciles* (D_1, . . . , D_9) divide a set of observations into ten equal portions.

If 25% of the observations are always below P_{25}, the 25th percentile, and the same is true for Q_1, the first quartile, then P_{25} must equal Q_1. Figure 3.1

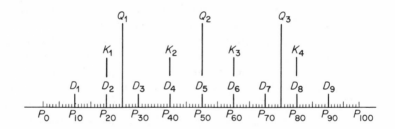

FIG. 3.1   Relationships among quantiles.

shows the relationships among the various quantiles defined so far and still another type called *quintiles*. (*Quint* for *five*.) The four quintiles divide a group into fifths. We shall denote them K_1, K_2, K_3, and K_4 since the letter Q was used for quartiles.

Quantiles are very useful for summarizing data. Simply reporting that P_5 is 10.75 and P_{15} is 16.80 tells immediately that 5% of the observations are less than 10.75 and that 10% of them lie between 10.75 and 16.80. For some large groups of data that are familiar, the entire collection of observations can be pictured in a reader's mind if he knows only the values of three or four percentiles, for example. All too often, more complicated summary measures (such as those to be encountered soon) are used to describe data when certain quantiles are more easily calculated and more readily understood. It is regrettable that quantiles are not more widely used by persons attempting simply to describe a set of data.

3.3
DETERMINING PERCENTILES

Because of the relationships among various quantiles noted in Fig. 3.1, one need know only how to determine percentiles to find the values of any quantiles desired. (Typically, no one ever wishes to divide a group of observations into more than 100 quantiles.)

The definition of a *percentile* is simple: the Pth percentile is the point below which P percent of the scores lie. Calculating a given percentile is slightly more complicated than the definition might lead you to believe.

Before beginning the calculation of any percentile in a group of scores one must arrange the scores from smallest to largest. This may be a time-consuming operation in large groups of scores, and it may be more convenient to tabulate the scores in a grouped frequency distribution. The method we will present for finding a percentile point is general and applies to either a ranking or a grouped frequency distribution of the scores.

A teacher administered a 40-item achievement test to his 125 students. The test score was taken to be the number of questions answered correctly. An ungrouped frequency distribution of the 125 test scores appears in Table 3.5.

What is the 25th percentile in the group of 125 test scores, i.e., what is the value of P_{25}? P_{25} is the point below which 25% of the 125 scores lie.

The calculation of any percentile will be facilitated if a *cumulative frequency distribution* is constructed. The *cumulative frequency* up to any given score is the total number of frequencies at or below that score. In the third column in Table 3.5 you will find the cumulative frequencies for the 125 achievement test scores. Notice, for example, that there are 106 persons with test scores of 33 or less. The cumulative frequency *through* the test score of 33 is 106.

The calculation of P_{25} can be accomplished in five steps:

Step 1. Find $(.25)n$ by dividing n by 4:

$$\frac{125}{4} = 31.25.$$

Step 2. Determine the lower real limit L of the score class containing the 31.25th person from the bottom.

Because 16 persons scored at or below a score of 28, and 34 persons scored at or below a score of 29, the 31.25th frequency lies on the score-class interval 28.5–29.5.

It will be assumed that the 18 frequencies at a score of 29 are evenly spread along the score class 28.5–29.5. Each frequency occupies (1/18)th

TABLE 3.5   DETERMINATION OF P_{25}, THE 25th PERCENTILE, IN A FREQUENCY DISTRIBUTION
WHERE THE SCORE-CLASS INTERVAL IS ONE

Test score	Frequency	Cumulative frequency	Calculations
38	1	125	Step 1. $0.25n = \dfrac{n}{4} = \dfrac{125}{4} = 31.25.$
37	1	124	
36	3	123	Step 2. Find lower real limit of score class
35	5	120	containing 31.25th score:
34	9	115	$L = 28.5.$
33	8	106	
32	17	98	Step 3. Subtract the cumulative frequency up to
31	23	81	L from 31.25:
30	24	58	$31.25 - 16 = 15.25.$
29	18	34	
28	10	16	Step 4. Divide the result of Step 3 by the
27	3	6	frequency f in the interval containing
26	1	3	the 31.25th score:
25	0	2	$\dfrac{15.25}{18} = 0.85.$
24	2	2	
	$n = \overline{125}$		Step 5. Add the result of Step 4 to L: $P_{25} = 28.5 + 0.85 = 29.35.$

of a unit. Determining how much of the interval the 31.25th score cuts off
is a problem of *interpolation* within the interval. Steps 3 and 4 accomplish
the interpolation.

Step 3. Subtract the cumulative frequency (*cum.f*) up to L
from .25n. L is 28.5, and 16 frequencies have accumulated up to L. Hence,

$$.25n - (cum.f) = 31.25 - 16 = 15.25.$$

In Step 3, one determines how many frequencies in the interval 28.5–29.5
lie below .25n.

Step 4. Divide the result of Step 3 by the frequency f in the
interval containing the .25nth frequency.

$$\frac{15.25}{18} = 0.85.$$

Step 4 is the determination of what fraction of the score-class interval
lies below the .25nth frequency. There are 18 frequencies in the interval
28.5–29.5, and $15.25/18 = 0.85$ of the interval is occupied by the first $15\frac{1}{4}$
frequencies.

Step 5. Add the result of Step 4 to L. The sum is P_{25}.

$$P_{25} = 28.5 + 0.85 = 29.35.$$

Under the conventions we have adopted for the presentation of the scores, $P_{25} = 29.35$; i.e., 25% of the 125 scores lie below 29.35. (Similarly, 75% of the 125 scores lie above 29.35.)

Steps 1 through 5 can be expressed in a single formula:

$$P_{25} = L + \frac{.25n - (cum.f)}{f}, \tag{3.1}$$

where L is the lower real limit of the score interval of length 1 containing the .25nth frequency from the bottom of the distribution,

$cum.f$ is the cumulative frequency up to L, and

f is the frequency within the score interval containing the .25nth frequency.

A more general form of Eq. (3.1) applies to the determination of any percentile in a frequency distribution whose score-class interval is 1. Suppose we wish to find the point which exceeds some proportion p of the frequencies. P_p represents the pth percentile.

$$P_p = L + \frac{pn - (cum.f)}{f}, \tag{3.2}$$

where L is the lower real limit of the score interval containing the $p$nth frequency,

$cum.f$ is the cumulative frequency up to L, and

f is frequency of scores in the interval containing the $p$nth score.

We shall illustrate the use of Eq. (3.2) by calculating P_{60} from the data in Table 3.5:

$$P_{60} = 30.5 + \frac{75 - 58}{23} = 31.24.$$

Calculation of any percentile point from a grouped frequency distribution is almost identical to the calculations for the ungrouped distribution. In fact, the formula for the grouped frequency distribution that will be developed includes Eq. (3.2) as a special case when the score interval is one unit wide.

The data in Table 3.6 are the ages to the nearest year of 1982 teachers who participated in special summer programs for the improvement of the teaching of selected high-school subjects.

The general formula for determining the pth percentile in a group of n scores is as follows:

$$P_p = L + \frac{pn - (cum.f)}{f}(W), \tag{3.3}$$

where L is the lower real limit of the interval containing the pnth frequency from the bottom,

$cum.f$ is the cumulative frequency up to L,

f is the frequency in the interval containing the pnth frequency, and

W is the width of any score interval.

Note that Eq. (3.3) is exactly the same as Eq. (3.2) when $W = 1$, i.e., when the score interval is one score wide, which means that scores are not grouped more finely than originally in constructing the frequency distribution.

Application of Eq. (3.3) will now be illustrated by finding P_{20} for the data in Table 3.6. The pnth score—the 396th score—lies in the interval 24–27 that has a lower real limit of 23.5. The difference between pn and the cumulative frequency up to 23.5 is $396.4 - 135$. Noting that the frequency in the interval including the 396th score is 295 and the interval width is 4 units, we obtain:

$$P_{20} = 23.5 + \frac{396.4 - 135}{295} \cdot 4 = 27.04.$$

Under the conventions adopted for the calculation of percentiles, we can say that 20% of the teachers were younger than 27.04 years. We do not expect this statement to be exactly true. Errors have entered the process of determining the percentiles at two points. First, ages were reported to the

TABLE 3.6   ILLUSTRATION OF THE CALCULATION OF P_{50} IN A GROUPED FREQUENCY DISTRIBUTION

Age interval	Frequency	Cumulative frequency	Calculations
64–67	4	1982	Step 1. $0.50n = 0.50(1982) = 991$.
60–63	38	1978	
56–59	82	1940	Step 2. Find lower real limit of score class
52–55	120	1858	containing 991st score:
48–51	125	1738	$L = 31.50$.
44–47	160	1613	
40–43	221	1453	Step 3. Subtract the cumulative frequency
36–39	204	1232	$cum.f$ up to L from 991:
32–35	307	1028	$991 - 721 = 270$.
28–31	291	721	Step 4. Divide the result of Step 3 by the
24–27	295	430	frequency f in the interval containing
20–23	135	135	the 991st score:
$n = 1982$			$\frac{270}{307} = 0.88$.

Step 5. Multiply the result of Step 4 by the width W of the score class:
$(0.88)(4) = 3.52$.

Step 6. Add the result of Step 5 to L:
$P_{50} = 31.50 + 3.52 = 35.02$.

nearest year instead of to the nearest month, day, hour, or minute. Second, it was assumed that the frequencies within each score interval were evenly distributed over the entire interval. Undoubtedly this assumption was false: at the younger ages frequencies are probably stacked up at the upper end of each score interval; at the older ages, frequencies are probably stacked up at the lower end of each interval. In making the assumption of evenly distributed frequencies, a compromise between computational labor and errors of approximation was made. The error made in approximating P_{20} or any other percentile is probably immaterial relative to the difficulties that would arise if we assumed that the frequencies were distributed in any manner other than evenly on each score interval.

That percentiles are fractional (e.g., 27.04) in measuring age is reasonable. We have no difficulty imagining that someone is precisely 27.04 years of age. What if the variable being measured is discrete? Suppose we build a frequency distribution of sizes of kindergarten classes in a large city school system. This variable, "size of class," can take only values such as 25, 26, 27, 28, etc. It is absurd to speak of a class with 27.31 students. Yet if we were to build a frequency distribution of class sizes and calculate percentile points by the methods in this chapter, we would most certainly obtain fractional values. Can such fractional percentile points be taken seriously? Isn't it utterly false that 81% of the classes can have a size of 32.41 while 89% have a size of 32.78? Of course, it is utterly false. The same percent of the classes have 32.41 or fewer students and 32.78 or fewer students, and this percent is exactly the number of classes with 32 or fewer students. Even though fractional percentiles in distributions of discrete variables cannot be reconciled with common sense, they are useful and widely employed. The alternative to using them is to abandon this convenient and helpful process of converting scores to percentiles and adopt some more cumbersome procedure. No one seems willing to do this just because a class with 32.50 students seems a little ridiculous.

3.4
GRAPHING DATA

There can be little doubt that the graphical representation of educational data is a valuable supplement to statistical analysis and summarization. A graph or chart tends to attract the reader's attention. The average casual reader is likely to give scant attention to the ordinary printed matter in a research report and to be unimpressed by the mass of tabular data often piled up at the end. However, his eye is likely to be arrested by any picture or chart that may happen to be included, and this may lead him to read the entire discussion.

A graph is often an effective method of clarifying a point. One small graph will often make a point more clearly than a dozen tables or paragraphs.

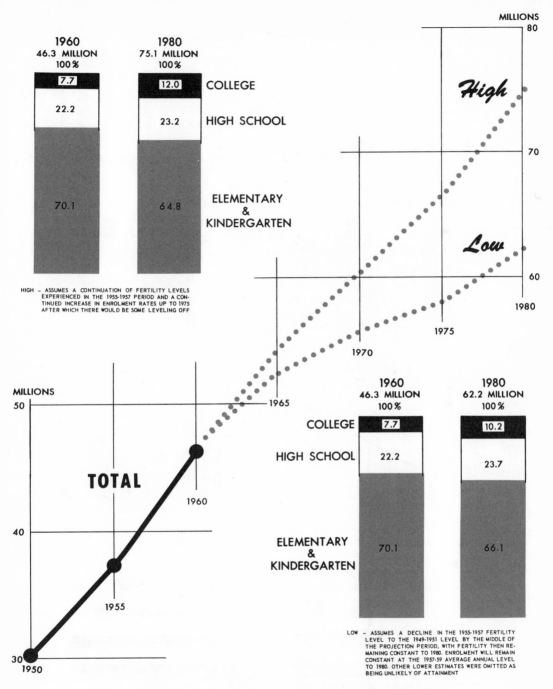

FIG. 3.2(a) Projected school enrollments, 1965–1980. Data refer to the civilian noninstitutional population five to 34 years old. *Copyrighted; reproduced with permission of the National Industrial Conference Board, 845 Third Avenue, New York, N.Y. 10022.*

WHICH CHART TO USE?
THE DATA

Motor Buses in Operation in United States

Year	Intercity Buses	Local Buses[1]	Charter and Sightseeing	School Buses[2]	Total Buses
1941	18,420	37,855	2,383	87,400	146,058
1942	22,710	44,101	2,400	79,000	148,211
1943	28,504	45,610	2,000	77,850	153,964
1944	28,000	48,525	3,300	75,500	155,325
1945	29,000	45,955	1,033	83,228	159,216
1946	30,260	47,760	1,475	82,500	161,995
1947	31,900	54,100	3,000	85,900	174,900
1948	31,775	57,175	3,200	90,400	182,550
1949	30,200	57,800	3,500	97,600	189,100

[1]Omits trolley buses.   [2]Exclusive of common carrier buses doing schoolwork.
SOURCE: "Bus Transportation" as of December 31st.

THE CURVE CHART

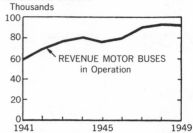

THE GROUPED COLUMN

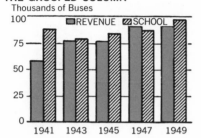

THE BAR CHART

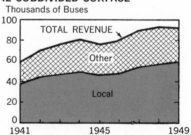

THE CUMULATIVE CURVE

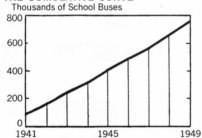

THE SUBDIVIDED SURFACE

THE SLIDING BAR

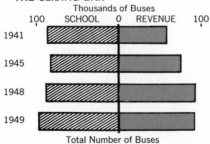

THE PICTOGRAM

FIG. 3.2(b)   The same data plotted in 15 different ways. *From Mary E. Spear, Charting Statistics (New York: McGraw-Hill Book Company, 1952), endpapers, by permission of the publisher. © 1952 McGraw-Hill Book Company.*

THE INDEX CHART

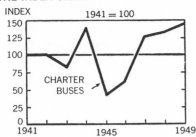

INDEX 1941 = 100

THE LOGARITHMIC CHART

Thousands of Buses

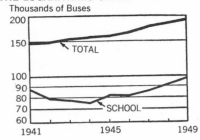

THE SUBDIVIDED COLUMN

Thousands of Buses

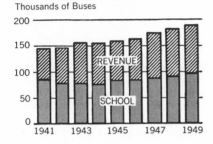

THE PAIRED BAR

Thousands of Buses   Percent School Buses

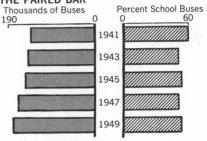

THE BAR and SYMBOL

Thousands of Buses

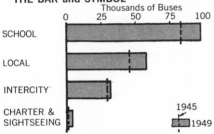

THE COLUMN and CURVE

Thousands of Buses

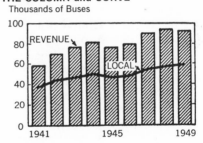

THE PICTORIAL SURFACE

THOUSANDS OF INTERCITY BUSES

THE PIE CHART

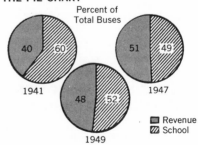

Percent of Total Buses

Revenue
School

41

It is sometimes said that the facts speak for themselves. In reality, statistics often stand speechless and silent, tables are sometimes tongue-tied, and only the graph cries aloud its message. Ordinary numerical data are quite abstract; they convey their meaning vaguely and with effort to the average mind. The picture or graph is a more concrete representation.

A wide variety of graphs and charts are shown in Fig. 3.2(a) and (b). In Fig. 3.2(b) basic information concerning motor buses in operation in the United States is given first in tabular form, followed by 15 different black and white graphs. Each graph conveys a unique point in an impressive manner.

Spear's description of the function of graphs is a fitting conclusion to this introduction:

> In the present day, when visual education in all aspects has become, not only an aid to, but also a vital basis of learning, our attention is called more than ever before to the almost limitless possibilities in this field. The eye absorbs written statistics, but only slowly does the brain receive the message hidden behind written words and numbers. The correct graph, however, reveals that message briefly and simply. Its purposes, which follow, are clear from its context:
>
> **1.** Better comprehension of data than is possible with textual matter alone
> **2.** More penetrating analysis of subject than is possible in written text
> **3.** A check of accuracy
>
> This triple purpose of the chart can be carried out through careful planning and familiarity with the functions of all types of graphs and media. The following six steps are fundamental to the development of graphic presentation that will describe statistical data with clarity and dramatic impact:
>
> **1.** Determine the significant message in the data.
> **2.** Be familiar with all types of charts and make the correct selection.
> **3.** Meet the audience on its own level; know and use all appropriate visual aids.
> **4.** Give detailed and intelligible instructions to the drafting room.
> **5.** Know the equipment and skills of the drafting room.
> **6.** Recognize effective results.*

3.5
REPRESENTING A FREQUENCY
DISTRIBUTION GRAPHICALLY

The ordinary frequency distribution does not give a very clear picture of the situation. There are three common methods of representing a distri-

---

* From Mary E. Spear, *Charting Statistics* (New York: McGraw-Hill Book Company, 1952), pp. 3–4, by permission of the publishers. © 1952 by the McGraw-Hill Book Company.

bution of scores graphically: the histogram or column diagram, the frequency polygon, and the smooth curve.

The Histogram or Column Diagram

The histogram is a series of columns, each having as its base one class interval and as its height the number of cases, or frequency, in that class.   Figure 3.3

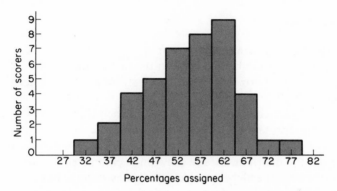

FIG. 3.3   A histogram, or column diagram, representing the percentage values assigned to an arithmetic paper by 42 scorers.

represents a histogram showing the distribution of percentage values assigned to an arithmetic paper by 42 scorers. Since the greatest frequency is 9, in the 59.5–64.5 class, it is not necessary to extend the vertical or frequency scale at the left above 9. And since the scores range from the 29.5–34.5 class to the 74.5–79.5 class, it is necessary to represent the horizontal scale only through that distance. For clarity, however, it is customary to extend

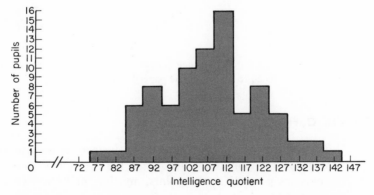

FIG. 3.4   A histogram, or column diagram, representing the distribution of the 83 IQ's in a small junior high school.

the scale one class interval above and below that range. In order to avoid having the figure be too flat or too steep, it is usually well to arrange the scales so that the width of the histogram itself is about one and two-thirds times its height—that is, the ratio of height to width should be approximately 3:5. A column is centered around the midpoint of the score-class interval. In actual practice it is customary to represent the histogram in outline form, rather than to show the full length of the columns. Figure 3.4 illustrates the shaded outline form of the histogram.

The Frequency Polygon

The process of constructing a frequency polygon is very much like that of constructing the histogram. In the histogram, the top of each column is indicated by a horizontal line, the length of one class interval, placed at the proper height to represent the frequency in that class. But in the polygon a point is located above the *midpoint* of each class interval and at the proper height to represent the frequency in that class. These points are then joined by straight lines. As the frequency is zero at the classes above and below those in the distribution, the polygon is completed by connecting the points that represent the highest and lowest classes with the base line at the midpoints of the class intervals next above and below. Figure 3.5 shows a polygon for the same data represented by a histogram in Fig. 3.4.

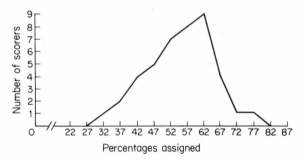

FIG. 3.5   A frequency polygon representing the percentage values assigned to an arithmetic paper by 42 scorers.

The Smooth Curve

Sometimes a smooth curve is drawn instead of a histogram or frequency polygon. The only difference is that for the former a smooth line is drawn as close as possible to the points, and for the latter two figures an angular or jagged line is used.

A smooth curve widely used in representing test scores is the *percentile curve* or *ogive*. Figure 3.6 shows a percentile curve used to represent the percentage data already used to illustrate the histogram and the polygon. The points that determine the percentile curve are located on the horizontal line at the upper limit of each class, at the position that indicates on the horizontal scale the percentage of scores up to and including that class. Notice, also, that two columns have been added to the ordinary frequency table. The cumulative frequency column indicates the number of scores up to and including each class. For example, there is one score in the 30–34 class, and there are two in the 35–39 class, making a cumulative frequency of 3 in the two lowest classes. The cumulative percent column shows what percentage each of these cumulative frequencies is of the total. In the

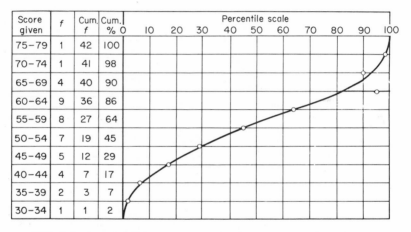

Score given	f	Cum. f	Cum. %	Percentile scale
75–79	1	42	100	
70–74	1	41	98	
65–69	4	40	90	
60–64	9	36	86	
55–59	8	27	64	
50–54	7	19	45	
45–49	5	12	29	
40–44	4	7	17	
35–39	2	3	7	
30–34	1	1	2	

FIG. 3.6   A percentile curve representing the percentage values assigned to an arithmetic paper by 42 scorers.

illustration, the total, *n*, is 42. The first entry in this column is, of course, 100; the second is 98, because 41 is 98% of 42; the third is 95, because 40 is 95% of 42; and so on for the others. Each value in the cumulative percent column is represented as a point on the upper limit of that class interval (the horizontal line separating that class from the class above it), since it includes the percentage of scores up through that class. These points determine the curve. As a rule, especially in small groups where irregularities are most likely to occur, it is best to miss some of the points in order to obtain a smooth and regular curve; but care should be taken in order to leave about as many points on one side of the line as on the other. In this way the ogive will fit the trend of the points as closely as possible.

IQ	f	Tally
145–149	1	X
140–144	2	XX
135–139	2	XX
130–134	5	XXXXX
125–129	8	XXXXXXXX
120–124	5	XXXXX
115–119	16	XXXXXXXXXXXXXXXX
110–114	12	XXXXXXXXXXXX
105–109	10	XXXXXXXXXX
100–104	8	XXXXXXXX
95–99	6	XXXXXX
90–94	8	XXXXXXXX
85–89	6	XXXXXX
80–84	1	X
75–79	1	X
	91	

FIG. 3.7 Bar graph made on a type-writer, showing the distribution of 91 IQ's in a junior high school.

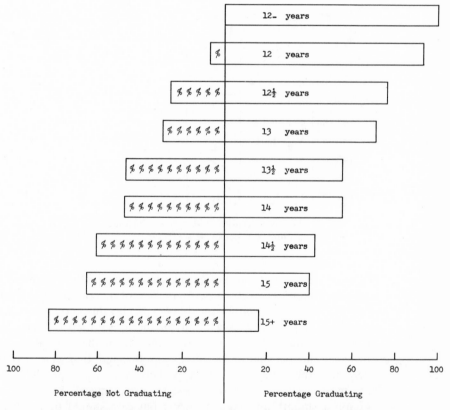

FIG. 3.8 Bar graph made on a typewriter, showing the percentage of pupils of each age group who were graduated from high school and the percentage who entered high school at that age but did not graduate.

Typewriter Graphs

A satisfactory bar graph can be made on the typewriter. Figures 3.7, 3.8, and 3.9 illustrate this type of graph. Other graphs, such as the circle or pie graph, and various picture graphs, or pictographs, are occasionally used in educational measurement; these are discussed especially by Spear (1952).

Score	Frequency for Grade			Bar Graph for School Grade		
	7	8	9	Seventh	Eighth	Ninth
200–219			3			999
180–199	1	4	5	7	8888	99999
160–179	3	3	7	777	888	9999999
140–159	4	9	7	7777	888888888	9999999
120–139	11	7	11	77777777777	8888888	99999999999
100–119	4	7	2	7777	8888888	99
80– 99	4	2	1	7777	88	9
60– 79	1	3		7	888	
40– 59		1			8	
20– 39		1			8	

FIG. 3.9 Graph made on a typewriter, showing the overlapping of grades seven, eight, and nine in reading comprehension.

Which Graph is Best?

As we might expect, no one type of graph is equally good for all purposes. The histogram is the easiest of all to understand and therefore is usually best if no more than one distribution is being represented. But if two or more distributions are to be compared, frequency polygons (or relative frequency polygons) are usually better, since so many lines coincide when histograms are superimposed that the picture is likely to be confusing. The percentile curves have many advantages not possessed by other curves. An important one is that from them it is possible to estimate with a high degree of accuracy the quartiles, medians, and other similar points. As we will see in the next section, by means of percentile curves several groups can be presented, for convenient comparison, on a single graph. The main value of bar graphs, circle graphs, and picture graphs lies probably in school publicity and in the motivation of learning. "A successful graph," as the prominent educator Douglas Scates pointed out long ago, "depends far more on careful thought and judgment than on techniques" (Scates, 1942).

Representing Two or More
Distributions Graphically

It is often desirable to compare two or more distributions. For example, school administrators may wish to compare the entire distribution of verbal ability test scores of the pupils in one school with that of pupils in another school. Also, the overlapping of scores among the various grades within a single building is a striking way to present the need for individualized instruction and varied materials within the same grade.

Representing Entire Distributions

When it is important to compare two or more entire distributions, as would be the case in a study of the status of a school or school system, the choice will usually be between the frequency polygon and the percentile curve. We have already pointed out the difficulty of superimposing two or more histograms. A series of polygons may be drawn on the same sheet one above the other, or alongside each other. In Fig. 3.9, a method of showing overlapping by using bar graphs made on the typewriter is illustrated. (Perhaps the scores there are grouped too coarsely. According to the conventional rule it would be better to have 12 to 15 score classes, instead of the 7, 9, and 7 actually used in Fig. 3.9.)

The Use of Polygons

The distinct advantage of polygons over histograms for representing a series of distributions is that polygons can be superimposed on each other with less crossing of lines. In this form, comparisons among distributions are more easily made. Figure 3.10 illustrates this possibility with the distribution of reading comprehension scores for the 100 seventh, 100 eighth, and 100 ninth graders of a certain school. (For some purposes it could be quite misleading to graph overlapping frequency polygons for different sizes of groups. In these instances, frequencies should be converted to relative frequencies— proportions—before graphing.) The great overlapping in reading ability of the three grades stands out clearly. But even with only three distributions, the lines cross and recross so many times that it becomes difficult to make any accurate comparison of one grade with another. More than three classes can hardly be represented in the same graph by frequency polygons without considerable confusion.

The Use of Percentile Curves

For the graphic comparison of two or more distributions the percentile curve has some distinct advantages. Since the frequencies are reduced to

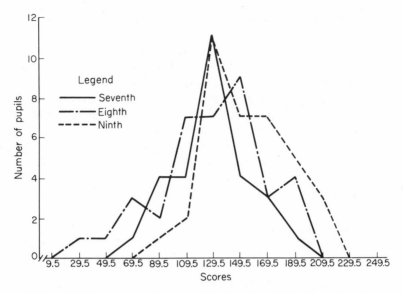

FIG. 3.10　Frequency polygons representing the distribution of reading comprehension scores on a reading test for the seventh, eighth, and ninth grades of a certain school (100 students in each grade).

Test score	Seventh			Eighth			Ninth			Percentile scale
	f	Cum. f	Cum. %	f	Cum. f	Cum. %	f	Cum. f	Cum. %	0　10 20 30 40 50 60 70 80 90 100
200							3	36	100	
180	1	28	100	4	37	100	5	33	92	
160	3	27	96	3	33	89	7	28	78	
140	4	24	86	9	30	81	7	21	59	
120	11	20	71	7	21	57	11	14	39	
100	4	9	32	7	14	38	2	3	8	
80	4	5	18	2	7	19	1	1	3	
60	1	1	4	3	5	14				
40				1	2	5				
20				1	1	3				
										Q_1　　Q_2　　Q_3

FIG. 3.11　Comprehension scores on a reading test for the seventh, eighth, and ninth grades.

percents, it is possible to compare groups of unequal size.　Another important advantage is that several distributions can be represented in a single graph without difficulty or confusion.　Figure 3.11 shows the distribution of reading comprehension scores, for the same grades as in Figs. 3.9 and 3.10, in the form of percentile curves.

From these percentile curves we can observe several relationships that were not apparent in the polygons. It is clear that although the seventh and eighth grades have almost exactly the same average scores, the eighth grade has greater variability. This is evident since the upper half of the eighth grade exceeds the upper half of the seventh grade, while the lower half of the eighth grade falls behind the lower half of the seventh.

Furthermore, although the ninth grade runs consistently above the other two grades, about 15 percent of the ninth-grade pupils fall below the median of the seventh and eighth grades.

3.6
MISLEADING GRAPHS

So far in this chapter we have stressed correct procedures in the construction of graphs and have presented many examples of good graphs. The unwary researcher or the propagandist can construct graphs which seriously mislead the reader, however. Perhaps the best protection against committing these errors is to study several examples of poor graphs.

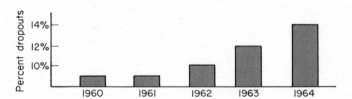

FIG. 3.12   Percent of drop-outs at the end of grade 11 for the years 1960–1964.

Figure 3.12 is a graph of the percent of high school juniors dropping out of school in a particular district at year's end for the period 1960 through 1964. The percent of drop-outs shows a steady rise from 9% in 1960 to 14% in 1964, but has not even doubled over the five-year span. However, because the vertical scale of the graph does not start at 0%, as it should, the impression is given that the percent of drop-outs is six times as great in 1964 as it was in 1960. The true ratios of percents of drop-outs by years are perceived when the percent drop-outs scale extends from 0% at its base up to 14%.

In Fig. 3.13, the school bonds for three mythical school districts are graphed. The *diameter* of each circle represents the amount of the bond in a district.

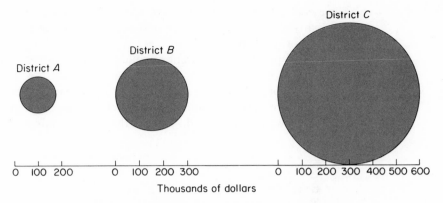

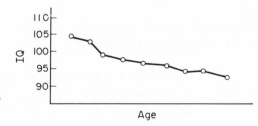

FIG. 3.13   School bonds for districts *A*, *B*, and *C*.

The school bond for district *B* is twice that for district *A*, as can be seen by comparing the diameters of the two circles. However, one's eye is drawn to the *areas* of the circles in Fig. 3.13. Although the diameter of circle *B* is *twice* the diameter of circle *A*, the area of *B* is *four times* as great as the area of circle *A*. The circle for district *C* has 16 times the area of the circle for district *A*, although it is intended to depict a school bond which is only four times as great. Geometric figures can be misleading when used to depict magnitudes, especially when their areas are measured by squares or higher powers of the magnitude being portrayed.

An especially serious error in the presentation of figures and graphs is improper description of the axes of a graph or even total failure to describe them. Although unlabeled axes are rare in published works, they appear all too frequently in preliminary drafts of unpublished research reports. It is to the credit of editors that such graphs are seldom tolerated for any length of time or published. Much time can be saved and communication can be improved if you never construct a graph without a complete and comprehensible description of the axes. Notice how the graph in Fig. 3.14 is unintelligible without calibration of the horizontal axis. One cannot even be sure that "age" increases from left to right on the horizontal scale.

FIG. 3.14   Average IQ (Stanford-Binet, Form LM) in a sample of 1000 persons by age.

The meaning that might attach to the descending curve in Fig. 3.14 would change greatly if the youngest and oldest chronological ages were 6 and 60 years instead of 4 and 6, say.

Figure 3.15 presents the percent of children in a group of 3-, 4-, 5-, and 6-year-olds who could correctly answer the question, "Who discovered America?" Figure 3.15 may appear to be clear and correct; however, close inspection reveals an anomalous occurrence. A greater percentage of 5-year-olds knew who discovered America than 6-year-olds. This is indeed

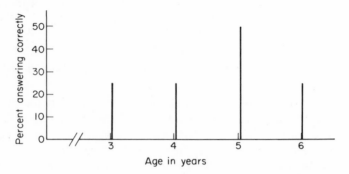

FIG. 3.15   Percent of children answering correctly for four different ages.

unexpected. However, one important piece of information is missing from the graph: the number of cases on which the percents are based. If you are told that the percents for each age in Fig. 3.15 are based on four children, then you see that two 5-year-olds and one 6-year-old knew the answer. We do not expect this result to be stable, since the percents are computed on so few cases. Large groups of 5- and 6-year-olds would probably yield a greater percent of correct answers among 6-year-olds than among those age 5. Figure 3.15 fails because it does not give the number of cases for each age upon which the percents are based.

Space does not permit our listing more hazards in the construction of graphs and figures. You will find Darrell Huff's (1954) treatment of this subject in *How to Lie with Statistics* entertaining, informative, and well worth your attention.

3.7
GENERAL SUGGESTIONS FOR CONSTRUCTING GRAPHS

A wide diversity of practice will be found in the construction of graphs as used in psychology and education. The title is sometimes placed above the graph, though usually it is placed below. In nearly all books and periodicals the graph title is placed below, but in unpublished charts such as wall charts the title is often more effective when lettered above. The figures are numbered consecutively with Arabic numerals placed at the beginning of the title. Sometimes the title is written in capital letters, as often done in tables; sometimes only the initial letters of all important words are capitals. A third method capitalizes only the first word in the title, unless there are proper names, in which case the usual rules for capitalization apply. The second of these three methods is perhaps most common.

Suggested Standards

In 1915 a committee of representatives of groups interested in graphical methods prepared a report* recommending standards for constructing graphs. The problems of graphic representation have changed little through the years, and this report still covers most of the points required for the proper representation of data. The following rules are taken from it:

1. The general arrangement of a diagram should proceed from left to right.
2. Where possible represent quantities by linear magnitudes, as areas or volumes are more likely to be misinterpreted.
3. For a curve, the vertical scale, whenever practicable, should be so selected that the zero line will appear on the diagram.
4. If the zero line of the vertical scale will not normally appear on the curve diagram, the zero line should be shown by the use of a horizontal break in the diagram.
5. The zero lines of the scales for a curve should be sharply distinguished from the other coordinate lines.
6. For curves having a scale representing percentages, it is usually desirable to emphasize in some distinctive way the 100% line or other line used as a basis of comparison.
7. When the scale of a diagram refers to dates, and the period represented is not a complete unit, it is better not to emphasize the first and last ordinates, since such a diagram does not represent the beginning or end of time.
8. When curves are drawn on logarithmic coordinates, the limiting lines of the diagram should each be at some power of ten on the logarithmic scales.

* W. C. Brinton, Chairman, Preliminary Report. Joint Committee on Standards of Graphic Representation, *Quarterly Publications of the American Statistical Association*, 14 (1915), 790–97.

9. It is advisable not to show any more coordinate lines than necessary to guide the eye in reading the diagram.

10. The curve lines of a diagram should be sharply distinguished from the ruling.

11. In curves representing a series of observations, it is advisable, whenever possible, to indicate clearly on the diagram all the curves representing the separate observations.

12. The horizontal scale for curves should usually read from left to right and the vertical scale from bottom to top.

13. Figures for the scales of a diagram should be placed at the left and at the bottom or along the respective axes.

14. It is often desirable to include in the diagram the numerical data or formulae represented.

15. If numerical data are not included in the diagram, it is desirable to give the data in tabular form accompanying the diagram.

16. All lettering and all figures on a diagram should be placed so as to be easily read from the base as the bottom, or from the right-hand edge of the diagram as the bottom.

17. The title of a diagram should be made as clear and complete as possible. Subtitles or descriptions should be added if necessary to insure clearness.

Also see Arkin and Colton (1936), Walker and Durost (1936), and Kelley (1947) for more on graphing and tabulating data.

PROBLEMS AND EXERCISES

1. This problem is an exercise in constructing a grouped frequency distribution. The following data are Stanford-Binet intelligence test scores for 75 adults:

141	104	101	130	148
92	87	115	91	96
100	133	124	92	123
132	118	98	101	107
97	124	118	146	107
110	111	138	121	129
106	135	97	108	108
107	110	101	129	105
105	110	116	113	123
83	127	112	114	105
127	114	113	106	139
95	105	95	105	106
109	102	102	102	89
108	92	131	86	134
104	94	121	107	103

a. Determine the inclusive range of the above set of scores.
b. Divide the inclusive range [found in (a)] by 12 and by 15, separately.
c. Choose the class size to be the whole number which lies between the two quotients found in (b) above.
d. Using the class size found in (c) above, construct a grouped frequency for the 75 scores:

Interval	Score interval	Tally	Frequency	Cumulative freq.
14	145–149			75
13				
12				
11				
10				
9				
8				
7				
6				
5				
4				
3				
2				
1	80–84			

$$n = \overline{75}$$

2. Find the 50th percentile, P_{50}, for the 75 intelligence-test scores from the grouped frequency distribution constructed in Prob. 1.

3. Complete the frequency polygon started below for the grouped frequency distribution in Prob. 1. Be sure to label the horizontal axis with the midpoints of the 14 score intervals.

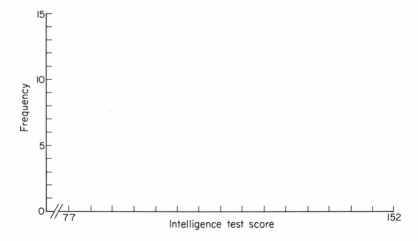

4. Plot two *relative frequency* polygons on the same graph from the following grouped frequency distributions of Scholastic Aptitude Test Verbal scores for the 903 men and the 547 women in the freshman class of a large Eastern university:

SAT-V score interval	Men Frequency	Men Relative frequency	Women Frequency	Women Relative frequency
750–799	1	.001	4	.007
700–749	27	.030	28	.051
650–699	63	.070	56	.102
600–649	138	.153	85	.155
550–599	174	.193	117	.214
500–549	202	.226	128	.234
450–499	171	.189	86	.157
400–449	96	.106	32	.059
350–399	25	.028	9	.016
300–349	4	.004	1	.002
250–299	1	.001	1	.002
200–249	1	.001	0	.000
	$n_m = 903$	1.00	$n_w = 547$	1.00

4

MEASURES
OF
CENTRAL TENDENCY

4.1
INTRODUCTION

We saw in Chapter 3 how the properties of a collection of scores can be depicted graphically or in tabular form. Frequently a graph or table of data tells us more than we want or need to know, and the message it conveys may be time-consuming to communicate. Usually we single out for description just two or three properties of a set of scores. These properties (e.g., the typical "size" of the scores and their spread) may be describable by indexes known as *summary statistics*. In this chapter we shall study summary statistics which describe the typical "size" of a set of scores.

The descriptive indexes that will be developed in this chapter would be used to answer a question like "How tall is the typical male graduate student in this university?" If the scores in a set are thought of as positioned along a number line, the property of the set that we now want to describe is where along that line the scores tend to lie. Are they bunched around a score of 71, or do they center about a score of 67? Different measures of the *central tendency* of a set of scores imply different definitions of a "central score." There are only a few summary measures of central tendency in common use, and in the following sections we shall study them in detail.

4.2
THE MODE

The most easily obtained measure of central tendency is the *mode*. The *mode* is the score in a set of scores that occurs most frequently. Not every set of scores has a single mode by a strict interpretation of this definition, so the working definition of the mode contains some qualifications and conventions that will be discussed after an illustration.

In the set of scores (2, 6, 6, 8, 9, 9, 9, 10) the mode is 9 because it occurs more often than any other score. Note that the mode is the most frequent *score* (9 in this example) and not the frequency of that score (3 in this example).

4.3
CONVENTIONAL USE OF
THE MODE

1. When all of the scores in a group occur with the same frequency, it is customary to say that the group of scores has *no mode*. Thus there is no mode in the group (0.5, 0.5, 1.6, 1.6, 3.9, 3.9).

2. When two adjacent scores have the same frequency and this common frequency is greater than that for any other score, the mode is the average of the two adjacent scores. Thus, the mode of the group of scores (0, 1, 1, 2, 2, 2, 3, 3, 3, 4) is 2.5.

3. If in a group of scores two nonadjacent scores have the same frequency and this common frequency is greater than that for any other score, *two modes* exist. In the group of scores (10, 11, 11, 11, 12, 13, 14, 14, 14, 17), both 11 and 14 are modes; the group of scores is said to be *bimodal*. Large sets of scores are often referred to as bimodal when they present a frequency polygon that looks like a Bactrian (two-humped) camel's back even though the frequencies at the two peaks are not strictly equal. This slight twisting of the definition is allowed because the term *bimodal* is so convenient and nicely descriptive. A convenient distinction can be made be-

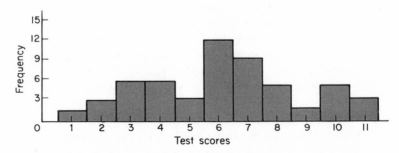

FIG. 4.1   A frequency distribution of test scores with a major mode at 6 and minor modes at 3.5 and 10.

tween *major* and *minor modes*. In a group of scores the major mode is the single score which satisfies the definition of the mode. However, several minor modes might exist at points throughout the group of scores. These minor modes are essentially local peaks on the frequency distribution. For example, in Fig. 4.1 the major mode is at 6 and minor modes exist at 3.5 and 10.

4.4
THE MEDIAN

You have already encountered the *median* (though it wasn't called by that name) and learned how to find it in Sec. 3.2 on quantiles.

Definition: The *median*, *Md*, is the 50th percentile in a group of scores. It is the score that divides the ranked scores into halves, such that half of the scores are larger than the median, and the other half are smaller.

4.5
CALCULATION OF THE
MEDIAN

1. If the data are an odd number of untied scores, e.g., 11, 13, 18, 19, 20, the median is the middle score when they are ranked; $Md = 18$.

2. If the data are an even number of untied scores, e.g., 4, 9, 13, 14, the median is the point halfway between the two central values when the scores are ranked: $Md = (9 + 13)/2 = 11$.

3. If tied scores occur in the data, particularly at or near the median, a frequency tabulation of the scores will probably be necessary. Interpolation within a score class will often be necessary in such instances. For example, suppose that 36 scores ranging from 7.0 to 10.5 have the following ungrouped frequency distribution:

Score	Frequency	Cumulative frequency
10.5	2	36
10.0	3	34
9.5	2	31
9.0	6	29
8.5	10 = 5 + 5	23
8.0	8⎫	13
7.5	4⎬13	5
7.0	1⎭	1
	$n = \overline{36}$	

The median score will be the $n/2 = 18$th score from the bottom. We see, however, that the 18th score lies in the interval from 8.25 to 8.75. Since 13 scores have been accumulated up to the lower limit of this interval, we wish to move through $18 - 13 = 5$ frequencies in the interval. Since there are a total of 10 frequencies in the interval, the median will be taken to be the point half of the way through the interval $(.50 = 5/10)$. The interval extends from 8.25 to 8.75, a width of one-half unit; half this distance is one-fourth unit. Hence, the median is the value $8.25 + 0.25 = 8.50$.

You may have recognized that the above process is nothing but a special case of the method of determining percentiles in a grouped frequency distribution which was presented in Sec. 3.2. If we call the score interval which contains the $n/2$nd largest score when they are ordered by size the *median interval*, then the following formula will yield the median:

$$Md = \left(\begin{array}{c} \text{Lower real} \\ \text{limit of} \\ \text{median interval} \end{array}\right) + \left(\begin{array}{c} \text{width of} \\ \text{median} \\ \text{interval} \end{array}\right) \left[\frac{(n/2) - \left(\begin{array}{c} \text{Cumulative} \\ \text{frequency } up \\ to \text{ the} \\ \text{median interval} \end{array}\right)}{\begin{array}{c} \text{frequency in} \\ \text{median interval} \end{array}}\right].$$

$$(4.1)$$

The above formula will produce the median for any grouped frequency distribution as well as for ungrouped distributions.

4.6
THE MEAN

We have n individuals whom we measure on some characteristic and obtain the scores $X_1, X_2, \ldots, X_n$. Two measures of central tendency have already been defined for a set of n scores, namely the mode (the most frequent score) and the median (the score that divides the set of scores into two equally frequent halves). We now define a third measure of central tendency, the *sample mean* (variously called "the mean," and "the arithmetic mean").

Definition: The mean of a set of n scores is denoted by $\bar{X}_.$ and is defined as

$$\bar{X}_. = \frac{(X_1 + X_2 + \ldots + X_n)}{n}.$$

As pointed out earlier, we replace the cumbersome sum $X_1 + X_2 + \ldots + X_n$ by the economical $\sum_{i=1}^{n} X_i$. With this notation, the mean has the formula

$$\bar{X}_. = \frac{1}{n}\sum_{i=1}^{n} X_i.$$

$$(4.2)$$

The mean is no more than the familiar "average." People often use the word "average" for any one of the three above-mentioned "measures of central tendency." The name "mean," being less ambiguous, is preferred.

You may begin to question this proliferation of measures of central tendency, especially when someone is holding you responsible for learning them. However, each measure has characteristics that make it uniquely valuable.

The mode is easiest to calculate—it can be found literally at a glance. Moreover, in very large groups of scores it is a fairly stable measure of the center of the distribution. In many distributions of large numbers of measures taken in educational and psychological research, the mode is close to two other measures of central tendency, the median and the mean.

The median stands between the mode and the mean in computational effort, if the calculation is done by hand. This measure is obtained almost entirely by counting and can be easily calculated once the data have been arranged in numerical order. For a large number of scores, the data can first be arranged in a grouped frequency distribution (which is considerably easier than ranking the data), and then the median can be easily obtained. For purely descriptive purposes, classroom teachers and others working with small samples will find that percentile measures of central tendency and variability will serve them well enough.

The mean of a set of data involves the most arithmetic computation. The value of the mean is affected by the individual values of all of the scores in the set of data. The median and mode may not be affected by all of the values. For example, observe what happens to the values of the mean, median, and mode when the largest score in the following set is doubled:

	Mean	*Median*	*Mode*
Set 1: 1, 3, 3, 5, 6, 7, 8	$\frac{33}{7}$	5	3
Set 2: 1, 3, 3, 5, 6, 7, 16	$\frac{41}{7}$	5	3

The value of the mean is especially affected by what might be called "outliers," i.e., scores which lie far from the center of the group of scores. Whether this is an advantage depends upon the particular questions you are asking of the data.

4.7
CALCULATION OF THE MEAN

The definition of the mean is so well known and the calculations by which it is found are so simple that you may wonder why its calculation deserves special attention. Part of the reason is that, traditionally, statistical calculations were performed by hand without the aid of machines. Under these circumstances, various methods of simplifying the operations in finding $\bar{X}$.

were necessary, or at least helpful. These procedures, known as "coding techniques," have outlived their usefulness and survive in some modern texts as vestiges of the early history of statistics. In short, the "coding techniques" require more effort to learn than they are worth and serve no useful function in an age of mechanical computation.

Quite simply, the mean is found by summing all scores and dividing by the number of scores summed. This process can be carried out easily on any adding machine or desk calculator. A slight simplification of the process can be achieved when some scores occur several times. Consider the group of scores in the first column in Table 4.1.

TABLE 4.1   ILLUSTRATION OF THE CALCULATION OF THE MEAN WHEN SOME SCORES OCCUR SEVERAL TIMES

Original scores	Score (X_i)	Frequency count f_i	$X_i f_i$	Final calculations
2 6 10	2	1	2	
3 6 10	3	2	6	$\bar{X}_. = \dfrac{\sum_{i=1}^{10} X_i f_i}{n}$
3 6 11	5	4	20	
5 8 11	6	3	18	
5 8 11	8	2	16	$= \dfrac{166}{21} = 7.90,$
5 9 15	9	2	18	
	10	2	20	where $i = 1, 2, \ldots, 10$
5 9 18	11	3	33	*different* scores.
	15	1	15	
	18	1	18	
	$n = \sum_{i=1}^{10} f_i = 21$		$\sum X_i f_i = 166$	

A group of 21 scores, only 10 of them different, is recorded in the first column. In the second column, each unique score (X_i) and the number of times it occurs in the group (f_i) are recorded in the third column. You will recall that multiplication is repeated addition; for example, $2 + 2 + 2 = 3 \cdot 2$. Thus in finding the sum of the original scores one would form $2 + 3 + 3 + 5 + 5 + 5 + 5 + \ldots + 18$, which is the same as $2 + (2 \cdot 3) + (4 \cdot 5) + \ldots + 18$. Consequently, the sum of all the scores in a group is found by multiplying each score X_i by its frequency f_i to form $X_i f_i$, and then obtaining the sum of the resulting products $(\Sigma\, X_i f_i)$. The sum of the ten $X_i f_i$'s in Table 4.1 is 166; you may wish to add all 21 scores in the first column of the table to assure yourself that their sum is 166. The final step in obtaining $\bar{X}$ is to divide $\Sigma\, X_i f_i$ by n (in Table 4.1, $166/21 = 7.90$).

The principle which has just been illustrated is sometimes applied to approximate the mean of a collection of scores when only their grouped frequency distribution is available. Suppose that all that is known about a group of scores is that they have the group frequency distribution shown in the left portion of Table 4.2.

TABLE 4.2   ILLUSTRATION OF CALCULATION OF THE MEAN FROM A GROUPED
FREQUENCY DISTRIBUTION

Score interval	f_i	Midpoint of score interval	$f_i \cdot midpoint$
70–74	1	72	72
65–69	0	67	0
60–64	3	62	186
55–59	2	57	114
50–54	6	52	312
45–49	10	47	470
40–44	8	42	336
35–39	8	37	296
30–34	4	32	128
25–29	2	27	54
20–24	4	22	88
15–19	1	17	17
10–14	1	12	12
	$n = \sum_{i=1}^{13} f_i = 50$		$\sum f_i (midpoint) = 2085$

Lacking better information and for the sake of simplicity, we assume that the scores in any score interval are evenly distributed along the interval. This assumption is usually false and for this reason the value we shall calculate is only an approximation (a rather close one) to the mean of the ungrouped data. [The degree of error introduced into the calculation of many statistics by this assumption was the subject of some theoretical work by Sheppard (e.g., see Keeping, 1962, p. 107) to which you may wish to refer at some point later in your statistical training.] Under the assumption, the sum of the f_i scores in any score interval equals the product of f_i and the midpoint of the interval. These products appear as the last column in Table 4.2. The grand sum of all of the scores in the group is approximately equal to the sum of these products. Thus, the mean of the ungrouped scores is approximately equal to this grand sum divided by n, i.e.,

$$\bar{X}_. \cong \frac{\Sigma f_i(\text{midpoint})}{n}, \tag{4.3}$$

and the summation extends over all of the score intervals.

For Table 4.2, the following approximation to the mean of the scores is obtained:

$$\bar{X}_. \cong \frac{2085}{50} = 41.70.$$

4.8
PROPERTIES OF THE MEAN

We shall now investigate a few of the interesting properties of the mean. Recall that

$$\bar{X}_. = \frac{1}{n}(X_1 + X_2 + \ldots + X_n) = \frac{1}{n}\sum_{i=1}^{n} X_i.$$

What if we subtracted $\bar{X}_.$ from the score X_1? The resulting difference is a *deviation score*—it can be either negative or positive. If we were to find the deviation score for each of the n scores in the set, *the sum of all n deviation scores would be exactly zero.* We illustrate this property:

Data: $(0, 1, 1, 3, 5)$; $n = 5$; $\bar{X}_. = 2$.

Score $-$ Mean $=$ Deviation score

0	$-$ 2	$=$	-2
1	$-$ 2	$=$	-1
1	$-$ 2	$=$	-1
3	$-$ 2	$=$	1
5	$-$ 2	$=$	3
			$\overline{0}$

The general proof of the fact that the sum of the deviation scores from their mean is zero is this:

$$\text{Sum of deviations} = \sum_{i=1}^{n}(X_i - \bar{X}_.) = \sum_{i=1}^{n} X - \sum_{i=1}^{n} \bar{X}_. = \sum_{i=1}^{n} X_i - n\bar{X}_.$$

$$= \sum_{i=1}^{n} X_i - n\frac{\sum_{i=1}^{n} X_i}{n} = \sum_{i=1}^{n} X_i - \sum_{i=1}^{n} X_i = 0.$$

What would happen to the value of the mean if some one number (a constant) were added to every score in a set of scores? Suppose we take the above five scores and add 3 to each score. We obtain the scores 3, 4, 4, 6, 8, whose mean is $(3 + 4 + 4 + 6 + 8)/5 = 25/5 = 5$. The mean is 3 units greater, and this is no coincidence.

If a constant, c, is added to each score in a group whose mean is $\bar{X}_.$, the resulting scores will have a mean equal to $\bar{X}_. + c$.
We shall prove that this statement is true:

$$\frac{1}{n}\sum_{i=1}^{n}(X_i + c) = \frac{1}{n}\sum_{i=1}^{n} X_i + \frac{1}{n}\sum_{i=1}^{n} c = \bar{X}_. + \left(\frac{1}{n}\right)nc = \bar{X}_. + c.$$

If each score in a set whose mean is $\bar{X}$. is multipled by a constant c, the mean of the resulting scores is $c\bar{X}$., because $\sum_{i=1}^{n} cX_i/n = c\sum_{i=1}^{n} X_i/n = c\bar{X}$.

A fourth property of the mean concerns the n deviation scores. *The sum of the squared deviations of scores from their arithmetic mean is less than the sum of the squared deviations around any point other than $\bar{X}$.*

That is, $(X_1 - \bar{X}.)^2 + (X_2 - \bar{X}.)^2 + \ldots + (X_n - \bar{X}.)^2$ is smaller in value than $(X_1 - b)^2 + (X_2 - b)^2 + \ldots + (X_n - b)^2$, where b is any number other than $\bar{X}$., the mean.*

For example, the sum of the squared deviations of 0, 1, 1, 3, 5 around 2, their mean, is $(0 - 2)^2 + (1 - 2)^2 + (1 - 2)^2 + (3 - 2)^2 + (5 - 2)^2 = (-2)^2 + (-1)^2 + (-1)^2 + (1)^2 + (3)^2 = 16$. The sum of the squared deviations of 0, 1, 1, 3, 5 around 1 is equal to 21, which is greater than 16.

4.9
MEAN, MEDIAN, AND MODE
OF COMBINED GROUPS

We might know the means, medians, and modes of three separate classrooms in a school and wish to find the same measures for all three classrooms combined. This will be a simple matter in the case of the mean, but for the median and mode it will be necessary to go back to the original data and make new calculations. The ease with which the mean of the combined groups is found reveals one of the advantages of definite summary statistics in terms of simple algebraic operations, such as adding and dividing, and having every score in a group exert an influence on the measure of central tendency. The median and mode are found by the operations of ranking and inspecting the data, respectively.

The means and frequencies for classrooms A, B, and C are as follows:

$$\bar{X}_A = 11.9 \qquad n_A = 24.$$

$$\bar{X}_B = 14.2 \qquad n_B = 30.$$

$$\bar{X}_C = 10.8 \qquad n_C = 28.$$

* Proof:

$$\sum_{i=1}^{n} [X_i - (\bar{X}. + c)]^2 = \sum_{i=1}^{n} [(X_i - \bar{X}.) - c]^2$$

$$= \sum_{i=1}^{n} (X_i - \bar{X}.)^2 - 2c\sum_{i=1}^{n} (X_i - \bar{X}.) + nc^2 = \sum_{i=1}^{n} (X_i - \bar{X}.)^2 + c^2,$$

because $\sum_{i=1}^{n} (X_i - \bar{X}.) = 0$; since $c_2 \geqq 0$,

$$\sum_{i=1}^{n} (X_i - \bar{X}.)^2 \leq \sum_{i=1}^{n} [X_i - (\bar{X}. + c)]^2 = 0.$$

The total n of all three classes combined is equal to $n = n_A + n_B + n_C = 82$. The mean of the combined groups is simply the sum of all 82 scores divided by 82. The sum of the 24 scores in class A is simply $n_A \cdot \bar{X}_A = 24(11.9) = 285.6$, because the mean is the sum of the scores divided by the number of scores, i.e., $\Sigma X = n\bar{X}$. Similarly for groups B and C, the sums of the scores are $30(14.2) = 426.0$ and $28(10.8) = 302.4$, respectively. $285.6 + 426.0 + 302.4 = 1014.0$. If we combine all 82 scores and sum them, we will also obtain 1014.0. Thus, the mean of all three classes combined is $(1014.0)/82 = 12.4$. Symbolically, the mean of the combined groups is:

$$\bar{X} = \frac{n_A \bar{X}_A + n_B \bar{X}_B + n_C \bar{X}_C}{n_A + n_B + n_C}. \tag{4.4}$$

You should now be able to write the formula for the mean of four combined groups when you are given only the four means and numbers of scores per group.

Notice that if each group is based on the same number of frequencies, $n_A = n_B = n_C = n$, then Eq. (4.4) becomes

$$\bar{X} = \frac{n(\bar{X}_A + \bar{X}_B + \bar{X}_C)}{3n} = \frac{\bar{X}_A + \bar{X}_B + \bar{X}_C}{3}. \tag{4.5}$$

This shows that if the three groups are the same size, the mean of the combined group is the same as the unweighted average of the three means. Of course, this is true for combining any number of means of equal-size groups.

Attempting to find the median or the mode of a combination of groups is a different matter, however. Suppose you know that group A has six scores and the mode is 17 and that group B also has six scores and a mode of 19. What is the mode of groups A and B combined? Would you guess that it is $18 = (17 + 19)/2$? If you did you might be wrong, because groups A and B might look like this:

A	B
15	15
15	15
17	16
17	19
17	19
18	19

When A and B are combined, the score of 15 occurs four times and is the mode of the combined groups. There was no way of knowing that this might happen when you were told only the modes for A and B individually. For both the mode and the median, you must have the original data in hand before you can find these measures of central tendency on combined groups.

4.10
INTERPRETATION OF MODE, MEDIAN, AND MEAN

Each of the measures of central tendency we have presented has an interesting interpretation in terms of errors which result when a single statistic takes the place of each score in the group. The sense in which the mode is the most representative score or the score which best "takes the place of all of the scores" is fairly obvious. If we were forced to select one score to stand for every score in a group, the selected score would equal the score for which it stands the greatest number of times if it (the selected score) is the mode of the group. Or similarly, if we were being paid one dollar for each time we correctly guessed which score in a group would be selected by chance, we should make most money in the long run by always guessing the mode.

One interpretation of the median of a group is not so obvious. Suppose that the scores in a group are placed along the real-number line. (1, 3, 6, 7, 8) appear on the line below:

The *Md* indicates the median of the group, 6. The distance between 6 and 1 is 5 units; between 6 and 3, 3 units; between 6 and 6, 0 units; between 6 and 7, 1 unit; between 6 and 8, 2 units. The sum of these distances, $5 + 3 + 0 + 1 + 2 = 11$, is smaller than would be the sum of the distances of the five points from any other point on the line. (Try it and see for yourself.) *The median of a group of scores is that point on the number line such that the sum of the absolute (i.e., unsigned) distances of all scores in the group to that point is smaller than the sum of distances to any other point.* If the median is taken in place of every score in the group, the *least error* results—provided "error" is defined as the sum of the absolute distances of each score to the score which will take its place.

The interpretation of the mean has already been noted. *The mean of a group of scores is that point on the number line such that the sum of the squared distances of all scores to that point is smaller than the sum of the squared distances to any other point.* If the mean is taken in place of every score in the group, the *least error* results—provided "error" is defined as the sum of the squared distances of each score to the score that will take its place.

* For a proof of this property of the median, see Horst (1931).

4.11
CHOICE OF A MEASURE OF
CENTRAL TENDENCY

Calculation of the mode, median, or mean is purely mechanical. Machines do it with far greater accuracy and speed than humans. However, the choice among these three measures and their interpretation may sometimes require judicious thought. Here are some considerations to keep in mind when you are faced with the choice:

1. In small groups the mode can be quite unstable. The mode of the group (1, 1, 1, 3, 5, 7, 7, 8) is 1; but if one of the 1's is changed to 0 and the other to 2, the mode becomes 7.

2. The median is *not* affected by the *size* of the "large" and "small" scores above or below it. For example, in a group of 50 scores the median will not change when the largest score is tripled.

3. The mean *is* influenced by the size of every score in the group. If any one score is changed by c units, $\bar{X}$ will be changed in the same direction by c/n units. For example, if 100 is added to the third largest score in a group of 10, the mean of the group is increased by 10 units.

4. Some groups of scores simply do not "tend centrally" in any meaningful way, and it is often misleading to calculate one measure of central tendency. This is particularly true of groups of scores that have more than one mode. For example, an acquaintance of the authors' who is a researcher on curriculum development maintains that he can build achievement tests composed of eight multiple-choice items that can separate a group of students into those who have acquired the concept of adding two-digit numbers and those who have not. The "haves" will make scores of 6, 7, and 8; the "have-nots" will make scores of 0, 1, and 2. Suppose a typical group of students produced scores yielding the histogram shown in Fig. 4.2.

The mean of the scores depicted in Fig. 4.2 is approximately 3.85, even though no person scored 3.85 or within two units of that

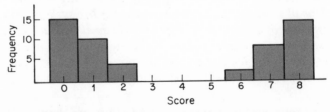

FIG. 4.2 Histogram of scores on a 10-item test of adding two-digit numbers ($n = 53$).

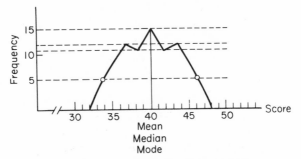

FIG. 4.3   A symmetrical, unimodal group of scores.

score. The median of the group is approximately 2.17, even though the score that is two ranks above the middle score is 6! Neither the mean nor the median depicts this group of scores well. Perhaps the best simple summary of the size of the scores is the statement that "the histogram is bimodal and U-shaped with one mode at 0 and the other at 8."

5. The central tendency of groups of scores which contain extreme values is probably best measured by the median if the scores are unimodal. As pointed out previously, each score in a group influences the mean. Thus, one extreme value can move the mean of the group far away from what would generally be regarded as the central region. For example, if nine persons have incomes ranging from $4500 to $5200, with an average of $4900, and the tenth person's income is $20,000, the average income of the group of 10 is $6410. This figure does not do justice to either group, though it would be an impressive figure for the president of a small company (whose salary was $20,000) to report as the average salary on his payroll. The median would be preferred as a measure of central tendency in this instance. Demographers, economists, and journalists often choose to report "median income" because they wish to avoid the problem just illustrated.

6. In unimodal groups of scores that are symmetrical (i.e., the half of the histogram below the mode is the mirror image of the half above the mode), the mean, median, and mode are equal. For an example, see Fig. 4.3. The frequency polygon shows that the mean, median, and mode are all 40.

   Lack of perfect symmetry in the frequency polygon or histogram of a group of scores generally has a regular effect on the relationships among the mean, median, and mode. Suppose that a preponderance of the scores in some group lie above a peak in the frequency polygon as in Fig. 4.4.

   In Fig. 4.4 the mode (Mo) equals 100, the median (Md) equals 104.6 and the mean ($\bar{X}$) equals 105.98. If a preponderance of the scores lie lower than the peak of a frequency polygon, it would

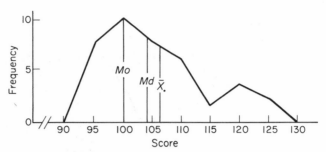

FIG. 4.4   An asymmetrical frequency polygon illustrating the relationships among the mean, median, and mode.

generally be true that the mean would be the smallest number, the median would be next largest, and the mode would be the largest number.

7. An additional consideration which bears on one's choice of a measure of central tendency can be discussed only superficially with the concepts developed thus far. When the group of scores in hand is considered to be a sample from a much larger symmetrical group, the mean of the sample is probably closer to the center of the large group of scores than is either the median or the mode of the scores in hand. We shall return to this important point in Sec. 11.4.

The following anecdote summarizes many of the problems that arise in the use of measures of central tendency:

An improbable anecdote should make this problem of heterogeneity [i.e., that no measure of central tendency is an adequate description of all of the scores in a group] plain. Five men once sat near each other on a park bench. Two were vagrants, each with total worldly assets of 25 cents. The third was a workman whose bank account and other assets totaled $2000. The fourth man had $15,000 in various forms. The fifth was a multi-millionaire with a net worth of $5,000,000. Therefore, the modal assets of the group were 25 cents. This figure describes [the financial assets of] two of the persons perfectly, but is grossly inaccurate for the other three. The median figure of $2000 does little justice to anyone except the workman. The mean, $1,003,400.10, is not very satisfactory even for the multimillionaire. If we *had* to choose one measure of central tendency, perhaps it would be the mode, which describes 40 percent of this group accurately. But if told that "the modal assets of five persons sitting on a park bench are 25 cents," we would be likely to conclude that the total assets of the group are approximately $1.25, which is more than five million dollars lower than the correct figure. Obviously, no measure of central tendency whatsoever is adequate for these "strange benchfellows," who simply do not "tend centrally."*

* Quoted from page 73 of Julian C. Stanley, *Measurement in Today's Schools*, 4th Ed., © 1964. Reprinted by permission of Prentice-Hall, Inc., Englewood Cliffs, N.J.

Another escape from the contradictions in this anecdote is to point out that no summary statistic is needed for a group of five scores.

4.12
OTHER MEASURES OF
CENTRAL TENDENCY

Numerous other ways of locating a "central value" in a group of scores exist. A few of these measures will be presented here despite the rarity of their appearance in the literature of educational research.

The Geometric Mean

Undoubtedly you recall that $\sqrt{4} = 2$ and that, more generally, if $b = \sqrt{a}$, then $b^2 = a$. Perhaps your memory is somewhat more vague on the general question of roots of numbers. $\sqrt[3]{a}$ is read "the cube root" of the number a and is that number which when raised to the third power equals a, i.e., if $\sqrt[3]{a} = b$, then $b \cdot b \cdot b = b^3 = a$. The nth root of a, denoted $\sqrt[n]{a}$, is that number which when raised to the nth power (i.e., multiplied by itself n times) equals a. For example, $\sqrt[4]{16} = 2$ because $2 \cdot 2 \cdot 2 \cdot 2 = 2^4 = 16$.

Definition: The *geometric mean* of the n positive numbers $X_1, \ldots, X_n$ is given by

$$gm = \sqrt[n]{X_1 \cdot X_2 \cdot \ldots \cdot X_n}, \qquad (4.6)$$

i.e., the geometric mean of $X_1, \ldots, X_n$ is the nth root of the grand product of all n of the X's.

The definitional formula for gm is not computationally convenient. If you find that you need to calculate gm for four, five, or more scores, refer to Senders (1958, p. 316).

It is necessary to restrict the definition of gm to positive numbers; if any single X_i were zero, the grand product of $X_1, \ldots, X_n$ would also be zero and hence gm would equal zero even if zero was (by any other definition) far from a central value of the group.

The geometric mean is useful for describing the central location of rate-of-change scores (see Ferguson, 1959, p. 50).

The Harmonic Mean

This measure of central tendency is sometimes applied when a group of ratios is being averaged.

Definition: The *harmonic mean* of the *positive* scores $X_1, \ldots,$ X_n is given by

$$hm = \frac{1}{[(1/X_1) + (1/X_2) + \ldots + (1/X_n)]/n}$$

$$= \frac{n}{\sum\limits_{i=1}^{n} 1/X_i} .$$

It is thus their reciprocals (where $1/X_i$ is the reciprocal of X_i). To find *hm*, each score is divided into 1, the resulting reciprocals are summed, and this sum is divided into *n*.

The harmonic mean has very limited application. A *contraharmonic mean* is thought to have broader application than either the geometric or harmonic mean (see Senders, 1958, pp. 317–18); however, it is doubtful that any of these three measures is sufficiently familiar to most readers that the use of them in written reports would pass without considerable confusion.

The Ratio of Means and the Mean of Ratios

An IQ score, as computed from most of the earlier intelligence tests, is 100 times the ratio of a person's mental age to his chronological age: IQ = 100(MA/CA). At first sight, it might appear that the average IQ of a group of persons could be found by dividing the average mental age of the group by the average chronological age and multiplying by 100, i.e., that $\overline{IQ} = 100(\overline{MA/CA})$. However, this is not generally true.

Only under very special conditions will it be true that

$$\frac{1}{n} \sum_{1}^{n} \frac{X_i}{Y_i} = \frac{\bar{X}.}{\bar{Y}.} ,$$

i.e., that the mean of the ratios is the ratio of means (see Stanley, 1957b). This seems like such a simple fact, but in a slightly more complicated form the error of assuming that the mean of ratios is the ratio of means sneaks into statistical literature (e.g., see Winer, 1962, pp. 61 and 119; Ferguson, 1959, p. 258).

PROBLEMS AND EXERCISES

1. Find the mean, median, and mode of the following set of scores: 1.2, 1.5, 1.6, 2.1, 2.4, 2.4, 2.7, 2.8, 3.0, 3.0, 3.0, 3.1, 3.1, 3.1, 3.4.

2. Suppose the number 0.5 is added to each of the 15 scores in Prob. 1 above. What will be the value of the mean and median of these 15 augmented scores?

3. Find the mean and median of the 100 scores in the following grouped frequency distribution:

Score interval	Frequency
20–22	8
17–19	14
14–16	41
11–13	26
8–10	7
5–7	4
	$n = 100$

4. Suppose that each of the 100 scores in the grouped frequency distribution in Prob. 3 is multiplied by 3. What would be the values of the mean and median of the 100 resulting scores?

5. Find the mean and median in the following grouped frequency distribution:

Score interval	Frequency
20–24	2
15–19	11
10–14	17
5–9	13
0–4	9
(-5)–(-1)	7
	$n = 59$

6. Group A contains 10 scores, the mean and median of which are 14.5 and 13, respectively. Group B contains 20 scores, the mean and median of which are 12.7 and 10, respectively. What are the mean and median of the 30 scores obtained from combining Groups A and B?

7. The seven members of the Sunday Afternoon Picnic Society (SAPS) live along a straight stretch of Highway 101. Their homes are positioned along the highway as follows:

The cost of gas—3.5 cents per mile—for the travel of all members to the Sunday outing is taken out of the club treasury. Since any point along Highway 101 is a fine place for a picnic, where along the road should the members hold their picnic so as to spend the minimum amount of money for travel?

8. Find the mean SAT-V score from the $n = 903$ scores for men in Prob. 4 at the end of Chapter 3. (Hint: a quick way to find the mean is to multiply the midpoint of each score interval by the relative frequency of the scores in that interval, and then add up these products for all 12 intervals.)

5

MEASURES
OF
VARIABILITY

5.1
INTRODUCTION

Measures of central tendency tell us about the concentration of a group of scores on a number scale. A particular measure of central tendency gives a score that "represents" in one of several senses all of the scores in the group. This process disregards the differences that exist among separate scores. Other descriptive statistics are required to measure the variation of scores within a group. In this chapter, several statistics that measure, in different ways, the variability (heterogeneity, dispersion, scatter) in a group of scores will be presented and discussed.

Later in this text, you should begin to see that some of the most important functions of statistics relate to procedures by which variability, which is in a sense uncertainty, can be reduced, explained, or accounted for. The whole scientific enterprise is concerned with notions of variability. When much unexplained variability exists, predictions can never be very accurate. But when explanations can be fashioned for *why* people or things differ, uncertainty can be reduced and portions of variability can be removed.

For example, if nothing is known about why people differ in intelligence, one is faced with great uncertainty when attempting to predict intelligence; some people would appear "bright" and others "dull" and no one would know why. However, if it is known that heredity and environment produce quantifiable influences on measured IQ, then knowing a child's ancestry and early upbringing would permit a more accurate prediction of his adult intelligence. In other words, the variability of IQ's for persons with like heredity and environment is less than it is for people in general. But before we can continue with these loftier matters, we must learn about conventional indices of variability.

5.2
THE RANGE

The *range* simply measures the full distance along the number scale over which the scores vary. Because slightly different definitions of the range have been given in the past, it will be necessary to distinguish two types of range: the *inclusive* and the *exclusive range*.

Definition: The *exclusive range* is the difference between the largest and smallest scores in a group.

For example, the exclusive range of the scores 0, 2, 3, 3, 5, and 8 is $8 - 0 = 8$. The scores -0.2, 0.4, 0.8, and 1.6 have an exclusive range of $1.6 - (-0.2) = 1.8$.

Definition: The *inclusive range* is the difference between the *upper real limit* of the interval containing the largest score and the *lower real limit* of the interval containing the smallest score.

For example, the heights of six boys are measured to the nearest inch. The following heights are obtained: 59", 61", 62", 65", and 66". The actual height of the shortest boy is somewhere between 58.5" and 59.5", the lower real limit being 58.5". The upper real limit of the interval containing the largest score is 66.5". Thus, the inclusive range equals $66.5" - 58.5" = 8"$, which is 1 larger than $66 - 59$ (see Fig. 5.1).

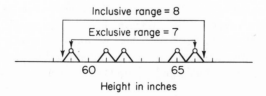

FIG. 5.1 Illustration of the inclusive and the exclusive range.

The exclusive range is the distance between the smallest and largest reported scores in a group, and is thus likely to *exclude* an actual score that lies above the largest or below the smallest reported score (see Sec. 2.3 for definitions of actual and reported scores).

The inclusive range is sufficiently large to include all actual scores as well as all reported scores.

In the future, if we refer to "the range" without specifying inclusive or exclusive, the point being made will be equally valid for either. Although the meaning of the range as a measure of variability is quite clear, it has certain drawbacks. Because the range is determined by just two scores in the group, it ignores the spread of all scores except the largest and smallest. For example, if 100 scores are spread evenly from 1 through 10, the inclusive range is $10.5 - 0.5 = 10$. But if one score is at 1 and one score is at 10 and the remaining 98 scores are at 5, the inclusive range is still equal to 10. For almost any purpose, these two types of heterogeneity (one in which 100 scores are uniformly distributed over a ten-unit interval and the other in which all but two of the 100 scores are clustered at the same point) have different meaning; but they cannot be distinguished by merely inspecting the range. The range is by far the crudest measure of variability commonly employed.

5.3
D, THE 90TH-TO-10TH PERCENTILE RANGE

A second measure of variability is D, the range between the 10th and 90th percentiles in a group of scores. It was defined by an educational statistician, Truman Kelley (1921), as

$$D = P_{90} - P_{10}.$$ (5.1)

D is somewhat more stable than the range because it is directly affected by a greater number of scores. It is easier to compute than other measures of variability we shall meet later in this chapter. Neither of these advantages has been great enough to make D a popular measure of variability. It is seldom used.

5.4
THE SEMI-INTERQUARTILE RANGE

In Sec. 3.2 we considered the three quartiles of a distribution of scores: Q_1, the point on the scale below which 25% of the scores lie, Q_2 (the median), and Q_3, the point above which 25% of the scores lie. The distance between the first and third quartiles of a group of scores, i.e., $Q_3 - Q_1$, is called the *interquartile range*. The *semi*-interquartile range is half this distance.

Using Q to denote the semi-interquartile range, we have the following:

Definition: The *semi-interquartile range* Q is half the distance between the third and first quartiles, i.e.,

$$Q = \frac{Q_3 - Q_1}{2}. \qquad (5.2)$$

Q is an easily obtained and useful measure of variability. For descriptive purposes it is superior to the range on any criterion except computational simplicity. If two groups of scores have the same value of Q, they are much more likely to possess similar patterns of heterogeneity than are two groups with the same range.

In distributions that are nearly symmetrical around the mean or median, Q can be used to reconstruct the score limits between which approximately 50% of the scores are contained. If it is known that 250 scores which are approximately symmetrically distributed around a median of 63 have a semi-interquartile range of 11, then approximately 50% (125) of the scores lie between

$$Md - Q = 63 - 11 = 52$$

and

$$Md + Q = 63 + 11 = 74.$$

If the distribution of scores is very asymmetrical around the median, then as many as 70% of the scores might lie within the range $Md - Q$ to $Md + Q$. The symmetric and asymmetric cases and the use of Q are illustrated in Fig. 5.2.

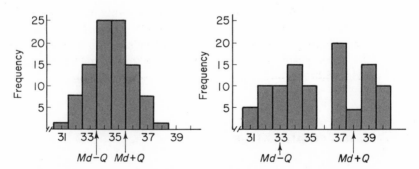

FIG. 5.2 Interpretation of Q. Exactly 50% of the scores lie between $Md - Q$ and $Md + Q$ in the symmetric distribution on the left. 52.5% of the scores lie between $Md - Q$ and $Md + Q$ in the somewhat asymmetric distribution on the right.

5.5
THE VARIANCE

The range, the semi-interquartile range Q, and $D = P_{90} - P_{10}$ are three measures of dispersion, scatter, heterogeneity, or variation met thus far. Each increases in value as the set of scores on which it is computed shows greater dispersion—less homogeneity. Note that, as with the mode and median, calculation of these three measures does not involve every individual score in a group of scores. We shall now encounter a fourth measure in the calculation of which, like the mean, every score is utilized.

Deviation scores, scores of the form $X_i - \bar{X}$, reflect something about the variation in a set of scores. A set of scores with great heterogeneity will have some large deviation scores. What would the deviation scores be if all the scores in the set were 9? The mean would be 9, hence every deviation score would be $9 - 9 = 0$. In the most homogeneous set of scores that it is possible to achieve, all the deviation scores equal zero. Some combination of the deviation scores might be a useful measure of variation.

If we were to sum all of the deviation scores, would that sum reflect the variation in the original scores? No, since this sum is always exactly zero: $\sum_{i=1}^{n} (X_i - \bar{X}) = 0$. To overcome this we could square each deviation score and sum the resulting squared scores. Hence, for a given set of scores a measure of the form

$$\sum_{i=1}^{n} (X_i - \bar{X})^2 = (X_1 - \bar{X})^2 + \ldots + (X_n - \bar{X})^2$$

will be large when the scores are heterogeneous and small when they are homogeneous. We would not have had to square the deviation scores to get rid of their signs; we could have simply regarded all of them as positive (i.e., taken their absolute value). This method would have led to a different measure of variation called the *mean deviation*, which you will encounter in Sec. 5.9. The value of the above expression also depends upon how many scores are considered. The larger n, the larger the sum tends to be. This is a limitation if one wishes to compare the variability in two sets that differ in numbers of scores. This limitation is overcome by dividing the expression by $n - 1$. The resulting measure of variability is called the *variance* (denoted by s_x^2) and has the formula

$$s_x^2 = \frac{\sum_{i=1}^{n} (X_i - \bar{X})^2}{n - 1}. \tag{5.3}$$

Why did we divide by $n - 1$ instead of simply n? A satisfactory answer cannot be given at this point because as yet in this chapter we have not developed the concepts necessary to give the explanation much meaning. You will learn in Sec. 12.4 why $n - 1$ was chosen instead of n.

We shall use the following data to illustrate the calculations of the variance of a set of six scores:

Score	Score — Mean	(Score — Mean)²
1	$1 - 2 = -1$	1
3	$3 - 2 =\ \ \ 1$	1
3	$3 - 2 =\ \ \ 1$	1
0	$0 - 2 = -2$	4
4	$4 - 2 =\ \ \ 2$	4
1	$1 - 2 = -1$	1
$\overline{12}$	$\overline{0}$	$\overline{12}$

$$s_x^2 = \frac{12}{6-1} = \frac{12}{5} = 2.4$$

Suppose we had a second, more heterogeneous set of six scores with the same mean, 2. These data, and the calculations, are as follows:

X	$X - \bar{X}.$	$(X - \bar{X}.)^2$
0	$0 - 2 = -2$	4
0	$0 - 2 = -2$	4
0	$0 - 2 = -2$	4
0	$0 - 2 = -2$	4
6	$6 - 2 =\ \ \ 4$	16
6	$6 - 2 =\ \ \ 4$	16
$\sum_{i=1}^{6} X_i = \overline{12}$	$\sum_{i=1}^{n}(X_i - \bar{X}.) = \overline{\ 0\ }$	$\sum_{i=1}^{n}(X_i - \bar{X}.)^2 = \overline{48}$

$$\bar{X}. = \frac{12}{6} = 2 \qquad s_x^2 = \frac{48}{6-1} = \frac{48}{5} = 9.6$$

In the above examples, s_x^2 was easily calculated because each score and the mean were whole numbers. Computation of s_x^2 as above would be tedious, however, if the mean were 17.697, for example. For this reason we seek, by algebraic manipulation, an expression for s_x^2 that is computationally simpler in such instances.

$$s_x^2 = \frac{\sum_{i=1}^{n}(X_i - \bar{X}.)^2}{n-1} = \frac{\sum_{i=1}^{n}(X_i^2 - 2\bar{X}.X_i + \bar{X}.^2)}{n-1} = \frac{\sum_{i=1}^{n}X_i^2 - 2\bar{X}.\sum_{i=1}^{n}X_i + \sum_{i=1}^{n}\bar{X}.^2}{n-1}.$$

If we recall that $\sum X = n\bar{X}.$, we can write the above expression as follows:

$$\frac{\sum\limits_{i=1}^{n} X_i^2 - 2n\bar{X}.^2 + n\bar{X}.^2}{n-1} = \frac{\sum\limits_{i=1}^{n} X_i^2 - n\bar{X}.^2}{n-1}.$$

Since the square of the mean is the square of the sum of all the scores divided by the square of n, we have

$$s_x^2 = \frac{\sum\limits_{i=1}^{n} X_i^2 - \left(\sum\limits_{i=1}^{n} X_i\right)^2 \Big/ n}{n-1}. \qquad (5.4)$$

We can also multiply both sides of Eq. (5.4) by a fancy form of the number 1, namely n/n, to obtain another formula for s_x^2 that does not contain the mean:

$$s_x^2 = \frac{n\sum\limits_{i=1}^{n} X_i^2 - \left(\sum\limits_{i=1}^{n} X_i\right)^2}{n(n-1)}.$$

5.6
CALCULATION OF THE
VARIANCE s^2

The calculation of s_x^2 by means of Eq. (5.4) will be illustrated on the six scores used in the first example above: 1, 3, 3, 0, 4, 1.

X	X^2	*Final calculations*
1	1	
3	9	$\sum\limits_{1}^{n} X^2 - \dfrac{\left(\sum\limits_{1}^{n} X\right)^2}{n} = 36 - \dfrac{12^2}{6} = 36 - \dfrac{144}{6}$
3	9	
0	0	$= 36 - 24 = 12$
4	16	
1	1	
$\sum\limits_{i=1}^{6} X_i = 12$	$\sum\limits_{i=1}^{6} X_i^2 = 36$	$s_x^2 = \dfrac{12}{6-1} = \dfrac{12}{5} = 2.4$

When one or more of the possible values a variable can assume occurs more than once in a group of scores, a simplification of the calculation of s_x^2 is possible, as was the case in the calculation of $\bar{X}.$ (see Sec. 4.7). In the above illustration, the number 3 appeared twice. The amount contributed to the sum of the scores ($\sum X$) by the two threes was $3 + 3 = 2(3)$. The amount contributed to the sum of the squared scores ($\sum X^2$) by the two threes was $9 + 9 = 2(9)$. If the value X_i has a frequency in the group of f_i, then this value will contribute $f_i X_i$ to the sum of the scores and $f_i X_i^2$ to the sum of the squared scores. Consequently, in finding $\sum X^2$, for example, it is not necessary to square the value X_i each time it occurs. Instead, X_i^2 is found once and multiplied by the number of times X_i occurs in the group.

Using the same data upon which the calculation of $\bar{X}$ was illustrated in Sec. 4.7, we shall find s_x^2 by this shortened method, where

$$s_x^2 = \frac{\sum\limits_{i=1}^{k} f_i X_i^2 - \left[\left(\sum\limits_{i=1}^{k} f_i X_i\right)^2 / n\right]}{n - 1},$$

k is the number of *different* scores, and $\sum\limits_{i=1}^{k} f_i = n$.

TABLE 5.1   ILLUSTRATION OF THE CALCULATION OF THE VARIANCE WHEN SOME SCORES OCCUR SEVERAL TIMES

Original scores	X	X_i^2	f	fX	fX²	Final calculations
2 6 10	2	4	1	2	4	$\sum\limits_{i=1}^{21} X_i = \sum\limits_{i=1}^{10} f_i X_i = 166.$
3 6 10	3	9	2	6	18	
3 6 11	5	25	4	20	100	$\sum X_i^2 = \sum f_i X_i^2 = 1632.$
5 8 11	6	36	3	18	108	
5 8 11	8	64	2	16	128	$\sum X_i^2 - \dfrac{(\sum X_i)^2}{n}$
5 9 15	9	81	2	18	162	
5 9 18	10	100	2	20	200	$= 1632 - 1312.19 = 319.81.$
	11	121	3	33	363	
	15	225	1	15	225	$s_x^2 = \dfrac{319.81}{20} = 15.991.$
	18	324	1	18	324	
			$\sum f_i = 21$	$\sum f_i X_i = 166$	$\sum f_i X_i^2 = 1632$	

5.7
THE STANDARD DEVIATION s

A measure of variability closely related to the variance is the standard deviation. The *standard deviation*, denoted by s, is defined as the positive square root of the variance. To find s, one first finds s^2 and then finds the square root of s^2.

$$s_x = \sqrt{\frac{\sum X^2 - [(\sum X)^2/n]}{n - 1}} \tag{5.5}$$

If the variance is 16, what is the standard deviation?

$$s_x = \sqrt{s_x^2} = \sqrt{16} = 4.$$

The standard deviation is often a useful measure of variation because in many distributions of scores we know approximately what percent of the scores lie within one, two, three, or more standard deviations of the mean. For example, we may know that 70% of the scores lie between $\bar{X}_. - s_x$ and $\bar{X}_. + s_x$.

5.8
SOME PROPERTIES OF THE VARIANCE

Suppose we added a constant number to every score in a set of scores. How would the variance of the scores be affected? In Sec. 5.6 we found that the scores 1, 3, 3, 0, 4, 1 have variance equal to 2.4. Let's add 2 to each score and then calculate s_x^2:

(*Original score* + 2)		− *Mean*		(*Deviation score*)^2
3	−4 =	−1		1
5	−4 =	1		1
5	−4 =	1		1
2	−4 =	−2		4
6	−4 =	2		4
3	−4 =	−1		1
Sum = $\overline{24}$	Sum of deviations =	$\overline{0}$		$\overline{12}$
Mean = 4				

$$s_x^2 = \frac{12}{6-1} = \frac{12}{5} = 2.4$$

Adding 2 to each score did not change the value of s_x^2. In general, adding a constant c to each score in a group will not change the variance (nor the standard deviation) of the scores:

$$\frac{\sum_{i=1}^{n}\left\{(X_i + c) - \left[\sum_{i=1}^{n}(X_i + c)\Big/n\right]\right\}^2}{n-1} = \frac{\sum_{i=1}^{n}[X_i + c - (\sum X_i/n) - (nc/n)]^2}{n-1}$$

$$= \frac{\sum_{i=1}^{n}(X_i + c - \bar{X}_. - c)^2}{n-1}$$

$$= \frac{\sum_{i=1}^{n}(X_i - \bar{X})^2}{n-1} = s_x^2.$$

What would happen to s_x^2 if each score were multiplied by a constant, say 2?

(*Original score* × 2) − *Mean*	(*Deviation score*)²

2	− 4 = −2	4
6	− 4 = 2	4
6	− 4 = 2	4
0	− 4 = −4	16
8	− 4 = 4	16
2	− 4 = −2	4

Sum = $\overline{24}$ $\overline{0}$ $\overline{48}$

Mean = 4

$$s_x^2 = \frac{48}{6-1} = \frac{48}{5} = 9.6$$

Note also 9.6 equals $(2^2) \cdot (2.4)$ In general, multiplying each score by a constant c makes the variance of the resulting scores equal to $c^2 s_x^2$:

$$\frac{\sum_{i=1}^{n}\left[cX_i - \left(\sum_{i=1}^{n}cX_i/n\right)\right]^2}{n-1} = \frac{\sum_{i=1}^{n}\left[cX_i - \left(c\sum_{i=1}^{n}X_i/n\right)\right]^2}{n-1} = \frac{\sum_{i=1}^{n}[c(X_i - \bar{X})]^2}{n-1}$$

$$= \frac{\sum_{i=1}^{n}c^2(X_i - \bar{X})^2}{n-1} = \frac{c^2\sum_{i=1}^{n}(X_i - \bar{X})^2}{n-1} = c^2 s_x^2.$$

In Chapter 4, the mean of a set of scores formed by pooling scores from two separate groups was found to be a simple weighted average of the means of the two groups (see Sec. 4.9).   The comparable situation for variances is more complicated.   It will be seen that the variance of the set of scores formed by pooling scores from groups a and b depends on both the variances and means of the two groups.   Notice that if group a comprises the scores 3, 3, 3 and 3 and group b is 6, 6, 6, 6, then the variance of groups a and b combined (3, 3, 3, 3, 6, 6, 6, 6) is not zero even though $s_a^2 = s_b^2 = 0$.

Suppose that a and b denote two separate sets of scores:

	Group a	Group b
Group size	n_a	n_b
Mean	$\bar{X}_{.a}$	$\bar{X}_{.b}$
Variance	s_a^2	s_b^2

The variance of the group of $n_a + n_b$ scores formed by combining groups a and b is

$$s^2 = \frac{[(n_a - 1)s_a^2 + (n_b - 1)s_b^2 + n_a(\bar{X}_{.a} - \bar{X}_{..})^2 + n_b(\bar{X}_{.b} - \bar{X}_{..})^2]}{n_a + n_b - 1}, \quad (5.6)$$

where

$$\overline{X}_{..} = \frac{n_a \overline{X}_{.a} + n_b \overline{X}_{.b}}{n_a + n_b}.$$

5.9
THE MEAN DEVIATION

An additional measure of variability, the *mean* (or *average*) *deviation* is somewhat easier to calculate than the standard deviation but is less useful. The *deviation* of each score in a group from the *mean* is denoted by $X_i - \overline{X}_.$. The collection of all n of these deviations is descriptive of the amount of variability in the original scores. As we saw in Sec. 4.8, however, the sum of these positive and negative deviations is not in the least descriptive of the total amount of variability in the group of scores because it is always precisely zero. If the deviations are regarded as distances of the scores from $\overline{X}_.$ without regard to sign, the sum of these distances is descriptive of the variability in the scores.

The distance of each X_i from $\overline{X}_.$ is found by a process known as *taking the absolute value* of a number. The absolute value of 4.65 is denoted $|4.65|$ and equals 4.65. In fact the absolute value of any positive number is that positive number itself. Thus $|2| = 2$, and $|105| = 105$. The absolute value of any negative number is found by changing the minus sign to a plus sign: $|-3| = 3; |-1.69| = 1.69$. Finally, $|0| = 0$.

$$|5| = 5,$$
$$|0| = 0,$$
$$|-5| = 5.$$

Another way to think of the process of taking absolute values—though one would be foolish to do it this way in calculations—is that $|a| = \sqrt{a^2}$, i.e., the absolute value of a number is the positive square root of the square of the number!

The distance of the score X_i from the mean is given by $|X_i - \overline{X}_.|$. The average of the n distances of the scores from their mean is called the *mean deviation*, MD. (Do not confuse MD, the mean deviation, with Md, the median.)

$$MD = \frac{\sum_{i=1}^{n} |X_i - \overline{X}_.|}{n}.$$

There is no simpler expression for the *mean deviation* that might be used for purposes of calculation. An illustration of the calculation of MD appears in Table 5.2. The mean deviation has not often been used as a measure of

TABLE 5.2   ILLUSTRATION OF THE CALCULATION OF THE MEAN DEVIATION

Scores	$X - \bar{X}.$	$|X - \bar{X}.|$	Final calculations
10	$10 - 12 = -2$	2	$MD = \dfrac{\sum |X_i - \bar{X}.|}{n}$
12	$12 - 12 = \ \ 0$	0	
13	$13 - 12 = \ \ 1$	1	
10	$10 - 12 = -2$	2	$= \dfrac{8}{5} = 1.60$
15	$15 - 12 = \ \ 3$	3	

$$\sum_{i=1}^{n} X_i = 60$$
$$\bar{X}. = 12$$

$$\sum_{i=1}^{n} |X_i - \bar{X}.| = 8$$

variability, even though it is easily calculated and has a logical simplicity. One reason for this is that the mean deviation does not have a theoretical undergirding comparable to that of the variance, for example. The mathematical statistician finds that the process of "taking absolute values" presents special difficulties for certain mathematical derivations. The mean deviation has been defined and discussed at this point, however, because of the role it will play later in this text in a novel approach to testing hypotheses about variabilities in populations.

5.10
STANDARD SCORES

It is frequently desirable to describe the position of a score in a set of scores by measuring its deviation from the mean of all scores in standard deviation units. For example, a particular set of 100 scores has a mean of 18.75 and a standard deviation of 2.60. If you know only that a certain one of these 100 persons has a score of 20, his relative position in the collection of 100 scores is not immediately apparent. It can be determined by a series of calculations that 20 lies 1.25 units $(20 - 18.75 = 1.25)$ above the mean and that this distance is $1.25/2.60 = 0.48$ standard deviation units. Thus his score is 0.48 standard deviations above the mean.

For any arbitrary score X_i in the set of 100 scores, the deviation of the score from the mean measured in standard deviation units is given by

$$\frac{X_i - 18.75}{2.60}.$$

All 100 such original scores could be so transformed. What would be the mean and standard deviation of the resulting 100 transformed scores?

The mean of the 100 values of $X - 18.75$ is equal to the mean of the 100 original X scores minus 18.75, since subtracting a constant from each score subtracts that same constant from the mean. But since the mean of X is 18.75, the mean of $X - 18.75$ must be zero. If $X - 18.75$ has a mean of zero, then $(X - 18.75)/2.60$ must also have a mean of zero, since multiplying a variable with a zero mean by a constant produces a variable with mean equal to zero times the constant.

To find the standard deviation of $(X - 18.75)/2.60$, it is convenient first to write the standardized score as

$$\left(\frac{1}{2.60}\right)X_i - \frac{18.75}{2.60}.$$

It is well known that the additive constant $-18.75/2.60$ does not alter the standard deviation of X. The multiplicative constant $1/2.60$ does affect the standard deviation of the $100 \, X$ scores, however. Multiplying each score in a set of scores with standard deviation s_x by a constant c produces a new set of scores cX, with standard deviation $|c| \, s_x$. The absolute value of $1/2.60$ is simply $1/2.60$, of course. Since the 100 original scores had a standard deviation of 2.60, the standard deviation of $X/2.60$ is $(1/2.60)2.60 = 1$. Hence the 100 values of

$$\frac{X}{2.60} - \frac{18.75}{2.60} = \frac{X - 18.75}{2.60}$$

have a standard deviation of 1. To summarize, the $100 \, X$ scores with a mean of 18.75 and a standard deviation of 2.60 have a mean and standard deviation of 0 and 1, respectively, when transformed by $(X - 18.75)/2.60$.

Any set of n scores with mean $\bar{X}$ and standard deviation s_x can be transformed into a different set of scores with mean 0 and standard deviation 1 so that the transformed score immediately tells one the deviation of the original score from the mean measured in standard deviation units. The transformation is accomplished by subtracting $\bar{X}$ from the score X_i, and dividing the difference by s_x. The resulting set of scores are called z scores:

$$z_i = \frac{X_i - \bar{X}}{s_x}.$$

We can confirm that these z scores have a mean of 0 and a variance (and also a standard deviation) of 1:

$$\bar{z} = \frac{\left[\sum_1^n (X_i - \bar{X})\right] / s_x}{n} = \frac{1}{ns_x} \sum_1^n (X_i - \bar{X}) = \frac{1}{ns_x}(0) = 0.$$

$$s_z^2 = \frac{\sum_1^n (z_i - \bar{z})^2}{n-1} = \frac{\sum_1^n z_i^2}{n-1} = \frac{\sum_1^n (X_i - \bar{X})^2 / s_x^2}{n-1}$$

$$= \frac{1}{s_x^2}\left[\frac{\sum_1^n (X_i - \bar{X})^2}{n-1}\right] = \left(\frac{1}{s_x^2}\right)s_x^2 = 1.$$

Aside from being a convenient means of communicating the position of a person's score relative to the mean and measured in standard deviation units, z scores are a step toward transforming a set of X scores to an arbitrary scale with a convenient mean and standard deviation. For some purposes, for example, the z scores themselves may not be convenient. The negative scores might be bothersome, and a collection of z scores will undoubtedly be full of decimal numbers. A transformation of the z scores can eliminate these minor problems.

Since the n z scores have mean zero and standard deviation 1, we know that cz—formed by multiplying each z score by the constant c—will have a standard deviation of $|c|$, and $cz + d$ will have a mean of

$$c\bar{z} + d = c(0) + d = d.$$

For example, a set of 250 X scores has mean 79.65 and standard deviation 5.71. Suppose we wish to transform these scores so that their mean is 50 and their standard deviation is 10. We could first transform them to z scores by forming the 250 values of $z = (X - 79.65)/5.71$. Next, we could calculate $10z + 50$ for each of the 250 z scores. The resulting set of 250 transformed scores has a mean of 50 and a standard deviation of 10. A person with a transformed score of 59 lies $(59 - 50)/10 = 9/10$ of a standard deviation above the mean of the 250 scores; furthermore, we know that this same person's X score is approximately $79.65 + 0.9(5.71) = 85$. The transformed score of 59 is more immediately informative than the X score of 85.

There are many scales of measurement (arbitrary means and standard deviations) that are popular in education and the social sciences. A set of scores can be placed along any such scale, i.e., they can be given a desired mean and standard deviation, merely by letting c be the desired standard deviation and d the desired mean in the expression $cz + d$. Intelligence-test scores are often transformed to a scale with mean 100 and standard deviation 15 or 16. T scores formed by $10z + 50$ find wide application. These and other popular scales are shown in Fig. 6.5 in Chapter 6.

5.11
SKEWNESS

The degree of asymmetry of a frequency distribution is one of its more important properties. Exactly symmetrical frequency polygons and histograms almost never occur with real data. The degree to which the frequency distribution of a group of scores is asymmetrical is its *skewness*. The nature and extent of asymmetry will be apparent if a frequency polygon or histogram is observed, but such observation is not always possible or convenient. Consequently, various summary statistics measuring the type and degree of asymmetry of a group of scores have been devised.

The best measure of the skewness of a set of scores has the formula

$$\text{skewness} = \frac{\sum_{i=1}^{n}(X_i - \bar{X})^3/n}{s_x^3}. \tag{5.7}$$

As was seen in Sec. 5.10, it is standard practice to denote the directed distance which a score lies from the mean of the group it is in, measured in units of the standard deviation of that group, by z_x; i.e.,

$$z_x = \frac{X_i - \bar{X}}{s_x}.$$

If we recognize that

$$\frac{(X_i - \bar{X})^3}{s_x^3} = \left[\frac{(X_i - \bar{X})}{s_x}\right]^3 = z_x^3,$$

then the measure of skewness in (5.7) becomes

$$\text{skewness} = \frac{\sum_{i=1}^{n} z_{xi}^3}{n} = \overline{z^3}. \tag{5.8}$$

Thus, one measure of skewness is simply the average of the z scores which have been raised to the third power. (In mathematical statistical work this measure of skewness is denoted by $\sqrt{\beta_1}$. The measure is due to Karl Pearson and its properties have been widely studied.)

Suppose the skewness of the two distributions in Fig. 5.3 is being measured. The mean of the scores for distribution A in Fig. 5.3 is about 16.

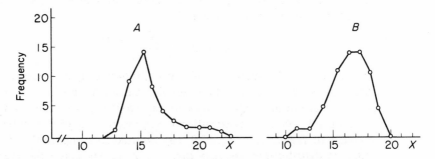

FIG. 5.3   Two skewed frequency distributions.

When the z scores for A are formed there will be some very large positive ones (because the largest X score is 22, which is 6 units above the mean) that will be larger in absolute value than any of the negative ones (the smallest

X score, 13, lies only 3 units below the mean). Now the algebraic sign of a number remains the same when it is cubed; $(-2)^3 = -8$. Hence, for distribution A, the contribution of the cubed negative z scores to $\sum z_x^3/n$ will be less than the contribution of the cubes of those large positive z scores. Consequently, the value of $\sum z_x^3/n$ in Eq. (5.8) will be large and positive. We say that distribution A is *positively skewed* because its measure of skewness is positive. A positively skewed frequency distribution has scores that extend further above the mean than the small scores extend below it.

Distribution B in Fig. 5.3 is *negatively skewed*. The value of $\sum z_x^3/n$ for distribution B is negative. Try to convince yourself that this is true. Distribution A is more markedly positively skewed than distribution B is negatively skewed.

In a symmetric distribution the value of the measure of skewness in Eq. (5.8) is zero. This is true because exact symmetry implies that every negative z score can be paired with a positive z score of equal size. Since the cubes of negative scores are still negative, the sum of the cubes of each pair of positive and negative z scores is zero.

Unfortunately, the value of $\sum z_x^3/n$ is laborious to obtain, even on a desk calculator, for any sizable group of scores. A quick method for measuring the skewness of a distribution grows out of the fact that the mean is more affected by extreme scores than the median. In the chapter on measures of central tendency we saw that in unimodal positively skewed distributions the mean is larger than the median, which is in turn larger than the mode. In negatively skewed distributions, the mean is smaller than the median, which is in turn smaller than the mode. This suggests that the position of the mean relative to the median tells something about the skewness of the distribution. This is indeed so for reasonably large groups of scores, say n of 50 or greater. A simple measure of skewness that makes use of these facts has the following definition:

$$\text{skewness} = \frac{3(\bar{X} - Md)}{s_x}. \tag{5.9}$$

In words, the skewness of a distribution can be measured by taking three times the difference between the mean and median, divided by the standard deviation. The values of Eq. (5.9) will generally range between -3 and $+3$. When a distribution is symmetric, Eq. (5.9) will be zero. The measure of skewness in Eq. (5.9) can be used to compare the skewnesses of different distributions because division by s_x has made the measure independent of the variability of the distribution.

5.12
KURTOSIS

We have seen how statisticians describe three properties or features of groups of scores. These three properties are central tendency, variability, and

FIG. 5.4 "Peaked," "flat," and "mesokurtic" curves (*A*, *B*, and *C*, respectively).

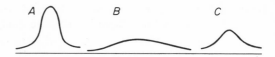

symmetry. A fourth property completes the set of features of distributions of scores that are generally of interest in analyzing data. One may wish to know something about how peaked or flat a frequency polygon or histogram is. *Kurtosis* is a Greek word and refers to the quality of "peakedness" of a curve. (Karl Pearson is credited with formalizing the concept of kurtosis in statistics and proposing a method of measuring it.)

In Fig. 5.4 three curves differing in "peakedness" or kurtosis appear. The first (*A*) is quite peaked; such a curve is called *leptokurtic*. (The prefix "lepto" means "slender" or "narrow.") The second curve (*B*) is relatively flat; such curves are called *platykurtic*. (The prefix "platy" means "flat" or "broad.") The "peakedness" or degree of kurtosis of the third curve (*C*) is a standard against which the kurtosis of other curves is measured. The third curve in Fig. 5.4 is the normal curve, which will be discussed at length in Chapter 6, and is said to be *mesokurtic*, "meso" meaning "intermediate."

We shall now learn how the statistician measures the kurtosis of a curve. First it is necessary to point out, however, that the concept of kurtosis applies only to unimodal distributions and concerns the steepness of the curve in the vicinity of the single mode. (If a distribution has two modes, it would be acceptable to talk about the kurtosis of the curve in the vicinity of each mode.)

The customary measure of kurtosis has the following definitional formula:

$$\text{kurtosis} = \frac{\sum\limits_{i=1}^{n}(X_i - \bar{X}.)^4/n}{s_x^4}. \tag{5.10}$$

If we recognize that $(X_i - \bar{X}.)^4/s_x^4$ is simply

$$\left[\frac{(X_i - \bar{X}.)}{s_x}\right]^4 = z_{x}^4,$$

then we see that a measure of kurtosis is given by the formula

$$\text{kurtosis} = \frac{\sum\limits_{i=1}^{n} z_{x_i}^4}{n} = \bar{z.}^4. \tag{5.11}$$

That is, kurtosis is measured by taking the average of the fourth powers of the *z* scores. The relationships between the size of the kurtosis statistic and the "peakedness" of the distribution on which it is calculated are recorded in Table 5.3.

TABLE 5.3   RELATIONSHIP OF THE VALUE OF THE KURTOSIS STATISTIC TO
THE "PEAKEDNESS" OF THE FREQUENCY DISTRIBUTION

Nature of distribution	Description of "peakedness"	Value of kurtosis statistic (Eq. 5.11)
Normal, e.g., curve C in Fig. 5.4	Mesokurtic	3
Peaked, e.g., curve A in Fig. 5.4	Leptokurtic	Greater than 3 (can become very large)
Flat, e.g., curve B in Fig. 5.4	Platykurtic	Less than 3 (must be zero or greater)

PROBLEMS AND EXERCISES

1. Calculate the inclusive range, variance, standard deviation, and mean deviation of the following set of scores:

102	112	116
106	114	119
111	115	120
112	115	122

(Hint: To simplify calculations, first subtract 100 from all scores; this will not change the values of any of the measures of variability.)

2. Find the semi-interquartile range for the IQ scores in the following grouped frequency distribution:

Score interval	Frequency	Cumulative frequency
150–159	5	100
140–149	7	95
130–139	9	88
120–129	12	79
110–119	17	67
100–109	21	50
90–99	12	29
80–89	8	17
70–79	6	9
60–69	1	3
50–59	2	2

The median of the above set of scores is 109.5. Determine the proportion of scores that lie in the range determined by subtracting and adding Q to the median, i.e., what proportion of the scores lie between $109.5 \pm Q$?

3. Find s_x^2 and s_x for the following grade-placement scores arranged in an ungrouped frequency distribution:

Score	Frequency
6.9	2
6.8	4
6.7	5
6.6	9
6.5	14
6.4	10
6.3	6
6.2	3
6.1	2
6.0	1

(Hint: Subtract 6.0 from each of the ten score values to simplify calculations.)

4. Indicate whether each of the following distributions of measures is probably negatively or positively skewed:

a. ages of students in U.S. universities;
b. numbers of children in U.S. families;
c. population of cities in the United States;
d. ages at death of females in the United States.

5.

Group A	Group B
13	28
11	26
10	25
9	24
7	22

The variances of both groups A and B equal 5. Will the variance of the ten scores formed by pooling together groups A and B be less than, greater than, or equal to 5?

6. For the 290 students taking a 50 item social studies achievement test the mean is 32.50 and the standard deviation is 4.80. Find the z scores corresponding to the following:

	Test scores X	z score
a.	28	−0.94
b.	36	
c.	45	
d.	20	

7. Two vocabulary tests were administered to the 40 students in a beginning French class. The means, the standard deviations on the two tests, and the raw scores obtained by students A and B were as follows:

	$\overline{X}$	s_x	A's scores	B's scores
Test 1	54.10	14.28	45	60
Test 2	21.25	3.52	30	21

a. Which student has the larger total raw score on tests 1 and 2?

b. Calculate the z scores for both students on each test.

c. Which student has the larger total of his two z scores?

d. Which student has a better knowledge of French vocabulary? (This question has no easy answer; attempt to raise the issues involved.)

8. Prove that $\sum\limits_{i=1}^{n} z_i^2 = n - 1$.

6

THE NORMAL
DISTRIBUTION

6.1
INTRODUCTION

This chapter is an interruption, but a very necessary one. It must stand alone and fail to be immediately integrated into the statistics we have developed to this point because we are attempting here to gain knowledge of techniques that rest on essential concepts we shall not present in detail because of their complexity. This is the price that all of us pay for attempting to master the upper layer of statistics before establishing a foundation in bedrock. Obviously, we feel that the present venture is worth the price.

6.2
HISTORY OF THE NORMAL
DISTRIBUTION

The brief history of the discovery and study of the normal distribution given here does not do the topic justice. Even the mathematically naïve student will find Helen Walker's account of the history of the normal distribution informative and rewarding reading (Walker, 1929, Chap. II).

In Europe in the seventeenth century, a handful of mathematicians were pursuing small, private researches which would one day be incorporated into the theory of probability. (See Chapter 10.) These studies, by such men as Blaise Pascal (1623–1662) and Pierre de Fermat (1601–1665), were undertaken at the request of Chevalier de Mere, a gambler to whom the nature of chance must have been particularly urgent.

One of the single greatest events in the early history of probability was the publication in 1713 of *Ars Conjectandi* by the Swiss mathematician Jacob Bernoulli (1654–1705). A central issue in probability theory during its infancy was determining the probability that an event would occur some number of times if it were given several independent opportunities to occur. For example, if a fair coin is flipped 20 times, what is the probability that 15 "heads" will occur? Or, if a die is cast 10 times, what is the probability that the face of the die on which six dots appear will turn up exactly twice? The solutions to these problems were known at the time *Ars Conjectandi* was published (we will develop the solutions in Chapter 10), and the formal properties of these solutions were the main concern of this great work. However, the computations involved in obtaining the solutions for large problems were enormous. No reasonable man would attempt to calculate directly the probability that 10,000 tosses of a coin will result in 8000 or more "heads," for example. Although it would be clear to him what calculations are necessary, they would be too laborious to carry out.

Some activity in the early eighteenth century was directed toward finding convenient mathematical approximations to many of the calculations that problems in probability involved. In 1730, James Stirling published a formula that gave an approximation to the grand product of the first n integers, i.e., $(1)(2)(3) \ldots (n - 1)(n)$, a term that appears often in probability theory. (Whether Stirling actually derived the approximation himself is currently being disputed by mathematicians.) With Stirling's approximation, the stage was then set for the solution of the grandest problem of all. How does one approximate the probability that n independent trials of an event with probability P of producing one (a "success") of its two outcomes will yield r "successes"? The man equal to the task at the time was Abraham De Moivre (1667–1754).

Before returning to De Moivre's work, let us take a closer look at the problem he sought to solve. Suppose that a coin is to be flipped 10 times. Assume that the coin is just as likely to come up "heads" as "tails." We can ask, what is the probability that 0 "heads" will result, or what is the probability that 1 "head" will result, . . . , or what is the probability that 10 "heads" will result from the 10 flips? The exact answers to all eleven of these questions can be calculated, even though for just 10 tosses the calculations are already becoming arduous. (For as many as 1000 flips of a coin the calculations border on being impossible.) The probabilities that

0, 1, 2, . . . , 9, or 10 "heads" will result in 10 flips of a fair coin are graphed in Fig. 6.1.

The problem De Moivre sought to solve was how to find a mathematical curve that would approximate closely the curve obtained by connecting the tops of the columns in Fig. 6.1. If such a curve could be found, the nearly impossible calculations of the probability problem could be replaced by simply reading off points on mathematical curves or looking up numbers in a mathematical table.

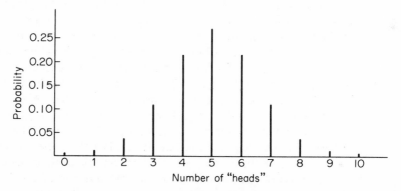

FIG. 6.1   Graph of the distribution of probabilities of obtaining certain numbers of "heads" in 10 flips of a fair coin.

De Moivre was able to show that a mathematical curve which came very close to the curve that connects the tops of the lines in Fig. 6.1 (and the curve for almost any other such problem) has the following formula:

$$u = \frac{1}{\sqrt{2\pi}\,\sigma}\, e^{-(X-\mu)^2/2\sigma^2}, \tag{6.1}$$

where u is the height of the curve directly above any given value of X in the plotted frequency distribution,

π is the ratio of the circumference of any circle to its diameter, which is approximately 3.142,

e is the base of the system of natural logarithms, approximately 2.718, and

μ and σ are numbers that locate the curve along the number line and control its spread.

Equation (6.1) is the formula for the *normal distribution*. It is certainly ominous looking, but do not let that frighten you. We shall have little to do with the formula as such.

6.3
THE NORMAL CURVE

The graph of Eq. (6.1) yields the familiar, symmetric, bell-shaped curve known as the *normal curve*. We speak of *a* normal curve, because Eq. (6.1) imparts a characteristic shape to the graph. However, by changing the values of μ and σ we can move *the* normal curve up and down the scale and change its spread. The value μ corresponds to the mean of a large frequency distribution that would look like the normal curve, and σ corresponds to the standard deviation of the distribution. In Fig. 6.2, the graph of the normal distribution for $\mu = 0$ and $\sigma = 1$ appears. We shall use the letter z as the symbol for a normally distributed variable with $\mu = 0$ and $\sigma = 1$.

The curve in Fig. 6.2 does not meet the z-axis at the points 3 and -3; in fact, although it gets closer and closer to the z-axis as X gets larger than 3, it never touches the axis. The highest point on the curve is above the z value of 0; at this point u is approximately .3989. Notice that the curve is symmetric around the vertical line drawn through $z = \mu = 0$. The normal curve will always be symmetric around μ. The *area* of the space under the curve and above the z-axis is exactly 1. The skewness of the normal curve is zero, because the curve is perfectly symmetric around the central value μ. The kurtosis of the normal curve, i.e., the average of the fourth powers of the z-scores, is 3. As we noted earlier, distributions with a measure of kurtosis greater than 3 are more peaked than the normal distribution and are said to be *leptokurtic*. Distributions which are flatter than the normal have a measure of kurtosis less than 3 and are called *platykurtic*. The normal distribution is said to be *mesokurtic* (see Sec. 5.11).

Another feature of the normal curve is the special way in which it bends. On either side of μ, which is 0 in Fig. 6.2, the curve ceases to bow away from the X-axis and begins to bow toward it, i.e., the curve has a point of inflection, at exactly a distance of one σ from μ, which is one unit in Fig. 6.2.

The normal curve in Fig. 6.2 is a special one because it has been chosen as a standard. It is called the *unit normal curve* because the area under the curve is 1. Its mean and standard deviation are convenient ($\mu = 0$, $\sigma = 1$), and any other normal curve can be moved along the number scale and stretched or compressed by a simple transformation (i.e., subtract μ and divide by σ) so that it coincides with the unit normal curve.

It will often be necessary to find the ordinate u (the height of the curve above the z-axis) for any value of z on the unit normal curve or the area under the curve between any two values of z. Solving Eq. (6.1) for u when z is given is far too inconvenient; and even though we know that the area under the curve from $z = -\infty$ to $z = \infty$ is 1, the area between any other two values of z is difficult to find. Statistical tables are a necessity at this point. Table B in the Appendix gives the area under the unit normal curve to the

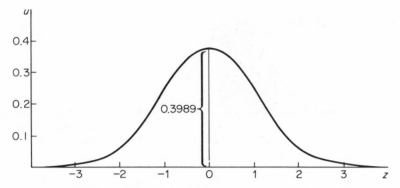

FIG. 6.2   The normal distribution for $\mu = 0$ and $\sigma = 1$.

left of any point on the z-axis from -3.00 to $+3.00$. Also given in Table B is the ordinate u of the unit normal curve for values of z from -3.00 to $+3.00$.

A few examples will illustrate the use of Table B. Suppose one desires to find the area under the unit normal curve to the left of $z = -2.50$. The value -2.50 is found in the first column of Table B. To the right of this entry in the second column, titled "Area," the number .0062 is found. Thus, only 62 ten-thousandths of the area under the unit normal curve is contained to the left of $z = -2.50$. The height of the unit normal curve at the point $z = -2.50$ is found in the "Ordinate" column to the right of the "Area" column. For $z = -2.50$, $u = .0175$.

Check and see if you can look up these areas and ordinates correctly in Table B in the Appendix.

Value of z	Area to the left of z	Ordinate at z
0.00	.5000	.3989
0.50	.6915	.3521
−1.27	.1020	.1781
1.96	.9750	.0584

Since the total area under the curve is 1, the above areas (but not the ordinates) can be read as proportions or percents of the total. 97.5% of the area under the unit normal curve lies to the left of 1.96.

Table B is also used to find the area under the unit normal curve between any two values of z. For example, the area to the left of $z = -1.27$ is .1020 and the area to the left of $z = 0.50$ is .6915. Therefore, the area *between* -1.27 and 0.50 is $.6915 - .1020 = .5895$. In other words, about 59% of the area lies between these two points. This is illustrated in Fig. 6.3.

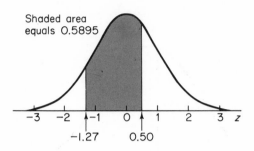

Shaded area
equals 0.5895

FIG. 6.3 Determining the area under the unit normal curve between two values of z.

6.4
THE FAMILY OF NORMAL CURVES

Actually there are infinitely many normal curves, a different one for each different pair of values for μ and σ. The curve in Fig. 6.4 has a mean μ of 20 and a standard deviation σ of 5, but it is a normal curve nonetheless.

What do all of these normal curves have in common? For our purposes, their most important common property is the amount of area under the curve between any two points expressed in standard deviations. For example, in *any* normal distribution approximately

   1. 68% of the area under the curve lies within *one* σ of the mean either way (i.e., $\mu \pm 1\sigma$),
   2. 95% of the area under the curve lies within *two* σ's of the mean, and
   3. 99.7% of the area under the curve lies within *three* σ's of the mean μ.

You can check these relationships and obtain the exact areas by finding the areas under the *unit normal curve* between -1 and $+1$, -2 and $+2$, and -3 and $+3$ in Table B of the Appendix.

The normal curve and its relationship to various transformed scales which are widely used in educational and psychological measurement appear in Fig. 6.5.

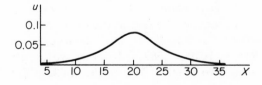

FIG. 6.4 The normal curve for $\mu = 20$ and $\sigma = 5$.

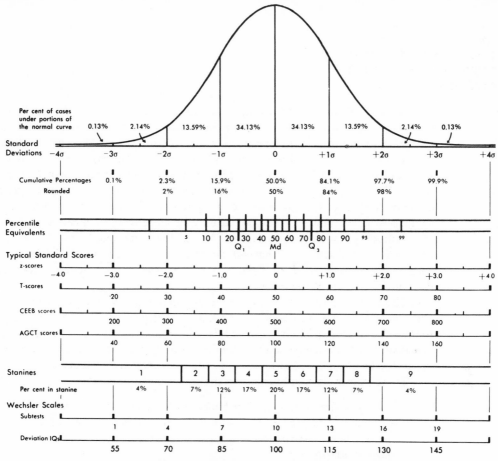

Per cent of cases under portions of the normal curve	0.13%	2.14%	13.59%	34.13%	34.13%	13.59%	2.14%	0.13%

Standard Deviations -4σ -3σ -2σ -1σ 0 +1σ +2σ +3σ +4σ

| Cumulative Percentages | 0.1% | | 2.3% | | 15.9% | | 50.0% | | 84.1% | | 97.7% | | 99.9% | |
| Rounded | | | 2% | | 16% | | 50% | | 84% | | 98% | | | |

Percentile Equivalents 1 5 10 20 30 40 50 60 70 80 90 95 99
Q₁ Md Q₃

Typical Standard Scores

z-scores -4.0 -3.0 -2.0 -1.0 0 +1.0 +2.0 +3.0 +4.0

T-scores 20 30 40 50 60 70 80

CEEB scores 200 300 400 500 600 700 800

AGCT scores 40 60 80 100 120 140 160

Stanines 1 2 3 4 5 6 7 8 9

Per cent in stanine 4% 7% 12% 17% 20% 17% 12% 7% 4%

Wechsler Scales

Subtests 1 4 7 10 13 16 19

Deviation IQs 55 70 85 100 115 130 145

THE NORMAL CURVE, PERCENTILES AND STANDARD SCORES

Distribution of scores of many standardized educational and psychological tests approximate the form of the NORMAL CURVE shown at the top of this chart. Below it are shown some of the systems that have been developed to facilitate the interpretation of scores by converting them into numbers which indicate the examinee's relative status in a group.

The zero (0) at the center of the baseline shows the location of the mean (average) raw score on a test, and the symbol σ (sigma) marks off the scale of raw scores in STANDARD DEVIATION units.

Cumulative percentages are the basis of the PERCENTILE EQUIVALENT scale.

Several systems are based on the standard deviation unit. Among these STANDARD SCORE scales, the z-score, the T-score and the stanine are general systems which have been applied to a variety of tests. The others are special variants used in connection with tests of the College Entrance Examination Board, the World War II Army General Classification Test, and the Wechsler Intelligence Scales.

Tables of NORMS, whether in percentile or standard score form, have meaning only with reference to a specified test applied to a specified population. The chart does not permit one to conclude, for instance, that a percentile rank of 84 on one test necessarily is equivalent to a z-score of +1.0 on another; this is true only when each test yields essentially a normal distribution of scores and when both scales are based on identical or very similar groups of people.

The scales on this chart are discussed in greater detail in Test Service Bulletin No. 48, which also includes the chart itself in smaller size. Copies of this Bulletin are available on request from the Psychological Corporation, 304 East 45th St., New York 17, N.Y.

FIG. 6.5 From Test Service Bulletin No. 48, courtesy The Psychological Corporation.

6.5
THE UNIT NORMAL
DISTRIBUTION AS A
STANDARD

The value of X for the unit normal distribution locates a point X units from the mean. It will be most useful in the future if all references to scores in normal distributions are in terms of deviations from the mean μ, in standard deviation σ units. For almost any application of the normal curve, we shall want to know how many standard deviations a score lies above or below the mean. Knowing this, questions about the area between points on any normal curve or heights of the curve above any point can be answered by reference to the unit normal curve. The deviation of a score from its mean is $X - \mu$; the number of standard deviations X lies from its mean is $(X - \mu)/\sigma$. $(X - \mu)/\sigma$ is called the *unit normal deviate*. If X has a normal distribution with mean μ and standard deviation σ, $(X - \mu)/\sigma$ has the unit normal distribution, but not otherwise.

The *shape* of the normal curve does not change when we subtract μ and divide by σ. If we would like to know what proportion of the area lies to the left of a score of 20 in a normal distribution with mean 25 and standard deviation 5, we can translate this question into "What proportion of the area lies to the left of $(20 - 25)/5 = -1$ in the unit normal distribution?"

These points are summarized in the following statement:

> If X has a normal distribution with mean μ and standard deviation σ, then $z = (X - \mu)/\sigma$ has a normal distribution with mean 0 and standard deviation 1, i.e., $z = (X - \mu)/\sigma$ has the unit normal distribution.
>
> The area between X_1 and X_2 in the normal distribution with mean μ and standard deviation σ is the same as the area between $z_1 = (X_1 - \mu)/\sigma$ and $z_2 = (X_2 - \mu)/\sigma$ in the unit normal distribution.

6.6
USES OF THE NORMAL CURVE

De Moivre invented the normal curve for a particular use; namely, to provide an easy, approximate solution to applications of probability theory. Surely he was never aware that his discovery would find applications in practically every corner of science that now exists. Indeed, the wide application and occurrence of the normal distribution are a wonder.

The normal distribution plays an important role in both descriptive and inferential statistics. We must defer any discussion of the normal distribution in inferential statistics until the later chapters in this text.

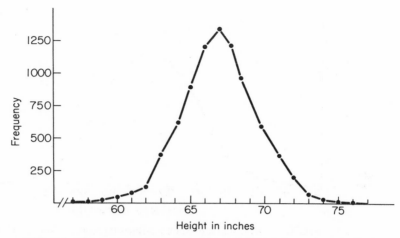

FIG. 6.6   Frequency polygon for heights of 8585 adult men born in Great Britain during the nineteenth century.

The normal curve is an excellent approximation to the frequency distributions of large numbers of observations taken on a variety of variables. The frequency polygons of heights of adult males and adult females both look quite like a normal curve.   The frequency polygon in Fig. 6.6 shows the distribution of heights of 8585 adult men born in Great Britain during the nineteenth century.

The frequency polygon in Fig. 6.6 is based on the frequency distribution shown in Table 6.1 (see Rugg, 1917):

TABLE 6.1   FREQUENCY DISTRIBUTION FOR FIG. 6.6

Height	Frequency	Height	Frequency	Height	Frequency
58″	4	64″	669	70″	646
59″	14	65″	990	71″	392
60″	41	66″	1223	72″	202
61″	83	67″	1329	73″	79
62″	169	68″	1230	74″	32
63″	394	69″	1067	75″	16
				76″	5

Psychometric tests of general and special mental abilities often yield distributions of scores that conform closely to the normal distribution.   It is fairly well known that IQ's from the Stanford-Binet Intelligence Test are approximately normally distributed with a mean (μ) of 100 and standard deviation (σ) of 16 for people in general (see Fig. 6.7).   Tests of educational

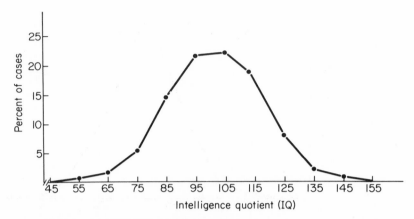

FIG. 6.7   Distribution of Stanford-Binet IQ scores. *From L. M. Terman and M. A. Merrill, Measuring Intelligence (Boston: Houghton Mifflin, 1937).*

attainment which are constructed in accord with the same psychometric principles upon which ability tests rest usually produce frequency polygons that resemble the normal curve. Measures of human ability in general are frequently nearly normally distributed. Whether or not some ties can be drawn between this fact and the relationship of the normal curve to the probability distribution of groups of binomial trials for chance events is a task we leave gladly to the more philosophically inclined.

Somehow the misapprehension arises in the minds of many students that there is a necessary link between the normal distribution—an idealized description of *some* frequency distributions—and practically any data they might collect. The normal curve is a mathematician's invention that is a reasonably good description of the frequency polygon of measurements on several different variables. A collection of scores that are *exactly* normally distributed has never been gathered and never will be. But much is gained if we can tolerate the slight error in the statement and claim from time to time that scores on a variable are "normally distributed." (On this point, see Boring, 1920, and Kelley, 1923.)

The mathematical statistician has greatly contributed to the eminence of the normal distribution. Although many different mathematical curves would fit empirical frequency polygons tolerably well, special mathematical advantages are gained when the normal curve can be assumed to "fit the data." Certain mathematical properties of the normal curve, Eq. (6.1), produce simple and elegant proofs to many inferential statistical problems. Without the normal curve, mathematical statisticians would have to labor under extreme complications that arise when other mathematical curves are used to represent data.

6.7
THE BIVARIATE NORMAL
DISTRIBUTION

The theory of correlation, which will be the subject of Chapter 7, has close historical ties with the normal distribution and the *bivariate normal distribution*. One preoccupation of statistics since its inception as a formal discipline has been the description of the way variables are related. Do tall fathers tend to have tall sons? Will a plot of land produce a higher yield of corn if we increase the amount of nutrients in the soil? Are bright children less athletic than less intellectually able children? Each of these questions can be studied abstractly as the problem of describing the way in which scores on a variable X are paired with scores on a second variable Y for the same persons. Thus, these questions concern *bivariate relationships*, i.e., relationships between two variables.

If we measure a large group of persons in two ways, e.g., we might measure each person's IQ (X) and physical strength (Y), the data can be represented in a *bivariate frequency distribution*. For each person there is a pair of scores, his score on X and his score on Y. A bivariate frequency distribution is a picture of the frequency with which different pairs of X and Y scores occur in a group of persons. Figure 6.8 is a bivariate frequency distribution for a group of persons measured on IQ (X) and physical strength (Y).

From Fig. 6.8, we can see that approximately 20 persons scored 125 on the IQ variable X and 30 on the physical strength variable Y. The height of the line at the intersection of 125 and 30 must be measured against the vertical scale of frequencies.

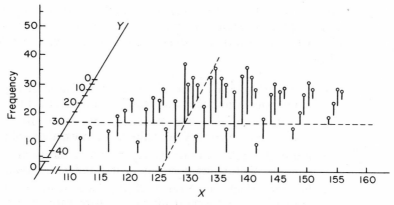

FIG. 6.8 Bivariate frequency distribution for a large group of persons measured on IQ (X) and physical strength (Y).

A large number of bivariate frequency distributions built from data gathered in educational and psychological settings show a characteristic shape. A surface drawn through the end points of the columns which represent the frequencies in a bivariate frequency distribution often looks like a bell—in three dimensions—that has been stretched in the X and Y directions and rotated around its center in the X-Y plane. Much was to be gained if the mathematical statistican could find a set of mathematical curves that gave a good description of many bivariate frequency distributions. The mathematical surface which was found to accomplish this objective is called the *bivariate normal distribution*. This smooth, continuous, bell-shaped surface provides a mathematically convenient and satisfactory representation of numerous bivariate frequency distributions.

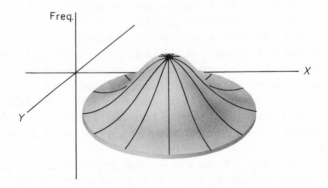

FIG. 6.9   One of the family of bivariate normal distributions (a section of the surface.

As was true of *the* normal distribution, the bivariate normal distribution is a family of three-dimensional surfaces. One member of this family appears in Fig. 6.9. All bivariate normal distributions have the following characteristics:

1. The distribution of the X scores, completely disregarding the Y scores with which they are paired, is a normal distribution.
2. The distribution of the Y scores, completely disregarding the X scores with which they are paired, is a normal distribution.
3. For each single score on X, say X_1, the Y scores of persons with a score on X of X_1 are normally distributed with variance $\sigma^2_{y.x}$.
4. For each single score on Y of Y_1, the X scores of persons with a score of Y_1 are normally distributed with variance $\sigma^2_{x.y}$.
5. The means of the Y scores for each separate score on X fall on a straight line.

We shall refer to the bivariate normal distribution on several occasions, but we shall not explore further properties of it.   For a more advanced discussion see Walker and Lev (1953, pp. 248–49).

PROBLEMS AND EXERCISES

1. Let z stand for the unit normal variable, i.e., the normally distributed variables with mean 0 and standard deviation 1.   Find the area under the unit normal curve which lies:

a. above $z = 1.00$;
b. below $z = 2.00$;
c. above $z = 1.64$;
d. below $z = -1.96$;
e. between $z = 0$ and $z = 3.00$;
f. above $z = -0.50$;
g. between $z = -1.50$ and $z = 1.50$.

2. Find the ordinates of the unit normal distribution above each of the following z scores:

a. $z = 1.00$;
b. $z = -1.00$;
c. $z = 2.25$;
d. $z = -0.15$.

3. Find the z scores which are exceeded by the following proportions of the area under the unit normal distribution:

	Proportion of area above z score	z score
a.	0.50	0
b.	0.16	+1.00
c.	0.84	
d.	0.05	
e.	0.005	
f.	0.995	
g.	0.10	

4. If in the general population of children Stanford-Binet IQ's have a nearly normal distribution with mean 100 and standard deviation 16, find the percentile equivalent of each of the following IQ's:

	I.Q.	Percentile equivalent
a.	100	
b.	120	
c.	75	
d.	95	
e.	140	

5. X and Y have a bivariate normal distribution. Both X and Y have means of zero and variances of 1. Suppose that for $X = 1.25$ the variance of the associated Y variable is 0.50. What is the variance of the Y variable associated with a value of 1.50 for the X variable?

7

MEASURES
OF
RELATIONSHIP

7.1
INTRODUCTION

In this chapter we shall begin the study of the description of relationships between variables. Before we leave this general topic at the end of Chapter 9, we hope that the major portion of the description of relationships between variables which you will find useful will have been covered. A complete discussion of the measurement of relationship or *correlation*, a subject that has undergone almost a century of research, would easily require a book ten times as long as this chapter. The topics we shall purposely overlook in this text can be found in references cited in Sec. 7.10 at the end of this chapter.

7.2
THE PEARSON
PRODUCT-MOMENT
CORRELATION COEFFICIENT

Researchers are often concerned with the way in which two variables relate to each other for a given group of persons (classrooms, schools, nations, etc.). For example, do students who tend to read earlier than others also tend to have higher achievement in science in the sixth grade? Do large classrooms show lesser gains in knowledge over a semester than smaller classrooms? Is the average length of employment of teachers in a school directly related to the average salary for teachers? Obviously, to answer such questions we must make observations on each variable for a group of units (typically persons, but they might be classrooms, schools, counties, etc.). The data gathered to answer one such question might take the following form:

Student no.	Stanford-Binet IQ score (X)	Raw score on chemistry achievement test (Y)
1	120	31
2	112	25
3	110	19
4	120	24
5	103	17
6	126	28
7	113	18
8	114	20
9	106	16
10	108	15
11	128	27
12	109	19

In this example, the variables observed on 12 students were IQ as determined by the Stanford-Binet Intelligence Scale in grade 6 and achievement in high-school chemistry as measured by a 35-item teacher-made test.

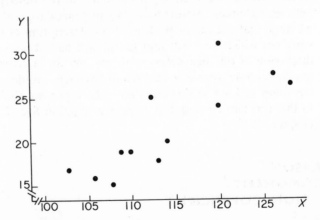

FIG. 7.1   Scatter diagram showing relationship of IQ (X) to achievement in chemistry (Y) for 12 students.

The relationship between the two variables can be depicted graphically in a presentation of the data called a *scatter diagram*. The scatter diagram for the above data appears as Fig. 7.1.

Each unit (person in this example) is represented by a point on the scatter diagram. A dot or mark is placed for each person at the point of intersection of straight lines drawn through his IQ score perpendicular to the X axis and through his chemistry-test score perpendicular to the Y axis. The scatter diagram in Fig. 7.1 shows a moderate positive relationship between X and Y. As yet, however, we have no summary measure of this relationship.

The general question of "relationship" must be given a somewhat more precise meaning. Is high relative standing on X of a person with respect to a group paired with high or low relative standing of that person on Y, or is there no systematic pairing off of high and low relative standings?

The standing of a person relative to others in a group on X and Y relative to the means of two distributions is reflected in the size and algebraic sign of the deviation scores $(X_i - \bar{X})$ and $(Y_i - \bar{Y})$, respectively. If a person is high on both variables, as is student 11 above, the product of $(X_i - \bar{X})$ and $(Y_i - \bar{Y})$ will be large and positive for him. Similarly, if a person is relatively low on both X and Y, $(X_i - \bar{X})(Y_i - \bar{Y})$ will be large and *positive* for him also (because the product of two negative numbers is a positive number). Now if X and Y are *directly* related (high paired with high and low with low) substantially, most of the products $(X_i - \bar{X})(Y_i - \bar{Y})$ will be positive; consequently, the sum of these products for all persons $\left[\text{i.e., } \sum_{i=1}^{n} (X_i - \bar{X})(Y_i - \bar{Y})\right]$ should be large and positive.

If X and Y bear an *inverse* relationship to each other (high X paired with low Y and vice versa), many persons with positive $(X_i - \bar{X})$ scores will tend to have negative $(Y_i - \bar{Y})$ scores, and negative $(X_i - \bar{X})$ scores will tend to be paired with positive $(Y_i - \bar{Y})$ scores. In this case, the products $(X_i - \bar{X})(Y_i - \bar{Y})$ will generally be negative. Hence,

$$\sum_{i=1}^{n} (X_i - \bar{X})(Y_i - \bar{Y})$$

will be *negative* when X and Y are inversely related.

If X and Y bear no systematic relationship to each other (high X's are as likely to be paired with low Y's as with high Y's, and the same is true of low X's), then of the people with large positive $(X_i - \bar{X})$ scores some will have positive $(Y_i - \bar{Y})$ scores and others will have negative $(Y_i - \bar{Y})$ scores. When the products $(X_i - \bar{X})(Y_i - \bar{Y})$ are formed, some will be positive and others will be negative. The sum of the products,

$$\sum_{i=1}^{n} (X_i - \bar{X})(Y_i - \bar{Y}),$$

should contain about an even balance of positive and negative terms of the same size and should therefore be relatively close to zero.

Thus we have the quantity $\sum_{i=1}^{n} (X_i - \bar{X}.)(Y_i - \bar{Y}.)$ being large and positive when X and Y are strongly related directly, being near zero when X and Y are unrelated, and being large and negative when X and Y are strongly related inversely. However, this sum of the products of deviation scores is still not an adequate summary measure of relationship. For one thing, its size depends on how many pairs of scores are included in its calculation. Since we may wish to compare the degree of relationship between X and Y in two groups of different size, we shall want to make the measure of relationship independent of the size of the group on which it is calculated. A simple averaging procedure will accomplish this. Two means calculated on different size groups are comparable in terms of locating central scores, but the simple sums of the two groups of scores are not. This is why we take an average if we want a statistic to be independent of group size. However, for the same reason that s_x^2 was defined by dividing the sum of squared deviations by $n - 1$ instead of n, we should divide

$$\sum_{i=1}^{n}(X_i - \bar{X}.)(Y_i - \bar{Y}.) \quad \text{by} \quad n - 1.$$

The quantity $\sum_{i=1}^{n} (X_i - \bar{X}.)(Y_i - \bar{Y}.)/(n - 1)$ is a measure of the relationship between X and Y and is called the *covariance* of X and Y. The covariance of X and Y is denoted by s_{xy}:

$$s_{xy} = \frac{\sum_{i=1}^{n}(X_i - \bar{X}.)(Y_i - \bar{Y}.)}{n - 1}. \tag{7.1}$$

Notice that the covariance of X with itself is simply the variance of X:

$$s_{xx} = \frac{\sum_{i=1}^{n}(X_i - \bar{X}.)(X_i - \bar{X}.)}{n - 1} = \frac{\sum_{i=1}^{n}(X_i - \bar{X}.)^2}{n - 1} = s_x^2.$$

The covariance is a perfectly good measure of association in many problems in the physical sciences and engineering. (In fact, physicists call the hallowed "correlation coefficient" of the behavioral sciences—which we shall encounter presently—the "dimensionless covariance.") And it is an adequate measure as long as the scale (mean and variance) of the variables are not arbitrary and contain some meaning. Many variables with which we deal are measured on an arbitrary scale: the mean and variance may be whatever anyone wishes since we are usually interested only in relative positions in a group. This is particularly true of psychological and educational test data.

The process of deviating both the X and Y scores around their respective means has made s_{xy} independent of the means of the scores. To make the desired measure of relationship independent of the standard deviations of the two groups of scores, one need only divide s_{xy} by s_x and s_y. The result is the desired measure of relationship between X and Y. It is called the *Pearson product-moment correlation coefficient* and is denoted by r_{xy}:

$$r_{xy} = \frac{s_{xy}}{s_x s_y} \tag{7.2}$$

The designation r comes from the word *regression*. In the early applications of the coefficient by Francis Galton and Karl Pearson (1857–1936), it played an important role in the study of association of physical characteristics in humans, a study that first pointed up the regressive nature of physical measurements from one generation to the next. Although Pearson played the most important role in establishing the mathematical properties of r_{xy}, the notion of a correlation coefficient equal to $s_{xy}/(s_x s_y)$ can be traced through the writings of Galton back to an article published in 1846 by the Frenchman Bravais.

7.3
A COMPUTATIONAL
FORMULA FOR r_{xy}

Equation (7.2) is definitional and not convenient for computing r_{xy}. We shall now derive a form more convenient for calculating r_{xy} on a desk calculator, given the raw scores X and Y. Begin with

$$r_{xy} = \frac{s_{xy}}{s_x s_y} = \frac{\sum_{i=1}^{n}(X_i - \bar{X})(Y_i - \bar{Y})/(n-1)}{\sqrt{\sum_{i=1}^{n}(X_i - \bar{X})^2/(n-1)}\sqrt{\sum_{i=1}^{n}(Y_i - \bar{Y})^2/(n-1)}}. \tag{7.3}$$

Note that $1/(n-1)$ can be factored out of the two terms $(1/\sqrt{n-1}$ from each term) in the denominator of Eq. (7.3), and it cancels the $1/(n-1)$ in the numerator of Eq. (7.3). Also recall that since $\sqrt{a}\sqrt{b} = \sqrt{ab}$, the terms in the denominator of Eq. (7.3) can be combined under the radical.

$$r_{xy} = \frac{\sum_{i=1}^{n}(X_i - \bar{X})(Y_i - \bar{Y})}{\sqrt{\left[\sum_{i=1}^{n}(X_i - \bar{X})^2\right]\left[\sum_{i=1}^{n}(Y_i - \bar{Y})^2\right]}}. \tag{7.4}$$

Consider just the numerator of (7.4):

$$\sum_{i=1}^{n}(X_i - \bar{X})(Y_i - \bar{Y}) = \sum_{i=1}^{n}X_i Y_i - \bar{X}\sum_{i=1}^{n}Y_i - \bar{Y}\sum_{i=1}^{n}X_i + n\bar{X}\bar{Y}. \tag{7.5}$$

Several steps were involved in moving from Eq. (7.4) to Eq. (7.5): expanding a binomial, moving constants (e.g., $\bar{X}$) outside of summation signs, and summing constants. Try to fill in the details.

Recalling that $\sum Y = n\bar{Y}$ and $\sum X = n\bar{X}$, we can write the right side of Eq. (7.5) as follows:

$$\sum_{i=1}^{n} X_i Y_i - n\bar{X}\bar{Y} - n\bar{Y}\bar{X} + n\bar{X}\bar{Y} = \sum_{i=1}^{n} X_i Y_i - n\bar{X}\bar{Y}. \qquad (7.6)$$

If we had chosen to replace $\bar{X}$ by $\sum X/n$ and similarly for Y, we would have obtained

$$\sum_{i=1}^{n} (X_i - \bar{X})(Y_i - \bar{Y}) = \sum_{i=1}^{n} X_i Y_i - \frac{(\sum X_i)(\sum Y_i)}{n}. \qquad (7.7)$$

Either Eq. (7.6) or Eq. (7.7) provides a simple formula for the numerator of r_{xy}. We already know a simple way to compute the denominator of r_{xy}.

$$\sum (X_i - \bar{X})^2 = \sum X_i^2 - \frac{(\sum X_i)^2}{n}. \qquad (7.8)$$

$$\sum (Y_i - \bar{Y})^2 = \sum Y_i^2 - \frac{(\sum Y_i)^2}{n}. \qquad (7.9)$$

Combining Eqs. (7.7), (7.8), and (7.9) produces the following formula for r_{xy},

$$r_{xy} = \frac{\sum X_i Y_i - (\sum X_i)(\sum Y_i)/n}{\sqrt{[\sum X_i^2 - (\sum X_i)^2/n][\sum Y_i^2 - (\sum Y_i)^2/n]}}, \qquad (7.10)$$

which can be simplified further to become the *computational formula*

$$r_{xy} = \frac{n\sum X_i Y_i - (\sum X_i)(\sum Y_i)}{\sqrt{[n\sum X_i^2 - (\sum X_i)^2][n\sum Y_i^2 - (\sum Y_i)^2]}}. \qquad (7.11)$$

Equation (7.11) is more convenient than Eq. (7.10) for finding r_{xy} on a desk calculator on which "negative multiplication" is possible. It will then be possible to calculate the numerator of Eq. (7.11) without divisions and without writing any numbers down on paper. This is also true for both terms in brackets in the denominator of Eq. (7.11).

7.4
ILLUSTRATION OF THE
CALCULATION OF r_{xy}

Some ability-test data will be used here to illustrate the calculation of r_{xy} from Eqs. (7.10) and (7.11). A researcher is studying the relationship between two types of reasoning ability in high-school juniors: abstract reasoning and verbal reasoning. Two tests are constructed, one measuring abstract reasoning (X) and the other measuring verbal reasoning (Y). The two tests were administered to 40 high-school juniors from the junior class

of the only high school in an Illinois town of about 30,000 residents. The
test scores for the 40 students appear in Table 7.1. Each test was 50 items

TABLE 7.1   RAW SCORES ON 50-ITEM TESTS OF ABSTRACT AND VERBAL
REASONING ABILITY FOR 40 ILLINOIS HIGH-SCHOOL JUNIORS*

Student	X Abstract reasoning	Y Verbal reasoning	Student	X Abstract reasoning	Y Verbal reasoning
Linda J.	19	17	Martin T.	38	30
Peggy Y.	32	7	Sharon L.	25	18
Deane L.	33	17	Julie E.	35	26
Constance L.	44	28	Natalie J.	22	17
William P.	28	27	Maryjean K.	40	17
Roger D.	35	31	Larry N.	42	26
Caroline E.	39	20	Michael B.	41	16
Trudy R.	39	17	Carleen M.	41	37
Peter A.	44	35	Scott C.	37	26
David E.	44	43	Sigrid K.	30	21
Cheryl G.	24	10	Jan W.	31	16
Georgia S.	37	28	Roger B.	41	37
Erma J.	29	13	Richard H.	42	37
Ronald L.	40	43	Bonita G.	24	14
Pamela J.	42	45	Rex N.	43	41
Edward B.	32	24	Richard S.	36	19
Rosa L.	48	45	Maurice D.	39	18
Karen M.	43	26	Warren W.	39	39
Roger W.	33	16	Jack G.	39	37
Richard T.	47	26	Stanley L.	48	47

* We wish to express our appreciation to Dr. J. Thomas Hastings, Director of
the Illinois Statewide Testing Program, who made these data available.

in length, and the test score was the number of correct answers given. A
scatter diagram of the bivariate data in Table 7.1 appears in Fig. 7.2.

The intermediate and final calculations of r_{xy} for both formulas (7.10)
and (7.11) appear in Table 7.2. All calculations were performed on a desk
calculator. (Without mechanical computation, the calculation of product-
moment correlation coefficients is usually tedious.) Perhaps the only quantity
in Table 7.2 whose origin is doubtful in your mind is $\sum_{i=1}^{40} X_i Y_i$. This quantity
is the sum over all persons of the *product* of each person's X and Y scores.
For the first student in Table 7.1, Linda J., $X_1 = 19$ and $Y_1 = 17$; for the
second student, Peggy Y., $X_2 = 32$ and $Y_2 = 7$. The quantity

$$\sum_{i=1}^{40} X_i Y_i = (19 \cdot 17) + (32 \cdot 7) + \ldots + (48 \cdot 47) = 40{,}798.$$

The final calculations on the right-hand side of Table 7.2 show r_{xy} to

TABLE 7.2 ILLUSTRATION OF THE CALCULATION OF r_{xy} FOR THE DATA IN TABLE 7.1

Intermediate calculations	*Final calculations*
$n = 40$	Equation (7.10): $$r_{xy} = \frac{40{,}798 - (1465)(1057)/40}{\sqrt{[55{,}725 - (1465)^2/40]}\ \times [32{,}551 - (1057)^2/40]}$$
$\displaystyle\sum_{i=1}^{40} X_i = 1465 \qquad \sum_{i=1}^{40} Y_i = 1057$	$$= \frac{2085.375}{3091.932} = 0.67.$$
$\displaystyle\sum_{i=1}^{40} X_i^2 = 55{,}725 \qquad \sum_{i=1}^{40} Y_i^2 = 32{,}551$	Equation (7.11): $$r_{xy} = \frac{40(40{,}798) - (1465)(1057)}{\sqrt{[40(55{,}725) - (1465)^2]}\ \times [40(32{,}551) - (1057)^2]}$$
$\displaystyle\sum_{i=1}^{40} X_i Y_i = 40{,}798$	$$= \frac{83{,}415}{123{,}761.128} = 0.67.$$

be 0.67, by either Eq. (7.10) or Eq. (7.11). It will always be true that the two formulas will yield the same value, within rounding error. Thus, there appears to be a strong, direct relationship between abstract and verbal reasoning ability as measured by the two tests.

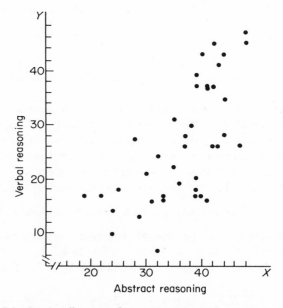

FIG. 7.2 Scatter diagram of the 40 pairs of test scores in Table 7.1.

7.5
RANGE OF VALUES OF r_{xy}

It is somewhat difficult to prove, but r_{xy} *can never take on a value less than* −1 *nor a value greater than* +1.* (If you are dismayed by the apparent

TABLE 7.3   INTERPRETATION OF VALUES OF r_{xy}

Value of r_{xy}	Description of linear relationship	Scatter diagram
+1.00	Perfect, direct relationship	
About +.50	Moderate, direct relationship	
.00	No relationship (i.e., 0 covariation of X with Y)	
About −.50	Moderate, inverse relationship	
−1.00	Perfect, inverse relationship	

* To prove that the value of r_{xy} cannot exceed +1, expand $\sum_{1}^{n} (z_x - z_y)^2$, which is always greater than or equal to zero, and use the fact that

$$\sum z_x^2 = \sum z_y^2 = n - 1 \quad \text{and} \quad r_{xy} = \frac{\sum z_x z_y}{(n-1)}.$$

To show that r_{xy} cannot be less than −1, work with $\sum (z_x + z_y)^2$.

difficulty of the proof suggested in the footnote, you can at least take con-
solation in the fact that the simpler proof often given in elementary textbooks
is fallacious.) Table 7.3 is a listing of various values of r_{xy} with illustrations
of the type of *linear* relationship that exists between X and Y for the given
values of r_{xy}.*

In Table 7.4 some representative correlation coefficients are presented.

TABLE 7.4   TYPICAL VALUES OF r_{xy}

Descriptions of variables		*Nature of*	*Typical value*
X	*Y*	*subjects*	*of r_{xy}*
Iowa Test of Educational Development, Grade 9	Freshman grade-point average in college	Over 600 college students	.58
The Stanford-Binet Intelligence Test IQ	The same test given one week later	Elementary-school pupils	.90
Verbal reasoning ability (as measured by the Differential Aptitude Test)	Nonverbal reasoning ability	High-school juniors	.65
Height	Achievement in college physics	Male college seniors	.00

After a little experience with actual data, you will begin to develop a "feel"
for the degree of relationship that is indicated by any particular value of r.
You will probably learn to associate in your mind a scatter diagram of points
and the approximate value of r that corresponds to it. We hesitate to apply
descriptive adjectives to values of r, such as calling an r of .80 "high" or an
r of .20 "low." Whether or not a particular r is "high," "low," or "moderate"
depends upon how the two variables being correlated have been related in
the past, what use one intends to make of the relationship between the
variables, etc. Moreover, why use a vague and ambiguous adjectival description for a value of r when it is so simple merely to report the value?

Erlenmeyer-Kimling and Jarvik (1963) presented data that are enlighten-
ing illustrations of the use of r. They found typical values of r for large
classes of studies published in the literature in which the intelligence-test
scores of children were correlated with those of siblings, related children,
or unrelated children. For example, the typical value of the correlation

---

* The sort of relationship r_{xy} is designed to measure is a special type, to be discussed
in Chapter 8. For more on this point, see Sec. 7.7 on curvilinear relationships between X
and Y in this chapter.

coefficient between a child's IQ (X) and the IQ of his identical twin (Y) for a large set of identical-twin pairs was .88 when the twins were reared together. The typical correlation between IQ's of identical twins reared apart was .75. These and other data are reported in Table 7.5.

TABLE 7.5   CORRELATIONS BETWEEN IQ's OF RELATED OR UNRELATED CHILDREN AS A FUNCTION OF GENETIC SIMILARITY AND SIMILARITY OF ENVIRONMENT

Nature of pairing	Typical value of r_{xy}
Identical twins, reared together	.88
Identical twins, reared apart	.75
Fraternal twins of same sex	.53
Fraternal twins of opposite sex	.53
Siblings, reared together	.49
Siblings, reared apart	.46
Parent with own child	.52
Foster parent with child	.19
Unrelated, reared together	.16

7.6
THE EFFECT ON r_{xy} OF
TRANSFORMING SCORES

Often the mean and variance of the scores on X and Y are arbitrary. We can change them at will without consequence, it seems. But does the value of r_{xy} depend on the means and variances of X and Y? The answer is *No*. This answer was implicit in our development of the formula for r_{xy}; now we wish to make it more explicitly.

The mean and variance of X (or Y) can be changed to any value we desire by multiplying X by a constant $b \neq 0$, and adding a constant a to the product, i.e., by forming $bX + a$. This process is called "taking a *linear transformation* of X." Suppose we take another (or perhaps the same) linear transformation of Y, $dY + c$, where $d \neq 0$. Is the correlation coefficient between X and Y the same as that between $bX + a$ and $dY + c$?

The correlation of $bX + a$ and $dY + c$ is the covariance of the two divided by the product of the standard deviations. We know that adding a constant to a variable does not change its standard deviation and that multiplying a variable by a constant multiplies the standard deviation of that variable by the absolute value of the constant. Thus, the standard deviation of $bX + a$ is $|b|\, s_x$, and $dY + c$ has a standard deviation of $|d|\, s_y$.

$$s_{bX+a} = |b|\, s_x, \quad \text{and} \quad s_{dY+c} = |d|\, s_y. \tag{7.12}$$

The covariance of $bX + a$ and $dY + c$ is

$$S_{(bX+a)(dY+c)} = \frac{\sum_{i=1}^{n} [bX_i + a - (b\bar{X} + a)][dY_i + c - (d\bar{Y} + c)]}{n - 1}.$$

This expression reduces to the following:

$$\frac{\sum_{1}^{n} (bX_i - b\bar{X})(dY_i - d\bar{Y})}{n - 1} = \frac{bd \sum_{1}^{n} (X_i - \bar{X})(Y_i - \bar{Y})}{n - 1} = bds_{xy}. \quad (7.13)$$

In words, the covariance of $bX + a$ and $dY + c$ equals bd times the covariance of X and Y. We can combine the results in Eqs. (7.12) and (7.13) into an expression for the correlation of $bX + a$ and $dY + c$.

$$r_{bX+a,dY+c} = \frac{bds_{xy}}{|b|\,|d|\,s_x s_y} = \frac{bd}{|b|\,|d|} r_{xy}. \quad (7.14)$$

In words, the correlation between $bX + a$ and $dY + c$ equals r_{xy} times the product of b and d over the product of the absolute values of b and d. As an example, suppose that X is transformed into $3X + 5$ and Y into $2Y + 8$.

$$r_{3X+5,2Y+8} = \frac{3 \cdot 2}{|3| \cdot |2|} r_{xy} = r_{xy}.$$

This particular transformation of X and Y had no effect on the correlation r_{xy}. In fact the ratio of bd to $|b|\,|d|$ in Eq. (7.14) can never be anything but $+1$ or -1. Hence, no linear transformation of either X or Y (provided b or d is not zero) can change the *size* of the correlation between X and Y, though it may change the *sign* of the correlation. If either b or d, but not both, is negative, the correlation of $bX + a$ and $dY + c$ will equal $-r_{xy}$. These results are summarized in Table 7.6.

TABLE 7.6   THE EFFECT OF LINEAR TRANSFORMATIONS OF X AND Y ON THE VALUE OF r_{xy} [SPECIAL CASES OF EQ. (7.14)]

$bX + a$	$dY + c$	Value of $r_{bX+a,dY+c}$
b is positive	d is positive	r_{xy}
b is negative	d is positive	$-r_{xy}$
b is positive	d is negative	$-r_{xy}$
b is negative	d is negative	r_{xy}

7.7
INTERPRETING CORRELATION
COEFFICIENTS

A. Causation and Correlation

The presence of a correlation between two variables does not necessarily mean there exists a causal link between them. Even though concomitance (correlation) between events can be useful in identifying causal relationships when coupled with other methodological approaches, it is a dangerous and potentially misleading test for causation when used alone. First, even when one can presume that a causal relationship does exist between the two variables being correlated, r_{xy} can tell nothing by itself about whether X causes Y or Y causes X. Second, often variables other than the two under consideration are responsible for the observed association. Third, the relationships that exist among variables in education and the social sciences are almost always too complex to be explained in terms of a single cause. Achievement in school is the resultant of numerous influences, in addition to being a complex concept itself which cannot be described adequately by any single measurement.

We shall examine some examples of the problems that arise in attempts to unearth causal relationships with correlational techniques. It is probably true that in the United States there is a positive correlation between the average salary of teachers in high schools and the percent of the school's graduates who enter college. Does this imply that a well-paid teaching staff *cause* better trained high-school graduates? Would the percent of high-school graduates entering college rise if we increased the pay of teachers? Certainly affirmative answers to these questions are not justified by the associational relationship alone. The relationship between the two factors is not simple, but one prominent variable not yet mentioned is the financial and economic condition of the community that largely determines its ability to pay *both* teachers' salaries and college tuitions. Moreover, the economic and financial condition of the community is in part dependent upon the intellectual powers of its citizens, another variable that contributes to both higher teachers' salaries and greater college attendance among the young people.

It has been found that the percent of "dropouts" in each of a number of high schools is negatively correlated with the number of books per pupil in the libraries of those schools. But common sense tells us that piling more books into the library will no more affect the dropout rate than hiring a better truant officer will bring about a magical increase in the holdings of the school library. If only common sense always served us so well!

Many researchers do not stop with one fallacious conclusion, i.e., that correlation is *prima facie* evidence for causation, but draw a second one as well. They assume a certain direction for the causal relationship. This is only natural, since their minds are generally made up as to the nature of a causal relationship between two phenomena before they gather data and compute r_{xy}. Let's investigate a plausible example more closely. Suppose that among a large group of pupils the correlation coefficient is $-.60$ between anxiety while taking an intelligence test (X) and performance on the intelligence test (Y). Does this imply that high anxiety has caused the pupils to perform poorly on the test, whereas low-anxiety pupils, not being handicapped by fear, were able to perform up to the full measure of their ability? This conclusion has tempted some researchers. Why is it not equally plausible that the intelligence test is the factor that causes anxiety? Might not dull pupils become anxious when their intelligence is tested, while bright students find the experience pleasant and not anxiety-producing? What is involved here is the question of whether X can be said to cause Y or Y to cause X. A simple correlation coefficient between X and Y cannot lend evidence in support of either claim. Suffice it to say here that studies of association alone, without experimental substantiation, are often difficult to interpret convincingly. A manipulative experimental approach to this same problem would involve making one group of pupils anxious and comparing their scores on the intelligence test with those of a control group.

Failure to recognize that correlation may not mean causation is a widespread logical error. Going to Sunday School is generally believed to be valuable in many ways, but a positive relationship between the rate of Sunday School attendance and honesty, for example, does not *necessarily* imply that children are honest *because* they attend Sunday School. Under-lying rate of attendance and honesty and causing them both may be early childhood training in the home. A crucial—but ethically repugnant test of the hypothesis that Sunday School makes children more honest would involve prohibiting a group of children from attending Sunday School to see if an increase in dishonesty results.

While correlation does not directly establish a causal relationship it may furnish clues to causes. When it is feasible, these clues can be formalized as hypotheses that can be tested in experiments in which influences other than the few whose interrelationships are being studied can be controlled. Also, there are elaborate procedures, especially in sociology, for inferring causation from associational data.

Sometimes lack of correlation can have a more profound impact on our hypothesis of a causal relationship than the presence of a high corre-lation. A zero correlation between two variables may mean that there exists no influence of one upon the other, provided that we have faith in the measurements we've taken of the variables and that the Pearson product-moment r—which measures only a special type of relationship—is appro-priate for measuring a more general type of relationship called "causal." But all of this is little help; what is needed are techniques to discover causal relationships, not techniques to demonstrate noncausal ones. There are only relatively few of the former and they are valuable, but noncausal relationships exist in superabundance and the discovery of one is little cause for celebration. For further discussion, see Blalock (1964) and Campbell and Stanley (1963).

B. Presence of Identifiable Groups of Subjects with Different Means

A substantial correlation between two variables is a fact that can be explained differently in different situations. Some correlations result from measuring a cause and its effect, e.g., when X is food intake in a period of one month and Y is weight gain over the same period. Other correlations result from measuring two variables with a common cause or influence, e.g., when X is achievement in English and Y is achievement in social studies. Still other correlations result when two distinct groups of persons within which X and Y are unrelated are pooled together.

Suppose that girls report greater anxiety than boys on an inventory such as Taylor's Manifest Anxiety Scale. It is well known that girls tend to score higher than boys on achievement tests in English, especially in the intermediate grades. The scatter diagram of the anxiety and English achievement scores for 15 boys and 15 girls might look like the one in Fig. 7.3.

The scatter diagram in Fig. 7.3 shows a moderately strong positive relationship between anxiety and English achievement when boys' and girls' scores are pooled. Does this mean that anxiety (tension) makes a student work harder and thus achieve more? Not at all. For if it did, why would one obtain no relationship between the two variables for boys and girls separately?

Figure 7.3 shows that nonzero correlations can result when distinct groups, e.g., boys and girls, with different average values on the two variables are pooled together. Either positive or negative relationships can result from this pooling. Sketch the scatter diagram that would result if one pools two groups for which X and Y are uncorrelated and for which group A

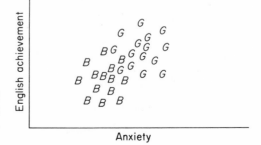

FIG. 7.3 Scatter diagram of anxiety and English achievement scores for 15 boys (B's) and 15 girls (G's).

has a high mean on X and a low mean on Y and group B has a low mean on X and a high mean on Y. Does the resulting scatter diagram correspond to a zero, a positive, or a negative correlation between X and Y?

The identification of subgroups with differing means on X and Y does not negate the fact that X and Y correlate. However, it may provide a more rational explanation of why r_{xy} is substantially different from zero.

C. Curvilinearity and the Shapes of Marginal Distributions

Of all the possible ways in which measurements on two variables can be related, r_{xy} measures only one type. The value of r_{xy} is a measure of the degree of *linear relationship* between X and Y. If X and Y are perfectly linearly related, the points in the scatter diagram will fall on a single straight line, as was illustrated in Table 7.3. If we scatter the points in such a scatter diagram above and below the line in a haphazard manner and about the same distance in each direction, we obtain various degrees of basically linear relationships between X and Y. If the points in a scatter diagram look as though they depart in a haphazard manner from a *curved* line, the relationship between X and Y may be basically *curvilinear*. To say that r_{xy} measures only the linear relationship between X and Y means that different sorts of curvilinear relationships between X and Y may produce values of r_{xy} that are misleadingly close to 0 if interpreted without reference to a scatter diagram of the data. X and Y can be closely related *curvilinearly* and yet r_{xy} can be zero. If we know that X and Y are generally linearly related, the meaning of r_{xy} is fairly unequivocal. However, if X and Y have some sort of curvilinear relationship, values of r_{xy} near zero can be obtained even though X and Y are highly related. Figure 7.4 shows two different scatter diagrams, each of which has correlation coefficients of approximately zero.

However, even though the scatter diagrams A and B in Fig. 7.4

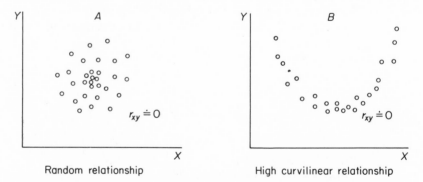

FIG. 7.4 Two instances of approximately zero product-moment correlation.

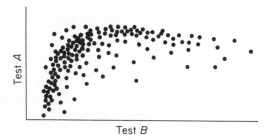

FIG. 7.5 The scatter diagram of scores for test A (which is too easy) and test B (which is too difficult for the group tested).

both have correlation coefficients of zero, there is considerable relationship present in B, while any systematic relationship between X and Y is lacking in A. The single illustration in Fig. 7.4 should be sufficient warning never to draw a rash conclusion that two variables are *unrelated* merely because r_{xy} is zero. Various degrees of curvilinearity of relationship between measures of variables are not uncommon. Educational and psychological test scores frequently show "ceiling" or "cellar" effects with atypical groups of persons, i.e., the tests may be too easy or too difficult with the result that many persons obtain the highest or the lowest test score. The scatter diagram of test scores for test A, which shows a "ceiling effect," and test B, which shows a "cellar effect," might look like the one in Fig. 7.5.

The value of r_{AB} for the data in Fig. 7.5 is not large; it is probably only about .30. In the range for which both tests are of appropriate difficulty, the two tests appear to be more highly related. One suspects that if test A was made more difficult and Test B easier without radically affecting the content of either test, the value of r_{AB} for these persons would increase. The scatter diagram of the test scores for such altered tests would probably show less curvilinearity than now. (This example illustrates another important point: the degree of relationship obtained between any two variables—regardless of how the relationship is expressed—depends on the nature of the measurement of the variables. For example, we generally think of the characteristics *weight* and *height* as being rather closely related in adult human beings; but it is not difficult to conceive ways of measuring each variable that are so poor—e.g., measurement by the sober subjective judgments of four-year olds—that weight and height scores would show almost no correlation.)

7.8
FURTHER REMARKS ON THE
INTERPRETATION OF r_{xy}

Carroll (1961) presented a readable account of how the interpretation of r_{xy} is dependent upon the shapes of the distributions of X and Y and of their joint distribution. Carroll's article is an excellent statement of many points touched only briefly here and parts of it will be clear to the student whose acquaintance with correlation does not extend beyond this and the next two chapters. He made the following observation on both the problem of interpreting r_{xy} and the statistical training of students:

> "Students are not adequately informed that these limits $[-1$ to $+1]$ and meanings ["highly related," "moderately related," "not related"] strictly have reference to certain statistical models. Two of the most frequently used models are the normal bivariate surface [see Sec. 6.6] and the linear regression model [see Chapter 8].... No assumptions are necessary for the computation of a Pearsonian coefficient, but the interpretation of its meaning certainly depends upon the extent to which the data conform to an appropriate statistical model for making this interpretation. As actual data depart from a fit to such a model [e.g., the bivariate normal surface], the limits of the correlation coefficient may contract, and the adjectival interpretations are less meaningful."

As an example of how the maximum value of r_{xy} might bound away from $+1$ when the frequency distributions of X and Y are skewed in different directions, consider 99 scores on X and on Y with the following frequency distributions:

Score on X:	0	1	2	3	4	5	6	7	8	9	10
Frequency:	21	12	14	14	13	10	7	4	2	1	1

Score on Y:	0	1	2	3	4	5	6	7	8	9	10
Frequency:	0	0	1	1	2	2	4	5	6	7	71

X is highly positively skewed, and Y is highly negatively skewed. The maximum possible value of r_{xy} is about .60. In other words, even if the maximum possible linear relationship between X and Y exists, r_{xy} will be only about .60. This reflects no weakness in r_{xy} as a descriptive measure; it cannot be blamed for not doing what it was not designed to do. In fact, that r_{xy} cannot be much larger than .60 in the above example should actually be rather comforting. When X has so many values below its mean and Y has so many values above its mean, it is impossible for all positive deviations of the Y_i around $\bar{Y}$ to be associated with positive deviations of the X_i around $\bar{X}$. In fact r_{xy} *cannot* attain the extreme values of $+1$ or -1 unless the X and Y distributions have identical shapes.

This dependence of the maximum value of r_{xy} on the distributions of X and Y places one in a difficult position. Suppose that an r_{xy} of .60 is obtained. What does it reflect? Moderate relationship between two variables whose joint frequency distribution looks like a bivariate normal surface, or the maximum possible relationship between a positively skewed X and a negatively skewed Y? Earlier we saw how similar doubts surround a zero value for r_{xy}. Are X and Y actually unrelated or is the relationship between them non-linear? The most satisfactory resolution of all of these doubts can be made by looking at a scatter diagram of the X and Y scores. From such a diagram it can be seen immediately whether or not X and Y have a pronounced curvilinear relationship and whether X and Y are markedly skewed. Regrettably, researchers are too hesitant to construct scatter diagrams. One would think that one beneficial effect of electronic data processing would be increased plotting of scatter diagrams in correlational problems, either by hand or by computer. This has not yet happened. In the authors' judgment, building and inspecting the scatter diagram so that r_{xy} can be interpreted more intelligently are well worth the little effort they take.

7.9
THE VARIANCE OF SUMS AND DIFFERENCES OF VARIABLES

Quite often in education and psychology one wishes to find the variance of a group of summed X and Y scores. Moreover, simply inspecting the formula that related s^2_{x+y}, the variance of the summed X and Y scores, to s^2_x, s^2_y, and r_{xy} can illuminate the way in which influences combine to produce joint effects. In the history of mental test theory, a general expression for the variance of a sum of variables has played an important role (a total test score is the sum of scores on the individual items of the test).

The variance of $X + Y$, where each of the n sums is $X_i + Y_i$, has the following definition:

$$s^2_{x+y} = \frac{\sum_1^n [X_i + Y_i - (\bar{X} + \bar{Y})]^2}{n - 1}. \tag{7.15}$$

The terms inside the brackets in Eq. (7.15) can be rearranged to produce

$$s^2_{x+y} = \frac{\sum_1^n [(X_i - \bar{X}) + (Y_i - \bar{Y})]^2}{n - 1}. \tag{7.16}$$

If the bracketed expression in the numerator of Eq. (7.16) is expanded and the summation sign is distributed over the terms after expansion, one obtains

$$s^2_{x+y} = \frac{\sum_1^n (X_i - \bar{X})^2}{n - 1} + \frac{2\sum_1^n (X_i - \bar{X})(Y_i - \bar{Y})}{n - 1} + \frac{\sum_1^n (Y_i - \bar{Y})^2}{n - 1}. \tag{7.17}$$

You will recognize immediately that the first and last terms on the right-hand side of Eq. (7.17) are s_x^2 and s_y^2, respectively. The middle term is simply 2 times the covariance of X and Y, s_{xy}. Thus,

$$s_{x+y}^2 = s_x^2 + s_y^2 + 2s_{xy}. \qquad (7.18)$$

One way of denoting r_{xy} is by $s_{xy}/(s_x s_y)$. Obviously then, $s_{xy} = r_{xy}s_x s_y$. Therefore, replacing s_{xy} by an equivalent expression gives

$$s_{x+y}^2 = s_x^2 + s_y^2 + 2r_{xy}s_x s_y. \qquad (7.19)$$

Equations (7.18) and (7.19) relate the variance of the sum of two arrays of scores to the variance of each array and the covariance of the arrays.

An important special case of Eq. (7.19) is that in which X and Y are *uncorrelated*, i.e., $r_{xy} = 0$. If this is true, then

$$s_{x+y}^2 = s_x^2 + s_y^2. \qquad (7.20)$$

What is an expression equivalent to s_{x-y}^2?

$$s_{x-y}^2 = \frac{\sum_1^n [(X_i - Y_i) - (\bar{X}. - \bar{Y})]^2}{n-1}$$

$$= \frac{\sum_1^n (X_i - \bar{X}.)^2 + \sum_1^n (Y_i - \bar{Y})^2 - 2\sum_1^n (X_i - \bar{X}.)(Y_i - \bar{Y})}{n-1}$$

$$= s_x^2 + s_y^2 - 2s_{xy} = s_x^2 + s_y^2 - 2r_{xy}s_x s_y.$$

This is an interesting development. The variance of the differences between a group of persons' scores on X and Y equals the variance of X *plus* the variance of Y *minus* twice the covariance of X and Y (or twice r_{xy} times s_x and s_y). Again, if X and Y are uncorrelated, then

$$s_{x-y}^2 = s_x^2 + s_y^2. \qquad (7.21)$$

You may find it difficult to reconcile Eq. (7.20) with Eq. (7.21) and this is not surprising. Perhaps the following argument will help:

If X and Y are uncorrelated, then surely X and $-Y$ are uncorrelated, since $-Y$ is just a linear transformation of Y (see Sec. 7.6). If we let Y^* stand for $-Y$, we know that $s_{x+y*}^2 = s_x^2 + s_{y*}^2$ because X and Y^* are uncorrelated. The effect of multiplying Y by -1 to form Y^* gives Y^* a mean of $-\bar{Y}$ but leaves the variance at s_y^2. Therefore, $s_{x+y*}^2 = s_x^2 + s_y^2$; but of course, $X + Y^*$ is just $X - Y$. Hence, $s_{x-y}^2 = s_x^2 + s_y^2$.

The above results are not only useful in more advanced statistics—they can be illuminating also. For example, we know that

$$s_{x+y}^2 - s_x^2 - s_y^2 = s_x^2 + s_y^2 + 2r_{xy}s_x s_y - s_x^2 - s_y^2 = 2r_{xy}s_x s_y.$$

Therefore, if we divide the above equation through by $2s_x s_y$, we find that

$$\frac{s_{x+y}^2 - s_x^2 - s_y^2}{2s_x s_y} = r_{xy}.$$

Suppose one has *three* variables X, Y, and Z. What would be the variance of the sums formed by adding together a person's scores on these three variables to secure the sum $X_i + Y_i + Z_i$?

$$s_{x+y+z}^2 = \frac{\sum_{1}^{n} [(X_i + Y_i + Z_i) - (\bar{X}_. + \bar{Y}_. + \bar{Z}_.)]^2}{n-1}. \qquad (7.22)$$

The terms in brackets in Eq. (7.22) can be rearranged to yield

$$s_{x+y+z}^2 = \frac{\sum_{1}^{n} [(X_i - \bar{X}_.) + (Y_i - \bar{Y}_.) + (Z_i - \bar{Z}_.)]^2}{n-1}. \qquad (7.23)$$

The numerator of Eq. (7.23) is a *trinomial* squared. You may recall from high-school algebra that $(a + b + c)^2 = a^2 + b^2 + c^2 + 2ab + 2ac + 2bc$. Hence,

$$s_{x+y+z}^2 = \frac{\sum (X_i - \bar{X}_.)^2}{n-1} + \frac{\sum (Y_i - \bar{Y}_.)^2}{n-1}$$

$$+ \frac{\sum (Z_i - \bar{Z}_.)^2}{n-1} + \frac{2 \sum (X_i - \bar{X}_.)(Y_i - \bar{Y}_.)}{n-1}$$

$$+ \frac{2 \sum (X_i - \bar{X}_.)(Z_i - \bar{Z}_.)}{n-1} + \frac{2 \sum (Y_i - \bar{Y}_.)(Z_i - \bar{Z}_.)}{n-1}.$$

All of the terms to the right of the equal sign in the above equation are variances or covariances. The entire expression can be reduced to

$$s_{x+y+z}^2 = s_x^2 + s_y^2 + s_z^2 + 2s_{xy} + 2s_{xz} + 2s_{yz},$$

which is the same as

$$s_{x+y+z}^2 = s_x^2 + s_y^2 + s_z^2 + 2r_{xy}s_x s_y + 2r_{xz}s_x s_z + 2r_{yz}s_y s_z.$$

The problems of variances of sums of and differences between variables are very important in intermediate and advanced statistics. A thorough understanding of these concepts is requisite to most work in mental test theory, factor analysis, and many other areas which lie outside of statistics. You would do well to thoroughly understand the material in this section before moving on. If you need further instruction in this area, Edwards (1964, pp. 15–23) should be helpful.

7.10
OTHER MATERIAL ON
CORRELATION

This chapter does not contain the entire treatment of correlation in this text. Chapter 8 has as its subject the problem of least-squares estimation, which is closely related to correlation (see Sec. 8.4). In Chapter 9, correlation coefficients are presented for correlating scores that are nominal and ordinal. These three chapters by no means exhaust the subject of measuring relationships. Those aspects of the subject which have been slighted here can be covered adequately by consulting Ezekiel and Fox (1963), DuBois (1957), and Kruskal (1958).

PROBLEMS AND EXERCISES

1. Prove that the correlation of X and Y equals $+1$ when $z_x = z_y$.

   (Hint: Start with the equation $r_{xy} = \sum z_x z_y / (n-1)$. Since a person's z score on X is assumed to be identical to his z score on Y, substitute z_x for z_y in the formula for r_{xy}. Then prove that $\sum_{1}^{n} z_x^2/(n-1) = +1$. See Prob. 8 in Chapter 5.)

2. Brown calculated the covariance of height in inches X and running speed in seconds Y. He obtained a value of 27.60 on a sample of 50 students. Smith calculated the covariance of height in feet X ($5\frac{1}{2}'$, $5\frac{7}{12}'$, etc.) and running speed Y from the same original data that Brown collected. Smith obtained a value of 2.30. Will Brown or Smith obtain a larger value for the correlation between X and Y with this one set of measures?

3. Indicate whether the covariance and, hence, the correlation of the two designated variables would probably be positive or negative in the population of all elementary-school pupils in the United States:

   a. X, height in inches; Y, weight in pounds.
   b. X, age in months between 6 and 16 years; Y, time in seconds required to run 50 yards.
   c. X, reading achievement in grade-placement units; Y, arithmetic achievement in grade-placement units.
   d. X, I.Q. of student; Y, "citizenship" rating of student on a 10-point scale by his teacher.
   e. X, arithmetic achievement in grade-placement units; Y, number of days absent from school during the year.

4. For a particular set of data, $s_x = 5$ and $s_y = 4$. What is the largest that s_{xy} could possibly be? [Hint: r_{xy} cannot be larger than $+1$; $r_{xy} = s_{xy}/(s_x s_y)$.]

5. The correlation of X with Y is .60; the correlation of X with Z is $-.80$. Is X more closely linearly related to Y or to Z?

6. A researcher demonstrated a correlation of $-.52$ between average teacher salary X and the proportion of students who drop out of school before graduation Y, across 120 high schools in his state. He concluded that increasing teachers' salaries would reduce the "drop-out rate." Comment on his conclusion.

7. a. Find the value of the correlation coefficient r for the following data:

Person	X	Y
1	100	28
2	90	25
3	126	19
4	112	24
5	80	23
6	115	21
7	105	27
8	110	25
9	99	26
10	97	25
11	87	23
12	76	18
13	100	29
14	80	20
15	120	18

   b. Plot a scatter diagram for the above data.

   c. Does the relationship between X and Y—if there is a nonzero one—appear to be predominantly linear or curvilinear?

8. Compute the r for data set a, below, and the r for data set b. Why do the r's differ in magnitude?

a. Person number	IQ		b. Person number	Test score gen. vocab.	Arith. reasoning
	Test A	Test B			
1	80	83	1	96	104
2	105	101	2	111	121
3	121	117	3	89	84
4	93	100	4	107	91
5	99	96	5	102	114
6	107	112	6	115	96
7	119	123	7	98	109
8	103	99	8	83	94
9	102	110	9	104	116
10	115	110	10	100	86
11	87	81	11	117	101
12	96	98	12	94	99

9. It has been shown that women tend to score much higher (i.e. have more "accepting" attitudes) than men on the Minnesota Teacher Attitude Inventory.

A researcher correlated the MTAI scores of a group of 100 experienced secondary teachers with the number of students each teacher failed in a year. He obtained an r of $-.39$. He concluded that teachers tend to fail students because they do not have "accepting" attitudes toward students. Comment on the researcher's methods and conclusions.

10. $\displaystyle\sum_{i=1}^{n} (X_i - \bar{X})(Y_i - \bar{Y}) = \sum_{i=1}^{n} [X_i(Y_i - \bar{Y}) - \bar{X}(Y_i - \bar{Y})]$

$\displaystyle = \sum_{i=1}^{n} X_i(Y_i - \bar{Y}) - \bar{X} \sum_{i=1}^{n} (Y_i - \bar{Y}) = \sum_{i=1}^{n} X_i(Y_i - \bar{Y}) - \bar{X}(0).$

In words, the sum of the cross products of the X and Y scores, both in *deviation score form*, equals the sum of the cross products of X, *not* in deviation score form, and the Y's in deviation score form. This seems paradoxical. Has a mistake been made in the proof? Or is it truly a fact?

11. Is it true that $\displaystyle\sum_{i=1}^{n} X_i(Y_i - \bar{Y}) = \sum_{i=1}^{n} Y_i(X_i - \bar{X})$?

Hint: Show that $\displaystyle\sum_{i=1}^{n} [X_i(Y_i - \bar{Y}) - Y_i(X_i - \bar{X})] = 0.$

8

PREDICTION
AND
ESTIMATION

8.1
PRELIMINARIES

The concepts and procedures involved in the simplest form of statistical prediction are best illustrated by means of a few elementary notions in analytic geometry. We shall develop little more than the idea of a two-dimensional coordinate system and the equation for a straight line in this system.

A *cartesian** coordinate system is depicted in Fig. 8.1. The axes of the coordinate system—the mutually perpendicular X and Y lines—divide the plane (the flat, two-dimensional surface having length and width, but not depth) into four quadrants: I, II, III, and IV. This coordinate system is a means of marking off the plane in such a way that every point in the plane can be identified by a pair of numbers, (X, Y). The point $(0, 0)$ is called the *origin* of the system and lies at the point where the X and Y lines cross, i.e., where the two axes intersect. The first number of any pair is the distance

* Named after the French philosopher-mathematician René Descartes.

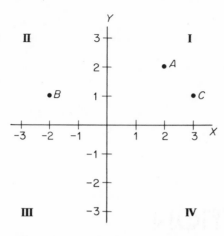

FIG. 8.1   Two-dimensional   (*X* and   *Y*)   cartesian   coordinate system.

one must travel *horizontally* from the origin (the *X* distance) to reach the point, and the second number is the distance the point lies *vertically* from the origin.   The point *A* in Fig. 8.1 corresponds to the pair of numbers (2, 2). The first number is called the *X-coordinate*; the second number is called the *Y-coordinate*.   The point *B* corresponds to the pair of numbers (−2, 1); it lies two units to the *left* of the origin along the *X* axis and one unit above the origin along the *Y* axis.   Points in quadrant I correspond to pairs of numbers both of which are positive; points in quadrant II correspond to pairs of numbers the first of which is negative, the second of which is positive.
What are the signs of the numbers describing points in the third

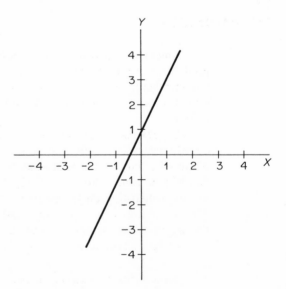

FIG. 8.2   Graph of the straight line $Y = 2X + 1$.

quadrant? The fourth quadrant? What is the pair of numbers that determine the location of point C in Fig. 8.1?

You should realize that any point in a plane corresponds to a pair of real numbers and that any pair of real numbers identifies a point. Thus, $(-100, 3.67)$ determines a point, as does $(-41.65, 214.6)$.

Eventually, we shall arrive at a method of predicting a set of scores that uses a straight line in a plane to describe the set of predicted scores. It will be useful to know the manner in which any straight line in a plane can be completely described by a simple equation.

In Fig. 8.2 the straight line L crosses the Y axis at the point $(0, 1)$, and the X axis at the point $(-0.5, 0)$. For each unit on the X axis that the moving point which describes the line moves to the right, it rises two units on the Y axis. The following points lie on the line L: $(-2, -3)$, $(-1, -1)$, $(0, 1)$, $(1, 3)$, etc. The value of Y in the description of the point (X, Y) is systematically related to the value of X. For the line L in Fig. 8.2, the Y value of any point on the line equals twice the X value plus 1, i.e., $Y = 2X + 1$. The equation $Y = 2X + 1$ is the equation for the straight line in Fig. 8.2. The number 1 is called the Y *intercept* because it is the distance above the X axis at which the line intersects with the Y axis. The number 2 is the *slope* of the straight line. The slope is the number of units the line rises for each unit of movement to the right on the X axis, here $2:1$.

The equation $Y = b_1 X + b_0$ is called the "*general equation for a straight line.*" It says simply that the pairs of points (X, Y) that lie on any straight line are related in such a way that for any X value the Y value paired with it can be found by multiplying X by some number b_1, and adding a second number b_0 to this product. This is a linear transformation of X to secure Y; b_1 is a multiplicative constant, the same for every X, and b_0 is an additive constant, the same for every X.

8.2
THE PROBLEM OF
ESTIMATING Y FROM X
(OR X FROM Y)

Given an individual's score on characteristic (variable) X, what information can be gained about his score on characteristic (variable) Y? Some examples of the estimation problem are:*

    1. How, and how well, can we *predict* college English grades from high-school English grades? (The high-school grades precede the college grades, so we can predict the latter.)

* When X precedes the Y we wish to estimate from it, then we predict (i.e., tell in advance) Y from X, once we know the relationship between X and Y based on an earlier group.

2. How well can we estimate Stanford-Binet IQ scores from California Test of Mental Maturity IQ scores? (No antecedent-consequent order is implied, so this is estimation to determine how nearly equivalent the z scores of each examinee are on the two tests.)

3. How well can we *predict* income at age 35 from rank in high-school graduating class?

4. How well can we estimate achievement from intelligence?

To derive a means of estimating the score of a person on one variable (which we shall denote by Y) from a different variable (X), we must know how X and Y are related. The variable we wish to estimate is called the *dependent variable* (Y), and the variable that will be used to estimate it is the *independent variable* (X). For example, we might wish to predict achievement in ninth-grade mathematics (dependent variable Y) from a group intelligence test given at the end of grade eight (independent variable X). Measures of Y might be scores on a 50-item achievement test in ninth-grade math. We must first gather data on some number n of students whose intelligence we test in grade eight and whose achievement in ninth-grade math we measure. We next establish an equation that relates X and Y in this group; we would then use this equation in the future with students whose score on X we know and whose score on Y we would like to estimate.

Illustrative data can be tabulated as in Table 8.1, and graphed as in Fig. 8.3. It is apparent in Table 8.1 that five sums and the number of pairs (there, $n = 20$) are required to determine b_1, which is the slope of the straight regression line needed to estimate Y (mathematics scores in grade 9) from X (IQ's in grade 8). The five statistics, shown at the upper right section of Table 8.1, are: the sum of the 20 X scores—that is, $X_1 + X_2 + \ldots + X_n = 2165$; the sum of the 20 Y scores (824); the sum of the *squared* X scores, which is $X_1^2 + X_2^2 + \ldots + X_n^2 = 235{,}091$; the sum of the 20 squared Y scores (34,442); and the sum of the 20 products of the X scores and their paired Y scores, which is

$$X_1 Y_1 + X_2 Y_2 + \ldots + X_n Y_n = 95(33) + 100(31) + \ldots + 118(48)$$

$$= 89{,}715.$$

By means of these six statistics one finds that $b_1 = .708$, and that $b_0 = -35.441$. Thus, the equation for estimating Y's from X's is $.708X + (-35.441) = .708X - 35.441$. The straight line that follows this formula is shown in Fig. 8.3. It has a slope of $+.708$, because for every increment of $.708$ in Y there is an increment of 1.000 in X: $.708/1.000 = .708$.

$b_0 = -35.441$ means that if Fig. 8.3 were drawn with the X axis extending all the way back to $X = 0$ IQ, we would see that the regression line at the X of 0 crosses the Y axis at -35.441, the cartesian pair there being $(0, -35.441)$.

TABLE 8.1   DATA FOR THE DETERMINATION OF A PREDICTION LINE

X Independent variable (*IQ in grade 8*)	Y Dependent variable (*math score in grade 9*)	Calculations
95	33	$\sum X = 2165 \qquad \sum Y = 824$
100	31	
100	35	$\sum X^2 = 235{,}091 \qquad \sum Y^2 = 34{,}442$
102	38	
103	41	$\sum XY = 89{,}715$
105	37	$n = 20$
106	37	
106	39	$b_1 = \dfrac{n \sum XY - \sum X \sum Y}{n \sum X^2 - (\sum X)^2}$
106	43	
109	40	
		$\dfrac{20(89{,}715) - (2165)(824)}{20(235{,}091) - (2165)^2} = \dfrac{10{,}340}{14{,}595} = .708.$
110	41	
110	44	
111	40	$b_0 = \bar{Y}. - b_1 \bar{X}. = \dfrac{824}{20} - .708\left(\dfrac{2165}{20}\right) =$
112	45	
112	48	-35.441
		Least-squares prediction line:
114	45	$\hat{Y} = .708X - 35.441$
114	49	
115	47	Other descriptive statistics:
117	43	
118	48	$s_x = 6.198,\ s_y = 5.095,\ s_{xy} = 27.211$
		$r_{xy} = .861$

What criteria led to the formulas for b_1 and b_0 used in Table 8.1? This is an important question that deserves a detailed answer, as given below.

Suppose we found an equation for predicting Y from X that had satisfactory properties. We would have two constants, b_1 and b_0, such that multiplying X by b_1 and adding b_0 would give us an estimated value of Y. That is,

$$\hat{Y}_i = b_1 X_i + b_0,$$

the predicted value of Y for the ith person, denoted by $\hat{Y}_i$, equals b_1 times his X score plus b_0. Obviously, $\hat{Y}_i$ will not always equal Y_i, i.e., even with the "best" straight-line prediction equation we shall usually make errors in predicting Y from X. We say, then, that $Y_i = b_1 X_i + b_0 + e_i$, where e_i is an error of estimating Y from $\hat{Y}$ for the ith person:

$$e_i = Y_i - \hat{Y}_i. \qquad (8.1)$$

Another name for e_i is the *error of estimate*. The nature of the error of estimate in the prediction problem is illustrated in Fig. 8.4 for a person

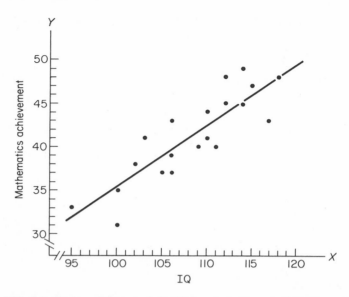

FIG. 8.3   Scatter diagram of X (IQ in grade 8) and Y (mathematics achievement in grade 9) for 20 students (see Table 8.1), with least-squares prediction line superimposed.

whose actual Y score is 4.36 units below the estimated Y for him that lies on the regression line.

How should we go about choosing b_1 and b_0?   Usually, b_1 and b_0 are found by choosing them so that

$$\sum e_i^2 = e_1^2 + e_2^2 + \ldots + e_n^2$$

is as small as possible—that is, the sum of the *squared* errors of estimate is minimal.

This choice of a criterion for selecting b_0 and b_1 is arbitrary to some extent. It has historical precedent, and computationally it is convenient. Moreover, it is preferred on statistical inferential grounds, but just why it is preferred on these grounds cannot be known until you have learned considerably more statistics.   However, the criterion of *least squares* (i.e., minimal sum of squared errors of estimate) is not the only criterion possible. Although there has never been a serious contender with it for the role of criterion for fitting the regression line, other criteria exist.   One is that b_0 and b_1 should be chosen so that the sum of the *absolute* values of errors made in prediction is as small as possible, i.e., so that $|e_1| + \ldots + |e_n|$ is minimized. This criterion leads to a "median-regression line."   (You will recall that the median of a group of scores is the point around which the sum of the absolute deviations of the scores from that point is minimal.)   Although the median-regression line is easily calculated, it does not have the inferential theoretical superstructure that the least-squares regression line has.

The use of the criterion of least squares for establishing a prediction line is over 150 years old. Karl Gauss (1777–1855), a famed German mathematician, physicist, and astronomer, is generally credited with having invented the criterion of least squares. In one form or another it underlies a large portion of theoretical and applied statistical work.

We noted earlier that e_i is the difference between a person's actual Y score and the Y score we predict for him:

$$e_i = Y_i - \hat{Y}_i = Y_i - (b_1 X_i + b_0). \tag{8.2}$$

We choose b_1 and b_0 so that

$$[Y_1 - (b_1 X_1 + b_0)]^2 + [Y_2 - (b_1 X_2 + b_0)]^2 + \ldots + [Y_n - (b_1 X_n + b_0)]^2$$

is as small as it can possibly be. The exact manner in which one determines the values of b_1 and b_0 that minimize the above quantity is too complicated for us to detail. (See McNemar, 1962, pp 119–24.) We shall simply report the results here, and in Sec. 8.5 present a verification of the reported solutions.

b_1 is given by the following equation:

$$b_1 = \frac{n \sum_{i=1}^{n} X_i Y_i - \left(\sum_{i=1}^{n} X_i \right) \left(\sum_{i=1}^{n} Y_i \right)}{n \sum X_i^2 - (\sum X_i)^2}. \tag{8.3}$$

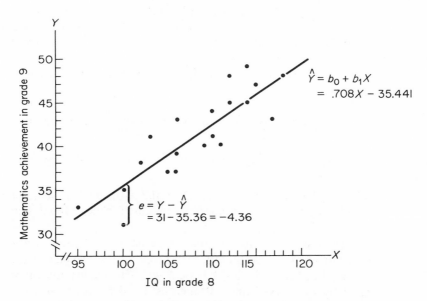

FIG. 8.4   Illustration of the error of estimate, e, for the person scoring 100 on variable X and 31 on variable Y.

b_0 is given by the equation

$$b_0 = \bar{Y}_. - b_1 \bar{X}_. . \tag{8.4}$$

The values of b_1 and b_0 found in this way give the "best" prediction equation in the sense that the sum of the squared differences between the Y_i and the $\hat{Y}_i = b_1 X_i + b_0$ is as small as it can possibly be for these data. In the last section in this chapter a simple algebraic verification that this is in fact true is presented.

Suppose that we seek the "best" equation for estimating Y from X by means of a straight line best fitting (in the least-squares sense) the dots of the scatter diagram and that we have the X and Y scores for 20 persons as given in Table 8.1.

Nothing has been said to this point about whether the dependent and independent variables are normally distributed or distributed in any other special way. No knowledge of the shapes of the frequency distributions of X and Y was needed to derive the least-squares regression coefficients b_0 and b_1. Equations (8.3) and (8.4) for b_0 and b_1 produce the straight line that minimizes the sum of squared residuals regardless of the nature of the scatter diagram of the X and Y scores.

If we make some plausible assumptions about the distributions of large numbers of X and Y scores, we are likely to be rewarded by being able to perform a more penetrating prediction study. Our study does gain much, in fact, if we assume that X and Y have a *bivariate normal distribution* (see Sec. 6.7). It is assumed, then, that the n pairs of X and Y scores in hand form a random sample of a very large collection of X and Y scores that have a bivariate normal distribution.

The properties of the bivariate normal distribution now of importance are:

1. The population means of the Y's for each separate value of X lie on a straight line;

2. For any single value of X the associated Y scores are normally distributed;

3. For any single value of X the associated Y scores have variance $\sigma^2_{y \cdot x}$, and this variance is the same for all of the X scores.

If we can be confident that the n pairs of X and Y scores are from a bivariate normal distribution, then property 1 above tells us that the use of a straight line for predicting Y from X was reasonable and cannot be improved upon by any curved line. Properties 2 and 3 above can be combined into a very useful technique that adds greatly to Y-from-X prediction and estimation problems. This technique will be developed next.

8.3
HOMOSCEDASTICITY AND THE STANDARD ERROR OF ESTIMATE

Property 3 of the bivariate normal distribution leads us to believe that, if we have, say, 19 persons with a score of 75 on X and 21 persons with a score of 80 on X, the variances of the two groups of associated Y scores should be about the same. This condition of equal variance of Y scores for each value of X is known as *homoscedasticity* (the roots of this word mean *equal spread*). The scatter diagram in Fig. 8.5 should help you gain an understanding of this condition.

It is important to note that *homoscedasticity* is a property of very large bodies of bivariate data. One should not expect equality of variances of Y scores for any two values of X when the n's are small, say of the order of 100 or less. For n's of 19 and 21 the variances of the Y scores for $X = 75$ and $X = 80$ in Fig. 8.5 are $s_{y\cdot75}^2 = 5.54$ and $s_{y\cdot80}^2 = 6.85$. These two variances are not equal, but they are reasonably close. With such small numbers of persons we cannot ascertain very well whether the condition of homoscedasticity is satisfied, but at least it seems somewhat plausible for X equals 75 and 80 after inspection of the data of Fig. 8.5.

Obviously the sizes of the errors made in estimating Y from X are an indication of the accuracy of estimation. For the data in hand, i.e., the n pairs of X and Y scores, the differences between the actual Y scores and the predicted Y scores are measures of the errors that would result if X is used to estimate Y. These errors are called *errors of estimate*. The formula for the error of estimate for the ith person is

$$e_i = Y_i - \hat{Y}_i = Y_i - b_1 X_i - b_0. \qquad (8.5)$$

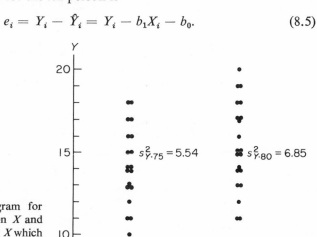

FIG. 8.5 Scatter diagram for 19 persons scoring 75 on X and 21 persons scoring 80 on X which exhibits nearly the same variance of Y scores for both values of X.

Would the mean of these n errors of estimate, $\bar{e}_{\cdot}$, be a suitable measure of how well Y is predicted from X? No, because it so happens that $\bar{e}_{\cdot}$ is always exactly zero:

$$n\bar{e}_{\cdot} = \sum_{1}^{n} e_i = \sum_{1}^{n} (Y_i - b_1 X_i - b_0) = \sum_{1}^{n} Y_i - b_1 \sum_{1}^{n} X_i - \sum_{1}^{n} b_0$$

$$= n\bar{Y}_{\cdot} - n b_1 \bar{X}_{\cdot} - n b_0 = n\bar{Y}_{\cdot} - n b_1 \bar{X}_{\cdot} - n(\bar{Y}_{\cdot} - b_1 \bar{X}_{\cdot}) = 0. \quad (8.6)$$

(Recall that $b_0 = \bar{Y}_{\cdot} - b_1 \bar{X}_{\cdot}$.)

Therefore, *the average error of estimate is always zero* when it is calculated on the same n pairs of scores that produced b_0 and b_1. For this reason it is not a suitable measure of the accuracy of predicting Y from X.

You will remember that the sample mean had the property that $\sum_{1}^{n} (X_i - \bar{X}_{\cdot}) = 0$. The principle of estimation that makes the least-squares regression line a minimum-variance estimator of Y scores is the same principle that makes $\bar{X}_{\cdot}$ a minimum-variance summary measure of central tendency. If a single score had to be used in place of, or to estimate, every score in a group, the sample mean $\bar{X}_{\cdot}$ would do so with the smallest sum of squared errors of estimate.*

One of several possibilities for a measure of the accuracy of predicting Y from X is the variance of the n errors of estimate, e_i. This quantity will be independent of the mean of the errors, which is always zero, and the number of such errors, because it involves division by $n - 1$. The variance of the n scores $e_i = Y_i - \hat{Y}_i$ is called the *variance error of estimate* and is denoted by s_e^2.

$$s_e^2 = \frac{\sum_{1}^{n} (e_i - \bar{e}_{\cdot})^2}{n - 1} = \frac{\sum_{1}^{n} e_i^2}{n - 1}. \quad (8.7)$$

There is a means of expressing s_e^2 in terms of s_y^2 and the correlation between X and Y, r_{xy}, that illuminates some of the relationships between correlation and prediction. We can write

$$s_e^2 = \frac{\sum_{1}^{n} e_i^2}{n - 1} = \frac{\sum_{1}^{n} (Y_i - b_1 X_i - b_0)^2}{n - 1}$$

$$= \frac{\sum_{1}^{n} (Y_i - b_1 X_i - \bar{Y}_{\cdot} + b_1 \bar{X}_{\cdot})^2}{n - 1} = \frac{\sum_{1}^{n} [(Y_i - \bar{Y}_{\cdot}) - b_1(X_i - \bar{X}_{\cdot})]^2}{n - 1}$$

* Formally, $\sum_{i=1}^{n} [X_i - (\bar{X}_{\cdot} + P)]^2 > \sum_{i=1}^{n} (X_i - \bar{X}_{\cdot})^2$ when $P \neq 0$. Confirm this for yourself by squaring the left-hand member of the inequality, "distributing the summation sign," and simplifying algebraically. Hint: $X_i - (\bar{X}_{\cdot} + P) = (X_i - \bar{X}_{\cdot}) - P$.

$$= \frac{\sum_1^n (Y_i - \bar{Y})^2}{n-1} + \frac{b_1^2 \sum_1^n (X_i - \bar{X})^2}{n-1} - 2\left[\frac{b_1 \sum_1^n (X_i - \bar{X})(Y_i - \bar{Y})}{n-1}\right]$$

$$= s_y^2 + b_1^2 s_x^2 - 2b_1 s_{xy}. \tag{8.8}$$

We know, however, that $b_1^2 = (r_{xy}s_y/s_x)^2 = r_{xy}^2 s_y^2 / s_x^2$ (see Sec. 8.4). Therefore, Eq. (8.8) can be written

$$s_e^2 = s_y^2 + r_{xy}^2 s_y^2 - 2b_1 s_{xy}.$$

Let us take a closer look at $2b_1 s_{xy}$.

$$2b_1 s_{xy} = \frac{2r_{xy}s_{xy}s_y}{s_x}.$$

Since $r_{xy} = s_{xy}/(s_x s_y)$, the quantity s_{xy}/s_x must equal $r_{xy}s_y$. Therefore,

$$2b_1 s_{xy} = 2r_{xy}^2 s_y^2.$$

Finally,

$$s_e^2 = s_y^2 + r_{xy}^2 s_y^2 - 2r_{xy}^2 s_y^2 = s_y^2(1 - r_{xy}^2). \tag{8.9}$$

Equation (8.9) gives the variance error of estimate in terms of the variance of Y and r_{xy}.

The positive square root of the variance error of estimate is called the *standard error of estimate*:

$$s_e = s_y\sqrt{1 - r_{xy}^2}. \tag{8.10}$$

The standard error of estimate can be used to set limits around a predicted score $\hat{Y}$, within which a person's actual score is likely to fall. If it can be assumed that the persons whose scores determined the prediction line $b_0 + b_1 X$ came from what is roughly a bivariate normal distribution (see Sec. 6.7), then the following statements can be made. In a large group of persons to which the prediction equation is applied:

1. Approximately 68% will have actual scores that lie within one s_e of their predicted score $\hat{Y}$;

2. Approximately 95% will have actual scores that lie within two s_e's of their $\hat{Y}$;

3. Approximately 99.7% will have actual scores that lie within three s_e's of their $\hat{Y}$.

These statements are valid because if the bivariate normality assumption is correct, the distribution of actual Y scores is normal around a mean of $b_0 + b_1 X$ and with a standard deviation of s_e for any X.* (Notice that although the *mean* of the normal distribution of the Y scores differs from one

---

* For the *exact* estimation procedures that remove the "approximately" from statements 1–3, see Dixon and Massey (1969, pp. 199–200).

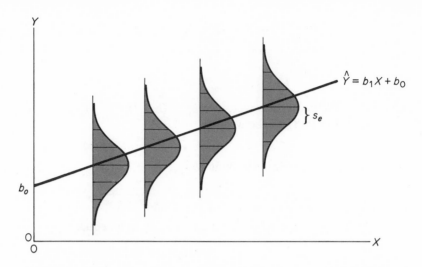

FIG. 8.6   Illustration of the standard error of estimate, s_e, at four levels of X when a bivariate-normal distribution of X and Y can be assumed.

value of X to the next, the standard deviation s_e does not depend on X.) These relationships are illustrated in Fig. 8.6.

8.4
RELATIONSHIPS BETWEEN b_0
AND b_1 AND OTHER
DESCRIPTIVE STATISTICS

Both the problems of finding a "best" prediction line and of measuring the correlation between two variables are concerned with pairs of measures for a group of persons. In both instances, the data can be represented in a scatter diagram. In this section we shall see that there exist several interesting relationships between r_{xy}, s_x, s_y, and the coefficients b_0 and b_1 for the least-squares prediction line. Some of these relationships will illuminate the nature of both the problems of linear estimation and the measurement of correlation; others will only be correspondences at the level of calculating b_0, b_1, and r_{xy}.

First, let us look at the formula for b_1 in estimating Y from X. We saw that the n pairs of scores (X_i, Y_i) produce the coefficient b_1, for X used to estimate Y:

$$b_1 = \frac{n \sum XY - (\sum X)(\sum Y)}{n \sum X^2 - (\sum X)^2}.$$

If we multiply the above equation by

$$\frac{1/n(n-1)}{1/n(n-1)} = \frac{1/n(n-1)}{1/n(n-1)},$$

where $n > 1$ (an operation equivalent to multiplying by $1 = 1$ that does not change the value of either side, of course), the following results:

$$b_1 = \frac{\{\sum XY - (\sum X)(\sum Y)\ /n\}/(n-1)}{\{\sum X^2 - (\sum X)^2\ /n\}/(n-1)}. \tag{8.11}$$

The numerator of Eq. (8.11) is s_{xy}, the covariance of X and Y. The denominator of Eq. (8.11) is s_x^2, the variance of X. Therefore,

$$b_1 = \frac{s_{xy}}{s_x^2}. \tag{8.12}$$

That is, b_1 *equals the covariance of X and Y divided by the variance of X.* The covariance of X and Y for the data in Table 8.1 is 27.211, and s_x^2 equals 38.408. The ratio s_{xy}/s_x^2 equals .708, the value of b_1 as calculated from Eq. (8.3).

You will recall that $r_{xy} = s_{xy}/(s_x s_y)$. Thus, if we simply multiply this equation by

$$\frac{s_y}{s_x} = \frac{s_y}{s_x},$$

we obtain b_1:

$$r_{xy}\frac{s_y}{s_x} = \frac{s_{xy}}{s_x^2} = b_1. \tag{8.13}$$

Suppose that X and Y have the same variance. If this is true, then s_y/s_x is 1 and

$$r_{xy}\frac{s_y}{s_x} = r_{xy} = b_1. \tag{8.14}$$

In words, *if X and Y have the same variance, b_1 equals r_{xy}.*

Equations (8.13) and (8.14) will be useful in exploring the range of possible values that b_1 can assume. We shall see that the largest and smallest possible values of b_1 depend on the sizes of s_y and s_x. We know, of course, that r_{xy} has a maximum value of $+1$ and a minimum value of -1.* Since r_{xy} is independent of s_x and s_y, b_1 will assume its maximum value when $r_{xy} = +1$ and its minimum value when $r_{xy} = -1$. By substituting these two

---

* But $r_{xy} = -1$ indicates the same degree of inverse relationship that $r_{xy} = 1$ indicates direct relationship.

values into Eq. (8.14), we see that the largest possible value of b_1 is

$$(+1)\frac{s_y}{s_x}$$

and the smallest possible value of b_1 is

$$(-1)\frac{s_y}{s_x}.$$

Hence, b_1 *can never be larger than* s_y/s_x. For example, the data in Table 8.1 yield an s_y of 5.095 and an s_x of 6.198. Therefore, the largest possible value of b_1 for estimating Y from X is $5.095/6.198 = .822$. The smallest possible value is $-.822$.

If there is no linear relationship between X and Y, then r_{xy} is zero. In this case,

$$b_1 = r_{xy}\frac{s_y}{s_x} = 0\frac{s_y}{s_x} = 0.$$

Hence, if X and Y are not linearly related the "best" estimation line has zero slope. It is a straight line, *parallel* to the X axis. The value of b_0 will be $\bar{Y}.$, as can be seen by setting b_1 equal to zero in Eq. (8.4). Thus,

$$\hat{Y}_i = b_0 + b_1X_i = \bar{Y}. - b_1\bar{X}. + b_1X_i = \bar{Y}. - 0(\bar{X}.) + 0(X_i) = \bar{Y}. ;$$

everyone's predicted score is the same. This is particularly unsatisfactory in most practical applications of the estimation technique. One generally obtains the prediction equation so that individual differences can be antici-pated and accommodated. (Who will need special attention? Who is likely to experience nothing but failure?) When X and Y are uncorrelated, X gives no information on the basis of which persons can be distinguished on Y. Regardless of whether a person has an exceptionally high score or an exceptionally low score on X, we cannot predict whether he would score higher or lower on Y than any other person.

The equation for the least-squares prediction line for z scores is partic-ularly interesting. Since both

$$z_x = \frac{X_i - \bar{X}.}{s_x} \quad \text{and} \quad z_y = \frac{Y_i - \bar{Y}.}{s_y}$$

have a variance of 1, the coefficient of z_x for predicting z_y is

$$b_1 = \frac{r_{z_xz_y}s_{z_x}}{s_{z_y}} = \frac{r_{xy}(1)}{1} = r_{xy}.$$

We know, of course, that $\bar{z}_y = \bar{z}_x = 0$. Therefore, the constant b_0 in esti-mating z_y from z_x is

$$b_0 = \bar{z}_y - b_1\bar{z}_x = 0 - b_10 = 0.$$

Consequently, the best estimate of z_{y_i} from z_{x_i} is $r_{xy}z_x$.

In other words, the distance which $\hat{Y}$ lies from $\overline{Y}$ in standard-deviation units is $r_{xy}z_{x_i}$:

$$z_{\hat{y}} = r_{xy}z_x. \tag{8.15}$$

Is $(\hat{Y}_i - \overline{Y})/s_y$ in Eq. (8.15) a z score? No. Its mean is 0, but its variance is r_{xy}^2, rather than 1. From Eq. (8.15) you can easily prove this. Note that

$$s^2_{(\hat{y}-\bar{y}\cdot)}/s_{y_i} = s^2_{r_{xy}z_x} = r_{xy}^2 s_{z_x}^2 = r_{xy}^2.$$

This means that the Y's as predicted from the X's in the manner of Eq. (8.15) are less variable—and hence closer together—than are the z_y's themselves unless $r_{xy}^2 = 1$. Such "regression" toward the mean $(\overline{Y})$ is characteristic of the Y-from-X estimation technique, as indicated by Eq. (8.16) below.

Equation (8.15) is easily remembered. From it you can quickly determine the Y-from-X formula by multiplying each side of Eq. (8.15) by s_y and adding $\overline{Y}$ to both sides of the same equation.

There is an illuminating relationship between the variances of $\hat{Y}$ and Y and the correlation coefficient. Of course, the variance of Y is denoted by s_y^2; the variance of $\hat{Y}$ is denoted by $s_{\hat{y}}^2$. Let us explore the expression $s_{\hat{y}}^2$ further. $\hat{Y}_i$ equals $b_0 + b_1X_i$, i.e., $\hat{Y}$ is a linear transformation of X. We can determine another form for $s_{\hat{y}}^2$ by applying what we know about the effect of a linear transformation on the variance of X. Adding a constant to X does not change its variance; multiplying X by a constant (e.g., b_1) has the effect of multiplying s_x^2 by the square of the constant (e.g., b_1^2). These points can be summarized thus:

$$s_{\hat{y}}^2 = s_{b_0+b_1x}^2 = b_1^2 s_x^2.$$

We have seen that $b_1 = r_{xy}(s_y/s_x)$; therefore,

$$s_{\hat{y}}^2 = \left(r_{xy}^2 \frac{s_y^2}{s_x^2}\right) s_x^2 = r_{xy}^2 s_y^2. \tag{8.16}$$

The variance of the predicted scores, i.e., the $\hat{Y}_i$'s, equals the square of the correlation between X and Y times the variance of Y. For example, the value of r_{xy} for the data in Table 8.1 is .861; s_y^2 is equal to 25.958. Therefore, the variance of the 20 predicted Y scores is

$$s_{\hat{y}}^2 = (.861)^2 25.958 = 19.243.$$

If $r_{xy} = 0$, then the variance of the predicted Y scores is zero; in fact each predicted Y score is $\overline{Y}$. If r_{xy} is $+1$ or -1, Y and $\hat{Y}$ have the same variance, s_y^2.

If we divide both sides of Eq. (8.16) by s_y^2, we obtain the following:

$$\frac{s_{\hat{y}}^2}{s_y^2} = r_{xy}^2. \tag{8.17}$$

In words, *the ratio of the variance of the predicted Y scores, Ŷ, to the actual Y scores is equal to the square of the correlation coefficient between X and Y.* Notice that this ratio tells nothing about the direction of the relationship; the ratio is never negative. For the data in Table 8.1, $s_y^2 = 25.958$ and $s_{\hat{y}}^2 = 19.243$. The ratio 19.243/25.958 equals .741, which corresponds to the square of the value of r_{xy} for these same data. It is often said in an attempt to explain the meaning of r_{xy} that r_{xy}^2 is the "amount of variance in Y explained by variance in X." This is ambiguous and nearly meaningless language without explicit definitions of what it means for a variable to have its "variance explained," and yet explicit definitions are usually lacking. Such "explanations" of r_{xy} are attempts to verbalize Eq. (8.17) beyond the italicized sentence above.

The most significant formula for "understanding" what the correlation coefficient describes is Eq. (8.17). We shall try to interpret the meaning of r_{xy}^2 in a slightly different way.

Suppose we wanted to predict each person's score on variable Y but no variable X was available. The predicted score that minimizes the sum of the squared errors of prediction in predicting Y happens to be $\overline{Y}$ for each person. That is, if no X variable is available and nothing is known about how individuals score on Y, the *best* prediction can be attained by predicting that everyone will score at the mean $\overline{Y}$ on Y. A measure of the goodness of such prediction without an X variable is given by

$$\frac{\sum_{1}^{n} (Y_i - \overline{Y})^2}{n - 1},$$

which happens to equal s_y^2.

Now suppose that knowledge of a person's status on X is available for predicting his Y score. The sum of the squared errors of prediction made in predicting Y from X with the least-squares regression line is given by

$$\frac{\sum_{1}^{n} (Y_i - \hat{Y}_i)^2}{n - 1},$$

which is s_e^2.

Now we know that $s_{\hat{y}}^2 + s_e^2 = s_y^2$. The quantity s_y^2 is the error made in prediction before knowledge of X is used; s_e^2 is the error made when knowledge of X is used. The amount of error *eliminated* from s_y^2 by knowledge of X must then equal $s_{\hat{y}}^2$. Recall that

$$\frac{s_{\hat{y}}^2}{s_y^2} + \frac{s_e^2}{s_y^2} = 1.$$

Noting that $s_{\hat{y}}^2/s_y^2 = r_{xy}^2$, the above equation can be written as:

$$r_{xy}^2 = 1 - \frac{s_e^2}{s_y^2} = \frac{s_y^2 - s_e^2}{s_y^2} = \frac{s_{\hat{y}}^2}{s_y^2}. \tag{8.18}$$

The following interpretation of r_{xy}^2 can be extracted from Eq. (8.18):

The value r_{xy}^2 equals the proportion of the variance of squared errors, s_y^2, made in predicting Y without knowledge of X that is eliminated when Y is predicted by the least-squares method from a knowledge of X.

For example, suppose $r_{xy}^2 = .75$ and $s_y^2 = 100$. We know, then, that $s_e^2 = 25$. The total error that would be made in predicting Y without knowledge of X, in which case everyone is predicted to have a Y score of $\bar{Y}$, is equal to

$$\frac{\sum_{1}^{n} (Y_i - \bar{Y})^2}{n-1} = s_y^2 = 100.$$

The total error made in predicting Y from X with the least-squares regression line is

$$\frac{\sum_{1}^{n} (Y_i - \hat{Y}_i)^2}{n-1} = s_e^2 = 25.$$

Therefore, $100 - 25 = 75$ is the percent of error eliminated from s_y^2 by knowledge of X. We note also that $r_{xy}^2 = .75$.

8.5
VERIFICATION THAT THE LEAST-SQUARES CRITERION IS SATISFIED BY b_1 AND b_0

This algebraic derivation is placed in Appendix C because it will probably not be of interest to all students. Earlier we stated without proof or verification that Eqs. (8.3) and (8.4) give the values of b_1 and b_0 that minimize $\sum [Y_i - (b_0 + b_1 X_i)]^2$, the sum of squared errors of estimate. Appendix C gives a relatively simple algebraic verification of the fact that Eqs. (8.3) and (8.4) for b_1 and b_0 produce the smallest possible sum of squared errors of estimate. Hopefully, this demonstration will satisfy some curious minds while imparting a deeper understanding of the least-squares criterion to all. We emphasize that the proof is *not* the means by which Eqs. (8.3) and (8.4) were originally derived. Our proof is an after-the-fact verification, given the Eqs. (8.3) and (8.4) for b_0 and b_1.

8.6
MEASURING NONLINEAR RELATIONSHIPS BETWEEN VARIABLES; THE CORRELATION RATIO η^2

This section appears here for the sake of completeness and logical continuity. You may find it more comprehensible after having studied Chapter 15 on the one-factor analysis of variance.

Although we have repeatedly pointed out that the Pearson product-moment r measures only the degree of *linear* relationship between X and Y, we have yet to indicate a descriptive measure to use when the relationship between X and Y is predominantly nonlinear. As an example of a non-linear relationship, consider the data in Fig. 8.7 relating age X to performance Y on the Digit Symbol subtest of the Wechsler Adult Intelligence Scale. The data depicted in Fig. 8.7 are tabulated in Table 8.2. It is obvious from

TABLE 8.2   WAIS DIGIT-SYMBOL-SUBTEST SCALED SCORES OF 28 PERSONS IN EIGHT EQUALLY SPACED AGE GROUPS

			Age to nearest year				
10	14	18	22	26	30	34	38
7	8	9	11	9	8	7	8
8	9	10	11	10	9	9	
9	10	11	12	11	9	10	
9	11	12	12		10		
10							

Age-group means:

8.60	9.50	10.50	11.50	10.00	9.00	8.67	8.00

$$\text{Grand mean of all scores} = \frac{269}{28} = 9.61$$

Fig. 8.7 that the scores on this subtest rise in straight-line fashion from age 10 to a peak at age 22 and then decline rather rapidly.

A measure of the linear *or* nonlinear relationship between X and Y is denoted by η^2 (read "eta squared"), also called the *correlation ratio*. The correlation ratio has the following definitional form:

$$\eta^2_{y,x} = 1 - \frac{SS_{within}}{SS_{total}}, \tag{8.19}$$

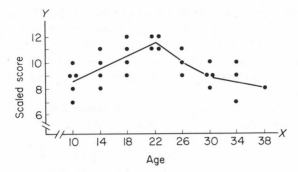

FIG. 8.7   Relationship between age and performance of 28 persons on the digit symbol subtest of the WAIS.

where $SS_{total} = \sum\limits_{i=1}^{n} (Y_i - \bar{Y})^2$, i.e., the sum of squared deviations of each Y score from the mean of *all n* Y scores, and SS_{within} is obtained in the following manner.

For the first value attained by X, the corresponding Y scores are deviated around their own mean and the sum of the squared deviations is calculated. For example, in Table 8.2 this first sum of squares is $(7 - 8.60)^2 + (8 - 8.60)^2 + (9 - 8.60)^2 + (9 - 8.60)^2 + (10 - 8.60)^2$. This process is repeated for each distinct value that X assumes. For example, for $X = 14$, one calculates $(8 - 9.50)^2 + (9 - 9.50)^2 + (10 - 9.50)^2 + (11 - 9.50)^2$. For the last group, $X = 38$, the sum of the squared deviations of the Y "scores" around their mean is $(8 - 8)^2 = 0$, since there is only one score. Finally, these sums of squared deviations for the separate values of X are summed. The result is SS_w. (If you are reading this section after having read Chapter 15, it will help you to note that SS_{within} is the "sum of squares within" for a one-factor analysis of variance with unequal *n*'s.) For the data in Table 8.2, the value of SS_{total} is 54.68 and the value of SS_{within} is 24.87. Hence the value of $\eta_{y,x}^2$ is

$$\eta_{y,x}^2 = 1 - \frac{24.87}{54.68} = 1 - .455 = .545.$$

The following considerations bear on the interpretation of $\eta_{y,x}^2$. The coefficient $\eta_{y,x}^2$—notice that Y precedes the comma and X follows it—is a measure of the extent to which Y is predictable from X by a "best-fitting" line that may be either straight or curved.

It is important to note that $\eta_{y,x}^2$ and $\eta_{x,y}^2$ will generally have different values. This is contrary to our experiences with *r*, for which $r_{xy} = r_{yx}$. We can give the fact that $\eta_{y,x}^2$ may not equal $\eta_{x,y}^2$ some intuitive appeal with the data in Table 8.2. If a person's age is 10, his Digit Symbol score can be fairly confidently predicted to be about 8.60. However, if we know that a person's Y score is 8, his age X may either be low, around 10, or high, around 38. Hence, Y can be predicted from X reasonably well; but X cannot be predicted well from Y. These facts are reflected in the values of $\eta_{y,x}^2 = .545$ and $\eta_{x,y}^2$, which we have not calculated but which is close to zero.

The value of $\eta_{y,x}^2$ should be compared with the value r_{xy}^2 instead of r_{xy}. We saw that $r_{xy}^2 = 1 - (s_e^2/s_y^2)$, which is equal to

$$r_{xy}^2 = 1 - \frac{\sum\limits_{i=1}^{n}(Y_i - \hat{Y}_i)^2}{\sum\limits_{i=1}^{n}(Y_i - \overline{Y})^2}. \tag{8.20}$$

Equation (8.20) shows r_{xy}^2 to be 1 minus (the sum of squared deviations of the Y scores around a straight prediction line divided by $(n-1)s_y^2$). Equation (8.19) shows $\eta_{y,x}^2$ to be 1 minus (the sum of squared deviations of the Y scores around a *curved* prediction line that passes through the mean of the Y's for each value of X divided by $(n-1)s_y^2$). The curvilinear prediction line for predicting Y from X appears in Fig. 8.7.

As with r_{xy}^2, $\eta_{y,x}^2$ must always be less than or equal to 1 and greater than or equal to 0. Furthermore, $\eta_{y,x}^2 \geqslant r_{xy}^2$. The difference, $\eta_{y,x}^2 - r_{xy}^2$, is a measure of the degree of nonlinearity of a best-fitting line for predicting Y from X. (See Glass and Hakstian, 1969.)

8.7
ADDITIONAL READING ON PREDICTION

A comprehensive and excellent textbook for the student who wishes to pursue the study of statistical prediction beyond this text is William Rozeboom's *Foundations of the Theory of Prediction* (Homewood, Illinois: The Dorsey Press, 1966). The study of the correlation ratio and related matters can be pursued in E. A. Haggard's *Intraclass Correlation and the Analysis of Variance* (1958).

PROBLEMS AND EXERCISES

1. Draw the graphs of the lines corresponding to each of the following equations:
 a. $Y = -2 + 3X$.
 b. $Y = \frac{1}{2} - 1/3X$.
 c. $2Y = 4 + 2X$. (Hint: Divide both sides by 2.)
 d. $Y = 2(1 + 2X)$. (Hint: Multiply the right side out.)

2. What are the values of the Y intercept b_0 and the slope b_1 of the straight line that passes through the points $(X = 2, Y = 2)$ and $(X = 3, Y = 1)$?

3. A particular high school has determined a prediction equation for predicting college grade-point-average at the state university from high-school grade-point-average. The equation is $\hat{Y} = .76 + .62X$. Predict the college grade-point-average which would be earned by students with the following high-school grade-point-averages:

a. 3.50   b. 1.68   c. 2.10   d. 4.00

4. The following are arithmetic test scores and final-exam scores for 12 students in an elementary statistics course:

Student number	X, Arithmetic test	Y, Final exam
1	33	65
2	36	51
3	39	53
4	29	42
5	41	50
6	38	53
7	42	64
8	35	54
9	23	50
10	37	45
11	28	63
12	25	50

Find b_0 and b_1 in the least-squares prediction equation $\hat{Y}_i = b_1 X_i + b_0$. Predict the final-exam score of person 13, whose arithmetic test score was 36. (For your curiosity, his final-exam score was 68. What was the error of estimate?)

5. Find the value of the standard error of estimate s_e for the data in Prob. 4.

6. For the data in Table 8.1, calculate the error of estimate, $Y - \hat{Y}$, for that person whose X score is 100 and whose Y score is 35.

7. In a particular estimation problem, $\hat{Y} = 6.4X + 32.5$, and the standard error of estimate equals 4.25. Assuming that X and Y have a bivariate normal distribution, determine the limits within which lie the middle 50% of the Y scores of a population of persons whose score on X is 10, i.e., determine Y_1 and Y_2 in the following figure:

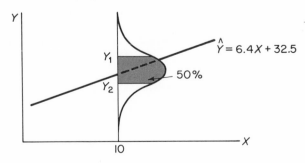

8. Is it true that the larger the value of b_1 the higher the product-moment correlation coefficient between X and Y?

9. Brown uses Scholastic Aptitude Test scores X on the verbal section to predict Graduate Record Examination scores Y on the verbal section at the end of four years of college. His prediction equation is $\hat{Y} = .50X + 250.00$. The mean and standard deviations of each variable are 500 and 100, respectively. Smith wants to predict GRE verbal scores from SAT verbal scores also. However, all of the SAT verbal scores he has available were transformed to the T-scale that has a mean of 50 and a standard deviation of 10. Adapt Brown's formula for Smith's purpose. (Hint: For Brown, $s_y = s_x = 100$; thus $b_1 = r_{xy}$. For Smith, $s_y = 100$, but $s_x = 10$. Smith's regression line slope will equal $r_{xy}(s_y/s_x)$.)

10. In Chapter 7, it was demonstrated that a linear transformation of X and/or Y will not change the value of r_{xy}. What is the effect of the transformation $cX + d$ on the values of b_1 and b_0? (Hint: For estimating Y from X, $b_1 = r_{xy}(s_y/s_x)$. The linear transformation of X leaves r_{xy} unchanged, and it obviously doesn't change the value of s_y. Hence, consider only the influence on s_x of forming $cX + d$. Now express b_0 as $\bar{Y} - b_1\bar{X}$. Having already determined the effect of $cX + d$ on b_1, combine this knowledge with the knowledge of what happens to $\bar{X}$ when X is transformed into $cX + d$.)

9

ADDITIONAL
MEASURES OF
RELATIONSHIP

9.1
INTRODUCTION

In the Chapter 7 discussion of the Pearson product-moment correlation coefficient, we saw that the use and interpretation of r_{xy} depend on the type of data being correlated: whether it is somewhat bivariate normally distributed, whether both X and Y can assume numerous values, whether the two distributions have the same shape. Now we wish to study measures of relationship that can be applied to variables not as nicely quantifiable as weight, age, intelligence, and others to which r_{xy} is readily applied. In particular, we shall develop correlation coefficients that apply to dichotomous $(0, 1)$ data, rank $(1, 2, \ldots, n)$ data, and other types. Some of these coefficients will be the result of applying the formula for r_{xy} to the new types of data directly. Others will be used in attempts to estimate what the value of r_{xy} would be if the data were not in the crude form given. Also, new coefficients will be developed that entail new concepts of what a "relationship" is and how it should be measured.

Partial, part, and multiple correlation will be discussed briefly in the latter sections of this chapter.

9.2
AN OVERVIEW OF THE
CHAPTER

Four types of measurement of variables will be distinguished:

1. Nominal-dichotomous measurement. The mere presence or absence of something is noted. The data are 0's and 1's. The order of the scoring is generally arbitrary. Examples: Republican (1) – Democrat (0); sibling in school (1) – no sibling in school (0); male (1) – female (0); married (1) – not married (0).

2. Nominal-dichotomous measurement with underlying normal distribution. It is assumed that more sophisticated, extensive, or refined measuring techniques could produce an approximately normal distribution of measures, *but* the data in hand tell only whether a person stands above (1) or below (0) some point in this normal distribution. If in a large group of students it was known only whether a child's IQ exceeded a score of 120 (call this 1) or fell below (call this 0), the 1's and 0's would be dichotomized data with an underlying normal distribution. Of course, it usually would be inefficient to discard original scores on persons and record 1's and 0's instead, and this is not normally done (although in the early history of factor analysis it was computationally convenient). Generally, one assumes that a more highly developed measuring device would produce normally distributed scores even though the device in hand allows only dichotomous observation. Examples: IQ above 100 (1), below 100 (0); above average height (1), below average height (0).

3. Ordinal measurement. The data are the n consecutive and untied ranks $1, 2, \ldots, n$. These ranks may be converted measures from some other sort of observations (as when the raw scores 136, 124, 97 are ranked 1, 2, 3), or they may be the first translation of perceptions into numbers (as when a judge ranks 10 contestants from most proficient, 1, down to least proficient, 10). Example: the 94 members of a graduating class are ranked from 1 to 94 on the basis of their 94 grade-point averages.

4. Interval or ratio measurement. A unit of measurement exists, e.g., degree on the centigrade scale, inch, day, etc., and (in the case of ratio measurement) a zero point on a scale of measurement corresponds to the absence (i.e., zero amount) of the variable being measured. Any real number may result

from the act of measurement, and differences between scores reflect on the differences in amount of the characteristic possessed.   In this chapter we shall generally regard the interval and ratio scores to be approximately normally distributed, though of course in some situations they may not be. Examples: height; intelligence-test scores; achievement-test scores; certain measures in psychological experiments.

If measurement can be accomplished at the interval- or ratio-scale level, the scores can be transformed into any of the other three levels above.   For example, suppose that ten students earned scores on a test of verbal reasoning, which is believed to produce an approximately normal distribution of measurements roughly on an interval scale; see Table 9.1.

TABLE 9.1   CHANGING TEN INTERVAL-SCALE SCORES INTO RANKS
(ORDINAL SCALE) AND 0, 1 (NOMINAL SCALE)

Student no.	Verbal reasoning scores	Rank scores	Dichotomized scoring— normal distribution underlying
1	17	3	1
2	10	7	0
3	29	1	1
4	16	4	1
5	3	10	0
6	14	5	1
7	9	8	0
8	26	2	1
9	6	9	0
10	11	6	0

The first column gives an identification number for the student.   The raw scores that are assumed to come from an approximately normal distribution appear in the second column.   These ten scores were ranked to obtain the third column.   In the fourth column, the top five raw scores were given a 1; the bottom five raw scores were given a 0.   It does not seem proper in this example for nominal-dichotomous scores to be assigned (though they would be identical to the scores in the fourth column), because we have reason to believe that a normal distribution underlies the dichotomy, or at least we *know* that a ten-category distribution does.

Where there are two sets of scores, X_i and Y_i, for each of n individuals, either X or Y could be measured in any one of the four manners outlined above.   Thus there are $4 \times 4 = 16$ possible pairs of descriptions of the measurement of two variables that are to be correlated.   These 16 possible pairs of conditions on X and Y can be represented as in Table 9.2.

TABLE 9.2 TEN DIFFERENT BIVARIATE SITUATIONS RESULTING FROM COMBINATIONS OF FOUR SCALES OF MEASUREMENT

Measurement of variable Y	*Measurement of variable X*			
	Dichotomous	Dichotomized, with underlying normal	Ordinal	Interval or ratio
Dichotomous	A	(B)	(C)	(D)
Dichotomized, with underlying normal	B	E	(F)	(G)
Ordinal	C	F	H	(I)
Interval or ratio	D	G	I	J

It is necessary to consider only 10 of the 16 possible pairs, since the designation of the two variables being correlated as X or Y is entirely arbitrary (because $r_{xy} = r_{yx}$). In terms of correlational theory, the six cells with letters in parentheses in Table 9.2 are the same as the cells with the same letters not in parentheses. Table 9.2 will be the structure upon which the following discussion of several specific measures of relationship will be built. One appropriate correlational measure for *two* interval or ratio variables (J) was the subject of the previous chapter. This is an instance in which the Pearson product-moment coefficient r_{xy} is used. We shall consider some of the remaining nine cases (A–I) below.

9.3
MEASURES OF RELATIONSHIP

Case A

Both variables yield nominal-dichotomous measures: the phi coefficient, ϕ. In this case, both X and Y have been measured dichotomously. The data can be thought of as arranged in two columns of 0's and 1's where each row corresponds to one person's two scores. For example, 12 students in academic trouble in their sophomore year of college might be observed on the variables marital status and "dropped out of college"; see Table 9.3. Arbitrarily 1 means married and 1 means dropped out, with 0 for not married and 0 for remaining in school. One measure of the relationship between X and Y is simply r_{xy}, the Pearson product-moment coefficient. The Pearson product-moment coefficient calculated on nominal-dichotomous data is called the *phi coefficient* and is denoted by ϕ. The value of ϕ for the data in Table 9.3 is .507; but this was not found with the usual computation formula for r_{xy}. That formula can be replaced with a still simpler but algebraically identical formula when the data on X and Y are dichotomous.

TABLE 9.3   ILLUSTRATION OF THE CALCULATION OF THE PHI
COEFFICIENT, ϕ

Student no.	X Marital status (married, 1; not married, 0)	Y Attrition (dropped out, 1; remained, 0)	Calculations
1	0	0	$p_x = .4167 \qquad q_x = .5833$
2	1	1	
3	0	1	$p_y = .5000 \qquad q_y = .5000$
4	0	0	
5	1	1	$p_{xy} = .3333$
6	1	0	
7	0	0	$\phi = \dfrac{.3333 - (.4167)(.5000)}{\sqrt{(.4167)(.5833)(.5000)(.5000)}}$
8	1	1	
9	0	0	$= .507$
10	0	1	
11	0	0	
12	1	1	

Let p_x be the proportion of people scoring 1 on X; q_x, the proportion scoring 0 on X, will be equal to $1 - p_x$. The proportion scoring 1 on Y is denoted by p_y, and $q_y = 1 - p_y$. One more definition is necessary: p_{xy} is the proportion of people scoring 1 on *both* X and Y. If we were to operate on the formula for r_{xy} with these new definitions, we would find that it simplifies algebraically to the following convenient form:

$$\phi = \frac{p_{xy} - p_x p_y}{\sqrt{p_x q_x p_y q_y}}. \tag{9.1}$$

Equation 9.1 is a convenient way to compute the phi coefficient. The following derivation shows that ϕ is the Pearson product-moment correlation between two variables, each of which is scored 0, 1.

If both the numerator and the denominator of Eq. (7.10) on page 114 are divided by n, the expression for r_{xy} becomes

$$r_{xy} = \frac{(1/n) \sum X_i Y_i - \bar{X}.\bar{Y}.}{\sqrt{[(1/n) \sum X^2 - \bar{X}.^2][(1/n) \sum Y^2 - \bar{Y}.^2]}}. \tag{9.2}$$

If X and Y are measured dichotomously, $\bar{X}.$ and $\bar{Y}.$ are simply the proportions of 1's on each variable. For example,

$$\bar{X}. = \frac{(0 + 1 + 0 + \ldots + 0 + 1)}{12} = \frac{5}{12},$$

in the illustration in Table 9.3. Thus, we can replace $\bar{X}.$ and $\bar{Y}.$ with p_x and p_y, respectively. Now, $X_i Y_i$ will be different from zero only when the ith person scores 1 on each variable, in which case $X_i Y_i = 1 \cdot 1 = 1$. Surely, then, $\sum X_i Y_i$ is simply a count of the number of persons scoring 1 on both X and Y; hence $(1/n) \sum XY = p_{xy}$. Since X is 0 or 1 and because $0^2 = 0$ and $1^2 = 1$,

$$\frac{\sum X^2}{n} = \frac{(0^2 + 1^2 + \ldots + 0^2 + 1^2)}{n} = p_x.$$

Therefore, substituting such expressions into Eq. (9.2) produces

$$r_{xy} = \frac{p_{xy} - p_x p_y}{\sqrt{(p_x - p_x^2)(p_y - p_y^2)}} = \frac{p_{xy} - p_x p_y}{\sqrt{p_x(1 - p_x)p_y(1 - p_y)}} = \frac{p_{xy} - p_x p_y}{\sqrt{p_x q_x p_y q_y}}. \quad (9.3)$$

When one has no particular interest in the proportions p_x and p_y and finds it more convenient to tabulate dichotomous bivariate data in a *contingency table* (a table showing the joint occurrences of pairs of scores on two variables in a group), ϕ can be calculated with a convenient raw score formula. The data in Table 9.3 can be represented as in Fig. 9.1.

Attrition	Marital status		Totals
	Not married (0)	Married (1)	
Dropped out (1)	2	4	6
Remained (0)	5	1	6
Totals	7	5	12

FIG. 9.1 Contingency table for the data in Table 9.3.

Figure 9.1 presents the frequencies of persons, showing the four possible pairs of characteristics in Table 9.3. For example, five persons in Table 9.3 were *not married* and *remained in school* during their sophomore year. The marginal totals for rows show the numbers of persons at both levels of "attrition," irrespective of their marital status. What is the interpretation of the column totals?

Suppose that in each cell of a contingency table of the above sort we substitute a letter for the actual frequencies so that we can deal with the computation of ϕ more generally. See Fig. 9.2.

The number of persons scoring 0 on X and 1 on Y is denoted by a. The total number of persons scoring 0 on X is $a + c$. The total number of persons represented in the table is n. How many people scored 0 on Y and 0 on X?

It can be shown by substituting such equivalences as $p_x = (b + d)/n$, $p_y = (a + b)/n$, and $p_{xy} = b/n$ into Eq. (9.1) that the phi coefficient for the

		Variable X		Totals
		O	1	
Variable Y	1	a	b	$a+b$
	O	c	d	$c+d$
	Totals	$a+c$	$b+d$	n

FIG. 9.2   General form of a 2 × 2 contingency table.

data arranged in a contingency table like that of Fig. 9.2 is

$$\phi = \frac{bc - ad}{\sqrt{(a+c)(b+d)(a+b)(c+d)}}. \qquad (9.4)$$

Equation (9.4) was first derived by Karl Pearson in 1901 in a paper, published in the Philosophical Transactions of the Royal Society of London, that dealt with the correlation between variables that cannot be measured quantitatively.   To illustrate the calculation of ϕ by Eq. (9.4), the data in Fig. 9.1 will be used.

$$\phi = \frac{20 - 2}{\sqrt{(7)(5)(6)(6)}} = \frac{18}{6\sqrt{35}} = \frac{3}{\sqrt{35}} = .507.$$

This value of ϕ is exactly equal to the value found in Table 9.3 for the same data.   This equivalence must always result, because Eqs. (9.1) and (9.4) are algebraically equivalent.

Properties of ϕ

The meaning of the phi coefficient in a correlational sense is quite clear; it is simply the Pearson product-moment coefficient of correlation for dichotomous data. However, the interpretation of ϕ can present special problems. In Chapter 7 it was seen that for the purpose of interpreting r_{xy}, certain assumptions, several of which can be checked by construction a scatter diagram of the data, must be made. The dichotomous data involved in the calculation of ϕ are quite a departure from the two-variable normal surface to which the interpretation of r_{xy} has reference. Consequently, it is wrong to think that the interpretive meaning of a r_{xy} of .60 and a ϕ of .60 is the same.

Especially pertinent here is the fact that ϕ can assume the value $+1$ only when $a + b$ and $b + d$ are equal (and hence $a = d$) in the 2 × 2 contingency table, i.e., when there are the same proportions of 1's on both X and Y.* Notice that in Fig. 9.3, where $p_x = .8$ and $p_y = .4$, no higher

---

* Or, what is the same, when $a + c = c + d$,' and therefore $a = d$. This is one necessary condition for $\phi = +1$. The other is that $a = d = 0$. The 0, 1, and 1, 0 quadrants must be empty.

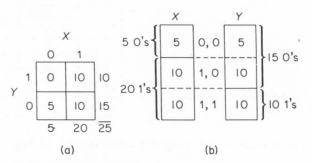

FIG. 9.3 The greatest possible positive association when $p_x = .8$ and $p_y = .4$.

positive relationship between X and Y than is shown can be obtained. All of the ten 1's on Y are paired with 1's on X, but because there are 20 1's on X but only 10 1's on Y, there must be 10 1's on X that are paired with 0's on Y. Y cannot be predicted perfectly from X because knowledge that a person scores a 1 on X does not rule out the possibility that his score on Y is 0. The value of ϕ in Fig. 9.3 is .41. In other words, so long as 10 of the 25 scores on Y are 1's and 20 of the 25 scores on X are 1's (or vice versa), the value of ϕ cannot exceed .41. This is regarded by some statisticians as a great disadvantage in the use of ϕ. In an attempt to sidestep this undesirable property of ϕ, Cureton (1959) and others have divided the obtained value of ϕ by the maximum value ϕ can attain, ϕ maximum, for the distribution of 1's and 0's obtained. This produces a coefficient, ϕ/ϕ_{max}, that can always range between -1 and $+1$, regardless of how discrepant the proportions of 1's on X and Y are. Carroll (1961) discussed ϕ/ϕ_{max} at length and found it wanting. The basic principle involved here is that a product-moment r can attain the value $+1$ only if the distribution of the X's has the same shape as that of the Y's. The value -1 can be obtained only if the shape of the distribution of the X's is exactly the reverse of that of the Y's; for ϕ this would mean that $p_x = q_y$. These conditions of identical or reversed distributions are necessary to attain the limits $+1$ or -1, but they are by no means sufficient. Even if X and Y are distributed identically, they can correlate 0 with each other, of course.

Case B

X is dichotomous; Y is dichotomous, with an underlying normal distribution. We know of no one satisfactory coefficient for correlating variables measured in these ways. Perhaps for most such situations, likely to be infrequent, one should forego the normality assumption and calculate ϕ. Quilling (1969) has discussed this problem.

Case C

X is dichotomous and Y is ordinal. The only available coefficients for this situation are due to Cureton (1956) and Glass (1966). (Also see Stanley, 1968*b*.) Because these coefficients build upon rationales first proposed for correlating two ordinal variables, they can best be discussed after Case I later in this section.

Case D

One variable yields nominal-dichotomous measures, the other yields interval or ratio measures: the point-biserial correlation coefficient. In this case, one variable is measured dichotomously (e.g., sex, marital status), and the measurement of the other variable produces a collection of scores with interval or ratio properties. For example, in a group of high-school juniors, we might observe whether a student drops out of college (0) during the freshman year or remains in college (1), and also measure his intelligence. Observation of the two variables, *intelligence* (X) and *attrition* (Y), will produce two scores for each student.

One means of describing the relationship between X and Y is simply to calculate the Pearson product-moment coefficient on the data as they are. Such a coefficient is called a *point-biserial correlation coefficient* and is denoted by r_{pb}. (The term *biserial* refers to the fact that there are *two series* of persons being observed on X: those who scored 0 on Y, and those who scored 1 on Y. Both the name and the rationale for this coefficient are due to Karl Pearson. The expression *product-moment biserial* is sometimes used instead of *point-biserial*.) A simplified formula for r_{pb} follows:

$$r_{pb} = \frac{\bar{X}_{.1} - \bar{X}_{.0}}{s_x} \sqrt{\frac{n_1 n_0}{n(n-1)}}, \tag{9.5}$$

where $\bar{X}_{.1}$ is the mean on X of those who scored 1 on Y,
        $\bar{X}_{.0}$ is the mean on X of those who scored 0 on Y,
        s_x is the standard deviation of all n scores on X,
        n_1 is the number of persons scoring 1 on Y,
        n_0 is the number of persons scoring 0 on Y, and
        $n = n_1 + n_0$.

Equation (9.5) represents an algebraic simplification of the Pearson product-moment correlation coefficient formula when Y is a dichotomous variable. Equation (9.5) is only one of several simplifications that could have resulted. Each of the following formulas is equivalent to Eq. (9.5), and one of them will probably be more convenient than the others for a particular problem.

$$r_{pb} = \frac{\bar{X}_{.1} - \bar{X}_{.}}{s_x} \sqrt{\frac{n_1 n}{n_0(n-1)}}, \qquad (9.6)$$

where $\bar{X}_{.}$ is the mean of all n scores on X.

$$r_{pb} = \frac{\bar{X}_{.} - \bar{X}_{.0}}{s_x} \sqrt{\frac{n_0 n}{n_1(n-1)}}. \qquad (9.7)$$

As is particularly evident from consideration of Eq. (9.5), r_{pb} is a measure of the difference between the average scores on X of the persons scoring 1 on Y and the persons scoring 0 on Y. Because r_{pb} is nothing more than the product-moment correlation coefficient calculated on particular types of data, it must take on some value from -1 to $+1$, inclusive. When those scoring 1 on Y have the same average value on X as those scoring 0 on Y, r_{pb} will be zero. Of course, r_{pb} is not defined if either n_0 or n_1 equals n; "covariation" cannot be studied if variation (on Y, in this case) does not exist.

The calculation of r_{pb} is illustrated in Table 9.4 on data gathered to

TABLE 9.4   ILLUSTRATION OF THE CALCULATION OF THE POINT-BISERIAL CORRELATION COEFFICIENT

Person	Y Sex (1, male; 0, female)	X Height (in inches)	Calculating r_{pb}
A	1	59	
B	0	67	
C	1	63	
D	1	65	
E	0	55	1. Equation (9.5):
F	1	72	
G	0	62	$\dfrac{64.25 - 61.14}{3.91}\sqrt{\dfrac{8(7)}{15(14)}} = .41.$
H	0	60	
I	1	64	
J	1	66	2. Equation (9.6):
K	1	63	
L	0	61	$\dfrac{64.25 - 62.80}{3.91}\sqrt{\dfrac{8(15)}{7(14)}} = .41.$
M	1	62	
N	0	63	
O	0	60	3. Equation (9.7):

$n_1 = 8 \qquad \bar{X}_{.1} = 64.25$

$n_0 = 7 \qquad \bar{X}_{.0} = 61.14$

$n = 15 \qquad \bar{X}_{.} = 62.80$

$\qquad\qquad s_x = 3.91$

$$\frac{62.80 - 61.14}{3.91}\sqrt{\frac{7(15)}{8(14)}} = .41.$$

relate sex (the nominal-dichotomous variable) and height for 15 adolescents— eight boys and seven girls. The boys are taller than the girls, on the average

(64.25 versus 61.14 inches), but the relationship found between sex and height is only moderate (.41). Just one girl is taller than the average boy, but six of the seven girls are taller than the shortest boy.

Case E

Both variables are dichotomous with underlying normal distributions: the tetrachoric correlation coefficient, r_{tet}. In some instances, we think we know a great deal about the variable being measured, even though we can make only very crude measurements of it. For example, a test item is written to measure syllogistic reasoning power. The writer of the item believes that the ability to draw correct conclusions in a variety of syllogisms is a normally distributed trait, but the single test item will allow him to identify only a group of those who answer correctly (all of whom will be given a score of 1) and a group who do not (all of whom will be given a 0). As a second example, suppose that the heights of 1000 boys are approximately normally distributed. The researcher may choose to give a 1 to those taller than 5'2" and a 0 to those under that height, as in Fig. 9.4. Surely he is discarding information, but he may gain a great amount of computational ease with tolerable loss of information, specially if his n is large. (This device was frequently used in psychometrics before the wide availability of mechanical computing equipment. Faced with the problem of computing several hundred correlation coefficients, it proved to be expedient to employ the methods discussed below as a short-cut approximation.)

Two variables X and Y are measured dichotomously on a group of persons, although it is believed that more costly and extensive operations could produce nearly normal distributions of measurements. Only 0 and 1 data are available, but the researcher's interest is in the correlation of X and Y he *would have* obtained if he had gathered the normally distributed measures. (The phi coefficient will usually underestimate this relationship.) If he feels that his understanding of the underlying variables (i.e., that they produce normally distributed measurements) entitles him to more information,

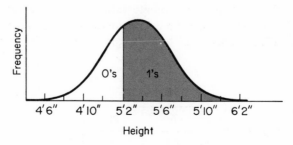

FIG. 9.4   Transforming normally distributed scores into dichotomous scores.

he will choose to calculate the *tetrachoric coefficient of correlation*, r_{tet}, between X and Y.

The observable data are dichotomous scores (0 or 1) for each person on X and Y. At this first stage, the data are in the same form as when a phi coefficient is calculated. All of the explicit information in the data is preserved when they are placed in a 2×2 contingency table like that of Fig. 9.2.

The most exact formula for r_{tet} uses the frequencies a, b, c, and d in the 2×2 contingency table to obtain an approximation to the value of r_{xy} that could be calculated if more sophisticated measurement of X and Y were possible. This formula was derived by Karl Pearson in 1900. Unfortunately, it is very complex, so we must settle for a more convenient though less exact approximation.

If you have some facility with trigonometry, you will have no trouble understanding the following formula for approximating r_{tet}:

$$ r_{tet} \doteq \text{cosine } \frac{180°}{1 + \sqrt{bc/ad}}. \tag{9.8} $$

After calculating the term to the right of "cosine" in the above equation, you can refer to a table of trigonometric functions to find the cosine of the angle measured in degrees. Undoubtedly, you will find it more convenient to refer a function of the value of $(ad)/(bc)$ to Table H in Appendix A, in which all of the operations in Eq. (9.8) have been carried out. It is entered with $(bc)/(ad)$, provided that this ratio is greater than 1. *If $(bc)/(ad)$ is less than 1, the table is entered with $(ad)/(bc)$, and the value of r_{tet} is negative.*

Two examples will illustrate the use of Table H in finding r_{tet}.

Two test items were administered to 100 persons. Each person was given a score of 1 if he answered an item correctly and a 0 if he answered it incorrectly or omitted it. Figure 9.5 contains a tabulation of the numbers of persons scoring each combination of correct and incorrect on the two items. The number of persons answering *both* items *incorrectly* was 64; five persons answered item 2 correctly and item 1 incorrectly. The value of $(bc)/(ad)$ for the table (Fig. 9.5) is $(64)(25)/(5)(6) = 53.33$. Since this ratio is greater than 1, it is referred directly to Table H in the Appendix. From Table H, we find that the approximate value of r_{tet} for a value of $(bc)/(ad)$ equal to 53.33 is .93. This is an approximation to the value of the product-moment correlation coefficient between the normally distributed variables for which

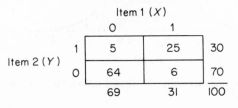

FIG. 9.5 Frequencies of pairs of scores on two test items.

test items 1 and 2 provided only dichotomous measures. As a second example, suppose that for a certain 2×2 contingency table, $a = 31$, $b = 10$, $c = 5$, and $d = 14$. If you draw this contingency table you will see a negative relationship between the two variables. Now $(bc)/(ad)$ equals .115. Consequently, Table H is entered with $(ad)/(bc)$, which equals 8.68, and the value of r_{tet} is negative. From Table H we see that the value of r_{tet} is $-.70$.

The reader must be warned that the use of Eq. (9.8) and, what is equivalent, of Table H can result in substantial errors (see Bouvier *et al.*, 1954). Neither method should be used if $(a + b)/n$ or $(b + d)/n$ (i.e., p_y or p_x) departs greatly from .50. If both ratios equal .50, Table H will not be in error by more than .04 for values of r_{tet} between $-.90$ and $+.90$. When the ratios deviate from .50, the tabled values are over-estimates of the true value of r_{tet}, when it is positive. If either $(a + b)/n$ or $(b + d)/n$ is greater than .70 or less than .30, the methods in this text for finding r_{tet} should not be used. Tables prepared by Jenkins (1955) should be used in such cases. The illustration in Fig. 9.5 of the use of Table H represents about the most extreme proportion of 1's on either X or Y for which Table H should be used.

An interesting development in the theory of correlation was the derivation of a "polychoric" correlation coefficient. Instead of transforming two normal distributions into dichotomies (i.e., just two scoring categories), each could be transformed into polychotomies having more than two categories. The problem is then one of estimating r_{xy} between the normally distributed variables given only the contingency table, with several rows and several columns, relating the categorical data. The solution to this problem is in the work of Lancaster and Hamdan (1964); and though it fills a theoretical gap, the computational labor involved requires the use of electronic computers.

The limits on the value of r_{tet} are -1 to $+1$. One particularly advantageous feature of this coefficient is that its maximum and minimum values are $+1$ and -1 regardless of how far $(a + b)/n$ or $(b + d)/n$ depart from equality. This property alone makes r_{tet} superior to the phi coefficient as a measure of relationship when normal distributions underlying the dichotomies can be assumed. (See Carroll, 1961.)

Case F

X is dichotomous, with an underlying normal distribution, and Y is ordinal. We know of no coefficient appropriate for describing the relationship between variables measured in this unorthodox combination of ways. If such measurements do arise, we suggest that you forego the assumption of a normal distribution underlying the dichotomy on X and proceed with the calculation of Cureton's rank-biserial correlation coefficient, which is discussed after **Case H**, below.

Case G

One variable yields dichotomous measures with an underlying normal distribution, the other yields interval or ratio measures; the biserial correlation coefficient. Suppose that variable Y is measured dichotomously even though one might think that more extensive or refined techniques could produce a nearly normal distribution of scores on Y. We say that the measurement of Y has produced a dichotomy with an underlying normal distribution. Thus Y is measured in precisely the same way as either of the variables involved in the calculation of a tetrachoric correlation coefficient. However, in this instance the data produced by measurement of X can be thought of as scores on an interval or ratio scale that are approximately normally distributed. For example, the X scores might be scores on the Scholastic Aptitude Test, and the Y scores might be 0's and 1's on a test item measuring cognitive flexibility. With more elaborate tests of cognitive flexibility, it might be possible to produce a wide range of cognitive flexibility scores (Y scores) that are nearly normally distributed. These two arrays of normally distributed scores on X and Y could be correlated and r_{xy} found. What do the X scores and the dichotomous scores on Y tell about the value of r_{xy}? The answer to this question lies in the biserial correlation coefficient r_{bis}. (In r_{bis} we meet another product of the genius of Karl Pearson.)

The biserial correlation coefficient is an estimate of the product-moment correlation between X and the normally distributed scores on Y that are assumed to underlie the dichotomous (0 or 1) scores. This situation is similar to the conditions out of which r_{tet} arose, except that for r_{tet} *both* variables were dichotomous with underlying normal distributions.

The data gathered for the computation of r_{bis} consist of an X score, which can be any one of several different values, and a Y score, which is either 0 or 1, for each of n persons.

Suppose that a teacher wishes to relate the amount of time (X) students spend studying balancing chemical equations and their ability (Y) to balance such equations. Measurements of X are gathered by students' own reports of the homework time they gave to the study of the subject. Although Y could probably be measured by an extensive achievement test in such a way that a nearly normal distribution of scores would result, suppose that the teacher's time available for testing will allow the administration of only one item, a chemical equation to be balanced. Thus a normal distribution of ability is assumed to underlie the 0-incorrect and 1-correct scores on the test item. Data that might result from such a study appear in Table 9.5. They show that 11 of the 18 students balanced the equation correctly and that they scored higher than did the 7 students who balanced the equations incorrectly.

The rationale that underlies the derivation of r_{bis} is taken from regression theory. The regression coefficient for predicting X from the *normally* distributed Y is

$$b_1 = \frac{r_{xy}s_x}{s_y},$$

where s_y is the standard deviation of the hypothetically normally distributed Y, *not* of the dichotomous measures taken on Y. The slope of the least-squares regression line for predicting X from Y can be approximated by the slope of the line that passes through the mean X score for those scoring 0 on Y (which is denoted $\bar{X}_{.0}$) and the mean X score for those scoring 1 on Y (which is denoted by $\bar{X}_{.1}$). This latter line is drawn on the scatter diagram in Table 9.5. This line is a least-squares line in a sense, because the mean of a group is the point around which the sum of squared deviations is at a minimum.

The slope of this line is equal to $(\bar{X}_{.1} - \bar{X}_{.0})$ divided by the distance between the mean scores on the normally distributed Y for those scoring 0 and 1 on the dichotomy. This latter distance is difficult to find in any elementary manner (see Walker and Lev, 1953, for a more advanced discussion). The desired distance turns out to involve the height u of the unit normal curve above the point on the abscissa (i.e., the Y axis *here*) above which $100(n_1/n)$ percent of the area lies. (n_1 is the number of persons scoring 1 on the dichotomy.) Combining these facts appropriately yields the following computational formula for r_{bis}:

$$r_{bis} = \frac{\bar{X}_{.1} - \bar{X}_{.0}}{s_x} \cdot \frac{n_1 n_0}{un\sqrt{n^2 - n}}, \qquad (9.9)$$

where $\bar{X}_{.1}$ and $\bar{X}_{.0}$ are the mean X scores for those scoring 1 and 0 on Y, respectively;

s_x is the standard deviation of the X scores;

n_1 and n_0 are the numbers of 1's and 0's on Y, respectively ($n_1 + n_0 = n$); and

u is the ordinate (i.e., the height) of the unit normal distribution at the point above which lies $100(n_1/n)$ percent of the area under the curve (see Table B in Appendix A).

The calculation of r_{bis} from Eq. (9.9) will be illustrated with the data in Table 9.5.

Since $n_1/n = 11/18 = .61$, the ordinate u of the unit normal curve for the point above which lies 61% of the area must be found. In Table B in Appendix A this height is found to be .3836. The summary statistics from Table 9.5 are substituted into Eq. (9.9):

$$r_{bis} = \frac{12.36 - 10.00}{2.55} \cdot \frac{11 \cdot 7}{(.3836)18\sqrt{18^2 - 18}} = .60.$$

TABLE 9.5   ILLUSTRATION OF THE CALCULATION OF THE BISERIAL
CORRELATION COEFFICIENT

Time spent in study X	Scores on test item Y	Scatter diagram
16	1	
12	0	
11	0	
7	1	
15	1	
14	1	
10	0	
11	0	
15	1	
9	0	
13	1	
7	0	
13	1	
11	1	
10	0	
11	1	
10	1	
11	1	

Summary statistics

$$n_1 = 11, \quad n_0 = 7, \quad n = 18$$
$$\bar{X}_{.1} = 12.36, \quad \bar{X}_{.0} = 10.00, \quad \bar{X}_{.} = 11.44$$
$$s_x = 2.55, \quad u = .3836$$

$$r_{bis} = \frac{\bar{X}_{.1} - \bar{X}_{.0}}{s_x} \cdot \frac{n_1 n_0}{un\sqrt{n^2 - n}}$$

$$= \frac{12.36 - 10.00}{2.55} \cdot \frac{11 \cdot 7}{(.3836)18\sqrt{18^2 - 18}} = .60$$

It may be simpler to calculate r_{bis} from the following equivalent but slightly different formula that will always give the same value as Eq. (9.9):

$$r_{bis} = \frac{\bar{X}_{.1} - \bar{X}_{.}}{s_x} \cdot \frac{n_1}{u\sqrt{n^2 - n}} \cdot \tag{9.10}$$

The only symbol present in Eq.(9.10) which was missing from Eq. (9.9) is $\bar{X}_.$, the mean of all n X scores.

A word or two about the range of possible values for r_{bis} is in order. Unlike almost any other commonly used correlation coefficient, r_{bis} can sometimes take on values below -1 and above $+1$. The only significance of these extreme values of r_{bis} is that they reflect either incorrectness of the assumption that the multi-categorized X scores are normally distributed, or sampling fluctuation when n is small that produces a markedly platykurtic distribution of X's in the sample. If small n's are involved, the line that passes through $\bar{X}_{.1}$ and $\bar{X}_{.0}$ is probably a poor estimate of the regression line for the normally distributed X and Y. The unpleasant fact remains that for n's of 15 and smaller, values of r_{bis} exceeding 1.25 are occasionally obtained. Also, the limits of r_{bis} may be *less* than -1 to $+1$ if the distribution of the X's is leptokurtic. For a fuller explanation, see Stanley (1968b).

You have probably already noticed that the data on which both r_{pb}, the point-biserial coefficient, and r_{bis} are calculated are alike. The only difference between the statements of the two problems is that in the case of r_{bis} something about a distribution underlying the dichotomous measures is assumed. In terms of what is *assumed* about the data, r_{pb} and r_{bis} are quite different. Thus it is somewhat pointless to ask, "How do r_{pb} and r_{bis} compare on a single set of data?" The two coefficients do not compete for use; each is appropriate for its intended purpose. However, relating the values of r_{pb} and r_{bis} for the same set of data will reveal something about the returns to which one is entitled when he is familiar with his data.

For the same set of data, the ratio of r_{bis} to r_{pb} is

$$\frac{r_{bis}}{r_{pb}} = \frac{\sqrt{n_1 n_0}}{un}. \tag{9.11}$$

The minimum value of the ratio in Eq. (9.11) is 1.25, as long as neither r_{bis} nor r_{pb} is zero. Hence, if r_{pb} is positive, r_{bis} will be positive and larger; if r_{pb} is negative, r_{bis} will be negative and closer to -1. If r_{pb} is zero, r_{bis} is zero also. Thus the same data will give evidence for a stronger relationship between X and Y if more is assumed about it, i.e., if the dichotomy is assumed to have an underlying normal distribution.

The concepts underlying biserial correlation lead to such generalizations as triserial and other polyserial correlation. If Y is measured trichotomously (0, 1, 2), a triserial correlation coefficient can be used to estimate the product-moment correlation between X and the normally distributed Y assumed to underlie the trichotomy. The generalization of r_{bis} to polyserial correlation is the work of Jaspen (1946). A readable account of Jaspen's work appears in the textbook by Wert, Neidt, and Ahmann (1954). It has been the authors' experience that often the magnitude of a polyserial correlation coefficient is little different from the value of r_{bis} that would be obtained by coalescing the several categories of Y into just two (as when a trichotomous variable is changed into a dichotomous variable by combining two adjacent categories).*

Case H

Both variables yield ordinal measures. *Spearman Rank-Correlation Coefficient.* Raw data may be converted to ranks, or ranks may be gathered as the original data. "Rank in graduating class" is an example of the conversion of ordered scores to ranks: grade-point averages are computed for each of 500 students, say a rank of 1 is assigned the highest GPA, 2 to the next highest, . . . , 500 to the lowest. "Judges' rankings of excellence of a recitation" is an example of gathering ranks as original data: 10 students recite a passage, and a judge assigns the rank 1 to the best recitation, 2 to the second best recitation, . . . , and 10 to the worst recitation. Data are often gathered in this form when more refined measurements are not convenient, needed, or possible. Regardless of how the ranks $1, 2, \ldots, n - 1$, n are generated, two sets of ranks for the same n persons can be correlated in the same way.

Suppose that 12 students are ranked by a single judge on the basis of both overt hostility toward their teacher (X) and overt hostility toward other students (Y). A rank of 1 is given to the student showing the greatest hostility toward the teacher; 12 indicates that student who showed the least hostility toward the teacher. The same ranking procedure is used for hostility toward other students.

Hypothetical data appear in Table 9.6. Student A was ranked second on X and sixth on Y. An obvious method of describing the relationship between the two sets of ranks, X and Y, is to compute the product-moment correlation coefficient between the n paired ranks, i.e., simply substitute the data of Table 9.6 into the formula for r_{xy}. This rather obvious technique was employed first by Francis Galton. Charles Spearman, the British psychologist, made more use of it. He has been rewarded by having the coefficient named in his honor, even though Karl Pearson apparently felt that the honor was due Galton (see Walker, 1929, p. 103). *The product-moment correlation coefficient computed on two sets of the n consecutive, untied ranks* $1, \ldots, n$ *is known as the Spearman rank-correlation coefficient.* We shall symbolize this coefficient by r_s.

Before you begin to calculate r_s using any of the usual formulas for r_{xy}, take note. The constraints that exist on $\bar{X}_.$, $\bar{Y}_.$, s_x^2, and s_y^2 because X and Y take on only the values $1, 2, \ldots, n$ lead to enormous simplifications in the

---

* To avoid spuriously high r_{bis}'s, however, one should be careful about such coalescing when done *after* the data (i.e., the X's and Y's) are collected. The particular combining of categories that works well in one sample might not do so in another, if the combining is done to maximize r_{bis} in the first sample. Problems of crossvalidation and "shrinkage" are involved.

TABLE 9.6   THE TWO SETS OF RANKS ASSIGNED BY A JUDGE TO TWELVE STUDENTS ON HOSTILITY TOWARD THEIR TEACHER (X) AND HOSTILITY TOWARD OTHER STUDENTS (Y)

	Hostility toward		Computations		
Student	*Teacher (X)*	*Students (Y)*	X^2	Y^2	$(X - Y)^2$
A	2	6	4	36	16
B	8	5	64	25	9
C	12	10	144	100	4
D	3	7	9	49	16
E	1	3	1	9	4
F	6	4	36	16	4
G	7	9	49	81	4
H	10	8	100	64	4
I	4	1	16	1	9
J	9	11	81	121	4
K	11	12	121	144	1
L	5	2	25	4	9
Sums	$\sum X = \overline{78}$	$\sum Y = \overline{78}$	$\sum X^2 = \overline{650}$	$\sum Y^2 = \overline{650}$	$\sum (X - Y)^2 = \overline{84}$

formula for r_{xy}. Notice in Table 9.6 that $\sum X = \sum Y$ and $\sum X^2 = \sum Y^2$. You should realize immediately that these equalities must always hold, as long as no tied ranks are allowed. It can be shown that

$$\sum X = 1 + 2 + \ldots + n = \frac{n(n + 1)}{2}.$$

In Table 9.6, we have

$$\frac{n(n + 1)}{2} = \frac{12(13)}{2} = 78.$$

The famous German mathematician and astronomer Karl Gauss is reputed to have demonstrated this fact as a child for his astonished tutor in the following manner:
If

$$\sum_{1}^{n} X = 1 + 2 + \ldots + (n - 1) + n,$$

then of course

$$\sum_{1}^{n} X = n + (n - 1) + \ldots + 2 + 1$$

also (i.e., the same series in reverse order). Add the two equations together vertically and obtain

$$2 \sum_{1}^{n} X = (n + 1) + (n + 1) + \ldots + (n + 1) = n(n + 1),$$

because there are n of the $(n + 1)$'s. Divide both sides of the equation by 2; you obtain

$$\sum_{1}^{n} X = \frac{n(n + 1)}{2},$$

the sum of the n consecutive, untied ranks $1, 2, \ldots, n$. Divide both sides of the above equation by n and you have

$$\bar{X}_{.} = \frac{n + 1}{2}, \tag{9.12}$$

the mean of the n consecutive, untied ranks $1, 2, \ldots, n$.

Using similar, but slightly more complicated techniques, it can be shown (see Siegel, 1956, or Edwards, 1964) that if X takes on the n consecutive and untied ranks $1, 2, \ldots, n$, the variance of the X's is

$$s_x^2 = \frac{n^2 - 1}{12}. \tag{9.13}$$

Taking Eqs. (9.12) and (9.13) into consideration and performing other minor simplifications, we obtain the following formula for r_s (see Pearson, 1907; Siegel, 1956, pp. 203–4):

$$r_s = 1 - \frac{6 \sum_{i=1}^{n} (X_i - Y_i)^2}{n(n^2 - 1)}. \tag{9.14}$$

$X_i - Y_i$ is the difference between the ith person's rank on X and his rank on Y. The 12 values of $(X_i - Y_i)^2$ for the data in Table 9.6 appear in the last column of the table. Their sum is 84.

The value of r_s for the two sets of ranks in Table 9.6 is found as follows:

$$r_s = 1 - \frac{6(84)}{12(144 - 1)} = 1 - \frac{42}{143} = .71.$$

This value of r_s indicates a fairly strong direct relationship between the students' overt hostility toward the teacher and toward other students as ranked by the judge.

When calculations are being performed on a desk calculator, the following formula, which is equivalent to Eq. (9.14), will be more convenient:

$$r_s = \frac{3}{n - 1} \left[\frac{4 \sum_{i=1}^{n} X_i Y_i}{n(n + 1)} - (n + 1) \right]. \tag{9.15}$$

$X_i Y_i$ is the product on person i's ranks on X and Y. Equation (9.15), which gives exactly the same value as Eq. (9.14), does not require the calculation of $X_i - Y_i$, which may need to be written down when calculations are made on a desk calculator. Each journey of a datum from machine to paper and back to machine is an opportunity to err.

Often, though, the deviations can be squared and summed mentally, without writing down anything except the sum of the squared deviations [needed in Eq. (9.14)]. Stanley (1964, pp. 375–78) offers a table from which r_s can be secured readily when one knows $\sum_{1}^{n} (X_i - Y_i)^2$ and n, for any value of n from 2 through 10. For further discussion of the use of r_s in practical situations, see Stanley (1964, pp. 98–100 and 379–81).

The Problem of Tied Ranks

Ties in measurements often occur. When they do, there is a special rule for assigning ranks. For example, if the 12th and 13th highest ranking students in a graduating class of 245 each has a grade-point average of 4.76, it is customary to assign both students the average of the two ranks: $(12 + 13)/2 = 12.5$. Or a judge may find it impossible to discriminate between the quality of the handwriting of the top three students, so he gives all three students the average of the top three ranks, $2 = (1 + 2 + 3)/3$. (As a generous gesture, some judges would give all three a rank of 1, but that fails to preserve the sum of the 3 untied ranks 1, 2, 3.)

When tied ranks occur, neither Eq. (9.14) nor Eq. (9.15) is equivalent to the r_{xy} between the ranks. Even though the mean of the numbers $1, 2, \ldots, n$ does not change when ties in the ranks occur [it is still $(n + 1)/2$], the variance of the ranks is less than $(n^2 - 1)/12$. Consequently, the variance simplifications in the formula for r_{xy} that led to Eqs. (9.14) and (9.15) cannot be made.

There are three possible ways to proceed in the calculation of r_s when tied ranks occur: (a) use the computational formula for r_{xy} on the data—this will always give r_s, whether any ranks are tied or not; (b) use a formula (see Kendall, 1955) that incorporates corrections of s_x^2 and s_y^2 for the ties in the ranks; (c) compute an approximation to r_s via Eq. (9.14) or (9.15), if there are few ties. With the current availability of fully automatic desk calculators and electronic computers we suggest method (a)—that you compute the r_{xy} between the ranks, having assigned ranks to tied measurements by the averaging method described above.

Interpretation and Use of r_s

No special interpretation can be given to r_s over and above the statement that it equals the product-moment correlation coefficient calculated on ranks. The value of r_s can never be less than -1 nor greater than $+1$. It equals $+1$ only if each person has exactly the same ranks on both X and Y.

The Spearman rank-correlation coefficient is especially useful when the original data are ranks, as when judges rank persons or things. It is sometimes regarded as a quick means of estimating r_{xy}. The original data are ranked, r_s is computed, and a trigonometric function of r_s is supposed to convert r_s back into the value of r_{xy}. This procedure does *not* accomplish this except approximately so for very large n. Desk calculators and electronic computers have taken enough of the labor out of calculation so that there is no longer any reason not to calculate r_{xy} on unranked data.

The Spearman rank-correlation coefficient r_s is very closely tied to the concept of a product-moment correlation coefficient. Another coefficient of correlation exists for data that are ranks on both X and Y; it involves a rather different concept of what "relationship" is and how it should be measured.

Kendall's Tau, τ

All of the coefficients of correlation met in this book so far employ the product-moment rationale of Pearson in one form or another. Some coefficients are merely the Pearson product-moment formula applied to dichotomous or ordinal data, e.g., ϕ, r_s, and r_{pb}; others are attempts to approximate the Pearson r, e.g., r_{tet} and r_{bis}. The English statistician Maurice Kendall made one of the few attempts at conceptualizing the measurement of relationships between variables in a manner other than by use of the product-moment principle. His efforts have resulted in one of the few basically new approaches to statistical description in modern times. For a readable account of his work see Kendall (1955).

As was the case with the Spearman coefficients, the observations on both X and Y are the n consecutive and untied ranks $1, 2, \ldots, n$. Kendall based his coefficient of correlation on the numbers of pairs of ranks that are ordered in the same direction on both X and Y. Thus, his measure, called *tau* and denoted τ, is merely an enumerator of the extent of disagreement in the rankings on X and Y

Suppose that the ranks in Table 9.7 were assigned to eight persons on X and Y. Suppose we select any pair of persons, e.g., A and B. A is ranked above B on X, but B is ranked above A on Y. This represents a departure from a direct relationship between X and Y; this inversion of the relative status of A and B as we move from X to Y argues for an inverse relationship between X and Y, at least as far as A and B are concerned. There are $n(n-1)/2$ pairs of n persons, and the contribution of each pair to the relationship between X and Y must be studied. For any pair of persons, an *agreement* is counted if their order on X and Y is the same. For example, persons A and H contribute one agreement because A ranks higher than H on X (1 vs. 4) *and* on Y (3 vs. 5). For any pair of persons, an *inversion* is counted if their order on X and Y is different. Persons A and B contribute

TABLE 9.7   ILLUSTRATION OF THE CALCULATION OF KENDALL'S TAU, τ
(I IS THE HIGHEST RANK)

Person	X	Y	Agreements	Inversions	
A	1	3	5	2	
C	2	1	6	0	$n = 8$
B	3	2	5	0	
H	4	5	3	1	$\tau = \dfrac{P-Q}{n(n-1)/2} = \dfrac{21-7}{28}$
E	5	7	1	2	
F	6	8	0	2	
D	7	4	1	0	$= \dfrac{14}{28} = .50$
G	8	6	0	0	
			$P = \overline{21}$	$Q = \overline{7}$	

an inversion; note that F and D also contribute one inversion: F has a higher rank than D on X but a lower rank than D on Y.

With no tied ranks, all $n(n-1)/2$ pairs of persons will contribute either an agreement or an inversion. When the rankings on both X and Y are identical, there will be $n(n-1)/2$ agreements and no inversions. What will be the total numbers of agreements and inversions when Y is the reverse of X? Zero and $n(n-1)/2$, respectively.

These facts can be pieced together in various ways to define a coefficient of the relationship between X and Y. Kendall chose the following definition for his coefficient τ:

$$\tau = \frac{(\text{total number of ``agreements''}) - (\text{total number of ``inversions''})}{n(n-1)/2}.$$

$$(9.16)$$

The process of counting the agreements and inversions in the ranks on X and Y for all $n(n-1)/2$ pairs of persons can be laborious. Fortunately, it can be simplified.

The first simplification occurs by algebraic manipulation of Eq. (9.16). Let us call the total number of agreements P and the total number of inversions Q. In this notation, Eq. (9.16) becomes

$$\tau = \frac{P-Q}{n(n-1)/2}.$$

It is customary to denote $P - Q$ by the symbol S so that τ may be written

$$\tau = \frac{S}{n(n-1)/2}. \qquad (9.17)$$

Since the sum of P and Q must be $n(n-1)/2$, we can write Eq. (9.17) as

$$\tau = \frac{P-Q}{n(n-1)/2} = \frac{[n(n-1)/2 - Q] - Q}{n(n-1)/2} = 1 - \frac{4Q}{n(n-1)}. \qquad (9.18)$$

Another formula exactly equivalent to Eq. (9.17) is

$$\tau = \frac{4P}{n(n-1)} - 1. \tag{9.19}$$

Now we shall illustrate a simple means of obtaining either P or Q or both. The n persons are ordered from 1 down to n on variable X, as in Table 9.7. Starting with the first person, count the number of times his rank on Y is smaller in magnitude than the ranks below it. This number is recorded in the column headed "Agreements." In Table 9.7, the top person has a "score" of 3 on Y; 3 is less than five of the scores below it on Y, namely the scores 5, 7, 8, 4, and 6, so a 5 is recorded under "Agreements" for the first person. The entry in the column headed "Inversions" is the number of times a score on Y is greater than a score below it in column Y. For person A this number of inversions is 2. The second person on X—person C in Table 9.7—is considered. The entry in the "Agreements" column for the second person is the number of times his Y score is less than a Y score below it in the column. The number of inversions for the second person is the number of times his Y score is greater than a Y score below his in the column. In this way the numbers of agreements and inversions are obtained for all n persons. The total of the "Agreements" column is P; the total of the "Inversions" column is Q. For the data in Table 9.7, these values substituted into Eq. (9.17) yield a value of .50. Of course, either Eq. (9.18) or Eq. (9.19) will produce the same value for τ.

Comparison of Kendall's and Spearman's Coefficients

By way of contrasting the values obtained on the same data using τ and r_s, we found that the data in Table 9.7 produced a value of r_s equal to .667. Surprising as it may seem when one considers the computational techniques for obtaining τ and r_s, there is a close logical connection between the two. Those who wish to explore these aspects of statistics should start with articles by Durbin and Stuart (1951) and Kruskal (1958).

Kendall's τ has an interesting interpretation for which there is nothing comparable in the case of r_s. If two persons are drawn at random (by chance) from the group of n, the difference between the probability that they will have the same order on both X and Y and the probability that they will have different orders on X and Y is equal to the value of τ. Mathematical statisticians find this a particularly pleasing property for such a coefficient to have (see Kruskal, 1958). They tend to prefer τ to r_s on these grounds and on the grounds that it is somewhat easier to work with in the realms of inferential statistics. Computational ease and historical precedent constitute the weak case that can be made for use of r_s.

Kendall's τ With Tied Ranks

When ties occur in the ranks on either X or Y, P and Q are still determined as indicated in Table 9.7. The only alteration in the formula for τ occurs in the denominator. The correction of the denominator of τ involves the quantities K_x and K_y (both of which are functions of the numbers of persons tied at the various ranks on X and Y).

The following formula is applied when ties occur in the ranks on X and Y:

$$\tau = \frac{P - Q}{\sqrt{[n(n-1)/2] - K_x}\,\sqrt{[n(n-1)/2] - K_y}}, \qquad (9.20)$$

where $K_x = (\frac{1}{2}) \sum f_i(f_i - 1)$ (where f_i is the number of tied observations in each group of ties on X), and
$K_y = (\frac{1}{2}) \sum f_i(f_i - 1)$ (where f_i is the number of tied observations in each group of ties on Y).

For an illustration of the application of Eq. (9.20), see Siegel (1956, pp. 218–19) or a more recent textbook on nonparametric statistics.

Case I

X is ordinal and Y is interval or ratio. No coefficient has been developed and studied for this particular case. If you find yourself with variables measured in these ways, it would be advisable to convert the Y scores to ranks and proceed with the calculation of either Spearman's or Kendall's rank-correlation coefficients.

Return to Case C

Rank-biserial correlation. At this point it is appropriate to discuss the coefficient first mentioned under Case C, above. One notable coefficient for correlating a dichotomous variable X and an ordinal variable Y has been investigated by Cureton (1956) and Glass (1966b). This coefficient is closely related to Kendall's τ and incorporates in its definition the concepts of agreements and inversions. We shall denote this coefficient by r_{rb}, the rank-biserial r.

Let X be a dichotomous variable and Y a variable comprising the n untied ranks $1, 2, \ldots, n$. Cureton sought a coefficient descriptive of the relationship between X and Y such that (a) it would have attainable limits ± 1 under all circumstances, (b) it would be $+1$ when the n_1 highest ranks are all 1 on the dichotomy, and (c) it would be strictly nonparametric, i.e., defined wholly in terms of inversions and agreements without such concepts as mean, variance, regression, etc. Suppose that the following data are gathered on X and Y for $n = 10$ persons:

Person	X	Y
A	0	1
B	1	10
C	0	2
D	1	9
E	0	5
F	0	8
G	1	4
H	1	7
I	0	3
J	0	6

To compute r_{rb} the data are arranged in the following manner:

Ranks on Y for			
X = 1	X = 0	Agreements	Inversions
10		6	
9		6	
	8		2
7		5	
	6		1
	5		1
4		3	
	3		
	2		
	1		
		$P = \overline{20}$	$Q = \overline{4}$

There is an *agreement* at any given rank under column 1 for every smaller rank under column 0. There is an *inversion* at any given rank under column 0 for every smaller rank under column 1. Thus there are three agreements corresponding to the rank "4" under column 1 since there are three smaller ranks, 3, 2, and 1, under column 0. P is the sum of all agreements in the data, and Q is the sum of all inversions.

Cureton defined r_{rb} as follows:

$$r_{rb} = \frac{P - Q}{P_{max}}.$$
(9.21)

When no ties exist, $P_{max} = n_0 n_1$, where n_0 is the number of persons at 0 on the dichotomy and n_1 is the number of persons at 1.   Hence

$$r_{rb} = \frac{P - Q}{n_0 n_1}. \tag{9.22}$$

For the above data,

$$r_{rb} = \frac{20 - 4}{(4)(6)} = \frac{16}{24} = \frac{2}{3} = .67.$$

Glass (1966b) has shown that r_{rb} is algebraically equivalent to a coefficient analogous to r_{bis} for ordinal variables. The practical importance of this equivalence is that it provides an easy means of computing r_{rb} without counting agreements and inversions. The following formula can be shown to yield the same value as that given by Eq. (9.22):

$$r_{rb} = \frac{2}{n} (\bar{Y}_1 - \bar{Y}_0), \tag{9.23}$$

where $\bar{Y}_1$ is the average rank of those scoring 1 on X and
        $\bar{Y}_0$ is the average rank of those scoring 0 on X.

The data on which the calculation of r_{rb} by Eq. (9.22) was illustrated will be used to illustrate use of Eq. (9.23).

Ranks on Y for		*Calculations*		
$X = 1$	$X = 0$			
10	8	$n_1 = 4$	$n_0 = 6$	
9	6			
7	5	$\bar{Y}_1 = \frac{30}{4} = 7.500$	$\bar{Y}_0 = \frac{25}{6} = 4.167$	
4	3			
	2	$r_{rb} = \frac{2}{10}(7.500 - 4.167) = \frac{3 \cdot 333}{5} = .67$		
	1			

When no ties occur in Y, Eq. (9.23) can always be used in place of Eq. (9.22).   For a discussion of the case when there are ties in Y see Cureton (1968).

Whitfield (1947) derived a coefficient for correlating one dichotomous and one ordinal variable.   His rationale was to consider the dichotomous variable to be a ranking variable tied at two ranks.   He then applied Kendall's τ formula for tied ranks.   The resulting coefficient has the same numerator as r_{rb} but a different denominator.   The rank-biserial coefficient is to be preferred as a measure of correlation because Whitfield's coefficient may not attain $+1$ when some perfect relationships between X and Y exist.   For example, when $n = 5$, $n_1 = 2$, and $n_0 = 3$ and the fourth- and fifth-ranking persons on Y have the two scores of 1 on X, $r_{rb} = 1$, but Whitfield's coefficient equals only .77.

9.4
PART CORRELATION AND
PARTIAL CORRELATION

Concepts from simple linear regression and correlation are combined in *part correlation* and *partial correlation*. We shall begin this section with the development of part correlation, since partial correlation is its generalization—statistically, at least.

A researcher wishes to determine the correlation between a measure of intelligence X and learning performance during an instructional unit in social studies. He chooses to measure X with the Kuhlmann-Anderson intelligence test; however, he faces some important decisions about how to measure learning performance. He can construct a respectable achievement test of the content being learned. But to give the test and score it for "number of correct answers" is not what this researcher means by the words "learning performance." A large correlation of X with the achievement-test score might result even though no learning at all took place during instruction, because variability on the achievement test could be due to intelligence and test-wiseness and not be at all due to differential learning during instruction. Administering the achievement test both before and after instruction and subtracting each student's initial score from his post-instruction score produces a measure that is far closer to the researcher's notion of a measure of "learning performance." One slight difficulty remains. Such "posttest minus pretest" measures of learning would have a predictable negative correlation with intelligence due, in part, to the manner in which measurement errors are combined by subtracting one fallible measure from another. In fact, it is almost certain that these "difference scores" will have a negative correlation with the pretest scores upon which they are based. This is considered a defect of such "difference scores" when we have reason to believe that amount of learning should not necessarily correlate negatively with pretest status. An alternative method is to measure learning or change by fitting a straight regression line to the pretest and posttest achievement-test data and taking the deviation from the regression line (errors of estimate) measured along the posttest axis. This deviation, called a *residual change score*, is illustrated in Fig. 9.6 where Y and Z denote the posttest and pretest, respectively. (The Z here is not the standard score z mentioned earlier.)

The residual gain score is denoted by $e_{y \cdot z}$ because it is precisely the same as the error made in predicting Y from Z by the least-squares regression line. We know from previous experience with the regression model that the correlation of $e_{y \cdot z}$ with Z is always zero. As a measure of learning, then, $e_{y \cdot z}$ has the property that the measure of how much has been learned is

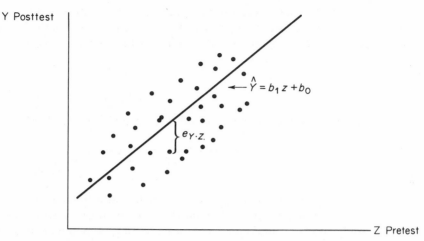

FIG. 9.6   Illustration of the definition of the residual gain score.

unrelated ($r = 0$) with initial performance. The researcher may consider this property desirable.*

The correlation of X with $e_{y \cdot z}$ is called a *part correlation*. In a sense, it is the correlation of X with Y after the portion of Y that can be predicted linearly from Z has been removed from Y. However, such an ambiguous verbal definition will not substitute for the unequivocal definition embodied in the symbol $r_{xe_{y \cdot z}}$.

Of course, the part-correlation coefficient $r_{xe_{y \cdot z}}$ could be found by actually calculating the values of $e_{y \cdot z}$ from the regression line of Y on Z and correlating these values with X. However, we shall now see how this computational labor can be bypassed.

By definition, $r_{xe_{y \cdot z}}$ is given by

$$r_{xe_{y \cdot z}} = \frac{s_{xe_{y \cdot z}}}{s_x s_{e_{y \cdot z}}} ,$$ (9.24)

i.e., by the ratio of the covariance of X with $e_{y \cdot z}$ to the product of the two standard deviations.

From Sec. 8.3, we know $s_{e_{y \cdot z}} = s_y \sqrt{1 - r_{yz}^2}$. It remains to evaluate the numerator of Eq. (9.24)

$$s_{xe_{y \cdot z}} = s_{x(y - b_0 - b_1 z)} = s_{xy} - 0 - b_1 s_{xz}.$$ (9.25)

---

* The properties of residual gain scores have been extensively studied; see Bereiter (1963), Lord (1963), and Tucker, Damarin, and Messick (1966).

(The zero occurs because the covariance of X with the constant b_0 is 0.)

The regression slope b_1 in Eq. (9.25) is for predicting Y from Z; thus $b_1 = r_{yz}s_y/s_z$. Combining these facts in Eq. (9.25) produces

$$r_{xe_{y \cdot z}} = \frac{s_{xy} - r_{yz}(s_y/s_z)s_{xz}}{s_x s_y \sqrt{1 - r_{yz}^2}}. \tag{9.26}$$

Dividing the numerator and denominator of Eq. (9.26) by $s_x s_y$ yields

$$r_{xe_{y \cdot z}} = \frac{s_{xy}/(s_x s_y) - r_{yz}s_{xz}/(s_x s_z)}{\sqrt{1 - r_{yz}^2}} = \frac{r_{xy} - r_{xz}r_{yz}}{\sqrt{1 - r_{yz}^2}}. * \tag{9.27}$$

Thus we see that $r_{xe_{y \cdot z}}$ can be calculated directly from r_{xy}, r_{xz}, and r_{yz}. For example, let X be the measure of intelligence from the Kuhlmann-Anderson test and Z and Y the measures of pretest and posttest achievement, respectively. Suppose that $r_{xy} = .70$, $r_{xz} = .50$, and $r_{yz} = .80$. The value of $r_{xe_{y \cdot z}}$ is

$$r_{xe_{y \cdot z}} = \frac{.70 - (.50)(.80)}{\sqrt{1 - (.80)^2}} = \frac{.70 - .40}{.60} = .50.$$

Thus, although the correlation r_{xy} between X and Y is .70, when one eliminates the linear relationship of Y with Z, the residual relationship of X with $e_{y \cdot z}$ is only .50.

By no means is part correlation limited to applications in which Z and Y are "pretests" and "posttests." One could, for example, apply the part-correlation technique with X a measure of reading speed, Y a measure of reading comprehension, and Z a measure of intelligence. In this instance, $r_{xe_{y \cdot z}}$ measures the relationship between reading speed X and that part of reading comprehension $e_{y \cdot z}$ that is unrelated to intelligence.

In one sense, *partial correlation* is a simple extension of part correlation. To find the partial correlation of X and Y with Z "held constant" or "partialed out," we merely calculate the two arrays of errors of estimate for predicting X from Z and Y from Z and correlate them. Symbolically, the partial correlation of X and Y with Z partialed out is given by

$$r_{xy \cdot z} = r_{e_{x \cdot z}e_{y \cdot z}},$$

where $e_{x \cdot z} = X - (b_0 + b_1 Z)$ and
$\qquad e_{y \cdot z} = Y - (b_0^* + b_1^* Z)$.

---

* In the numerical-subscript notation sometimes used this becomes

$$r_{1(2\ 3)} = \frac{r_{12} - r_{13}r_{23}}{\sqrt{1 - r_{23}^2}}.$$

Notice that there are two distinct regression lines involved in calculating the two sets of errors of estimate (or "residuals"): the line for predicting X from Z—which has constants b_0 and b_1—and the line for predicting Y from Z—the constants for which have been labeled b_0^* and b_1^* to distinguish them from those for the X and Z regression line.

As in the case of part correlation, the actual calculation of the errors of estimate for all n persons is unnecessary in the calculation of $r_{xy \cdot z}$. The partial correlation coefficient can be calculated directly from r_{xy}, r_{xz}, and r_{yz}.

It can be shown, in a manner analogous to the derivation of Eq. (9.27) for the part-correlation coefficient, that $r_{xy \cdot z}$ is given by the following formula:

$$r_{xy \cdot z} = \frac{r_{xy} - r_{xz} r_{yz}}{\sqrt{1 - r_{xz}^2}\, \sqrt{1 - r_{yz}^2}} \, . \qquad * \qquad\qquad (9.28)$$

Next we shall see what interpretation may be given to a calculated value of $r_{xy \cdot z}$. One might hypothesize that there exists a positive correlation between reading performance X and visual perceptual ability Y (as evidenced by eye coordination, scanning speed, etc.). Suppose a sample of 30 children, ranging in age (Z) from 6 years to 15 years, yields a correlation of X with Y, r_{xy}, of .64. The conclusion that some children read better than others because of greater perceptual abilities is tempting, but the cautious researcher will avoid drawing it. It is obvious that as children grow older they develop greater eye coordination and other perceptual abilities as a part of natural maturation. Moreover, the same children receive instruction in school which helps make them better readers year after year, up to a point. Could it not be that measures of both X and Y increase (improve) with age, in the one case as a consequence of physical maturation and in the other case as a function of mental maturation and increased exposure to instruction? This certainly could be the case. If the correlation of X and Y were zero at any one level of chronological age (instead of over the range from 6 years to 15 years), the r_{xy} of .64 for the sample of 30 children has far different implications. Indeed, even the cautious researcher would be tempted to conclude that the observed r_{xy} of .64 was due to a common relationship of both reading performance X and visual perceptual ability Y to chronological age Z, and was *not* due to any direct relationship between X and Y. How can we find what the value of r_{xy} would be for any single value of the chronological age variable Z? Under suitable assumptions, this desired correlation equals the partial correlation of X and Y with Z held constant: $r_{xy \cdot z}$.

---

* $r_{xy \cdot z}$ is called a *first-order* partial-correlation coefficient, because the linear influence of *one* variable, Z, is partialed out. r_{xy} is a *zero*-order correlation coefficient, because nothing is partialed out.

Provided that Z has a linear relationship with both X and Y and that the strength of the linear relationship between X and Y is the same for persons at any level of Z, then $r_{xy \cdot z}$ equals the value of r_{xy} we would obtain by correlating X and Y for a group of persons having identical scores on Z. For example, in the above illustration suppose that $r_{xy} = .64$, $r_{xz} = .80$, and $r_{yz} = .80$. The value of $r_{xy \cdot z}$ from Eq. (9.28) is

$$r_{xy \cdot z} = \frac{.64 - (.80)(.80)}{\sqrt{1 - .80^2}\sqrt{1 - .80^2}} = \frac{.64 - .64}{(.60)(.60)} = 0.$$

Thus we would estimate the value of r_{xy} for children of the *same chronological age* to be zero. If enough children of the same chronological age were available, we could calculate r_{xy} for them alone to check the above result. However, in our example there was not a sufficient number of children of the same age; there were 30 who ranged from 6 to 15 years of age. The partial-correlation coefficient serves the purpose of estimating r_{xy} for a single level of chronological age when there is an insufficient number of persons at any single chronological age to do the estimating by direct calculation.

More than one variable can be "partialed out," using the techniques of multiple regression to be discussed in the next section. For formulas and explanations, see Ezekiel and Fox (1959). With partial correlation, especially, it is well to keep in mind that correlation does not necessarily mean causation. In the behavioral sciences causation is usually complex and indirect. One must be quite nimble intellectually to avoid assuming that he has isolated causal influences when other explanations of one's results are at least as plausible. For discussions of pitfalls see Lerner (1965).

9.5
MULTIPLE CORRELATION
AND PREDICTION

The last correlational technique to be presented in this chapter is known as *multiple correlation*. As was true with the ordinary Pearson product-moment correlational technique of Chapter 7, multiple correlation has a second side known as *multiple prediction*. Stated broadly, the purpose of multiple prediction is the estimation of a variable Y, the dependent variable, from a linear combination of m independent variables $X_1, X_2, \ldots, X_m$.

You will recall from Chapter 8 that when one variable X was used to estimate a second variable Y, the estimation criterion of "least squares" was equivalent to choosing values for b_0 and b_1 so that

$$\sum_{i=1}^{n} (Y_i - b_0 - b_1 X_i)^2$$

was as small as possible. The equation $b_0 + b_1 X_i$ provides the least-squares estimate $\hat{Y}_i$ of the ith person's score on the variable Y. This type of estimation is sometimes termed *univariate* estimation or prediction because there is only one "predictor variable." A *multivariate* prediction of the Y variable given scores on m independent variables is

$$\hat{Y} = b_0 + b_1 X_1 + b_2 X_2 + \ldots + b_m X_m. \tag{9.29}$$

Equation (9.29) provides a *multiple-prediction* or *multiple-regression* equation. Equation (9.29) is sometimes referred to as a *linear* regression equation since the b's appear only with exponents of 1 and never appear as squared terms, cubed terms, etc. Of course, Eq. (9.29) alone is of no value; the procedure by which "good" values for the b's are chosen must be specified. Again the least-squares criterion is invoked, and those values of $b_0, b_1, \ldots, b_m$ are chosen that minimize the quantity

$$\sum_{i=1}^{n} (Y_i - b_0 - b_1 X_{i1} - b_2 X_{i2} - \ldots - b_m X_{im})^2 \tag{9.30}$$

for a given set of values of Y and the X's.

The values $b_0, \ldots, b_m$ that minimize the above quantity provide us with $b_0 + b_1 X_1 + \ldots + b_m X_m$ as a good estimate of Y:

$$\hat{Y}_i = b_0 + b_1 X_{i1} + \ldots + b_m X_{im}.$$

The Pearson product-moment correlation between Y and $\hat{Y}$ is a measure of how well the "best" linear weighting of the independent variables $X_1, \ldots, X_m$ predicts or correlates with the single dependent variable Y. This special case of Pearson's r is called the *multiple correlation coefficient* and is denoted by $R_{y \cdot 1, 2, \ldots, m}$. A second sense in which the values $b_0, \ldots, b_m$ that minimize Eq. (9.30) are "best" is as follows: the *maximum possible positive correlation* between Y and any linear combination of $X_1, \ldots, X_m$ is attained when the X's are combined into

$$b_0 + b_1 X_1 + \ldots + b_m X_m,$$

the b's being those values that minimize Eq. (9.30). Thus,

$$b_0 + b_1 X_1 + \ldots + b_m X_m$$

not only provides the least-squares estimate of Y but it also correlates higher with Y than could any other linear combination of the X variables. (As a consequence of how the weights for the X variables are derived, the multiple correlation coefficient will always be positive or zero.)

The theory and techniques of multiple prediction and correlation are involved and complex. A comprehensive treatment of these subjects would occupy many pages. Fortunately, there is no lack of excellent treatments of these topics in the pedagogical literature of applied statistics. You will find the theoretical and applied aspects of *multiple regression* developed fully in such texts as DuBois (1957), Rozeboom (1966), Draper and Smith (1966), and Acton (1959). For a briefer treatment see Williams (1968).

In the remainder of this section we shall illustrate multiple prediction and correlation for the case in which two variables X_1 and X_2 are used to predict the criterion variable Y. Suppose that Y is grade-point average for college freshmen at the end of two semesters. One wishes to predict Y from X_1, high-school grade-point average, and X_2, verbal ability as measured by the Scholastic Aptitude Test. Many details of the following discussion will be simplified if it is assumed that Y, X_1, and X_2 are transformed to standard scores with mean zero and variance 1. Thus Y, X_1, and X_2 become z_y, z_1, and z_2. We seek the values of b_0, b_1, and b_2 that minimize the quantity

$$\sum_{1}^{n} (z_y - b_0 - b_1 z_1 - b_2 z_2)^2$$

for a group of n students for whom freshman GPA, Y, high-school GPA, X_1, and SAT Verbal scores, X_2, are available.

Without substantiating the claim here, we state that the least-squares estimates b_0, b_1, and b_2 are as follows:

$$b_0 = 0, \qquad b_1 = \frac{r_{y1} - r_{y2} r_{12}}{1 - r_{12}^2}, \qquad b_2 = \frac{r_{y2} - r_{y1} r_{12}}{1 - r_{12}^2}. \tag{9.31}$$

The fact that b_0 is zero is a consequence of having transformed Y, X_1, and X_2 to standard scores; b_0 would not be 0 if these variables had not been standardized. The quantities r_{y1}, r_{y2}, and r_{12} are simply the correlation coefficients between Y and X_1, Y and X_2, and X_1 and X_2 calculated on the data from the n students.

The best (in the least-squares sense) estimate of the ith person's standard score on Y given his standard scores on X_1 and X_2 is

$$\hat{z}_y = b_1 z_1 + b_2 z_2, \tag{9.32}$$

where b_1 and b_2 are as defined in Eq. (9.31). Transforming Eq. (9.32) back into the scale of the original variables gives the multiple-regression equation for estimating Y from X_1 and X_2:

$$\hat{Y}_i = \left(b_1 \frac{s_y}{s_1}\right) X_{i1} + \left(b_2 \frac{s_y}{s_2}\right) X_{i2} + \left(\bar{Y}. - b_1 \frac{s_y}{s_1} \bar{X}_{.1} - b_2 \frac{s_y}{s_2} \bar{X}_{.2}\right). \tag{9.33}$$

The correlation coefficient between the n actual freshman grade-point averages (Y) and the n predicted freshman grade-point averages ($\hat{Y}$) obtained from Eq. (9.33) is the multiple correlation coefficient $R_{y \cdot 1,2}$ between freshman grade-point average and the best linear composite of high-school grade-point average and SAT Verbal scores. One could compute $R_{y \cdot 1,2}$ directly from the n pairs of values of Y_i and $\hat{Y}_i$. However, once r_{y1}, r_{y2}, and r_{12} are known, the multiple correlation coefficient is given conveniently by the following equation:

$$R_{y \cdot 1,2} = \sqrt{b_1 r_{y1} + b_2 r_{y2}}. \tag{9.34}$$

The values of b_1 and b_2 in the above equation are, of course, obtained from the formulas in Eq. (9.31). Note that the positive square root is taken so that R will never be negative. It is not as simple to see that the term under the radical will never be negative, but such is the case.

Data from a study conducted by Dizney and Gromen (1967), shown in Table 9.8, will be used to illustrate multiple prediction and correlation for

TABLE 9.8 SUMMARY DATA FROM A MULTIPLE-PREDICTION STUDY (DIZNEY AND GROMEN, 1967) *

	Intercorrelations				Standard
	X_1	X_2	Y	Means	deviations
X_1 (MLA—Reading)	1.00	.58	.33	25.55	10.20
X_2 (MLA—Writing)		1.00	.45	63.22	11.91
Y (German grade)			1.00	2.61	0.50

the case of two independent variables. Dizney and Gromen studied the relationship of reading proficiency X_1 and writing proficiency X_2 (both as measured by the Modern Language Association Foreign Language Proficiency Tests) to course grades in the second quarter of a college German class. A total of $n = 111$ students participated.

The values of b_1 and b_2 for predicting *standard scores* on Y from *standard scores* on X_1 and X_2 are found from Eq. (9.31) as follows:

$$b_1 = \frac{r_{y1} - r_{y2}r_{12}}{1 - r_{12}^2} = \frac{.33 - .45(.58)}{1 - (.58)^2} = .104$$

$$b_2 = \frac{r_{y2} - r_{y1}r_{12}}{1 - r_{12}^2} = \frac{.45 - .33(.58)}{1 - (.58)^2} = .390.$$

Hence, the best estimate of standard scores on Y given z_1 and z_2 is

$$\hat{z}_y = .104z_1 + .390z_2.$$

From Eq. (9.33) and the data in Table 9.8 we can construct the multiple-prediction equation for raw scores.

$$b_1 \frac{s_y}{s_1} = .104\left(\frac{0.50}{10.20}\right) = .005 \qquad b_2 \frac{s_y}{s_2} = .390\left(\frac{0.50}{11.91}\right) = .016,$$

$$\hat{Y} = .005X_1 + .016X_2 + [2.61 - (.005)25.55 - (.016)63.22]$$

$$= .005X_1 + .016X_2 + 1.47.$$

* Dizney and Gromen report their statistics to too few significant figures for the desirable level of accuracy in the computations here. The r's, for example, should be to the nearest four decimal places, rather than only two. They probably used more figures in their computations than they reported to the reader, however.

The multiple correlation coefficient $R_{y \cdot 1,2}$, which is the product-moment correlation between Y and the best-weighted composite of X_1 and X_2, could either be calculated directly or found more conveniently by Eq. (9.34):

$$R_{y \cdot 1,2} = \sqrt{b_1 r_{y1} + b_2 r_{y2}} = \sqrt{(.104).33 + (.390).45} = .46.$$

Notice that the best combination of X_1 and X_2 is scarcely any better as a predictor of Y than is X_2 alone. Combining X_1 with X_2 in an optimal way increases the correlation of X_2 with Y from .45 to .46. This "expendability" of X_1 arises from the fact that X_1 and X_2 correlate about equally with Y (with X_2 correlating slightly higher), and X_1 and X_2 are substantially correlated themselves ($r_{12} = .58$). The net effect of combining two predictors X_1 and X_2 increases when X_1 and X_2 are both substantially correlated with Y but have a low correlation with each other. Note below how the value of $R_{y \cdot 1,2}$ depends upon the value of r_{12}:

	Case 1					*Case 2*		
	X_1	X_2	Y			X_1	X_2	Y
X_1	1.0	0	.50		X_1	1.0	.5	.5
X_2		1.0	.50		X_2		1.0	.5
Y			1.0		Y			1.0

$$b_1 = .50 \qquad b_2 = .50 \qquad\qquad\qquad b_1 = .33 \qquad b_2 = .33$$
$$R_{y \cdot 1,2} = \sqrt{.50^2 + .50^2} = .71 \qquad\qquad R_{y \cdot 1,2} = \sqrt{.33(.50) + .33(.50)} = .57$$

The multiple R is substantially larger in the case in which $r_{12} = 0$. As you explore the relationships between the correlations of X_1 and X_2 with Y, the correlation of X_1 with X_2, and the value of $R_{y \cdot 1,2}$, you may have need of an inequality that relates r_{y1} and r_{y2} to r_{12}. If r_{y1} and r_{y2} are given, then r_{12} must satisfy the following inequality:

$$r_{y1} r_{y2} - \sqrt{(1 - r_{y1}^2)(1 - r_{y2}^2)} \leq r_{12} \leq r_{y1} r_{y2} + \sqrt{(1 - r_{y1}^2)(1 - r_{y2}^2)}. \quad (9.35)$$

This result comes readily by algebraic manipulation of the inequality $-1 \leq r_{12 \cdot y} \leq 1$, where $r_{12 \cdot y}$ is the $r_{xy \cdot z}$ of Eq. (9.28). More generally the correlation between variables 1 and 2 cannot be outside the limits

$$r_{13} r_{23} \pm \sqrt{(1 - r_{13}^2)(1 - r_{23}^2)}.$$

For $r_{13} = r_{23} = 0$, the limits that r_{12} may attain are the conventional ± 1. For $r_{13} = r_{23} = 1$ or $r_{13} = r_{23} = -1$, r_{12} must be 1. For $r_{13} = -1$ and $r_{23} = 1$, r_{12} must be -1. Try putting these equations into words to be sure you understand what they mean. See Stanley and Wang (1969) and Glass and Collins (1969) for further details.

Interpreting multiple-regression results causally is fraught with hazards. Probably sociologists have struggled with this problem more than have psychologists or educators. For example, see Coleman *et al.,* (1966). Helpful methodological articles have been provided by Werts (1968) and Pugh (1968).

PROBLEMS AND EXERCISES

1. The following are characteristics of people and methods of measuring them:

Characteristic	*Measurement*
A. Sex	Dichotomous; males—1, females—0
B. Age	Measured in months to nearest month
C. Height	Measured to nearest inch
D. Political preference	Dichotomous; Democrat—1, Republican—0
E. Anxiety	Measured by the judgment of clinical psychologists in ranks from 1 through n for a group of n persons.
F. Intelligence	Measured by converting IQ scores to the ranks 1 through n for a group of n persons.

In each of the following instances, identify one or more correlation coefficients appropriate for describing the relationship between the two variables in question:

a. Sex and height.
b. Anxiety and intelligence.
c. Sex and anxiety.
d. Age and height.
e. Sex and political preference.
f. Political preference and intelligence.

2. The following data are illustrative of data gathered by Kennedy, Van de Riet, and White (1963) and Terman and Merrill (1960). (Also see Jensen, 1968.) A sample of $n = 100$ ten-year-old children was drawn from the population of ten-year-olds. Fifty of the children were Negro, and 50 were white. The children were given both digit-span and vocabulary subtests. The following data were obtained:

		Digit span				Vocabulary		
		Fail (0)	Pass (1)			Fail (0)	Pass (1)	
Race	White (1)	25	25	50	White (1)	22	28	50
	Negro (0)	29	21	50	Negro (0)	39	11	50
		54	46	100		61	39	100

a. Calculate the phi coefficient between race X and performance on the digit-span test Y.
b. Calculate the phi coefficient between race X and performance on the vocabulary test Y.

   c. Calculate the maximum possible phi that could occur in each of the two
      situations for the p's there. Hint: $p_{race} = .5$ each time, but $p_{digit\text{-}span} = .46$
      and $p_{vocabulary} = .39$.
   d. Compare the two values of ϕ calculated above and attempt to interpret
      the difference, both statistically and substantively.

3. In a sample of 100 adults, the mean score on an object-assembly test is 104.00
   and the unbiased estimate of the *variance* of the scores is 256.00. The 50
   women in the group have a mean score of 100.00. Scoring females 0 and
   males 1, calculate the point-biserial coefficient of correlation between sex and
   object-assembly ability.

4. Data were gathered on a test of writing skill (Y) and dichotomously on verbal
   reasoning (X). The variable X was scored 0 for "below average" and 1 for
   "above average"; Y was measured by taking raw scores on a 70-item test:

Student	X	Y
A	0	52
B	1	52
C	0	44
D	0	55
E	1	58
F	0	52
G	0	61
H	0	38
I	1	53
J	0	29
K	0	40
L	0	40
M	0	45
N	1	59
O	1	57
P	1	50

   Calculate r_{bis} as an approximation to the correlation between the "underlying"
   verbal-reasoning scores and writing skill.

5. Equation (9.11) shows that the ratio of r_{bis} to r_{pb} is given by

$$\frac{r_{bis}}{r_{pb}} = \frac{\sqrt{n_1 n_0}}{un}.$$

   You are told that $n_1 = 25$, $n = 50$ and $r_{pb} = -.60$. Find the value of r_{bis}.

6. A clinical psychologist and a speech therapist jointly ranked $n = 20$ children
   on two variables: X—emotional adjustment (1 = best adjustment, 20 = worst
   adjustment); Y—severity of stuttering (1 = least severe, 20 = most severe).
   There are $C_2^{20} = 190$ distinct pairs of children in this group. In 80% of these
   pairs, the child in the pair who had a higher rank on X also had a higher rank

on Y; in the remaining 20 % of the pairs, the child with the higher rank on X had a lower rank on Y than the other child of the pair. What is the value of Kendall's τ for these data?

7. For a sample of 89 children, Kabot (see Delacato, 1966, Chap. 14) gathered dichotomous data on reading performance X and laterality Y (consistency with which one "side"—eye, hand, foot—of the body is used). Data were in the form of judgments of poor (0) and good (1) reading performance and low (0) and high (1) consistency in the use of one side of the body:

		Reading performance Poor (0)	Good (1)	
Laterality	High (1)	18	31	49
	Low (0)	28	12	40
		46	43	89

Assume that normally distributed variables underlie both dichotomies and that their joint distribution is bivariate-normal. Calculate the value of r_{tet} for the above data as an approximation to the product-moment correlation of reading performance and laterality.

8. The raw scores of 12 high-school students on tests of abstract and verbal reasoning are reported below:

Student	Abstract reasoning	Verbal reasoning
A	40	37
B	49	42
C	44	25
D	42	40
E	24	19
F	48	39
G	36	27
H	25	14
I	45	43
J	28	16
K	31	20
L	39	35

a. Convert the raw scores to ranks (1–12) for each variable and calculate r_s.
b. Using the same ranks generated in (a), calculate τ.

9. Themes written by ten pupils were judged to be either "creative" ($X = 1$) or "not creative" ($X = 0$). A ranking of the same students on intelligence Y was available (10 = highest, 1 = lowest). Calculate the rank-biserial

correlation coefficient from these data:

Student	X	Y
A	1	2
B	1	6
C	1	1
D	0	7
E	0	3
F	0	10
G	1	9
H	1	5
I	0	4
J	0	8

10. In a group of female physical-education students Leyman (1967) found the following intercorrelations of measures of grade-point average X, the Scott Motor Ability Test Y, and intellectual aptitude Z:

	X	Y	Z
X	1.00	.30	.22
Y		1.00	−.04
Z			1.00

a. Find the correlation of the Scott Motor Ability Test Y and GPA in physical education X, with intelligence Z partialed out.

b. Determine the value of the multiple correlation coefficient $R_{x \cdot y, z}$, i.e., the correlation of physical education GPA with the optimal linear combination of intelligence and motor ability.

c. Try to interpret these results.

11. Goolsby (1967) found the following correlations among the School and College Ability Test (SCAT), the Florida Twelfth Grade Achievement Test (FTGAT), and freshman Grade-Point Average (GPA):

	Intercorrelations		
	SCAT	FTGAT	GPA
SCAT	1.00	.70	.40
FTGAT		1.00	.34
GPA			1.00

Find the value of the multiple correlation coefficient $R_{y \cdot 1, 2}$ between GPA Y, and the best linear combination of SCAT X_1 and FTGAT X_2. In the process, determine the weights b_1 and b_2 for obtaining the least-squares estimate of the ith person's standard score on Y from his standard scores on X_1 and X_2.

12. The correlation of Y with X_1 is .91; the correlation of Y with X_2 is .87. Can the correlation of X_1 with X_2 be as low as .10?

10

PROBABILITY

10.1
INTRODUCTION

The scientist is always attempting to go beyond his data. Even when he is most objective and wants least to generalize, he makes tacit assumptions that his set of data has some stability; if he gathered more data tomorrow it would reflect approximately, though not exactly, the same trend. When least objective, he makes wide, general inferences from what he sees today to what he will see in different places, under different conditions, tomorrow.

Every inference contains some degree of uncertainty. The likelihood of an inference's being true often does not rush upon us, as when we hear: "The Yankees will beat the Sox tomorrow because I saw them beat the Sox today." Other inferences are much more cogent: "I've noted that the sun has risen every day for the past twenty years, hence it will also rise tomorrow morning." Inferences differ in their likelihood of being valid all the way from "extremely unlikely" to "almost certain." By its very nature, no inference is certain to be valid, although some approach certainty.

Much of the work of the statistician is derivation of methods that assign probabilities to inferences. This is indeed an important occupation. Inferential reasoning is the method of science; what a clumsy method it would be if scientists had no objective and systematic means of assigning probabilities to the inferences they make. The language of everyday life with which people refer to inferences as "extremely unlikely" or "almost certain" does not serve science adequately. These subjective estimates vary from person to person depending on the words chosen to express the likelihood and on what the words themselves mean. It is far better for communication among scientists that they can independently arrive at the same statement of the probability of the validity of an inference, and that the statement can be made in unambiguous terms carrying the same meaning for all scientists.

We have idealized the actions of scientists only slightly in the above paragraphs to make the point stronger. Scientists and statisticians are not unanimous on the questions how to assign probabilities to statements and to which statements should probabilities be assigned. Nonetheless, although they may construct adjacent but nonintersecting systems, their preference for one system springs from a value judgment about what the role of the scientist is and ought to be. Their systems are open for all to see, and anyone who is capable of understanding them may. Although statisticians do not always agree on the proper method, their methods of assigning probabilities to inferences are far better than the use of everyday language and unquantified subjective estimates.

Much of the remaining material in this text deals with assigning a probability value to an inference. We shall examine the methods the statistician has developed that allow him to state, for example, "The relationship between IQ and grade-point average is not random in children 11 years of age, and I make this statement with probability .99 that it is true." Obviously, you must set yourself to the task of learning the mathematical conventions that constitute the beginnings of probability theory. You cannot expect to learn all about probability in the space that is available, for probability is a large and complex body of knowledge. Hopefully, you can learn enough to make elementary statistical methodology meaningful.

10.2
PROBABILITY AS A
MATHEMATICAL SYSTEM

We shall begin by being entirely arbitrary. Probability will be looked at as a system of definitions and operations pertaining to a *sample space*. The idea of a sample space is basic. We shall never make a probability statement

that is not related to a sample space of some sort.   Indeed, statements of probability are simply statements about sample spaces and their characteristics.*

A *sample space* is a set of points.   These points can represent anything:
persons, numbers, balls, etc.   An *event* is an observable happening like the
appearance of "heads" when a coin is flipped or the observation that a person
whose name you have selected at random from a telephone book is watching
television.   There may be several points in the sample space, each of which is
an example of an event.   For instance, the sample space may be a set of 6
white and 3 black balls in an urn.   This sample space has 9 points.   An event
might be "A ball is white."   This event has 6 sample-space points.   How
many points in the sample space does the event "A ball is black" have?
The event "A ball in this urn is red" has no sample points.   "A ball in this
urn is either white or black" is also an example of an event.   Notice that
many different events can be defined on the same sample space.

A statement of probability is made about the occurrence of an event
that is associated with a sample space.   For the next few pages, we shall let a
capital letter, A, B, C, . . . , stand for an event; the "probability of the event
A" will be denoted by $P(A)$.

Definition: *The probability of the event A, $P(A)$, is the ratio of
the number of sample points that are examples of A
to the total number of sample points, provided all
sample points are equally likely.*

Let A be the event "A ball is white," where the sample space is the set
of 9 balls (6 white, 3 black) in an urn.   How many sample points are examples
of the event A?   Obviously, the answer is 6.   What is the total number of
sample points? 9.   Hence, the probability of the event A ("A ball is white") is

$$P(A) = \frac{\text{number of examples of } A}{\text{total number of sample points}} = \tfrac{6}{9} = \tfrac{2}{3}.$$

If B is the event "A ball is black" in our example, find $P(B)$.   Add
together $P(A)$ and $P(B)$.   In our example, what is $P(C)$ if C is the event "A
ball is red" ? D is the event "A ball is *either* white *or* black."   What is
$P(D)$? E is the event "A ball is *both* white *and* black."   Find $P(E)$.

Suppose you have a second urn which has 4 white balls in it and an
unspecified number of black balls.   What is the probability of the event
that a ball is white?   You cannot know; at least, within the system we have
developed so far, the question cannot be answered.   A probability statement

---

* The notion of a sample space is actually a relatively recent development in probability
theory, dating back only to the 1920's and the work of von Mises (1931).

can be made if you know fully the characteristics of the sample space, but in this example you do not.

There exists an alternative route by which we may establish the definition of the probability of an event. Consider a sample space composed of a countable number of *elementary events*. An *elementary event* is a sample point. Denote each sample point by a lower case letter "a": $a_1, a_2, \ldots, a_n$. Every event defined on the sample space is composed of a set of elementary events.

Definition: *A probability function is a rule of correspondence that associates with each event A in the sample space a number P(A) such that* (1) $P(A) \geqslant 0$, for any event A; (2) the sum of the probabilities for all distinct events is 1; (3) if A and B are mutually exclusive events, i.e., have no sample points in common, then $P(A \text{ or } B) = P(A) + P(B)$.

If we assume that the probability of an elementary event a_i is $1/n$, where n is the total number of sample points, then the probability of the event A that is composed of n_1 sample points is

$$P(A) = \frac{1}{n} + \frac{1}{n} + \ldots + \frac{1}{n} = \frac{n_1}{n}.$$

n_1/n is the ratio of the number of sample points that are examples of A to the total number of sample points.

Both routes bring us to the same definition for $P(A)$. While the latter definition might have the preference of the mathematician, the former definition of $P(A)$ will probably seem clearer to you.

10.3
COMBINING PROBABILITIES

Suppose we have an urn that contains 4 red, 3 white, and 3 black balls. Three events might be of interest to us: (1) A, a ball is red; (2) B, a ball is white; (3) C, a ball is black. These three events are mutually exclusive: each sample point is an example of one and only one event.

The question arises, "What is the probability that a ball is red *or* white?" We shall denote this event by the symbol $A \cup B$ and its probability by $P(A \cup B)$.

First Addition Rule of Probabilities

When the events A and B are mutually exclusive, $P(A \cup B)$, the probability of either A or B, is $P(A) + P(B)$.

In our example,

$$P(A \cup B) = P(A) + P(B) = \tfrac{4}{10} + \tfrac{3}{10} = \tfrac{7}{10}.$$

Find $P(A \cup C) = P(A) + P(C)$. What is the value of $P(B \cup C)$?

In some sample spaces two events may not be mutually exclusive, i.e., a single sample point may be an example of both events A and B. Let's consider the possible outcomes ("heads" or "tails") of flipping a coin three times in a row. We consider these outcomes abstractly; as yet we don't want to talk about the physical act of flipping a coin. The eight possible outcomes are the sample space:

1. $H H H$	5. $T T T$
2. $H H T$	6. $T T H$
3. $H T H$	7. $T H T$
4. $H T T$	8. $T H H$

Assuming that all of the eight outcomes are equally likely, i.e., each has probability 1/8, what is the probability of "heads" on the first "flip"? What is the probability of "heads" on flips 1 and 2?

We shall now define two events A and B on the above sample space:

A: "heads" on flips 1 and 2
B: "heads" on flips 2 and 3

The sample points that are examples of event A are the first two outcomes (numbers 1 and 2 above). Two sample points are examples of event B. Which two are they?

We shall let the symbol $A \cap B$ denote the new event, "A and B." In our example $A \cap B$ is the event "heads" on flips 1 and 2 *and* "heads" on flips 2 and 3. If we assume that all the eight sample points are equally likely, then the probability of the event $A \cap B$ is as follows:

$$P(A \cap B) = \frac{\text{number of sample points that are examples of } A \cap B}{\text{total number of sample points}}.$$

The total number of sample points is 8. Only one sample point is an example of the event "heads" on flips 1 and 2 *and* "heads" on flips 2 and 3. Which one is it? So the probability of the event $A \cap B$ is 1/8.

Look back at the First Addition Rule of Probabilities and you'll see the assumption that the two events A and B are mutually exclusive. In the example just discussed A and B were not mutually exclusive. The outcome $H H H$ was an example of both events A and B. Keep the same definitions for A and B and let's see what the probability of A or B, $A \cup B$, is when A and B are *not* mutually exclusive.

Second Addition Rule of Probabilities .

The probability of either event A or event B or both, $P(A \cup B)$, is $P(A) + P(B) - P(A \cap B)$.

This expression might look strange; a Venn diagram, an illustration of the relationship between events defined on sample spaces, should help clear up the mystery of the term "$-P(A \cap B)$." See Fig. 10.1 where the events A and B, two overlapping groups of sample points, are depicted in the sample space S. We'll assume that the probability of event A is the area of circle A, and that the probability of event B is the area of circle B.

The probability of A or B or both is that area covered by the intersecting circles A and B. The shaded portion in Fig. 10.1 is that set of sample points in both events A and B, i.e., those points that are examples of $A \cap B$.

How do we find the area covered by A and B? We first find the area of A that is not shared by B, add to it the area of B not shared by A, and then add the area of A *and* B:

$$P(A \cup B) = [P(A) - P(A \cap B)] + [P(B) - P(A \cap B)] + P(A \cap B).$$

The first two terms on the right side of the above equation give the area of A minus the area in common with B. Terms three and four give the area of B minus its area in common with A. We complete the area we wish to find by adding in the area common to A and B, $P(A \cap B)$. The above equation simplifies to:

$$P(A \cup B) = P(A) + P(B) - P(A \cap B).$$

Hence, we have established the Second Addition Rule of Probabilities. Notice that if we had simply added $P(A)$ and $P(B)$ to find $P(A \cup B)$, the portion in common to A and B, $P(A \cap B)$, would contribute twice to the sum. It must contribute only once, so consequently it must be subtracted once.

Even though we have presented two separate rules for the addition of probabilities, the first rule is just a special case of the second rule—that is, the case when $P(A \cap B) = 0$.

If A and B are mutually exclusive events in S, then they don't overlap. See Fig. 10.2; there is no area in common to A and B, so $P(A \cap B) = 0$.

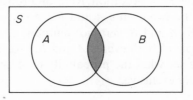

FIG. 10.1 Venn diagram of the intersecting events A and B in the sample space S.

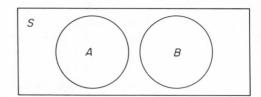

FIG. 10.2 Venn diagram of the mutually exclusive events A and B in the sample space S.

In general, $P(A \cup B) = P(A) + P(B) - P(A \cap B)$. If A and B are mutually exclusive, then $P(A \cap B) = 0$. Therefore, if A and B are mutually exclusive, then

$$P(A \cup B) = P(A) + P(B) - 0 = P(A) + P(B).$$

So far we have treated probability rather abstractly. In much the same manner as the mathematical systems of geometry and algebra, probability theory can be developed from a small set of axioms and definitions. But also in the same manner as geometry and algebra, probability theory can serve as a model for what is going on in a certain class of events in the world around us. Geometry has applications to surveying and architecture. The numerous applications of algebra are obvious. Probability theory also applies to a certain group of events.

The principle that relates probability statements to physical events is due to James Bernoulli (1654–1705). An example of the application of a formal probability statement to an actual set of actions should suffice to show the relationship between theory and application.

Suppose we have an urn that contains 4 white and 6 black balls. The balls are identical in size, shape, and weight and thoroughly mixed so that if we were to reach in and pull one out, it is equally likely that any one of the ten balls would be selected; each ball has one chance in 10 of being chosen. We reach into the urn, pull out a ball, and record its color. The ball is returned to the urn, the balls in the urn are stirred thoroughly, and the act is repeated under the same conditions. We perform this act a very large number of times, say 10,000. After the 10,000th drawing of a ball, suppose we count the number of times a white ball was drawn. Your intuition would tell you that the ratio of the number of times a white ball is drawn to 10,000 will be very close to 4/10. The ratio will very probably not be exactly 4/10 but it will be close.

If we regard the 10 balls as a sample space, and if we say that A is the event "a ball is white," then $P(A)$ is 4/10, exactly. The question arises, Will the formal probability of an event as calculated from theory correspond closely to the relative frequency of the occurrence of the event? The answer to this question is the key to the relationship of probability theory and its application, and the answer is "yes."

We shall attempt a formal statement of this relationship. Suppose an event A either does or does not occur on every trial of an act. The probability that A will occur is the same for all trials of the act and equals $P(A)$. For example, the act may be flipping a symmetrical coin, A may be the event "heads," and it is assumed that the probability of heads, 1/2, is the same from one flip to the next. It is also assumed that every trial is independent of (in no way affected by) every other trial. Now after n trials of the act, the proportion of times A has occurred is p. It can be proved (the proof is so difficult there is no point presenting it here) that p gets closer and closer to $P(A)$ as n becomes larger and larger. We can make the proportion of times A occurs as close as we want to $P(A)$, the probability calculated from the sample space, by performing the act enough times. So $P(A)$ tells what will happen in the long run if we actually performed the actions under the conditions laid down above.

The preceding paragraph is a verbal statement of the *law of large numbers*. The law of large numbers is important for the application of probability and since statistics is one such application, it is important for statistical inference. In spite of its importance, we shall have little more to say about the law of large numbers.

Multiplicative Rule of Probabilities

There exists a multiplicative rule for probabilities that will be of considerable importance to us in later work. Suppose we are flipping a coin five times in a row. Assume that the probability of "heads" is 1/2 on each flip and that the flips are independent. The *multiplicative rule for probabilities* states that the probability of getting five straight "heads" is $1/2 \cdot 1/2 \cdot 1/2 \cdot 1/2 \cdot 1/2 = 1/32$. A general statement of the rule follows:

> *Multiplicative Rule of Probabilities: The probability that A, which has probability $P(A)$ of occurring on any one trial, will occur n times in n independent trials is*
>
> $$P(A) \cdot P(A) \cdot \ldots \cdot P(A) = P(A)^n.$$

The following examples will illustrate the probability rules developed so far. Suppose one rolls a die (singular of dice) on which the probability of any one of the 6 faces coming up is 1/6. What is the sample space of outcomes for one toss? The sample space is the set of 6 outcomes 1, 2, 3, 4, 5, and 6. What is the probability of the die's coming up 2? What is the probability that an even number will appear on a single toss of the die?

$$P(\text{even number}) = P(2) + P(4) + P(6) = \tfrac{1}{6} + \tfrac{1}{6} + \tfrac{1}{6} = \tfrac{3}{6} = \tfrac{1}{2}.$$

What is the probability of an even or odd number appearing on a single toss? Suppose we consider two rolls of the die. The sample space of possible

FIG. 10.3   Sample   space   of   outcomes of tossing a die twice.

1, 1	2, 1	3, 1	4, 1	5, 1	6, 1
1, 2	2, 2	3, 2	4, 2	5, 2	6, 2
1, 3	2, 3	3, 3	4, 3	5, 3	6, 3
1, 4	2, 4	3, 4	4, 4	5, 4	6, 4
1, 5	2, 5	3, 5	4, 5	5, 5	6, 5
1, 6	2, 6	3, 6	4, 6	5, 6	6, 6

outcomes has 36 points, as shown in Fig. 10.3. Let event A be "a 1 on toss 1"
and event B "a 2 on toss 2." Find $P(A \cap B)$ by dividing the number of
sample points that are examples of $A \cap B$ (both A *and* B) by 36. Verify
that $P(A \cap B)$ is equal to $P(A) \cdot P(B)$. Find $P(A \cup B)$, the probability of
event A or event B, remembering that $P(A \cup B) = P(A) + P(B) - P(A \cap B)$. Here, this is $6/36 + 6/36 - 1/36 = 11/36$; the point 1, 2 is common
to A and B.

We shall accept as a definition the statement that *two events are independent if and only if* $P(A \cap B) = P(A) \cdot P(B)$. Independence is an important concept in statistics and probability, and we shall have more to say
about it later.

10.4
PERMUTATIONS AND
COMBINATIONS

Two additional concepts that crop up repeatedly when one begins examining
the outcomes of experiments are *permutations* and *combinations*.

A *permutation* of a set of objects (the letters A, B, C, and D, for example)
is an arrangement of them in which their order is considered. A different
ordering of the objects is a different permutation. How many different
permutations (orderings) are there of the letters A, B, C, and D? To find
out we can set about the task of writing them down and counting them, as
shown in Table 10.1.

The first letter can be either A, B, C, or D. Suppose it is A (this puts
us in the top fourth of Table 10.1). If the first letter is A, the second letter
can be either B, C, or D. If the second letter is B, then the third letter can
be either C or D. If the third letter is C, then the fourth letter must be D.
So $ABCD$ is one possible permutation. There are four possible letters for
the first position; after one letter is assigned to the first position, there are
three possible letters for the second position; etc. Hence, the number of
possible permutations of the four letters A, B, C, and D is $4 \cdot 3 \cdot 2 \cdot 1 = 24$.

If we have n distinct objects we can make $n(n-1)(n-2)\ldots 2 \cdot 1$
different permutations of them. Instead of writing $n(n-1)(n-2)\ldots 2 \cdot 1$
we can denote this product by $n!$, read "n factorial." $n!$ is the product of
the numbers from 1 through n and equals the number of permutations of n
distinct objects. (We agree to let $0!$ equal 1.)

TABLE 10.1   FINDING THE 24 PERMUTATIONS OF 4 THINGS TAKEN 4 AT A TIME

First letter	Second letter	Third letter	Fourth letter	Permutation
A	B	C	D	ABCD
A	B	D	C	ABDC
A	C	B	D	ACBD
A	C	D	B	ACDB
A	D	B	C	ADBC
A	D	C	B	ADCB
B	A	C	D	BACD
B	A	D	C	BADC
B	C	A	D	BCAD
B	C	D	A	BCDA
B	D	A	C	BDAC
B	D	C	A	BDCA
C	A	B	D	CABD
C	A	D	B	CADB
C	B	A	D	CBAD
C	B	D	A	CBDA
C	D	A	B	CDAB
C	D	B	A	CDBA
D	A	B	C	DABC
D	A	C	B	DACB
D	B	A	C	DBAC
D	B	C	A	DBCA
D	C	A	B	DCAB
D	C	B	A	DCBA

The value of $n!$ increases exceedingly rapidly as n increases. At first glimpse, $10! = 10 \cdot 9 \cdot 8 \cdot 7 \ldots 2 \cdot 1$ seems like an innocuous number; but if you were to calculate it you would find that $10! = 3{,}628{,}800$. To give an idea of the size of $12!$, imagine that you have one dozen eggs in a carton and that you want to form every possible permutation (arrangement) of them. Assume you can make a new arrangement every minute of your eight-hour working day. If you keep at this job five days a week, 52 weeks a year, you would require longer than 3500 years to make every possible arrangement! Successive members of a family who began at the start of the Roman Empire would not be through yet.

The concept of *combinations* arises when one is selecting some number of objects from a larger or equally large set of objects. A *combination* of objects is a distinct set of objects in which order is not considered. When n objects are selected from n objects, i.e., all the objects are selected, there is only one combination. If one object is selected from n objects, there are n combinations. The problem is to find a general expression for the number of combinations that exist when n_1 things are selected from n.

Consider four objects, A, B, C, and D. How many different combinations can be made by selecting two letters at a time from these four? The answer is six: AB, AC, AD, BC, BD, CD. Notice that for combinations order is *not* considered; AB is one combination, and BA is the same combination. Write down the four possible combinations that can be formed by selecting *three* letters at a time from A, B, C, and D. (The first is ABC.)

Suppose n_1 objects are being selected from n objects. How many different combinations are there? For the time being let us regard order as important and then later collapse together all those sets of selections that are different only because of order. If n_1 objects are being selected from n, then there are n choices for the first object, $n - 1$ choices for the second, $n - 2$ for the third, $n - 3$ for the fourth, and so on until there are $n - n_1 + 1$ choices for the n_1th object. So the total number of different selections (i.e., permutations) of n_1 from n where order is important is equal to

$$n(n - 1)(n - 2) \ldots (n - n_1 + 1).$$

There are n_1 terms in this product corresponding to the n_1 objects selected. However, corresponding to each distinct combination of n_1 objects are $n_1!$ permutations of them. Hence, the number of combinations of n_1 objects selected from n such that order is not considered is

$$\binom{n}{n_1} = \frac{n(n - 1)(n - 2) \ldots (n - n_1 + 1)}{n_1!}.$$

The symbol $\binom{n}{n_1}$ denotes "the number of combinations of n_1 things taken from n things."

It can be shown fairly easily, and you should satisfy yourself that it is true, that

$$n(n-1)(n-2)\ldots(n-n_1+1) = \frac{n!}{(n-n_1)!}\;;$$

merely write $n!$ as

$$n(n-1)(n-2)\ldots[(n-n_1)+1](n-n_1)[(n-n_1)-1]\ldots 1.$$

Write out $n!$ in the numerator and $(n-n_1)!$ in the denominator and cancel the terms that are common to both numerator and denominator and express $(n-n_1)[(n-n_1)-1]\ldots 1$ as $(n-n_1)!$ Then perform the division.

Consequently,

$$\binom{n}{n_1} = \frac{n!}{n_1!\,(n-n_1)!}.$$

To summarize, *the number of permutations of n objects is n!. The number of permutations of n objects taken n_1 at a time is*

$$n(n-1)\ldots(n-n_1+1).$$

The number of combinations of n things taken n_1 at a time is given by

$$\binom{n}{n_1} = \frac{n!}{n_1!\,(n-n_1)!}.$$

How many different *combinations* are there of 3 things taken from 5 things? In this problem $n=5$ and $n_1=3$.

$$\binom{5}{3} = \frac{5!}{3!\,(5-3)!} = \frac{5!}{3!\,2!} = \frac{5\cdot4\cdot3\cdot2\cdot1}{(3\cdot2\cdot1)(2\cdot1)} = \frac{5\cdot4}{2\cdot1} = \frac{20}{2} = 10.$$

Note that there are $5\cdot4\cdot3 = 60$ *permutations* of 5 things taken 3 at a time because each of the 10 combinations of 5 things taken 3 at a time has $3\cdot2\cdot1$ permutations.

Ten men are eligible to serve on a committee. The committee must be composed of only seven men. How many different committees could be formed from the 10 available men? Let $n=10$ and $n_1=7$; then evaluate $\binom{10}{7}$.

An ice cream manufacturer has six different flavors of ice cream. He can sell them individually, he can mix any two different flavors, or he can mix any three different flavors to make new flavors. How many different flavors (and combinations of flavors) can he make? You must evaluate three separate quantities of the form $\binom{n}{n_1}$ to solve this problem.

10.5
BINOMIAL DISTRIBUTION

Practically every topic discussed so far in this chapter can be applied to the solution of a problem in statistics. The following problem concerns the repeated independent performance of an act that can result in either "success" or "failure" with a constant probability. We shall develop a *binomial distribution* that will describe one aspect of the results of such a series of acts, namely, the probability of a given number of successes.

Suppose a fair coin, i.e., symmetrical and of homogeneous composition, is to be flipped five times in succession. Each flip is independent of every other flip in the sense that if the first flip results in "heads," then a "heads" on the second flip is no more nor less likely than if the first flip had given a "tails." Assume further that the probability of "heads" is the same from the first to the fifth flip. The five flips are five "trials"; independent trials that can result in one of two outcomes with a constant probability are called *Bernoulli* or *binomial trials*. (James Bernoulli was a 17th-century mathematician whose *Ars Conjectandi* was one of the first treatises on probability theory.) The five coin flips are five binomial trials. How does one find the probability that three "heads" will result in five trials?

One possible outcome of the five flips that gives three "heads" and two "tails" is H, H, H, T, T. From the multiplicative rule of probabilities, we know that the probability of H, H, H, T, T is $1/2 \cdot 1/2 \cdot 1/2 \cdot 1/2 \cdot 1/2 = 1/32$ since the probability of "heads" and the probability of "tails" are both $1/2$. However, the sample space of outcomes of the five flips has 32 points $(2 \cdot 2 \cdot 2 \cdot 2 \cdot 2)$, and several of these outcomes are examples of the event "three 'heads' and two 'tails'." We can find the number of different points that are examples of the event in question by using the concept of combinations. Further examples of the event are H, H, T, T, H and H, T, T, H, H. The total number of distinct outcomes that have three "heads" and two "tails" is the number of combinations of five things taken three at a time,

$$\binom{5}{3} = \frac{5!}{3! \, 2!} = \frac{4 \cdot 5}{2 \cdot 1} = 10.$$

There are 10 sample points that are examples of the event and each has probability $1/32$; consequently, we use the addition rule of probabilities so that the probability of obtaining three "heads" in five flips of a fair coin is $10(1/32) = 10/32$.

In summary, $10/32$ was found by multiplying out $\binom{5}{3}\left(\frac{1}{2}\right)^3\left(\frac{1}{2}\right)^2$.

In general, the probability of obtaining n_1 "successes" in n binomial trials is equal to

$$\binom{n}{n_1} p^{n_1} q^{n-n_1},$$

where p is the probability of a "success" on any one trial,
  q is the probability of a "failure" and equals $1 - p$, and
  $n_1 = 0, 1, 2, \ldots, n$.

Note that "binomial trials" refers only to trials that have only two possible outcomes: *yes* or *no*, *success* or *failure*, *heads* or *tails*, *red* or *not red*, etc.

A die is tossed four times, and we wish to find the probability of three "sixes." In this example, $n = 4$, $n_1 = 3$, and we take the probability of a "six" on any trial, p, to be $1/6$. Hence, $q = 1 - p = 5/6$, the probability of *not a* 6. The probability of 3 "sixes" thus equals

$$\binom{4}{3}\left(\frac{1}{6}\right)^3\left(\frac{5}{6}\right)^1 = \frac{4!}{3!\,1!}\left(\frac{1}{6}\right)^3\left(\frac{5}{6}\right) = \frac{4\cdot5}{6^4} = \frac{20}{1296}.$$

You can see that the probability of three "sixes" in four tosses of a die is small, less than .02.

The expression

$$\text{probability } (n_1) = \binom{n}{n_1} p^{n_1} q^{n-n_1}$$

is the formula for the *binomial distribution*. This distribution has many important uses in theoretical and applied statistics.

An interesting relationship exists between the term $\binom{n}{n_1}$ in the binomial distribution and a table known as Pascal's triangle [after the French mathematician and philosopher Blaise Pascal (1623–1662)]. Each row in Pascal's triangle (see Fig. 10.4) is formed by adding together certain numbers in the row above it. Each number is the sum of the two numbers diagonally above it. Thus, the 6 in row 4 is the sum of the two 3's above it. You could easily construct the eighth, ninth, tenth, and subsequent rows yourself.

It can be proved that $\binom{n}{n_1}$ equals the $n_1 + 1$st number in the nth row of Pascal's triangle. For example, $\binom{3}{1}$ equals the second, $(n_1 + 1)$st, number in row 3:

$$\binom{3}{1} = \frac{3!}{1!\,2!} = 3.$$

$\binom{5}{0} = 1$ is the first, $(n_1 + 1)$st, number in row 5; it is the number of combinations of zero things, taken from 5. Note that the first and the last

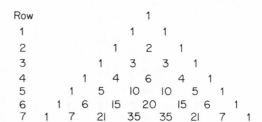

FIG. 10.4   Pascal's triangle.

number in each row is 1; because $\binom{n}{0} = \binom{n}{n} = 1$.

Calculating, for example, the probability of 14 successes in 30 trials when $p = 3/8$ and $q = 5/8$ would be an arduous task. Fortunately, excellent tables for the binomial distribution exist. We recommend you use them whenever your calculations are more complicated than the elementary ones in this chapter. A brief table for the binomial distribution appears in Pearson and Hartley (1966). Much more extensive tables have been published. See Staff, Harvard University Computational Laboratory (1956) and "Tables of the Cumulative Binomial Probabilities" (1953). (The "cumulative binomial" is simply the sum of successive terms in the binomial distribution and gives the probability of *at least* n_1 successes in n trials.)

Figure 10.5 illustrates the entire binomial distribution for eight trials when $p = q = 1/2$. Note that when $p = q$ the distribution is symmetrical. For $p > q$ it will be skewed to the left because high values will predominate. How will it be skewed for $p < q$?

In Fig. 10.6 the binomial distribution for $n = 5$ and $p = .30$, $q = .70$ appears. You can see from Fig. 10.6 that the probability of five successes when $n = 5$ and $p = .30$ is very small. It is only $(.30)^5 = .00243$, i.e., 243 times in 100,000. If you watched five trials of some event and you had no idea what the probability of success was (p was unknown), and you observed five successes, would you think it likely that $p = .30$? What values of p would make five successes in five trials likely—say, would yield a probability of at least .5? (Hint: Solve $p^5 = .5$ for p. Use logarithms, if you know how. Otherwise, try various large values of p. Then find $p^5 \geqslant .5$.)

The binomial distribution affords a good example of the general type of reasoning used in testing statistical hypotheses. A statistician may feel

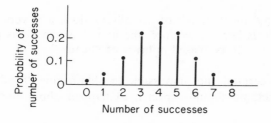

FIG. 10.5   Binomial distribution for $n = 8$, $p = 1/2$.

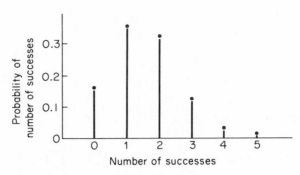

FIG. 10.6   Binomial distribution for $n = 5$, $p = .30$.

that the process by which the data he has observed were generated was a series of binomial trials. Suppose he has flipped a coin ten times and observed nine "heads." He is suspicious that the coin is not fair, i.e., the probability of getting "heads" is not 1/2. His observations appear to be evidence that the coin is unfair. He formalizes his evidence in the following manner:

1. Entertain the notion temporarily that the probability of "heads" for this coin truly is 1/2. This is a *hypothesis*.

2. If the probability of "heads" is 1/2, what is the probability that I would have observed the event that I did (nine "heads") or one more extreme (10 "heads")?

3. This probability is

$$\binom{10}{9}\left(\frac{1}{2}\right)^9\left(\frac{1}{2}\right)^1 + \binom{10}{10}\left(\frac{1}{2}\right)^{10}\left(\frac{1}{2}\right)^0 = .0107.$$

   (Recall that any number with an exponent of zero equals 1.)

4. If this coin is fair, I have observed an event that is extremely unlikely.

5. If this coin is biased in favor of "heads," the event I observed would be more probable. For example, if the probability of "heads" for this particular coin were actually 8/10, then the probability of getting nine or 10 "heads" in 10 flips would be

$$\binom{10}{9}\left(\frac{8}{10}\right)^9\left(\frac{2}{10}\right)^1 + \binom{10}{10}\left(\frac{8}{10}\right)^{10}\left(\frac{2}{10}\right)^0 = .3758.$$

6. It appears that on the basis of my observations it is very unlikely that this coin is fair. Therefore, the hypothesis in (1) is rejected; the coin appears to be biased in favor of "heads."

Notice that it is certainly not impossible to obtain nine "heads" in 10 flips of a coin; in fact, we should expect it to happen about once (1.07) in every 100 sets of 10 flips. The *possibility* exists that the coin that yielded nine "heads" actually is a fair coin, but the *probability* that this is true is small.

The experimenter's logic often follows the same pattern as the reasoning above. He hypothesizes that certain features of a model for his experiment (the binomial distribution is one such model) have certain values (e.g., the probability of "heads" is 1/2). He needn't believe this hypothesis; he only entertains it temporarily to see where it leads him. The experimenter then takes his observations (e.g., flips the coin 10 or 20 times), after which he calculates the probability of obtaining the actual result he did obtain, or a more extreme one, if his original hypothesis was true. If this probability is very small (say, .05 or .01), he questions the truth of the hypothesis. If his original hypothesis was false and some alternative hypothesis was true (e.g., the coin is biased), his results might be much more likely. This process, called "hypothesis testing," is one of rejecting or failing to reject some explanation (hypothesis) for the obtained results on the basis of the probability of obtaining the particular results if the hypothesis were true. If the probability of the obtained results (or more extreme ones) is large (for example, .30 or more) when one calculates this probability under a certain hypothesis, then the hypothesis is not rejected at that moment. If the probability of the obtained results (or more extreme ones) is small (.05 or less) when this probability is calculated under another hypothesis, then this hypothesis is rejected. It has not been proven that the hypothesis is false; there is some small probability (.05 or less) that it is true. However, the evidence for its falsity is great.

The study of probability can be interesting and entertaining. Historically, probability concepts arose in connection with games of chance. Those who make use of probability theory are generally awed by the intricacy and excitement of the system and the way in which it produces results quite in disagreement with intuition, unless one's intuition has been developed by experience with calculated probabilities. A few examples of surprising results will convince you of the untrustworthiness of your intuition at this stage.

What is the probability that at least two people in a group of 23 have the same birthdate? (Assume that the people are drawn randomly from a population of persons in which all 365 birthdates (not counting February 29) are equally likely.) Is the probability .001 or .0001 or even smaller? Actually, the probability that at least two people out of 23 have the same birthdate is .507! You should expect multiple birthdates to occur in slightly more than half the groups of size 23. It is practically certain that in a group of 150 persons at least two people will have the same birthdate! (See Feller, 1957, pp. 31–32.)

Suppose John and Jim have a fair coin (probability of "heads" is 1/2) and each has an equally large stockpile of marbles. John flips the coin; each time a "heads" comes up, he wins one of Jim's marbles. Jim wins one of John's marbles whenever a "tails" appears. Does it not seem clear that John and Jim will have equally large stockpiles about half the time during a large series of coin flips? Shouldn't Jim be in the lead half the time and John be in the lead the other half? Actually, this is the least probable occurrence. It is much more probable that either Jim or John will lead for the entire game.

10.6
RANDOMNESS AND
RANDOM SAMPLING

The concept of *random sampling* is closely tied to probability; this is an appropriate place to deal with the topic.

Inference is the process of reasoning from "some" (meaning "not none, and perhaps all") to "all." The validity of the inference will depend on how representative the "some" is of the "all." If you were interested in evaluating the voting preferences of all voters in the United States, common sense would tell you not to interview only corporation presidents. In this example, the "some" (corporation presidents) are not representative of "all" (all voters in the U.S.). How does one go about obtaining a representative sample?

There are several different methods, but we shall study only one at any length. At a later stage of your education in statistics, time spent with textbooks dealing expressly with sampling methods will be valuable (especially see Cochran, 1963). We shall deal only with *simple random sampling*. Often the adjective "simple" is dropped when there is no need to distinguish between different sampling methods. When "random sampling" is referred to here, "simple random sampling" is implied.

Simple random sampling is the process of selecting observations from a larger group in such a way that each observation in the larger group has an *equal and independent* probability of being selected. The larger group is called a *population*; the smaller group of those observations selected is a *sample*. If the sampling is random, then the process by which the observations are selected will give each observation in the population an equal chance of being selected for the sample. Furthermore, if the sampling is truly random, the result of one selection is independent of (is not affected by nor has any effect on) the result of any other selection.

The condition of independence of the selections is an important one, and one which is often not given sufficient attention. Lack of independence between the observations sampled is one of the most prevalent errors in educational and psychological research.　Careful study of the proper random-sampling procedure and how it can be abused will be worthwhile.

The condition of *equiprobability* in the definition of random sampling states that at each stage in the sampling process all of the remaining elements have the same probability of being chosen.　Suppose two cards are to be selected at random from a deck of 52.　If the first choice is to be random, then all 52 cards must have an equal chance of being chosen, namely 1/52. If the second choice is to be random, all of the 51 remaining cards must have the same probability of being chosen, namely 1/51.　How do you achieve this goal of equiprobability in practice?　There are numerous ways in which equiprobability is approximated; some are much better than others.　Probability statements about various "hands" in poker and bridge assume that the cards are shuffled in a purely random manner.　The greater incidence of "royal flushes" and "perfect hands" than would be predicted by probability attests to the fact that a casual shuffling of the cards is a poor approximation to randomness.　Drawing names from a hat is an equally bad attempt to approximate randomness.　The best method of achieving random sampling available to the practitioner of statistics is use of a table of random numbers.

Tables of random numbers are tables of digits, 0 through 9, ordered by a mechanical process that approximates equal probability of the occurrence of any one digit as nearly as technology can.　If you select your sample with the aid of a well-known table of random digits and if you use an approximate procedure, you need have no worry that your sample will not be random. A table of random digits appears as Table A in Appendix A.

The following is an example of random sampling using a table of random digits.　From the 900 male members of the PTA, Principal Jones wishes to estimate the percent of fathers with high-school diplomas from a random sample of 200.　The percent with diplomas in the random sample of 200 will not differ much from the corresponding percent in the population of 900.　Jones instructs his secretary to assign a three-digit number from 001 to 900 by starting at the beginning of the alphabetical file of PTA members. He then goes to his table of random numbers to make his selection.　With the book open to the first page, he lays the point of his pencil on the page of random digits with his eyes closed.　The two digits closest to his pencil point are 3 and 6.　He moves to the intersection of row 3 and column 6 of the table to begin selections.　Moving along row 3 starting with column 6 Jones sees the digits 7 8 2 1 2 1 6 9 9 3 3 5 9 0 2 9 1 3 . . . .　By grouping digits into groups of three, he obtains the numbers 782, 121, 699, 335, 902, 913, ...　His secretary will now pull the cards of those persons who have identification numbers 782, 121, 699, 335, etc.　But what about 902 and 913?　There are only 900 persons, so no one has identification numbers 902 and 913.　These numbers are simply disregarded.　What happens when 782 comes up again, if it does, or the number of any other person who has already been selected?

That number is disregarded; the sampling continues as though nothing had happened. In this manner, Principal Jones can be assured of the randomness of his sample.

Why should Jones have gone through this process of obtaining a random sample? Why didn't he just go through the files and choose 200 persons he thought would be representative of all 900? Wouldn't his judgment give a more representative sample than leaving the process to chance? The random sample will probably be better than a judgmental sample. Numerous factors can operate on the principal's judgment to make his judgmental sample unrepresentative. The most active PTA members are known best by him; they are also more likely to be high-school graduates. Possibly a greater proportion of nongraduates do not attend PTA meetings regularly and have never met the principal. If the principal were more likely to select those he had met or knew by name, his judgmental sample would have a greater proportion of high-school graduates than the population of 900 fathers. If Jones selects his sample via the random-number table, these biases will not affect the selection. Randomized selection prevents any *systematic* biases.

Independence

An example of sampling in which the observations are *not* independent will illustrate what must be avoided in random sampling. Suppose a researcher wants to estimate the average IQ of children who have a twin brother or sister. Assume that 100 children (50 pairs of twins) constitute the available population, and the researcher can administer intelligence tests to 30 children. He decides that his work will be simplified if each time he chooses one child at random, he also tests the child's twin. He feels that he would then have a random sample of 30 children. He would not. The 30 observations have not been selected independently. If they were, the selection of one child would not have made the selection of his twin any more likely than the selection of any other child. As it was, the selection of a child made the probability of the selection of his twin equal to 1 a certainty. The researcher does not have a simple random sample of 30 children from the population of 100. He is justified in saying, however, that he has obtained a simple random sample of 15 twin pairs from a population of 50 pairs; and he could average the two IQ's in the twin set to obtain an observation appropriate to his sampling technique. Drawing twin pairs is an example of *cluster* sampling.

Nonindependence of the observations in a supposedly random sample is a prevalent fault in experimentation, too. An intolerable number of experiments in education are analyzed incorrectly because the experimenter was not aware of what is and what is not a random sample. Countless studies at the master's and doctor's level and many others that are published in journals stumble on this basic problem. Examples of proper and improper analyses will be given throughout this text; you are best advised, however, to seek expert advice concerning your sampling technique when you are designing an experiment.

A common fault of naïve researchers in education is to choose "classrooms" randomly to participate in an experiment and then to analyze the data as if "students" had been chosen randomly. If classroom A is chosen for method A of teaching and classroom B for method B, then surely the selection of "students" has not been an independent one. If John and George are both in classroom A, then John and George must both receive method A. There's no chance for John to receive A and George to receive B. Any analysis that treats the 30 students in both A and B as though they constituted 60 separate observations is quite likely to be wrong because the two classrooms are just two "clusters" of students. The average of the 30 observations in A may be treated as independent of the average of the 30 observations in B, if other conditions are met. Hence, one has *two* observations that constitute a random sample. This is a difficult point to comprehend. The general problem assumes a slightly different form for all of its special instances. The proper method of sampling and analysis sometimes manages to elude the most sophisticated researchers. We hope to throw more light on the problem later in this text.

We conclude this section on random sampling with an alternative statement of the definition of simple random sampling. Try to satisfy yourself that this statement is equivalent to the one given at the beginning of this section.

> *Simple random sampling: If sampling from n observations is random, then regardless of what the first n_1 choices were, the probability of any particular observation's being chosen on the $(n_1 + 1)$st selection is $1/(n - n_1)$.*

10.7
RANDOM VARIABLE

A random variable is defined in terms of two concepts, one of which has already been introduced: *sample space* and *function*. We have already discussed the meaning of a sample space. It is a collection (finite or infinite) of objects or events. *A function is any set of ordered pairs of elements, no two of which have the same first element.* As you can see, the definition of a function is quite general; $\{(a, 1), (b, 2), (c, 3)\}$ is a function, so is $\{(\text{John}, \text{Alice}), (\text{Joe}, \text{Mary}), (\text{Ted}, \text{Sharon}), (\text{Jim}, \text{Joyce})\}$. A function is formed when we specify a rule that associates a unique element with every element of some set. We form a function when we associate every person with his age: (Mr. Jones, 37), (Mark Smith, 5), ... *A random variable is a function such that all of the first elements are points in a sample space.* The previous example is a random variable. The sample space is all persons; each is associated with his age.

The following are all examples of random variables (the random variables of most interest to statisticians and to us in this text are those in which the elements of a sample space are associated with numbers):

1. Sample space: outcomes of the flip of a coin ("heads," "tails").

Random variable X

1st element	2nd element
"heads"	1
"tails"	0

2. Sample space: the 6 different outcomes of rolling a die.

Random variable Y

1st element	2nd element
the face with 1 dot	1
the face with 2 dots	2
.	.
.	.
.	.
the face with 6 dots	6

3. Sample space: a bushel of oranges.

Random variable Z

1st element	2nd element (the weight of the orange in ounces)
Orange #1	3
Orange #2	5
Orange #3	2
.	.
.	.
.	.

The idea of a random variable is so simple and seems so obvious that a fancy definition appears to be "window dressing." Confusion can arise, however, if the definition is not made explicit.

We shall speak later of "the value of the random variable Z." If Z is the random variable as defined in (3) above, then Z assumes a value, the weight in ounces, for each element of the sample space, each orange. For the first orange, Z assumes the value 3.

You have already met a random variable in this chapter, but no attempt was made to point it out. The binomial distribution is that of a random variable. The sample space is the collection of points that are the distinct outcomes of n binomial trials. The random variable X takes on the values $0, 1, 2, \ldots, n$ according to the number of "successes" that occur in n trials. If a coin is flipped four times and a "heads" is called a "success," then X has the value 3 for the event H, T, H, H, since 3 "successes" occurred.

A sample space can become complex conceptually. For example, a child is to read a given page of a reader. He is to do this a large number of times; each separate reading of the page is a sample point in the sample space of all readings. A random variable X can be defined on this sample space by associating with each reading the time from beginning to end. X takes on a value for each reading: reading 1—3 min 5 sec; reading 2—2 min 48 sec; . . . . X is a random variable that takes on values expressed in "minutes" and "seconds."

In subsequent chapters we shall see how probabilities are associated with values of a random variable. For example, suppose a fair coin is being flipped. The random variable X is the same as example (1) above. The probability that X will take on the value 1 is 1/2, the probability that the event "heads" associated with 1 will occur. The probability that the random variable X will assume the value 0 is 1/2.

10.8
TYPES OF RANDOM
VARIABLES

The statistician finds the distinction between *discrete* and *continuous* random variables a useful one. We have had no need to use this distinction yet; it becomes a useful one when certain operations on random variables are defined and performed.

The distinction between discrete and continuous refers to the nature of the numbers that are associated as second elements of the random-variable function with sample-space points. *A discrete random variable is one that can assume only certain values on the real-number line.* We can think of all real numbers as points on a line that extends from $-\infty$ to $+\infty$, as in Fig. 10.7. Between two points on the real-number line, a discrete random variable

$$\longleftarrow \quad \text{to} \; -\infty \quad -2 \quad -1 \quad 0 \quad 1 \quad 2 \quad \text{to} \; +\infty \longrightarrow$$

FIG. 10.7   The real number line.

can assume some values but not others. An example of a discrete random variable is X in (1) in Sec. 10.7 above. It can assume only the values 0 and 1; it is impossible for X to equal 1/2. *A continuous random variable is one that can assume any value on the real-number line between two points.* An example of a continuous random variable is age. The value of the random variable "age" for a person can equal 5 years, 6 months, 4 days, 11 hours, 14 minutes, 6.132 . . . seconds. A person who has just become 10 years old has possessed an age equal to every possible number on the real number line from 0 to 10 years.

Which of the following random variables are discrete and which are continuous?

1. Number of "heads" in six flips of a coin.

2. Time required to solve a concept formation task.

3. Height of mercury in a barometer.

4. Highest temperature of the air during the daylight hours.

5. The number of teeth in an infant's mouth.

6. The amount of money in the pocket of a corporation president.

Variables 1, 5, and 6 are discrete; the others are continuous. Can a corporation president have 11.5 cents (not counting trading stamps) in his pocket? Can a subject require 51.23 seconds to solve a concept formation task? Can he require 46.721 seconds or 38.50 seconds?

A distinction must be made between the values that a random variable can assume *theoretically* and the values that one's measuring instruments yield. A variable such as length can assume theoretically any possible real number between $0''$ and $5''$, say. For example, analytic geometry tells us that the hypotenuse of a right triangle both sides of which are $1''$ in length has length $\sqrt{2}''$. The number $\sqrt{2}$ is an unending number the first few digits of which are 1.414 . . . . No physical act of measurement will yield a value exactly equal to $\sqrt{2}$. The most sensitive measuring instrument must finally give up in its attempt to add more figures after 1.414 . . . . Perhaps a finely calibrated ruler could give lengths to the nearest 1/128th of an inch; if so, length as measured by this ruler could not assume a value between $6/128''$ and $7/128''$, for example. Although "length" is theoretically a continuous random variable, any measurement of it yields discrete values. Nonetheless, it will be helpful to retain the distinction between discrete and continuous while remembering that the physical act of measurement yields discrete numbers.

10.9
PROBABILITY AS AN AREA

The probabilities of observing values of continuous variables, e.g., height, are conveniently represented by mathematical curves known as *probability distributions*. Suppose we have a continuous random variable X that can

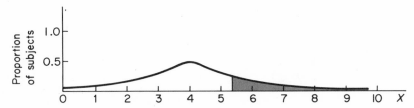

FIG. 10.8 The probability density function of the variable X, time required to solve a puzzle.

take on values from 0 to 10. For example, X could be the time required for subjects to solve a certain puzzle. They may solve it almost immediately, or they may take as long as 10 minutes but no longer. Presumably the length of time required to solve the problem is known for a huge number of different subjects. A graph is drawn in which the "time to solution" is graphed against "proportion of subjects requiring that time" (see Fig. 10.8).

The proportion of subjects requiring between 2 and 4 minutes to solve the puzzle can be regarded as *the probability that a subject selected at random from the population will require between 2 and 4 minutes to solve the puzzle.* The area under the curve in Fig. 10.8 is 1, so the area under the curve between any two points X_1 and X_2 is the probability that a randomly selected subject will require between X_1 and X_2 minutes to solve the puzzle. The probability that a randomly selected subject will take more than 5.3 minutes is equal to the shaded area in Fig. 10.8. What area corresponds to the probability that a randomly selected subject will take less than 0.5 minutes? (Theoretically, the probability of a subject's taking *exactly* 4 minutes, say, is zero because there is no area between 4 and itself.) If the area under the curve in Fig. 10.8 between 6 and 10 were .07, then in a group of 100 randomly chosen subjects we would expect about 7 of them to take between 6 and 10 minutes to solve the puzzle.

The statistician frequently plots the values a continuous random variable can assume in such a way that the area between any two values of the variable equals the probability that the variable will assume a value between those two values. The resulting graph is called a *probability density function.* The graph can often be expressed as a mathematical function in such a way that the ordinate $P(X)$ can be found by substituting any value of the random variable X. For example, assume X is a random variable that can take on any value between 0 and 2 *with equal probability.* If we let $P(X) = 1/2$ for all X, then the resulting graph (Fig. 10.9) will be the probability density function of X.

The area under the curve, e.g., of the rectangle in Fig. 10.9, is exactly 1 ($0.5 \cdot 2.0$). The shaded area is the probability that X takes on a value between 0 and 1. What does this probability equal?

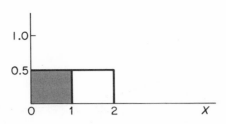

FIG. 10.9 Probability density function of the variable X that assumes all possible values between 0 and 2 with equal probability.

10.10
EXPECTATIONS AND MOMENTS

Moments are characteristics of distributions defined in terms of expectations. We shall consider the definition of the expectation of a random variable X first.

Definition: If X is a discrete random variable that takes on the values $X_1, X_2, \ldots, X_n$ with probabilities $p_1, p_2, \ldots, p_n$, then the expectation of X denoted by $E(X)$ is defined as

$$E(X) = p_1X_1 + p_2X_2 + \ldots + p_nX_n = \sum_{j=1}^{n} p_j X_j,$$

where $p_1 + p_2 + \ldots + p_n = 1$.

Note how similar this is to a formula for computing the mean from grouped data:

$$\bar{X} = \left(\frac{f_1}{N}\right) X_1 + \left(\frac{f_2}{N}\right) X_2 + \ldots + \left(\frac{f_n}{N}\right) X_n.$$

However, expectations are only for infinite populations, not for samples.

Another symbol denoting the expectation of X is μ, the Greek letter "mu." $\mu = E(X)$, the mean of the infinite population of X's.*

* The mathematically sophisticated reader may note that

$$\mu = E(X) = \lim_{N \to \infty} \left(\frac{\sum_{i=1}^{N} X_i}{N} \right),$$

i.e., the mean of the infinite number of X_i's. In this notation,

$$p_j = \lim_{N \to \infty} \left(\frac{f_j}{N} \right),$$

the proportion of all the scores that are X_j's. n, the number of different X's, may be finite, but N must be infinite in order to define the p_j's, or the p_j's may be theoretical values, such as $p_H = .5$ for one random flip of an unbiased coin.

The names "expectation" and "expected value" are synonymous. Some examples of expectations are as follows:

1. Suppose X is the random variable that has 6 possible values, $1, 2, \ldots, 6$. The events of the sample space could be the 6 sides of a die. *Assume* that a probability of $1/6$ is associated with each value of X. What is the value of $E(X)$?

$$E(X) = \tfrac{1}{6}1 + \tfrac{1}{6}2 + \tfrac{1}{6}3 + \tfrac{1}{6}4 + \tfrac{1}{6}5 + \tfrac{1}{6}6 = \tfrac{1}{6}(1 + 2 + \ldots + 6)$$
$$= \tfrac{21}{6} = 3.5,$$

halfway between the smallest value, 1, and the largest value, 6:

$$\frac{1 + 6}{2} = 3.5.$$

In this example, $E(X) = \mu = 21/6 = 3.5$. In repeatedly rolling the die, one can "expect" to average 3.5 points.

2. A particular slot-machine has payoffs of $0.00, $0.50, $1.00, and $2.00. The probabilities associated with each of these occurrences are .80, .15, .04, and .01, respectively. Define a random variable X that takes on the four values 0, 50, 100, and 200 cents with probabilities .80, .15, .04, and .01. What is the value of $E(X)$?

$$\mu = E(X) = .80(0) + .15(50) + .04(100) + .01(200)$$
$$= 0 + 7.5 + 4.0 + 2.0 = 13.5.$$

If it costs $0.25 for each trial on this slot-machine, would you like to play?

3. Let X be the random variable that corresponds to the number of "heads" in 4 flips of a fair coin. X can take on the values 0, 1, 2, 3, and 4. Find $E(X)$.

   First we must calculate the probabilities that X will take on each of the values from 0 to 4, i.e., the probabilities that there will be 0 "heads," $\ldots$, 4 "heads" in 4 flips of a fair coin.

$$\text{Probability } (X = 0) = \binom{4}{0}\left(\frac{1}{2}\right)^0\left(\frac{1}{2}\right)^4 = \frac{4!}{0!\,4!} \cdot 1 \cdot \frac{1}{16} = \frac{1}{16}.$$

$$\text{Probability } (X = 1) = \binom{4}{1}\left(\frac{1}{2}\right)^1\left(\frac{1}{2}\right)^3 = \frac{4!}{1!\,3!} \cdot \frac{1}{16} = \frac{4}{16} = \frac{1}{4}.$$

If you have forgotten how to compute the remaining three probabilities, refer back to the relevant sections of this chapter. Then show that $E(X) = \mu = 2$.

   Actually, one need not compute the mean of a binomial distribution this long way, because that mean is always merely np, where n is the number of trials and p is the probability per trial. Here, $np = 4(1/2) = 2$, which agrees with the result computed above via the $\sum_{j=1}^{4} p_j X_j$ formula.

How does this result differ from that for example 1, above? If we had wanted to know the average value that would be obtained in repeatedly flipping an unbiased coin, where $T = 0$, $H = 1$, and $p_T = p_H = 1/2$, we would have computed $1/2(0) + 1/2(1) = 1/2$, not the 2 found above for a different problem.

Analogously, if in example 1 we had wanted to know the number of, say, 5's to be expected in rolling an unbiased die 4 times, we would have been working with the binomial expansion $(1/6 + 5/6)^4$; $1/6$ is the probability of securing a 5 on any roll of the die. The number 5 can occur 0, 1, 2, 3, or 4 times in 4 rolls of the die. The answer would be

$$p_0(0) + p_1(1) + p_2(2) + p_3(3) + p_4(4) = \tfrac{1}{6}(4) = 2/3,$$

not the 3.5 found in example 1 for another problem.

If we rolled a die 4 times, and then 4 more times, etc., until we had rolled it 6 sets of 4 times each, we would expect a total of $(2/3)$ (6 sets of rolls) $= 4$ fives to appear. This is reasonable, for we would have rolled the die independently $4(6) = 24$ times, each time with a probability of $1/6$ of rolling the number five; $24(1/6) = 4$.

Obviously, one must state his probability problem carefully and then solve *it*, rather than a similar-sounding but different problem. This can be quite tricky, as even some eminent mathematicians have regretfully learned.

If X is a continuous variable instead of a discrete one, then an algebraic function describes the form of its probability distribution. As we saw earlier, if X is continuous we cannot assign a probability to a single value of X. Instead, we make statements about the probability that X lies in an interval. For these reasons, the definition given above for $E(X)$ cannot be applied to a continuous random variable. Unfortunately for those who have no knowledge of calculus, there seems to be no sensible way to define the expectation of a continuous variable without recourse to the calculus concept of integration. We shall attempt to sketch heuristically the idea of $E(X)$ when X is continuous so that those without a knowledge of calculus will not be at any disadvantage in our later discussions.

Suppose X is a continuous random variable and the probability distribution of X looks like the one in Fig. 10.10. There is an algebraic rule that gives the height of the curve in Fig. 10.10 for every value of X. The area under the curve is 1 unit. The probability that X will assume a value between, for example, 2 and 3 is equal to the area under the curve between those two points.

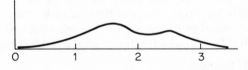

FIG. 10.10   Probability distribution of X.

Definition: The *expectation* of the continuous random variable
X is the sum of the products formed by multiplying
each value that X can assume by the height of the
probability function curve above that value of X.

Since X can take on infinitely many values, you might wonder how you
could physically multiply each of the separate values of X by the height of
the curve at X to find its expectation. This is the problem that recourse to
the integral calculus solves. We ask that you take it on faith that it can be
done, in a precise but somewhat indirect way, by "integration."

The expectation of a continuous random variable X is denoted by $E(X)$
or μ, as is the expectation of a discrete variable.

Moments

Moments are quantities that describe the distributions of variables.

Definition: The *first moment* of a random variable X is μ, the
expectation of X.

The first moment is also called the "population mean." μ, the first
moment of X, describes the general location of the distribution along a line.
For some distributions (for most met in practice), $E(X)$, or μ, is a good
indicator of the central point toward which the values of X tend. Suppose
X and Y are both normally distributed random variables, but $E(X) = \mu_x = 10$
and $E(Y) = \mu_y = 5$. Then we know that the distribution of X is generally
to the right, on the number line, of the distribution of Y, as in Fig. 10.11.

FIG. 10.11   Distributions of X and Y where $E(X) = 10$ and $E(Y) = 5$.

Definition: The *second moment* of a random variable X is
$E(X^2)$.

$$E(X^2) = p_1 X_1^2 + p_2 X_2^2 + \ldots + p_n X_n^2$$

if X is discrete.

We have little use for the second moment directly. The idea of a "second
moment" is used to define a very important concept, however.

Definition: The *variance*, or second moment about the mean, of a random variable X is $E(X - \mu)^2$.

If X is a discrete variable, then

$$E(X - \mu)^2 = p_1(X_1 - \mu)^2 + p_2(X_2 - \mu)^2 + \ldots + p_n(X_n - \mu)^2.$$

The quantity $E(X - \mu)^2$ is denoted by σ^2 (read "sigma squared"). σ, the positive square root of the variance, is called the *standard deviation*. σ^2 describes the dispersion, spread, heterogeneity, or scatter of a random variable X.

Suppose X and Y are two random normally distributed variables with the same mean, $\mu = 0$, but σ^2 for X is 1 and for Y, σ^2 is 4. The two distributions appear in Fig. 10.12. Notice that for the two distributions in Fig. 10.11 the variances are the same. The values of X and Y are equally heterogeneous.

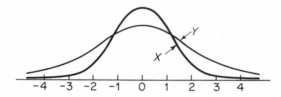

FIG. 10.12 Distributions of X and Y with $\mu = 0$ for both, but $\sigma^2 = 1$ for X and $\sigma^2 = 4$ for Y.

There are many more moments to any distribution, but we shall have use only for the first moment, μ, and the second moment about the mean, σ^2. We shall leave the discussion of expected values and moments at this point. If you wish to extend your knowledge of this topic or study another source, see Edwards (1964).

PROBLEMS AND EXERCISES

1. Let a pack of 52 playing cards be the sample space, S, of interest. Determine the probabilities of each of the following events:

a. A is the event that "a card is a spade." Find $P(A)$.

b. A is "a card is the ace of clubs." Find $P(A)$.

c. A is "a card is a diamond" and B is "a card is a spade." Find $P(A \cap B)$.

2. Suppose that in a certain locale, 3% of the children of kindergarten age have severe perceptual problems and that 6% of the children of the same age have emotional problems. Also, 1.5% of the same group of children are suffering from *both* perceptual and emotional problems. Children suffering from either problem or both must receive special teaching apart from normal pupils. What is the probability that a child entering kindergarten will require special teaching, i.e., will have either perceptual or emotional problems or both?

3. a. Find 4!.
   b. Find 15!/13!.
   c. Find $6!/[3! (6 - 3)!]$.
   d. For what value of n is $(n + 1)!$ exactly twenty times larger than $n!$?

4. An experimenter wishes to have subjects learn a list of paired associations in all possible orders of the pairs. There are 10 paired associates and 150 subjects; each subject can learn the list only once. Are there enough subjects so that at least one subject can learn every possible ordering of pairs?

5. a. Find $\binom{6}{3}$.

   b. Find $\binom{4}{0}$.

   c. Find $\binom{15}{15}$.

6. The varsity basketball team has 13 members. How many possible "starting fives"—the five players who start the game—could the coach form from his team of 13 players?

7. Verify that $\binom{4}{0} + \binom{4}{1} + \binom{4}{2} + \binom{4}{3} + \binom{4}{4}$ is equal to 2^4. $\left(\text{In general, }\right.$

$$\sum_{i=0}^{n} \binom{n}{i} = 2^n. \Bigg)$$

8. In how many ways may a ten-item test be split into two tests of five items each? (Hint: Find the number of ways to select five items from ten to comprise one half. Since *selecting* five items for one half is the same as *not selecting* them for the other half, divide the first quantity you calculated by 2.)

9. A pupil takes a 10-item true-false test in which half of the statements are true. If he guesses randomly between "true" and "false" on each item, what is the probability that he will earn a score X of 4 or more correct? (Hint: Find the probabilities of either 0, 1, 2, or 3 items correct and subtract the sum of these probabilities from 1.00.)

10. Graph the expected distribution of total test scores X that would be obtained by 256 completely ignorant examinees who will guess at random the answers to each of four four-option multiple-choice items. (Hint: Regard the test items as four binomial trials in which the probability of success is 1/4. Multiply each term of the binomial distribution with $n = 4$ and $p = 1/4$ by 256 to obtain the number of examinees that would be expected to obtain each test score from 0 to 4.) Stanley (1964, p. 197) shows the distribution of chance scores for 90 five-option items. Compare the skewness of your results with that of his Curve 2.

11. It can be proved that if n binomial trials result in n_1 successes, then the probability of this happening is maximal if p, the probability of success on any one trial, equals n_1/n. (When p is unknown and the outcome of n trials is n_1 successes, the ratio n_1/n is termed the "maximum likelihood estimate" of the unknown p because this value of p, namely n_1/n, makes the outcome more probable than does any other value of p.) Suppose 4 binomial trials yield 3 successes. Verify that this outcome has higher probability if $p = 3/4$ than if $p = 1/2$ or $4/5$.

12. Ten convicts volunteered for an experiment on the relationship between smoking and lung cancer. The convicts were matched into five matched pairs so that both pair mates are of the same age. Within each pair of convicts a coin was flipped to determine which convict would smoke two packs of cigarettes a day and which one would not smoke for the duration of the experiment. At the end of the 30-year experimental period the five smokers in each pair had lung cancer; none of the nonsmokers had lung cancer. (This experiment is pure fiction.) Suppose that at the outset of the experiment, five convicts either had lung cancer or were destined to develop it in the next 30 years whether they smoked or not. What is the probability that if smoking is truly unrelated to lung cancer, the five initially cancerous convicts were totally by chance assigned to be the five experimental smokers?

13. In the general population, Stanford-Binet IQ's are nearly normally distributed with a mean of 100 and a standard deviation of 16. By referring to Table B in Appendix A, determine the following probabilities to two decimal places:

    a. That a randomly sampled person will have an IQ between 80 and 120.
    b. That a randomly sampled person will have an IQ above 140.
    c. That three independently randomly sampled persons will all have IQ's above 92.

14. The variable X takes on the values 0, 1, 2, 3, and 4 with probabilities 0, 2/5, 1/5, 1/5, and 1/5, respectively. What is the value of $E(X)$, the expected value of X?

15. The variable X is binomially distributed with $n = 4$ and $p = 1/2$, i.e., X takes on the following values with the following probabilities:

X	Probability (X)
0	$\frac{1}{16}$
1	$\frac{4}{16}$
2	$\frac{6}{16}$
3	$\frac{4}{16}$
4	$\frac{1}{16}$

    a. Determine the value of $E(X)$. Compare this value with $np = 4(1/2) = 2$.
    b. Determine the variance of X, which is

$$\sigma_x^2 = \sum_{i=0}^{4} [X_i - E(X)]^2 \text{ probability } (X_i).$$

Compare this value with $npq = 4(1/2)(1/2) = 1$.

16. Trials of an event that can happen in one of *three* ways are called *trinomial*. If the event A can occur in three possible ways (a_1, a_2, a_3) with probabilities $p_1, p_2,$ and p_3 $(p_1 + p_2 + p_3 = 1)$, respectively, then it can be shown that the probability that n trials of A will produce r occurrences of a_1, s occurrences of a_2, and t occurrences of a_3 is given by the general formula for the *trinomial distribution*:

$$P(r, s, t) = \frac{n!}{r!\, s!\, t!} p_1^r p_2^s p_3^t.$$

a. Show that if $p_3 = 0$ the formula for the trinomial distribution reduces to the formula for the binomial distribution. (Hint: If p_3 is zero, t can never be anything except zero and s must equal $n - r$.)

b. The First Methodist Church is planning a Sunday evening pot-luck supper. Each of 20 families is asked to bring either a salad or a "hot dish" or a dessert. Assume that the families make their choice of a contribution to the supper independently and with the following probabilities: for salad, $p_1 = .10$; for "hot dish," $p_2 = .60$; for dessert, $p_3 = .30$. Calculate the probability that—to the chagrin of the parents and to the delight of the children—each of the 20 families brings a dessert to the pot-luck supper.

11

THEORETICAL DISTRIBUTIONS FOR USE IN STATISTICAL INFERENCE

11.1
INTRODUCTION

Part of the "working tools" of inferential statistical methods are a group of theoretical distributions of some special variables. In this section we shall study four such distributions: the normal, which was the subject of Chapter 6; the chi-square distribution; the t-distribution; and the F-distribution.

11.2
NORMAL DISTRIBUTION

In Chapter 6 we learned that a normal distribution is a particular type of mathematical curve. The graph of a normal distribution is symmetric about its mean, μ; it is unimodal; it has a kurtosis of 3.0, etc.

The normal distribution—in fact there are many, one for every different set of values of μ and σ—is very important in statistical inference. Many inferential statistical techniques rest on the assumption that the frequency distribution of scores on a variable in a population is adequately described as a normal distribution with a certain mean and standard deviation. It will be seen in this section that the other theoretical distributions build upon the normal distribution.

This primacy of the normal distribution probably can be attributed to three facts, one empirical, the other two mathematical. First, the normal distribution happens to be a fairly accurate representation of the frequency distributions of scores on a large number of different variables. In Sec. 6.6 we saw that the normal distribution was a good representation of the frequency polygon of heights of 8585 adult men born in Great Britain during the 19th century and of the distribution of scores on the Stanford-Binet Intelligence Test.

Second, it is a mathematical fact that averaging individual scores that are *not* normally distributed results, in many instances, in an average that *is* nearly normally distributed. This fact—stated and proved as the "Central Limit Theorem" of mathematical statistics—finds important applications in modern inferential statistical techniques, although it does not play the crucial role it once did. (See Sec. 12.3.)

Third, the normal distribution is mathematically convenient. A most convenient feature of the normal distribution is that when samples are drawn from a normal distribution and μ and σ are estimated in a certain way, the two estimates produced for repeated samples are independent.

11.3
CHI-SQUARE DISTRIBUTIONS

Imagine a huge population of scores that are essentially normally distributed with mean 0 and standard deviation 1. Suppose that a single score X_1 is selected at random from this population and the standard score $z = (X_1 - 0)/1$ is formed. Over repeated selections of an X score, z will have a normal distribution with mean 0 and standard deviation 1. Denote the *square* of z as follows:

$$\chi_1^2 = z^2, \tag{11.1}$$

i.e., the square of a standardized score selected from a normal distribution is symbolized by χ_1^2, where the superscript 2 tells us that squaring has taken place and the subscript 1 tells us that only one score has been "combined" to produce χ^2. We can conceive of repeating an unlimited number of times the process by which a value of χ_1^2 was found. Each time a new X score is randomly selected, standardized, and squared. We can build a frequency polygon of the values of χ_1^2 so obtained. If this frequency polygon is smoothed off after many thousand values of χ_1^2 have been recorded and if the scale of the ordinate is adjusted so that the area under the resulting curve is 1, the graph of the *chi-square distribution with one degree of freedom* would be obtained. A graph of this distribution appears in Fig. 11.1.

The mathematical curve that is graphed in Fig. 11.1 and that describes the distribution of χ_1^2 has a complex formula we will not study. (If interested in this formula, see Graybill, 1961, p. 31.) We denote the mathematical

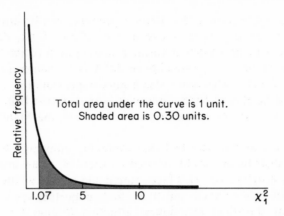

FIG. 11.1 Graph of the chi-square distribution with one degree of freedom. (The shaded area comprises 30% of the area under the curve.)

curve in Fig. 11.1 by χ_1^2. The curve takes its name from the Greek letter χ used to denote it. (The mathematical curve for the chi-square distribution was derived by Karl Pearson in 1900.)

The area under the curve for χ_1^2 is set equal to one unit so that χ_1^2 is a probability distribution, e.g., the probability of obtaining a value of χ_1^2 between 0.5 and 2.5 equals the area under the curve between 0.5 and 2.5. In Fig. 11.1 we see that .30 or 30% of the area under the curve lies to the right of 1.07. Thus, we know that the probability of obtaining a value of $z^2 = \chi_1^2$ that exceeds 1.07 is .30. In other words, 30% of the z scores randomly selected from a normal distribution will have squares that exceed 1.07. An equivalent statement of this fact is that the 70th percentile in the chi-square

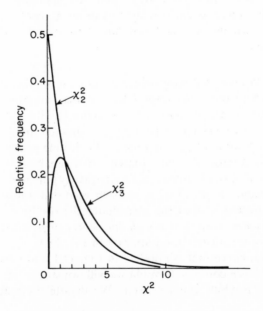

FIG. 11.2 Graphs of χ_2^2 and χ_3^2, the chi-square distributions with two degrees and three degrees of freedom.

distribution with one degree of freedom equals 1.07. We also write this as:

$$._{70}\chi_1^2 = 1.07,$$

where χ_1^2 denotes the chi-square distribution with one degree of freedom and .70 indicates the 70th percentile of that distribution.

Now we shall develop the chi-square distribution with two degrees of freedom, χ_2^2. Suppose we go back to the original normal distribution of X. Instead of drawing out just one X score, draw two X scores at random and independently. Standardize each of these scores by subtracting μ from it and dividing the difference by σ. Call the first (by order of selection, not by size) standardized score z_1 and the second z_2. Now square and sum the two z's to form the quantity

$$\chi_2^2 = \left(\frac{X_1 - \mu}{\sigma}\right)^2 + \left(\frac{X_2 - \mu}{\sigma}\right)^2 = z_1^2 + z_2^2. \tag{11.2}$$

This process of determining a χ_2^2 could be repeated thousands of times with new pairs of z scores. A frequency polygon of these χ_2^2 scores could be constructed, smoothed, and reduced so that the area under the curve was one unit. The resulting curve would look like the graph of the mathematical curve χ_2^2, the chi-square distribution with two degrees of freedom. Fig. 11.2 shows a graph of χ_2^2.

The Chi-Square Distribution with
n Degrees of Freedom, χ_n^2

A chi-square variable with n degrees of freedom, χ_n^2, is formed by adding together the squares of n independent z scores from a normal distribution:

$$\chi_n^2 = z_1^2 + z_2^2 + \ldots + z_n^2. \tag{11.3}$$

If a large number of these χ_n^2 values are generated from separate sets of n z scores, their frequency polygon will have the same shape as the mathematical curve χ_n^2. Figure 11.3 illustrates the graphs of χ_6^2 and χ_{10}^2.

The area under each curve in Fig. 11.3 is one unit. One-half the area under χ_{10}^2 lies above the point 9.34. Hence, we know that the probability is .50 that the sum of the squares of ten z scores drawn at random from a normal distribution will exceed 9.34. Equivalently $._{50}\chi_{10}^2 = 9.34$, the median of the chi-square distribution with ten degrees of freedom.

There is a different chi-square distribution for each integer value of n $(1, 2, 3, \ldots)$. The properties of the curve χ_n^2 depend upon the value of n. The following facts provide a partial description of the family of chi-square distributions:

1. The mean of a chi-square distribution with n degrees of freedom is equal to n. For example, the average value of χ_{12}^2 one would

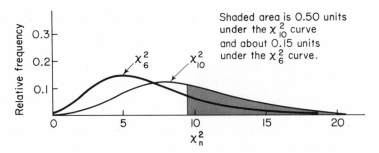

FIG. 11.3   Graphs of χ^2_6 and χ^2_{10}.

expect to obtain by squaring and summing 12 independent, standardized normal scores is 12.

2. The mode of χ^2_n is at the point $n - 2$ for $n = 2$ or greater.

3. The standard deviation of χ^2_n is $\sqrt{2n}$.

4. The skewness of χ^2_n is $\sqrt{8/n}$.   Hence, every chi-square distribution is positively skewed, but the asymmetry becomes very slight for large n.

5. As n becomes large, χ^2_n approaches more nearly a normal distribution with mean n and standard deviation $\sqrt{2n}$.

An important theorem concerning combinations of chi-square variables can be stated as follows:

If $\chi^2_{n_1}$ has a chi-square distribution with n_1 degrees of freedom and if $\chi^2_{n_2}$ has a chi-square distribution with n_2 degrees of freedom and is independent of $\chi^2_{n_1}$, then $\chi^2_{n_1} + \chi^2_{n_2}$ has a chi-square distribution with $n_1 + n_2$ degrees of freedom.

The pth percentile in the chi-square distribution with n degrees of freedom is denoted by $_p\chi^2_n$.   The percentiles of the chi-square distribution play a prominent role in inferential statistical techniques, particularly as applied to nominal data.   Various percentiles in chi-square distributions for $n = 1$ up to $n = 30$ appear in Table C of Appendix A to this text.   The following is an example of how Table C is read: Suppose one wishes to find the 50th percentile in the chi-square distribution with four degrees of freedom, i.e., $_{.50}\chi^2_4$.   First, the *row* labeled 4 in Table C is located.   Second, the *column* headed "50th percentile" is found; it is near the center of the table.   At the intersection of the appropriate row and column, the number 3.357 is found. This is the value of $_{.50}\chi^2_4$, the median of the chi-square distribution with four degrees of freedom.

11.4
F-DISTRIBUTIONS

Imagine that a chi-square variate with five degrees of freedom χ_5^2 is formed from $z_1^2 + \ldots + z_5^2$. Now suppose a second, *independent* chi-square variate with 10 degrees of freedom χ_{10}^2 is formed by sampling values from a unit normal distribution, squaring, and summing the 10 squared terms. A variate called an *F-ratio* with 5 and 10 degrees of freedom is formed as follows:

$$F_{5,10} = \frac{\chi_5^2/5}{\chi_{10}^2/10} . \tag{11.4}$$

By repeatedly determining values of χ_5^2 and χ_{10}^2, dividing each by its respective degrees of freedom, and forming the ratio $F_{5,10}$, the distribution of $F_{5,10}$ could be determined. It is known from mathematical statistics that the distribution of $F_{5,10}$ is an *F-distribution* with 5 degrees of freedom for the numerator and 10 degrees of freedom for the denominator. The *F*-distribution with 5 and 10 degrees of freedom is a positively skewed distribution with mean $(10)/(10 - 2) = 1.25$ and a median less than 1. Because of the squaring, only nonnegative values of $F_{5,10}$ may occur; hence the $F_{5,10}$ distribution has all of its area to the right of zero. The area under the $F_{5,10}$ distribution between any two values of $F_{5,10}$ is equal to the probability of obtaining an *F*-ratio between these two values. Later in this text selected percentile points in *F*-distributions will be useful. Certain percentile points in the *F*-distributions were tabulated long ago for easy reference. We know, for example, that the 90th percentile in the *F*-distribution with 5 and 10 degrees of freedom, $_{.90}F_{5,10}$, is equal to 2.52. That is, the probability is .90 of obtaining a value of $F_{5,10}$ between 0 and 2.52. $_{.95}F_{5,10}$ equals 3.33, and $_{.99}F_{5,10}$ equals 5.64.

There exists a different *F*-distribution to describe the distribution of each *F*-ratio with a unique combination of degrees of freedom for the chi-square variates in the numerator and denominator. In general, if two *independent* chi-square variates, one with n_1 degrees of freedom $\chi_{n_1}^2$, and the other with n_2 degrees of freedom $\chi_{n_2}^2$, are combined as

$$F_{n_1, n_2} = \frac{\chi_{n_1}^2/n_1}{\chi_{n_2}^2/n_2} , \tag{11.5}$$

then F_{n_1, n_2} has an *F*-distribution with n_1 and n_2 degrees of freedom. Such an *F*-distribution with n_1 degrees of freedom for the numerator and n_2 degrees of freedom for the denominator has the following properties:

1. It is positively skewed.
2. It is unimodal.

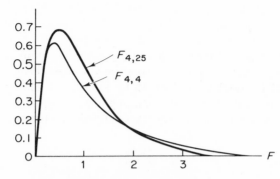

FIG. 11.4 Graphs of the distributions $F_{4,25}$ and $F_{4,4}$.

3. It has a median of 1 or less.
4. It has a mean equal to $n_2/(n_2 - 2)$ for $n_2 \geqslant 3$.

The F-distributions with 4 and 4 degrees of freedom and 4 and 25 degrees of freedom appear in Fig. 11.4.

Percentiles above the 50th in the distribution F_{n_1,n_2} are related to those percentiles below 50 in the following manner:

$$_{1-p}F_{n_1,n_2} = \frac{1}{_{p}F_{n_2,n_1}}.$$ (11.6)

For example, the fifth percentile in the distribution $F_{10,5}$ equals

$$\frac{1}{_{.95}F_{5,10}} = \frac{1}{3.33} = 0.30.$$

Table E of Appendix A is a tabulation of the upper percentile points in the F-distributions for numerous values of n_1 and n_2. The columns of Table E correspond to values of n_1; the rows of Table E correspond to values of n_2. Check the table to see if you can verify that the 99th percentile in $F_{10,20}$ is 3.37, i.e., $_{.99}F_{10,20} = 3.37$.

11.5
t-DISTRIBUTIONS

Imagine that a unit normal distribution and a chi-square distribution with 10 degrees of freedom are at hand. One observation is randomly sampled from each distribution: z and χ_{10}^2. Next, the following ratio is formed:

$$t_{10} = \frac{z}{\sqrt{\chi_{10}^2/10}}.$$ (11.7)

The quantity t_{10} in Eq. (11.7) is an observation from the t-distribution with 10 degrees of freedom. In other words, if the process of randomly drawing one observation each from the unit normal distribution and from χ_{10}^2 and forming $t_{10} = z/\sqrt{\chi_{10}^2/10}$ was repeated an infinite number of times, the values of t_{10} would form a t-distribution with ten degrees of freedom.

The t-distribution with 10 degrees of freedom is described by a symmetric, unimodal curve. The mean of the distribution is 0; the standard deviation is slightly greater than 1, approaching 1 as the degrees of freedom increase. The distribution is somewhat leptokurtic, i.e., it has kurtosis greater than 3; hence, it is more peaked and has more area in the extreme "tails" of the distribution than the normal distribution.

There is not just one t-distribution; as was true of the χ^2 and F-distributions, there exists a family of t-distributions. There is a different t-distribution for every distinct number of degrees of freedom for the chi-square variable in the denominator of Eq. (11.7). If the denominator of Eq. (11.7) involves a chi-square variable with 5 degrees of freedom, then

$$t_5 = \frac{z}{\sqrt{\chi_5^2/5}}$$

has a t-distribution with 5 degrees of freedom. In general, if z has a unit normal distribution and χ_n^2 is a chi-square variable with n degrees of freedom and is independent of z, then

$$t_n = \frac{z}{\sqrt{\chi_n^2/n}} \tag{11.8}$$

has a t-distribution with n degrees of freedom.

All of the t-distributions are described by symmetric, unimodal curves with a mean of 0. The variance of the t-distribution with n degrees of freedom is $n/(n-2)$. They are all slightly leptokurtic. As n becomes larger and larger, the distribution t_n begins to look more and more like a normal distribution. When n is infinitely large—a theoretical possibility that is empirically impossible—the t-distribution is the same as the normal distribution. The t-distributions with degrees of freedom 1, 5, and 25 appear along with the normal distribution in Fig. 11.5.

In subsequent discussions of statistical inference, selected percentile points in a t-distribution will have to be found. The pth percentile in the t-distribution with 10 degrees of freedom will be denoted by $_p t_{10}$. The most often used percentiles in the t-distributions appear in Table D in Appendix A. There we read, for example, that the 95th percentile in the t-distribution with 10 degrees of freedom, i.e., $_{.95}t_{10}$, is equal to 1.812.

Only the upper-percentile points in the t-distributions appear in Table D. Because of a simple relationship it is unnecessary to tabulate both upper- and lower-percentile points. The symmetry of all t-distributions implies that

$$_{1-p}t_n = -_p t_n, \tag{11.9}$$

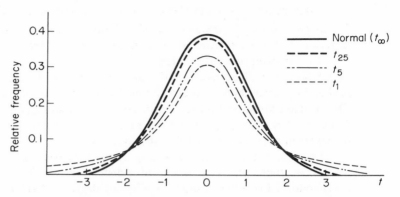

FIG. 11.5   The t-distributions with 1, 5, and 25 degrees of freedom and the unit-normal distribution.

i.e., the negative of the pth percentile in the t-distribution with n degrees of freedom equals the $(1 - p)$th percentile in the same distribution.   For example,

$$_{.95}t_{10} = 1.812, \quad \text{therefore} \quad _{.05}t_{10} = -1.812,$$

$$_{.99}t_{20} = 2.528, \quad \text{therefore} \quad _{.01}t_{20} = -2.528,$$

$$_{.90}t_{5} = 1.476, \quad \text{therefore} \quad _{.10}t_{5} = -1.476.$$

11.6
RELATIONSHIPS AMONG THE NORMAL, t-, CHI-SQUARE, AND F-DISTRIBUTIONS

The t-, χ^2, and F-distributions are all based on the normal distribution. In each instance, sampling from a normal distribution underlies the new distribution.   For example, a chi-square variable is formed by summing squared, unit normal variables; in turn, chi-square variables are combined to form F-variables.   In this section, the relationships among the various families of distributions will be made explicit.

We have already seen that a t-distribution with infinite degrees of freedom is the same as the normal distribution.   Suppose we look at the *square* of the t-variable with n degrees of freedom:

$$t_n^2 = \frac{z^2}{\chi_n^2/n}. \tag{11.10}$$

In the numerator of Eq. (11.10) we find the square of a unit normal variable *divided by* 1; in the denominator is an independent chi-square variable

Degrees of freedom, n_1, for numerator

		1	2	$\bullet\ \bullet\ \bullet$	n_1	$\bullet\ \bullet\ \bullet$	∞
	1	t_1^2	$F_{2,1}$	$\bullet\ \bullet\ \bullet$	$F_{n_1,1}$	$\bullet\ \bullet\ \bullet$	$F_{\infty,1}$
	2	t_2^2	$F_{2,2}$	$\bullet\ \bullet\ \bullet$	$F_{n_1,2}$	$\bullet\ \bullet\ \bullet$	$F_{\infty,2}$
	$\vdots$	$\vdots$	$\vdots$		$\vdots$		$\vdots$
	n_2	$t_{n_2}^2$	F_{2,n_2}	$\bullet\ \bullet\ \bullet$	F_{n_1,n_2}	$\bullet\ \bullet\ \bullet$	F_{∞,n_2}
	$\vdots$	$\vdots$	$\vdots$		$\vdots$		$\vdots$
	∞	t_∞^2 $\dfrac{\chi_1^2}{z^2}$	$\dfrac{\chi_2^2}{2}$	$\bullet\ \bullet\ \bullet$	$\dfrac{\chi_{n_1}^2}{n_1}$	$\bullet\ \bullet\ \bullet$	$\dfrac{\chi_\infty^2}{\infty}=1$

Degrees of freedom, n_2, for denominator

FIG. 11.6　The family of *F*-distributions and their relationship to the normal, *t*-, and χ^2 distributions.

divided by its degrees of freedom. Stated in slightly different form,

$$t_n^2 = \frac{\chi_1^2/1}{\chi_n^2/n}. \tag{11.11}$$

We recognize, however, that Eq. (11.11) is an *F*-variable with 1 and *n* degrees of freedom. *Therefore, the square of a t-variable with n degrees of freedom is an F-variable with 1 and n degrees of freedom.*

It is somewhat more difficult to prove another interesting fact, which we shall simply state: *Any F-distribution with n degrees of freedom for the numerator and infinite degrees of freedom for the denominator is the same as the χ_n^2 distribution divided by the constant n:* i.e.,

$$F_{n,\infty} = \frac{\chi_n^2}{n}. \ *$$

All of these facts are depicted in Fig. 11.6. Figure 11.6 is a cross-classification of the family of *F*-distributions with respect to the degrees of

* The proof depends on the fact that $\lim\limits_{n_2 \to \infty} \dfrac{\chi_{n_2}^2}{n_2} = 1$.

freedom (1 through ∞) of numerator and denominator. Each cell in Fig. 11.6 corresponds to an F-distribution. When a cell happens to coincide with a special case of either the normal, t-, or χ^2 distributions, the symbol for the F-distribution does not appear; this should not be taken to mean that no such F-distribution exists for that cell, however, for an F-distribution could be shown in every cell.

The pth percentile in the χ_n^2 distribution is the same as the pth percentile in the $n(F_{n,\infty})$ distribution. However, if you square the pth percentile in the t-distribution with n degrees of freedom, you obtain the $2p - 1$ percentile in the distribution $F_{1,n}$. For example, the 95th percentile of the t_n-distribution is the $2(.95) - 1 = .90 = 90$th percentile of the $t_n^2 = F_{1,n}$-distribution. (This is true because 5% of the cases exceed the 95th percentile in t_n and 5% lie below the 5th percentile. When the t values are squared both the top 5% and the bottom 5% take on a positive sign; hence, 10% of the values in $F_{1,n}$ exceed the square of $_{.95}t_n$.)

PROBLEMS AND EXERCISES

1. Complete the following table by finding the value of the designated percentile in the tables in Appendix A:

Distribution	Degrees of freedom	Percentile	Value of the percentile
a. Normal		54th	
b. t	20	97.5th	
c. Normal		90th	
d. t	120	90th	
e. Chi-square	6	1st	
f. F	4 and 60	99th	
g. Chi-square	15	99.9th	

2. Compare the 95th percentile in the F-distribution with 8 and infinite degrees of freedom with the 95th percentile of the chi-square distribution with 8 degrees of freedom divided by 8.

3. What is the probability that a randomly selected observation from a chi-square distribution with 21 degrees of freedom will exceed 36.34? (Refer immediately to Table C in Appendix A.)

4. Recall that the pth percentile in the F-distribution with n_1 and n_2 degrees of freedom is equal to the reciprocal of the $(100 - p)$th percentile in the F-distribution with n_2 and n_1 degrees of freedom. Find the 5th percentile in the F-distribution with 4 and 8 degrees of freedom.

5. The mean of the F-distribution with n_1 and n_2 degrees of freedom equals $n_2/(n_2 - 2)$. When $n_1 = n_2$, the median of the F-distribution is 1. In which

direction is the *F*-distribution with 12 and 12 degrees of freedom skewed? (Report your reasoning.)

6. The mean of the chi-square distribution with n degrees of freedom is n. The one and only mode is at $n - 2$ for n greater than 2. We know that the chi-square distribution is positively skewed. Is the median of the chi-square distribution with n degrees of freedom *above*, *below*, or *equal to n*?

7. For reasonably large n, the chi-square distribution with n degrees of freedom is nearly a normal distribution. The mean and standard deviation are n and $\sqrt{2n}$, respectively, regardless of the size of n. For $n = 20$, find the 95th percentile in the chi-square distribution from Table C in Appendix A and compare it with the 95th percentile in a normal distribution with mean $n = 20$ and standard deviation $\sqrt{2n} = \sqrt{40}$.

8. Prove that the variance of the *t*-distribution with n degrees of freedom is $n/(n - 2)$. (Hint: t_n^2 is the same as the *F*-distribution with 1 and n degrees of freedom. Since $E(t_n) = 0$, and $\sigma_t^2 = E[t - E(t)]^2$, the variance of t_n is $E(t_n^2)$.)

12

STATISTICAL
INFERENCE:
ESTIMATION

12.1
POPULATIONS AND SAMPLES;
PARAMETERS AND STATISTICS

The *inferential statistical problem* present in most scientific and much technological research is one of gaining knowledge about a large class of objects, persons, or events from a relatively small class of the same sorts of elements. In short, inferential statistical reasoning is reasoning from the particular to the general, from the seen to the unseen. (Inference is the counterpart of deduction, which is reasoning from the general to the particular as, for example, in syllogistic reasoning.) Inferential statistical reasoning would help answer such a question as "What do I know about the average reading speed of ten-year-olds (the large class) after having seen that these 100 ten-year-olds (the small class) average 84.8 words per minute?" Any large (finitely or infinitely) collection or aggregation of things that we wish to study or about which we wish to make inferences is called a *population*. This definition is so all-inclusive as to be practically worthless. The term *population* takes on genuine meaning when coupled with the definition of a *sample* from a population.   A *sample* is a part, or subset, of a population. The sample is generally selected in a deliberate fashion from the population in order that the properties of the population can be studied.   Theoretically, populations can be either *infinitely large* or *finite* in size.   The truly infinite populations that come easily to mind are somewhat artificial or conceptual: the collection of all positive numbers, the collection of all possible lengths of a stick, the collection of tosses of two dice which could be made throughout eternity.   Almost any interesting population of physical items—as opposed to conceptual possibilities—is finite in size: all persons in the Western Hemisphere, the refrigerators produced in Canada in the last decade, the school districts in the United States of America.   A finite population may be extremely large, e.g., the proverbial "grains of sand on earth" or 150!, but if it is conceivable that the process of counting the elements of the population could be completed, then the population is finite.   At times, but not often, in inferential statistics it is important to distinguish between finite and infinite populations.   However, for the purposes of statistical inference it is generally not necessary to worry about the distinction between finite and infinite populations whenever the size of the population is more than 100 times greater than the sample taken from the population.   If the ratio of population size to sample size is larger than 100, the techniques appropriate to making inferences to finite populations and those appropriate for infinite populations give essentially the same results.   It is customary to use statistical techniques based on the assumption that infinite populations are being sampled whenever the population is reasonably large (containing several hundred or more elements) and the sample from the population does not constitute an appreciable proportion of the population.   It is common to speak of a population as being "virtually infinite" when one means to say that it is huge but finite and that statistical techniques that assume infinite populations will be used on it.   We shall not discuss inferential statistical techniques that have been developed for "finite populations," i.e., for small populations or when a sample being studied is more than 1/100, say, of the population. An excellent treatment of these "finite techniques" can be found in William G. Cochran's *Sampling Techniques* (1963).

Measurements taken on populations of things can be described in the ways we have discussed in the preceding chapters.   We can compute means, medians, variances, and percentiles on the data gathered from a population; we might calculate the correlation between height and weight for the population of high-school sophomores in the United States of America.   The values of various descriptive measures computed for *populations* are called *parameters*.   For samples, these same descriptive measures are called *statistics*.   The *parameter* describes a *population* in the way a *statistic* describes a *sample*.   It is customary to denote statistics by Roman letters and parameters by Greek letters.   The symbol $\bar{X}$ stands for the sample mean, and the Greek letter μ stands for the population mean.   The sample variance is denoted by s^2; the population variance by σ^2.

A statistic computed on a sample can be regarded as estimating a parameter in the population. An *estimator* is some function of the scores in a sample that produces a value, called the *estimate*; an estimate gives us some information about a parameter. For example, the sample mean $\bar{X}$ is an estimator of the mean or average score in the population. A random sample of 100 eight-year-olds might yield 104.65 for a sample mean on the California Test of Mental Maturity; this value, 104.65, would be an *estimate* of the mean test score in the population from which the pupils were sampled.

12.2
RANDOM SAMPLING

Samples, and estimates calculated from them, give us some idea about the characteristics of the population sampled. There are many different ways in which samples can be chosen from a population. Simple random sampling, which was discussed at length in Sec. 10.6, is just one of many ways, though it happens to be the most widely used. Other sorts of sampling plans can become quite elaborate and lead to complex methods of estimation. We shall restrict our attention in this text to simple random sampling. It is so common to speak of only simple random samples in elementary statistics that we will occasionally use only the word "sample" when we mean a "simple random sample." More sophisticated sampling plans, such as stratified sampling, cluster sampling, and two-stage sampling, are dealt with in more advanced statistical textbooks (Cochran, 1963).

Before a sample will serve well as a basis for making estimates of population parameters, it must be representative of the population. However, this criterion of representativeness presents a problem. How would one know whether a sample is representative of a population unless the characteristics of the population are known? And if the characteristics of the population are known, why does one need a sample with which to estimate them? This quandary is a genuine one. It is resolved when one realizes that random sampling of a population will produce samples which *in the long run* are representative of the population. It will happen that some random samples from a population will not be very representative of it. A random sampling of 20 from the population of all high-school teachers in California might yield—though it is unlikely—20 female French teachers. Some random samples will not be very representative of the population; others will be. One never knows whether the sample one has chosen is representative. If it is a random sample, the most that can be said is that it is *randomly representative* of the population in all respects.

An important feature of a random sample is that one can determine what sorts of nonrepresentativeness are to be expected in the long run or in a large group of random samples. This is not possible or feasible with many other types of sampling plan. For example, if one were to choose the first 50 men to walk down the street whose names began with the letter "T," one would not have a random sample of the population of adult Americans. Furthermore, this sample of 50 is nonrepresentative of the population, *and* it is nonrepresentative in unknown ways and to unknown extents. However, if 50 persons were randomly sampled from the population of adult Americans it would be mathematically possible to answer such questions as "How likely is it that a randomly drawn sample of 50 adult Americans will have a mean height that is more than one inch above the mean height of all adult Americans?"

The process of inferential statistical reasoning involves finding an estimate of a parameter from a sample and then determining how representative such a sample can be expected to be for the purpose of estimating the parameter. It is not surprising, then, that inferential statistics is based on assumptions of random sampling from populations.

12.3
THE CONCEPT OF A
SAMPLING DISTRIBUTION

The statistician assesses the representativeness to be expected from random samples by studying *sampling distributions*. The concept of a sampling distribution is basic to one entire branch of inferential statistics. A statistic or estimator calculated on a sample is said to possess a certain sampling distribution. You can imagine the process of choosing sample after sample of size n from a certain population and recording for each sample the value of some estimator, e.g., the sample mean $\bar{X}$. If this process of drawing a sample from the population were repeated thousands of times, it would be possible to construct a frequency distribution of the thousands of sample means that were obtained. The frequency distribution so constructed would look like the sampling distribution of the mean of samples of size n for the population being sampled. If a frequency polygon were drawn for the data to a scale so that the area under the curve was one unit, the curve would be almost identical to the sampling distribution of the sample mean.

Suppose, for example, that a certain population has several thousand elements and that measurement of any one element will yield a score of $0, 1, 2, \ldots, 9$ with equal probability. Hence, the random variable X takes on any one of the values $0, 1, 2, \ldots, 9$ with probability .10. A probability distribution for the population has the form shown in Fig. 12.1.

One hundred random samples of size $n = 2$ were drawn from the above population. For each sample, the mean was calculated. The first sample contained the digits $(3, 2)$, which yield a mean of $(3 + 2)/2 = 2.5$. Ninety-nine other sample means were calculated, and all 100 means were graphed.

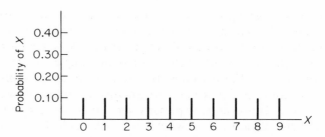

FIG. 12.1   Probability distribution for a population.

The frequency polygon of the 100 sample means appears in Fig. 12.2.

Figure 12.2 gives us some idea of what the actual sampling distribution of $\bar{X}$ looks like for samples of size 2 from the population in Fig. 12.1. The graph in Fig. 12.2 is an empirical approximation to the sampling distribution of $\bar{X}$ in this situation.

Generally, the statistician does not have to rely on empirical procedures (such as were reported in Fig. 12.2) to determine the sampling distribution of a statistic. Advanced mathematical techniques can be used to answer such questions as "What is the distribution of the mean of samples of size n from a normal distribution?" or "What is the distribution of the product moment coefficient of correlation of X and Y in samples of size n from a population in which the correlation of X and Y is zero?" Because of the difficult mathematics underlying the derivations of most of the sampling distributions we shall use, we shall simply report the results without proof.

One of the principal theorems of inferential statistics concerns the sampling distribution of the sample mean $\bar{X}$. This theorem is called the

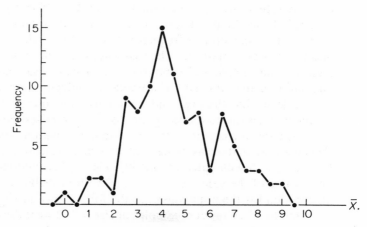

FIG. 12.2   Frequency distribution of 100 means of 100 samples ($n = 2$) from the population in Fig. 12.1.

central limit theorem. Suppose that samples are being drawn from an infinitely large population. The mean of this population is denoted by μ and the variance by σ^2. Random samples of size n will be drawn from the population. What will the sampling distribution of the sample mean $\bar{X}$ look like? If n is "sufficiently large" (and it is not possible to be more specific about the size of n), the sample mean will be very nearly *normally distributed.* Furthermore, the mean of all of the sample means will equal μ, the population mean; and the variance of the sample means will equal σ^2/n, where σ^2 is the population variance.

The following example will be used to illustrate the central limit theorem. Suppose that the population in Fig. 12.3 has a mean μ equal to 15 and a variance σ^2 equal to 100. Random samples of size 100 will be drawn from the population in Fig. 12.3. The central limit theorem tells us that the distribution of the means $\bar{X}$ of these samples will be nearly normal with a mean of 15 and a variance of $\sigma_x^2/n = 100/100 = 1$. The sampling distribution of $\bar{X}$ in this instance is depicted in Fig. 12.4.

It may seem incredible to you at first that, regardless of the shape of the population being sampled, the means of "sufficiently large" samples will have a normal distribution. Such is the case, however. This is one of three reasons why the normal distribution is so important in statistics. Just how large n must be before the sampling distribution of $\bar{X}$ is nearly normal depends on the shape of the population. Samples of size 100 are probably large enough to yield nearly normal sampling distribtuions of $\bar{X}$ for most populations one might meet in practice.

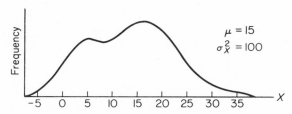

FIG. 12.3   Distribution of X for a population.

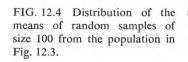

FIG. 12.4 Distribution of the means of random samples of size 100 from the population in Fig. 12.3.

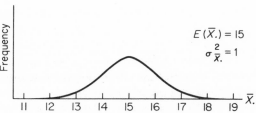

A proof of the fact that the sampling distribution of $\bar{X}$ has a mean of μ and variance of σ^2/n, where μ and σ^2 are the mean and variance of the population sampled and n is the sample size, is not too difficult to develop. X is the variable being measured on the population; its mean is μ and its variance is σ^2. A random sample of size n has a first element X_1, a second element $X_2, \ldots$, and an nth element X_n. The ordering of the subscript is not indicative of the size of the score in the sample; X_1 is merely the *first* score chosen in each sample. Therefore, the collection of all possible X_1's, i.e., all first scores chosen in all possible random samples from the population, forms a population with mean μ and variance σ^2. In other words, X_1, $X_2, \ldots, X_n$ are each random variables with a mean of μ and a variance of σ^2.

The sample mean equals $(X_1 + X_2 + \ldots + X_n)/n$. The mean of the sampling distribution of $\bar{X}$ equals the *expected value* of $\bar{X}$.

$$E(\bar{X}) = E[(X_1 + X_2 + \ldots + X_n)/n]$$

$$= \frac{1}{n} E(X_1 + X_2 + \ldots + X_n)$$

$$= \frac{1}{n} [E(X_1) + E(X_2) + \ldots + E(X_n)]. \tag{12.1}$$

Now X_1, the arbitrarily chosen first observation in a sample, has the same distribution over samples as does X_2 or any other X_i. Its mean is μ and its variance is σ_x^2. Hence, the last term in Eq. (12.1) equals

$$\frac{1}{n} (\mu + \mu + \ldots + \mu) = \frac{1}{n} (n\mu) = \mu.$$

Stated in words, *the expected value of $\bar{X}$, which is the population mean of the sampling distribution of the sample means, is equal to μ, the mean of the population being sampled.*

How much will $\bar{X}$ vary randomly from sample to sample? In other words, if a population (sampling distribution) were formed that consisted of the means of random samples of size n from a population with mean μ and variance σ^2, what would the variance of this population of sample means be? You might expect that the variance of the sample means will be smaller than the variance of the population sampled. This will certainly be true if each sample contains two or more observations (i.e., $n > 2$). Notice that if we chose samples with an n of 1, the sample mean would be the same as the single observation drawn. If we then took repeated samples with $n = 1$ and built a sampling distribution of these "sample means," we would simply be building a sampling distribution of the original population. In this case, the variance of the original population, σ^2, and the variance of the sampling distribution of the "means" of samples of size 1 would be the same ($\sigma^2/n = \sigma^2/1 = \sigma^2$).

Suppose we try to find the variance of the means of samples of size $n = 2$ from a population. Let the population variance be σ^2. For each sample, $\bar{X}_. = (X_1 + X_2)/2$ is calculated. X_1 and X_2 are arbitrary designations for the first and second observations randomly drawn and are not related to the size of the scores. Consequently, over all random samples, X_1 has variance σ^2 and so does X_2. Because the samples are randomly drawn, there is no relationship between the sizes of the first and second observations in any sample. If we were to construct a scatter diagram for graphing the points (X_1, X_2) from sample to sample, after hundreds of samples the scatter diagram would show no correlation between X_1 and X_2. This is depicted in Fig. 12.5.

Clearly, X_1 and X_2 are uncorrelated. Thus, the correlation coefficient and covariance between the first and second observations in a sample over infinitely many random samples from a population is zero.

Now the variance over random samples of $\bar{X}_. = (X_1 + X_2)/2$ is denoted as follows:

$$\sigma^2_{\bar{x}_.} = \sigma^2_{(x_1+x_2)/2}. \tag{12.2}$$

The σ^2's are simply the expected, long-run average values of s^2; $E[s^2_x] = \sigma^2_x$. Equation (12.2) shows that the variance of $\bar{X}_.$ is the same as the variance of $1/2$ times the sum of X_1 and X_2. We saw in Sec. 5.8 that the effect on the variance of a variable of multiplying the variable by a constant was to multiply the variance by the square of the constant. Therefore,

$$\sigma^2_{(x_1+x_2)(1/2)} = (\tfrac{1}{2})^2 \sigma^2_{(x_1+x_2)}. \tag{12.3}$$

In Sec. 7.9 we learned that if two variables are uncorrelated then the variance of the sum of the two variables is the sum of their variances. Above we argued that X_1 and X_2 are uncorrelated. Hence,

$$(\tfrac{1}{2})^2 \sigma^2_{x_1+x_2} = \tfrac{1}{4}(\sigma^2_{x_1} + \sigma^2_{x_2} + 2\rho_{x_1x_2}\sigma_{x_1}\sigma_{x_2}) = \tfrac{1}{4}(\sigma^2_{x_1} + \sigma^2_{x_2}). \tag{12.4}$$

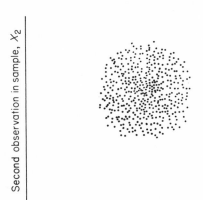

FIG. 12.5 Scatter diagram of the relationship between the first (X_1) and second (X_2) observations in random samples from a population.

Second observation in sample, X_2

First observation in sample, X_1

The variance of X_1 over repeated random samples is σ_x^2, and so is the variance of X_2. Therefore, we can write Eq. (12.4) as follows:

$$(\tfrac{1}{4})(\sigma_{x_1}^2 + \sigma_{x_2}^2) = (\tfrac{1}{4})(2\sigma_x^2) = \sigma_x^2/2. \qquad (12.5)$$

Equation (12.5) expresses the conclusion of the argument: the variance of the mean of samples of size 2 from a population with variance σ^2 is equal to $\sigma^2/2$. In this instance, $n = 2$ and $\sigma_{\bar{x}.}^2 = \sigma^2/2$. This is no coincidence. It is true in general that for random samples of size n, $\sigma_{\bar{x}.}^2 = \sigma^2/n$. Let's explore this general statement further.

If random samples of size n are taken from a population with variance σ^2, then the variance of the mean, $\bar{X}. = (X_1 + X_2 + \ldots + X_n)/n$, over samples is given by

$$\sigma_{\bar{x}.}^2 = \sigma_{(x_1+x_2+\ldots+x_n)/n}^2. \qquad (12.6)$$

The right-hand side of Eq. (12.6) shows $\sigma_{\bar{x}.}^2$ to be the variance of $(1/n)$ times the sum of the n *uncorrelated* variables $X_1, X_2, \ldots, X_n$. Therefore,

$$\sigma_{\bar{x}.}^2 = \left(\frac{1}{n}\right)^2 \sigma_{(x_1+x_2+\ldots+x_n)}^2.$$

Each variable X_i $(i = 1, 2, \ldots, n)$ has a variance of σ^2 and is uncorrelated with the other $n - 1$ variables. Therefore, the variance of the sum of the n uncorrelated variables is the sum of the variances of the variables, because each of the $n(n - 1)/2$ covariances is 0. Thus

$$\left(\frac{1}{n}\right)^2 \sigma_{(x_1+x_2+\ldots+x_n)}^2 = \left(\frac{1}{n}\right)^2 (\sigma_{x_1}^2 + \sigma_{x_2}^2 + \ldots + \sigma_{x_n}^2). \qquad (12.7)$$

Because each variable has the same variance σ^2, Eq. (12.7) can be written as

$$\left(\frac{1}{n}\right)^2 (\sigma^2 + \sigma^2 + \ldots + \sigma^2) = \left(\frac{1}{n}\right)^2 (n\sigma^2) = \frac{\sigma^2}{n}. \qquad (12.8)$$

A fundamental relationship is expressed in Eq. (12.8). *The variance of the means of random samples of size n from a population with variance σ^2 is equal to σ^2/n.*

The expression σ^2/n has traditionally been called the *variance error of the mean*. The positive square root of Eq. (12.8) is another important expression known as the *standard error of the mean*,

$$\sigma_{\bar{x}.} = \sigma/\sqrt{n}. \qquad (12.9)$$

The standard error of the mean, Eq. (12.9), is the standard deviation of the sampling distribution of the means of an infinite number of samples, each of size n, from a population with variance σ^2. Notice that in Figs. 12.3 and 12.4 the population from which samples were drawn had a standard deviation of 10, and the standard deviation of the sampling distribution of means of random samples of size 100 from that population was 1. This is consistent with Eq. (12.9):

$$\sigma_{\bar{x}.} = \frac{10}{\sqrt{100}} = 1.$$

The estimation of a population correlation coefficient provides another illustration of the concept of a sampling distribution. Probably the variables "verbal intelligence" X and "reaction time" Y are virtually uncorrelated in the population of all twelve-year-olds in the U.S.A. Imagine for the moment that someone administered the Wechsler Intelligence Scale for Children to measure X and a reaction time test to measure Y to all children age 12 in the country. With these measures, a scatter diagram of the X and Y scores could be constructed and, also, the correlation between X and Y could be calculated. Suppose, further, that the normal bivariate surface (see Sec. 6.7) proved to be an adequate description of the scatter diagram for the X and Y scores. Also, suppose that the value of the product-moment correlation coefficient, which we will denote by the Greek letter ρ, turned out to be zero, i.e., $\rho_{xy} = 0$. (Since the correlation coefficient describes the population in which we are interested, it is a parameter instead of a sample statistic. We have followed the widely accepted custom of denoting all parameters by Greek letters; statistics are denoted by Roman letters. Hence, ρ is the correlation coefficient in a population, and r is a correlation coefficient in a sample from the population.) A sample of 80 children could be drawn randomly from the population and their X and Y scores observed. For this sample, the value of r_{xy}, the sample correlation of "verbal intelligence" and "reaction time," could be computed. The sample of 80 could then be returned to the population. A second sample of 80 could then be drawn at random, r_{xy} computed, and the sample returned to the population. This process could be repeated indefinitely; a large number of values of r_{xy} for samples of size 80 from a bivariate normal population in which ρ_{xy} equals 0 could thus be accumulated. What would the frequency distribution of the large collection of sample correlation coefficients look like? The statistician can answer this question without going through the actual process of drawing thousands of samples and computing r each time. He can show mathematically that the distribution of these values of r for random samples of size 80 from a bivariate normal population in which $\rho = 0$ is nearly a normal distribution with mean 0 and variance $1/(n-1) = 1/79$. The theoretical *sampling distribution* of r for random samples of size 80 from a population with $\rho = 0$ appears in Fig. 12.6.

The standard deviation of the sampling distribution of r is called the *standard error of the correlation coefficient*. In this particular case *only*, it happens to be equal to 0.11. The standard error of r is denoted by σ_r.

Approximately 68% of the samples will yield values of r between $-.11$ and $+.11$. About 95% of the samples will yield values of r between $-.22$

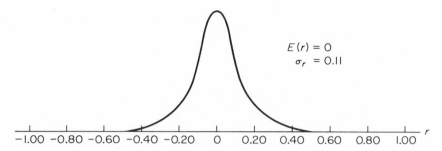

FIG. 12.6   Theoretical sampling distribution of r for random samples of
size 80 from a bivariate normal population in which ρ is zero.

and +.22. Most, but not all, samples will yield a value of r between
−.33 and +.33. If you were investigating the relationship between X and Y
and obtained a value of r equal to .08 on a random sample of 80 persons from
a population for which the value of ρ was unknown to you, would you be
prepared to declare categorically that the unknown value of ρ was not zero?
If you were rational about it, you probably would not. If you will measure
the proportion of the area under the curve in Fig. 12.6 to the right of a value
of r of .08, you will find that about 23 % of the samples of size 80 *from a
population for which* ρ = 0 will produce values of r larger than .08. Note
also that 23 % of the samples of 80 will give values of r *less* than −.08—in
other words, 46 % of the samples will yield values of r more discrepant from
zero in either direction than yours when in fact ρ = 0; you thus see that
there is no good reason to believe that an r of .08 on a sample of 80 makes a
population value of ρ equal to zero unlikely. This line of reasoning closely
parallels one theory of inferential statistics that will be studied in greater
detail later in this chapter.

12.4
PROPERTIES OF ESTIMATORS

In spite of the general importance of statistical estimation, attempts at
formalizing the properties of estimators were not pursued seriously until the
early twentieth century. The most successful single attempt was the work
of Sir Ronald Fisher. The concepts of consistency and relative efficiency
that will be met in this section are due to Fisher.

It was pointed out earlier that an estimate is a value of a statistic for a
sample which gives information about a population parameter. For example,
the sample mean $\bar{X}$ is an estimator of the population mean μ. There is a
close analogy between the way in which a sample mean is calculated and the
way in which one might calculate a population mean. It is logical to think
of $\bar{X}$ as estimating μ. However, there are other ways of treating sample
data to arrive at a value that estimates μ. Why not use the sample median or

the sample mode as an estimate of μ? It is certainly possible to do this; we shall see, however, that by the criteria used in assessing the properties of an estimator, $\bar{X}$ turns out to be a better estimator of μ than either the sample median or the sample mode.

In this section we shall also be concerned with the properties of estimators of a population median, variance (σ^2), standard deviation (σ), and correlation coefficient (ρ). What are the different ways in which these parameters can be estimated? Is one estimator to be preferred over all others for estimating a certain parameter, and why? We shall look closely at three properties of estimators.

Unbiasedness

An estimator is said to be *unbiased* for estimating a parameter if the mean of the sampling distribution of the estimator equals the value of the parameter being estimated.

Regardless of the nature of the population being sampled, the sample mean $\bar{X}$ is an unbiased estimator of the population mean μ. Notice in Figs. 12.3 and 12.4 that the value of the population mean μ is 15 and that the mean of the sampling distribution of $\bar{X}$ is also 15. This example illustrates the unbiasedness of $\bar{X}$ as an estimator of μ. If samples are drawn randomly from a normal distribution (or any other symmetric distribution), then the sample median is also an unbiased estimator of the population mean μ. In other words, the average of the medians of an infinite number of random samples from a normal distribution equals μ, the mean of the normal distribution (which is, of course, also its median and its mode).

There are many examples of *biased* estimators. Suppose we wish to estimate ρ, the correlation between two variables that have a bivariate normal distribution in the population. Imagine that for a particular population $\rho = .75$. The mean of the sampling distribution of the sample correlation coefficient r will be *less than* .75 for any finite sample size. Thus, r is in general a *biased* estimator of ρ. If you have already looked back at Fig. 12.6, you might doubt this statement. In Fig. 12.6, we saw that the mean of the sampling distribution of r was 0 for samples of size 80 from a population in which $\rho = 0$. Consequently, r was then an unbiased estimator of ρ. It so happens that r estimates ρ unbiasedly only when $\rho = 0$. If ρ is any other value from -1.00 to $+1.00$, there will be a bias in r as an estimator of ρ. (Olkin and Pratt, 1958, have derived the unbiased estimator of ρ. Its calculation on a sample is rather complex. Olkin and Pratt provided tables for finding an unbiased estimate of the population correlation coefficient.)

Though we are formally dealing with the property of unbiasedness of estimators here for the first time in this text, this property influenced the methods used to describe variation in Chapter 5. In Sec. 5.5 we chose to measure the variation in a sample by the quantity $s_x^2 = \sum (X_i - \bar{X}.)^2/(n - 1)$. It might have been more natural to measure variability by simply taking the *average* of the squared deviations around the sample mean, but instead it was decided to place $(n - 1)$ and not n in the denominator of s^2. Now we are in a position to elaborate on the motivation of this choice. *The quantity s_x^2 is an unbiased estimator of the population variance σ^2, whereas $\sum (X_i - \bar{X}.)^2/n$ is negatively biased as an estimator of σ^2.* That is,

$$E\left[\sum \frac{(X_i - \bar{X}.)^2}{n} \right] \leqslant \sigma^2,$$

approaching equality only as $n \to \infty$.

Suppose that we took random samples from any population with variance σ^2 and calculated s_x^2 each time. The average of a huge number of these sample variances would be exactly equal to σ^2. Hence, s_x^2 is an unbiased estimator of σ^2. If $\sum (X_i - \bar{X}.)^2/n$ had been calculated on each sample instead, the average of these quantities would have been smaller than σ^2, namely $[(n - 1)/n]\sigma^2$. Of course, if n was quite large—100 or more, for example—the difference between s_x^2 and $\sum (X_i - \bar{X}.)^2/n$ would be quite small, because the value of $(n - 1)/n$ would approach 1. Nonetheless, the latter would contain some small bias as an estimator of σ^2. It is sometimes said that $\sum (X_i - \bar{X}.)^2/n$ is "asymptotically unbiased" as an estimate of σ^2 because the bias becomes smaller as n increases.

Suppose that one has a normal distribution with mean $\mu = 0$ and variance $\sigma^2 = 100$. If an infinite number of random samples of size $n = 6$ were drawn from the population and both s_x^2 and $\sum (X_i - \bar{X}.)^2/6$ were calculated for each sample, the two sampling distributions in Fig. 12.7 would be obtained.

Notice that the mean of the sampling distribution of s_x^2 is 100, the value of σ^2. This illustrates the unbiasedness of s_x^2 in this instance. The mean of the sampling distribution of $\sum (X_i - \bar{X}.)^2/6$ is equal to 83.33. In this instance, the bias introduced into the estimation of σ^2 by using n in place of $n - 1$ in the denominator of the sample variance is sizable—i.e., $(n - 1)/n = 5/6$ here.

You are probably wondering how it was determined that the denominator of the sample variance should be $n - 1$ and not $n - 2$, or $n - 3$, or $n - \frac{1}{2}$. It was *not* determined empirically that $n - 1$ gives the unbiased estimator. There are several ways of proving mathematically that s_x^2 is an unbiased estimator of σ^2. The algebraic proof is cumbersome, although not as difficult to comprehend as you might imagine. We shall not present the proof here. It can be found in Edwards (1964, pp. 29–36).

The quantity s_x^2 is an unbiased estimator of σ^2. Does this imply that s_x, the sample standard deviation, is an unbiased estimator of σ, the population standard deviation? As a matter of fact, it does not. A nonlinear transformation of an unbiased estimator is not itself an unbiased estimator,

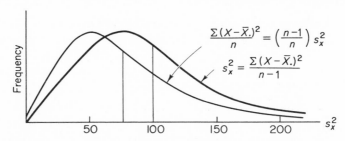

FIG. 12.7   Sampling distributions of s_x^2 and $\sum(X_i - \bar{X}.)^2/6$ for random samples of size 6 from a normal distribution with variance $\sigma^2 = 100$.

so the sample standard deviation is a *biased* estimator of the population standard deviation.   The amount of bias depends on the shape of the population being sampled.   *If the population is normal*, the mean of the sampling distribution of s is slightly less than σ. Specifically, ˙

$$E(s) = \mu_s = \left(\frac{4n - 4}{4n - 3}\right)\sigma. \qquad (12.10)$$

If n is fairly large, the bias in s is quite small.   Nonetheless, s remains a biased (but consistent) estimator of σ.   As $n \to \infty$, the expression in parentheses in Eq. (12.10) approaches 1 and the bias disappears.

TABLE 12.1   BIASEDNESS OR UNBIASEDNESS OF VARIOUS ESTIMATORS OF PARAMETERS OF VARIOUS POPULATIONS

Parameter	Nature of population	Estimator	Status of the estimator
μ	Any population	$\bar{X}$.	Unbiased
μ	Symmetric	Median	Unbiased
μ	Symmetric and unimodal	Mode	Unbiased
μ	Skewed	Median	Biased
μ	Skewed	Mode	Biased
σ^2	Any population	s_x^2	Unbiased
σ	Normal	s_x	Biased negatively*
ρ_{xy}	Bivariate-normal	r_{xy}	Biased negatively

* For interesting discussion of unbiased estimation of the standard deviation, see Cureton (1968b), Jarrett (1968), Cureton (1968c), and Bolch (1968) in that order.

Table 12.1 presents some parameters, their estimators, and statements that the estimator is biased or unbiased.   As you study Table 12.1, remember that several different sample statistics may be used to estimate the same parameter and that whether an estimator is biased or unbiased depends in part upon the shape of the distribution of measures in the population from which samples are drawn.

Consistency

A second property of estimators is their *consistency*. A consistent estimator, even though it may be biased, tends to get closer and closer to the value of the parameter it estimates as the sample size becomes larger and larger. Some estimators that are biased are consistent. For example, the sample standard deviation is a biased but consistent estimator of σ. By taking a large sample, s will be close to σ in value; the larger the sample becomes, the closer s gets to σ. This can be seen algebraically if you let n approach infinity in Eq. (12.10). In an inexact sense, the condition of consistency implies that a consistent estimator of a parameter is calculated on a sample in such a way that if the same calculation was performed on the entire population it would yield the value of the parameter. The sample mean is a consistent estimator of μ since, if the sample were made as large as the population, $\bar{X}$ would equal μ. (The sample mean is also an unbiased estimator of μ.) This requirement of consistency makes good sense. It is difficult to find any estimators that are taken seriously which are not consistent. The few examples of inconsistent estimators that might be presented are quite contrived.

Relative Efficiency

The third property of estimators we shall consider is their *efficiency*. "Efficiency" refers to the precision with which an estimator estimates a parameter; it refers to the variability of the estimate from sample to sample. In a few previous examples we have measured this variability (or efficiency) by taking the variance or standard deviation of the sampling distribution of the statistic. The variance error of the sample mean, $\sigma_{\bar{x}}^2$, is a measure of the efficiency of $\bar{X}$ as an estimator of μ. The variance error of the sample correlation coefficient, σ_r^2, is a measure of the efficiency of r as an estimator of ρ.

The variance error of an estimator is one of its most important properties. The *variance error* of any statistic is the variance of the sampling distribution of the statistic.

Suppose we wish to estimate the value of the population mean of a particular normal distribution. One way of estimating μ is to find the mean $\bar{X}$ of a sample of size n. However, the sample median Md is also an unbiased estimator of μ. Both are consistent estimators of μ. Which is to be preferred? This question could be answered by considering the *relative efficiencies* of the two estimators. Which estimator of μ, the sample mean or the sample median, varies less from sample to sample? Which has a smaller variance error?

If the variance σ^2 of the normal population being sampled is 50 and sample size n is 10, then the variance of $\bar{X}$ over repeated random samples is $\sigma^2/n = 50/10 = 5$. What about the variance error of the sample median, σ^2_{Md}? If thousands and thousands of random samples, each of size n, are drawn from a normal population with mean μ and variance σ^2, and the median Md is calculated for each sample, the frequency distribution of these sample medians will be normal with mean μ and variance $(1.57)\sigma^2/n$. Hence, the variance error of the sample median is $(1.57)\sigma^2/n$. Figure 12.8 depicts the sampling distributions of $\bar{X}$ and Md for samples of size 10 from a normal distribution with variance 50.

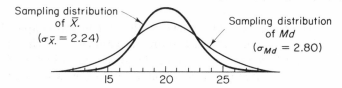

Sampling distribution of $\bar{X}$.
$(\sigma_{\bar{X}} = 2.24)$

Sampling distribution of Md
$(\sigma_{Md} = 2.80)$

15   20   25

FIG. 12.8   Sampling distributions of the sample mean $\bar{X}$ and the sample median Md for random samples of size 10 from a normal population with mean $\mu = 20$ and variance $\sigma^2 = 50$.

The variance error of the sample median in Fig. 12.8 is equal to $(1.57)\sigma^2/n = (1.57)(5) = 7.85$. This figure reveals that the sample median will vary more than the sample mean over repeated samples. Note that while only 16% of the sample means will be larger than 25, about 26% of the sample medians will be larger than 25. $\bar{X}$ is a more efficient estimator of μ than Md. Seeking greater descriptive precision, the statistician defines the *efficiency* of $\bar{X}$ *relative* to Md as the ratio of their variance errors. In this instance,

$$\text{relative efficiency} = \frac{\sigma^2/n}{(1.57)\sigma^2/n} = \frac{1}{1.57} = .637 = 63.7\%,$$

meaning that for normally distributed measures the median is less than two-thirds as efficient as the arithmetic mean, regardless of the magnitude of n.

One interpretation of the coefficient of relative efficiency is that if the median of a sample of 100 observations is used to estimate μ, the same degree of precision of estimation could be attained by drawing a sample of 64 observations and computing $\bar{X}$.

Statisticians have generally combined the criteria of unbiasedness and efficiency when making their choice of a "best" estimator of a parameter. For example, the sample mean, median, and mode might all be worthy contenders for "best estimator" of μ in a normal population. The first question a statistician would probably ask is "Which ones are unbiased estimators?" All three qualify on this criterion. The next question would probably be "Which one is the most efficient?", i.e., "Which one has the smallest variance error?" The sample mode is least efficient, and we saw that the sample median is less efficient than the sample mean. The sample mean wins. In fact, the sample mean wins relative to any competition. The primary reason that $\bar{X}$ is used almost exclusively to estimate the population mean μ of any population is that *it has a smaller variance error than any other unbiased estimator of μ.* In this sentence you can see that both the properties of unbiasedness and efficiency are important.

12.5
INTERVAL ESTIMATION

The topics we have discussed thus far in this chapter belong to one branch of the theory of estimation of parameters. That branch is called *point estimation* because we considered as the estimate of a parameter a single value or number—a *point* on a line, if you will. For example, a sample of 100 teachers might be drawn from the population of all female elementary-school teachers in the nation for the purpose of estimating the average number of years in service for the population. For the sample, $\bar{X}$ might equal 3.47 years. The number 3.47 is a single point on the number line and thus provides a *point estimate* of μ, the population mean.

The other type of estimate that is typically used builds on the concept of the point estimate and is called an *interval estimate*. Interval estimation is a highly useful inferential statistical technique. We shall encounter it repeatedly in the remainder of this text.

An interval estimate of a parameter is a segment on the number line, and the value of the parameter is thought to lie somewhere on that interval. For example, the result of drawing a sample from a population in order to estimate μ might be the interval (25.91, 38.65), which probably contains between its bounds—lower bound 25.91 and upper bound 38.65—the value of μ. Instead of calculating a single point as an estimate of a parameter, we have now found a whole set of adjacent points, an *interval*, and one of those points is *probably* the value of the parameter. The complication that arises to make interval estimation a difficult notion to comprehend is the way in which one determines exactly how probable it is that the parameter lies on the interval. The remainder of this section is concerned with the mechanics of constructing an interval estimate of a parameter in such a way that it has a known probability of including the value of the parameter between its limits.

For our first example of interval estimation, let us go back to $\bar{X}$ as an estimator of μ and what the central limit theorem tells us about the sampling

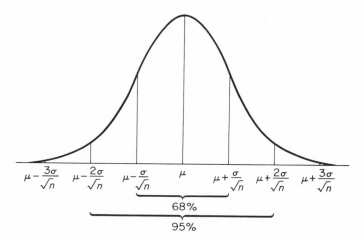

FIG. 12.9   The sampling distribution of $\bar{X}$ for random samples of size
n from a population.

distribution of $\bar{X}$. . We have seen that if random samples of size n are drawn
from a population with mean μ and variance σ^2, the sampling distribution
of $\bar{X}$ will have mean μ and variance σ^2/n, and will be nearly normal if n is
sufficiently large.   The sampling distribution of $\bar{X}$ is shown in Fig. 12.9.

In Fig. 12.9 the standard deviation of the sampling distribution of $\bar{X}$,
the standard error of the mean, is $\sigma/\sqrt{n}$.   Since the distribution is normal,
68% of the observations lie within one standard deviation of μ, i.e., 68%
of the sample means that would be obtained in repeated random sampling
would lie on the interval $\mu - (\sigma/\sqrt{n})$ to $\mu + (\sigma/\sqrt{n})$.   Approximately 95%
of the means lie on the interval $\mu - (2\sigma/\sqrt{n})$ to $\mu + (2\sigma/\sqrt{n})$, since about 95%
of the area under the normal curve lies within two standard deviations of
the mean.   By referring to a table of the unit normal distribution, we can
determine exactly how many standard deviations we must go out from μ in
each direction to establish an interval that includes 80%, 90%, 99%, or any
other percent of the area under the curve.   For example, we can see from
Table B in Appendix A that 5% of the area under the normal curve lies
above a z score of 1.64, and 5% lies below a z score of -1.64.   In other words,
90% of the area under the normal curve lies within 1.64 standard deviations
on either side of the mean μ, i.e., within the range $\mu \pm 1.64\sigma$.   For Fig. 12.9,
this means that 90% of the sample *means* obtained in repeated random
sampling would lie on the interval $\mu - (1.64\sigma/\sqrt{n})$ and $\mu + (1.64\sigma/\sqrt{n})$.
Stated in probabilistic terms, the probability is .90 that a randomly drawn
sample will have a mean $\bar{X}$ that is larger than $\mu - (1.64\sigma/\sqrt{n})$ and smaller
than $\mu + (1.64\sigma/\sqrt{n})$.

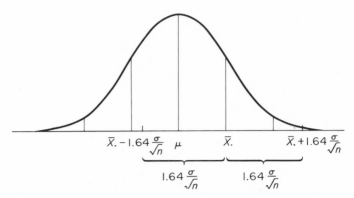

FIG. 12.10   Illustration of how the interval established around $\bar{X}$. captures μ within its limits.

We know, then, that 90% of the random samples which could be drawn from the normally distributed population will produce a sample mean that lies a distance of $1.64\sigma/\sqrt{n}$ or less from μ.   Now comes the important step in the reasoning underlying interval estimation.   *If 90% of the $\bar{X}$.'s lie within a distance of $1.64\sigma/\sqrt{n}$ of μ, then adding and subtracting $1.64\sigma/\sqrt{n}$ from any $\bar{X}$. produces an interval, $\bar{X}. - (1.64\sigma/\sqrt{n})$ to $\bar{X}. + (1.64\sigma/\sqrt{n})$, that has a 90% chance of including μ between its limits.*   Figure 12.10 is an attempt to illustrate this.

The sample mean that happened to result from the random sample of size n from the population lies one standard deviation, $\sigma/\sqrt{n}$, above μ. This is not unlikely, since before it was drawn the probability was .90 that the sample mean obtained would lie within a distance of $1.64\sigma/\sqrt{n}$ of μ. Because this particular $\bar{X}$. is within $\sigma/\sqrt{n}$ of μ, when we add and subtract $1.64\sigma/\sqrt{n}$ from $\bar{X}$. the resulting interval will include μ.   In fact, the resulting interval, $\bar{X}. - (1.64\sigma/\sqrt{n})$ to $\bar{X}. + (1.64\sigma/\sqrt{n})$, includes every point within a distance of $1.64\sigma/\sqrt{n}$ of $\bar{X}$. .   Since μ lies only a distance of $\sigma/\sqrt{n}$ below $\bar{X}$. , it is included on the interval.   How big or how small must $\bar{X}$. be before μ will not lie within $1.64\sigma/\sqrt{n}$ units of $\bar{X}$.?   Obviously, if $\bar{X}$. is above $\mu +$ $(1.64\sigma/\sqrt{n})$ or below $\mu - (1.64\sigma/\sqrt{n})$, then $\bar{X}$. lies further away from μ than a distance of $1.64\sigma/\sqrt{n}$.   How likely is it that a sample mean will lie further than $1.64\sigma/\sqrt{n}$ from μ?   The probability of this happening is .10.   We chose $1.64\sigma/\sqrt{n}$ because we wondered how far one would have to go above and below μ in the sampling distribution of $\bar{X}$. to include 90% of the sample means.   Of course, then, 10% of the sample means lie outside of the interval $\mu - (1.64\sigma/\sqrt{n})$ to $\mu + (1.64\sigma/\sqrt{n})$.   This implies that in 10% of the random samples which might be drawn from the population, adding $1.64\sigma/\sqrt{n}$ to $\bar{X}_.$ and subtracting $1.64\sigma/\sqrt{n}$ from $\bar{X}_.$ will establish an interval that does *not* contain μ between its lower and upper limits. Such an interval is depicted in Fig. 12.11.

Suppose we now consider the entire collection of means of random samples of size n from the population in question. This is an infinitely large collection and any single element of it is denoted by $\bar{X}_.$. We can think of constructing an interval around each of these sample means by adding and subtracting $1.64\sigma/\sqrt{n}$ from each mean. Now we have an infinite collection of intervals. Ninety percent of these intervals contain μ between their lower and upper limits; ten percent do not. What is the probability that a randomly selected interval from this infinite collection of intervals will contain μ between its lower and upper limits? Of course this probability is .90. The probability must be .10, then, that an interval randomly selected in this manner will *not* contain μ between its bounds.

The mathematical statement of what we have been discussing is concise, unambiguous, and very revealing. Since $\bar{X}_.$ is distributed normally with mean μ and variance σ^2/n, the variable $(\bar{X}_. - \mu)/(\sigma/\sqrt{n})$ has a normal distribution with mean 0 and variance 1. We know, then, that

$$\text{probability}\left(-1.64 < \frac{\bar{X}_. - \mu}{\sigma/\sqrt{n}} < 1.64\right) = .90. \qquad (12.11)$$

Stated in words, the probability that the distance of $\bar{X}_.$ from μ in units measured by $\sigma/\sqrt{n}$ is greater than -1.64 and less than 1.64 is .90. Multiplying the inequality inside the parentheses by $\sigma/\sqrt{n}$, subtracting $\bar{X}_.$ throughout the inequality, and then multiplying by -1—which changes the direction of the inequality—changes Eq. (12.11) into the following:

$$\text{probability}\left\{\left[\bar{X}_. - \left(1.64\,\frac{\sigma}{\sqrt{n}}\right)\right] < \mu < \left[\bar{X}_. + \left(1.64\,\frac{\sigma}{\sqrt{n}}\right)\right]\right\} = .90.$$

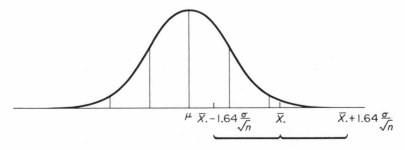

FIG. 12.11   Illustration of how an interval established around $\bar{X}_.$ may not capture μ within its limits.

Thus, the probability is .90 that μ is greater than $\bar{X} - (1.64\sigma/\sqrt{n})$ and less than $\bar{X} + (1.64\sigma/\sqrt{n})$.

When an interval estimate of a parameter is constructed so that it has a certain known probability of including the value of the parameter between its limits, the interval is called a *confidence interval*. The probability that the confidence interval "captures" the parameter between its limits should be used in identifying the interval. In the example developed above, a ".90 confidence interval," or "90% confidence interval" was constructed. The *confidence coefficient* is the probability that a randomly selected interval from the collection of all possible confidence intervals as defined in the above way (i.e., $\bar{X} \pm z\sigma/\sqrt{n}$) will capture the parameter. In the above example, the confidence coefficient we chose to use was equal to .90. Another way of saying this is as follows: "A confidence interval with confidence coefficient .90 was constructed." Finally, we speak of constructing a confidence interval *around* a sample statistic and *on* a parameter, because for a given population the parameter assumes just one value. For example, $\bar{X} \pm (1.64\sigma/\sqrt{n})$ is the .90 *confidence interval around $\bar{X}$ and on μ*.

Example of the construction and use of a confidence interval. We will now present an example of how interval estimation would be applied. The example will be developed in considerable detail so that more can be learned about the rationale of applying the theory we have developed.

A researcher has set out to determine, as well as he can with his limited resources, the average IQ, as measured by the Wechsler Intelligence Scale for Children (WISC), of the 35,000 fifth-grade pupils in his state. The WISC is an individual intelligence test that yields measures of performance and verbal intelligence and a total IQ that is a combination of both; it must be administered by trained examiners. The available funds for this research will cover 900 test administrations, but no more.

The researcher has good reason to believe that the fifth-grade pupils in his state are as heterogeneous as the pupils used to norm the WISC, but he has some reason to believe that their average score might deviate from that of the norm group. Hence, he is willing to believe that the variance of WISC total IQ's in his state is 225—the same as the variance in the norm group.*

---

* You may have sensed that our argument as to why σ^2 is known and μ is not known is somewhat artificial. In almost all instances, both are either known or unknown. We assumed here that σ^2 is known and μ is unknown in order to keep the problem of interval estimation simpler than it would be if both σ^2 and μ had to be estimated from the same sample. This latter case, in which both σ^2 and μ are unknown, is by far the more realistic situation. The distribution theory that led to the solution of the problem of interval estimation of μ when σ^2 is unknown might well be taken as the dawn of modern inferential statistical methods; this solution was not presented until early in this century. It is due to W. S. Gosset who wrote under the pseudonym of "Student" (1908). We will return to "Student" and his epoch-making research in a later chapter.

Our researcher is in the position of taking a random sample of 900 WISC Total IQ scores from a population of 35,000 scores in which the variance is 225. He will calculate $\bar{X}.$ as an estimate of the unknown μ. He wishes to establish a confidence interval around $\bar{X}.$, and he would like the confidence coefficient for this interval to be .99. With samples as large as 900, one can be confident in this situation that in repeated random samples $\bar{X}.$ is very nearly normally distributed around μ with a standard error of $\sigma/\sqrt{n} = \sqrt{225/900} = 0.5$. From Table B in Appendix A, it can be determined that 99% of the area under the unit normal curve lies within 2.58 standard-deviation units of the mean. The sampling distribution of $\bar{X}.$ for samples of 900 from a population with $\sigma^2 = 225$ appears in Fig. 12.12, where distance along the baseline is in terms of $\sigma_{\bar{x}.} = 0.5$. Thus, 99% of the area under this curve lies within $\mu \pm 1.29$ because $2.58(0.5) = 1.29$.

Confusion often arises in the interpretation of a confidence interval. For example, some persons believe mistakenly that if the 95% confidence interval on μ around a sample mean of 46.25 extends from 36.25 to 56.25, then 95% of the sample means would be expected to fall between 36.25 and 56.25. This is an incorrect interpretation of a confidence interval. If 46.25 happens to lie far (perhaps $3\sigma_{\bar{x}.}$) above (or below) μ—and there is no way of knowing this from the sample—then less than half of the subsequent sample means would fall between 36.25 and 56.25.

It is correct to state that "the probability is .95 that $\bar{X}. \pm (1.96\sigma/\sqrt{n})$ will span μ," or to write the same in symbols:

$$\text{prob}\left\{\left[\bar{X}. - \left(1.96\frac{\sigma}{\sqrt{n}}\right)\right] < \mu < \left[\bar{X}. + \left(1.96\frac{\sigma}{\sqrt{n}}\right)\right]\right\} = .95. \quad (12.12)$$

It is understood that the probability statement refers to the sample space of all intervals that could be formed by computing one interval for each sample.

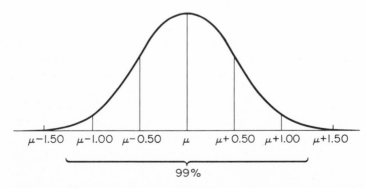

FIG. 12.12 Sampling distribution of $\bar{X}.$ for random samples of size 900 from a population with unknown mean μ and known variance $\sigma^2 = 225$.

The mathematical statement in Eq. (12.12) makes perfect sense because it involves a variable $\bar{X}$ about which probability statements can be made. However, after a single sample has been drawn and a single value like 46.25 attached to $\bar{X}$, it is incorrect to say that $46.25 \pm 1.96\sigma/\sqrt{n}$ has probability .95 of spanning μ. It is *not* legitimate to write

$$\text{prob}\left\{\left[46.25 - \left(1.96\frac{\sigma}{\sqrt{n}}\right)\right] < \mu < \left[46.25 + \left(1.96\frac{\sigma}{\sqrt{n}}\right)\right]\right\} = .95.$$

The above statement of a probability makes no sense because there is no quantity that varies from sample to sample.

The chances are 99 in 100 that the mean of a random sample will lie less than $2.58\sigma/\sqrt{n}$ units from μ. In this case, $2.58\sigma/\sqrt{n} = 2.58(0.5) = 1.29$. The researcher knows this is true even though we do not know the value of μ. Consequently, if he conceives of adding and subtracting 1.29 from all sample means he would obtain in a series of random samples, he would have a probability of .99 of capturing the true value of μ between the limits of the confidence intervals he so constructed. Suppose now that he draws his single sample and obtains a mean of 103.72. The .99 confidence interval on μ around $\bar{X}$ is calculated as follows:

$$\bar{X} \pm 2.58\frac{\sigma}{\sqrt{n}} = 103.72 \pm 1.29 = (103.72 - 1.29,\ 103.72 + 1.29)$$

$$= (102.43,\ 105.01).$$

It is sometimes said that "the probability that (102.43, 105.01) captures μ is .99." This is a confusion and is not true. The value of μ either does or does not lie between 102.43 and 105.01. Since the value of μ is unknown, we do not know whether it does or does not lie in this interval; we know, however, that only these two possibilities are logical. The interval (102.43, 105.01) is not a sample space (see Sec. 10.2), and it does not make sense to speak of probabilities in connection with it. Probabilities and the confidence coefficient apply to the *repeated process* of constructing confidence intervals. R. von Mises, one of the two or three persons most responsible for modern, statistical notions of probability, has said (1939, pp. 11–14): "Our probability theory has no relation to questions such as: 'Is there a probability of Germany being again involved in a war with Liberia?' . . . we may say that in order to apply the theory of probability we must have a practically unlimited sequence of similar observations." If the researcher in the above example were to repeat his actions of drawing samples and constructing confidence intervals on μ indefinitely, then 99% of the intervals he would produce would contain the value of μ. The sample space to which the probability statement applies is the collection of all possible confidence intervals.   But any real-life researcher draws only a few samples, typically just one.   Whether or not the confidence interval he constructs captures the parameter he is interested in *cannot be known by him.* It may and then it may not.   All he knows is that he has performed an action that would result, if he were to repeat it thousands of times, in the parameter being captured between the limits of his confidence interval 99% (or 95%, or 90%, or any other percent he chooses) of the time.   If his confidence coefficient is large enough, he cannot help but believe that *this* particular interval he has just calculated has captured the value of the parameter. (This is one good reason for keeping the confidence coefficient large—.90, .95, .99, or even larger—as is typically done.)   However, if he is rational, he will acknowledge the slight probability (.01, or .05, or .10, or any other value he chooses) that his belief is mistaken.

Summary of the construction of a confidence interval on μ **around** $\bar{X}$ **for large samples when** σ^2 **is known.** Samples of size n, sufficiently large to insure the near normality of the sampling distribution of $\bar{X}$, are drawn from a population with unknown mean μ and known variance σ^2. A confidence interval on μ is to be constructed around $\bar{X}$.   A confidence coefficient of $1 - \alpha$ is chosen.   For example, if a confidence coefficient of .95 is desired, $\alpha = .05$.   (This rather backward way of denoting the confidence coefficient, namely as $1 - \alpha$, has a purpose that will become evident after more work in statistical inference.   The notation is due partly to historical precedent, however. In Sec. 13.4, the origin of the α notation will be presented.)

From Table B in Appendix A, the value of the z score above which $100(\alpha/2)\%$ of the area under the unit normal curve lies is found.   Denote this z score by $z_{1-(\alpha/2)}$.   The $1 - \alpha$ confidence interval around $\bar{X}$ is given by the following formula:

$$\left(\bar{X} - z_{1-(\alpha/2)} \frac{\sigma}{\sqrt{n}} , \ \bar{X} + z_{1-(\alpha/2)} \frac{\sigma}{\sqrt{n}} \right). \tag{12.13}$$

An expression equivalent to Eq. (12.13) is the following:

$$\bar{X} \pm z_{1-(\alpha/2)} \frac{\sigma}{\sqrt{n}} . \tag{12.14}$$

Equations (12.13) and (12.14) will be illustrated on the following data:

1. $n = 400$, $\sigma^2 = 36$, and the confidence coefficient is arbitrarily chosen to equal .95; i.e., $1 - \alpha = .95$, so $\alpha = .05$.   From Table B in Appendix A we see that $100(\alpha/2)\% = 2.5\%$ of the area under the unit normal curve lies above a z score of 1.96.   Hence, $z_{.975} = 1.96$.

2. The mean of the sample of 400 observations equals 51.04.

The .95 confidence interval on μ around $\bar{X}$ is found from Eq. (12.14) as follows:

$$51.04 \pm (1.96) \frac{6}{20} = (50.45, 51.63).$$

Construction of confidence intervals around sample correlation coefficients. This final illustration of the theory of interval estimation provides a far more useful technique than the classical techniques presented above. Here we are concerned with the interval estimation of the correlation coefficient ρ in a *bivariate normal population*. (See Sec. 6.7.)

The usual method of estimating ρ is to find the point estimate r for a random sample from the population. Even though r is a biased estimator of ρ, it is almost always chosen in practice as the estimator of ρ. Actually, the bias in r as an estimator of ρ is not great for even moderately large samples, and the bias becomes smaller as n, the sample size, becomes larger. (In fact, r is said to be an "asymptotically unbiased" estimator of ρ because the bias vanishes as n becomes infinitely large.)

How can we establish a confidence interval around r so that we can say, for example, that "intervals constructed in this manner will include ρ between the lower and upper limits 95% of the time"? The theory of interval estimation is the same in this instance as it was in the estimation of μ. One or two complications arise in applying the theory, and we must deal with these now.

The theory of interval estimation directs us to: (1) find the sampling distribution of r; (2) find the standard error of r; (3) add and subtract some multiple of the standard error of r from r to determine the limits of the confidence interval. However, this approach breaks down before we can finish the first step. Here is the dilemma with which mathematical statisticians were faced early in this century when they sought to solve the statistical inferential problems concerning r: if statistical inferences about ρ are to be made, the standard error of r must be known; before the standard error of r can be known, ρ must be known. Indeed this is a hopeless situation. To find the standard error of r we must know ρ; but if we know ρ, there is no point in constructing a confidence interval as an estimate of it.

For all values of ρ, the distribution of r over random samples from the bivariate normal population with correlation coefficient ρ is known. When $\rho = 0$ and samples of size 30 or greater are taken, the sampling distribution of r is nearly normal with mean 0 and standard deviation σ_r equal to $1/\sqrt{n-1}$. However, when $\rho = .60$, the sampling distribution of r is not normal; its mean, μ_r or $E(r)$, is not equal to .60; its standard deviation σ_r is equal to $.80/\sqrt{n-1}$; and the sampling distribution is quite negatively skewed. What is the sampling distribution of r when $\rho = 1$? If in the population X and Y are perfectly linearly related—as they must be if $\rho_{xy} = 1$—is it possible to select a sample of any size in which r is not equal to 1?

The standard deviation of the sampling distribution of r for random samples of size n from a bivariate normal population with correlation coefficient ρ is

$$\sigma_r = \sqrt{\frac{1-\rho^2}{n-1}}.$$

As ρ increases from 0 to $+1$, the sampling distribution of r becomes increasingly negatively skewed. As ρ decreases from 0 to -1, the sampling distribution becomes increasingly positively skewed.

Perhaps you can appreciate the impossible state of affairs that would exist if we tried to use the above sampling distribution information about r to construct confidence intervals on ρ. If you can, you will surely be impressed by the insightful solution to these problems that the English statistician Sir Ronald A. Fisher (1890–1962) produced in 1921. Fisher determined that a particular mathematical transformation of the sample correlation coefficient would yield a quantity with a sampling distribution that would have the same variance regardless of the value of ρ. This transformation is called *Fisher's Z-transformation*. The Z-transformation of any r is denoted by Z_r; the Z-transformation of the value of ρ is denoted by Z_ρ. Z_r has the following formula:

$$Z_r = \log_e \sqrt{(1+r)/(1-r)}. \tag{12.15}$$

If we want to find the Z-transformation of the value of ρ, we simply substitute ρ for r in Eq. (12.15).

$$Z_\rho = \log_e \sqrt{(1+\rho)/(1-\rho)}.$$

The mathematical symbolism in Eq. (12.15) may look baffling to you. Virtually no one ever computes Z_r from Eq. (12.15), but uses a table instead; the calculations have been performed and tabulated for convenience in Table G in Appendix A. In Table G the value of Z_r is given for values of r from 0 to $+1.000$ in steps of .001. If r is negative, simply give Z_r a minus sign. Verify that a Z_r of .418 corresponds to an r of .395, and that $r = -.775$ gives a Z_r of -1.033. The r to Z transformation is graphed in Fig. 12.13.

Suppose we set out to build a sampling distribution of r by taking thousands of random samples each of size n from a bivariate normal population with correlation ρ and by computing r for each. Instead of building up a frequency distribution of the r's, however, suppose a frequency distribution of the Z_r's was built. How would such a frequency distribution look? *The sampling distribution of the Z_r's would be nearly normal with mean Z_ρ and variance $1/(n-3)$.* The sampling distribution would look like the distribution in Fig. 12.14.

Fisher's Z-transformation provides what is needed for a solution to the problem of placing confidence intervals around r. The standard deviation of

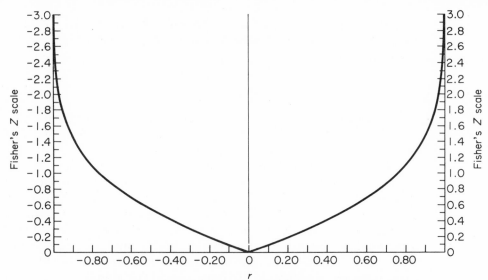

FIG. 12.13   Relationship between r and Fisher's Z-transformation of r. (Redrawn from Fig. 3-10 in Julian C. Stanley, *Measurement in Today's Schools*, 4th Ed., © 1964, by permission of Prentice-Hall, Inc., Englewood Cliffs, N.J.)

Z_r over repeated random samples is $1/\sqrt{n-3}$, regardless of the value of ρ. Hence, 90% of the Z_r's obtained in repeated random samples will lie within 1.64 standard deviations—a distance of $1.64(1/\sqrt{n-3})$—of Z_ρ; 95% of the Z_r's will lie within a distance of $1.96(1/\sqrt{n-3})$ of Z_ρ; etc. The distribution of Z_r is approximately normal regardless of the size of n. Consequently, if we add and subtract some multiple of $1/\sqrt{n-3}$ from Z_r we will have a

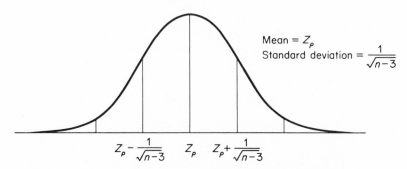

FIG. 12.14   Sampling distribution of Fisher's Z-transformation of r for random samples of size n from a bivariate normal distribution with correlation coefficient ρ.

specified probability of capturing Z_ρ within these intervals. The following is another way of conceptualizing the problem. Since Z_r is normally distributed with mean Z_ρ and standard deviation $1/\sqrt{n-3}$, then

$$\frac{Z_r - Z_\rho}{1/\sqrt{n-3}}$$

is normally distributed with mean 0 and standard deviation 1. Consequently,

$$\text{prob}\left[-1.96 < \frac{Z_r - Z_\rho}{1/\sqrt{n-3}} < 1.96\right] = .95,$$

or

$$\text{prob}\left[-2.58 < \frac{Z_r - Z_\rho}{1/\sqrt{n-3}} < 2.58\right] = .99.$$

Therefore, the interval

$$Z_r - 1.96\,\frac{1}{\sqrt{n-3}},\ Z_r + 1.96\,\frac{1}{\sqrt{n-3}} \tag{12.16}$$

captures Z_ρ with probability .95; and the interval

$$Z_r - 2.58\,\frac{1}{\sqrt{n-3}},\ Z_r + 2.58\,\frac{1}{\sqrt{n-3}} \tag{12.17}$$

captures Z_ρ with probability .99.

To illustrate Eqs. (12.16) and (12.17) suppose that a sample of $n = 84$ observations is drawn at random from what is believed to be a bivariate normal population and that r equals .245. A confidence interval with confidence coefficient .95 is desired.

First, r is transformed into Z_r by reference to Table G in Appendix A:

$$Z_{.245} = .250.$$

Second, 1.96 times the standard error of Z_r is found:

$$1.96\,\frac{1}{\sqrt{84-3}} = \frac{1.96}{9} = .218.$$

The 95% confidence interval on Z_ρ is found by substituting into Eq. (12.16). The lower and upper limits of the interval are

$$Z_r - 1.96\,\frac{1}{\sqrt{n-3}} = .250 - .218 = .032$$

$$\text{and}\quad Z_r + 1.96\,\frac{1}{\sqrt{n-3}} = .250 + .218 = .468,$$

respectively.

The interval (.032, .468) was generated by a process having a probability of .95 of producing an interval that captures the Z-transformation of ρ. *We can interpret the confidence interval more intelligibly if everything is transformed back from Fisher Z scores into correlation coefficients.* So we read Table G backwards and find the values of r which correspond to Z scores of .032 and .468. An r of .032 corresponds to a Z of .032 and an r of .436 corresponds to a Z of .468. *Therefore, the 95% confidence interval around an r of .245 extends from .032 to .436.* We feel quite confident that the value of ρ, the population correlation coefficient, is between .032 and .436.

12.6
CONCLUSION

Our purpose in this chapter has been to present the theory and a portion of the practice of interval estimation. We have done so in considerable detail, because it is important that you comprehend the rationale of this highly useful inferential statistical technique. In subsequent chapters, you will come across numerous examples of the construction of confidence intervals. In each instance, some of the particulars of the calculation of the confidence interval will be different from those we have presented in this chapter. New theoretical distributions that describe the sampling distributions of some important statistics will have to be described. The solution to the important problem of placing a confidence interval around $\bar{X}$. when σ^2 is unknown will be shown. We shall also see how it is possible to place a confidence interval around the difference between two sample estimates, e.g., $\bar{X}_{.1}$ and $\bar{X}_{.2}$ (the means of two separate groups of observations on the same variable), for the purpose of estimating the difference between two parameters, e.g., μ_1 and μ_2. (This technique will provide a flexible tool for answering important questions about the superiority of one population over another.) But for almost every example presented in subsequent chapters, the basic rationale is the same. (The only exception to this will be found in Chapter 16.)

In Chapter 13 we introduce a second major branch of the subject of inferential statistics: "hypothesis testing," a statistical inferential methodology that has been widely applied in research in education and the other behavioral sciences. We shall find that it is closely related to interval estimation. In fact, though the close relationships are occasionally obscured to the eyes of the student of statistics, interval estimation and hypothesis testing are actually two sides of the same coin.

PROBLEMS AND EXERCISES

1. By using the table of random digits (Table A in Appendix A), draw a random sample of eight students from the following set of sixteen:

John	Al	Joan	Phil
Mary	Tom	Susan	Paul
Alice	Maurice	Martha	Edith
Bob	Barbara	Jack	Warren

2. In which of the following pairs of terms do the two terms in the pair stand for exactly the same thing?
   a. 1: the standard error of $\bar{X}_\cdot$; 2: the standard deviation of the random-sampling distribution of $\bar{X}_\cdot$.
   b. 1: σ_x^2/n; 2: the standard error of $\bar{X}_\cdot$.
   c. 1: the variance error of $\bar{X}_\cdot$; 2: the variance of the sampling distribution of $\bar{X}_\cdot$.
   d. 1: the population variance σ^2; 2: n times the variance error of $\bar{X}_\cdot$.
   e. 1: the mean of the sampling distribution of s_x; 2: σ_x.

3. In general, the sampling distribution of s_x^2 is positively skewed with a mean of σ_x^2 (see Fig. 12.7). Recall the relationship between the mean and median in a positively skewed distribution. Is the probability of obtaining a value of s_x^2 that exceeds σ_x^2 greater or less than .50?

4. A sample of size n is to be drawn from a population with mean 220 and variance 50. Complete the following table by calculating the variance error and standard error of $\bar{X}_\cdot$ for various sample sizes:

n	$\sigma_{\bar{X}_\cdot}^2$	$\sigma_{\bar{X}_\cdot}$
a. 2		
b. 4		
c. 8		
d. 16		
e. 32		
f. 64		
g. 1000		
h. 2000		

5. When samples of size n are drawn from a normal population with mean μ and variance σ^2, the variance error of $\bar{X}_\cdot$ is σ^2/n but the variance error of the sample median Md is $1.57\sigma^2/n$. Suppose that for a particular problem, $\mu = 100$, $\sigma^2 = 25$, and $n = 25$, and $\bar{X}_\cdot$ is used to estimate μ; the variance error of $\bar{X}_\cdot$ is $\sigma^2/n = 25/25 = 1$. If one chose to estimate μ with Md, how large a sample would have to be taken so that the variance error of Md, σ_{Md}^2, would also equal 1?

6. A sample of size n is to be drawn at random from a population with mean μ and variance σ^2. The sample size is sufficiently large that $\bar{X}_\cdot$ can be assumed to have a normal sampling distribution. Determine the probabilities with which

$\bar{X}$, will be between the following pairs of points:

a. $\mu + \sigma/\sqrt{n}$ and $\mu - \sigma/\sqrt{n}$

b. $\mu + 1.64\sigma/\sqrt{n}$ and $\mu - 1.64\sigma/\sqrt{n}$

c. $\mu + 2.58\sigma/\sqrt{n}$ and $\mu - 2.58\sigma/\sqrt{n}$

d. $\mu + 0.675\sigma/\sqrt{n}$ and $\mu - 0.675\sigma/\sqrt{n}$

e. $\mu + 3\sigma/\sqrt{n}$ and $\mu - 3\sigma/\sqrt{n}$

7. A sample of 100 persons was randomly drawn from a population with variance 16 but with an unknown mean μ. The value of $\bar{X}$, obtained was 106.75. Construct the 95% confidence interval on μ around $\bar{X}$.

8. Construct the 95% and 99% confidence intervals on p for the following cases:
a. $n = 28$, $r = +0.36$ b. $n = 12$, $r = -0.65$ c. $n = 300$, $r = +0.14$

9. Which one of the following sample statistics has the *smaller* variance over random samples of size n ("variance error")?

a. $\bar{X} = \dfrac{X_1 + \ldots + X_n}{n}$ b. $\bar{X} = \dfrac{X_1 + \ldots + X_n}{(n + 1)}$

13

STATISTICAL INFERENCE: HYPOTHESIS TESTING

13.1
INTRODUCTION

In Chapter 12 the statistical inferential technique known as interval estimation was developed for a few examples in detail. Interval estimation is just one part, though at present probably the most useful and important one, of the body of statistical inferential techniques. In this chapter we shall encounter a second statistical inferential technique: hypothesis testing. Hypothesis testing has become an almost omnipresent feature of empirical research in education and the behavioral sciences. Reported research can be read only with difficulty and partial comprehension if the reader is not trained in the theory and some of the techniques of statistical hypothesis testing. Empirical research is seldom executed in education and the behavioral sciences without the utilization of either interval estimation or, where it is appropriate, hypothesis testing. This state of affairs is partly a reflection of rigid and uncritical standards imposed by some anxious persons who administer research (as in the case of the academic adviser who demanded that his advisee use statistical inferential techniques on data from all 50 states which exhausted the population of interest) and partly—the greater part, we hope—an indication of the genuine utility and necessity for employing such techniques.

The number of new concepts to be introduced and comprehended in connection with hypothesis testing will make the discussion to follow a challenge. Fortunately, some of the concepts of interval estimation also play central roles in hypothesis testing. We shall find that the concepts of random samples, the sampling distributions of statistics, and probability values applying to statements are building blocks for hypothesis testing as well as for interval estimation. Hypothesis testing and interval estimation are carried out with different languages, but we shall see that they usually produce equivalent results or results that are easily converted from one technique to the other. The basic problem, however, remains "How does one infer properties of the population from observation of a sample?"

13.2
SCIENTIFIC AND
STATISTICAL HYPOTHESES

The history of statistical hypothesis testing began in the early eighteenth century. The earliest example of a formal statistical hypothesis test appears in a publication dated 1710 and written by John Arbuthnot (1667–1735); it is titled "An Argument for Divine Providence, Taken from the Constant Regularity Observed in the Births of Both Sexes." Noting that for 82 consecutive years the records showed a greater number of males born than females, Arbuthnot argued that the hypothesis that male and female births are equally likely (each with a probability of 1/2) was refuted by these data; for if the probability of a male birth were precisely 1/2, then the probability of 82 consecutive years in which more males than females were born would be infinitesimally small, $(1/2)^{82}$ to be exact. Arbuthnot concluded that the greater proportion of male births than female births was an act of Divine Providence; the sacred institution of monogamy was being maintained since males were more likely to be killed in war or work before reaching adulthood. Arbuthnot's statistics were unimpeachable, but his theology failed to account for polygamous societies. Like Arbuthnot, the modern researcher is much concerned with the probabilistic consequences of various hypotheses.

A researcher is interested in studying the relationship between creativity and anxiety in fifth- and sixth-grade pupils (this entire example is based on a study by Ohnmacht, 1966). His search of the literature has disclosed one group of persons believing that the creative thinker should be less anxious than the uncreative thinker and another group believing that the two characteristics are not related in any way. Our researcher has not yet joined either camp. He is undecided on this matter and intends to satisfy his curiosity with a small empirical study of his own. First he must decide how he will measure creativity and anxiety. Two tests that appear to have some validity for measuring the two characteristics are found: Getzels and Jackson's test "Uses of Things" is taken as a measure of creativity, and the "Children's Manifest Anxiety Scale" by Castenada, McCandless, and Palermo is taken as the measure of anxiety. There are over 20,000 fifth- and sixth-grade pupils available for study, but the resources available to our researcher make it possible for him to observe only about 200 of them. Being an excellent student of statistics, our researcher plans to draw a random sample of 200 pupils from the population of 20,000 so that he can draw statistical inferential conclusions about the population based on his sample observations. Each of the 200 pupils in the sample will be given the Uses of Things test and the Children's Manifest Anxiety Scale. The sample product-moment correlation coefficient between the measure of creativity and the measure of anxiety will be computed. Our researcher could proceed to establish a confidence interval around this sample r by the techniques outlined in Sec. 12.5. However, he has been trained in a somewhat different school of statistical thought, one in which *decisions* are paramount; this being so, he proceeds differently.

The *decision* that the researcher will supposedly make is a decision about the truth or falsity of a statistical hypothesis. There are at least two types of hypotheses it would be well to identify and distinguish: *scientific hypotheses* and *statistical hypotheses*. A *scientific hypothesis* is a suggested solution to a problem. It is an intelligent, informed, and educated guess. A scientific hypothesis is generally stated as a proposition. "It is an empirical proposition in the sense that it is testable by experience; experience is relevant to the question as to whether or not the hypothesis is true. . ." (Braithwaite, 1953). The formulation of a good scientific hypothesis is truly a creative act. On the other hand, a *statistical hypothesis* is merely a statement about an unknown parameter. For the next few pages we shall use H: (statement) to denote a statistical hypothesis. "$H: \mu = 125$" is a statistical hypothesis; it is an assertion that the unknown mean of a particular population is 125. Clearly, such a statement is either true or false. The decision "$H: \mu = 125$ is false" is an example of the type of decision with which hypothesis testing is concerned. "$H: \rho = 0$, where ρ is the correlation coefficient in a bivariate normal distribution," is another example of a statistical hypothesis. "$H: \sigma_1^2 = \sigma_2^2$" is a statistical hypothesis stating that the variances of populations 1 and 2 are equal. How would you denote the hypothesis that the means of populations 1, 2, and 3 are all equal to each other?

It is important to distinguish scientific and statistical hypotheses. It is quite possible to test statistical hypotheses about very mundane matters that possess limited generality and not a whit of scientific importance. For example, the question of whether School District 108 has a greater pro- portion of pupils taking "milk lunch" than School District 214 might correctly be stated and tested as a statistical hypothesis; however, it is difficult to imagine that the outcome of the investigation could be of much scientific importance. It is increasingly apparent that many researchers are under the impression that, since a major activity of science is formulating and empirically testing hypotheses (scientific ones), they are engaged in a scientific activity because they are testing hypotheses (statistical ones). This is not necessarily true. Not all scientific hypotheses need to be tested statistically; and by no means are all statistical hypotheses of scientific interest. Edu- cational researchers and others should realize that stating and testing a statistical hypothesis does not automatically make their work scientific. A good scientific hypothesis is the result of creative and, at times, inspired thought, whereas a statistical hypothesis is often just a standardized ex- pression of one step in the empirical testing of a scientific hypothesis.

A psychologist studying the relationship between anxiety and creativity in children might have reasoned on the basis of experience and previous research that there should be a negative relationship between measures of anxiety and creativity. That is, high scorers on the creativity test Uses of Things should be low scorers on the Children's Manifest Anxiety Scale, and low scorers on the Uses of Things should be high scorers on the CMAS. He may conceptualize creativity as an ability or perhaps an inclination that strives to find expression in work and play. Any inhibition of the expression of a child's creativity is likely to frustrate the child, and the frustration of this impulse may manifest itself as anxiety, he might suppose. Now this is not a very daring hypothesis—it is full of loopholes through which the psychologist can easily escape if challenged—but it is a crude example of a scientific hypothesis. We shall contrast it with the statistical hypothesis our researcher will test.

13.3
TESTING A STATISTICAL
HYPOTHESIS

The researcher has drawn a random sample for the purpose of investigating the relationship between two variables in a population. Aware that at this point it is a mathematical necessity, he *assumes* (note that we did *not* say that he *hypothesizes*) that his sample is a random sample of size 200 from a virtually infinite population in which the data for anxiety and creativity have a *bivariate normal distribution*. This is an assumption he will probably not test explicitly even though he could if he so chose. The interest of the re- searcher centers on ρ, the product-moment correlation between the anxiety and creativity tests in the population he sampled. Being an inveterate hypothesis tester, he views the statistical inferential problem of reasoning from the sample and r to the population and ρ as one of *making a decision about a hypothesis that asserts ρ is a particular number*. Partly out of habit, partly because of tradition, and partly because it is a sensible choice, this researcher establishes the hypothesis he wishes to test as $H: \rho = 0$, i.e., that the correlation between creativity and anxiety in the population is zero. *This is his statistical hypothesis*. On the basis of the observations he will make on a random sample of 200 pupils from the population, he will *decide* to accept his hypothesis as true or reject it as false. The techniques he will use to make a decision about the truth of the statistical hypothesis comprise what is called the *hypothesis test*.

What constitutes a legitimate and rational test of the hypothesis $H: \rho = 0$ in this situation? Should the researcher compute r for his sample of 200 and decide that H is true if r is zero and decide that H is false if r is not zero? Obviously not; we know too much about the erratic behavior of sample estimates to agree to such a plan. It is quite possible for ρ to equal 0 in the population and for r to be substantially different from 0 in a sample of 200. In fact, it is not even an *impossibility* that a sample of 200 from a population with $\rho = 0$ will yield an r of $+1$ or -1! It is extremely improbable, but it is certainly possible. This presents a perplexing problem. Even if $\rho = 0$ in the population, any value of r from -1 to $+1$ is a "possibility" in a random sample of 200. Consequently, regardless of the value of r for the sample of 200, the researcher cannot *with certainty* conclude that ρ is or is not zero. This is an important principle that underlies all tests of statistical hypotheses, and we shall restate it: *In testing any statistical hypothesis the researcher's decision that the hypothesis is true or that it is false is never made with certainty; he always runs a risk of making an incorrect decision*. The essence of statistical hypothesis testing is that it is a means of controlling and assessing that risk. As we elaborate the example introduced, we shall learn the rationale of controlling and assessing the risk of deciding incorrectly about the truth of a hypothesis.

The next step after stating the hypothesis to be tested is to draw a sample from the population and make the observations that will reflect on the hypothesis. The researcher has drawn a random sample of 200 pupils, measured them on both the anxiety and creativity tests, and correlated the scores. The value of r for the sample was $+.09$.

The uncertainty in making a decision about $H: \rho = 0$ arises from the phenomenon of sampling fluctuation, usually called *sampling error*. This is not a new idea to us in this text. Our entire discussion of inferential statistics has been concerned with the problem of how to handle estimation of a parameter by a sample value that is almost certainly in error to a greater or lesser degree. As before, we attack the inferential problems of hypothesis testing with the concept of a sampling distribution.

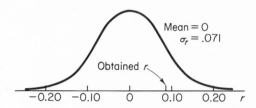

FIG. 13.1 Sampling distribution of r for samples of size 200 from a bivariate normal population with $\rho = 0$.

After stating the hypothesis, one must determine the sampling distribution of the estimator of the parameter about which the hypothesis is made. Furthermore, *one finds that sampling distribution that would result if the hypothesis being tested were true.* In our example, we must determine the sampling distribution of r for random samples of size 200 from a bivariate normal population in which $\rho = 0$. Fortunately, this has been done before and the result is a convenient one. The sampling distribution of r for samples of size 200 under these circumstances is nearly normal, with mean 0 and standard deviation $1/\sqrt{200 - 1} = .071$.

Figure 13.1 is the sampling distribution of r when the hypothesis $H: \rho = 0$ is true. This sampling distribution, when considered in connection with the actual sample r obtained ($r = .090$), will throw light on the possibility that the hypothesis being tested is true.

We have given up any hope of making either of the decisions "H is true" or "H is false" with certainty. Such certainty is not possible without knowing the entire bivariate population. Instead we must ask the question, "Is the decision 'H is true' plausible after observing an r of .09?" An equivalent question is "Is it reasonable to expect a value of r as deviant from zero as .09 when H is true?" If "yes" is the answer to these questions, then the researcher will decide to accept the hypothesis being tested; if "no" is the answer to the questions, H is rejected. But how do we give exact meaning to "plausible" and "reasonable"? This is an arbitrary matter. Suppose that in a certain locale it rains on 90% of the days. Is it "reasonable" to wake up one morning and announce for no reason whatsoever that today it will rain? Yes, it probably is. If on the other hand it rains on only 10% of the days, it is not very reasonable to go around saying it will rain every day. Ninety per cent makes it plausible to predict rain every day; 10% makes it implausible. These are crude definitions of "plausible" and "reasonable," but the arbitrary logic differs little from that which the statistician uses when he says it is unreasonable to assert at random that "today it will rain" if it rains only on 10%, 5%, or 1% of the days.

Suppose we agree that if an event has a probability of .05 of occurring at random it would be unreasonable or implausible to expect it to occur on the single trial of the event which you observe. We could have chosen the probability of .10 or .01 or .001. Our choice of .05 was arbitrary. It begins

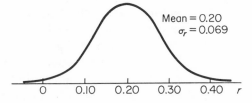

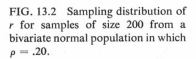

FIG. 13.2 Sampling distribution of r for samples of size 200 from a bivariate normal population in which $\rho = .20$.

to become *reasonable* to expect to observe an event on a single trial when the probability of the event increases above .10, say.

If the hypothesis being tested, $H: \rho = 0$, is false, then ρ is either greater or less than 0. If ρ is not zero, we would *expect* to obtain a sample r which is somewhat above or somewhat below the major portion of the distribution in Fig. 13.1. For example, if ρ is .20, the sampling distribution in Fig. 13.2 would result from repeated sampling of the population.

Consequently if $H: \rho = 0$ is true, the sampling distribution in Fig. 13.1 will hold. If $H: \rho = 0$ is false, the distribution of r will lie generally higher on the scale, if ρ is above 0, or generally lower on the scale, if ρ is below 0, than the distribution in Fig. 13.1. Hence, a very large value of r, e.g., $r = .50$, is an unlikely event if the hypothesis $H: \rho = 0$ is true, but it is much more likely to happen if ρ is above zero, e.g., if $\rho = .40$ or .59. Similarly, a very small value of r, e.g., $r = -.60$, is unlikely to occur if $\rho = 0$ and somewhat more likely to occur if ρ is below zero. For these reasons, the values of r that make the truth of $H: \rho = 0$ unlikely or implausible lie to the right of some point above zero and to the left of some point below zero in Fig. 13.1. Now we want to determine some such points exactly.

The standard deviation σ_r of the distribution in Fig. 13.1 is .071; thus, the probability that a value in the distribution exceeds $(1.96)\sigma_r = .140$ is .025. The probability that a value is below $-.140$ is also .025. Therefore, the probability is .05 that a value sampled from the distribution in Fig. 13.1

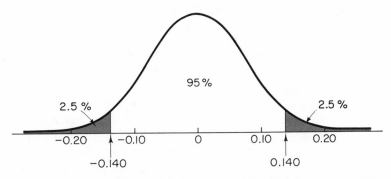

FIG. 13.3 Sampling distribution in Fig. 13.1 with the extreme 5% (2.5% in each tail) of the area under the curve shaded.

will lie above .140 or below —.140. In less precise terms, it is unlikely to expect a value of r greater than .140 or less than —.140 to be sampled from the distribution in Fig. 13.3.

In repeated random samples of size 200 from a population in which $\rho = 0$, a value of r above .140 or below —.140 will occur one time in twenty samples on the average, i.e., the probability is .05 that a random sample will produce an r greater than .140 or less than —.140. When we consider jointly the decisions our researcher can make about the hypothesis and the possible outcomes of selecting a sample and computing r, we find that there are four possibilities. Two possible decisions (after observing the data) are reasonable, and the other two are unreasonable, as the accompanying table shows.

	The sample produced an r which was	
	Between −0.140 and 0.140	Above 0.140 or below −0.140
The researcher decided that — *H* was true	The researcher's decision was reasonable	The researcher's decision was unreasonable
H was false	The researcher's decision was unreasonable	The researcher's decision was reasonable

Let us see what is implied when a researcher decides $H: \rho = 0$ is true after an r on a sample of 200 is observed that lies either above .140 or below —.140. In the table we have called such a decision in the light of such evidence "unreasonable." Why is it "unreasonable"? The decision is unreasonable because values of r deviating from 0 by more than .140 are not normally to be expected—they will occur in only 5% of all possible random samples—when $H: \rho = 0$ is true. If one continues to maintain that the hypothesis $H: \rho = 0$ is true after observing an r of .30 for a sample of 200, he is forced to admit that the event observed, namely an r of .30 or larger, is relatively rare. Naturally we expect to observe likely events, even though unlikely ones do occur. But common sense tells us to expect likely events and not unlikely ones. Consequently, if we are forced to acknowledge an event as unlikely in order to decide that $H: \rho = 0$ is true, we find it far more reasonable to alter our decision. A more reasonable decision is that $H: \rho = 0$ is false; for only values of ρ other than 0 make it reasonable to expect a sample r either below —.140 or above .140.

Consequently, *the reasonable action is to decide H: $\rho = 0$ is true if r for a sample of 200 lies between —.140 and .140, and to decide H: $\rho = 0$ is false if r lies below —.140 or above .140.* We call this our *decision rule.*

Will our decision rule ever lead us into error? Most certainly, the possibility of making an incorrect decision with this rule does exist. The heart of the problem of hypothesis testing is the formulation of such decision rules and the assessment of the probability that they will lead us into error.

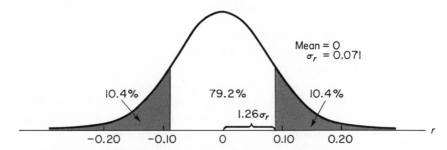

FIG. 13.4   Representation of the area in the sampling distribution of r for samples of 200 when $\rho = 0$ which lies more than 1.26 standard deviation units from the mean.

Suppose that in fact, but unknown to us, ρ is exactly 0. We have agreed to decide that $H: \rho = 0$ is false whenever an r outside the interval $-.140$ to $.140$ is obtained. In what percentage of an infinite number of random samples of size 200 will an r deviating from 0 by at least .140 be obtained when ρ is actually 0? In exactly 5% of the samples. Consequently, if $H: \rho = 0$ is true, the decision rule we adopted would cause us to decide that $H: \rho = 0$ was false in 5% of the samples—or with probability .05—when in fact the hypothesis was true.

The researcher investigating the relationship between creativity and anxiety found a correlation of .090 between the Uses of Things test and the Children's Manifest Anxiety Scale in a random sample of size 200. This value of r lies 1.26 standard-deviation units $(.090/.071 = 1.26)$ above 0. If $H: \rho = 0$ is true, our researcher has drawn an r which lies 1.26 standard deviations from the mean of the sampling distribution of r (see Fig. 13.4). How often would one expect to obtain an r for a sample of 200 that lies 1.26 standard deviations above or below the mean of this normal distribution? From Table B in Appendix A we see that 20.8% of the area under a normal curve lies more than 1.26 standard-deviation units from the mean. Therefore, a value of r deviating from 0 by at least .090 is to be expected in over 20% of the samples of size 200 from a population in which $\rho = 0$. It is not un- likely, then, to obtain an r of .090 from a population with $\rho = 0$. Conse- quently it would be unreasonable to conclude that $H: \rho = 0$ was false on the basis of an r of .090 in a sample of 200.

13.4
TYPE I ERROR, LEVEL OF SIGNIFICANCE, AND CRITICAL REGION

In this section we shall summarize the points made in the preceding section and give the conventional names for many of the concepts presented there.

From the discussion in Sec. 13.3 we shall reconstruct four steps:

Step 1: A hypothesis to be tested is stated. In our example that hypothesis was H: $\rho = 0$. It has long been customary to call the hypothesis to be tested the *null hypothesis*. This convention arises from the fact that statistical hypothesis testing procedures arose within a philosophy of science that conceived of its role as gathering evidence in attempts to *nullify* hypotheses. We shall not use the term "null hypothesis" until later in this chapter, when it will be necessary to distinguish between different hypotheses.

Step 2: Assumptions are made that are necessary for determining the sampling distribution of the statistic that estimates the parameter about which something is hypothesized. The sampling distribution of this statistic is determined for the case in which the hypothesis of step 1 is true.

Step 3: A degree of risk of incorrectly concluding on the basis of sample evidence that H is false is adopted. This risk, stated as a probability, is denoted by α and is called the *level of significance* of the hypothesis test (or, occasionally, the "size" of the test). This usage has made "significance test" synonymous with "hypothesis test." From the risk adopted, a set of values of the sample statistic is determined that will lead one to decide H is false if the sample yields such a value. This set of values is called the *critical region*.

For example, in the illustration in Sec. 13.3 it was decided that a risk of .05 was acceptable. In other words, since no decision about ρ could be made with certainty, it was considered acceptable to make the probability equal to .05 of deciding H: $\rho = 0$ was false when in fact it was true. The *level of significance* α of the hypothesis test was thus taken to be .05.

By determining the point (.140) above which and the point ($-.140$) below which 2.5% of the r's in repeated samples of size 200 from a population with $\rho = 0$ would fall, we found the two regions of "unlikely r's given a true hypothesis H: $\rho = 0$." These two regions, which constitute the most unlikely 5%

of the sample r's one could obtain by sampling from a population with $\rho = 0$, are the *critical regions*. The critical regions for the illustration in Sec. 13.3 are indicated in Figure 13.3. One portion of the critical region lies from .140 to $+1.00$, and the second portion lies from $-.140$ to -1.00. A critical region is sometimes called a *region of rejection* because the occurrence of a sample value that lies in the critical region leads one to *reject* the hypothesis $H: \rho = 0$.

Step 4: A single sample is drawn from the population, the value of a statistic is observed, and a decision about the truth of H is made. This is the final step in the testing of the hypothesis stated in step 1.

The sample data must lead us to make one of two decisions about H: "H is true" or "H is false." The former decision is spoken of as "accepting H," the latter as "rejecting H." From any sample it can never be concluded with certainty that $H: \rho = 0$ is true or false; the best one can do is to make a decision about H that has a high probability of being true.

If H is true and our sample leads us to accept H, a correct decision is made. If H is true and our sample leads us to reject H, an incorrect decision is made. Such an incorrect decision is called a *type I error* or *error of the first kind*. (Later we shall meet a type II error.) A type I error is made when a true hypothesis H is rejected. It is, of course, impossible for a person to know whether his decision to reject H is correct or a type I error. To know this, it is necessary to know whether H is true or false; but if the truth is known about H, there is no need for inferential statistics. At best, one knows the probability—or proportion of times in the long run—of making a correct decision or a type I error.

In the hypothesis test of $H: \rho = 0$, a decision process was set up that would cause one to reject H erroneously five times in 100—or with probability .05—in a long series of similar hypothesis-testing situations if H were true. Hence, it is known that if H were true a type I error would occur with probability .05 if any sample r outside the interval $-.140$ to .140 was regarded as evidence that $H: \rho = 0$ was false. If H is indeed true, what would be the probability of making a correct decision about it, i.e., accepting it? Since under these circumstances 95% of the r's for samples of size 200 will fall between $-.140$ and .140, the probability of accepting H when it is true is .95.

The size of the probability of a type I error can be controlled. We shall denote the probability of a type I error for any unspecified hypothesis-testing situation by α. In the test of $H: \rho = 0$, α was set equal to .05. We can make α equal to such values as .20, .10, .01, .001, or even .125, if we choose.

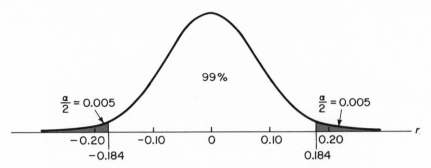

FIG. 13.5 The critical region for testing the hypothesis that $\rho = 0$ with an α of .01($n = 200$).

Since α stands for the probability of making a certain type of incorrect decision, we would prefer to keep it small. It would probably rarely be acceptable to decide to accept or reject H with a plan that would commit a type I error with probability much greater than .10, i.e., with α greater than .10. It is customary to let α equal .05, .01, or .001. We shall now see how we could have tested H: $\rho = 0$ with an α of .01.

If $\rho = 0$, then the distribution of r for samples of size 200 is approximately normal with mean 0 and standard deviation .071, as we saw before. Both "large" and "small" values of r will cause us to question the truth of the assertion that $\rho = 0$. So that we shall run a risk of exactly .01 of rejecting H: $\rho = 0$ if it is true, we must determine the two numbers between -1 and $+1$ that are exceeded by only 1% of the sampling distribution of r when $\rho = 0$. These two halves of the critical region are depicted in Fig. 13.5.

It can be determined from the table of the unit normal distribution that the probability is .005 that a normally distributed variable will lie more than 2.58 standard deviations *above* the mean. Similarly, the probability is .005 that a normally distributed variable will lie more than 2.58 standard deviations *below* the mean. Hence, if we establish the critical region from $(2.58)(.071) = .184$ to 1.00 and from -1.00 to $(-2.58)(.071) = -.184$, we shall have a probability of only .01 of rejecting H: $\rho = 0$ if it is true.

It might be instructive to some who read this to see the above argument in its mathematical form. If H: $\rho = 0$ is true, then

$$\frac{r - 0}{\sigma_r} = \frac{r}{.071} \sim N(0, 1),$$

where "$\sim N(0, 1)$" means "is distributed normally, with population mean 0 and population variance 1." Therefore,

$$\text{prob}\left(-2.58 < \frac{r}{.071} < 2.58\right) = .99.$$

Multiplying the inequality in parentheses by .071 gives the following expression:

$$\text{prob}(-.184 < r < .184) = .99.$$

Consequently, if the correlation coefficient for a sample of size 200 from a bivariate normal distribution is above .184 or below $-.184$, the null hypothesis $H: \rho = 0$ can be rejected at the .01 level of significance. Suppose that for a sample of size 200, the value of r is .340. The obvious decision can be stated in several equivalent ways:

1. "Reject $H: \rho = 0$ at the .01 level of significance."
2. "Reject $H: \rho = 0$ with an α of .01."
3. "Reject $H: \rho = 0$ at the 1% level of significance."
4. "Reject $H: \rho = 0$ with a probability of .01 of making a type I error."

The importance of the assumption that the sample comes from a bivariate normal distribution has been investigated by various researchers: Norris and Hjelm (1961), Nefzger and Drasgow (1957), Binder (1959), Furfey (1958), LaForge (1958), and Milholland (1958). If you read one of these references, you would be well advised to read them all since no single reference on this topic presents a balanced picture.

13.5
TYPE II ERROR, β, AND POWER

Quite literally, so far in this chapter we have related only half the story of statistical hypothesis testing. In this section, we shall present the rest of our account.

The standard technique for testing the hypothesis $H: \rho = 0$ is to select a level of significance α, determine the critical values of r or $z = (r - 0)/\sigma_r$ (whichever you wish), draw a sample and compute r, and then accept or reject H. In the previous section, we showed how to measure the probability that H would be rejected when it was in fact true, i.e., the probability of a type I error. It was acknowledged that the decision "H is false" could be incorrect. Now we acknowledge that the decision to accept H, i.e., to conclude that "H is true," could also be incorrect. In other words, we could falsely accept H, e.g., conclude that $\rho = 0$ when in fact $\rho = .20$. The error of accepting a false H is termed an *error of the second kind* or a *type II error*. Having acknowledged the possibility of committing a type II error, we now proceed to a discussion of the techniques for measuring the probability of an error of the second kind.

If the hypothesis H: $\rho = 0$ is false, some other hypothesis—an *alternative* hypothesis—about the value of ρ must be true. We shall now make use of the term *null hypothesis* for the original hypothesis $\rho = 0$ and the term *alternative hypothesis* to describe some other hypothesis we could make about the value of ρ, e.g., that $\rho = .20$. Henceforth, *the null hypothesis will be denoted by H_0 and the alternative hypothesis by H_1.* We can seldom specify a single alternative value of the parameter. Generally (though not always) the alternative hypothesis is *composite*, i.e., it specifies many possible values of the parameter, instead of *simple*, like the null hypothesis, in which a single value is hypothesized. The following illustrate a simple null hypothesis and a composite alternative:

$$\text{null hypothesis:} \quad H_0: \rho = 0;$$

$$\text{alternative hypothesis:} \quad H_1: \rho \neq 0.$$

In the theory of hypothesis testing, it is held that one of two "states of nature" may exist: either H_0 is true or H_1 is true; and it is agreed that after inspecting a sample, one of two decisions will be reached: H_0 will be accepted (hence, H_1 is rejected), or H_1 will be accepted (hence, H_0 is rejected). The four possible combinations of these states of nature and decisions are illustrated here along with a description of the validity of the decision.

		State of nature	
		H_0 is true	H_1 is true
	Reject H_0	Type I error	Correct decision
	(Accept H_1)	(Probability $= \alpha$)	(Probability $= 1 - \beta$)
Decision			
	Reject H_1	Correct decision	Type II error
	(Accept H_0)	(Probability $= 1 - \alpha$)	(Probability $= \beta$)

We have adopted the convention of calling the probability of committing a type I error α. *The probability of committing a type II error, i.e., of accepting H_0 when H_1 is true, will be denoted by β.* We will now look at an example of how β would be calculated.

Suppose that an investigator wishes to test the null hypothesis H_0: $\rho = 0$. Also assume that the investigator has no particular reason to suppose that ρ is any more likely to be one nonzero value than any other. He can afford to draw a sample of $n = 200$ persons and it is reasonable to assume that the variables observed have a bivariate normal distribution. Furthermore, he wishes to risk rejecting H_0: $\rho = 0$ when it is true only five times per 100; hence, $\alpha = .05$.

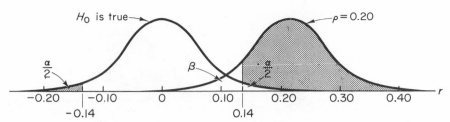

FIG. 13.6   Illustration of the power of the test of H_0: $\rho = 0$ against H_1: $\rho \neq 0$ for the case in which $\rho = .20$ ($n = 200$ and $\alpha = .05$).

The investigator would establish critical regions of r that lead to the rejection of H_0 as was done in Fig. 13.3. A sample r of .140 or larger or $-.140$ or smaller would be taken as evidence of the falsity of H_0. We know, then, that if ρ is actually zero, there is one chance in twenty ($\alpha = .05$) that the investigator will reject H_0.

However, what if ρ is really .20? In this case, H_0: $\rho = 0$ should be rejected in favor of the conclusion that ρ is different from zero. But what is the probability that H_0 will be rejected? This probability is the power of the test $\rho = .20$, and is depicted by the shaded area in Fig. 13.6.

The upper critical region for r is all values from .140 to 1.00. Hence, the power of the hypothesis test to reject H_0 when $\rho = .20$ is the area above .140 under the curve that represents the sampling distribution of r for samples of size 200 when $\rho = .20$. This area is approximately 82% of the total area under the curve on the right in Fig. 13.6. Thus the power is approximately .82. [Actually there also exists an infinitesimal chance that H_0 will be rejected in favor of H_1 when $\rho = .20$ due to a sample r below $-.140$! We disregard this improbability here; however, see Kaiser (1960).] The area under the curve on the right in Fig. 13.6 (the sampling distribution of r when $\rho = .20$) *below* .140 is a measure of the probability that r will fail to exceed the critical value even though H_0 is false; this area measures β, the probability of a type II error. The area in question is about 18% of the total area under the curve. Hence, β is approximately .18. Since if ρ is actually .20 we must either commit a type II error or not, the probability of not committing the error, i.e., the power of the test, is given by $1 - \beta = .82$. Now try to convince yourself that if ρ were equal to $-.20$, the same hypothesis-testing procedure would run the same risk of a type II error and have the same power, .82, as when $\rho = .20$.

It will further extend the notions being developed here if we determine the power of the test of H_0: $\rho = 0$ with $\alpha = .05$ and $n = 200$ when $\rho = .10$ instead of .20. The critical regions of the test remain the same: -1.00 to $-.140$ and .140 to 1.00. The sampling distribution of r for samples of size 200 is unchanged from previous discussions, and it appears along with the sampling distribution of r for $n = 200$ when $\rho = .10$ in Fig. 13.7.

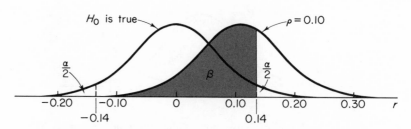

FIG. 13.7   Illustration of the power of the test of H_0: $\rho = 0$ against H_1: $\rho \neq 0$ for the case in which $\rho = .10$ ($n = 200$ and $\alpha = .05$).

Suppose one had chosen to test H_0: $\rho = 0$ against H_1: $\rho \neq 0$ with an α of .10 and a sample of 200 paired observations. By referring to Fig. 13.6, try to determine whether the power of this test is greater or less than the test with $\alpha = .05$ when $\rho = .20$.

From an exact measure of the area under the curve on the right above the critical value of .140 in Fig. 13.7 it can be shown that the power of the test of H_0: $\rho = 0$ when $\rho = .10$ is .29. Of course it follows that $\beta = .71$.

It seems almost never to be the case in research in education and psychology that the power of a hypothesis test for just one or two alternative values of the parameter is sufficient information. Generally one would want to determine the power of the test for several alternative values of the parameter, graph these values of the power against the values of the parameter, and then connect the points with a smooth line. The resulting curve provides an adequate determination of the power of the test against all alternative values of the parameter. The *power curve* for the test of H_0: $\rho = 0$ against H_1: $\rho \neq 0$ for $n = 200$ and $\alpha = .05$ appears as Fig. 13.8.

Note in Fig. 13.8 that the values of the power for $\rho = \pm.20$ and $\rho = \pm.10$ are .82 and .29, respectively, as they were calculated to be in Figs. 13.6 and 13.7. Notice also that the "power" is .05 when $\rho = 0$; that is, if H_0 is true, there is a probability equal to the level of significance of rejecting H_0 in favor of H_1.

It is apparent in Fig. 13.8 that the power of the test increases toward 1 as the value of ρ departs from 0. This is comforting to know, but it is a contingency not under the control of the investigator since he does not "set" the true value of ρ. However, the sample size n and the level of significance α *are* under his control, relatively speaking at least. For any given value of ρ other than zero, *the power of the test of H_0: $\rho = 0$ increases as n is increased* (e.g., from 10 to 100) *and also increases as α is increased* (from .01 to .05, say).

The following can be said about hypothesis-testing procedures in general:

1. For a given value of the parameter being tested, e.g., $\rho = .40$, the power of the test of H_0 increases as n, the sample size, increases.

2. For a given value of the parameter being tested, e.g., $\rho = .40$, the power of the test of H_0 increases as α, the probability of rejecting a true null hypothesis, increases, e.g., from .01 to .05.

These two relationships are quite important since to some extent α and n can be controlled by the investigator. It might be advisable in some circumstances to run a risk of a type I error as large as .10, i.e., $\alpha = .10$, to insure a reasonable power for a test. The third relationship we shall state is much less under the control of the investigator:

3. For fixed values of α and n, the power of the test of H_0 increases as the true value of the parameter being tested deviates further from the value hypothesized for it in H_0. For example, if $n = 100$ and $\alpha = .01$, the power of the test of H_0: $\rho = 0$ is greater when ρ actually equals .60 than when ρ equals .40 or $-.40$.

The popular notion among practicing researchers is that the statistician is a man who tells them "how large a sample to take." Presumably he derives this decision about sample size from studying cost per observation, costs of committing type I and type II errors, and the power of the test for different sample sizes and particular alternative values of the parameter about which a hypothesis is to be tested. The theory—known as the *Neyman-Pearson hypothesis-testing theory*—that gave us the notions of type II errors and power is very accommodating when these costs and specific alternative values of the parameter can be specified. However, in research in education and the social sciences it is rare that they can be specified with any confidence. We suspect that most statisticians consulting with researchers in these disciplines have had experiences similar to ours. We usually find ourselves advising

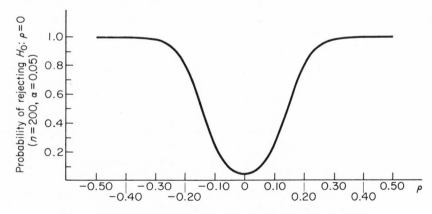

FIG. 13.8 Power curve for the test of H_0: $\rho = 0$ against H_1: $\rho \neq 0$ for $n = 200$ and $\alpha = .05$.

persons to draw the largest sample they can afford to take; then we determine whether the sample size they tell us they are capable of taking is unnecessarily large! If they can take a sample so large that the power of their test of H_0 is .97, say, even when the true value of the parameter is only slightly different from the value specified in H_0, then they can be safely advised not to draw such a wastefully large sample. It may well be true that the power of their test would drop to only .90 if they took a sample half as large as the largest possible sample. If so, we would not hesitate to advise them to reduce the size of their sample. Thus, as our inquiries in education and the social sciences are presently constituted, the concept of the power of a test is more useful as a signal that too large a sample may be drawn than it is useful as the "determiner of sample size."

13.6
NONDIRECTIONAL AND DIRECTIONAL ALTERNATIVES: "TWO-TAILED VS. ONE-TAILED TESTS"

An alternative hypothesis, H_1, can be designated as either *nondirectional* or *directional*. The alternative H_1: $\rho \neq 0$ is nondirectional in that it states only that ρ is not equal to zero and not in which direction (above or below) it deviates from zero. Consider the pair of hypotheses H_0: $\rho = 0$ and H_1: $\rho > 0$. In this instance, the alternative hypothesis is directional; it is maintained by the investigator stating this pair of hypotheses that either ρ equals zero or else it is greater than zero. The investigator believes that ρ could not possibly be less than zero; he will gather evidence that will either convince him ρ is positive or that will lead him to continue to believe ρ is zero.

One consequence of stating the directional alternative H_1: $\rho > 0$ to the null hypothesis is that now the critical region for rejection of H_0 in favor of H_1 is that value of r exceeded by $100(\alpha)\%$ of the area in the sampling distribution of r when $\rho = 0$. In other words, only large positive values of r will lead one to decide in favor of H_1 over H_0; hence the critical region for rejection of H_0 is in the right-hand tail of the sampling distribution of r for $\rho = 0$, as indicated in Fig. 13.9. In Fig. 13.9 the critical region extends from .117 to 1.00.

A very small value of r, say $-.40$, certainly does not favor the hypothesis that $\rho > 0$ over the hypothesis that $\rho = 0$. Since only the two conditions $\rho = 0$ or $\rho > 0$ are covered by the hypotheses, an r of $-.40$ would imply the truth of H_0 more than of H_1, even though it would be an extremely unlikely occurrence in a sample of $n = 200$ if ρ were zero. But such are the vagaries of directional hypothesis tests.

The fact that the critical region "lies in *one tail*" of the sampling dis-

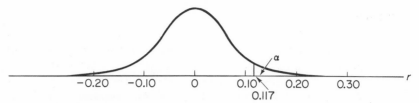

FIG. 13.9 Illustration of critical region for testing H_0: $\rho = 0$ against H_1: $\rho > 0$ for $n = 200$ and $\alpha = .05$.

tribution of the statistic under the null hypothesis has made popular the phrase *one-tailed test* for a significance test of a directional hypothesis. This usage is somewhat ambiguous and potentially misleading. The important distinction is between nondirectional and directional alternative hypotheses; whether a test statistic has grown out of the history of statistics in such a manner that one or two tails of a sampling distribution lie above the critical values of a statistic is quite arbitrary. We shall see in Chapter 15, for example, that a nondirectional hypothesis about a set of population means is tested by referring a test statistic to one tail of the F-distribution.

One sometimes reads that the hypotheses tested in a directional situation are H_0: $\rho \leqslant 0$ against H_1: $\rho > 0$. It is then maintained that sufficiently large sample r's favor H_1, and small or large negative r's favor H_0. Actually, logic does not support this particular statement of H_0 and H_1. H_0 must assert that $\rho = 0$, not that $\rho \leqslant 0$. Anything else leads to some interesting inconsistencies. Note that H_0: $\rho \geqslant 0$ and H_1: $\rho < 0$ are every bit as acceptable as H_0: $\rho \leqslant 0$ and H_1: $\rho > 0$. However, for fixed n and α, the probability of deciding in favor of H_0: $\rho \geqslant 0$ when ρ is actually .10 is far greater than the probability of deciding in favor of H_1: $\rho > 0$. It is indeed an unacceptable state of affairs when the power of a test to decide that ρ is above zero when ρ is .10 depends greatly on the arbitrary choice between H_0: $\rho \geqslant 0$, H_1: $\rho < 0$, or H_0: $\rho \leqslant 0$, H_1: $\rho > 0$. (See Rozeboom, 1960.)

A debate over the merits of testing directional versus nondirectional hypotheses in research in the behavioral sciences raged for a few years in the 1950's and 1960's. We shall not take the space to recapitulate the issues here. You will find the major issues presented in the following references: Burke (1953, 1954); Goldfried (1959); Hick (1952); Jones (1952, 1954); Kimmel (1957); Marks (1951, 1953); and Peizer (1967).

Our impression is that the potential for misusing directional hypothesis tests is great. To be perfectly legitimate, for example, one who hypothesizes that $\rho = 0$ against $\rho > 0$ must look the other way and refuse to budge from the belief that ρ is zero even if a sample of 1000 yields an r of $-.99$. We do not trust ourselves to be quite that orthodox, and we would not be astonished to observe others yielding to temptation.

13.7
POSTSCRIPT

Among recent attempts to clear away the practicing researcher's confusions about statistical hypothesis testing, the most successful in our opinion is William Kruskal's contribution to the *International Encyclopedia of the Social Sciences* (1968) entitled "Tests of Significance." You could probably profitably read Kruskal's article when you have finished studying this chapter and Chapter 14. Also see Nunnally (1960), Grant (1962), and Wilson and Miller (1964).

PROBLEMS AND EXERCISES

1. Give definitions of each of the following:
   a. Null hypothesis, H_0.
   b. Alternative hypothesis, H_1.
   c. Type I error.
   d. Type II error.
   e. Level of significance, α.
   f. Power of a test, $1 - \beta$.
   g. Critical region.

2. In which of the following instances can $H_0: \rho = 0$ be rejected with certainty, i.e., in which instances is the reported sample r an impossibility given that ρ is zero?
   a. $n = 10, r = .60$
   b. $n = 100, r = 1.00$
   c. $n = 1000, r = .50$

3. In each of the following instances, indicate whether a type I error, a type II error, or no error was committed by the researcher:

H_0	H_1	True value of ρ	Researcher's decision based on r
a. $\rho = 0$	$\rho \neq 0$	0	Reject H_0
b. $\rho = 0$	$\rho \neq 0$	.40	Reject H_0
c. $\rho = 0$	$\rho \neq 0$	0	Do not reject H_0
d. $\rho = 0$	$\rho \neq 0$	$-.50$	Do not reject H_0

4. The hypotheses $H_0: \rho = 0$ and $H_1: \rho \neq 0$ were tested with a sample of $n = 50$ at the .01 level of significance. The sample r was sufficiently large that H_0 was rejected in favor of H_1. What is the probability that a type II error was committed? (Hint: Can one commit a type II error when one rejects H_0?)

5. A researcher draws a sample of $n = 200$ paired observations from a bivariate normal distribution. He reasons correctly that if $\rho = 0$, then r will be distributed approximately normally with a mean of zero and a standard deviation of .071. Further, he decides to reject H_0: $\rho = 0$ if r is above .10 or below $-.10$. What is the probability that he will commit a type I error? (Hint: What percent of the area under a normal curve with mean zero and standard deviation .071 lies above .10 and below $-.10$?)

6. In each of the following instances indicate whether the critical region for rejection of H_0 lies in the upper (right) tail, lower (left) tail, or is divided between both tails of the sampling distribution of r for $\rho = 0$:

a. H_0: $\rho = 0$, H_1: $\rho \neq 0$
b. H_0: $\rho = 0$, H_1: $\rho > 0$
c. H_0: $\rho = 0$, H_1: $\rho < 0$

7. Researcher Rowe is testing H_0: $\rho = 0$ at the $\alpha = .05$ level with a sample of size $n = 25$, and he sets his critical values of r appropriately. Researcher Null is testing H_0: $\rho = 0$ at the $\alpha = .05$ level with a sample of $n = 100$ and he sets his critical values of r appropriately.

a. Does Rowe or Null have the larger probability of committing a type I error, or is this probability the same for both?
b. If ρ is actually .10, does Rowe or Null have the larger probability, β, of committing a type II error?
c. Which researcher is performing a significance test that has greater power to reject H_0 if $\rho = -.20$?

8. From Fig. 13.8, estimate the power of the test of H_0: $\rho = 0$ against H_1: $\rho \neq 0$ for $n = 200$ and $\alpha = .05$ when:

a. $\rho = .05$ b. $\rho = .25$ c. $\rho = -.25$ d. $\rho = .40$

9. Refer to Fig. 13.7. Suppose that in testing H_0: $\rho = 0$ against H_1: $\rho \neq 0$ with a sample of $n = 200$, the investigator sets his critical values at $r = -.30$ and below and $r = .30$ and above. Thus he is adopting an extremely small α. If ρ is actually .10, approximately how large is the probability that he will commit a type II error, i.e., accept H_0 even though it is false?

14

SELECTED INFERENTIAL TECHNIQUES

14.1
INTRODUCTION

At one time or another someone has studied the inferential properties of almost every statistic known. Using either strictly mathematical techniques or, occasionally, empirical methods, statisticians have derived sampling distributions to fill most practical needs. In this chapter, the inferential properties of only the more frequently used statistics will be presented; thus the word "selected" in the title of this chapter is appropriate. Where possible, the techniques of both testing the significance of a statistic and constructing a confidence interval around it will be given. The statistics with which we shall deal fall into four classes: means, variances, correlation coefficients, and frequency data.

The discussion of the inferential properties of each statistic will take the following form: (a) statement of the null hypothesis H_0 and the alternative hypothesis H_1—the alternative hypothesis will always be "nondirectional" so that modifications of critical values are necessary in the event a "one-sided" test is desired; (b) statement of the assumptions made in making the test;

(c) identification of the sample statistic employed in testing H_0 and H_1; (d) statement of the sampling distribution of the test statistic under both H_0 and H_1; (e) determination of critical values of the test; (f) construction of confidence intervals around the sample statistic; (g) an illustration; (h) special considerations, if any.

The first class of hypotheses we shall consider deals with population means.

14.2
INFERENCES ABOUT THE
MEAN, μ, OF A POPULATION

a. The hypothesis to be tested is that the mean μ of a population is equal to some real number a. The alternative hypothesis is, of course, that μ is different from a:

$$H_0: \mu = a$$

$$H_1: \mu \neq a.$$

b. It is assumed that the variable X has a normal distribution in the population sampled. One need not know the value of σ_x^2.

c. H_0 is tested by means of the test statistic

$$t = \frac{\bar{X}. - a}{s_x/\sqrt{n}}, \tag{14.1}$$

where

$$s_x = \sqrt{\frac{\sum (X_i - \bar{X}.)^2}{n-1}}.$$

d. If $H_0: \mu = a$ is true, t in Eq. (14.1) has the Student's t-distribution with $n-1$ df (degrees of freedom). When H_1 is true, i.e., when μ is actually equal to some value b that is different from a, then the sampling distribution of t in Eq. (14.1) has the shape and variability of Student's t-distribution with $n-1$ df but it has a mean approximately equal to $(b-a)/(\sigma_x/\sqrt{n})$. For example, the distribution of $t = (\bar{X}. - 0)/(s_x/\sqrt{n})$ is depicted in Fig. 14.1 both for the case in which $\mu = 0$ and $\mu = 2$; n and σ_x^2 are both equal to 30.

e. The critical values for testing H_0 at the α-level of significance with the test statistic $t = (\bar{X}. - a)/(s_x/\sqrt{n})$ are the $100[1 - (\alpha/2)]$ percentile point in Student's t-distribution with $n-1$ df and the negative of this percentile point:

$$-_{1-(\alpha/2)}t_{n-1} \quad \text{and} \quad _{1-(\alpha/2)}t_{n-1}.$$

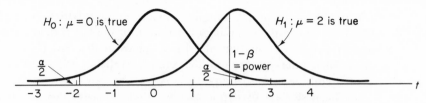

FIG. 14.1   Sampling distributions of $t = (\bar{X}. - 0)/(s_x/\sqrt{n})$ for the case in which $H_0: \mu = 0$ is true and the case in which $H_1: \mu = 2$ is true. The values of n and σ_x^2 are both 30 ($\alpha = .05$).

A value of $t = (\bar{X}. - a)/(s_x/\sqrt{n})$ falling below the negative critical value or above the positive critical value constitutes evidence for rejecting H_0: $\mu = a$ in favor of $H_1: \mu \neq a$.

f. The $100(1 - \alpha)\%$ confidence interval on μ is constructed as follows:

$$\bar{X}. \pm {}_{1-(\alpha/2)}t_{n-1} \frac{s_x}{\sqrt{n}}. \tag{14.2}$$

g. In the 1930's a study was performed on the effects on intelligence of placing illegitimate children born of average mothers into foster homes. The mean IQ (as measured by the Kuhlmann revision of Binet's tests) of some 175 children so placed between the ages of 6 months and 1 year was about 115. Critics raised the question of whether the mean score in the population of all infants is actually 100 as was presumed. (Studies revealed the population mean μ to be substantially above 100.)

We wish to test the hypothesis H_0 that the mean Kuhlmann IQ in the population of all infants in the United States is 100 against the alternative hypothesis that it is not:

$$H_0: \mu = 100 \qquad H_1: \mu \neq 100.$$

The probability of falsely rejecting H_0 will be set at .01.

A random sample of 25 infants yielded Kuhlmann IQ's with $\bar{X}. = 113.64$ and $s_x = 12.40$. Thus,

$$t = \frac{113.64 - 100}{12.40/\sqrt{25}} = 5.50.$$

The critical values for t are $-{}_{.995}t_{24} = -2.797$ and ${}_{.995}t_{24} = 2.797$.

Hence, we see that H_0 may be rejected in favor of H_1 at the .01 level of significance. Using Eq. (14.2) we find the 99% confidence interval on μ is

$$113.64 \pm 2.797 \frac{12.40}{\sqrt{25}} = 113.64 \pm 6.94 = (106.70, 120.58).$$

h. Although the assumption of a normal parent population is made in testing hypotheses about μ when σ_x^2 is not known, violations of the assumption have little effect upon either the level of significance or the power of the *two-tailed t*-test (see Srivastava, 1958). However, nonnormality of the population sampled can have serious effects on *one-tailed t*-tests of directional hypotheses.

Convenient tables for the calculation of the power of the *t*-test can be found in Wine (1964, pp. 254–60).

14.3
INFERENCES ABOUT $\mu_1 - \mu_2$
USING INDEPENDENT
SAMPLES

a. The hypothesis tested is that the difference between the means of two populations, $\mu_1 - \mu_2$, is equal to zero against the alternative hypothesis that it is different from zero:

$$H_0: \mu_1 - \mu_2 = 0$$

$$H_1: \mu_1 - \mu_2 \neq 0.$$

b. It is assumed that X_1 is *normally* distributed with mean μ_1 and variance σ_x^2 and that X_2 is *normally* distributed with mean μ_2 and *the same variance* σ_x^2. The assumption of equal variances in the two populations is referred to as the assumption of *homogeneous variances* or *homoscedasticity* (literally, "same spread"). Furthermore, it is assumed that a sample of size n_1 is randomly drawn from population 1 and that an *independent* sample of size n_2 is randomly drawn from population 2.

The major consequence of this assumption of independent samples is that the two sample means, $\bar{X}_{.1}$ and $\bar{X}_{.2}$, will be perfectly uncorrelated across infinitely many pairs of samples. The independence assumption would be violated if, for example, sample 1 was a random sample of 10-year-old boys and sample 2 was composed of their sisters. The two means of brother-sister paired samples would correlate on most variables one might observe.

c. H_0 is tested against H_1 by means of the following test statistic:

$$t = \frac{\bar{X}_{.1} - \bar{X}_{.2}}{\sqrt{\dfrac{(n_1 - 1)s_1^2 + (n_2 - 1)s_2^2}{n_1 + n_2 - 2}\left(\dfrac{1}{n_1} + \dfrac{1}{n_2}\right)}}, \tag{14.3}$$

where $\bar{X}_{.1}$ and $\bar{X}_{.2}$ are the means of the samples from populations 1 and 2, respectively,

s_1^2 and s_2^2 are the unbiased estimates from samples 1 and 2 of the common population variance σ_x^2, and

n_1 and n_2 are the sizes of samples 1 and 2.

d. When H_0 is true the distribution of t in Eq. (14.3) over pairs of samples is that of Student's t with $n_1 + n_2 - 2$ degrees of freedom. When H_1 is true and hence $\mu_1 - \mu_2$ is different from zero, the distribution of t in Eq. (14.3) has the shape and variability of Student's t-distribution but its mean is different from 0—the magnitude of this difference depends on the values of $\mu_1 - \mu_2$, σ_x^2, n_1, and n_2.

e. For testing H_0 against H_1 at the α-level of significance, the following critical values are determined and compared against the obtained value of t from Eq. (14.3):

$$-_{1-(\alpha/2)}t_{n_1+n_2-2} \quad \text{and} \quad _{1-(\alpha/2)}t_{n_1+n_2-2}.$$

f. The $100(1 - \alpha)\%$ confidence interval on $\mu_1 - \mu_2$ around $\bar{X}_{.1} - \bar{X}_{.2}$ is constructed as follows:

$$(\bar{X}_{.1} - \bar{X}_{.2}) \pm {}_{1-(\alpha/2)}t_{n_1+n_2-2}s_{\bar{x}_{.1}-\bar{x}_{.2}}, \tag{14.4}$$

where $s_{\bar{x}_{.1}-\bar{x}_{.2}}$ is the same as the denominator in Eq. (14.3).

g. Scandura and Wells (1967) performed an experiment on the effects of "advance organizers" (introductory material that organizes the material to be learned) on achievement in abstract mathematics. Fifty college students were randomly assigned to two groups: 25 Ss in group 1 studied a 1000-word essay on topology after having been exposed to an advance organizer on the subject; 25 Ss in group 2 read the same essay on topology after having read a 1000-word historical sketch of Euler and Riemann, two famous mathematicians. At the end of the experimental period, each group was given an objective test on the topological concepts. The dependent variable X was "number of correct answers." The following results were obtained:

Group 1 (*advance organizer*)	*Group* 2 (*historical sketch*)
$n_1 = 25$	$n_2 = 25$
$\bar{X}_{.1} = 7.65$	$\bar{X}_{.2} = 6.00$
$s_1^2 = 6.50$	$s_2^2 = 5.90$

The hypothesis can be tested that the two groups are random samples from normal populations with equal means. We shall test this hypothesis at the .05 level of significance. From Eq. (14.3)

$$t = \frac{\bar{X}_{.1} - \bar{X}_{.2}}{s_{\bar{x}_{.1}-\bar{x}_{.2}}} = \frac{7.65 - 6.00}{\sqrt{\dfrac{24(6.50) + 24(5.90)}{25 + 25 - 2}\left(\dfrac{1}{25} + \dfrac{1}{25}\right)}} = 2.34.$$

The critical values against which a t of 2.34 are compared are

$$-_{.975}t_{48} = -2.01 \quad \text{and} \quad _{.975}t_{48} = 2.01.$$

Hence we see that $H_0: \mu_1 - \mu_2 = 0$ can be rejected at the .05 level of significance. Indeed, a value of t deviating from 0 by more than 2.34 units has a probability p of approximately .03 if H_0 is true.

The 95% confidence interval on $\mu_1 - \mu_2$ can be constructed from Eq. (14.4):

$$(\bar{X}_{.1} - \bar{X}_{.2}) \pm _{.975}t_{48}s_{\bar{x}_{.1}-\bar{x}_{.2}} = 1.65 \pm 2.01(.705) = (0.23, 3.07).$$

h. Violation of the assumption of normality in the t-test of $H_0: \mu_1 - \mu_2 = 0$ has been shown to have only trivial effects on the level of significance and power of the test and hence should be no cause for concern (Boneau, 1960; Scheffé, 1959, chap. 10).

The effects of violation of the homogeneous variances assumption can be serious depending upon n_1 and n_2. *If n_1 and n_2 are equal, violation of the homogeneous variances assumption is unimportant and need not concern us* (Box, 1954a, b; Scheffé, 1959, chap. 10). This fact is a compelling motive for selecting samples equal in size when possible in using the technique in this section. Whenever the variances of populations 1 and 2 are different *and n_1 and n_2 are not equal*, probabilities of type I and type II errors may be quite different from what one imagines them to be (see Sec. 15.13). When a study in which $\mu_1 - \mu_2$ is to be estimated cannot be designed so that $n_1 = n_2$, and one suspects that the two populations have substantially different variances, recourse should be made to methods developed by Welch (1937) or Gronow (1951). The problem of testing the significance of the difference between two means when the population variances are unequal has been referred to as the Behrens-Fisher problem (see Fisher, 1959, pp. 93–97).

14.4
INFERENCES ABOUT $\mu_1 - \mu_2$
USING DEPENDENT SAMPLES

a. Population 1 has mean μ_1 and population 2 has mean μ_2. The null hypothesis to be tested is the same as in Sec. 14.3:

$$H_0: \mu_1 - \mu_2 = 0$$

$$H_1: \mu_1 - \mu_2 \neq 0.$$

b. It is assumed that samples 1 and 2 are randomly drawn from *normal* populations with the *same variance* σ_x^2. In this instance the samples need not be independent, i.e., there may exist a correlation between $\bar{X}_{.1}$ and $\bar{X}_{.2}$ over repeated pairs of samples. The following are examples of dependent samples: sample 1 is a sample of one-year-old infants and sample 2 consists of the fraternal twin-mates of the children in sample 1; sample 1 is a group of boys and sample 2 is the group of their sisters; sample 1 is the collection of scores on a reaction-time test made by a group of persons before administration of a drug and sample 2 is the collection of scores made by the same persons after taking the drug.

c. It will always be possible to "pair off" data from two dependent samples. The pairs may be defined by "brother-sister," "before-after," "twin 1, twin 2," "matched partner 1, matched partner 2," etc. Hence, data gathered from dependent samples will be in the form of n pairs of observations X_{i1} and X_{i2} for $i = 1, \ldots, n$. This pairing of the data from dependent samples will be used to test the hypothesis that $\mu_1 - \mu_2 = 0$. The hypothesis that X_1 and X_2 have the same mean, i.e., that $\mu_1 = \mu_2$, is equivalent to the hypothesis that $X_1 - X_2$ has a mean of 0 in the population. The difference $X_1 - X_2$ between the normally distributed variables X_1 and X_2 is itself normally distributed; thus the techniques in Sec. 14.2 can be employed to test the hypothesis that the n differences $X_{i1} - X_{i2}$ can be considered a random sample from a normally distributed population with mean $\mu_1 - \mu_2$ equal to zero.

Denote $X_{i1} - X_{i2}$ by d_i, the difference between the paired observations from samples 1 and 2. The test statistic is

$$t = \frac{\bar{d}_{.}}{s_d/\sqrt{n}}, \tag{14.5}$$

where

$$\bar{d}_{.} = \sum_{i=1}^{n} (X_{i1} - X_{i2})/n = \sum_{i=1}^{n} d_i/n,$$

the average of the n difference scores, and

$$s_d = \sqrt{\sum_{i=1}^{n} \frac{(d_i - \bar{d}_{.})^2}{n-1}},$$

the standard deviation of the n difference scores $X_{i1} - X_{i2}$, and n is the number of pairs of observations.

d. If $H_0: \mu_1 - \mu_2 = 0$ is true, then t in Eq. (14.5) will follow the Student's t-distribution with $n - 1$ df. If $H_1: \mu_1 - \mu_2 \neq 0$ is true, then t in Eq. (14.5) will have a distribution identical in shape to the Student's t-distribution with $n - 1$ df, but the distribution will have a mean that is different from zero in a direction and by an amount depending partially on the size of $\mu_1 - \mu_2$.

e. The critical values for testing H_0 against H_1 at the α-level of significance by means of the t-statistic in Eq. (14.5) are as follows:

$$-_{1-(\alpha/2)}t_{n-1} \quad \text{and} \quad _{1-(\alpha/2)}t_{n-1}.$$

f. The $100(1 - \alpha)\%$ confidence interval on $\mu_1 - \mu_2$ around $\bar{d}$ is constructed as follows:

$$\bar{d} \pm _{1-(\alpha/2)}t_{n-1}\frac{s_d}{\sqrt{n}}. \tag{14.6}$$

g. Webster and Bereiter (1963) reported data on personality changes in 100 college women from the Freshman to Senior year. A 60-item personality scale was administered in the Freshman and Senior years to the same 100 women. The first set of 100 scores constitutes sample 1; the 100 Senior-year scores constitute sample 2. There are 100 pairs of "before-after" scores. From these data 100 difference scores are formed by subtracting Senior scores from Freshman scores: $d_i = X_{i1} - X_{i2}$. The mean and standard deviation of these 100 d scores are:

$$\bar{d} = \sum_1^{100} \frac{X_{i1} - X_{i2}}{100} = -7.02.$$

$$s_d = \sqrt{\frac{\sum_1^{100}(d_i - \bar{d})^2}{99}} = 8.02.$$

We shall test $H_0: \mu_1 - \mu_2 = 0$ at the .01 level of significance. The value of t in Eq. (14.5) is

$$t = \frac{\bar{d}}{s_d/\sqrt{n}} = \frac{-7.02}{8.02/\sqrt{100}} = -8.75,$$

which lies far below the lower critical value of $-_{.995}t_{99} = -2.64$. In fact, the probability p of obtaining a t of -8.75 or less given a true null hypothesis is substantially smaller than even .001. Thus we can confidently reject the null hypothesis that these two dependent samples of 100 observations each could have been randomly sampled from two normal populations with the same mean. There is overwhelming evidence that a "gain" takes place on the personality inventory from the Freshman to the Senior years.

The 99% confidence interval on $\mu_1 - \mu_2$ can be found from Eq. (14.6):

$$\bar{d} \pm _{.995}t_{99}\frac{s_d}{\sqrt{n}} = -7.02 \pm (2.64)\frac{8.02}{\sqrt{100}} = (-9.14, -4.90).$$

h. A common misapplication of inferential statistical techniques is to apply the techniques of Sec. 14.3 when the techniques of this section are appropriate; in other words, researchers often have dependent samples, fail to recognize this fact, and inappropriately apply the t-test for independent groups to test the hypothesis that $\mu_1 - \mu_2 = 0$. The difference between the independent and dependent groups' t-tests becomes apparent when one observes the standard errors of the difference between uncorrelated and correlated means. If $\bar{X}_{.1}$ and $\bar{X}_{.2}$ are uncorrelated (estimated from independent groups), the standard error of the difference between the two means is

$$\sigma_{\bar{x}.1 - \bar{x}.2} = \sqrt{\frac{\sigma_x^2}{n_1} + \frac{\sigma_x^2}{n_2}},$$

which equals

$$\sigma_{\bar{x}.1 - \bar{x}.2} = \sqrt{\sigma_x^2 \frac{2}{n}} \tag{14.7}$$

when $n_1 = n_2$. When X_1 and X_2 have a nonzero correlation coefficient of ρ_{12} (as they will have with two dependent samples), the standard error of $\bar{X}_{.1} - \bar{X}_{.2}$ is

$$\sigma_{\bar{x}.1 - \bar{x}.2} = \sqrt{\frac{\sigma_x^2}{n} + \frac{\sigma_x^2}{n} - 2\rho_{12} \frac{\sigma_x^2}{n}} = \sqrt{\sigma_x^2 \left(\frac{2}{n} - \frac{2\rho_{12}}{n} \right)}. \tag{14.8}$$

The t-statistic for testing $\mu_1 - \mu_2 = 0$ with independent groups contains $\bar{X}_{.1} - \bar{X}_{.2}$ in the numerator and an estimate of Eq. (14.7) in the denominator. The t-statistic for dependent groups contains $\bar{d}_{.} = \bar{X}_{.1} - \bar{X}_{.2}$ in the numerator and an estimate of Eq. (14.8) in the denominator; note that

$$\frac{s_d}{\sqrt{n}} = \frac{s_{x_1 - x_2}}{\sqrt{n}} = \sqrt{\frac{s_{x_1 - x_2}^2}{n}} = \sqrt{\frac{s_{x_1}^2}{n} + \frac{s_{x_2}^2}{n} - 2r_{12} \frac{s_{x_1} s_{x_2}}{n}}.$$

If an inappropriate independent-groups t-test is performed with dependent groups for which X_1 and X_2 are substantially positively correlated, the standard error of $\bar{X}_{.1} - \bar{X}_{.2}$ will be greatly overestimated and significant differences between the two means will be branded "nonsignificant." The opposite error, mistaking nonsignificant differences for significant ones, would frequently be made if the independent-groups t-test is applied to dependent groups in which X_1 and X_2 have a substantial negative correlation. Thus we see that the ability to recognize and distinguish independent and dependent samples is an important activity in applying certain inferential statistical techniques. Knowing which test to apply requires a familiarity with the phenomena being studied plus a sensitivity to the statistical problems attendant upon drawing dependent samples.

14.5
INFERENCES ABOUT THE VARIANCE, σ_x^2, OF A POPULATION

Beginning with this section, we shall deal with testing hypotheses about population variances.

a. The hypothesis to be tested is that a population has a variance σ_x^2 equal to some number a versus the hypothesis that σ_x^2 is different from a:

$$H_0: \sigma_x^2 = a$$

$$H_1: \sigma_x^2 \neq a.$$

b. It must be assumed that the variable X has a *normal* distribution in the population and that a *random* sample of n observations has been selected from which σ_x^2 will be estimated.

c. The test statistic for testing H_0 against H_1 is

$$\chi^2 = \frac{(n-1)s_x^2}{a}, \tag{14.9}$$

where

$$(n-1)s_x^2 = \frac{(n-1)\sum_1^n (X_i - \bar{X})^2}{n-1} = \sum_1^n (X_i - \bar{X})^2.$$

d. When H_0 is true, the sampling distribution of χ^2 in Eq. (14.9) is the chi-square distribution with $n-1$ df, i.e., χ^2_{n-1}; when H_1 is true and σ_x^2 is actually equal to some number b different from zero, the sampling distribution of $(n-1)s_x^2/a$ will equal b/a times χ^2_{n-1}. For example, the graphs of $(n-1)s_x^2/10$ are drawn in Fig. 14.2 for the case in which $\sigma_x^2 = 10$, i.e., H_0 is true, and $\sigma_x^2 = 20$, i.e., H_1 is true—$n = 9$.

If, from a sample of size 9, a s_x^2 of 21.40 was obtained, the value of the test statistic in Eq. (14.9) would be

$$\chi^2 = \frac{(n-1)s_x^2}{10} = \frac{8(21.40)}{10} = 17.12.$$

In Fig. 14.2 we see that a value of the test statistic as large as 17.12 or larger is relatively improbable when $\sigma_x^2 = 10$ but is quite reasonable when $\sigma_x^2 = 20$ is true. On the basis of the evidence then, we are inclined to reject H_0 and support H_1.

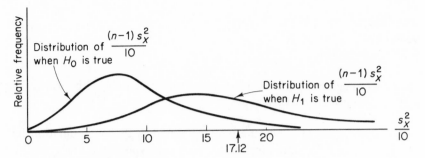

FIG. 14.2 Sampling distributions of $(n-1)s_x^2/10$ when H_0: $\sigma_x^2 = 10$ is true and when H_1: $\sigma_x^2 = 20$ is true ($n = 9$).

e. The critical values for testing H_0 against H_1 at the α-level of significance are the $\alpha/2$ and $1 - (\alpha/2)$ percentile points in the chi-square distribution with $df = n - 1$, i.e., χ_{n-1}^2:

$$\alpha/2\chi_{n-1}^2, \qquad 1-(\alpha/2)\chi_{n-1}^2.$$

f. The $100(1 - \alpha)\%$ confidence interval on the unknown value of σ_x^2 is constructed as follows:

$$\frac{(n-1)s_x^2}{1-(\alpha/2)\chi_{n-1}^2} < \sigma_x^2 < \frac{(n-1)s_x^2}{\alpha/2\chi_{n-1}^2}. \tag{14.10}$$

g. For several years the supervisor of curriculum and research in a large school system has observed a typical standard deviation of .80 yr. measured in grade placement units on a standardized test of arithmetic achievement given at the end of the third grade. Unlike previous years, this year saw the introduction of a programmed textbook for arithmetic study in the third grade. One of the highly touted features of programmed instruction is that it does a better job of accommodating individual differences in learning rate than do traditional methods. Hence, at the end of this year, third-grade students should show a different variance on the arithmetic achievement test than in past years. The curriculum supervisor selects a random sample of 25 pupils to whom he will administer the arithmetic achievement test. The data will be used to test the following hypotheses at the .10 level of significance:

$$H_0:\ \sigma_x^2 = (.80)^2 = .64$$

$$H_1:\ \sigma_x^2 \neq .64.$$

The variance of the sample of 25 test scores was found to equal 1.14.

The value

$$\chi^2 = \frac{24(1.14)}{.64} = 42.75$$

is compared with the critical values

$$_{.05}\chi^2_{24} = 13.85, \qquad _{.95}\chi^2_{24} = 36.42,$$

and is seen to be significant at the .10 level. The probability p of a value of χ^2 equal to 42.75 or more given that H_0 is true is approximately .01.

The 90% confidence interval on σ_x^2 is found by substituting the sample data into Eq. (14.10):

$$\frac{24(1.14)}{36.42} < \sigma_x^2 < \frac{24(1.14)}{13.85} \to 0.75 < \sigma_x^2 < 1.98.$$

The conclusion seems obligatory that the population of third graders taught by programmed instruction has a greater variance on the arithmetic achievement test than in past years. Notice that inferential statistical methods have made it unnecessary to administer the test to any more than 25 pupils.

h. Unlike hypothesis tests about means using Student's t-distribution, the assumption of sampling from a normal population cannot be taken lightly when testing hypotheses about population variances (see Scheffé, 1959, chap. 10). If the population is nonnormal—particularly if it departs substantially from mesokurtosis—the hypothesis test outlined above may be quite in error.

14.6
INFERENCES ABOUT σ_1^2/σ_2^2
USING INDEPENDENT
SAMPLES

a. The problem at hand possesses greater practical significance than that of testing whether a population has a variance equal to some hypothesized value a. For now we are concerned with two populations (1 and 2), and we wish to test whether their variances σ_1^2 and σ_2^2 are the same or different:

$$H_0: \sigma_1^2 = \sigma_2^2$$

$$H_1: \sigma_1^2 \neq \sigma_2^2.$$

b. It is assumed that a sample of size n_1 is drawn at *random* from a *normal* population with mean μ_1 and variance σ_1^2; an *independent random* sample of size n_2 is drawn from a second normal population with mean μ_2

and variance σ_2^2. The values of μ_1 and μ_2 are immaterial and of no interest in testing H_0.

c. The test statistic for testing H_0 against H_1 is the ratio of the two sample variances:

$$F = \frac{s_1^2}{s_2^2}. \tag{14.11}$$

d. When $H_0: \sigma_1^2 = \sigma_2^2$ is true, the sampling distribution of $F = s_1^2/s_2^2$ is the F-distribution with $n_1 - 1$ and $n_2 - 1$ df. When $H_1: \sigma_1^2 \neq \sigma_2^2$, the distribution of s_1^2/s_2^2 is equal to σ_1^2/σ_2^2 times the F-distribution with $n_1 - 1$ and $n_2 - 1$ df. Thus if in reality $\sigma_1^2/\sigma_2^2 = 2$, the distribution of s_1^2/s_2^2 will look like the F-distribution transformed by a multiplicative factor of 2.

e. The critical values against which F in Eq. (14.11) is compared in testing H_0 against H_1 at the α-level of significance are

$$_{\alpha/2}F_{n_1-1, n_2-1} \quad \text{and} \quad _{1-(\alpha/2)}F_{n_1-1, n_2-1},$$

i.e., the $100(\alpha/2)$ and $100[1 - (\alpha/2)]$ percentile points in the F-distribution with $n_1 - 1$ and $n_2 - 1$ df. The upper percentile points in the F-distributions can be read directly from Table E in Appendix A. The lower percentile points are related as follows to the upper percentiles:

$$_{\alpha/2}F_{n_1-1, n_2-1} = \frac{1}{_{1-(\alpha/2)}F_{n_2-1, n_1-1}}. \tag{14.12}$$

f. The $100(1 - \alpha)\%$ confidence interval on the *ratio* of σ_1^2 to σ_2^2 is constructed as follows:

$$_{\alpha/2}F_{n_1-1, n_2-1}\frac{s_1^2}{s_2^2} < \frac{\sigma_1^2}{\sigma_2^2} < _{1-(\alpha/2)}F_{n_1-1, n_2-1}\frac{s_1^2}{s_2^2}. \tag{14.13}$$

g. In a study by Sears (1940), children were given familiar arithmetic tasks, and upon completion, a randomly chosen half were told they had failed and the remaining half were told they did well. Each child was then asked to estimate the number of seconds it would take him to complete the next task. Observations were made by the experimenter of the difference between a child's goal (in seconds) on the task to be performed and his performance on the task just completed. It was felt that those who experienced failure on the preceding task might be erratic in establishing their goals.

The hypothesis to be tested at the .05 level of significance is that the *variance* in the population of children's estimates of future performance is the same whether they have been told they failed or successfully completed a preliminary task. Sears obtained the following data:

Group 1 (told they were successful)	Group 2 (told they were unsuccessful)
$n_1 = 12$	$n_2 = 12$
$s_1^2 = 8.16$	$s_2^2 = 90.45$

The value of the test statistic in Eq. (14.11) is

$$F = \frac{8.16}{90.45} = 0.090.$$

This value is compared with the critical values that are read approximately from Table E:

$$_{.975}F_{11,11} = 3.47 \quad \text{and} \quad _{.025}F_{11,11} = \frac{1}{_{.975}F_{11,11}} = \frac{1}{3.47} = 0.29.$$

Since $F = 0.09$ falls below the lower critical value, $H_0: \sigma_1^2 = \sigma_2^2$ is rejected at the .05 level of significance.

The 95% confidence interval on σ_1^2/σ_2^2 is constructed from Eq. (14.13):

$$(0.29)\frac{8.16}{90.45} < \frac{\sigma_1^2}{\sigma_2^2} < (3.47)\frac{8.16}{90.45} \rightarrow 0.03 < \frac{\sigma_1^2}{\sigma_2^2} < 0.31.$$

h. The choice of which sample to designate 1 and which to designate 2 is usually arbitrary *but it must not be made after observing which sample variance is larger.* To observe the larger sample variance and then designate it s_1^2 would effectively double the probability of a type I error over what that probability was believed to be. Determining which sample variance to designate s_1^2 might well be done by the flip of a coin. If one's purpose is solely to construct an interval estimate of the ratio of the population variances, the above concern over designating s_1^2 and s_2^2 is immaterial.

The assumption that s_1^2 and s_2^2 are derived from *independent* samples from *normal* populations cannot be taken lightly—unlike the normality assumption underlying the t-tests of means. If substantial nonnormality is expected the significance test in Sec. 15.14 should be used.

In the past it was customary to test $H_0: \sigma_1^2 = \sigma_2^2$ prior to performing a t-test of the hypothesis $H_0: \mu_1 - \mu_2 = 0$. The former hypothesis is a statement of the homogeneous variances assumption made in testing the latter hypothesis. One was advised in the textbooks of the time not to proceed with the simple t-test of Sec. 14.3 if s_1^2/s_2^2 led to rejection of $H_0: \sigma_1^2 = \sigma_2^2$. Although such advice stemmed from an admirable concern for meeting the assumptions of the tests employed, it proved to be generally poor advice. In particular, the preliminary test of the assumption of homogeneous variances can be largely invalidated by nonnormality of the populations; but this same nonnormality is of no consequence to the validity of the t-test of $\mu_1 - \mu_2 = 0$. In fact, if $n_1 = n_2$ there is no reason to be concerned about violation of the assumption of homogeneous variances. The only circumstance in which one might advisedly test H_0: $\sigma_1^2 = \sigma_2^2$ prior to testing H_0: $\mu_1 - \mu_2 = 0$ is when there is good evidence that the populations are normally distributed *and* n_1 and n_2 are quite unequal. It may be possible to find a simple transformation of the observations that will give them a more nearly normal distribution. The subject of "normalizing transformation" is dealt with in detail in P. O. Johnson's *Statistical Methods in Research* (1949, chap. 7).

14.7
INFERENCES ABOUT σ_1^2/σ_2^2
USING DEPENDENT SAMPLES

a. As in Sec. 14.6, the null hypothesis being tested here is that two populations have the same variance:

$$H_0: \ \sigma_1^2 = \sigma_2^2$$

$$H_1: \ \sigma_1^2 \neq \sigma_2^2.$$

b. It is assumed that two possibly *dependent* samples are drawn, one of size n from a *normal* population with variance σ_1^2 and the other of the same size n from a *normal* population with variance σ_2^2. The values of μ_1 and μ_2 are not of interest.

The nature of dependent samples was discussed in Sec. 14.4 on testing differences between means.

c. The test statistic used in testing H_0 against H_1 is

$$t = \frac{s_1^2 - s_2^2}{\sqrt{\dfrac{4s_1^2 s_2^2}{n-2}(1 - r_{12}^2)}} \tag{14.14}$$

where s_1^2 and s_2^2 are the variances of samples 1 and 2, respectively,
$\qquad$ n is the number of *pairs* of observations, pairing each observation of sample 1 with a single observation in sample 2, and
$\qquad$ r_{12} is the correlation coefficient calculated on the n paired observations.

As was pointed out in Sec. 14.4 it will generally be possible to "pair off" the observations in two dependent samples into n pairs ("before-after," "brother-sister," "husband-wife").

d. When $H_0: \sigma_1^2 = \sigma_2^2$ is true the sampling distribution of t in Eq. (14.14) is Student's t-distribution with $n - 2$ df.

e. The critical values for testing H_0 against H_1 at the α-level of significance are:

$$_{\alpha/2}t_{n-2} \qquad _{1-(\alpha/2)}t_{n-2}.$$

f. Constructing a confidence interval on $\sigma_1^2 - \sigma_2^2$ or σ_1^2/σ_2^2 when estimates of the variances are obtained from dependent samples presents difficulties beyond the scope of this textbook.

g. Lord (1963b) reported data gathered by William E. Coffman on the performance of a sample of 95 students on the Stanford Achievement Test in the seventh and eighth grades. One might wonder whether, in the population of students sampled, performance is more uniform (less variable) in the seventh or the eighth grade.

Sample 1 is the set of scores on the Stanford Achievement Test earned by the 95 students in grade seven, and sample 2 is the set of scores earned by the *same* 95 students in grade eight. Thus the two samples are not independent. The following data were obtained to test $H_0: \sigma_1^2 = \sigma_2^2$ at the .10 level of significance:

Sample 1 (grade 7)	Sample 2 (grade 8)
$n = 95$	$n = 95$
$s_1^2 = 134.56$	$s_2^2 = 201.64$

$$r_{12} = .876$$

The value of $r_{12} = .876$ is the product-moment correlation coefficient between the 95 students' performance in the seventh and eighth grades. From Eq. (14.14),

$$t = \frac{134.56 - 201.64}{\sqrt{\dfrac{4(134.56)(201.64)}{95 - 2}}\,(1 - .876^2)} = -4.07.$$

The critical values with which the obtained t of -4.07 is compared are

$$_{-.95}t_{93} = -1.66 \quad \text{and} \quad _{.95}t_{93} = 1.66.$$

Thus we see that evidence exists to conclude that in the populations sampled—seventh-grade students and eighth-grade students—the variances σ_1^2 and σ_2^2 are different. The probability of obtaining a value of t as discrepant from zero as that obtained is less than .001 if σ_1^2 is truly equal to σ_2^2. Performance on the Stanford Achievement Test is more variable among eighth-grade than among seventh-grade students.

14.8
INFERENCES ABOUT ρ, THE POPULATION PRODUCT-MOMENT CORRELATION COEFFICIENT

a. The hypothesis being tested is that the product-moment correlation coefficient between variables X and Y, i.e., ρ_{xy}, is equal to some value a—between -1 and $+1$, of course—in the population sampled:

$$H_0: \rho_{xy} = a$$

$$H_1: \rho_{xy} \neq a.$$

b. It is assumed that a *random* sample of n paired observations (X_i, Y_i) is drawn from a *bivariate normal population* (see Sec. 6.7) in which the correlation of X and Y is ρ_{xy}. The means and variances for the bivariate normal population are not of interest.

c. To test H_0 against H_1, one first calculates r_{xy}, the sample product-moment correlation coefficient. The value of r_{xy} is then transformed by means of Fisher's Z-transformation of r (see Table G in Appendix A) into Z_r. The test statistic for testing the null hypothesis that $\rho_{xy} = a$ is

$$z = \frac{Z_r - Z_a}{1/\sqrt{n-3}}, \tag{14.15}$$

where Z_r is the Z-transformed value corresponding to the sample value of r_{xy},
   Z_a is the Z-transformed value corresponding to a, the value hypothesized for ρ_{xy} in H_0, and
   n is the sample size.

d. When H_0 is true, i.e., ρ_{xy} is equal to a, then z in Eq. (14.15) is normally distributed with mean 0 and standard deviation 1, i.e., z has the unit normal distribution. If, on the other hand, H_1 is true and $\rho_{xy} = b$ that is different from a, then z in Eq. (14.15) has a normal distribution with standard deviation 1 and centering around a mean of $Z_b - Z_a$. For example, if $H_0: \rho_{xy} = 0$ is true, the distribution of $z = (Z_r - 0)/(1/\sqrt{n-3})$ for samples of size 12 is represented by the curve on the left in Fig. 14.3. If $H_1: \rho_{xy} = .60$ is true and $n = 12$, the sampling distribution of $z = (Z_r - 0)/(1/\sqrt{n-3})$ is the curve on the right in Fig. 14.3.

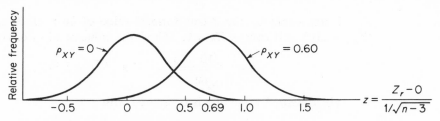

FIG. 14.3 Sampling distributions of $z = (Z_r - 0)/(1/\sqrt{n-3})$ for samples of size 12 when $\rho_{xy} = 0$ and when $\rho_{xy} = .60$.

e. The critical values against which z in Eq. (14.15) is compared in testing H_0 against H_1 at the α-level of significance are the $100(\alpha/2)$ and $100[1 - (\alpha/2)]$ percentiles in the unit normal distribution:

$$_{\alpha/2}z \quad \text{and} \quad _{1-(\alpha/2)}z.$$

For example, if H_0 is tested at the .05 level, the critical values are -1.96 and $+1.96$.

f. Confidence intervals are constructed on ρ_{xy} by first constructing a confidence interval on Z_ρ around Z_r and transforming the upper and lower limits on this interval back to the scale of r by reading Table G in reverse.

The first step in building the $100(1 - \alpha)\%$ confidence interval on ρ_{xy} is to calculate

$$Z_r \pm {}_{1-(\alpha/2)}z \frac{1}{\sqrt{n-3}}, \tag{14.16}$$

where Z_r and n are as defined in Eq. (14.15) above, and

$_{1-(\alpha/2)}z$ is the $100[1 - (\alpha/2)]$ percentile in the unit normal distribution.

Equation (14.16) will determine two points on the Z-transformation scale. Table G is entered with these two values and the two corresponding values of r_{xy} are determined. These two values of r_{xy} constitute the $100(1 - \alpha)\%$ confidence interval on ρ_{xy}.

g. Forehand and Libby (1962) gathered data on the correlation between "supervisors' ratings of innovative behavior," X, and scores on tests of divergent thinking ("flexibility" and "implications"—known in the vernacular as tests of "creativity"), Y, on $n = 60$ governmental administrators. An r_{xy} of .30 was obtained.

We shall test the null hypothesis with $\alpha = .05$ that ρ_{xy} is zero:

$$H_0: \rho_{xy} = 0$$

$$H_1: \rho_{xy} \neq 0.$$

From Table G, the Z-transformed value of an r of .30 is .310, i.e., $Z_{.30} = .310$. Of course, $Z_0 = 0$. Thus, the value of z in Eq. (14.15) is

$$z = \frac{.310 - 0}{1/\sqrt{60 - 3}} = .310(\sqrt{57}) = 2.34.$$

The obtained value of z is compared with

$$_{.025}z = -1.96$$

and

$$_{.975}z = 1.96.$$

Since 2.34 exceeds 1.96, H_0 can be rejected and H_1 accepted at the .05 level of significance. The 95% confidence interval on ρ_{xy} is constructed as follows:

$$Z_{.30} \pm (1.96) \frac{1}{\sqrt{60 - 3}} = .310 \pm .259 = (.051, .569).$$

From Table G, the values of r_{xy} corresponding to Z-values of .051 and .569 are found. These values are approximately .05 and .51, respectively. Thus the 95% confidence interval on ρ_{xy} is (.05, .51). (Also see Table J.)

h. In the vast majority of instances in practice the value of ρ_{xy} hypothesized in H_0 is 0. Hence, $(Z_r - 0)/(1/\sqrt{n - 3}) = Z_r(\sqrt{n - 3})$ is referred to a table of the unit normal distribution. An alternative test statistic exists that exactly describes the sampling distribution of r_{xy} when ρ_{xy} is 0. (The hypothesis test outlined above is an approximate one, but one which is so close to the exact test for even small n that the fact that it is an approximation should cause no concern.) When ρ_{xy} is 0,

$$t = \frac{r_{xy}}{\sqrt{(1 - r_{xy}^2)/(n - 2)}}$$

has the Student t-distribution with $n - 2$ df. This fact was used to construct a table of critical values of r_{xy} to facilitate testing $H_0: \rho_{xy} = 0$. Table I in Appendix A lists the values which r_{xy} must exceed in absolute value to constitute evidence for rejection of $H_0: \rho_{xy} = 0$. For example, with $n = 60$, a sample r_{xy} must lie above *approximately* .250 or below $-.250$ before $H_0: \rho_{xy} = 0$ can be rejected at the .05 level of significance. (Table I is entered for particular values of α and $df = n - 2$.) Hence, a sample r_{xy} of .30 leads to rejection, as was seen above. As a further example of how to read Table I, the critical values of r_{xy} for testing $\rho_{xy} = 0$ at the .01 level of significance with a sample of size 12 are .708 and $-.708$. An r_{xy} of $-.45$, say, for $n = 12$, would not lie sufficiently far from 0 to allow one to reject $H_0: \rho_{xy} = 0$.

For a study of the effects of violation of the assumption of bivariate normality, see Norris and Hjelm (1961) and Carroll (1961).

14.9
INFERENCES ABOUT $\rho_1 - \rho_2$
USING INDEPENDENT
SAMPLES

a. In this instance, inferences concern the possible difference between the correlation ρ_1 of X and Y in population 1 and the correlation ρ_2 of the same two variables in population 2. For example, are aptitude X and achievement Y more highly correlated for boys (population 1) than for girls (population 2)? The null hypothesis is generally that $\rho_1 = \rho_2$; the alternative hypothesis is that they are unequal:

$$H_0: \rho_1 = \rho_2$$

$$H_1: \rho_1 \neq \rho_2.$$

b. It is assumed that a *random* sample of size n_1 is drawn from a *bivariate-normal* population 1 in which the product-moment correlation coefficient is ρ_1 and that an *independent random* sample of size n_2 is drawn from a *bivariate-normal* population 2 with correlation ρ_2.

c. Again the inferential statistical problems are handled by means of Fisher's Z-transformation of r. Samples 1 and 2 are drawn from populations 1 and 2, respectively. The two sample correlation coefficients, r_1 and r_2, are calculated and then transformed to Z_{r_1} and Z_{r_2} by means of Table G. The test statistic for testing $H_0: \rho_1 = \rho_2$ is:

$$z = \frac{Z_{r_1} - Z_{r_2}}{\sqrt{\dfrac{1}{n_1 - 3} + \dfrac{1}{n_2 - 3}}}. \tag{14.17}$$

d. If in fact ρ_1 equals ρ_2, then z in Eq. (14.17) has a normal distribution with mean 0 and standard deviation 1 over repeated pairs of independent random samples. If ρ_1 and ρ_2 actually differ, then the mean of the sampling distribution of z in Eq. (14.17) will shift away from 0—it will become $Z_{\rho_1} - Z_{\rho_2}$—but the standard deviation will remain equal to 1.

e. To test $H_0: \rho_1 = \rho_2$ against $H_1: \rho_1 \neq \rho_2$ at the α-level of significance, the single calculated value of z in Eq. (14.17) is compared with the $100(\alpha/2)$ and $100[1 - (\alpha/2)]$ percentiles in the unit normal distribution:

$$_{\alpha/2}z \quad \text{and} \quad _{1-(\alpha/2)}z.$$

f. Confidence intervals on $\rho_1 - \rho_2$ are constructed by way of confidence intervals on the Z-transformation of ρ_1 and ρ_2. To find the $100(1 - \alpha)\%$

confidence interval on $\rho_1 - \rho_2$, one first calculates

$$(Z_{r_1} - Z_{r_2}) \pm {}_{1-(\alpha/2)}Z\sqrt{\frac{1}{n_1 - 3} + \frac{1}{n_2 - 3}}. \qquad (14.18)$$

The two values on the Z scale obtained from Eq. (14.18) are then transformed to the r scale by means of Table G. The resulting two values of r form the $100(1 - \alpha)\%$ confidence interval on $\rho_1 - \rho_2$. The problems of attaching meaning to a value for $\rho_1 - \rho_2$ will be discussed under (h) below.

g. The techniques of this section will be illustrated on data based loosely on studies by Hinton (1939) and Dispensa (1938). In a sample of 200 children ranging in age from six to 15, the correlation between intelligence (Stanford-Binet) X and basal metabolic rate Y was $r_1 = .71$. In a sample of 78 adults ranging in age from 18 to 25, intelligence and basal metabolic rate correlated $r_2 = .28$. We shall test H_0: $\rho_1 = \rho_2$ at the .01 level of significance. Hence, the critical values for z in Eq. (14.17) are -2.58 and 2.58.

$$Z_{.71} = .887 \qquad Z_{.28} = .288.$$

$$z = \frac{Z_{.71} - Z_{.28}}{\sqrt{\dfrac{1}{n_1 - 3} + \dfrac{1}{n_2 - 3}}} = \frac{.887 - .288}{\sqrt{\dfrac{1}{200 - 3} + \dfrac{1}{78 - 3}}} = \frac{.599}{.136} = 4.40.$$

We see that H_0: $\rho_1 = \rho_2$ can be rejected at the .01 level of significance. The 99% confidence interval on $\rho_1 - \rho_2$ is found from Eq. (14.18) as follows:

$$.887 - .288 \pm 2.58\sqrt{\frac{1}{200 - 3} + \frac{1}{78 - 3}} = .599 \pm .350 = (.249, .949).$$

Transforming these two Z-values back to the r-scale yields the 99% confidence interval on $\rho_1 - \rho_2$: .24, .74.

h. While testing the null hypothesis that $\rho_1 = \rho_2$ makes perfectly good sense, merely estimating the difference between the two coefficients with $r_1 - r_2$ and setting a confidence interval around this sample difference may lack meaning. Suppose, for example, that $\rho_1 - \rho_2$ is .20. Any one of the following conditions on ρ_1 and ρ_2 could hold: (1) $\rho_1 = .90$ and $\rho_2 = .70$; (2) $\rho_1 = .20$ and $\rho_2 = .00$; (3) $\rho_1 = .10$ and $\rho_2 = -.10$. Even though in each case the difference between ρ_1 and ρ_2 is the same, .20, the meaning that attaches to the three conditions is quite different. In (1) the .20 difference represents a much larger difference in the ability to predict one variable from the other than the .20 difference in (2). Moreover, the .20 difference between .10 and $-.10$ represents no difference in the ability to predict one variable from the other. Thus, the unadorned difference between ρ_1 and ρ_2

is of little interest, although testing hypotheses about that difference or merely noting the values of r_1 and r_2 are both meaningful approaches.

Hypothesis testing and inferential techniques exist for making inferences about a set of J correlation coefficients for variables X and Y when J independent estimates, r_{xy}, are available. For example, one might test the hypothesis that intelligence X and age at which a child begins to speak Y are equally highly correlated for the three populations of first-, second-, and third-born children. For a presentation of appropriate inferential techniques see Marascuilo (1966).

14.10
INFERENCES ABOUT $\rho_{xy} - \rho_{xz}$
USING DEPENDENT
SAMPLES

a. The null hypothesis to be tested is that a variable X has the same correlation with two other variables, Y and Z, against the alternative hypothesis that ρ_{xy} and ρ_{xz} are not equal:

$$H_0: \rho_{xy} = \rho_{xz}$$

$$H_1: \rho_{xy} \neq \rho_{xz}.$$

This situation would arise if one wished to predict "academic success" (as measured by a grade-point average) and had two potential predictors, Y and Z. If for financial reasons only one predictor (Y or Z) could be used, it would be wise to gather data, estimate r_{xy} and r_{xz}, and then test the hypothesis that the observed difference between the two sample r's represented a true difference between ρ_{xy} and ρ_{xz}.

b. It is assumed that there exist three bivariate-normal populations, one for each of the pairs of variables X and Y, X and Z, and Y and Z. A single *random* sample of n persons is drawn from which the three correlation coefficients r_{xy}, r_{xz}, and r_{yz} are calculated. Obviously, these three estimates of correlation are *not* independent.

c. The test statistic for testing H_0 against H_1 is:

$$z = \frac{\sqrt{n}(r_{xy} - r_{xz})}{\sqrt{(1 - r_{xy}^2)^2 + (1 - r_{xz}^2)^2 - 2r_{yz}^3 - (2r_{yz} - r_{xy}r_{xz})(1 - r_{xy}^2 - r_{xz}^2 - r_{yz}^2)}} \qquad (14.19)$$

where n is the sample size,

r_{xy} is the sample correlation of X and Y,

r_{xz} is the sample correlation of X and Z, and

r_{yz} is the sample correlation of Y and Z.

d. If H_0 is true, i.e., $\rho_{xy} = \rho_{xz}$, then z in Eq. (14.19) has a sampling distribution over repeated samples of size n that is closely approximated by the normal distribution with mean 0 and standard deviation 1 (see Olkin and Siotani, 1964, and Olkin, 1967). When H_1 is true, the mean of the sampling distribution of z in Eq. (14.19) shifts away from zero but the standard deviation remains approximately equal to 1.

e. As might be expected, the null hypothesis H_0: $\rho_{xy} = \rho_{xz}$ is tested at the α-level of significance by comparing the observed value of z in Eq. (14.19) with the $100(\alpha/2)$ and $100[1 - (\alpha/2)]$ percentile points in the unit normal distribution; the two critical values for the hypothesis test are

$$_{\alpha/2}z \quad \text{and} \quad _{1-(\alpha/2)}z.$$

f. Interval estimation of the difference $\rho_{xy} - \rho_{xz}$ is difficult to justify for the same reasons discussed at the end of Sec. 14.9. However, if such estimation can ever be justified, appropriate techniques may be found in Olkin (1967, p. 113).

g. Suppose that success in college X (as measured by grade-point average at the end of the first year) can be predicted either from test battery Y or test battery Z. Only one test battery can be employed because of the short available testing time. It is desired to test the hypothesis H_0: $\rho_{xy} = \rho_{xz}$ at the .05 level of significance.

For a random sample of 100 freshmen who were given both test batteries as high-school seniors, the three possible correlation coefficients among X, Y, and Z are:

$$r_{xy} = .56, \qquad r_{xz} = .43, \qquad r_{yz} = .52.$$

The value of z in Eq. (14.19) is found to be

$$z = \frac{\sqrt{100}(.56 - .43)}{\sqrt{(1 - .56^2)^2 + (1 - .43^2)^2 - 2(.52)^3 - [2(.52) - (.56)(.43)](1 - .56^2 - .43^2 - .52^2)}}$$

$$= \frac{10(.13)}{\sqrt{.6597}} = \frac{1.300}{.8122} = 1.60.$$

The obtained value of z falls far below the required critical value of 1.96. Thus the hypothesis that batteries Y and Z are alike with respect to accuracy in predicting X cannot be rejected. Unless a large sample would alter this conclusion, the decision to administer Y or Z in high school could not be made on the basis of relative predictive accuracies.

14.11
INFERENCES ABOUT OTHER
CORRELATION COEFFICIENTS

In this section, significance testing procedures for the correlation coefficients presented in Chapter 9 will be discussed. The presentation of inferential techniques will be greatly simplified since space does not permit detailed treatments such as those in the previous sections of this chapter. Procedures will be presented with which the null hypothesis of *no correlation* between variables X and Y can be tested against a nondirectional alternative hypothesis for most of the coefficients in Chapter 9. Where possible, a test statistic will be defined that has a known or approximately known sampling distribution *given that the two variables being correlated—whether they are measured dichotomously, with ranks, or otherwise—are unrelated, i.e., have a coefficient of zero in the population.* In each instance, the significance testing procedure will be illustrated with hypothetical data.

The Phi Coefficient, ϕ

Suppose that a random sample of n persons is drawn from a population in which two dichotomously scored variables, X and Y, have a population phi coefficient of zero. For large values of n (20 or greater, say) the sampling distribution of $\sqrt{n}\,\phi$, where ϕ is the *sample* phi coefficient, is approximately normal with mean 0 and standard deviation 1. (When the population phi coefficient is different from zero, the sampling distribution of $\sqrt{n}\,\phi$ becomes skewed and centers around a mean different from zero by an amount that increases as the population value of ϕ deviates further from 0.)

A random sample of $n = 25$ persons is observed on two dichotomous variables: X is the variable "sex" scored 0—female and 1—male; Y is the variable "attrition" scored 0—"dropped out of school" and 1—"remained in school." The sample value of ϕ is equal to $-.41$. The test statistic is found as follows:

$$z = \sqrt{n}\,\phi = \sqrt{25}\,(-.41) = 5(-.41) = -2.05.$$

This value of z lies just below the 2.5th percentile in the unit normal distribution ($_{.025}z = -1.96$). Hence, the hypothesis that sex and attrition from high school are unrelated in the population sampled can be rejected at the .05 level of significance. (It is interesting to note that a sample ϕ lying as far from zero as $-.30$ would not have led to rejection of the null hypothesis at the .05 level for a sample of 25 persons: $\sqrt{n}\,\phi = -1.50 > -1.96$.)

Spearman's Rank-Correlation Coefficient, r_s

The sampling distribution of r_s given zero correlation between two sets of ranks X and Y in the population cannot be characterized in terms of any well-known statistical distributions for n less than approximately 10. For $n > 10$, say, the sampling distribution of r_s when the population Spearman rank-correlation coefficient is zero is related approximately to Student's t-distribution. In fact, for $n > 10$

$$t = \frac{r_s}{\sqrt{(1 - r_s^2)/(n - 2)}} \tag{14.20}$$

is approximately distributed as Student's t-distribution with $n - 2$ df when the population value of r_s is zero.

Suppose, for example, that in a sample of $n = 22$, the value of r_s is .38. The value of t is

$$t = \frac{.38}{\sqrt{\dfrac{1 - .38^2}{22 - 2}}} = \frac{.38}{.207} = 1.84.$$

To test the hypothesis of no correlation in the population, at the .01 level, the above value of $t = 1.84$ is compared with $\pm_{.995}t_{20} = \pm2.845$. Since t lies between the .5th and 99.5th percentiles in the t-distribution with 20 df, the null hypothesis of no correlation in the population cannot be rejected at the .01 level.

For small n, the exact sampling distribution of r_s has been found for testing the null hypothesis of no relationship between the two ranked variables (see Kendall, 1962). Selected percentiles in the sampling distributions of r_s for various values of n have been determined and appear in Table K of Appendix A. As an example of how Table K is read, a value of r_s greater than .794 or less than $-.794$ is required for significance at the .01 level when $n = 11$.

Kendall's τ

The significance of a sample value of Kendall's τ is most conveniently tested in terms of one of the components in its calculation. As was seen in Sec. 9.3, for a sample of size n, τ is found from the formula

$$\tau = \frac{S}{n(n - 1)/2},$$

where $S = P - Q$ is the difference between the total number of "agreements"

P and the total number of "inversions" Q in the two arrays of ranks (see Sec. 9.3 for definitions of "agreements" and "inversions").

The sampling distribution of S is more conveniently studied than that of τ. When n is greater than or equal to 10, the sampling distribution of S is nearly normal when X and Y are uncorrelated in the population; the standard deviation of S is approximately

$$\sqrt{n(n-1)(2n+5)/18}.$$

The sampling distribution of S can be made more nearly normal by a simple "continuity correction" by which S is transformed into a quantity that will be denoted by S^*:

> If S is negative, $S^* = S + 1$.
>
> If S is positive, $S^* = S - 1$.

(In some textbooks, one is directed to calculate S^* by $|S| - 1$. This procedure is incorrect and approximately doubles the probability of a type I error.)

It follows that

$$z = \frac{S^*}{\sqrt{n(n-1)(2n+5)/18}} \tag{14.21}$$

closely follows the normal distribution with mean 0 and standard deviation 1 when $n \geqslant 10$ and the null hypothesis of no relationship between the two variables is true.

Suppose that $n = 10$ and $S = 9$ so that $\tau = 9/[10(9)/2] = .20$. Since S is positive, $S^* = S - 1 = 9 - 1 = 8$. The value of z is

$$z = \frac{8}{\sqrt{10(10-1)[(2 \cdot 10) + 5]/18}} = \frac{8}{\sqrt{125}} = 0.72.$$

The probability is greater than .40 that a z score will lie either above $+0.72$ or below -0.72. Hence we see that a $\tau = .20$ for a sample of size 10 gives no evidence that would lead one to conclude the value of τ is different from zero in the population sampled.

For values of n from 4 to 10, Kendall (1962) tabulated certain characteristics of the sampling distribution of S. Table L of Appendix A lists the probabilities of obtaining values of S equal to or greater than certain tabulated values when $n = 4, \ldots, 10$ and the population value of τ is zero. For example, when $n = 8$ and the population value of τ is zero, we see from Table L that the probability of obtaining a value of S equal to 14 or greater is .054. S attains a value of -14 or less with probability .054. Thus a value of $S = 16$ with an n of 8 is significantly different from zero with an α of .10 for a two-tailed test.

The Point-Biserial Correlation Coefficient, r_{pb}

By inspection of the formula for r_{pb} it can be seen that r_{pb} is equal to zero if and only if $\bar{X}_{.1} = \bar{X}_{.0}$:

$$r_{pb} = \frac{\bar{X}_{.1} - \bar{X}_{.0}}{s_x} \sqrt{\frac{n_1 n_0}{n(n-1)}}.$$

Testing the null hypothesis that a population value of the point-biserial correlation coefficient is zero is closely equivalent to testing the hypothesis that *in the population* those persons scoring 1 on the dichotomous variable have a mean equal to the *population mean* of the persons scoring 0 on the dichotomy, i.e., $H_0: \mu_1 = \mu_0$. If r_{pb} is zero in the population sampled, then

$$t = \frac{r_{pb}}{\sqrt{(1 - r_{pb}^2)/(n-2)}} \tag{14.22}$$

is approximately distributed as Student's t-distribution with $n - 2$ df.

Suppose that in a sample of size $n = 18$ the value of r_{pb} is .56. The value of t is found as follows:

$$t = \frac{.56}{\sqrt{\dfrac{1 - (.56)^2}{18 - 2}}} = \frac{.56}{\dfrac{\sqrt{.6864}}{4}} = 2.70.$$

A t value of 2.70 exceeds the 99th percentile in Student's t-distribution with 16 df. Hence, it appears unlikely that the point-biserial correlation coefficient is zero in the population sampled.

The Tetrachoric Correlation Coefficient, r_{tet}

When the null hypothesis of *no relationship* between X and Y (two normally distributed variables forced into dichotomies) is true, the sampling distribution of the sample tetrachoric correlation coefficient, r_{tet}, is approximately normal for n greater than about 20 with mean 0 and standard deviation

$$\sigma_{r_{tet}} \doteq \sqrt{\frac{p_x p_y q_x q_y}{n}} \frac{1}{u_x u_y}, \tag{14.23}$$

where n is the sample size,

$p_x = n_x/n$, the proportion of persons scoring 1 on the dichotomously measured X variable,

$p_y = n_y/n$, the proportion of persons scoring 1 on the dichotomously measured Y variable,

u_x is the ordinate above the z-score on the unit normal curve above which p_x proportion of the area lies (see Table B), and

X

	0	1	
1	4	19	23
0	21	6	27
	25	25	$n = 50$

Y (row label)

FIG. 14.4

u_y is the ordinate above the z-score on the unit normal curve above which p_y proportion of the area lies.

Thus, for moderately large and large n

$$z = \frac{r_{tet}}{\sigma_{r_{tet}}}$$

can be referred to the unit normal distribution to test the hypothesis that the population tetrachoric correlation coefficient is zero.

Suppose the data in Fig. 14.4 are gathered in studying the relationship between two variables X and Y that are believed to be normally distributed but can only be measured dichotomously.

The value of $(bc)/(ad)$ is $(21)(19)/(4)(6) = 399/24 = 16.625$. In Table H in Appendix A 16.625 is found to correspond to an r_{tet} of .81.

The standard error of r_{tet} is estimated from the following data:

$$p_x = \tfrac{25}{50} = .50 \qquad q_x = .50$$

$$p_y = \tfrac{23}{50} = .46 \qquad q_y = .54.$$

From Table B, the ordinate on the unit normal curve at the point above which $p_x = .50$ of the area lies is $u_x = .3989$; the ordinate on the curve at the point above which $p_y = .46$ of the area lies is $u_y = .3970$. Thus the value of z is

$$z = \frac{.81}{\sqrt{\dfrac{(.50)(.46)(.50)(.54)}{50} \cdot \dfrac{1}{(.3989)(.3970)}}} = 3.64.$$

A z score of 3.64 far exceeds even the 99.5th percentile in the unit normal distribution. We must conclude that the population tetrachoric correlation coefficient is nonzero.

The Biserial Correlation Coefficient, r_{bis}

The exact sampling distribution of r_{bis} is not known. It was never derived by Pearson, and the only substantial finding was that of Soper (1914), who derived the standard deviation of r_{bis} for large samples. McNamara and

Dunlap (1934) argued that when the population biserial correlation coefficient is zero, then for large samples r_{bis} should be approximately normally distributed with mean 0 and standard deviation

$$\sigma_{r_{bis}} \doteq \frac{\sqrt{n_1 n_0}}{un\sqrt{n}}, \tag{14.24}$$

where n is the sample size,

n_1 is the number of persons scoring 1 on the dichotomous variable $(n_0 = n - n_1)$, and

u is the ordinate on the unit normal curve at the point above which n_1/n proportion of the area under the curve lies.

When the population biserial correlation coefficient departs from zero, the value of $\sigma_{r_{bis}}$ is diminished by $1/\sqrt{n}$ times the square of the population value of r_{bis}. When the population value of r_{bis} is different from zero, the sampling distribution of r_{bis} becomes nonnormal, being skewed toward zero.

Empirical sampling studies by Lord (1963a) and Baker (1965) have shown that the above large-sample estimate of the standard error of r_{bis} is quite nearly exact; in Baker's case this was true even for samples of size 15.

Suppose that for a sample of size 36 in which $n_1 = 16$ and $n_0 = 20$, the value of r_{bis} is $-.145$. The value of $\sigma_{r_{bis}}$ when the population biserial coefficient is zero is

$$\sigma_{r_{bis}} = \frac{\sqrt{16 \cdot 20}}{(.3951)36\sqrt{36}} = .210.$$

If the population value of r_{bis} is zero, $r_{bis}/\sigma_{r_{bis}}$ will be approximately normally distributed with mean 0 and standard deviation 1 over repeated random samples of size n.

$$z = \frac{r_{bis}}{\sigma_{r_{bis}}} = \frac{-.145}{.210} = -.69.$$

A z value of $-.69$ appears to be a not unusual observation to obtain in sampling from a unit normal distribution. Hence, evidence does not exist to allow rejection of the null hypothesis of a population biserial correlation coefficient of zero.

The Rank-Biserial Correlation Coefficient, r_{rb}

For a discussion of significance tests for the rank-biserial correlation coefficient r_{rb} see Cureton (1956) and Glass (1966b).

The Partial Correlation Coefficient, $r_{xy \cdot z}$

The partial correlation coefficient between X and Y with variable Z "held constant" was developed in Sec. 9.4. There it was seen that the correlation of the errors of estimate when both X and Y are predicted individually from Z is

$$r_{xy \cdot z} = \frac{r_{xy} - r_{xz} r_{yz}}{\sqrt{(1 - r_{xz}^2)(1 - r_{yz}^2)}}.$$

The population partial correlation of X and Y with Z "partialed out" can be denoted by

$$\rho_{xy \cdot z} = \frac{\rho_{xy} - \rho_{xz} \rho_{yz}}{\sqrt{(1 - \rho_{xz}^2)(1 - \rho_{yz}^2)}}.$$

When $\rho_{xy \cdot z}$ equals zero, the test statistic

$$t = \frac{r_{xy \cdot z}}{\sqrt{(1 - r_{xy \cdot z}^2)/(n - 3)}} \qquad (14.25)$$

has Student's t-distribution with $n - 3$ df. Suppose that in a sample of $n = 12$, the value of $r_{xy \cdot z}$ is .80. Then

$$t = \frac{.80}{\sqrt{(1 - .80^2)/(12 - 3)}} = 4.00.$$

The 99.5th percentile in the t-distribution with 9 degrees of freedom is 3.250. The null hypothesis of a zero population partial correlation coefficient can be rejected at the .01 level of significance.

14.12
INFERENCES ABOUT P, THE POPULATION PROPORTION

a. We shall now be concerned with the proportion of "units" (persons, families, schools, counties, etc.) in a population that possess some characteristic (blue eyes, a late-model car, a "modern math" curriculum, a children's diagnostic center, etc.). The proportion of the units in the population that possess the characteristic in question will be denoted by P, which equals the number of the units possessing the characteristic divided by the total number of units in the population. For example, of the 60,000 pupils in a particular school system, 3000 are of Spanish-American descent; hence, $P = 3000/$

$60,000 = .05$ when the characteristic being observed is "Spanish-American vs. non-Spanish-American descent."

The hypothesis to be tested is that in a relatively large population, the proportion P possessing a particular characteristic is equal to a value a that lies between 0 and 1.0, inclusive:

$$H_0: P = a$$

$$H_1: P \neq a.$$

b. For purposes of testing H_0 against H_1 it need only be assumed that a *random* sample of size n is drawn from the population.

c. Within the sample of n units, the number f who possess the characteristic in question is observed. The sample proportion p is the ratio of f to n:

$$p = \frac{f}{n}.$$

The statistic p is an estimator of P. In fact, if we think of a dichotomously measured variable X that equals 1 when the unit observed possesses the characteristic in question and 0 when it does not, then p is to P as $\bar{X}$. is to μ. For example, suppose that "male gender" is the characteristic being measured. A child's score is denoted by X_i, which equals 1 if the child is male and 0 if female. If in a sample of n children there are f males ("1's scorers"), then

$$\sum_{i=1}^{n} X_i = X_1 + \ldots + X_n = f.$$

Hence,

$$\bar{X}. = \frac{\sum X}{n} = \frac{f}{n} = p.$$

The population mean of X will be P. Thus p possesses all the properties as an estimator of P which $\bar{X}$. possesses as an estimator of μ.

In this context it is also interesting to note that the *dichotomously* scored X variable has a *variance* in the population that equals

$$\sigma_x^2 = E(X - P)^2 = P(1 - P),$$

where P is the population proportion. This fact will be used below.

d. Suppose that the null hypothesis is true so that P equals a. You probably recall that the sampling distribution of $\bar{X}$. has a mean μ and standard deviation $\sigma_x/\sqrt{n}$. The same is true of p. For samples of size n, the sampling distribution of p has a mean of a—the population proportion—and a standard deviation of $\sigma_x/\sqrt{n} = \sqrt{a(1-a)/n}$:

$$E(p) = a$$

$$\sigma_p = \sqrt{\frac{a(1-a)}{n}}.$$

The question of the *shape* of the sampling distribution of p is answered by appealing to the central limit theorem. When n is *sufficiently large*, the sampling distribution of p is *normal* with mean P and standard deviation $\sqrt{P(1-P)/n}$. "Sufficiently large" can be taken to mean that before p can be considered normally distributed, the value of nP or $n(1-P)$, *whichever is smaller*, must be greater than 5. This rule-of-thumb depends on the sample size n and the unknown population proportion P. Suppose, for example, that an anthropologist wishes to make an inference about the proportion of left-handed persons in an African tribe. (P is as small as .02 in some African tribes, but P is greater than .10 in the United States.) The anthropologist would do well to draw a sample as large as 500 to guard against the possibility that P is as small as .01—$nP = 500(.01) = 5$.

If the value of P is a, i.e., if H_0 is true, and if na is greater than 5, then

$$z = \frac{p - a}{\sqrt{a(1-a)/n}} \tag{14.26}$$

is approximately normally distributed over random samples of size n with mean 0 and standard deviation 1.

If P is some value b different from a, p will, of course, be approximately normally distributed with mean b and standard deviation $\sqrt{b(1-b)/n}$, provided nb or $n(1-b)$, whichever is smaller, is greater than about 5.

e. To test H_0 against H_1 at the α-level of significance, the value of z in Eq. (14.26) is compared with the $100(\alpha/2)$ and $100[1-(\alpha/2)]$ percentiles in the unit normal distribution:

$$_{\alpha/2}z \qquad _{1-(\alpha/2)}z.$$

f. The 95% and 99% confidence intervals on P around p can be found most easily by reference to Table P in Appendix A. Suppose, for example, that in a sample of $n = 100$, the value of p is .60. The 95% confidence interval on P ranges approximately from .51 to .71. For large samples, the probability is only approximately $1 - \alpha$ that $p \pm {}_{1-(\alpha/2)}z\sqrt{p(1-p)/n}$ will include P between its limits.

g. The superintendent of a school district wishes to take a poll one month before a city election to determine the chances of the proposed school bond receiving a majority of the votes that will be cast.   The hypothesis to be tested at the .01 level of significance is that P, the proportion of the 25,000 registered voters favoring the school bond, is .50; the alternative hypothesis is that P is not .50.   A random sample of $n = 100$ registered voters is drawn; upon questioning, $f = 42$ voters indicated that they favored the school bond.

The value of p is $f/n = .42$.   The value of z in Eq. (14.26) is

$$z = \frac{p - a}{\sqrt{a(1 - a)/n}} = \frac{.42 - .50}{\sqrt{.50(.50)/100}} = -1.60.$$

The z value of -1.60 is compared with the critical values $_{.005}z = -2.58$ and $_{.995}z = 2.58$.   It cannot be concluded that $p = .42$ is significantly different from .50 at the .01 level.   In fact, even if the .05 level of significance had been adopted, evidence would not exist for rejecting $H_0: P = .50$ since the critical values of z are -1.64 and 1.64.

The 99% confidence interval on P is found (from Table P) to extend from approximately .28 to .55.

14.13
INFERENCES ABOUT $P_1 - P_2$
USING INDEPENDENT
SAMPLES

a. There are two large populations 1 and 2 in which the proportions of persons (or more generally, "units") possessing a certain characteristic are P_1 and P_2.   The hypothesis to be tested is that $P_1 = P_2$ against the alternative hypothesis that $P_1 \neq P_2$:

$$H_0: P_1 = P_2$$

$$H_1: P_1 \neq P_2.$$

For example, one might test the null hypothesis that the proportion P_1 of students receiving vocational counseling who plan to attend college is equal to the proportion P_2 of students *not* receiving vocational counseling who plan to attend college.

b. All that need be assumed is that a *random* sample of size n_1 is drawn from population 1 and that an *independent random* sample of size n_2 is drawn from population 2.

c. The number of persons in the sample from population 1 possessing the characteristic being observed is f_1 and the proportion is $p_1 = f_1/n_1$.   In the sample from population 2, f_2 possess the characteristic in question (planning to attend college, say) and the proportion is $p_2 = f_2/n_2$.   The following test statistic is defined:

$$z = \frac{p_1 - p_2}{\sqrt{\left(\dfrac{f_1 + f_2}{n_1 + n_2}\right)\left(1 - \dfrac{f_1 + f_2}{n_1 + n_2}\right)\left(\dfrac{1}{n_1} + \dfrac{1}{n_2}\right)}}. \tag{14.27}$$

The quantity $(f_1 + f_2)/(n_1 + n_2)$ is the proportion of persons in both samples 1 and 2 that possess the characteristic of interest. If the null hypothesis is true, then P_1 and P_2 equal a common value P that is estimated by $(f_1 + f_2)/(n_1 + n_2)$. And $(f_1 + f_2)/(n_1 + n_2)$ multiplied by 1 minus the same quantity is an estimate of the variance of X, a dichotomously scored variable with mean P. Hence, z in Eq. (14.27) bears a resemblance to

$$t = (\bar{X}_{.1} - \bar{X}_{.2})\Big/\sqrt{s_x^2\left(\frac{1}{n_1} + \frac{1}{n_2}\right)}$$

that would be used to test the hypothesis that $\mu_1 = \mu_2$.

d. If $H_0: P_1 = P_2$ is true and if, for both populations 1 and 2, $n_1 P_1$ [or $n_1(1 - P_1)$ whichever is smaller] and $n_2 P_2$ [or $n_2(1 - P_2)$ whichever is smaller] are greater than 5, then z in Eq. (14.27) has a normal distribution with mean 0 and standard deviation 1 over repeated pairs of independent samples.

e. To test H_0 against H_1 at the α-level of significance, the single calculated value of z in Eq. (14.27) is compared with $_{\alpha/2}z$ and $_{1-(\alpha/2)}z$, the $100(\alpha/2)$ and $100[1 - (\alpha/2)]$ percentiles in the unit normal distribution.

f. For large values of n_1 and n_2 (both equal to 100 or more, perhaps), the $100(1 - \alpha)\%$ confidence interval on $P_1 - P_2$ is given approximately by

$$(p_1 - p_2) \pm {}_{1-(\alpha/2)}z\sqrt{\left(\frac{f_1 + f_2}{n_1 + n_2}\right)\left(1 - \frac{f_1 + f_2}{n_1 + n_2}\right)\left(\frac{1}{n_1} + \frac{1}{n_2}\right)}. \tag{14.28}$$

g. A group of 200 students is randomly divided into two groups of 100 students each. Students in sample 1 are required to study instructional materials in which the concept of transitivity of the relationship "taller than" is first stated verbally then followed by several examples. In the instructional materials for sample 2, the examples are given first and are followed by the verbal statement of the concept. Underlying these two samples are hypothetical populations 1 and 2 of students who could have been selected to participate in the experiment. After studying the instructional materials, students in both samples are given one test item to determine whether they have mastered the transitivity concept. We wish to test whether the proportions P_1 and P_2 of students in the hypothetical populations who master the concept (as evidenced by correctly answering the test item) are equal.

Suppose we choose α to be .05 and that at the end of the experiment $f_1 = 68$ of the students in sample 1 mastered the concept and $f_2 = 54$ of the students in sample 2 mastered it. The value of z in Eq. (14.27) is

$$z = \frac{(68/100) - (54/100)}{\sqrt{\left(\dfrac{68 + 54}{100 + 100}\right)\left(1 - \dfrac{68 + 54}{100 + 100}\right)\left(\dfrac{1}{100} + \dfrac{1}{100}\right)}} = 2.03.$$

A z value of 2.03 exceeds the critical value of $_{.975}z = 1.96$ and, thus, constitutes evidence to reject $H_0: P_1 = P_2$. We can conclude in this hypothetical example that stating the concept first and then presenting examples of it is superior to the reverse order.

h. Appropriate techniques for making inferences concerning a set of J population proportions (in this section $J = 2$) exist. For example, one could be interested in the null hypothesis that in a large urban school system the proportion of Negroes, Puerto Ricans, and Orientals ($J = 3$) who leave school before graduation is the same. For a discussion of these techniques, see Marascuilo (1966) first and then Goodman (1964).

14.14
INFERENCES ABOUT $P_1 - P_2$
USING DEPENDENT SAMPLES

a. The hypotheses to be tested are identical to those in Sec. 14.13, namely, $H_0: P_1 = P_2$ against $H_1: P_1 \neq P_2$.

b. Two random samples both of size n are drawn from populations 1 and 2, respectively. In contrast to the procedures in Sec. 14.13, we do not require the two samples to be independent. Thus samples 1 and 2 could comprise matched pairs, twin mates, "before" and "after" observations, etc. The most frequent application of the procedures in this section are to problems in which samples 1 and 2 are the same group of persons observed at two different points in time. Thus, it has sometimes been referred to as a significance test of "change," but we shall see that this interpretation is not entirely correct.

c. As with all techniques involving dependent samples, it is possible to establish "pairs" of observations, one member of each pair from sample 1 and the other member from sample 2. Without losing any generality, we shall consider samples 1 and 2 to be observations of n persons at times 1 and

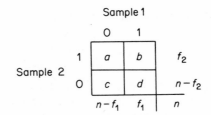

FIG. 14.5

2, respectively. The number of persons scoring 1 on the dichotomous variable, i.e., having the characteristic being observed, in sample 1 is f_1 and $p_1 = f_1/n$. In sample 2, f_2 persons have the characteristic, and $p_2 = f_2/n$. It is also necessary to determine the number of *pairs* of observations in which both members of the pair (one from sample 1 and one from sample 2) score 1, i.e., possess the attribute being observed. Such data can be tabulated in a 2×2 contingency table as shown in Fig. 14.5.

For example, b might be the number of persons out of n who possess the characteristic being observed at both times 1 and 2.

The following test statistic can be used to test H_0 against H_1:

$$z = \frac{d - a}{\sqrt{d + a}}. \tag{14.29}$$

d. When $H_0: P_1 = P_2$ is true, z in Eq. (14.29) is approximately normally distributed with mean 0 and standard deviation 1, *provided that $d + a$ is as large as* 10.

e. The critical values against which z in Eq. (14.29) is compared in testing H_0 at the α-level of significance are $_{\alpha/2}z$ and $_{1-(\alpha/2)}z$.

f. The question of placing a confidence interval on $P_1 - P_2$ will not be discussed.

g. A sample of $n = 60$ persons is asked to indicate whether or not they approve of capital punishment both before and after being exposed to a persuasive lecture on the abolition of capital punishment. The sample of 60 pre-lecture responses to the question on capital punishment constitutes sample 1; the 60 post-lecture responses constitute sample 2. The data obtained are tabulated in Fig. 14.6.

As an example of how the table in Fig. 14.6 is interpreted, one sees that 26 persons approved of capital punishment before hearing the lecture and disapproved after the lecture.

The null hypothesis that $P_1 = P_2$ will be tested at the .05 level of significance. The value of z in Eq. (14.29) is

$$z = \frac{d - a}{\sqrt{d + a}} = \frac{10 - 26}{\sqrt{10 + 26}} = \frac{-16}{6} = -2.67.$$

A z value of -2.67 lies considerably below the critical value of $_{.025}z = -1.96$. (Note that $d + a$ is far greater than 10.) Hence, the hypothesis that in the populations sampled (persons who had not heard an abolition of capital punishment lecture and persons who had) the proportions endorsing capital punishment are equal can be rejected at the .05 level of significance.

Sample 1

Pre-lecture

		Approve	Disapprove	
Sample 2 Post–lecture	Disapprove	$a = 26$	$b = 8$	34
	Approve	$c = 16$	$d = 10$	26
		42	18	$n = 60$

FIG. 14.6

h. The test outlined above must not be considered equivalent to testing the significance of "change." Notice that in the table in Fig. 14.7 the overwhelming changes taking place are apparent even though the test statistic in Eq. (14.29) is equal to zero.

$$z = \frac{d - a}{\sqrt{d + a}} = 0.$$

The significance test of this section is a test of the significance of the difference between $p_1 = f_1/n$ and $p_2 = f_2/n$ and not of a hypothesis about "change." Change is evaluated by the significance test presented here only as it may be reflected in the difference between P_1 and P_2.

The techniques presented in this section are due to McNemar (1947).

Time 1

		Agree	Disagree	
Time 2	Disagree	40	20	$60 = f_2$
	Agree	0	40	40
		40	$60 = f_1$	$100 = n$

FIG. 14.7

14.15 INFERENCES ABOUT THE INDEPENDENCE OF CLASSIFICATIONS IN A CONTINGENCY TABLE

Often observations are made that permit nominal measurement of each unit (person, group, etc.) with respect to two modes of classification. For example, students can be classified both with respect to sex (male-female) and academic major (humanities, social sciences, physical sciences, engineering, or education). Schools can be classified with respect to whether they are public or private and whether they offer an industrial arts curriculum or not.

Suppose that 120 persons were classified with respect to their political affiliation and their sex. The *frequencies* of the various combinations of attributes could be tabulated in a *contingency table* as shown in Fig. 14.8. As an example of how the table is interpreted, one sees that 14 of the 120 persons sampled are female Democrats.

In general, we can consider a contingency table with I rows and J columns. We shall denote the frequency of observations in the cell at the intersection of the ith row and jth column by f_{ij}. For example, in Fig. 14.9 the number of persons in the cell in row 1 and column 1 is f_{11}.

Note that in Fig. 14.8 the value of $f_{11} = 29, f_{12} = 36, f_{1.} = 80, f_{.3} = 17$, and $f_{..} = n = 120$.

a. The null hypothesis to be tested is that the two modes of classification upon which the contingency table is based are *independent*. This notion of *independence* requires some elaboration.

Consider again the problem of studying the relationship between sex and political affiliation in the population of all adults in a particular community. We shall denote the proportions of males in the population by $P_{.1}$ and the proportion of females by $P_{2.}$. The proportions of Democrats,

		Political affiliation			
		Democrat	Republican	Independent	
Sex	Male	29	36	15	80
	Female	14	24	2	40
		43	60	17	120

FIG. 14.8 Contingency table showing the relationship between sex and political affiliation.

Classification 2

		1	$\cdots$	j	$\cdots$	J	Row totals
	1	f_{11}	$\cdots$	f_{1j}	$\cdots$	f_{1J}	$f_{1.}$
Classification 1	i	f_{i1}	$\cdots$	f_{ij}	$\cdots$	f_{iJ}	$f_{i.}$
	I	f_{I1}	$\cdots$	f_{Ij}	$\cdots$	f_{IJ}	$f_{I.}$
Column totals		$f_{.1}$	$\cdots$	$f_{.j}$	$\cdots$	$f_{.J}$	$f_{..} = n$

FIG. 14.9

Republicans, and Independents in the population will be denoted by P_1, P_2, and P_3, respectively. If a sample of size n is drawn strictly at random from the population, these proportions can be interpreted as probabilities of obtaining males, females, or any one of the three political affiliations.

It was seen in Chapter 10 that the probability of the joint occurrence of two independent events is the product of their separate probabilities. For example, if sex and political affiliation are independent of each other, then the probability that an adult randomly selected from the population is a female Democrat is $P_{.2}P_{.1}$; the probability of randomly drawing a male Republican is $P_{.1}P_{.2}$ *if the two classifications are independent.* Testing the null hypothesis of independence is equivalent to testing the hypothesis that the probability of drawing a person who falls into cell ij of the contingency table is equal to the product of the probability that the person belongs to any cell in row i and the probability that he belongs to any cell in column j:

$$H_0: P_{ij} = P_{i.}P_{.j}, \quad \text{for all values of } i \text{ and } j.$$

The alternative hypothesis, H_1, is that $P_{ij} = P_{i.}P_{.j}$ is not true for at least one of the IJ cells in the contingency table.

b. All that is assumed is that a random sample of size n is drawn from the population in question.

c. The following test statistic is used to test H_0 against H_1:

$$\chi^2 = n\left[\sum_{i=1}^{I} \sum_{j=1}^{J} \frac{f_{ij}^2}{f_{i.}f_{.j}} - 1 \right], \tag{14.30}$$

where f_{ij} is the number of observations in the (ij)th cell of the contingency table,

$f_{i.}$ is the number of observations in the ith row of the table,
$f_{.j}$ is the number of observations in the jth column of the table, and
$n = f_{..}$, the total number of observations.

d. When the null hypothesis of independence of the two classifications is true, the statistic χ^2 in Eq. (14.30) has a chi-square distribution with $(I-1)(J-1)$ degrees of freedom over repeated random samples of size n from the population. For example, if sex and political affiliation are independent in the population from which the sample in Fig. 14.8 was drawn, then χ^2 for the data in that figure should appear to be a typical observation from a chi-square distribution with $(I-1)(J-1) = (2-1)(3-1) = 2$ degrees of freedom.

If H_0 is false, χ^2 in Eq. (14.30) will tend to be larger than the $\chi^2_{(I-1)(J-1)}$ distribution. In other words, nonindependence can be expected to produce large values of χ^2 in Eq. (14.30).

e. To test H_0 at the α-level of significance, the single computed value of χ^2 in Eq. (14.30) is compared with the $100(1-\alpha)$ percentile point in the chi-square distribution with $(I-1)(J-1)$ degrees of freedom, i.e., in the distribution $\chi^2_{(I-1)(J-1)}$. This percentile point is denoted by $_{1-\alpha}\chi^2_{(I-1)(J-1)}$. Selected percentile points in the chi-square distributions are presented in Table C of Appendix A.

f. The hypothesis tested is one involving several parameters (population proportions) and the question of interval estimation of some function of these does not arise.

g. The data in Fig. 14.8 will be used as an illustration. A random sample of $n = 120$ is drawn from the population of adults in a particular community. Each person is classified with respect to sex and political affiliation. The hypothesis of independence of the two modes of classification will be tested at the .01 level of significance.

Substituting the data in Fig. 14.8 into the formula for χ^2 in Eq. (14.30) yields the following value:

$$\chi^2 = 120\left(\frac{29^2}{80\cdot 43} + \frac{36^2}{80\cdot 60} + \frac{15^2}{80\cdot 17} + \frac{14^2}{40\cdot 43} + \frac{24^2}{40\cdot 60} + \frac{2^2}{40\cdot 17} - 1\right)$$

$$= 4.776.$$

The obtained value of $\chi^2 = 4.776$ is compared with the critical value of $_{.99}\chi^2_2 = 9.210$. The null hypothesis of independence cannot be rejected at the .01 level. However, the probability of obtaining a value of χ^2 as large as 4.776 or larger when the null hypothesis is true is slightly less than .10. The evidence for an association other than chance between sex and political affiliation is rather weak.

We shall consider a second illustration in which $I = J = 2$. A sample was drawn at random from the population of first-year graduate students in several large universities by the Committee on the Undergraduate Program

Academic area

		Psychology	Sociology	
Undergraduate mathematics	None	$f_{11} = 25$	$f_{12} = 34$	$f_{1.} = 59$
	Some	$f_{21} = 151$	$f_{22} = 49$	$f_{2.} = 200$
		$f_{.1} = 176$	$f_{.2} = 83$	$f_{..} = 259$

FIG. 14.10

in Mathematics of the Mathematical Association of America. The $n = 259$ students in either psychology or sociology were classified as having either "no credit" or "some credit" in undergraduate mathematics. The contingency table shown in Fig. 14.10 was obtained.

The null hypothesis to be tested is that there is no association between academic area and undergraduate mathematics training. In a 2×2 contingency table, the formula for χ^2 in Eq. (14.30) can be simplified considerably:

$$\chi^2 = \frac{n(f_{11}f_{22} - f_{12}f_{21})^2}{f_{1.}f_{2.}f_{.1}f_{.2}}. \tag{14.31}$$

The value of χ^2 with $(I - 1)(J - 1) = (2 - 1)(2 - 1) = 1$ degree of freedom for the data on mathematics training is found by Eq. (14.31) as follows:

$$\chi^2 = \frac{259(25 \cdot 49 - 34 \cdot 151)^2}{59 \cdot 200 \cdot 176 \cdot 83} = 22.96.$$

From Table C in Appendix A it is seen that the probability of obtaining a χ^2 as large as 22.96 or larger is less than .001 if academic area (psychology vs. sociology) and undergraduate mathematics training (no credit vs. some credit) are independent. We can conclude that there is a tendency for first-year psychology graduate students to have more undergraduate mathematics training than first-year sociology graduate students.

h. The discussion in this section of the chi-square test of independence of the classifications in a contingency table is sketchy in the extreme. Space permits only the mention of several important considerations in the application of this technique and the presentation of references in which they are examined.

When the number of observations in *any* cell of a 2×2 contingency table is small (less than 10), use of a correction to the formula for χ^2 in Eq. (14.31) due to Yates (1934) is advisable. The purpose of Yates's *continuity correction* is to improve the approximation of the sampling distribution of χ^2 to the chi-square distribution with one degree of freedom. For discussions of Yates's correction in textbooks in applied statistics see McNemar (1962), Ferguson (1966), or Hays (1963), among others.

There exists a conceptually distinct interpretation of the chi-square test of this section that is appropriate when the persons in the different rows (or columns) of the contingency table can be regarded as sampled from separate and distinct populations. The chi-square contingency table test presented above may then be regarded as a test of *homogeneous populations*. For a discussion of the chi-square test of homogeneous populations, see Keeping (1962) and Guenther (1965).

Techniques exist whereby the hypothesis of independence of three modes of classification in a three-way contingency table may be tested. See Tate and Clelland (1957).

The problem of determining which subset of cells in a contingency table contributes to a significant χ^2 statistic has been dealt with by Marascuilo (1966).

Finally, a valuable series of papers on the use and misuse of the chi-square contingency table test appears in the *Psychological Bulletin*: Lewis and Burke (1949), Edwards (1950), Lewis and Burke (1950), Pastore (1950), Peters (1950), Burke (1951).

14.16
RELATIONSHIP BETWEEN
INTERVAL ESTIMATION AND
HYPOTHESIS TESTING

A relationship exists in most instances between methods of interval estimation and hypothesis testing that allows one to determine from inspection of a $100(1 - \alpha)\%$ confidence interval what the results would be of a hypothesis test at the α-level of significance. For example, if the 95 % confidence interval around $\bar{X}_{.}$ on μ *includes* 0, then the hypothesis H_0: $\mu = 0$ *cannot* be rejected at the .05 level. If the $100(1 - \alpha)\%$ confidence interval around r on ρ *includes* 0, then the hypothesis H_0: $\rho = 0$ *cannot* be rejected at the α-level of significance. If the $100(1 - \alpha)\%$ confidence interval around $\bar{X}_{.1} - \bar{X}_{.2}$ *does not include* 0, then the hypothesis H_0: $\mu_1 - \mu_2 = 0$ *can* be rejected at the α-level. *In general, all values along a particular $100(1 - \alpha)\%$ confidence interval would lead to acceptance at the α-level of the null hypothesis that the parameter being estimated was equal to any one of those values. Conversely, any value outside the confidence interval would lead to rejection of the hypothesis that the parameter in question was equal to any one of those values.* For example, if the 99 % confidence interval around a particular $\bar{X}_{.}$ on μ extended from -4.86 to 8.41, then the same data would lead to *rejection* of any hypothesis that μ was any number less than -4.86 or greater than 8.41; if it had been hypothesized that μ was 0, the data would lead to *acceptance* of this hypothesis at the .01 level.

Suppose that the 95 % confidence interval on μ is being established around $\bar{X}$. by means of Eq. (14.2). Suppose further that the entire confidence interval is above zero. Hence, the lower limit of the confidence interval, namely $\bar{X}. - {}_{.975}t_{n-1}s_x/\sqrt{n}$, is greater than zero:

$$\bar{X}. - {}_{.975}t_{n-1}\frac{s_x}{\sqrt{n}} > 0.$$

It follows that

$$\bar{X}. > {}_{.975}t_{n-1}\frac{s_x}{\sqrt{n}}$$

and that

$$\frac{\bar{X}.}{s_x/\sqrt{n}} > {}_{.975}t_{n-1}.$$

The above inequality states that the test statistic [see Eq. (14.1)] for testing the hypothesis that $\mu = 0$ exceeds the 97.5 percentile in the t-distribution with $n - 1$ df. Hence, the hypothesis that $\mu = 0$ can be rejected at the $1 - .95 = .05$ level. Thus, the confidence interval contained the information necessary to make a hypothesis test as well.

PROBLEMS AND EXERCISES

1. Herman (1967) found Minnesota Teacher Attitude Inventory scores for a sample of 14 athletes and 28 nonathletes. His findings are summarized below:

Athletes	Nonathletes
$n_1 = 14$	$n_2 = 28$
$\bar{X}_{.1} = 116.00$	$\bar{X}_{.2} = 119.54$
$s_1 = 31.11$	$s_2 = 32.41$

Test the null hypothesis at the .01 level that in the populations of athletes and nonathletes sampled μ_1 equals μ_2.

2. Samuels (1967) performed an experiment to determine if the presence of pictures facilitated or interfered with young children's learning of words. Twenty pre-first-grade children were randomly assigned to either learn words which were illustrated with simple pictures or learn the same words without pictures. After several learning trials each child was tested on his knowledge of the words taught. The number of correct responses on the test trials for each group had the following means and standard deviations:

Nonpicture group	Picture group
$n = 10$	$n = 10$
$\bar{X}_{.1} = 19.20$	$\bar{X}_{.2} = 11.30$
$s_1 = 7.93$	$s_2 = 5.79$

Test the null hypothesis at the .05 level of significance that the two groups can be considered to be random samples from two populations with the same mean.

3. Herman (1967) studied the relationship between grade-point averages (X) in professional education courses and scores on the Minnesota Teacher Attitude Inventory (Y) on a sample of 42 prospective physical education teachers. An r_{xy} of $+.19$ was obtained. Construct the 99% confidence interval around this value of r_{xy} on ρ_{xy}. Does the interval include zero?

4. Yamamoto (1967) correlated IQ as measured by the Lorge-Thorndike Intelligence Test and creativity as measured by the Minnesota Tests of Creative Thinking on a sample of $n = 75$ ninth-grade pupils. An r_{xy} of .12 was obtained.

    a. Test the hypothesis H_0: $\rho_{xy} = 0$ at the .05 level of significance.

    b. Yamamoto also obtained a correlation between IQ and creativity of $-.01$ for $n = 84$ eleventh-grade pupils. Test the hypothesis that the population correlation coefficients between IQ and creativity are equal in the populations of ninth-grade and eleventh-grade pupils sampled. Test this hypothesis at the .05 level of significance.

5. Wallen and Campbell (1967) intercorrelated scores on the Miller Analogies Test (X), the Wide-Range Vocabulary Test (Y), and the Lorge-Thorndike Picture Reasoning Test (Z) on a sample of 60 graduate students. The following sample values were obtained:

$$r_{xy} = .58 \qquad r_{xz} = .17 \qquad r_{yz} = .10$$

Test the hypothesis at the .05 level of significance that ρ_{xy} equals ρ_{xz}, i.e., the hypothesis that the Miller Analogies Test is as closely related to a vocabulary test as it is to a nonverbal reasoning test. Interpret the results.

6. Thalberg (1967) intercorrelated intelligence (X), reading rate (Y), and reading comprehension (Z) in a sample of $n = 80$ college students. The following correlation coefficients were obtained:

	X	Y	Z
X		$r_{xy} = -.034$	$r_{xz} = .422$
Y			$r_{yz} = -.385$
Z			

Test the null hypothesis at the .05 level of significance that $\rho_{xy} = \rho_{xz}$, i.e., that intelligence is correlated with both reading rate and reading comprehension to the same degree.

7. North and Buchanan (1967) asked a sample of 69 teachers (29 Caucasian and 40 Negro) whether they perceived "poor children" to be generally responsible or irresponsible. A phi-coefficient of correlation was calculated between the race of the teacher, X, and the teacher's perception of "poor children," Y. A value of $\phi = .24$ seemed to indicate a weak relationship between the variables; Caucasian teachers tended to perceive "poor children" as irresponsible more than did Negro teachers. Using the techniques of Sec. 14.11, test the hypothesis at the .10 level of significance that in the population of teachers sampled "teacher's race" and "perception of 'poor children' as irresponsible" are uncorrelated.

8. Stennet (1967) sampled kindergarten pupils from rural Minnesota. In a random sample of $n_1 = 873$ boys, the proportion who were absent from school 20 or more days during the year was $p_1 = .28$. The proportion of girls absent 20 or more days in a sample of $n_2 = 837$ was $p_2 = .27$. Test the null hypothesis at the .01 level of significance that, in the populations of boys and girls sampled, the proportions of pupils missing 20 or more days of school are equal. (See Sec. 14.13.)

9. Brown (1964) investigated the relationship between student behavior and barometric pressure under conditions of high relative humidity. Assume that he sampled 413 classrooms divided among three different *barometric pressures* (high, medium, low) and had the teachers classify the *behavior of the class* as either normal, "squirmy," lethargic, or hyperproductive. (Actually Brown observed the same set of 47 classes on different occasions to generate 413 observations. This "repeated measuring" violates an assumption of independence of the observations in a cell that one must make in performing the chi-square contingency table test. We shall use his data for illustrative purposes nonetheless.) The following frequency data were obtained:

| | | Barometric pressure | | | |
		Low	Medium	High	Totals
	Hyperproductive	30	34	5	69
Class	*"Squirmy"*	79	39	16	134
behavior	*Normal*	60	97	23	180
	Lethargic	13	15	2	30
	Totals	182	185	46	413

Using the chi-square test in Sec. 14.15, test the null hypothesis at the .05 level of significance that *barometric pressure* and *class behavior* are independent in the population of classrooms sampled. [The number of observations in the cell "high-lethargic" contains only two classes. Small cell frequencies work against the validity of the chi-square test. The effect here should be negligible. See Hays (1963, pp. 596–97) for further discussion of the problem.]

10. Dyson (1967) studied the relationship between pupils' self-concepts (above average vs. below average) and whether they were members of a homogeneous or heterogeneous (with respect to classroom) group. The following data were obtained from a sample of $n = 568$ seventh-grade pupils:

| | | Self-concept | | |
		Below average	Above average	Totals
Classroom	*Homogeneous*	108	137	245
grouping	*Heterogeneous*	164	159	323
	Totals	272	296	568

Using the chi-square test for 2×2 contingency tables in Sec. 14.15, test the null hypothesis of independence of self-concept and classroom grouping in the population sampled at both the .10 and .05 levels of significance.

11. Asher and Schusler (1967) gathered data on IQ and access to an automobile on a sample of 190 senior girls in a suburban high school. The following

frequency data were obtained:

		None	Moderate	Great	Totals
			Access to car		
	111 *and up*	20	25	2	47
IQ	101–110	14	47	16	77
	Below 101	22	37	7	66
	Totals	56	109	25	190

Using the chi-square test of independence of classifications in a two-way contingency table (Sec. 14.15), test the null hypothesis at the .01 level of significance that IQ and access to a car are independent in the population of girls sampled.

12. Suppose that a particular 95% confidence interval on $\mu_1 - \mu_2$ based on $n_1 = n_2 = 10$ observations in each sample includes zero between its limits, i.e., zero is between

$$(\overline{X}_{.1} - \overline{X}_{.2}) \pm {}_{.975}t_{18}s_{\overline{x}_{.1}-\overline{x}_{.2}}.$$

Prove that the null hypothesis $H_0: \mu_1 = \mu_2$ cannot be rejected at the .05 level with the same data, i.e., prove that $t = (\overline{X}_{.1} - \overline{X}_{.2})/s_{\overline{x}_{.1}-\overline{x}_{.2}}$ is greater than $-{}_{.975}t_{18}$ and less than ${}_{.975}t_{18}$.

15

THE ONE-FACTOR
ANALYSIS OF VARIANCE—
FIXED EFFECTS

15.1
LAYOUT OF DATA

As an example of a one-factor experiment, assume that a researcher wants to know if four methods of studying a topic differ in their efficiency. He plans to let 10 students study the English monetary system by outlining the topic. A different 10 students will study by writing a summary of the topic; 10 other students will study a programmed textbook of the same material; the remaining 10 students will study the programmed material on a teaching machine. The four study conditions (treatments) represent increasing observable activity by the learner. The one factor in this experiment is "learner activity"; the factor is a concept that relates the four conditions. The treatments of the experiment are different types or amounts of that thing called the *factor*. A factor in an experiment might be "size of type," and the three treatments comprising this factor could be a passage printed in 6 point, 8 point, and 10 point type. The researcher wants to know if at least two of the study conditions produce a different amount of achievement (as measured by a multiple-choice test on English money).

338

Treatment

1	2	3	4
$X_{1,1}$	$X_{1,2}$	$X_{1,3}$	$X_{1,4}$
$X_{2,1}$	$X_{2,2}$	$X_{2,3}$	$X_{2,4}$
.	.	.	.
.	.	.	.
.	.	.	.
$X_{10,1}$	$X_{10,2}$	$X_{10,3}$	$X_{10,4}$

FIG. 15.1 Layout of data from an experiment comparing four levels of learner activity.

The data, multiple-choice test scores of the 40 students, can be tabulated as in Fig. 15.1.

You may wonder why the researcher doesn't simply look at the sums of the four treatments and see if any two are different. He does *not* do this because his attention doesn't focus only on the scores obtained for these particular persons at this particular time. What good would his results be if all he could say was that this group of 10 students did better than this other group on September 11 at this place? Although he has data on these 40 students taken at one particular time, if his experiment is to contribute any knowledge to science, his interest must focus on the populations of students from which these 40 are only a sample and on the population of experiments of which this is only one. The researcher seeks to answer the question, "Could I expect these same results if I had chosen a different 40 subjects and run the experiment at a different time under slightly different conditions?"

15.2
A MODEL FOR THE DATA

To answer this question is to make an inference to a population of students and a population of performances of the experiment. The researcher uses the methods of inferential statistics to answer the question. These methods are powerful tools for experimentation. Like many "servants" of man, however, they ask that certain concessions be made to them. The methods presented in this chapter are appropriate in making inferences to a hypothetical population of trials of the experiment if the population of scores, from which the 40 scores obtained are considered to have been sampled, has a certain form and the sampling is done in a certain way. We may at times speak as though the researcher samples a person when in fact the person's score on the test is that thing assumed to have been sampled from a certain population. As an example of the type of demands inferential statistical methods will make, the researcher must assume that he has drawn the 40 obtained scores at random (i.e., with equal and independent probabilities of being chosen) from four (one for each level of the treatment) normal distributions of scores with equal variances σ^2. These assumptions may appear quite restrictive; it will be pointed out later (Sec. 15.13) that certain violations of the assumptions have little effect on the results of the statistical analysis. Nevertheless, the assumptions should be remembered:

1. The scores were sampled at random
2. from normal populations
3. with equal variances σ^2,
4. and the different samples (four in our example) are independent.

Notice that no assumption is made about the mean μ of the normal populations. It will be seen that the researcher's question about the efficiency of the four methods will become a question about the four means, $\mu_1, \ldots, \mu_4$, of the four normal populations.

We must now phrase the question about the efficiencies of the four methods in more precise terms. Toward this end, we assume that any one of the 40 scores can be represented by a *linear model*, the sum of components (none of which has to be squared, cubed, etc.). The linear model is a decomposition of a score X_{ij} into a sum of terms that have a certain meaning to the statistician. We shall "tentatively entertain" the following linear model for the X_{ij}'s:

$$X_{ij} = \mu + \alpha_j + e_{ij}, \tag{15.1}$$

where X_{ij} is the ith score in the jth group,

μ is a term (equal to the average of the four population means) that is constant for all 40 scores and reflects the overall elevation of the scores,

α_j is a constant for all 10 scores in group j and reflects the elevation (or depression) in these 10 scores that results from the persons' being treated as they were (all 10 persons in group j were treated alike), and

e_{ij} is the "error" in the linear model. It is what remains to make up a person's score after μ and α_j have been taken out.

You must remember that μ, α_j, and e_{ij} are numbers. If in an experiment μ is 12, α_2 is -2, and e_{12} is 1, then X_{12} is $12 - 2 + 1 = 11$.

You might expect that interest focuses on the α_j's. The term μ is of little interest, and little can be done about the e_{ij}'s; but α_j reflects what effect level j of the treatment had on the scores. The researcher's original question, "Do the four methods differ?" can now be stated more precisely: "Is it *not* true that $\alpha_1 = \alpha_2 = \alpha_3 = \alpha_4$?" He wishes to know if he can safely say that the four levels of the treatment do *not* have the same effect. The methods to be developed will be appropriate for testing the hypothesis, called the *null hypothesis* (because there are *no* differences), that $\alpha_1 = \alpha_2 = \alpha_3 = \alpha_4$.

One needs a method of testing this hypothesis because such things as the e_{ij}'s exist. If there were no error in the linear model, the researcher could simply look at the sums of the scores in the four groups to see if they were different and thus test his null hypothesis. But the e_{ij}'s are there and they must be dealt with. How do the e_{ij}'s arise? They come about in various ways. First, persons or whatever is measured are inherently different even when they are treated alike. Of the 10 students who outline the English money material, some will score higher on the test than others simply because they are more intelligent. No amount of control over the conditions of study would result in all 10 students achieving the same degree of knowledge. Second, errors arise when an attempt is made to measure the students. These errors are due to unreliability of the measuring instrument, a multiple-choice test in this instance. A group of persons will not all earn the same test score today that they will tomorrow even if there were no forgetting. Third, errors arise from all manner of uncontrolled happenings during the experiment. A student may break his pencil and have to obtain a new one; someone may feel ill and not do well; someone else may not like the researcher's look and act uncooperatively. Additional error arises if the postulated linear model is not correct; it's possible that no linear model will give an exact description of the data.

All of these sources of error combine to make the results of the experiment today different from what would have been obtained yesterday or tomorrow on different groups of 40 students. The results of the experiment run at any one time will undoubtedly show differences between the four groups. It remains to be established, however, that the groups would be different if the experiment had been run on a different randomly chosen group of students under different conditions.

Let's go back to the original data and see how the null hypothesis that $\alpha_1 = \alpha_2 = \alpha_3 = \alpha_4$ can be tested. First we must develop some machinery. The sum of the scores under level one is denoted by

$$\sum_{i=1}^{10} X_{i1}.$$

The sum of the scores divided by 10, the number of scores summed, is the *arithmetic mean* of group one. The mean will be denoted as follows:

$$\bar{X}_{.1} = \frac{\sum_{i=1}^{10} X_{i1}}{10}.$$

As you'll recall the bar above the X indicates a *mean*; the dot in place of i means that the mean was found by summing over i. How do you find $\bar{X}_{.2}$?

We also need a *grand mean*, the mean of all 40 scores. To find the *grand mean*, we sum all 40 scores and divide by 40. The grand mean is denoted by

$$\bar{X}_{..} = \frac{\sum\limits_{j=1}^{4}\sum\limits_{i=1}^{10} X_{ij}}{40}.$$

Once again, the bar above X indicates a *mean*; the two dots in place of the i and j indicate that both i and j have been summed over.

If one takes the difference between each score in group one and $\bar{X}_{.1}$, squares this difference, and sums the squared differences, this sum has the form

$$\sum_{i=1}^{10} (X_{i1} - \bar{X}_{.1})^2.$$

This sum divided by 9, $(n-1)$, is the *sample variance* for group one and is denoted by s_1^2:

$$s_1^2 = \sum_{i=1}^{10} \frac{(X_{i1} - \bar{X}_{.1})^2}{9}.$$

s_1^2 is an unbiased estimator of σ_1^2, the variance of the population underlying group one. Since σ^2 is also the variance of the three other populations, s_1^2 is an unbiased estimator of this common variance σ^2. s_2^2, s_3^2, and s_4^2 are also unbiased estimators of σ^2. What does s_2^2 stand for?

$$s_2^2 = \sum_{i=1}^{10} \frac{(X_{i2} - \bar{X}_{.2})^2}{9}.$$

Now we have the machinery necessary to continue. Remember, we want to know if we can safely say that it is *not* true that $\alpha_1 = \alpha_2 = \alpha_3 = \alpha_4$.

15.3
ESTIMATES OF THE TERMS
IN THE MODEL

What one actually observes in an experiment are the 40 X_{ij}'s. The numbers μ, α_j, and e_{ij} are unknown and unobservable; but certain estimates of them are possible. The statistician has found a way to estimate the components of the linear model that has very useful and desirable properties. He obtains what are called *least-squares estimates* of μ, α_j, and e_{ij}. Denote these least-squares estimates by $\hat{\mu}$, $\hat{\alpha}_j$, and $\hat{e}_{ij}$. In the process of obtaining the least-squares estimates, the parameters of greatest interest, $\alpha_1, \ldots, \alpha_J$, are assumed to sum to zero, i.e., $\alpha_1 + \ldots + \alpha_J = 0$. This is an entirely reasonable sort of restriction to adopt since we have conceived of the α_j's as "elevators" or "depressors" above or below a general level that is embodied in the parameter μ. By placing this restriction on the α_j's, the statistician almost predestines that the α_j's will have the properties of deviations from a mean μ, since the sum of deviations around a mean is zero. The statistician has found that

$$\hat{\mu} = \bar{X}_{..},$$

$$\hat{\alpha}_j = \bar{X}_{.j} - \bar{X}_{..},$$

$$\hat{e}_{ij} = X_{ij} - \bar{X}_{.j}.$$

The estimates are made to fit the observed data in the sense that

$$X_{ij} = \hat{\mu} + \hat{\alpha}_j + \hat{e}_{ij}.$$

Notice that

$$X_{ij} = \bar{X}_{..} + (\bar{X}_{.j} - \bar{X}_{..}) + (X_{ij} - \bar{X}_{.j}). \qquad (15.2)$$

The first term on the right is $\hat{\mu}$, the second term is $\hat{\alpha}_j$, and the last term is $\hat{e}_{ij}$.

15.4
SUMS OF SQUARES

The motivation for the steps that follow won't be clear until much later in this chapter; let's proceed to do some arbitrary-looking manipulations on Eq. (15.2).

First, subtract the grand mean $\bar{X}_{..}$ from each side of Eq. (15.2):

$$X_{ij} - \bar{X}_{..} = (\bar{X}_{.j} - \bar{X}_{..}) + (X_{ij} - \bar{X}_{.j}).$$

Second, square each side of the above equation and sum both sides over j and i:

$$\sum_{j=1}^{4}\sum_{i=1}^{10}(X_{ij} - \bar{X}_{..})^2 = \sum_{j=1}^{4}\sum_{i=1}^{10}[(\bar{X}_{.j} - \bar{X}_{..}) + (X_{ij} - \bar{X}_{.j})]^2. \qquad (15.3)$$

The quantity on the left in Eq. (15.3) is called the *total sum of squares*. For the entire set of numbers obtained in an experiment, the sum of the squared deviation of each number from the grand mean is the *total sum of squares*.

Let's consider the right side of Eq. (15.3). Notice that if we let a stand for $(\bar{X}_{.j} - \bar{X}_{..})$ and b stand for $(X_{ij} - \bar{X}_{.j})$ then the right side involves the quantity $(a + b)^2$. You already know that $(a + b)^2 = a^2 + 2ab + b^2$. So it's easy to show that

$$\sum_{j=1}^{4}\sum_{i=1}^{10}(X_{ij} - \bar{X}_{..})^2$$

$$= \sum_{j=1}^{4}\sum_{i=1}^{10}[(\bar{X}_{.j} - \bar{X}_{..})^2 + 2(\bar{X}_{.j} - \bar{X}_{..})(X_{ij} - \bar{X}_{.j}) + (X_{ij} - \bar{X}_{.j})^2].$$

The right side of this equation is the same as

$$\sum_{j=1}^{4}\sum_{i=1}^{10}(\bar{X}_{.j}-\bar{X}_{..})^2 + 2\sum_{j=1}^{4}\sum_{i=1}^{10}(\bar{X}_{.j}-\bar{X}_{..})(X_{ij}-\bar{X}_{.j}) + \sum_{j=1}^{4}\sum_{i=1}^{10}(X_{ij}-\bar{X}_{.j})^2.$$

$$(15.4)$$

Consider for a moment only the middle term in Eq. (15.4). Since the quantity $\bar{X}_{.j}-\bar{X}_{..}$ has no i subscript, the $\sum$ sign for i can be moved past it; thus we may write the second term as follows:

$$2\sum_{j=1}^{4}(\bar{X}_{.j}-\bar{X}_{..})\sum_{i=1}^{10}(X_{ij}-\bar{X}_{.j}). \qquad (15.5)$$

Say for the moment that we are in group one and that we want to find

$$\sum_{i=1}^{10}(X_{i1}-\bar{X}_{.1}).$$

For this group, $\bar{X}_{.1}$ is a constant; using Rule 2 of Sec. 2.5, then, we can show that

$$\sum_{i=1}^{10}(X_{i1}-\bar{X}_{.1}) = \sum_{i=1}^{10}X_{i1} - 10\bar{X}_{.1} = \sum_{i=1}^{10}X_{i1} - \frac{10\sum_{i=1}^{10}X_{i1}}{10} = 0.$$

Going back to Eq. (15.5), we now see that

$$2\sum_{j=1}^{4}(\bar{X}_{.j}-\bar{X}_{..})\sum_{i=1}^{10}(X_{ij}-\bar{X}_{.j})$$
$$= 2[(\bar{X}_{.1}-\bar{X}_{..})\cdot 0 + \ldots + (\bar{X}_{.4}-\bar{X}_{..})\cdot 0] = 0.$$

Since the middle term of Eq. (15.4) is exactly zero—this is not an assumption, we have proved it, and it will be true for any set of numbers—we have shown that

$$\sum_{j=1}^{4}\sum_{i=1}^{10}(X_{ij}-\bar{X}_{..})^2 = \sum_{j=1}^{4}\sum_{i=1}^{10}(\bar{X}_{.j}-\bar{X}_{..})^2 + \sum_{j=1}^{4}\sum_{i=1}^{10}(X_{ij}-\bar{X}_{.j})^2. \quad (15.6)$$

Notice that in the first term on the right side of Eq. (15.6) no subscript i appears. The quantity $(\bar{X}_{.j}-\bar{X}_{..})^2$ is the same for all i from one to 10 when j has been fixed. For example, for the first, second, . . . , tenth scores in group one, $(\bar{X}_{.1}-\bar{X}_{..})^2$ is the same. Therefore,

$$\sum_{j=1}^{4}\sum_{i=1}^{10}(\bar{X}_{.j}-\bar{X}_{..})^2 = \sum_{j=1}^{4}10\cdot(\bar{X}_{.j}-\bar{X}_{..})^2.$$

Finally, we have broken the total sum of squares into two parts:

$$\sum_{j=1}^{4}\sum_{i=1}^{10}(X_{ij}-\bar{X}_{..})^2 = \sum_{j=1}^{4}10\cdot(\bar{X}_{.j}-\bar{X}_{..})^2 + \sum_{j=1}^{4}\sum_{i=1}^{10}(X_{ij}-\bar{X}_{.j})^2.$$

$$SS_{tot} = SS_{bet} + SS_{within}$$

The *total sum of squares* (SS_{tot}) has been partitioned (analyzed) into two additive components, the *sum of squares between groups* (SS_{bet}) and the *sum of squares within groups* (SS_{within}). SS_{tot} reflects variation in the scores obtained. This total variation has been *analyzed* into two components, SS_{bet} and SS_{within}. Thus the name "analysis of variance," (abbreviated ANOVA). You will soon see how this analysis is used to test the null hypothesis that $\alpha_1 = \alpha_2 = \alpha_3 = \alpha_4$.

I5.5
RESTATEMENT OF THE NULL HYPOTHESIS IN TERMS OF POPULATION MEANS

Before proceeding, let's phrase the null hypothesis that $\alpha_1 = \alpha_2 = \alpha_3 = \alpha_4$ in an equivalent but slightly different form. The estimator of α_1 was taken to be $\hat{\alpha}_1 = \bar{X}_{.1} - \bar{X}_{..}$. Since $\hat{\alpha}_1$ is an unbiased estimator of α_1, the expectation E (long-term average) of $\hat{\alpha}_1$ is α_1:

$$E(\hat{\alpha}_1) = E(\bar{X}_{.1} - \bar{X}_{..}) = E(\bar{X}_{.1}) - E(\bar{X}_{..}) = \mu_1 - \mu = \alpha_1.$$

Similarly, $\alpha_2 = \mu_2 - \mu$, $\alpha_3 = \mu_3 - \mu$, and $\alpha_4 = \mu_4 - \mu$.
The null hypothesis can be written as

$$(\mu_1 - \mu) = (\mu_2 - \mu) = (\mu_3 - \mu) = (\mu_4 - \mu).$$

Add μ to each of the four terms and you will see that this is obviously the same as saying that $\mu_1 = \mu_2 = \mu_3 = \mu_4$. *Hence, the null hypothesis that* $\alpha_1 = \alpha_2 = \alpha_3 = \alpha_4$ *in the linear model* $X_{ij} = \mu + \alpha_j + e_{ij}$ *is the same as the hypothesis that the means of the normal populations from which the samples are drawn are all equal*, i.e.,

$$\mu_1 = \mu_2 = \mu_3 = \mu_4.$$

We may state the null hypothesis in either form. A third equivalent form, when $n_1 = n_2 = n_3 = n_4$, is

$$H_0: \sum_{j=1}^{4}(\mu_j - \bar{\mu}_.)^2 = 0,$$

where $\bar{\mu}_.$ is the average of $\mu_1, \ldots, \mu_J$ and equals μ.

I5.6
DEGREES OF FREEDOM

Some more machinery is needed before we can show how the null hypothesis can be tested.

We must associate with each quantity in the partitioning of the total sum of squares (SS_{tot}, SS_{bet}, SS_{within}) an integer called the *degrees of freedom*.

"Degrees of freedom" is a name borrowed from the physical sciences where it denotes a characteristic of the movement of an object. If an object is free to move in a straight line only, it has one degree of freedom; an object that is free to move through any point in a plane, such as a bowling ball rolling down an alley, has two degrees of freedom; a ball in a handball court has three degrees of freedom: it can go from back to front, side to side, and floor to ceiling. You may be surprised to learn that the techniques we group under the rubric "analysis of variance" or ANOVA (the partitioning of SS_{tot} and testing the null hypothesis) have a geometric interpretation. The name "degrees of freedom" enters into analysis of variance (ANOVA) by way of its geometric interpretation.

First, let us discuss the degrees of freedom associated with SS_{bet}. Consider the definition of SS_{bet}:

$$SS_{bet} = \sum_{j=1}^{4} 10 \cdot (\bar{X}_{.j} - \bar{X}_{..})^2.$$

The four group means, $\bar{X}_{.1}, \ldots, \bar{X}_{.4}$, are related to $\bar{X}_{..}$ by the equation:

$$\frac{\bar{X}_{.1} + \bar{X}_{.2} + \bar{X}_{.3} + \bar{X}_{.4}}{4} = \bar{X}_{...} \qquad (15.7)$$

If $\bar{X}_{..} = 6, \bar{X}_{.1} = 3, \bar{X}_{.2} = 4$, and $\bar{X}_{.3} = 8$, what must $\bar{X}_{.4}$ be? $\bar{X}_{.4}$ must be 9. If $\bar{X}_{..} = 4, \bar{X}_{.2} = 3, \bar{X}_{.3} = 6$, and $\bar{X}_{.4} = 4$, what must $\bar{X}_{.1}$ be? $\bar{X}_{.1}$ must be 3. If $\bar{X}_{..}$ is a given number, then we are free to assign any values whatsoever to three of the group means, but having done so the last group mean is determined—it must have a value that satisfies Eq. (15.7). *The degrees of freedom for SS_{bet} is* $(4 - 1) = 3$, *one less than the number of group means, i.e.,* $J - 1$. We will abbreviate "degrees of freedom for SS_{bet}" to df_{bet}.

Consider now the degrees of freedom associated with SS_{within}.

$$SS_{within} = \sum_{j=1}^{4} \sum_{i=1}^{10} (X_{ij} - \bar{X}_{.j})^2.$$

For group one, the computation of SS_{within} involves

$$(X_{11} - \bar{X}_{.1})^2 + (X_{21} - \bar{X}_{.1})^2 + \ldots + (X_{10,1} - \bar{X}_{.1})^2.$$

How are $X_{11}, X_{21}, \ldots, X_{10,1}$ and $\bar{X}_{.1}$ related?

$$\frac{X_{11} + X_{21} + \ldots + X_{10,1}}{10} = \bar{X}_{.1}.$$

If $\bar{X}_{.1}$ were a fixed number, say 12.40, to how many of the 10 quantities X_{11} through $X_{10,1}$ could you assign any number you wished before you have to assign a value or values to make $\bar{X}_{.1}$ be 12.40? The answer is *nine*. Similarly,

$$(X_{12} - \bar{X}_{.2})^2 + (X_{22} - \bar{X}_{.2})^2 + \ldots + (X_{10,2} - \bar{X}_{.2})^2$$

is used in computing SS_{within}. Since $(X_{12} + X_{22} + \ldots + X_{10,2})/10 = \bar{X}_{.2}$, if $\bar{X}_{.2}$ is fixed, then *nine* of the 10 single numbers can be freely assigned before the tenth number must be assigned that gives the proper $\bar{X}_{.2}$. There are *nine* degrees of freedom for each of the four groups in the computation of SS_{within}; hence *the degrees of freedom for SS_{within} equals*

$$(10 - 1) + (10 - 1) + (10 - 1) + (10 - 1) = 40 - 4 = 36,$$

the total number of observations less the number of groups, i.e., $Jn - J =$ $J(n - 1)$. Space can be saved if "degrees of freedom for SS_{within}" is denoted by df_{within}.

SS_{tot} equals

$$(X_{11} - \bar{X}_{..})^2 + (X_{21} - \bar{X}_{..})^2 + \ldots + (X_{10,4} - \bar{X}_{..})^2;$$

41 terms are involved, and they are related as follows:

$$\frac{X_{11} + X_{21} + \ldots + X_{10,4}}{40} = \bar{X}_{..} \, .$$

Of the 40 quantities on the left of the equation, 39 can be assigned numbers without restriction before the fortieth one must be given that number that yields the preassigned $\bar{X}_{..}$. *The degrees of freedom for SS_{tot} equals* $40 - 1 =$ *39, the total number of observations minus 1, i.e., $Jn - 1$.*

15.7
MEAN SQUARES

A sum of squares (SS) divided by its degrees of freedom (df) is called a *mean square* (MS). In the one-factor ANOVA, only two mean squares will be of interest: the *mean square between*, MS_b, which equals SS_b/df_b, and the *mean square within*, MS_w, which equals SS_w/df_w.* A "mean square total" will not be defined because it would prove useless for the purpose of testing the null hypothesis. However, an important relationship to keep in mind is $SS_b + SS_w = SS_t$; another is $df_b + df_w = df_t = Jn - 1$.

15.8
EXPECTATIONS OF MS_b
AND MS_w

At this point, hopefully, you'll start finding the answers to some of the questions which must have arisen in your mind while studying the last few

---

* In the remainder of this chapter "between" will be abbreviated to b, "within" to w, and "total" to t. Thus we shall write SS_b, SS_w, SS_t, df_b, df_w, MS_b, and MS_w.

pages. Why partition SS_t into SS_b and SS_w? Why define degrees of freedom and mean squares? To test the null hypothesis H_0, of course; but by looking at the expectations of MS_b and MS_w, you'll begin to see how the machinery developed so far relates to H_0.

The *expectation of MS_w* means the long-term average of MS_w from experiment to experiment. The expectation of MS_w will be denoted by $E(MS_w)$. If in our learner-activity experiment we were to repeat the experiment an indefinitely large number of times and each time compute MS_w, then the average of all of these MS_w would be $E(MS_w)$. We can conceive of doing this even though it would be impossible to do so physically. $E(MS_w)$ is the average of all of the MS_w in that population of experiments about which we wish to make an inference from the data obtained this one time.

We can write $E(MS_w)$ in terms of a characteristic of the normal populations from which the scores obtained in the experiment are a random sample.

First, let's look at MS_w in a slightly different way.

$$MS_w = \frac{SS_w}{df_w} = \frac{\sum_{j=1}^{4} \sum_{i=1}^{10} (X_{ij} - \bar{X}_{.j})^2}{4 \cdot (10 - 1)}$$

$$= \frac{1}{4} \left[\frac{\sum_{i=1}^{10} (X_{i1} - \bar{X}_{.1})^2}{9} + \frac{\sum_{i=1}^{10} (X_{i2} - \bar{X}_{.2})^2}{9} \right.$$

$$\left. + \frac{\sum_{i=1}^{10} (X_{i3} - \bar{X}_{.3})^2}{9} + \frac{\sum_{i=1}^{10} (X_{i4} - \bar{X}_{.4})^2}{9} \right].$$

Isn't $\sum_{i=1}^{10} (X_{i1} - \bar{X}_{.1})^2/9$ the sample variance of group one? We shall denote it by s_1^2 and the sample variances of groups two, three, and four by $s_2^2, s_3^2,$ and s_4^2, respectively.

Therefore, $MS_w = \frac{1}{4}(s_1^2 + s_2^2 + s_3^2 + s_4^2)$, i.e., MS_w is the average of the sample variances of all the groups. We stated earlier that $E(s_1^2)$ was σ_1^2, the variance of the normal population from which the scores in group one were sampled. Since all of the normal populations had the same variance, σ^2, we can argue that

$$E(MS_w) = \tfrac{1}{4}E(s_1^2 + \ldots + s_4^2) = \tfrac{1}{4}[E(s_1^2) + \ldots + E(s_4^2)]$$

$$= \tfrac{1}{4}(\sigma^2 + \sigma^2 + \sigma^2 + \sigma^2) = \sigma^2.$$

The expectation of MS_w is σ^2.

The size of MS_w does *not* depend on the means of the populations underlying the groups in the experiment. MS_w is "mean-free," reflecting only the variability among the measures *within* groups. Such variability is around *each* group mean, rather than around the grand mean of all the groups. Whether all of the groups are samples from the same normal population or all the normal populations have different means, $E(MS_w)$ will be the same, σ^2.*

The same cannot be said for $E(MS_b)$, however. We shall show that *if all* of the normal populations underlying the samples in the experiment have the same mean (we've already assumed they have the same variance), then $E(MS_b)$ is σ^2. If, however, *at least two of the population means are different*, then $E(MS_b)$ will be *larger than* σ^2. If all the population means are equal, then the null hypothesis that $\mu_1 = \mu_2 = \mu_3 = \mu_4$ is *true*. If at least two population means are different, e.g., $\mu_1 = \mu_2$ but $\mu_3 \neq \mu_4$ or $\mu_1 \neq \mu_2 \neq \mu_3 \neq \mu_4$ (these are two of many possible examples), then the null hypothesis H_0 is false.

We shall state without proof that

$$E(MS_b) = \sigma^2 + \frac{n\sum\limits_{j=1}^{J}(\mu_j - \mu)^2}{J - 1}, \qquad (15.8)$$

where σ^2 is the variance in each population,

n is the number of subjects in each group (10 in our example),

J is the number of groups (four in our example),

μ_j is the population mean of the jth population, and

μ is the mean of the J population means.

Let us say for example that all four population means were 6.45. (This is a case where H_0 is true.) Then μ would be 6.45 and

$$\sum_{j=1}^{J}(\mu_j - \mu)^2 = 0.$$

Take an example where H_0 is not true and satisfy yourself that $E(MS_b)$ is greater than σ^2.

To summarize:

1. If H_0 is *true*, then

$$E(MS_w) = \sigma^2 \quad \text{and} \quad E(MS_b) = \sigma^2.$$

---

* Convince yourself that this is indeed true. Start with

$$E(MS_w) = E[(SS_{w_1} + SS_{w_2} + \ldots + SS_{w_J})/J(n - 1)].$$

For each SS_{w_j} substitute its equivalent, $(n - 1)MS_{w_j}$. Then distribute the expectations and simplify. Further, note that the definition of SS_{w_j} is $\sum\limits_{i=1}^{n}(X_{ij} - \bar{X}_{.j})^2$, which does not involve the overall mean, $\bar{X}_{..}$.

2. If H_0 is *false*, then

$$E(MS_w) = \sigma^2 \quad \text{and} \quad E(MS_b) = \sigma^2 + \frac{n \sum\limits_{j=1}^{J} (\mu_j - \mu)^2}{J - 1},$$

which is greater than σ^2.

In any experiment, MS_w and MS_b are known, but the values of their expectations are not. By comparing MS_b to MS_w, one can determine if H_0 is plausible. If MS_b is very large relative to MS_w, then it is likely that H_0 is false. But the test of the null hypothesis is not as simple as this. It can be shown that MS_b and MS_w are independent of one another (this is one reason for the original assumption of normal populations).

Suppose for the moment that you draw four samples at random of 10 scores each from a normal population. This is exactly what would be done if in our example experiment four conditions were equally efficient (in terms of the average score they produced). The 40 scores sampled could be placed in a table such as Table 15.1, and MS_w and MS_b could be computed. Remember this is a case of H_0 being true. Would MS_w and MS_b be equal? No. Their expectations would be equal; but from one sampling to the next, MS_w might be a little bigger than MS_b this time, and maybe a lot smaller next time. The sample value of MS_w and MS_b will fluctuate independently from one sampling of 40 scores to the next (the experiment that was actually run is considered to be one case of sampling 40 scores). The cases that vex the researcher are those in which MS_b is large relative to MS_w. He would like to regard such an occurrence as evidence that H_0 is false. (If H_0 is false, he would expect MS_b to be larger than MS_w.) But how can he be sure that a large value of MS_b relative to MS_w didn't occur simply by random fluctuations in scores sampled from the same normal population? The researcher can never be certain, but we shall see in the next section how he can control the proportion of times he will incorrectly conclude that H_0 is false.

15.9
SOME DISTRIBUTION THEORY

We saw in Chapter 11 that a chi-square variable with one degree of freedom has the form

$$\frac{(X - \mu)^2}{\sigma^2} \sim \chi_1^2,$$

i.e., the squared normal deviate is distributed as chi square with 1 degree of freedom.

Recall that X is a normally distributed variable with population mean μ and variance σ^2.

Suppose one randomly samples n scores from a normal distribution with mean and variance μ and σ^2. Since chi-square variables have the special additive property noted in Chapter 11, the quantity

$$\frac{(X_1 - \mu)^2}{\sigma^2} + \frac{(X_2 - \mu)^2}{\sigma^2} + \ldots + \frac{(X_n - \mu)^2}{\sigma^2} \sim \chi_n^2.$$

The sum of the squared z scores has a chi-square distribution with n degrees of freedom, i.e., this sum computed on repeated samples of n scores has a known frequency distribution χ_n^2.

We shall not prove the assertion; however, it is true (see, e.g., Wilks, 1962) that if $X_1, \ldots, X_n$ are n independent observations from a normal population with variance σ^2, then

$$\frac{(X_1 - \bar{X}.)^2}{\sigma^2} + \frac{(X_2 - \bar{X}.)^2}{\sigma^2} + \ldots + \frac{(X_n - \bar{X}.)^2}{\sigma^2} \sim \chi_{n-1}^2.$$

Therefore, $\sum_{i=1}^{n} (X_i - \bar{X}.)^2/\sigma^2 \sim \chi_{n-1}^2$. Also, $\sum_{i=1}^{n} (X_{ij} - \bar{X}._j)^2/\sigma^2 \sim \chi_{n-1}^2$.

Notice that $\bar{X}.$, the sample mean of the n observations, has replaced μ, the mean of the population from which the observations were selected. Also, the chi-square variable has $n - 1$ instead of n degrees of freedom.

For the experiment at the beginning of the chapter we defined SS_w:

$$SS_w = \sum_{i=1}^{10} (X_{i1} - \bar{X}._1)^2 + \sum_{i=1}^{10} (X_{i2} - \bar{X}._2)^2 + \ldots + \sum_{i=1}^{10} (X_{i4} - \bar{X}._4)^2.$$

If we divided the first quantity on the right of this equation by σ^2, it would have the distribution χ_9^2 (chi-square with 9 degrees of freedom). This is so because we assumed the scores in group one were *randomly* drawn from a *normal* population with *variance* σ^2. The same can be said for the other three quantities on the right of the equation. Since all four quantities are distributed as χ_9^2, then their sum divided by σ^2 is distributed as $\chi_{(9+9+9+9)}^2$ or χ_{36}^2 (chi-square with 36 degrees of freedom). Hence, for our example

$$\frac{SS_w}{\sigma^2} \sim \chi_{36}^2.$$

We can divide SS_w by 36 to obtain MS_w; then

$$\frac{MS_w}{\sigma^2} \sim \frac{\chi_{36}^2}{36}.$$

This fact will be saved for future use.

In general, how is the mean $\bar{X}.$ of a group distributed? That is, what frequency distribution would result if we sampled n scores at random from a population, computed $\bar{X}.$, then recorded only this one score, $\bar{X}.$? What would the distribution of these scores be like if this process of sampling, computing $\bar{X}$, and recording it would continue indefinitely? What would be the mean, variance, and shape of this distribution?

If the means, $\bar{X}$'s, are based on n scores randomly drawn from a normal population, they will:

1. be normally distributed themselves,
2. have mean μ, and
3. have variance σ^2/n.

Using the above facts, we can see that $(\bar{X}_. - \mu)/\sqrt{\sigma^2/n}$ has a mean of zero and a variance of 1; hence, it is a z score. Consequently

$$\frac{(\bar{X}_. - \mu)^2}{\sigma^2/n} = \frac{n(\bar{X}_. - \mu)^2}{\sigma^2} \sim \chi_1^2.$$

If the null hypothesis is true, then

$$\frac{\sum_{j=1}^{4} 10(\bar{X}_{.j} - \bar{X}_{..})^2}{\sigma^2} \sim \chi_3^2, \tag{15.9}$$

because under that condition $E(\bar{X}_{.1}) = E(\bar{X}_{.2}) = E(\bar{X}_{.3}) = E(\bar{X}_{.4}) = E(\bar{X}_{..}) = \mu$. That is, each of the four $\bar{X}_{.j}$'s is a random sample from a normally distributed, infinite population of $\bar{X}_{.j}$'s whose mean is μ. Our original assumption that the four populations sampled in our experiment had the same variance σ^2 allows us to make this statement. Dividing both sides of Eq. (15.9) by 3, we see that

$$\frac{\left[\sum_{j=1}^{4} 10(\bar{X}_{.j} - \bar{X}_{..})^2\right] / 3}{\sigma^2} = \frac{MS_b}{\sigma^2} \sim \frac{\chi_3^2}{3},$$

provided H_0, the null hypothesis, is true.

You'll remember from Chapter 11 that the ratio of two chi-square variables each of which is divided by its degrees of freedom has an F-distribution.

$$\frac{\left[\sum_{j=1}^{4} 10(\bar{X}_{.j} - \bar{X}_{..})^2\right] / 3\sigma^2}{\left[\sum_{j=1}^{4}\sum_{i=1}^{10} (X_{ij} - \bar{X}_{.j})^2\right] / 36\sigma^2} = \frac{\left[\sum_{j=1}^{4} 10(\bar{X}_{.j} - \bar{X}_{..})^2\right] / 3}{\left[\sum_{j=1}^{4}\sum_{i=1}^{10} (X_{ij} - \bar{X}_{.j})^2\right] / 36} \sim F_{3,36}.$$

Notice that since σ^2 appears in both numerator and denominator it cancels itself.

You should recognize that the numerator is MS_b and the denominator is MS_w. To summarize then, *if the null hypothesis is true*,

$$\frac{MS_b}{MS_w} \sim F_{3,36},$$

i.e., the ratio of the mean-square between, MS_b, to the mean-square within, MS_w, has an F-distribution with 3 and 36 degrees of freedom when $\mu_1 = \mu_2 = \mu_3 = \mu_4$.

The ratio MS_b/MS_w is called the *F-ratio*. The *F*-ratio is the statistic that will be used in the last steps of the test of H_0.

15.10
THE *F*-TEST OF THE NULL HYPOTHESIS: RATIONALE AND PROCEDURE

To coalesce the distribution theory that has been developed, consider the act of repeatedly sampling at random four groups of 10 scores each from the *same* normal distribution (note that under these conditions the null hypothesis is true). If each time this were done the *F*-ratio MS_b/MS_w were calculated and its value recorded, the frequency distribution of these *F*-ratios (many, many of them) would look like the mathematical curve $F_{3,36}$. This knowledge is extremely important, for with it the statistician can calculate the percent of *F*-ratios that will exceed 11.35 or 6.12; or he can determine the number that will be exceeded only by 5 % or 1 % of the *F*-ratios. He does this assuming H_0 is true. The *F*-ratios obtained in this procedure of repeatedly sampling, calculating, and recording would all be greater than zero and the largest would be infinitely large, theoretically.

What if the sampling of the four groups of 10 scores each was not done from the same normal population, i.e., what if sampling was done under the condition of a false null hypothesis? We saw earlier that under these conditions one expects MS_b to be larger than it would be if the null hypothesis were true. However, MS_w would have the same expectation, σ^2. When the null hypothesis is false, MS_b does not have a χ^2 distribution and the ratios MS_b/MS_w obtained from the sampling do *not* have an *F*-distribution. We do know, however, what effect this sampling under conditions of a false null hypothesis has on the distribution of the *F*-ratios. They will be *on the average* larger than the *F*-ratios obtained by random sampling from a single normal population.

Suppose we randomly sampled repeatedly four groups of 10 scores each from *one* normal population and calculated the *F*-ratio each time. The plot of the *F*-ratios obtained would look like the curve $F_{3,36}$ in Fig. 15.2. Now suppose we drew repeatedly two groups of 10 scores each from a normal

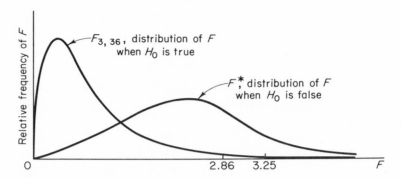

FIG. 15.2   Sampling distributions of $F = MS_b/MS_w$ when H_0 is true (curve $F_{3,36}$) and when H_0 is false (curve F^*).

population with mean μ_1, and two more groups of 10 scores from a normal population with a different mean μ_2. The null hypothesis is false, but we wouldn't in practice know this because μ_1 and μ_2 are unknown characteristics of populations. The distribution of the F-ratios obtained would look something like curve F^* in Fig. 15.2. Notice that in general the F-ratios shift to the right (are larger) when sampling is done under conditions of a false null hypothesis instead of a true null hypothesis. Even so, some of the values in the curve $F_{3,36}$ are larger than some of the values in curve F^*.

Is an F-ratio greater than 3.25 more likely to occur if one is sampling under conditions of a true or false null hypothesis? Compare the areas under the two curves to the right of the point 3.25 and see which area is larger (i.e., shows a greater probability of yielding a value of F greater than 3.25).

The statistician can find the percentile points of the curve $F_{3,36}$. He can calculate the value of F such that only 5% or 1% of the values in the curve $F_{3,36}$ are larger, i.e., he can find the 95th and 99th percentiles of the curve $F_{3,36}$. The 95th percentile in the curve $F_{3,36}$ is 2.86; the 99th percentile is 4.38. Table E of Appendix A shows the 75th, 90th, 95th, 97.5th, 99th, 99.5th, and 99.9th percentiles for various F-distributions. As we saw in Chapter 11 the F-distribution depends on two values: the degrees of freedom for the numerator and the degrees of freedom for the denominator of the F-ratio. To find the 95th percentile in the curve $F_{2,40}$, find the cell at the intersection of column 2 and row 40 for that portion of the table headed 95th percentile. The value of $_{.95}F_{2,40}$ is 3.23.

What if our experiment was run and an F-ratio of 6.51 was obtained with 3 and 36 degrees of freedom? Since the 95th percentile of the curve $F_{3,36}$ is 2.86, and under the null hypothesis the F-ratios form the curve $F_{3,36}$, if the null hypothesis were true, something very unlikely would have occurred. Less than five times in 100 a value as large or larger than 2.86 would be obtained if the null hypothesis were true. If the null hypothesis were false, then large values of *F* are more likely to be observed. The researcher agrees to reason thus:

If the value of the *F*-ratio obtained would occur less than five times in 100 (i.e., if it is greater than the 95th percentile of $F_{3,36}$) if the null hypothesis were true, then I'll conclude that the null hypothesis is false. It seems more likely that such a value indicates a false null hypothesis since large values are more likely if the null hypothesis is false.

Choosing the 95th percentile of the curve $F_{3,36}$ as the point on which the decision about H_0 hinges is rather arbitrary. One could have chosen the 90th, 99th or 99.9th percentile point. What if the 50th percentile point had been chosen? That is, what if one had agreed to reject the null hypothesis if the *F*-ratio was greater than the 50th percentile of $F_{3,36}$? If the null hypothesis were true, one would have a probability of $\frac{1}{2}$ of rejecting H_0 (calling it false). If researchers agreed on the 50th percentile point to make their decisions, half of them would be concluding that one method is better than another when the methods were actually no different. Scientists want to guard against these mistakes, type I errors; so they agree to conclude that the null hypothesis is false when values equal to or greater than the value of *F* obtained have a small probability of occurring when the null hypothesis is true. A "small probability" means .10, .05, or .01. These values correspond to using the 90th, 95th, and 99th percentile points, respectively.

Do not make the mistake of thinking that if the *F*-ratio obtained in our experiment were 6.51 the null hypothesis is certainly false. Such assertions are not possible in our situation. A researcher makes a conclusion of the form "I reject H_0 as a true statement about the means of the populations I've sampled" or "I fail to reject H_0 as . . . ." He is never certain of the truth of his conclusion. He does know, however, that his conclusions will be correct a certain percent (90%, 95%, 99%, etc.) of the times he makes them given the truth or falsity of H_0.

Suppose that the four learner activity levels were all alike with respect to the amount achieved under each. Suppose also that our researcher ran the same experiment, 40 subjects into four groups, a very large number of times. Each time he would compute an *F*-ratio and draw a conclusion about H_0. He is not aware that H_0 is true. The curve $F_{3,36}$ that the obtained *F*-ratios would follow has a known form. We know, for example, that 5% of the area under the curve lies to the right of the point 2.86. Our researcher has agreed that if the *F*-ratio he obtains exceeds 2.86, he will say that H_0 is false. He will expect 5% of the *F*-ratios he obtains to be greater than 2.86; hence, he will be expected to make the mistake of rejecting H_0 when it is really true 5% of the time.

Notice that the value (2.86) the researcher chooses, such that any *F*-ratio exceeding that number is regarded by him as evidence for the falsity of H_0, is arbitrary. If he had chosen 4.38, the 99th percentile point in the distribution $F_{3,36}$, and if H_0 is true, then on the average one time in 100 he will obtain an F-ratio exceeding 4.38 and conclude incorrectly that H_0 is false. The probability that the researcher will reject H_0 as the true state of nature when H_0 is actually true is called α (alpha). The size of α is under the researcher's control; he can make it as large or as small as he wishes by his selection of a number from the F-table that will govern his decision.

It is customary to assume (as we saw in Sec. 13.5) that there are two states of nature that can exist relative to our ANOVA model: H_0 can be *true*, or it can be *false*. A researcher agrees to make one of two conclusions after inspecting his data: *Reject H_0* as explaining my situation, or *do not reject* (continue to entertain) H_0 as an explanation of my situation. Four outcomes of an experiment are possible, as shown in the accompanying table.

	State of nature	
	H_0 is true	H_0 is false
Reject H_0	Type I error	No error is made
Do not reject H_0	No error is made	Type II error

If the researcher does *not* find evidence for the *falsity* of H_0 and H_0 is true (this situation is the lower left-hand cell in the table), then his thoughts will be in accord with the true state of nature: no error in his conclusion has been made. If the researcher *rejects H_0* when in reality H_0 is *false* (upper right-hand cell), he has not committed an error in making his conclusion. However, if he *rejects H_0* when it is *true*, we say he has made a "type I error" or an "error of the first kind." If H_0 is actually *false*, and the researcher fails to reject H_0, we say he has committed a "type II error" or an "error of the second kind." These names are merely a convenience; that one is a type I error and the other a type II error is of no significance.

The probability of committing a type I error is equal to α. The researcher can control the size of α, thus making his chances of incorrectly rejecting H_0 very large ($\alpha = .25$ or $.30$) or very small ($\alpha = .01$ or $.001$). It is customary to assign a value to α of .05 or .01; although .05 and .01 may be appropriate for industrial or agricultural research in which the ANOVA first enjoyed popularity, there is little reason to advocate their use exclusively in educational and psychological research. The value of α a researcher wishes to use should depend on certain aspects of his particular analysis. Values of $\alpha = .15$ or $.10$ might be justifiable if a small number of subjects are included in the experiment. As will be shown later, the size of α is related in an indirect way to the probability of making a type II error (failing to reject a false null hypothesis). The probability of failing to reject a false

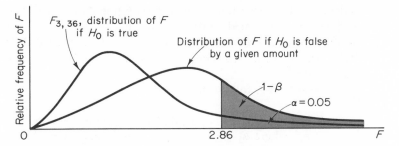

FIG. 15.3 Illustration of the probabilities of type I and type II errors for $J = 4$, $n = 10$, and a particular alternative hypothesis.

null hypothesis is under the control of the researcher to some extent. β depends on the number of subjects in the experiment and the value of α chosen, among other things. We shall denote the probability of correctly rejecting H_0 when it is false by some given amount by $1 - \beta$. *So the probability of type II error is β. $1 - \beta$ is the probability of rejecting H_0 when it is false; it is called the "power" of the test.* The larger α, the larger $1 - \beta$. The value of $1 - \beta$ is quite important to the researcher. All too often, people completely disregard "power." They invest large amounts of time and money in an experiment in which their probability of discovering differences between the treatments is only .2, say. That is, even if differences of a given magnitude exist, the researcher has two chances in 10 of rejecting H_0 ("discovering" that differences exist). There's a high probability that he won't find what he's looking for even when it is there.

It may happen that if a researcher set α at .05 the corresponding value of $1 - \beta$ would be .20; but if α were .10, $1 - \beta$ would be .50. Obviously, the prudent course of action is to accept a greater risk of making a type I error to increase the probability, $1 - \beta$, of finding differences between the treatments.

The definitions of α and β and their relationship are depicted in Fig. 15.3. The calculation of the power of the F-test of H_0 will be illustrated in Sec. 15.15.

15.11
THE ONE-WAY ANOVA WITH
n OBSERVATIONS PER CELL
(SUMMARY)

An experiment with one treatment factor and J levels of that factor is run. Under each of the J levels, n independent observations are taken. The researcher is willing to assume that the n observations in any one level are independent observations from a *normal* population with variance σ^2. The variance σ^2 is assumed to be *equal* in all J of the levels. (This assumption is often called the *assumption of homoscedasticity;* the word "homoscedasticity" derives from two Greek words meaning "same" and" scatter" or "dispersion.")

The ANOVA follows five steps:

1. A linear model is postulated to explain the data. $X_{ij} = \mu + \alpha_j + e_{ij}$, where $\alpha_1 + \ldots + \alpha_J = 0$ and the e_{ij} are all independent.

2. The null hypothesis H_0 and an alternative hypothesis H_1 are stated. $H_0: \alpha_1 = \alpha_2 = \ldots = \alpha_J$; $H_1:$ "At least two α_j's are different." Or equivalently

$$H_0: \mu_1 = \ldots = \mu_J \qquad H_1: \sum_1^J (\mu_j - \bar{\mu}_.)^2 \neq 0.$$

3. An α-level is selected, i.e., the researcher decides what probability he will assign to the event that he rejects H_0 when it is true (concludes there are differences between the levels of the treatment when there actually are none). This α-level is typically .10, .05, .01, or .001. Values of α much greater than .10 probably allow too great a risk of falsely rejecting H_0, and values of α much less than .001 are probably overly conservative.

4. Computations of sums of squares [parts (a) and (b) below], degrees of freedom [parts (c) and (d) below], and mean squares [part (e) below] are made.

The data from the experiment may be laid out as follows:

Treatments

1	2	...	J
X_{11}	X_{12}	...	X_{1J}
X_{21}	X_{22}	...	X_{2J}
.	.	...	.
.	.	...	.
.	.	...	.
X_{n1}	X_{n2}	...	X_{nJ}

a. $SS_w = \sum_{j=1}^{J} \sum_{i=1}^{n} (X_{ij} - \bar{X}_{.j})^2$. By algebraic manipulations, SS_w can be written in a form that is more efficient for computation:

$$SS_w = \sum_{j=1}^{J} \sum_{i=1}^{n} X_{ij}^2 - \frac{\sum_{j=1}^{J} \left(\sum_{i=1}^{n} X_{ij} \right)^2}{n}.$$

Step 1. To calculate SS_w, square each individual observation and sum these squared numbers. You then have

$$\sum_{j=1}^{J} \sum_{i=1}^{n} X_{ij}^2.$$

Step 2. Find the sum of the original observations for each of the J columns. The sum of the jth column is

$$\sum_{i=1}^{n} X_{ij}.$$

Square each of the J column sums and add these J squared numbers together. Divide this sum by n. You now have the quantity

$$\frac{\sum_{j=1}^{J} \left(\sum_{i=1}^{n} X_{ij} \right)^2}{n}.$$

Step 3. Find SS_w by subtracting the result of Step 2 from the result of Step 1.

b. $SS_b = \sum_{j=1}^{J} n(\bar{X}_{.j} - \bar{X}_{..})^2$. Again by algebraic manipulations it may be shown that

$$SS_b = \frac{\sum_{j=1}^{J} \left(\sum_{i=1}^{n} X_{ij} \right)^2}{n} - \frac{\left(\sum_{j=1}^{J} \sum_{i=1}^{n} X_{ij} \right)^2}{Jn}.$$

Step 1. Bring forward the value

$$\frac{\sum_{j=1}^{J} \left(\sum_{i=1}^{n} X_{ij} \right)^2}{n}$$

that was calculated in Step 2 of (a).

Step 2. Add together all of the Jn original observations and square this sum. Divide the squared sum by Jn. You now have the quantity $\left(\sum_{j=1}^{J} \sum_{i=1}^{n} X_{ij} \right)^2 \Big/ Jn$.

Step 3. Find SS_b by subtracting the result of Step 2 from the result of Step 1.

c. The degrees of freedom associated with SS_w are $J(n-1)$.

d. The degrees of freedom associated with SS_b are $J - 1$.

e. Calculate the MS_w and the MS_b as follows:

$$MS_w = \frac{SS_w}{J(n-1)}.$$

$$MS_b = \frac{SS_b}{J-1}.$$

5. The F-ratio MS_b/MS_w is calculated and compared to the $100(1 - \alpha)$ percentile point in the distribution $F_{J-1,J(n-1)}$.

The test of the null hypothesis is made by comparing the ratio MS_b/MS_w, an F-ratio with $J - 1$ and $J(n - 1)$ degrees of freedom, with a value obtained from an F-table that is the value exceeded by α per cent of F-ratios obtained under conditions of a true null hypothesis. If MS_b/MS_w exceeds that value (denoted by $_{1-\alpha}F_{J-1,J(n-1)}$), then the researcher rejects H_0 as a true statement.

To illustrate the above calculations, we shall return now to the example of Sec. 15.1 in which an experimenter sought to determine the relative effectiveness of four different levels of learner activity on learning about the English monetary system. Forty experimental subjects were randomly placed among the four levels (10 to each level) of learner activity: (1) outline the instructional material; (2) write a summary of the material; (3) study an instructional program of the material; (4) study the program on a teaching machine. Ten subjects studied English money under each of these conditions on five successive days; then a 100-item multiple-choice test on the English money system was given. A person's "score" was the number of items answered correctly on the 100-item test. These scores appear in Table 15.1.

TABLE 15.1 SCORES ON A 100-ITEM TEST OVER THE ENGLISH MONETARY SYSTEM FOR 40 SUBJECTS STUDYING UNDER FOUR LEVELS OF LEARNER ACTIVITY

1 Outline	2 Written summary	3 Program	4 Teaching machine
26	51	52	41
34	50	64	49
46	33	39	56
48	28	54	64
42	47	58	72
49	50	53	65
74	48	77	63
61	60	56	87
51	71	63	77
53	42	59	62

The calculations for obtaining SS_b, SS_w, MS_b and MS_w are performed in Table 15.2. In the upper portion of Table 15.2, the data in Table 15.1 are summarized by the necessary quantities.

TABLE 15.2   ILLUSTRATION OF CALCULATIONS FOR A ONE-FACTOR ANOVA WITH EQUAL n's; DATA FROM TABLE 15.1

1	2	3	4
$n = 10$	$n = 10$	$n = 10$	$n = 10$
$\bar{X}_{.1} = 48.40$	$\bar{X}_{.2} = 48.00$	$\bar{X}_{.3} = 57.50$	$\bar{X}_{.4} = 63.60$
$\sum_{i=1}^{10} X_{i1} = 484$	$\sum_{i=1}^{10} X_{i2} = 480$	$\sum_{i=1}^{10} X_{i3} = 575$	$\sum_{i=1}^{10} X_{i4} = 636$
$\sum_{i=1}^{10} X_{i1}^2 = 25{,}024$	$\sum_{i=1}^{10} X_{i2}^2 = 24{,}392$	$\sum_{i=1}^{10} X_{i3}^2 = 33{,}925$	$\sum_{i=1}^{10} X_{i4}^2 = 42{,}034$

$$\sum_{j=1}^{4}\sum_{i=1}^{10} X_{ij} = 2175 \qquad \sum_{j=1}^{4}\sum_{i=1}^{10} X_{ij}^2 = 125{,}375$$

$$SS_b = \frac{(484)^2 + (480)^2 + (575)^2 + (636)^2}{10} - \frac{(2175)^2}{40}$$

$$= 119{,}977.70 - 118{,}265.62 = 1712.08$$

$$SS_w = 125{,}375 - \frac{(484)^2 + (480)^2 + (575)^2 + (636)^2}{10}$$

$$= 125{,}275 - 119{,}977.70 = 5397.30$$

$$MS_b = \frac{SS_b}{J-1} = \frac{1712.08}{3} = 570.69 \qquad MS_w = \frac{SS_w}{J(n-1)} = \frac{5397.30}{36} = 149.93$$

The null hypothesis H_0, that $\mu_1 = \mu_2 = \mu_3 = \mu_4$, is tested by referring $F = MS_b/MS_w$ to the F-distributions in Table E of Appendix A. The obtained value of F is located relative to various percentile points of the F-distribution with 3 and 36 degrees of freedom to determine whether it could reasonably be regarded as an observation randomly sampled from that distribution—which it must be if H_0 is true.

The value of the F-ratio for the data in Tables 15.1 and 15.2 is $F = 570.69/149.93 = 3.81$. In Table E we can find the percentile points in $F_{3,30}$ and $F_{3,40}$ but not in $F_{3,36}$ since not all F-distributions are tabulated there. We can, however, interpolate between 30 and 40 to obtain approximate values of the percentile points in $F_{3,36}$. The interpolation is performed with the reciprocals of the degrees of freedom instead of the degrees of freedom themselves, e.g., to find $_{.95}F_{3,36}$ one solves the following equation:

$$\frac{\frac{1}{30} - \frac{1}{36}}{\frac{1}{30} - \frac{1}{40}} = \frac{_{.95}F_{3,30} - {}_{.95}F_{3,36}}{_{.95}F_{3,30} - {}_{.95}F_{3,40}}.$$

The following percentile points are obtained by interpolation in Table E:

$$_{.75}F_{3,36} = 1.43$$

$$_{.90}F_{3,36} = 2.25$$

$$_{.95}F_{3,36} = 2.86$$

$$F = 3.81 \leftarrow \begin{array}{l}\text{obtained value of}\\ F = MS_b/MS_w\end{array}$$

$$_{.99}F_{3,36} = 4.38$$

The single obtained value of F from the data in Table 15.1 lies between the 95th and the 99th percentiles in the F-distribution with 3 and 36 degrees of freedom. In fact it lies at about the 98th percentile in the $F_{3,36}$ distribution. Hence, if $H_0: \mu_1 = \mu_2 = \mu_3 = \mu_4$ were true, an F-ratio as large as 3.81 or larger would occur with a probability approximately equal to .02. If we were testing H_0 at the $\alpha = .05$ level in this instance, we would reject H_0 in favor of H_1 in which it is held that not all four μ's are equal. If we adhered rigidly to the $\alpha = .01$ level of significance we would not reject H_0. We would be inclined to proceed as though H_0 were true.

15.12
THE ONE-WAY ANOVA
WITH UNEQUAL n's

Not infrequently, the numbers of scores are unequal in the J cells of a one-factor ANOVA. For example, five persons might be observed under level 1 of the factor, and 10 and 20 persons might be observed under levels 2 and 3 respectively. The technique of analysis of variance that was developed in the preceding sections of this chapter can be easily modified to accommodate these "unequal n's designs." The theory is essentially the same; only slight modifications are made. The computational techniques are quite similar to those in the equal n's ANOVA.

Notation

You are accustomed by now to calling the ith score in the jth group, X_{ij}. When we said that i runs from 1 to n and j runs from 1 to J, we knew that there were J groups, each containing n measures.

Because in the present situation the groups may contain different numbers of scores, it will be necessary to refer to the number of scores in the first group as n_1, the number of scores in the second group as $n_2, \ldots,$ and the number of scores in the Jth group as n_J. Data gathered in a design that is to be analyzed with a one-factor unequal n's ANOVA could be depicted as follows:

Group 1	Group 2	Group 3
$X_{1,1}$	$X_{1,2}$	$X_{1,3}$
$X_{2,1}$	$X_{2,2}$	$X_{2,3}$
.	.	.
.	.	.
.	.	.
.	$X_{15,2}$	$X_{18,3}$
.		
$X_{20,1}$		

In the above example, group 1 contains 20 scores, group 2 contains 15 scores, and group 3 contains 18 scores. Consequently, $n_1 = 20$, $n_2 = 15$, and $n_3 = 18$.

The Model

The same assumptions about parent populations are made that were made for the equal n's ANOVA: the J samples are randomly drawn from normal populations with equal variances σ^2, and they are independent. As before, it is assumed that the scores X_{ij} can be thought of in terms of the following linear model:

$$X_{ij} = \mu + \alpha_j + e_{ij},$$

where X_{ij} is the ith score in the jth group,

μ is the average of the J population means,

α_j is the difference between the mean of the jth population, μ_j, and μ, and

e_{ij} is the difference between X_{ij} and μ_j, the mean of the jth population.

The subscript i runs from 1 to n_j in the jth group. We shall denote the total number of scores in all groups by N; of course, $N = n_1 + n_2 + \ldots + n_J$.

A restriction placed on the equal n's ANOVA was that $\alpha_1 + \ldots + \alpha_J = 0$. In the unequal n's ANOVA this assumption becomes $n_1\alpha_1 + n_2\alpha_2 + \ldots + n_J\alpha_J = 0$. This is the only substantial alteration of the theoretical model, and you should not be greatly concerned.

As before, the least-squares estimators of the treatment effects, α_j, are obtained and become the basis of tests of the hypothesis that in the population all $\alpha_j = 0$, i.e., all J population means are equal. The least-squares estimator of α_j is $\bar{X}_{.j} - \bar{X}_{..}$, i.e., the mean of the n_j scores in the jth group minus the mean of all scores.

$$\hat{\alpha}_j = \bar{X}_{.j} - \bar{X}_{..} = \frac{\sum\limits_{i=1}^{n_j} X_{ij}}{n_j} - \bar{X}_{..}.$$

Again, the least-squares estimator of μ is simply

$$\hat{\mu} = \bar{X}_{..} = \frac{\sum\limits_{j=1}^{J}\sum\limits_{i=1}^{n_j} X_{ij}}{N}.$$

The estimator of the error component, e_{ij}, is given by

$$\hat{e}_{ij} = X_{ij} - \bar{X}_{.j}.$$

The null hypothesis we wish to test is that in the population all of the α_j are equal, and hence equal zero. In symbols, the null hypothesis is as follows:

$$H_0: \alpha_j = 0 \quad \text{for all } j.$$

An equivalent statement of H_0 in terms of the J population means is $H_0: \mu_1 = \mu_2 = \ldots = \mu_J$.

Sums of Squares

As before, the route to a statistical significance test of H_0 goes by way of the sum of squared estimates of the treatment effects, α_j, and the sum of squared estimates of the errors, e_{ij}.

First, a sum of squares within, SS_w, and a sum of squares between, SS_b, are found. SS_w is simply a weighted sum of the J sample variances for each group:

$$SS_w = (n_1 - 1)s_1^2 + (n_2 - 1)s_2^2 + \ldots + (n_J - 1)s_J^2$$

$$= \sum_{i=1}^{n_1}(X_{i1} - \bar{X}_{.1})^2 + \sum_{i=1}^{n_2}(X_{i2} - \bar{X}_{.2})^2 + \ldots + \sum_{i=1}^{n_J}(X_{iJ} - \bar{X}_{.J})^2.$$

A simpler notation for the above weighted sum is:

$$SS_w = \sum_{j=1}^{J}\sum_{i=1}^{n_j}(X_{ij} - \bar{X}_{.j})^2.$$

Using sigma notation, SS_w can be written

$$SS_w = \sum_{j=1}^{J}\sum_{i=1}^{n_j} X_{ij}^2 - \sum_{j=1}^{J}\frac{\left(\sum\limits_{i=1}^{n_j} X_{ij}\right)^2}{n_j}.$$

In words,

1. Square each of the N scores and add them up to obtain the first term.

2. Sum the scores in the jth group, square this sum, and divide by n_j. Do this for all J groups.

3. Sum the J quantities obtained in step 2.

4. Subtract the sum found in step 3 from the quantity obtained in step 1.

The sum of squares between is the sum of squared weighted estimates of treatment effects, $\hat{\alpha}_j$:

$$SS_b = n_1(\bar{X}_{.1} - \bar{X}_{..})^2 + n_2(\bar{X}_{.2} - \bar{X}_{..})^2 + \ldots + n_J(\bar{X}_{.J} - \bar{X}_{..})^2.$$

Using sigma notation, SS_b can be written

$$SS_b = \sum_{j=1}^{J} \frac{\left(\sum_{i=1}^{n_j} X_{ij}\right)^2}{n_j} - \frac{\left(\sum_{j}^{J}\sum_{i}^{n_j} X_{ij}\right)^2}{N}.$$

The term on the left of the computational formula for SS_b was found in steps 2 and 3 in the calculation of SS_w. From this quantity, subtract the quantity found by squaring the sum of all N scores and dividing this product by N.

Degrees of Freedom and Mean Squares

The degrees of freedom for SS_b are the same in the equal n's and unequal n's ANOVA. SS_b has $J - 1$ degrees of freedom. As previously, $SS_b/(J - 1) = MS_b$, the mean square between.

The degrees of freedom for SS_w are equal to

$$(n_1 - 1) + (n_2 - 1) + \ldots + (n_J - 1) = n_1 + n_2 + \ldots + n_J - J = N - J.$$

The ratio of SS_w to $N - J$ is the mean square within, MS_w. Thus

$$MS_b = \frac{SS_b}{J - 1} \qquad MS_w = \frac{SS_w}{N - J}.$$

By looking at the expected values of MS_b and MS_w, i.e., the long-run average values of both quantities over replications of this one-factor, unequal n's experiment, we will be able to see how the relative sizes of MS_b and MS_w bear on the question "Is H_0 true?"

Expected Values of MS_b and MS_w

We have seen how SS_w is simply a weighted sum of the J sample variances:

$SS_w = \sum_{1}^{J} (n_j - 1)s_j^2$. Since each s_j^2 is an unbiased estimator of the *same* population variance σ^2, the value of $E(SS_w) = \sum_{1}^{J} (n_j - 1)\sigma^2$. Now

$$E(SS_w) = \sum_{1}^{J} (n_j - 1)\sigma^2 = \sigma^2 \sum_{1}^{J} (n_j - 1) = \sigma^2(N - J).$$

Therefore

$$E\left(\frac{SS_w}{N - J}\right) = E(MS_w) = \sigma^2.$$

Whether H_0 is true or false, the long-run average value of MS_w (which would be obtained by averaging the MS_w's from a huge number of instances of running the same experiment) is equal to σ^2, the common variance of each of the J populations.

The value of $E(MS_b)$ is somewhat more difficult to derive, so we state without proof that the following is true:

$$E(MS_b) = \sigma^2 + \frac{\sum_1^J n_j(\mu_j - \mu)^2}{J - 1}.$$

The formula for $E(MS_b)$ for the unequal n's ANOVA is quite similar to $E(MS_b)$ for the equal n's case. [See Eq. (15.8).] They differ only in that the factor n, by which all squared deviations $\mu_j - \mu$ are weighted in the equal n's case, becomes a differential weight n_j for each squared deviation in the unequal n's case.

The essential property of MS_b is the same as when n's were equal, and this property is best revealed by inspecting $E(MS_b)$. When H_0 is true, one expects MS_b and MS_w to be the same size, namely σ^2. When H_0 is false, one expects MS_b to be larger than MS_w. These considerations, and others concerning distribution theory quite like that in the equal n's case, provide the techniques for making the F-test of H_0.

The *F*-test of H_0: Rationale and Procedure

When the null hypothesis is true the ratio MS_b/MS_w will follow a central F-distribution with $J - 1$ and $N - J$ degrees of freedom. When the null hypothesis is false, the ratio MS_b/MS_w will follow a noncentral F-distribution, which has a larger mean than the central F-distribution and more of its area above the bulk of the area of $F_{J-1, N-J}$ (see Fig. 15.2).

The strategy by which H_0 is tested is no different from what it was in the equal n's case. One adopts an α, finds the $100(1 - \alpha)$ percentile point in the table of the F-distribution which has $J - 1$ and $N - J$ degrees of freedom, compares MS_b/MS_w with $_{1-\alpha}F_{J-1, N-J}$, and decides to accept or reject H_0. If MS_b/MS_w exceeds $_{1-\alpha}F_{J-1, N-J}$, then it is considered unlikely that H_0 is true; for to do so forces one to regard the obtained F-ratio as an unlikely event (in fact, an event with probability α or less of happening). It would make better sense to regard this large F-ratio as one of the typical values from a noncentral F-distribution that would describe the distribution of MS_b/MS_w if H_0 were false.

An Example

An experiment was performed in which the effects of perceived similarity to a social group on conforming behavior were observed. A group of 60 experimental subjects was divided at random into three groups: low similarity—subjects in this group were informed that their expressed opinions were generally at variance with those of college students in general; medium similarity—subjects were told that their opinions agreed with those of college students in general only moderately often; high similarity—subjects were told that their opinions were usually exactly like those of students in general. After subjects were thus informed, they were asked to express their opinions about 18 current issues (capital punishment, birth control, etc.). Before expressing their opinion, however, the subjects were told how students in general felt about each issue. The number of times out of 18 a subject's expressed opinion was the same as what was portrayed to be the opinion of students in general was taken to be the number of times the subject "conformed to majority opinion." The actual "conformity scores" for the 60 subjects are presented in Table 15.3.

TABLE 15.3   CONFORMITY SCORES OF SUBJECTS WHO WERE TOLD THAT THEY HELD OPINIONS OF LOW, MEDIUM, OR HIGH SIMILARITY TO STUDENTS IN GENERAL

1 *Low similarity*				2 *Medium similarity*		3 *High similarity*			
15	13	11	9	15	12	18	14	12	10
14	13	10	9	15	11	17	14	12	10
14	13	10	9	14	11	16	14	12	10
14	13	10	8	14	10	15	14	12	10
13	13	10	8	14	10	14	13	11	9
13	13	10	8	13	10	14	13	11	8

Twelve Ss were observed under the medium similarity condition; 24 were observed under low similarity and 24 under high similarity. The null hypothesis of interest is that in the populations from which these samples can be considered to have been drawn at random—these are hypothetical populations of comparable subjects participating in this same experiment—the means of the three conditions are equal. That is, if we number the groups 1, 2, and 3 from low similarity to high, then $H_0: \mu_1 = \mu_2 = \mu_3$.

The calculation of sums of squares is performed in Table 15.4.

The degrees of freedom for MS_b and MS_w are $J - 1 = 2$ and $N - J = 60 - 3 = 57$, respectively. Hence, $MS_b = 20.416/2 = 10.208$ and $MS_w = 304.167/57 = 5.336$. The ANOVA results are tabulated as follows:

Source of variation:	*df*	*MS*	*F*
Between groups	2	10.208	1.91
Within groups	57	5.336	

To test the null hypothesis H_0 that $\mu_1 = \mu_2 = \mu_3$ (or equivalently that $\sum_1^3 \alpha_j^2 = 0$), refer an obtained F-ratio of 1.91 to the F-distribution with 2 and 57 degrees of freedom. The 75th and 90th percentiles in the distribution $F_{2,57}$ are 1.42 and 2.40, respectively. In replications of the experiment in Table 15.3, F-ratios exceeding 2.40 will be obtained 10% of the time *when the null hypothesis is true*. The obtained F-ratio of 1.91 will not allow confident rejection of the null hypothesis.

TABLE 15.4   ILLUSTRATION OF CALCULATION OF SUMS OF SQUARES FOR A ONE-FACTOR ANOVA WITH UNEQUAL n's; DATA FROM TABLE 15.3

1	2	3
$n_1 = 24$	$n_2 = 12$	$n_3 = 24$
$\sum_{i=1}^{24} X_{i1} = 273$	$\sum_{i=1}^{12} X_{i2} = 149$	$\sum_{i=1}^{24} X_{i3} = 303$

$$\sum_{j=1}^{3} \sum_{i=1}^{nj} X_{ij} = 725 \qquad \sum_{j=1}^{3} \sum_{i=1}^{nj} X_{ij}^2 = 9085$$

$$SS_b = \frac{(273)^2}{24} + \frac{(149)^2}{12} + \frac{(303)^2}{24} - \frac{(725)^2}{60} = 8780.833 - 8760.417 = 20.416$$

$$SS_w = 9085 - \left[\frac{(273)^2}{24} + \frac{(149)^2}{12} + \frac{(303)^2}{24} \right] = 9085 - 8780.833 = 304.167$$

15.13
CONSEQUENCES OF FAILURE TO MEET THE ANOVA ASSUMPTIONS: THE "ROBUSTNESS" OF ANOVA

The problem of what happens (to levels of significance and power) when the assumptions underlying an analysis of variance model are violated presents considerable difficulty to the mathematical statistician. This is to be expected. Two criteria by which mathematicians select assumptions for their procedures are *credibility* and *manageability*. A credible assumption is one that is likely to be met by actual data, e.g., one would have little use for a procedure or model that depended heavily on the assumption that IQ test scores have a rectangular distribution (all scores equally likely) in a population of examinees. A manageable assumption is one that simplifies many mathematical derivations and operations. The widespread assumption of normality of observations on variables is perhaps the best example of an assumption that is both credible, in many instances, and manageable. Many groups of observations made in physical and social sciences have one mode, a large proportion of central scores, and very few scores deviating greatly from the central scores; and the fact that the mean and variance of samples from a normal distribution are statistically independent simplifies much of the statistical theory that rests upon the normality assumption.

It should be no surprise, then, that things quickly become difficult and involved when one inquires about the effects of violation of an assumption that has become important because it is credible and manageable. For to answer such inquiries, one must necessarily make other assumptions that, while possibly more credible, are certainly less manageable (mathematically). "... We realize that standards of rigor possible in deducing a mathematical theory from certain assumptions generally cannot be maintained in deriving the consequences of departures from these assumptions." (Scheffé, 1959, p. 331.)

Thus, easy mathematical generalizations will be scarce on the following pages, and tables reporting particular results must be relied upon.

You will recall that the following assumptions are made in a simple one-way fixed-effects model ANOVA:

1. $X_{ij} = \mu + \alpha_j + e_{ij}$.
2. $e_{ij} \sim$ NID $(0, \sigma^2)$, i.e., within each of the J groups the observations are *n*ormally and *i*ndependently *d*istributed about their mean μ_j, with variance σ^2.
3. $\sum\limits_{j=1}^{J} \alpha_j = 0$.

The first assumption is that an observation can be thought of as the simple sum of three components: one reflecting the overall elevation of the measurements (μ); a second reflecting the increment or decrement on the dependent variable resulting from all observations taken in group j being exposed to treatment j; and a component e_{ij} that comprises things usually referred to in the behavioral sciences as "individual differences" and "measurement error," among others. Various ways exist in which assumption 1 can fail to be met. One is that the effect of treatment j is not the same, α_j, for all persons exposed to the treatment. For example, some students may benefit more from a particular treatment than others. It appears that the facilitative effect of practicing a given mental ability test is greater for brighter students than for duller ones.

Assumption 2 states that the e_{ij}'s over repeated samples have a normal distribution with a population mean (expectation) of 0 and variance of σ^2 and are independent. We can consider three distinct violations of this assumption: (1) nonnormality, (2) different variances from group to group, and (3) nonindependence. It is a consequence of assumptions 1–3 that a huge number of observations taken under the J treatments should have within each group nearly a normal distribution and the variance of this distribution from one group to the next should be the same, σ^2 (but not necessarily the same mean, obviously). Furthermore, if repeated samples are drawn and a scatter diagram of the sample means for any one of the $[J(J-1)/2]$ pairs of treatments is constructed, it will show zero correlation of the means because of the independence assumption.

Assumption 3 is of no concern; it is not altogether necessary since it is merely a consequence of choosing to express X_{ij} in three terms (μ, α_j, e_{ij}).

Failure to satisfy the independence assumption can be serious. The correlated or dependent-groups t-test is an appropriate statistical technique (if only two treatments are being compared) when nonindependence of the e_{ij}'s exists. In the behavioral sciences, one often speaks of the problem of "repeated measures" (i.e., observing the same persons under more than one treatment) when working under conditions of nonindependent samples. [We shall not discuss the repeated-measures problem at this point. We shall come back to the problem briefly in Chapter 18. See Winer (1962, chaps. 4 and 7), and "Repeated measures" in the index; Greenhouse and Geisser (1959); and Lana and Lubin (1963).]

We shall concern ourselves exclusively with the effects on the level of significance of violations of the assumptions of normality and equality of variances. The paradigm for past research by mathematical statisticians has been somewhat like the following:

1. Given a true null hypothesis, find from the F-table the $1 - \alpha$ percentile point in the F-distribution with $J - 1$ and $N - J$ df ($_{1-\alpha}F_{J-1, N-J}$). (This percentile point will be the value exceeded by $(100\alpha)\%$ of the F-ratios obtained in an ANOVA when the null hypothesis is true *and the ANOVA assumptions are met.*)

2. By empirical or mathematical means, the *actual* percentage of F-ratios exceeding $_{1-\alpha}F_{J-1, N-J}$ is found when the null hypothesis is true and the variances are heterogeneous or the populations are nonnormal or both.

3. The *nominal* significance level α, and the *actual* significance level, the percentage of F's exceeding $_{1-\alpha}F_{J-1,N-J}$, are compared.

Box (1954*a*, *b*) and Box and Andersen (1955) obtained some of the early mathematical results to the problem of the effect on α of heterogeneous variances in the one-way ANOVA. Many of these results appear in Scheffé (1959, esp. p. 354). These (Scheffé's) results appear in Table 15.5.

TABLE 15.5   EFFECT OF HETEROGENEOUS VARIANCES ON THE PROBABILITY OF A TYPE I ERROR IN THE ONE-WAY ANOVA FOR A NOMINAL SIGNIFICANCE LEVEL OF .05

Number of groups, J	Ratio of σ^2's	Sample sizes, n_j	Actual probability of type I error
3	1:2:3	5, 5, 5	.056
		3, 9, 3	.056
		7, 5, 3	.092
		3, 5, 7	.040
3	1:1:3	5, 5, 5	.059
		7, 5, 3	.11
		9, 5, 1	.17
		1, 5, 9	.013
5	1:1:1:1:3	5, 5, 5, 5, 5	.074
		9, 5, 5, 5, 1	.14
		1, 5, 5, 5, 9	.025
7	1:1: ... :1:7	3, 3, ... , 3	.12

The following is an example of how Table 15.5 is read: If three treatments are compared and $n_1 = 9$, $n_2 = 5$, and $n_3 = 1$, and if the population variances are in the ratio 1:1:3 (e.g., $\sigma_1^2 = 10$, $\sigma_2^2 = 10$, $\sigma_3^2 = 30$), then the probability of a type I error is actually .17 when the experimenter thinks it is .05. In this case, violation of the assumption of equal variances has caused a shifting to the right (general increase of values) of the distribution of the F-ratio, MS_b/MS_w, when the null hypothesis is true. The experimenter is in the position of having far greater chances of rejecting a true null hypothesis than he realizes.

One important trend that emerges in the Box data concerns the relationship between the σ's and the distribution of n's. Note that when the n's are equal, the actual probability of a type I error is very close to the nominal probability α. It may be that the influence of violation of the assumption of homogeneous variances is not very great when the n's are equal.

Several research studies on the effect of heterogeneous variances have been executed. (See Hsu, 1938; Scheffé, 1959; Lindquist, 1953; Boneau, 1960; Cochran, 1947; Godard and Lindquist, 1940; Horsnell, 1953; Welch,

1937.) All of these corroborate in part or entirely the following conclusions:

1. When the sample sizes are equal, the effect of heterogeneous variances on the level of significance of the F-test is negligible.

2. When the sample sizes and variances are unequal and *fewer* persons are sampled from the populations with *larger* variances, the probability of a type I error is *greater* than α. In other words, the effect of heterogeneous variances in this case is to shift the distribution of F-ratios to the right.

3. When the sample sizes and variances are unequal and *greater* numbers of persons are sampled from the populations with *larger* variances, the probability of a type I error is *less* than α. The effect of heterogeneous variances in this case is to shift the distribution of F-ratios to the left.

Now let us inquire into the effect of failure to satisfy the assumption that the observations in an ANOVA are sampled from normal populations. Many years of study have shown clearly that the effects of nonnormality on the nominal level of significance of the F-test are extremely slight. Empirical results published by E. S. Pearson in *Biometrika* in 1929 and 1931 showed that for the ANOVA with two groups the actual and nominal probabilities of a type I error are nearly equal when skewed distributions are sampled. Departure from the mesokurtosis of the normal distribution had little effect. Pearson also compared the nominal α and empirical probabilities of a type I error for $J = 5$, 10 and $n = 4$, 5, 10 when the populations were highly positively skewed and not mesokurtic. Failure to meet the normality assumption gave no cause for concern. (See Pearson, 1931.) Box and Andersen (1955) reported exact mathematical comparisons of the nominal α-level and the actual probability of a type I error for various nonnormal distributions. Some of these results, which are reproduced in Scheffé (1959, p. 350, Table 10.32), appear in Table 15.6.

With respect to the probability of a type I error, we can safely conclude that the ANOVA assumption of normality is of almost no importance. It can be violated and the probability of a type I error remains almost exactly at the value specified by the experimenter, namely α.

Boneau (1960) reviewed much previous research and reported his own original work on violation of the t-test assumptions. Aside from the interest generated by Boneau's original contributions to the study of violation of ANOVA assumptions, his article is well known and often referenced because of its excellent review of the literature. A beginning student in this area would do well to study it carefully.

Boneau compared actual with nominal .05 and .01 significance levels for various sample sizes and violations of the assumptions of homogeneous

TABLE 15.6 APPROXIMATIONS TO ACTUAL PROBABILITIES OF A TYPE I ERROR IN A ONE-WAY ANOVA ($J = 5$, $n = 5$) FOR VARIOUS NONNORMAL POPULATIONS WHEN THE NOMINAL LEVEL OF SIGNIFICANCE IS .05

Kind of population*	Skewness of populations	Kurtosis of populations				
		2	2.5	3	3.5	4
Pearson	0	.053	.051	.05	.048	—
Edgeworth	0	.053	.051	.05	.049	.048
Pearson	+.5 or −.5	.052	.051	.050	.049	—
Edgeworth	+.5 or −.5	.053	.051	.050	.049	.048
Pearson	+1 or −1	.052	.050	.049	.048	.048
Edgeworth	+1 or −1	.053	.052	.050	.050	.049

* These names are descriptive of certain nonnormal distributions. If you are further interested, see Scheffé (1959, p. 349, footnote 30).

TABLE 15.7 ACTUAL PROBABILITIES OF TYPE I ERRORS WITH A TWO-TAILED t-TEST FOR VARIOUS NONNORMAL POPULATIONS AND VALUES OF THE POPULATION VARIANCES

Population 1			Population 2			Nominal level of significance	
Shape	σ_1^2	n_1	Shape	σ_2^2	n_2	.05	.01
Normal	1	5	Normal	1	5	.053*	.009*
Normal	1	15	Normal	1	15	.040*	.008*
Normal	1	5	Normal	1	15	.040*	.006*
Normal	1	5	Normal	4	5	.064	.018
Normal	1	15	Normal	4	15	.049	.011
Normal	1	5	Normal	4	15	.010	.001
Normal	4	5	Normal	1	15	.160	.060
Exponential†	1	5	Exponential	1	5	.031	.003
Exponential	1	15	Exponential	1	15	.040	.004
Rectangular‡	1	5	Rectangular	1	5	.051	.010
Rectangular	1	15	Rectangular	1	15	.050	.015
Rectangular	1	5	Rectangular	4	5	.071	.019
Normal	1	5	Rectangular	1	5	.056	.010
Normal	1	15	Rectangular	1	15	.056	.010
Exponential	1	5	Normal	1	5	.071	.019
Exponential	1	15	Normal	1	15	.051	.014
Exponential	1	25	Normal	1	25	.046	.013
Exponential	1	5	Rectangular	1	5	.064	.033
Exponential	1	15	Rectangular	1	15	.056	.016
Exponential	1	5	Exponential	4	5	.083	.017

* These cases, for which the ANOVA assumptions are met, were included as checks on the empirical sampling procedure.

† The exponential distribution looks something like the upper third of a normal distribution.

‡ The graph of a rectangular distribution is a straight, horizontal line, all values of the variable being equally likely.

variances and normality.   The actual significance levels are based on samples of 1000 t-ratios.   Entire frequency distributions of the t-ratios obtained when t-tests are performed on nonnormal populations or populations with unequal variances are reproduced in the 1960 article by Boneau.   These graphs are illuminating and ought to be studied.   We shall give only a few of the more easily reproduced findings from Boneau's work.   These results appear in Table 15.7.   Try to integrate Boneau's findings with those of Box and Pearson.

In summary, the fixed effects ANOVA appears to be remarkably insensitive to departures from normality; and when n's are equal, it is equally unaffected by heterogeneous variances.   Box has used the word "robustness" for this insensitivity of a statistical test to violation of its assumptions.

15.14
TESTING HOMOGENEITY OF VARIANCES

Two instances in which testing for heterogeneity of population variances is worthwhile come to mind: (1) when one wishes to make inferences about population variances because they are of scientific interest, and (2) when one suspects heterogeneity of variances in an analysis of variance in which not all factors have fixed effects.

The best known test of the homogeneity of a set of variances is due to M. S. Bartlett (1937).   Statisticians are sometimes reluctant to run Bartlett's test because the necessary calculations are arduous.   Bartlett's test requires the calculation of the J sample variances and their logarithms.   In addition to the drawback of laborious calculations, Bartlett's test has been found to be quite sensitive to violation of the necessary assumption that the J samples come from normal populations (Box, 1953).   If nonnormal populations are sampled, the probability of a type I error (rejecting a true H_0) with Bartlett's test may be far greater than the α chosen by the test user.   Bartlett's test is so sensitive to the assumption of normal populations that it may even be a good test of *normality* (Box, 1953)!   Scheffé's test of homogeneity of variances can be every bit as tedious arithmetically as Bartlett's.   It is much less sensitive to violation of the normality assumption, however (Scheffé, 1959).   A test devised by Hartley (see *Biometrika Tables for Statisticians*, pp. 60–61) is a useful short-cut test of H_0.   It consists of referring the ratio of the largest sample variance to the smallest variance to a special table (Table 31, *Biometrika Tables*).   Hartley's test does not use all of the information the observations provide about heterogeneity of variances, and it might be expected that far more powerful tests could be found.   Cochran (1951) proposed a test of H_0 that is simple to run and that uses more of the information in the data than does Hartley's.   Winer (1962, p. 96) maintained that there is evidence that the tests of Bartlett, Hartley, and Cochran are sensitive to the assumption, upon which each rests, that the J samples are from normal distributions. The two latter tests also require special tables for their execution.

Levene (1960) proposed a test of H_0 that is both simple to run (it uses ordinary analysis of variance techniques) and insensitive to violation of the normality assumption in most cases. Levene's test is simply a one-way analysis of variance on the absolute values of the differences between each observation and the mean of its group. For example, the data from an experiment have the following layout:

$$\textit{Treatment}$$

$$
\begin{array}{ccccc}
1 & 2 & \ldots & J \\
X_{11} & X_{12} & \ldots & X_{1J} \\
\cdot & \cdot & & \cdot \\
\cdot & \cdot & & \cdot \\
\cdot & \cdot & & \cdot \\
X_{n1} & X_{n2} & \ldots & X_{nJ}
\end{array}
$$

One wishes to test the hypothesis $H_0: \sigma_1^2 = \ldots = \sigma_J^2$. No assumption about the shapes of the distributions underlying the J samples is made. A statistic will be appropriate for testing H_0 on the above data provided that (1) one can approximate the 95th and 99th percentiles, say, in the distribution of the statistic when H_0 is true, and (2) the test based on the statistic has good power for rejecting H_0 when it is false. The test statistic for Levene's test is the ratio of MS_b to MS_w of transformed scores Z_{ij} that are related to the X_{ij}'s by $Z_{ij} = |X_{ij} - \bar{X}_{.j}|$. If this F-ratio exceeds the $1 - \alpha$ percentile point of the ordinary F-distribution with degrees of freedom $J - 1$ and $J(n - 1)$, one concludes with approximately $1 - \alpha$ confidence that the population variances are different.

Levene's paper (1960) reported on his investigation of the properties of the above test. Among other things, he studied the correspondence between the probability of obtaining a significant F-ratio on the Z_{ij}'s and the nominal probability adopted by the test user. That is, the correspondence between the sampling distribution of the F-ratio on the Z_{ij}'s and the F-distribution was examined. It was anticipated that this correspondence would be close due to the widely recognized "robustness" of the fixed-effects analysis of variance. Since the fixed-effects analysis of variance is robust for equal numbers of observations per group, Levene restricted attention to this case. The robustness of Levene's test has thus been examined only for equal n's. The mathematics for Levene's investigation proved to be intractable; thus empirical sampling distributions of F-ratios calculated on the Z_{ij}'s were compared with the F-distribution with $J - 1$ and $J(n - 1)$

degrees of freedom. In general, the agreement of the nominal (based on the F-distribution) and the empirical (based on 1000 observations) probabilities of rejecting a true H_0 was remarkably close.

Levene also investigated the power of his test for rejecting H_0. The power was found to be generally quite satisfactory. Assuming normal distributions and $J = 2$, the efficiency of Levene's test relative to the exact F-test was good. These efficiencies ranged between .75 and .96 for various values of α and various alternative hypotheses (σ_1^2/σ_2^2). For J samples the efficiency of Levene's test relative to the approximate efficiency of Bartlett's test, assuming normal distributions, ranged from .83 to .90.

In summary, Levene's test appears to be a "robust" test (for equal numbers of observations in J samples) of the hypothesis of equal population variances that has satisfactory power to reject alternative hypotheses. Its ease of calculation and use of standard tables of the F-distribution make it an attractive alternative for more laborious and less robust tests that have been in common use. (See Glass, 1966a.)

15.15
POWER OF THE F-TEST

The power of a particular F-test depends on four quantities: the degrees of freedom "between" denoted by n_1, the degrees of freedom "within" denoted by n_2, a quantity denoted by ϕ, which is a measure of the degree of "falseness" of the null hypothesis, and α, the level of significance of the test. Of course, in the one-factor ANOVA the value of n_1 is $J - 1$, and the value of n_2 is $N - J$. The power of the F-test is defined for a particular set of values of $\mu_1, \ldots, \mu_J$. The quantity ϕ has the following definition:

$$\phi = \sqrt{\frac{\sum_{j=1}^{J} n_j(\mu_j - \bar{\mu}_.)^2}{J\sigma^2}},$$

where $\bar{\mu}_. = (\mu_1 + \ldots + \mu_J)/J$, which also equals μ.

The calculation of ϕ involves σ^2, the population variance common to all J populations. Normally σ^2 will not be known; this necessitates either gathering preliminary data to estimate it, making a shrewd guess as to its value, or measuring the differences among the μ_j in σ-units so that σ^2 need not be known (e.g., what is the power of the F-test if $\mu_1 - \mu_2$ equals $\sigma/2$?).

Once ϕ, n_1, n_2, and α are known, the power of the F-test can be determined from Table N in Appendix A. For example, suppose that an experiment is performed comparing $J = 3$ treatments. Assume that there are $n = 11$ observations per group and that the F-test of the null hypothesis is to be performed at the $\alpha = .05$ level. We wish to calculate the power of the F-test for the following alternative hypothesis:

$$\mu_1 = 68, \qquad \mu_2 = 66, \qquad \mu_3 = 64.$$

Suppose that previous experiments on similar phenomena lead one to believe that σ^2 is reasonably close to 20. The value of ϕ is

$$\phi = \sqrt{\frac{11[(68 - 66)^2 + (66 - 66)^2 + (64 - 66)^2]}{3 \cdot 20}}$$

$$= \sqrt{\frac{11(8)}{3 \cdot 20}} = \sqrt{\frac{88}{60}} = \sqrt{1.47} = 1.21.$$

Table N is entered with $n_1 = (J - 1) = 2$, $n_2 = (N - J) = 30$, $\alpha = .05$, and $\phi = 1.21$. The power of the F-test of H_0 against the alternative hypothesis that $\mu_1 = 68$, $\mu_2 = 66$, and $\mu_3 = 64$ is approximately 0.40. Thus, there are four chances in 10 of rejecting H_0 in favor of H_1 if in fact $\mu_1 = 68$, $\mu_2 = 66$, and $\mu_3 = 64$.

Verify that for $n_1 = J - 1 = 1$, $n_2 = N - J = 60$, $\alpha = .01$, and $\phi = 3.00$, the power of the F-test is approximately 0.94.

PROBLEMS AND EXERCISES

1. Calculate the degrees of freedom for both MS_b and MS_w in each of the following instances:
   a. $J = 2, n = 4.$ b. $J = 5, n = 2.$
   c. $J = 3; n_1 = 3, n_2 = 6, n_3 = 4.$ d. $J = 3; n_1 = 4, n_2 = 1, n_3 = 5.$

2. Determine the critical value of $F = MS_b/MS_w$ for testing H_0 in each of the following instances:
   a. $J = 2; n = 6; \alpha = .01.$ b. $J = 5; n = 7; \alpha = .10.$
   c. $J = 3; n_1 = 4, n_2 = 6, n_3 = 8; \alpha = .05.$

3. Which one or more of the following statements are equivalent to the alternative hypothesis H_1 in the one-factor ANOVA?
   a. $\mu_j \neq \mu_{j*}$ for some j and j^*. b. $\mu_1 \neq \mu_2 \neq \ldots \neq \mu_{J-1} \neq \mu_J.$
   c. $\sum_{j=1}^{J} (\mu_j - \bar{\mu})^2 \neq 0.$ d. $\mu_j \neq \mu_{j*}$ for all pairs of j and j^*.

4. Given only the following data in an ANOVA table, determine MS_b, MS_w, and F.

Source of variation	df	SS	MS	F
Between groups	4	81.25		
Within groups				
Total	49	378.60		

5. The report of an experiment in which three treatment groups were compared contained only the following data:

$$n_1 = 10 \qquad n_2 = 10 \qquad n_3 = 10$$
$$\overline{X}_{.1} = 104.65 \qquad \overline{X}_{.2} = 112.41 \qquad \overline{X}_{.3} = 105.06$$
$$s_1 = 12.84 \qquad s_2 = 15.03 \qquad s_3 = 16.55$$

Using these summary statistics, calculate MS_b and MS_w and test H_0: $\mu_1 = \mu_2 = \mu_3$ at the .01 level of significance.

6. In Prob. 2 at the end of Chapter 14, a t-test of the significance of the difference between two means was called for on the following data:

Group 1	Group 2
$n_1 = 10$	$n_2 = 10$
$\overline{X}_{.1} = 19.20$	$\overline{X}_{.2} = 11.30$
$s_1 = 7.93$	$s_2 = 5.79$

The value of t was 2.55, which was significant at the .05 level. Perform a one-way ANOVA with $J = 2$ on the above data and show that $F = MS_b/MS_w$ equals $t^2 = (2.55)^2$ which is also significant at the .05 level. Thus, verify for one particular case that the one-way ANOVA for two groups is equivalent to a t-test of H_0: $\mu_1 = \mu_2$.

7. Guthrie (1967) studied the effectiveness of three different modes of training on deciphering cryptograms. Group I was trained by first being presented rules for deciphering cryptograms, then working examples. Group II worked examples first then was told the rules. Group III worked only examples. A control group studied Russian vocabulary during the training period. A group of 72 subjects was randomly split into four groups of 18 each and assigned to the four training conditions. After training, the S's were given a 10-item test comprising 10 new cryptograms like those studied during training. The means and standard deviations of the number of cryptograms solved on the criterion test in each group are as follows:

Group I (rule-example)	Group II (example-rule)	Group III (example)	Control
$n = 18$	$n = 18$	$n = 18$	$n = 18$
$\overline{X}_{.1} = 8.06$	$\overline{X}_{.2} = 6.94$	$\overline{X}_{.3} = 7.11$	$\overline{X}_{.4} = 4.73$
$s_1 = 2.37$	$s_2 = 2.31$	$s_3 = 2.42$	$s_4 = 2.27$

Perform a one-way ANOVA on Guthrie's data to test the null hypothesis that the means of the populations underlying the four groups are equal. Test H_0 at the .05 level of significance. (Save your calculations because they will be used again in the problems at the end of Chapter 16.)

8. Three methods of teaching foreign language vocabulary were compared in an experiment. To evaluate the instruction, a 50-item vocabulary test was administered to the 24 students in the experiment; eight students were in each group. The following data—expressed as number of correct items out of 50—were obtained:

Aural-oral method	Translation method	Combined methods
$X_{11} = 19$	$X_{12} = 21$	$X_{13} = 17$
$X_{21} = 37$	$X_{22} = 18$	$X_{23} = 20$
$X_{31} = 28$	$X_{32} = 15$	$X_{33} = 28$
$X_{41} = 31$	$X_{42} = 23$	$X_{43} = 30$
$X_{51} = 29$	$X_{52} = 20$	$X_{53} = 13$
$X_{61} = 25$	$X_{62} = 22$	$X_{63} = 18$
$X_{71} = 36$	$X_{72} = 26$	$X_{73} = 19$
$X_{81} = 33$	$X_{82} = 14$	$X_{83} = 23$

Perform an F-test of the null hypothesis that $\mu_1 = \mu_2 = \mu_3$ at the .05 level of significance. (Save your results for the exercises at the end of Chapter 17.)

9. Harrington (1968) experimented with the sequencing of instructional material and "organizers" that structured the material for the learner. A group of 30 persons were randomly split into three groups of 10 each. Group I received organizing material before studying instructional materials on mathematics; group II received the "organizer" after studying the mathematics; group III received no organizing material in connection with studying the mathematics instructional materials. On a 10-item test over the mathematics covered in the instructional materials, the following scores were earned:

Group I (pre-organizer)	Group II (post-organizer)	Group III (no organizer)
4	5	5
5	4	4
3	4	6
6	7	2
6	8	2
3	7	2
3	6	6
4	4	4
4	4	3
2	7	4

Perform a one-factor ANOVA; test the null hypothesis that $\mu_1 = \mu_2 = \mu_3$ at any level of significance you wish.

10. Perform an F-test of the null hypothesis $H_0 : \sum_{j=1}^{4} (\mu_j - \bar{\mu}.)^2 = 0$ at the .01 level on the following data which represent weight losses in pounds of subjects under four different diets.

Diet A	Diet B	Diet C	Diet D
$X_{11} = 6$	$X_{12} = 11$	$X_{13} = 21$	$X_{14} = 5$
$X_{21} = 8$	$X_{22} = 13$	$X_{23} = 20$	$X_{24} = 9$
$X_{31} = 3$	$X_{32} = 15$	$X_{33} = 17$	$X_{34} = 10$
$X_{41} = 5$		$X_{43} = 16$	$X_{44} = 7$
$X_{51} = 6$			$X_{54} = 7$

11. The null hypothesis $H_0: \mu_1 = \ldots = \mu_5$ is to be tested with an α of .05 and with samples of size $n = 5$. Suppose that unknown to the experimenter, $\mu_1 = 10$, $\mu_2 = 10$, $\mu_3 = 12$, $\mu_4 = 14$, and $\mu_5 = 14$; also, the value of σ^2 is 8.00. What is the power of the F-test of H_0 under these circumstances?

12. Ten samples of 20 scores each are drawn at random from a single normal population with mean μ and variance σ^2. The sample *means* of the 10 samples have a variance of 2.40, i.e.,

$$s_{\bar{x}.}^2 = \frac{\sum_{j=1}^{10} (\bar{X}_{.j} - \bar{X}_{..})^2}{9} = 2.40.$$

Find an estimate of σ^2, the variance of the original normal population sampled.

13. Unknown to the experimenter, the value of σ^2 is 20, and $\mu_1 = 10$, $\mu_2 = 15$, and $\mu_3 = 20$ in the three populations from which he has drawn samples of size $n = 10$. What is the expected value of MS_b in this experiment, i.e., what would be the average value of MS_b over an infinite number of replications of this same experiment?

14. Prove that $SS_w = \sum_{j=1}^{J} \left[\sum_{i=1}^{n} (X_{ij} - \bar{X}_{.j})^2 \right]$ is equal to its computational formula

$$SS_w = \sum_{j=1}^{J} \sum_{i=1}^{n} X_{ij}^2 - \sum_{j=1}^{J} \frac{\left(\sum_{i=1}^{n} X_{ij} \right)^2}{n}.$$ (Hint: First show that $\sum_{i=1}^{n} (X_{ij} - \bar{X}_{.j})^2$ equals

$$\sum_{i=1}^{n} X_{ij}^2 - \frac{\left(\sum_{i=1}^{n} X_{ij} \right)^2}{n},$$ as was done in Chapter 5. Then sum the J sums of squares for each group across j.)

15. Prove that the value of $F = MS_b/MS_w$ in a one-way ANOVA with $J = 2$ equals the square of the value of t for testing the significance of the difference between the two means, i.e., prove that

$$t^2 = \frac{(\bar{X}_{.1} - \bar{X}_{.2})^2}{[(s_1^2 + s_2^2)/2](2/n)}$$

equals

$$F = \frac{n[(\bar{X}_{.1} - \bar{X}_{..})^2 + (\bar{X}_{.2} - \bar{X}_{..})^2]}{(s_1^2 + s_2^2)/2}.$$

Start by noting that $\bar{X}_{..} = (\bar{X}_{.1} + \bar{X}_{.2})/2$, and then manipulate the numerator of F into the form $n(\bar{X}_{.1} - \bar{X}_{.2})^2/2$.

Reference

Now that you have completed this chapter on the analysis of variance for the one-factor, fixed-effects model, you may wish to read Stanley's (1968a) encyclopedia article to review some points already covered and to introduce certain other concepts that will be discussed in later chapters.

16

MULTIPLE COMPARISON PROCEDURES

16.1
INTRODUCTION

Generally, the conclusion of an ANOVA is a statement that the null hypothesis of no treatment differences is either true or false with an accompanying probability level (α) that gives the probability of a type I error. If the null hypothesis is rejected, the statement that "not all population means can be considered equal" (which is equivalent to "H_0 is false") is often not very informative. It is a tremendous improvement over simply pointing out that the sample means differed and making no inferential statement, but the decision to reject H_0 tells nothing about which population means of underlying treatment populations differ from which other population means. Suppose that for two experiments comparing four groups and involving large samples with a small MS_w, it so happens that $\mu_1 = \mu_2 = \mu_3 = 20$ and $\mu_4 = 30$ for the first experiment and $\mu_1 = 5$, $\mu_2 = 10$, $\mu_3 = 25$, and $\mu_4 = 50$ for the second experiment. In both instances the experimenter is likely to obtain a significant F-ratio in testing $H_0: \sum_{1}^{4} (\mu_j - \bar{\mu}.)^2 = 0$. Using no more than a simple one-factor ANOVA, both experimenters will end at precisely the same point, i.e., concluding that H_0 is false with a high level of significance (low α), although the patterns of the differences between the population means in the two experiments are quite different. This is indeed an unsatisfactory situation.

Most multiple comparison procedures are designed to be used after the null hypothesis of no treatment differences in an ANOVA has been rejected. The purpose of these procedures is the isolation of comparisons between means that are responsible for or contributed to the rejection of H_0. For example, in the first experiment above, comparing μ_1 and μ_2 by forming $\mu_1 - \mu_2 = 20 - 20 = 0$ reveals that these two means would not have given a high probability of rejecting H_0 if they were the only two treatment groups present. However, $\mu_4 - \mu_1 = 30 - 20 = 10$ was partly responsible for the significance of the obtained results. The application of multiple comparison procedures to large samples in the first experiment above should have a high probability of leading the experimenter to conclude that μ_1, μ_2, and μ_3 are the same and μ_4 is different from (and greater than) all three of them.

Your first reaction to this problem is probably the thought that t-tests performed on all possible pairs of means involved in the F-test will reveal where significant differences between means lie. This is an understandable first impression; however, it is quite unacceptable methodology. The t-test was not designed for this use and is invalid when so applied. The t-test is properly applied to *two* random samples. It is quite a different matter to expect the t-test to be valid for determining the significance of the difference between the smallest and largest sample means in a collection of J means. A t-test applied to the largest and smallest of J means takes no account of how large J is. Isn't it clear that if we take J to be 50 and we draw 50 samples randomly from the same normal population, a t-test will show the largest and smallest to be "significantly different" a large proportion of the time (a far larger proportion than the required α)? In spite of the patent invalidity of t-testing following a significant F-ratio in the analysis of variance, or multiple t-testing in lieu of the analysis of variance, this method has often been and continues to be used.

There are several multiple comparison procedures available, but we shall deal with just two of them in any detail. Such procedures are a relatively recent addition to statistical theory, having been developed during the 1950's; their use in research in the behavioral sciences dates from about 1957 (see McHugh and Ellis, 1955; Stanley, 1957a; Sparks, 1963; and Kenyon, 1965).

One of the earliest procedures grew out of Keuls's (1952) extension of some early work by Newman (1939) and is called, quite appropriately, the Newman-Keuls procedure (see Winer, 1962, p. 80 ff.). Another early worker in this field was Duncan (1955), who produced Duncan's New Multiple

Range Test. Duncan's procedure has probably been the most popular in the behavioral sciences and education; but until mathematical statisticians resolve their differences or satisfy one another that the derivation of the procedure is valid (see Scheffé, 1959, p. 78, fn. 16), it might be wise for persons in applied fields to observe a moratorium on Duncan's procedure.

If a researcher wishes to compare several treatment groups with a control group to decide which treatments differ from the single control, the procedure due to Dunnett (1955) is available (see Winer, 1962, pp. 90–91). One of the few published reports of educational research in which Dunnett's procedure was used is an article by Scannell and Marshall (1966). You should find this article informative as to the context in which the Dunnett procedure is used. The two most useful multiple comparison procedures are those developed by Tukey and Scheffé: the T-method and the S-method, respectively. Although the T-method and S-method have very general forms, we shall deal with specific cases that encompass almost all of the applications of these methods to problems you are likely to meet.

16.2
THE T-METHOD

The null hypothesis in a one-way ANOVA has been rejected at the α-level of significance. J treatments were compared, and the *number of observations, n, in each group was equal*. All assumptions for running the ANOVA were met—at least no evidence existed that any one was violated. Among the J treatments there are $J(J-1)/2$ pairs (i.e., combinations of J means taken two at a time). Each of these yields a simple comparison of the form $\bar{X}_{.j} - \bar{X}_{.j*}$, where $j \neq j*$. By observation of these $J(J-1)/2$ differences between sample means and application of the T-method, the experimenter wishes to decide whether he can regard each $\mu_j - \mu_{j*}$ as being different from zero. First we shall see how his decision is reached, then we shall discuss the probability values that apply to his decisions.

Step 1. All $J(J-1)/2$ comparisons between sample means of the form $\bar{X}_{.j} - \bar{X}_{.j*}$ are computed. For example, if three treatments are compared, then $\bar{X}_{.1} - \bar{X}_{.2}$, $\bar{X}_{.1} - \bar{X}_{.3}$, and $\bar{X}_{.2} - \bar{X}_{.3}$ are calculated.

Step 2. All comparisons $\bar{X}_{.j} - \bar{X}_{.j*}$ are divided by $\sqrt{MS_w/n}$, where MS_w is the mean-square within factor levels from the one-way ANOVA and n is the number of observations in any one group.

Step 3. The $100(1 - \alpha)$ percentile point in the Studentized range distribution with degrees of freedom J and $J(n - 1)$ is found from Table F in Appendix A. This percentile point is denoted $_{1-\alpha}q_{J,J(n-1)}$.

The Studentized range is the difference between the largest and the smallest means of J independent samples each of size n from a normal population, divided by $\sqrt{MS_w/n}$. There is a family of distributions of the Studentized range, since a different distribution results for all pairs of values of J and n. The two parameters used to identify a particular Studentized range distribution are J, the number of samples, and $J(n - 1)$, the degrees of freedom for MS_w.

Step 4. All $J(J - 1)/2$ differences $\bar{X}_{.j} - \bar{X}_{.j^*}$ divided by $\sqrt{MS_w/n}$ are compared with the percentile point. It is concluded that $\bar{X}_{.j}$ and $\bar{X}_{.j^*}$ are significantly different, i.e., present evidence that μ_j and μ_{j^*} are different, if $|\bar{X}_{.j} - \bar{X}_{.j^*}|$ over $\sqrt{MS_w/n}$ is greater than $_{1-\alpha}q_{J,J(n-1)}$.

An example of the application of the T-method is as follows. An experiment comparing three methods ($J = 3$), each having 11 observations per group ($n = 11$), yields $\bar{X}_{.1} = 22.60$, $\bar{X}_{.2} = 23.40$, $\bar{X}_{.3} = 28.50$, and $MS_w = 4.10$. An F-ratio significant at the .05 level is obtained.

Step 1. $\bar{X}_{.1} - \bar{X}_{.2} = -0.80.$
$\bar{X}_{.1} - \bar{X}_{.3} = -5.90.$
$\bar{X}_{.2} - \bar{X}_{.3} = -5.10.$

Step 2. Dividing the above differences by $\sqrt{4.10/11} = .610$, gives -1.311, -9.672, and -8.361.

Step 3. From Table F we see that $_{.95}q_{3,30} = 3.49$.

Step 4. Any *absolute* difference between means divided by $\sqrt{MS_w/n}$ that exceeds 3.49 is significant. Thus, it can be concluded—on the basis of the T-method—that the population means for groups 1 and 2 do not differ (because $1.311 < 3.49$), and the mean of population 3 differs from the means of both populations 1 and 2.

16.3
CONFIDENCE INTERVALS
AROUND CONTRASTS BY
THE *T*-METHOD

Establishing confidence intervals around the differences $\bar{X}_{.j} - \bar{X}_{.j*}$ should be considered as important, or perhaps more important, than the mere decision of whether the difference is significant. Using the *T*-method, one can establish a *set of simultaneous confidence intervals* for the differences between sample means. The confidence interval around $\bar{X}_{.j} - \bar{X}_{.j*}$ is found from the following formula:

$$(\bar{X}_{.j} - \bar{X}_{.j*}) \pm {}_{1-\alpha}q_{J,J(n-1)}\sqrt{MS_w/n}. \tag{16.1}$$

In the example used to illustrate the significance testing function of the *T*-method, $\bar{X}_{.1} = 22.60$, $\bar{X}_{.2} = 23.40$, $\bar{X}_{.3} = 28.50$, $\sqrt{MS_w/n} = .610$, and ${}_{.95}q_{3,30} = 3.49$. To establish confidence intervals around the three possible differences between means, one adds and subtracts $(3.49)(.610) = 2.13$ from each difference. These calculations are performed in Table 16.1.

TABLE 16.1 ESTABLISHING CONFIDENCE INTERVALS AROUND DIFFERENCES
BETWEEN THREE SAMPLE MEANS USING THE *T*-METHOD

$\bar{X}_{.j} - \bar{X}_{.j*}$	${}_{1-\alpha}q_{J,J(n-1)}(\sqrt{MS_w/n})$	Final calculations
$\bar{X}_{.1} - \bar{X}_{.2} = -0.80$	$(3.49)(.610) = 2.13$	$-0.8 \pm 2.13 = (-2.93, 1.33)$
$\bar{X}_{.1} - \bar{X}_{.3} = -5.90$	2.13	$-5.9 \pm 2.13 = (-8.03, -3.77)$
$\bar{X}_{.2} - \bar{X}_{.3} = -5.10$	2.13	$-5.1 \pm 2.13 = (-7.23, -2.97)$

Notice that the single confidence interval that includes zero between its bounds corresponds to the nonsignificant difference between the sample means $\bar{X}_{.1}$ and $\bar{X}_{.2}$, whereas the other two differences are significant.

Notice that the quantity added to and subtracted from the sample mean difference is the same for any value of j and j^*. Thus, one determines ${}_{1-\alpha}q_{J,J(n-1)}\sqrt{MS_w/n}$ and adds it to and subtracts it from each of the $J(J-1)/2$ mean differences to establish a set of simultaneous confidence intervals by the *T*-method. Of course, the purpose of any confidence interval of this type is to capture within its limits the value of $\mu_j - \mu_{j*}$. The *simultaneous* confidence intervals are constructed in such a way that the confidence coefficient for any single interval is *not* $1 - \alpha$, however. The meaning of the term *simultaneous* and the nature of the inference being made with such confidence intervals should become clearer in the following paragraph.

In an experiment comparing five groups, there are $5(4)/2 = 10$ comparisons of sample means that can be made. Confidence intervals can be established around all 10 of these sample mean comparisons by the T-method using Eq. (16.1) and an α of .05, for example. In the set of 10 confidence intervals, some of them will include $\mu_j - \mu_{j*}$ within their limits and some will not. The same experiment could be run again and again until thousands of sets of 10 confidence intervals are accumulated. The proportion of these thousands of experiments in which all 10 of the computed confidence intervals around the 10 comparisons $\bar{X}_{.j} - \bar{X}_{.j*}$ include within their limits the value of $\mu_j - \mu_{j*}$ is equal to .95, i.e., $(1 - \alpha)$. In other words, in $100(1 - \alpha)$ percent of the experiments in which J groups of n each are compared, the T-method will yield $J(J - 1)/2$ confidence intervals all of which include $\mu_j - \mu_{j*}$ within their limits. In some experiments, perhaps only one of the $J(J - 1)/2$ confidence intervals does not capture $\mu_j - \mu_{j*}$; in other experiments, more than one of the set of simultaneous confidence intervals will not capture $\mu_j - \mu_{j*}$. In the long run, only $100(\alpha)$ percent of the experiments will have one or more of the $J(J - 1)/2$ confidence intervals that do not capture $\mu_j - \mu_{j*}$.

The idea of a set of simultaneous confidence intervals is a radical departure from the simpler notions of confidence intervals met earlier in this text. Formerly, we spoke of the probability that a confidence interval of the form $\bar{X}_. \pm z\sigma/\sqrt{n}$ included μ within its limits. Now we are talking about the probability that for an experiment with J groups every one of a collection of confidence intervals captures the parameters of interest. In probability terms, a collection of intervals was the sample space to which the confidence coefficient, $1 - \alpha$, applied. With sets of simultaneous confidence intervals, the sample space is an infinite population of experiments, each experiment yielding $J(J - 1)/2$ sample mean differences.

Suppose that $J = 3$ groups of $n = 10$ persons are being compared on some variable, and that $\mu_1 = 13$, $\mu_2 = 10$, and $\mu_3 = 5$. There are $3(2)/2 = 3$ comparisons of means that can be made following the experiment. Imagine that T-method confidence intervals with $\alpha = .10$ are established around the three comparisons $\bar{X}_{.1} - \bar{X}_{.2}$, $\bar{X}_{.1} - \bar{X}_{.3}$, and $\bar{X}_{.2} - \bar{X}_{.3}$. Conceivably, the process of drawing three groups of 10 observations and establishing T-method intervals around the comparisons could be repeated indefinitely. The graph in Fig. 16.1 shows conceivable results of this process.

The small dots represent sample mean differences. The three dots above 1 on the horizontal scale in Fig. 16.1 represent the three differences between means obtained the *first* time the experiment was run. The lines that extend an equal distance above and below each dot represent the intervals established by the T-method. Notice that in the first experiment all three confidence intervals include the true value of $\mu_j - \mu_{j*}$. We should expect this to be true with $90\% = 100(1 - \alpha)$ of the experiments ($J = 3$, $n = 10$) performed. Notice that in the fifth experiment two of the three intervals do not cover the population mean differences. We would expect that one, two, or all

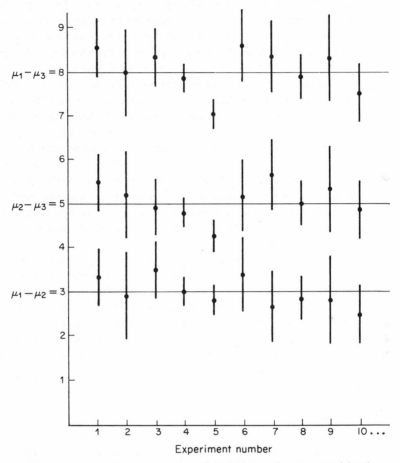

FIG. 16.1 Sets of simultaneous confidence intervals constructed by the *T*-method for 10 replications of an experiment comparing three treatments.

three of the intervals would fail to capture the population mean differences in about $10\% = 100(\alpha)$ of the experiments.

One weakness seems to exist in the adoption of an "experiment-wise" error rate when making multiple comparisons. This weakness relates to the concept of an experiment itself. Generally in research in education and the social sciences, the choice of the number of levels that will constitute a factor in an experiment is arbitrary. Seldom do compelling reasons exist for making this choice. The experimenter would willingly include any number of additional levels in the experiment for comparison if they presented themselves on his doorstep. Some experimenters choose to include a "control group" in any experiment, whereas others do not. The definition of a "factor" (a collection of levels to be compared) in an experiment is quite arbitrary. However, a *contrast* between method A and method B always means the same thing whether it stands alone or is imbedded in a factor with a dozen levels. (See Wilson, 1962 and Ryan, 1959 and 1962.)

Inspection of the Tukey method shows that the probability of detecting a significant contrast between two means (the *power* of the contrast) depends upon J, the number of groups compared in the experiment. The width of confidence intervals around individual contrasts depends upon J (as well as n and MS_w) in the Tukey method. It seems undesirable to allow either of these related conditions (power and widths of intervals) to be affected by the arbitrary choice of how many levels will constitute an "experiment." After all, isn't it a *contrast* that is primary? And shouldn't the probability of erring in concluding that $\mu_j - \mu_{j\bullet}$ is or is not different from zero be unaffected by how many and which other groups one happens to include in the "experiment?"

Although some case can be made for the pre-eminence of a *contrast* or *comparison* instead of the *experiment* as the choice for controlling the rate of errors of the first kind, the statistical techniques most commonly regarded as achieving this purpose—most notably the Newman-Keuls procedure (see Winer, 1962, pp. 80–81)—are not well understood. Suffice it to say that the Newman-Keuls procedure does *not* test the significance of the difference between means separately for all pairs of means with a contrast-wise error rate of α as is widely believed.

16.4
THE S-METHOD

The Scheffé method of multiple comparisons can be applied whenever the T-method is applicable, as well as in some situations where the T-method is not. The most comprehensive discussion of the S-method appears in Scheffé (1959).

The notion of a comparison ($\mu_1 - \mu_2$, say) that was met in the previous section is actually a special case of the more general concept of a *contrast*.

Definition: A *contrast* among the J population means $\mu_1, \ldots,$ μ_J is a linear combination

$$\psi = c_1\mu_1 + c_2\mu_2 + \ldots + c_J\mu_J,$$

such that $c_1 + c_2 + \ldots + c_J = 0$.

The constants $c_1, \ldots, c_J$ are simply positive and negative real numbers that sum to zero. Thus, $\psi = \mu_1 + \mu_2 - 2\mu_3$ is a contrast in the three means

μ_1, μ_2, and μ_3, where $c_1 = 1$, $c_2 = 1$, and $c_3 = -2$. The difference between any two means is a contrast by the above definition: $\psi = \mu_3 - \mu_6$ corresponds to $c_3 = 1$, $c_6 = -1$, and all other c's equal to 0.

Suppose there are five population means $\mu_1, \ldots, \mu_5$. Table 16.2 lists

TABLE 16.2

	Values of				
Contrast	c_1	c_2	c_3	c_4	c_5
1. $\mu_1 - \mu_2$	1	-1	0	0	0
2. $\mu_2 - [(\mu_1 + \mu_4)/2]$	$-\frac{1}{2}$	1	0	$-\frac{1}{2}$	0
3. $[(\mu_1 + \mu_3 + \mu_4)/3] - [(\mu_2 + \mu_5)/2]$	$\frac{1}{3}$	$-\frac{1}{2}$	$\frac{1}{3}$	$\frac{1}{3}$	$-\frac{1}{2}$
4. $\mu_3 - \mu_1$	-1	0	1	0	0

contrasts among the five means. Any contrast ψ can be estimated by replacing μ's with sample means, i.e., an estimate $\hat{\psi}$ of ψ is given by

$$\hat{\psi} = c_1 \bar{X}_{.1} + c_2 \bar{X}_{.2} + \ldots + c_J \bar{X}_{.J}. \tag{16.2}$$

For example, if $\psi = \mu_2 - \mu_3$, then an estimate of ψ is $\bar{X}_{.2} - \bar{X}_{.3}$.

Before the significance of any estimated contrast can be judged, it is necessary to estimate the variance of $\hat{\psi}$. If a one-way ANOVA has been performed and MS_w found, then an estimate of the variance of $\hat{\psi}$ is given by

$$\hat{\sigma}_{\hat{\psi}}^2 = MS_w \left(\frac{c_1^2}{n_1} + \frac{c_2^2}{n_2} + \ldots + \frac{c_J^2}{n_J} \right), \tag{16.3}$$

where MS_w is the "mean-square within,"

c_j is the constant that multiplies the jth mean, and

n_j is the number of observations in the jth group.

The degrees of freedom (df) associated with this estimate of variance are the df for MS_w, $N - J$, where N, the total number of observations in the *entire* one-factor ANOVA that precedes the *S*-method, is equal to $n_1 + n_2 + \ldots + n_J$.

For example, if $J = 4$, all n's equal 10, and $\hat{\psi} = \bar{X}_{.1} - \bar{X}_{.4}$, an estimate of the variance of $\hat{\psi}$ is

$$\hat{\sigma}_{\hat{\psi}}^2 = MS_w \left[\frac{1^2}{10} + \frac{0^2}{10} + \frac{0^2}{10} + \frac{(-1)^2}{10} \right] = MS_w \left(\frac{2}{10} \right).$$

The degrees of freedom for this estimate of variance are $N - J = 40 - 4 = 36$.

Usually, $\hat{\psi}$ will be obtained to test the significance of its difference from zero. This test answers questions like the following:

1. Is there any difference between overt and covert responding to a teaching program? $\mu_1 - \mu_2$

2. Is the average of overt responding with and without confirmation of response different from the same average for covert responding? $[(\mu_1 + \mu_2)/2] - [(\mu_3 + \mu_4)/2]$

3. Is the average of the three levels of positive reinforcement in an experiment different from the average of the two levels of negative reinforcement? $[(\mu_1 + \mu_2 + \mu_3)/3] - [(\mu_4 + \mu_5)/2]$

There are five steps to follow in testing the significance of a contrast among means:

Step 1. Specify and estimate ψ. The coefficients $c_1, \ldots, c_J$ that determine the contrast of interest must be specified. Once this is done, $\hat{\psi}$ is obtained by substituting sample means for population means, as in Eq. (16.2).

Step 2. Find an estimate of the variance of $\hat{\psi}$. The one-factor ANOVA that precedes application of the S-method contains a MS_w. This value, the c's, and the sample sizes are substituted into Eq. (16.3) to produce $\hat{\sigma}_{\hat{\psi}}^2$.

Step 3. Find $\hat{\sigma}_{\hat{\psi}}$. Take the positive square root of $\hat{\sigma}_{\hat{\psi}}^2$, which was found in step 2.

Step 4. Form the ratio of $\hat{\psi}$ to $\hat{\sigma}_{\hat{\psi}}$. The value of $\hat{\psi}$ obtained in step 1 is divided by the value of $\hat{\sigma}_{\hat{\psi}}$ found in step 3.

Step 5. Compare the absolute value of the ratio with the test statistic. The absolute value of the ratio found in step 4 is compared with the square root of $(J - 1)$ times the $100(1 - \alpha)$ percentile in the F-distribution with degrees of freedom $J - 1$ and $N - J$. That is, the absolute value of the ratio is compared with $\sqrt{(J - 1)_{1-\alpha} F_{J-1, N-J}}$. The hypothesis that $\psi = 0$ is rejected if the absolute value of the ratio exceeds the square root of $(J - 1)$ times the percentile point, i.e.,

$$\text{reject } H_0 \colon \ \psi = 0 \quad \text{if} \quad \frac{|\hat{\psi}|}{\hat{\sigma}_{\hat{\psi}}} > \sqrt{(J - 1)_{1-\alpha} F_{J-1, N-J}}.$$

Imagine that four ways of teaching the oxidation-reduction method of balancing chemical equations were compared. The data (scores on a 15-item achievement test) obtained in the experiment appear in Table 16.3.

TABLE 16.3

Group	Sample mean	n	
1	$\bar{X}_{.1} = 10.32$	$n_1 = 20$	
2	$\bar{X}_{.2} = 10.54$	$n_2 = 25$	$MS_w = 8.35$
3	$\bar{X}_{.3} = 12.86$	$n_3 = 20$	
4	$\bar{X}_{.4} = 7.17$	$n_4 = 15$	

The *F*-ratio in the analysis of variance of these data is significant at the .05 level. It is now the purpose of the *S*-method to uncover the groups contributing to this significant result.

Very likely, all possible pairs of differences between the sample means will be of interest. Thus, the significance of the following differences between sample means must be determined:

$$\bar{X}_{.1} - \bar{X}_{.2} \qquad \bar{X}_{.2} - \bar{X}_{.3}$$
$$\bar{X}_{.1} - \bar{X}_{.3} \qquad \bar{X}_{.2} - \bar{X}_{.4}$$
$$\bar{X}_{.1} - \bar{X}_{.4} \qquad \bar{X}_{.3} - \bar{X}_{.4}$$

Suppose in addition that a slightly more complicated contrast is of interest to the experimenter. It was the case that groups 1 and 2 were taught by two methods differing only in that group 1 actually observed the pre-

TABLE 16.4

Contrast	Estimate of contrast	Estimate of variance of contrast
A. $\mu_1 - \mu_2$	$\bar{X}_{.1} - \bar{X}_{.2}$	$MS_w\left(\dfrac{1}{n_1} + \dfrac{1}{n_2}\right)$
B. $\mu_1 - \mu_3$	$\bar{X}_{.1} - \bar{X}_{.3}$	$MS_w\left(\dfrac{1}{n_1} + \dfrac{1}{n_3}\right)$
C. $\mu_1 - \mu_4$	$\bar{X}_{.1} - \bar{X}_{.4}$	$MS_w\left(\dfrac{1}{n_1} + \dfrac{1}{n_4}\right)$
D. $\mu_2 - \mu_3$	$\bar{X}_{.2} - \bar{X}_{.3}$	$MS_w\left(\dfrac{1}{n_2} + \dfrac{1}{n_3}\right)$
E. $\mu_2 - \mu_4$	$\bar{X}_{.2} - \bar{X}_{.4}$	$MS_w\left(\dfrac{1}{n_2} + \dfrac{1}{n_4}\right)$
F. $\mu_3 - \mu_4$	$\bar{X}_{.3} - \bar{X}_{.4}$	$MS_w\left(\dfrac{1}{n_3} + \dfrac{1}{n_4}\right)$
G. $\dfrac{\mu_1 + \mu_2}{2} - \mu_3$	$\dfrac{\bar{X}_{.1} + \bar{X}_{.2}}{2} - \bar{X}_{.3}$	$MS_w\left(\dfrac{\frac{1}{4}}{n_1} + \dfrac{\frac{1}{4}}{n_2} + \dfrac{1}{n_3}\right)$

cipitation of silver chloride while group 2 did not. The data suggest that this experience for group 1 was irrelevant; in fact, groups 1 and 2 may not be different. The experimenter wishes to know whether the average of groups 1 and 2 differs significantly from group 3, which was taught by a substantially different method. This question suggests the contrast $[(\mu_1 + \mu_2)/2] - \mu_3$.

The contrasts in which the experimenter is interested appear in Table 16.4. These specifications complete steps 1 and 2 of the five steps to be followed. If we substitute the data into the formulas in Table 16.4 the estimates (see Table 16.5) of the contrasts and the variances of the contrasts result.

TABLE 16.5

Contrast	$\hat{\psi}$	$\hat{\sigma}^2_{\hat{\psi}}$
A. $\mu_1 - \mu_2$	-0.22	0.752
B. $\mu_1 - \mu_3$	-2.54	0.835
C. $\mu_1 - \mu_4$	3.15	0.969
D. $\mu_2 - \mu_3$	-2.32	0.752
E. $\mu_2 - \mu_4$	3.37	0.885
F. $\mu_3 - \mu_4$	5.69	0.969
G. $[(\mu_1 + \mu_2)/2] - \mu_3$	-2.43	0.605

As one example of how the calculations in Table 16.5 were made, consider contrast G. The contrast is $\psi = [(\mu_1 + \mu_2)/2] - \mu_3$; the estimate $\hat{\psi}$ of the contrast (step 1) is

$$\hat{\psi} = \frac{\bar{X}_{.1} + \bar{X}_{.2}}{2} - \bar{X}_{.3} = \frac{10.32 + 10.54}{2} - 12.86 = -2.43.$$

The estimate of the variance of this contrast (step 2) is

$$\hat{\sigma}^2_{\hat{\psi}} = MS_w \left(\frac{1}{4n_1} + \frac{1}{4n_2} + \frac{1}{n_3} \right) = 8.35(\tfrac{1}{80} + \tfrac{1}{100} + \tfrac{1}{20}) = 0.61.$$

Step 3. The positive square roots of the estimates of the variance of all six contrasts are now found:

Contrast	$\hat{\sigma}^2_{\hat{\psi}}$	$\hat{\sigma}_{\hat{\psi}}$
A	0.752	0.867
B	0.835	0.914
C	0.969	0.985
D	0.752	0.867
E	0.885	0.941
F	0.969	0.985
G	0.605	0.778

Step 4. The ratio of $\hat{\psi}$ to $\hat{\sigma}_{\hat{\psi}}$ is found for each of the six contrasts.

Contrast	$\hat{\psi}/\hat{\sigma}_{\hat{\psi}}$
A	$-0.22/0.867 = -0.25$
B	$-2.54/0.914 = -2.76$
C	$3.15/0.985 = 3.21$
D	$-2.32/0.867 = -2.67$
E	$3.37/0.941 = 3.59$
F	$5.69/0.985 = 5.81$
G	$-2.43/0.778 = -3.12$

Step 5. The absolute values of the ratios found in step 4 are compared with $\sqrt{(J-1)_{1-\alpha}F_{J-1,N-J}}$.

$$N = 20 + 25 + 20 + 15 = 80 \quad \text{and} \quad J = 4. \qquad _{.95}F_{3,76} = 2.72$$

$$\sqrt{(J-1)_{.95}F_{J-1,N-J}} = \sqrt{3(2.72)} = 2.86.$$

Therefore, if any ratio found in step 4 is greater than 2.86 in absolute value, i.e., if the ratio is above 2.86 or below -2.86, the corresponding contrast is significant. By this criterion, contrasts C, E, F, and G are significantly different from zero by the S-method with $\alpha = .05$. Thus the experimenter concludes that

$$\mu_1 - \mu_4, \quad \mu_2 - \mu_4, \quad \mu_3 - \mu_4, \quad \text{and} \quad \frac{\mu_1 + \mu_2}{2} - \mu_3$$

are not zero. It cannot be concluded that μ_1 and μ_2 differ, or that μ_1 and μ_3 differ, or that μ_2 and μ_3 differ. For a published application of the S-method to educational psychological research, see Travers *et al.* (1964).

16.5
CONFIDENCE INTERVALS AROUND CONTRASTS BY THE S-METHOD

The confidence interval around the estimate of a contrast is constructed as follows with the S-method:

$$\hat{\psi} \pm \hat{\sigma}_{\hat{\psi}}\sqrt{(J-1)_{1-\alpha}F_{J-1,N-J}}. \tag{16.4}$$

Of course, the purpose of this confidence interval is to capture between its extremes the true value of the contrast in the population means, ψ.

If $\psi = c_1\mu_1 + c_2\mu_2 + \ldots + c_J\mu_J$, then the confidence interval for ψ around $\hat{\psi}$ is

$$(c_1\bar{X}_{.1} + c_2\bar{X}_{.2} + \ldots + c_J\bar{X}_{.J})$$

$$\pm\sqrt{MS_w\left(\frac{c_1^2}{n_1} + \frac{c_2^2}{n_2} + \ldots + \frac{c_J^2}{n_J}\right)}\sqrt{(J-1)_{1-\alpha}F_{J-1,N-J}}. \quad (16.5)$$

Suppose, for example, that $\psi = \mu_1 - \mu_2$. The confidence interval around $\hat{\psi}$ would be

$$(\bar{X}_{.1} - \bar{X}_{.2}) \pm \sqrt{MS_w\left(\frac{1}{n_1} + \frac{1}{n_2}\right)}\sqrt{(J-1)_{1-\alpha}F_{J-1,N-J}}.$$

If the significance of the difference of the estimated contrasts from zero has been tested first, use of Eq. (16.4) for obtaining confidence intervals is quite convenient. The construction of the S-method confidence intervals will now be illustrated on the sample used in Sec. 16.4.

A sample contrast is significantly different from zero if the confidence interval around it does *not* span zero. Hence, contrasts C, E, F, and G in Table 16.6 correspond to contrasts that differ significantly from zero. In

TABLE 16.6   ILLUSTRATION OF THE CONSTRUCTION OF S-METHOD
CONFIDENCE INTERVALS BY EQ. (16.4)

$\hat{\psi}$	$\hat{\sigma}_{\hat{\psi}}$	$\hat{\psi} \pm \hat{\sigma}_{\hat{\psi}}\sqrt{(J-1)_{1-\alpha}F_{J-1,N-J}} = \hat{\psi} \pm \hat{\sigma}_{\hat{\psi}}(2.86)$
A. -0.22	0.867	$(-2.71, 2.27)$
B. -2.54	0.914	$(-5.17, 0.09)$
C. 3.15	0.985	$(0.35, 5.95)$
D. -2.32	0.867	$(-4.80, 0.16)$
E. 3.37	0.941	$(0.68, 6.06)$
F. 5.69	0.985	$(2.89, 8.49)$
G. -2.43	0.778	$(-4.66, -0.20)$

the case of contrast C, one can state with the confidence afforded by the S-method that the difference between μ_1 and μ_4 is some number greater than zero; indeed it probably lies between 0.35 and 5.95. Similarly, the confidence interval on contrast G tells us that the difference between μ_3 and the average of the population means μ_1 and μ_2 is very probably *not* zero. On the other hand, the S-method gives us no evidence to conclude with confidence that μ_1 and μ_2 differ (contrast A).

The confidence intervals established by the S-method must be regarded as a *set of simultaneous confidence* intervals. As was the case with intervals established by the T-method, no probability statement is made about each individual interval. On the contrary, the intervals are constructed in such a way that the entire set of those which can be constructed in any one experiment has a probability of $1 - \alpha$ of capturing the true value of the contrasts estimated within its bounds. In other words, if all possible contrasts among a set of means are formed by the *S*-method with a confidence coefficient of $1 - \alpha$, the statement that "all of these *S*-method confidence intervals contain the true value of the contrasts they estimate" will be true $100(1 - \alpha)$ percent of the times this experiment is run.

16.6
THE *T*- AND *S*-METHODS
COMPARED

The Scheffé method of multiple comparisons is generally regarded by mathematicians as superior to the *T*-method because of its generality (equal *n*'s are not necessary) and greater sensitivity when complex combinations of the sample means are being estimated. However, you will probably find greater use for the *T*-method.

An obvious criterion for the choice between use of the *T*-method or the *S*-method is the distribution of *N* among the *J* groups. A requirement of the *T*-method, which is *not* made with the *S*-method, is that the sample sizes are equal. Hence the *T*-method cannot be used when not all *n*'s are equal; the *S*-method must be used with unequal *n*'s. This dictum must be tempered with good sense. We shall see presently that if one is interested in only the differences among *pairs* of *J* sample means, the *T*-method is far superior—in terms of power to detect significant differences and shorter confidence intervals—to the *S*-method. If the *n*'s are only slightly unequal, e.g., $n_1 = 21$, $n_2 = 22$, and $n_3 = 20$, it is wiser to discard at random one person from group 1 and two persons from group 2 and apply the *T*-method than to apply the *S*-method. The random exclusion of three persons from the analysis will have a negligible effect on the results, and it allows you to use the more powerful *T*-method for comparing sample means. On the other hand, this strategy would not work well if, for example, $n_1 = 5$, $n_2 = 30$, and $n_3 = 40$ because too much data would have to be discarded to achieve equal *n*'s of 5. In this instance it would be better to use the *S*-method even if you were interested only in the three possible differences between sample means.

Suppose that after finding a significant *F*-ratio in an analysis of variance with equal *n*'s, the experimenter was interested in probing among the $J(J - 1)/2$ differences between sample means. Should he use the *T*-method or the *S*-method? Either *can* be applied, but which one is preferred? *The T-method is preferred because it produces a greater number of significant differences between means.* Equivalently, the *T*-method will give shorter confidence intervals around differences between means than the *S*-method.

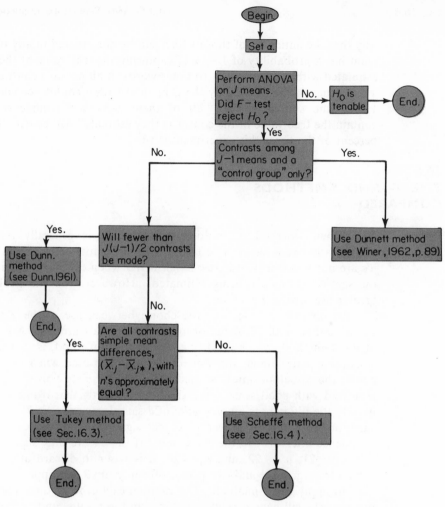

FIG. 16.2 Schema for making multiple comparisons among J group means. (Based on Hopkins and Chadbourn, 1967.)

As an example of the relative widths of the confidence intervals around $\bar{X}_{.j} - \bar{X}_{.j*}$ given by the T-method and the S-method, take the contrast between $\bar{X}_{.2}$ and $\bar{X}_{.3}$ in Table 16.1. The .95 confidence interval around $\bar{X}_{.2} - \bar{X}_{.3}$ was found to be $(-7.23, -2.97)$. Now let's establish a .95 confidence interval around the same difference using the S-method.

$$\bar{X}_{.2} - \bar{X}_{.3} = -5.1, \qquad MS_w = 4.1, \qquad n_2 = n_3 = 11.$$

$$\hat{\sigma}_{\hat{\psi}}^2 = 4.1(\tfrac{1}{11} + \tfrac{1}{11}) = 0.745, \qquad \sqrt{(J-1)_{.95}F_{J-1, N-J}} = \sqrt{2(3.23)} = 2.58.$$

The S-method confidence interval around $\bar{X}_{.2} - \bar{X}_{.3}$ is $-5.1 \pm (2.58)(.86) = (-7.32, -2.88)$.

This confidence interval is wider, but not by much, than the confidence interval around the same difference between means yielded by the T-method $(-7.23, -2.97)$. In some instances, the S-method will produce a confidence interval that includes zero—in which case the difference between the means is judged nonsignificant—while the T-method will produce a confidence interval around the same difference that does not include zero, thus leading to judgment of a significant difference between the two means.

When one is interested in contrasts that are more complex than a simple difference between means, e.g., $[(\mu_1 + \mu_2)/2] - \mu_3$, then the S-method has more power (and thus yields shorter confidence intervals around an estimate of the contrast) than an extension of the T-method appropriate for such contrasts. We have not discussed the extension of the T-method to contrasts other than $\mu_j - \mu_{j*}$ because it would only be a needless complication in view of the fact that we have developed the S-method, which is preferable with the more complex contrasts. You can find a readable account of the more general T-method in Guenther (1964, pp. 54–57) and a mathematical discussion of the method in Scheffé (1959, pp. 73–77).

The application of the T-method (or the S-method, when n's differ appreciably) to the differences between sample means accounts for almost all of the applications of multiple comparison procedures in educational research and the behavioral sciences. Interest in more complex contrasts— for which the S-method would be more appropriate—is not common. Undoubtedly, however, many opportunities for exploring interesting and worthwhile contrasts with the S-method are overlooked.

A recent textbook on simultaneous statistical inference by Miller (1966) is an excellent reference on these and related topics.

PROBLEMS AND EXERCISES

1. From Table F in Appendix A, determine the following percentile points:

   a. $._{.95}q_{4,30}$ b. $._{.99}q_{6,120}$ c. $._{.90}q_{10,10}$ d. $._{.99}q_{12,6}$ e. $._{.95}q_{2,60}$

2. Suppose that five samples each of size 7 are to be randomly drawn from a single normal distribution with mean μ and variance σ^2. The range between the largest, $\bar{X}_{.L}$, and smallest, $\bar{X}_{.S}$, sample mean will be found and divided by $\sqrt{MS_w/7}$, where MS_w is the average of the five sample variances.

   a. What is the probability that $(\bar{X}_{.L} - \bar{X}_{.S})/\sqrt{MS_w/7}$ will be larger than 4.102?

   b. If this sampling procedure were carried out thousands of times, what percent of the values of $(\bar{X}_{.L} - \bar{X}_{.S})/\sqrt{MS_w/7}$ would exceed 5.048?

3. If $(\bar{X}_{.j} - \bar{X}_{.j*}) \pm ._{.95}q_{J,J(n-1)}\sqrt{MS_w/n}$ does not contain zero, then the difference between $\bar{X}_{.j}$ and $\bar{X}_{.j*}$ is judged to be significant at the .05 level by the Tukey method. This procedure is equivalent to concluding that $\bar{X}_{.j}$ and $\bar{X}_{.j*}$ differ

significantly at the .05 level if

$$\frac{|\bar{X}_{.j} - \bar{X}_{.j*}|}{\sqrt{MS_w/n}} > {}_{.95}q_{J,J(n-1)}.$$

Suppose that in a particular experiment, $J = 6$, $n = 11$, and $MS_w = 44.00$. Which of the following means differ significantly from each other at the $\alpha = .05$ level by the T-method: $\bar{X}_{.1} = 61.25$, $\bar{X}_{.2} = 64.72$, $\bar{X}_{.3} = 70.57$, $\bar{X}_{.4} = 73.42$, $\bar{X}_{.5} = 81.66$, and $\bar{X}_{.6} = 82.17$?

4. In Prob. 7 at the end of Chapter 15, you performed an ANOVA on data gathered by Guthrie (1967) in an experiment on "discovery learning." Using the T-method, perform multiple comparisons on all pairs of means in Guthrie's experiment using an α of .05.

5. Jeffrey and Samuels (1967) compared phonic (letter) and look-say (word) methods of reading instruction on a measure of transfer of training. Twenty kindergarten pupils learned a list of eight words by the phonic method and 20 pupils learned the same words by the look-say method. A control group of 20 pupils did not learn the original list of words. All 60 pupils were subsequently taught a new list of eight words; the dependent variable in the experiment was the number of trials required to learn the second list. The following data were obtained.

Number of trials to learn second list

	Phonic method	*Look-say method*	*Control*
n	20	20	20
$\bar{X}_.$	13.50	27.20	29.25
s_x	9.94	10.37	9.99

The value of MS_w was 102.05. Perform multiple comparisons at the .01 level using the Tukey method. Determine which pairs of means differ significantly.

6. Four methods of teaching percentage (case method, formula method, equation method, unitary analysis method) to sixth graders were compared (Sparks, 1963). Twenty-eight sixth-grade classes were randomly assigned to the four methods; seven classes studied under each method. At the conclusion of the teaching unit a 45-item test on computing percentages was administered to each class and the class average recorded. The following data were obtained.

Average test score for each class

Case method (1)	*Formula method (2)*	*Equation method (3)*	*Unitary analysis method (4)*
14.59	20.27	27.82	33.16
23.44	26.84	24.92	26.93
25.43	14.71	28.68	30.43
18.15	22.34	23.32	36.43
20.82	19.49	32.85	37.04
14.06	24.92	33.90	29.76
14.26	20.20	23.42	33.88

a. Run a one-way analysis of variance on these data. Test the null hypothesis of no differences among the four teaching methods at the .05 level of significance.

b. After completing the F-test, use both the T-method and the S-method to determine which of the six pairs of means can be considered to be significantly different. Which method produces a greater number of significant differences?

c. Set up the 95% confidence interval for $[(\mu_2 + \mu_3)/2] - [(\mu_1 + \mu_4)/2]$ using the S-method.

7. Klausmeier (1963) studied the effects of accelerating bright older pupils from the second grade to the fourth grade, thus skipping the third grade. The following five groups of $n = 20$ pupils each were tested on the Metropolitan Achievement Test during their year in the fifth grade:

1. *Acc:* a group of 20 bright pupils who were promoted to the fourth grade from the second grade after a five-week special summer session. The *Acc* group is now in the fifth grade. Average age of this group is 9 years 6 months.

2. *SY:* a group of 20 pupils who did not skip the third grade and who are of superior (S) ability and are young (Y), i.e., below median age of fifth graders. The *SY* group is now in the fifth grade and has an average age of 10 years 0 months.

3. *SO:* 20 nonaccelerated pupils of superior (S) ability and who are older (O) than the median fifth grader. The *SO* group, now in the fifth grade, has an average age of 10 years 5 months.

4. *AY:* 20 nonaccelerated pupils of average ability who are younger than the median fifth grader. The *AY* group, now in the fifth grade, has an average age of 10 years, 0 months.

5. *AO:* 20 nonaccelerated fifth graders of average (A) ability who are above the age of the median fifth grader (average age, 10 years, 6 months).

The following table presents data for the Total Language scores on the Metropolitan Achievement Test for the five groups:

| | Group | | | | |
	Acc	*SY*	*SO*	*AY*	*AO*
n	20	20	20	20	20
$\bar{X}$	55.15	56.40	63.55	47.15	53.45
s_x	6.86	4.59	6.86	7.75	12.39

a. Perform an F-test at the .05 level of $H_0: \mu_1 = \ldots = \mu_5$ on the above data.

b. Follow the F-test in (a) with T-method multiple comparisons to determine which pairs of means differ significantly.

c. Use the S-method with $\alpha = .05$ to place a confidence interval on $\psi = \mu_1 - [(\mu_2 + \ldots + \mu_5)/4]$. In effect, then, test the hypothesis that μ_1, the mean for accelerated pupils, differs from the average of the remaining four means.

17

THE TWO-FACTOR
ANALYSIS OF VARIANCE—
FIXED EFFECTS

17.1
THE LAYOUT AND
SYMBOLIZATION OF DATA

The data gathered in a two-factor analysis of variance design are classified with reference to two factors. Such two-factor classifications of things are common in everyone's experience. For example, people can be classified both with respect to sex and race; automobiles can be classified with respect to "year" and "make."

Consider as an example of a two-factor design an experiment in which three methods of teaching beginning reading are compared. The pupils involved in this experiment can be classified in two ways (among others): with respect to the teaching method under which they study (factor A) and their sex (factor B). Factor A, teaching method, has three levels and factor B, sex, has two levels. Since both boys and girls study under each method in the experiment, six unique combinations of the levels of the two factors are possible. Suppose the variable that will be observed in the evaluation of the outcome of this experiment is reading comprehension, symbolized

Factor A, teaching method	Factor B, sex	
	Male (1)	Female (2)
1	X_{111} X_{112} X_{113} X_{114}	X_{121} X_{122} X_{123} X_{124}
2	X_{211} X_{212} X_{213} X_{214}	X_{221} X_{222} X_{223} X_{224}
3	X_{311} X_{312} X_{313} X_{314}	X_{321} X_{322} X_{323} X_{324}

FIG. 17.1   Layout of data in a 3×2 two-factor ANOVA design with four observations per cell (X_{ijk} notation, where $i = 1, 2, 3$ for method, $j = 1, 2$ for sex, and $k = 1, 2, 3, 4$ for pupil within method-sex group).

by X. Observations on X are taken by administering a standardized test of reading comprehension. If four boys and four girls were taught to read by method 1, four boys and four girls by method 2, etc., the data could be tabulated and symbolized as shown in Fig. 17.1.

A total of 24 pupils participated in this experiment. X_{111} represents the reading comprehension test score of the "first"—arbitrarily designated—boy who studied under method 1. X_{324} stands for the test score of the "fourth" girl who studied under method 3. The "3" stands for the method, the "2" for the sex (male—1, female—2), and the "4" designates the arbitrarily labeled fourth pupil in the group of four girls under method 3.

In general, an observation in a two-factor ANOVA design is denoted by X_{ijk}, where i is a subscript for factor A and takes on the values $1, 2, \ldots, I$; j is the subscript for factor B and takes on the values $1, 2, \ldots, J$; and k is the subscript that identifies the observations within a *cell* (combination of levels of factors A and B) of the design and takes on the values $1, 2, \ldots, n$. If we want to denote the score of the third (3) girl (2) studying under the first (1) method, we let $i = 1$, $j = 2$, and $k = 3$ to obtain X_{123}. Often with statistical notation one in effect reads subscripts or summation signs from right to left. To summarize, in X_{ijk},

$$i = 1, 2, \ldots, I \text{ for factor } A,$$

$$j = 1, 2, \ldots, J \text{ for factor } B, \text{ and}$$

$$k = 1, 2, \ldots, n \text{ for "within cells."}$$

This notation is a slight departure from the conventions established in Chapters 15 and 16. In particular, the right-most subscript now indexes observations within a cell, where previously the left index ranged over within-cell observations. Master this switch now so that it will not cause confusion later. Note also that now $k = 1, 2, \ldots, n$, whereas for the one-factor design $i = 1, 2, \ldots, n$.

17.2
A MODEL FOR THE DATA

Our interest in gathering the data was to determine how the size of the scores varies with the levels of the two factors, i.e., whether boys score higher than girls, whether method 2 gives higher scores than method 1, etc. Toward this end, we shall now devise a fairly abstract model—a generalization of that used with the one-factor ANOVA—to explain, in a general way, how the data are related to factors A and B.

Perhaps the simplest model for data in a two-factor ANOVA would be one that involved only four types of terms or "effects": a term μ, the same for each datum, which describes the general size of the scores; I terms α_i, one for each level of factor A, which describe the excess of the data above or below μ for those scores at the ith level of factor A; J terms β_j, one for each level of factor B, which describe the excess above or below μ for the scores at the jth level of factor B; and a term e_{ijk}, for each score that would essentially make up the difference between the score and the sum of the other terms in the model. Under this rudimentary model, a score X_{ijk} would be represented as follows:

$$X_{ijk} = \mu + \alpha_i + \beta_j + e_{ijk}. \tag{17.1}$$

For example, if adult males in general tend to be $5'7'' = \mu$, if feeding them yoghurt tends to add $1'' = \alpha_1$ to their height, if sleeping on a hard mattress tends to add $\tfrac{1}{2}'' = \beta_1$ to their height, and if Joe's unique individual history (environmental influences, heredity, errors of measurement, etc.) has taken $3''$ off the height he would have attained under standard conditions, then Joe's height is

$$X_{11(\text{Joe})} = \mu + \alpha_1 + \beta_1 + e_{11(\text{Joe})} = 5'7'' + 1'' + \tfrac{1}{2}'' - 3'' = 5'5\tfrac{1}{2}''.$$

Unfortunately, the most useful and widely applicable model for the data in a two-factor ANOVA is slightly more complex than the model in Eq.

(17.1). The more useful and descriptive model differs from Eq. (17.1) by a term that denotes the effect of the *unique* result of combining level i of factor A with level j of factor B. "Unique" in this context means that the outcome one would obtain from combining level i of A with level j of B may *not* be the simple sum of α_i and β_j. If not, perhaps a new $\alpha\beta_{ij}$, which is *not* the product of α_i and β_j, is needed to describe the scores in the ijth cell. Such a term is called an *interaction term*. [The concept of the interaction of two independent variables is due to the famed English statistician-geneticist, Ronald Fisher. It was Fisher's concepts of experimental control through randomization and the study of the effects of several factors and their interactions simultaneously that successfully overthrew the "one variable at a time" orthodoxy of experimental agriculture in the early 1900's. See Fisher (1925) and Stanley (1966b).] If an interaction term is needed in the model to describe the scores, then knowing the general effect of level i of A and of level j of B is not enough to predict the outcome in cell ij. An interaction is tenuously analogous to two polarized lenses: light passes through each lens individually, but when one is laid on top of the other (when they are combined) no light passes through the pair. The separate effects of the lenses differ from their combined effect.

The expanded model, the model upon which the analyses in this chapter are based, is

$$X_{ijk} = \mu + \alpha_i + \beta_j + \alpha\beta_{ij} + e_{ijk}. \tag{17.2}$$

Without any loss of generality the α, β, and $\alpha\beta$ terms in the above model are assumed to sum to zero over both i and j, i.e., $\sum_i \alpha_i = \sum_j \beta_j = \sum_i \alpha\beta_{ij} = \sum_j \alpha\beta_{ij} = 0$.

In Sec. 17.4 we shall take a closer look at the nature of an ANOVA interaction and examine some illustrations.

17.3
LEAST-SQUARES ESTIMATION
OF THE MODEL

With data in hand and having adopted a particular abstract model to explain them, we still have the task of relating the data to the model. What features of the data influence the value of μ in Eq. (17.2)? How can the data be manipulated to disclose information about the values of the α_i's, the β_j's and the $\alpha\beta_{ij}$'s?

This is the same general problem we faced when we sought to predict Y from X by means of a straight line or when we sought to explain the differences between factor levels in a one-factor ANOVA. The problem is basically the same, and our approach to its solution is no different. We fit the model in Eq. (17.2) to the data so that a criterion of least squares is satisfied. In this instance as in the others, the criterion of least squares is as

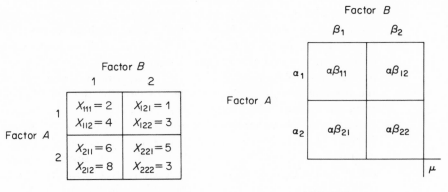

FIG. 17.2   FIG. 17.3

follows: (1) values are substituted into Eq. (17.2) for μ, $\alpha_1, \ldots, \alpha_I$, $\beta_1, \ldots, \beta_J$, $\alpha\beta_{11}, \ldots, \alpha\beta_{IJ}$; (2) these values along with the data X_{ijk} determine, by subtraction, values for the IJn errors e_{ijk}; (3) when the sum of the squared errors so determined is as small as it is possible to make it, the least-squares estimates of μ, the α_i's, the β_j's and the $\alpha\beta_{ij}$'s have been found.

For example, eight scores are gathered in a simple 2×2 design, with n also 2, as shown in Fig. 17.2. We postulate the following model for the data:

$$X_{ijk} = \mu + \alpha_i + \beta_j + \alpha\beta_{ij} + e_{ijk}, \qquad i = 1, 2$$

$$j = 1, 2$$

$$k = 1, 2$$

The hypothetical main and interaction effects underlie the data in Fig. 17.2 in the manner depicted in Fig. 17.3. Hence it is assumed, for example, that

$$X_{112} = \mu + \alpha_1 + \beta_1 + \alpha\beta_{11} + e_{112}.$$

By subtraction of appropriate terms, we see that

$$e_{112} = X_{112} - (\mu + \alpha_1 + \beta_1 + \alpha\beta_{11}). \qquad (17.3)$$

Suppose we let $\mu = 5$, $\alpha_1 = 2$, $\alpha_2 = 1$, $\beta_1 = 0$, $\beta_2 = 1$, and all the $\alpha\beta_{ij}$'s equal zero. Will this give us the smallest value for the sum of the eight squared errors? We can calculate e_{112} by Eq. (17.3):

$$e_{112} = 4 - (5 + 2 + 0 + 0) = -3.$$

Calculating the eight remaining e_{ijk}'s similarly, squaring each, and summing the squares produce a value of 132. Is this the smallest sum of squared errors possible? No, it so happens that the smallest sum of squared errors is produced by the following least-squares *estimates* of the parameters of the model:

$$\mu = 4 \qquad\qquad \alpha\beta_{11} = -.5$$
$$\alpha_1 = -1.5 \qquad \alpha\beta_{12} = .5$$
$$\alpha_2 = 1.5 \qquad\quad \alpha\beta_{21} = .5$$
$$\beta_1 = 1 \qquad\qquad \alpha\beta_{22} = -.5$$
$$\beta_2 = -1$$

The sum of the squared estimated errors, which were obtained by substituting the above least-squares estimates into Eq. (17.2) along with the data X_{ijk}, is equal to 8.00, the smallest possible value for any choices of μ, the α_i, the β_j, and the $\alpha\beta_{ij}$.

What manipulations of the data will produce the least-squares estimates? As was true in the one-factor ANOVA the least-squares estimates of the terms in the model for the data are obtained by simple averaging of the data in various ways. For example, the least-squares estimate of μ is just the mean of all eight scores in the 2×2 table. The least-squares estimate of α_1 is just the mean of the four scores in row 1 of the table minus the mean of all eight scores. The least-squares estimate of β_2 is the mean of the four scores in column 2 minus the mean of all eight scores. The least-squares estimate of $\alpha\beta_{11}$ is the mean of the two scores in the cell at the intersection of row 1 and column 1 minus the mean of row 1 minus the mean of column 1 *plus* the mean of all eight scores.

Let μ_{ij} be the mean of the population of scores from which those scores in the ith row and the jth column of the data layout were sampled. Let $\bar{\mu}_{i.}$ be the average of the J μ_{ij}'s in the ith row; let $\bar{\mu}_{.j}$ be the average of the I μ_{ij}'s in the jth column; and let μ be the average of all the μ_{ij}'s. For example, see Fig. 17.4.

The least-squares estimates of the terms in the model for the 2×2 ANOVA design can be characterized in terms of their definition in the sample and their long-range average (or expected) value that they attain in the population. This has been done in Table 17.1.

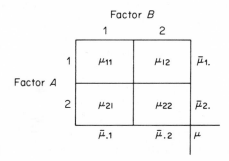

FIG. 17.4

TABLE 17.1   LEAST-SQUARES ESTIMATION IN THE TWO-FACTOR FIXED-EFFECTS ANOVA

Term in the model	Least-squares estimate	Population value
μ	$\hat{\mu} = \bar{x}_{...}$	μ
α_1	$\hat{\alpha}_1 = \bar{x}_{1..} - \bar{x}_{...}$	$\bar{\mu}_{1.} - \mu$
α_2	$\hat{\alpha}_2 = \bar{x}_{2..} - \bar{x}_{...}$	$\bar{\mu}_{2.} - \mu$
β_1	$\hat{\beta}_1 = \bar{x}_{.1.} - \bar{x}_{...}$	$\bar{\mu}_{.1} - \mu$
β_2	$\hat{\beta}_2 = \bar{x}_{.2.} - \bar{x}_{...}$	$\bar{\mu}_{.2} - \mu$
$\alpha\beta_{11}$	$\widehat{\alpha\beta}_{11} = \bar{x}_{11.} - \bar{x}_{1..} - \bar{x}_{.1.} + \bar{x}_{...}$	$\mu_{11} - \bar{\mu}_{1.} - \bar{\mu}_{.1} + \mu$
$\alpha\beta_{12}$	$\widehat{\alpha\beta}_{12} = \bar{x}_{12.} - \bar{x}_{1..} - \bar{x}_{.2.} + \bar{x}_{...}$	$\mu_{12} - \bar{\mu}_{1.} - \bar{\mu}_{.2} + \mu$
$\alpha\beta_{21}$	$\widehat{\alpha\beta}_{21} = \bar{x}_{21.} - \bar{x}_{2..} - \bar{x}_{.1.} + \bar{x}_{...}$	$\mu_{21} - \bar{\mu}_{2.} - \bar{\mu}_{.1} + \mu$
$\alpha\beta_{22}$	$\widehat{\alpha\beta}_{22} = \bar{x}_{22.} - \bar{x}_{2..} - \bar{x}_{.2.} + \bar{x}_{...}$	$\mu_{22} - \bar{\mu}_{2.} - \bar{\mu}_{.2} + \mu$

Before proceeding to the problem of testing hypotheses about the terms of the two-factor ANOVA model, it would be wise to dwell a little longer on the meaning of what has been called the interaction of factors A and B.

17.4
THE NATURE OF INTERACTION

In addition to being interested solely in the effect one variable (independent) has on another variable (dependent), investigators frequently ask whether this effect is the same for all levels of a second, independent variable. If this effect is not the same, an interaction between the two independent variables is said to exist. Suppose three different methods of teaching are being compared experimentally. It is found that one method is relatively best with high ability students whereas another method is relatively best with low ability students. We say that an *interaction* between teaching method and student ability exists.

In a study on test-wiseness, multiple-choice and free-response items were given to both American and Indonesian students. Interest was not focused on which type of item was harder or which group of students had the superior scores, but on the interaction between nationality and item type. Did one nationality do relatively better on one type of item and the other nationality do relatively better on the other type (interaction); or was the degree of superiority of one nationality over the other the same for both types of item (no interaction)?

An example of hypothetical data displaying an interaction effect between sex and type of reading material on reading speed is shown in Fig. 17.5. Notice that the boys read relatively faster with material of one type; girls, with material of another type. The difference between boys' and girls' reading speed is different for different reading matter. Notice that when

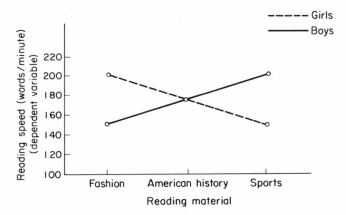

FIG. 17.5   Graphic representation of the mean reading speed scores for boys and girls on three types of reading material.

boys and girls are combined, i.e., the lines are averaged, the three word groups are equally difficult. We say that there is no main effect for "type of reading material." Further, when the three reading materials are combined, the boys and girls read equally fast.

Consider the data in Fig. 17.6. Here again the boys read *relatively* fastest with material on "sports." Even though the girls are clearly faster than the boys, their superiority is not the same for all reading materials. Thus, there is an interaction between sex and reading materials (as well as a difference between the sexes). Notice that the requirement for interaction is merely that the differences between the sexes on the different reading

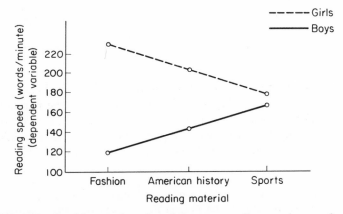

FIG. 17.6   Graphic representation of the mean reading speed scores for boys and girls on three types of reading material.

materials be different—they do not have to be reversed, as was the case in Fig. 17.5. This is why the words "relatively the same" and "relatively fastest" were used in the introductory paragraphs.

Differences across reading material in the difference between the sexes are reflected geometrically by nonparallel slopes. The fact that the solid and dotted lines are nonparallel reflects the presence of interaction.

A. Demonstration that Absence of Interaction Between Two Factors Implies Parallel Lines in the Graph of Cell Means

Suppose we have a 2×2 analysis of variance design as shown in Fig. 17.7. In this diagram, μ's represent population means for rows, columns, cells, and total. If no interaction exists between the two independent variables, then the cell mean equals the sum of the grand mean, the row main effect, and the column main effect, e.g.,

$$\mu_{11} = \mu + (\bar{\mu}_{1.} - \mu) + (\bar{\mu}_{.1} - \mu).$$

If interaction does exist, then this equality does not hold.

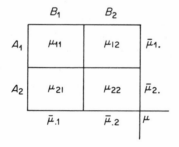

FIG. 17.7

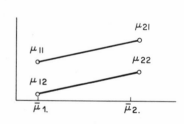

FIG. 17.8

Suppose we graph the four cell means in Fig. 17.7 in such a way that $(\mu_{11} - \mu_{12}) = (\mu_{21} - \mu_{22})$, which results in the parallel lines shown in Fig. 17.8. For the lines in Fig. 17.8 to be parallel, the vertical distance from one line to the other must be equal at all points. In particular, the distance from μ_{11} to μ_{12} must equal the distance from μ_{21} to μ_{22}.*

---

* The lines are not essential, of course, but just a convenient device to aid the reader in determining visually whether the differences differ. Also, it is not essential that the X axis be labeled with $\bar{\mu}_{1.}$ and $\bar{\mu}_{2.}$. A_1 and A_2, arbitrarily ordered and spaced, would suffice, but for *three* or more levels of factor A, the $\bar{\mu}_i$ may help one keep the results of the ANOVA for factor A in mind. See Stanley (1969).

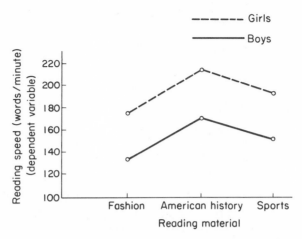

FIG. 17.9   Graphic representation of the mean reading speed scores for boys and girls on three types of reading material.

Assuming no interaction in the analysis of variance sense, we have

$$\mu_{11} = \mu + (\bar{\mu}_{1.} - \mu) + (\bar{\mu}_{.1} - \mu)$$

and

$$\mu_{12} = \mu + (\bar{\mu}_{1.} - \mu) + (\bar{\mu}_{.2} - \mu).$$

Also,

$$\mu_{21} = \mu + (\bar{\mu}_{2.} - \mu) + (\bar{\mu}_{.1} - \mu)$$

and

$$\mu_{22} = \mu + (\bar{\mu}_{2.} - \mu) + (\bar{\mu}_{.2} - \mu).$$

The distance from μ_{11} to μ_{12} is $\mu_{11} - \mu_{12}$, which you can easily show to be equal to $\bar{\mu}_{.1} - \bar{\mu}_{.2}$. The distance from μ_{21} to μ_{22} is $\mu_{21} - \mu_{22}$, which also equals $\bar{\mu}_{.1} - \bar{\mu}_{.2}$. The two distances between the pairs of means are equal. Thus, the lines are parallel.

Notice that the slopes of the lines for the boys (and, in turn, for the girls) is the same in Fig. 17.5 and in Fig. 17.6. Consequently, the degree or magnitude of the nonparallelism, and hence the degree of interaction, is identical in Fig. 17.5 and Fig. 17.6.

Figure 17.9 illustrates a situation in which no interaction is present. Notice that the lines for the boys and girls are parallel and thus the difference in reading speed between the sexes is the same for each type of reading material.

B. A Caution

One should not overlook artificial reasons for the existence of interaction. For example, consider Fig. 17.10, which illustrates the interaction

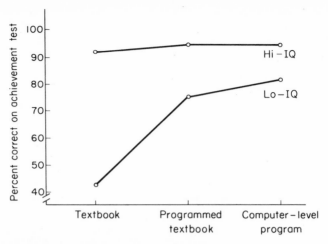

FIG. 17.10 Illustration of a possibly artificial interaction between intelligence and learning condition.

between intelligence and learning condition. In a sense, the definition of an interaction effect in terms of a simple sum of population means and the consequence that *"no interaction"* implies parallel lines when the means are graphed is an imperfect interpretation of our notion of a "unique" and "unpredictable" outcome resulting from combining the levels of two factors. Certainly, many graphs of means from a two-factor design evidence non-parallel lines, yet we feel uncomfortable talking about "unique and un-predictable" effects of the combining of two levels when the nonparallel lines result merely from a "ceiling" or "cellar" effect on a particular paper-and-pencil test. (For an example of such interaction, see Stanley, 1969a). This illustrates the fact that perhaps allowing our least-squares estimation procedure to determine that interaction effects would be measured by $\mu_{ij} - \bar\mu_{i.} - \bar\mu_{.j} + \mu$ did not capture the full richness of our intuitive notion of $\alpha\beta_{ij}$, the unique and unpredictable (from main effects, at least) result of combining factor levels. Such failure to see our intuitive notions reflected perfectly in our mathematical models is a hazard (or reality) of an attempt to represent the real world mathematically.

C. Two Types of Interaction

In the statistical literature, a useful distinction is made (e.g., by Lubin, 1962a) between two types of interaction: *ordinal* and *disordinal*. In the ordinal case, the rank order of the categories of one variable on the basis of their dependent variable scores is the same within each category of the second independent variable. In Fig. 17.6 we see an example of ordinal interaction. It is ordinal because the girls read faster than the boys on each type of reading material. Figure 17.10 also illustrates ordinal interaction. However, in Fig. 17.5 it is *not* the case that girls read faster than boys on each type of

410

reading material. Figure 17.5 presents an example of disordinal interaction. *When the lines do not cross, interaction is said to be "ordinal"; when the lines cross, interaction is said to be "disordinal."*

The importance of this distinction for interpretation is this. When interaction is ordinal, it makes sense to assume, for example, that when girls score higher than boys on the dependent variable the superiority exists for all types of reading material. That is, even though an interaction exists, it is still meaningful to make a single statement about boys and girls, over-all, without qualification or reference to some other variable. However, when there is a disordinal interaction, asserting that girls score higher (i.e., read faster) than boys cannot be understood to mean the superiority is maintained on all types of reading material. Disordinal interaction indicates that only in some situations are girls superior to boys on the dependent variable.

Let's consider an example in which teaching methods 1 and 2 are being tried out in either urban or rural settings. If there is a disordinal interaction between "teaching method" and "setting" and a significant difference between methods in favor of method 1, it would not be possible to claim that method 1 is better than 2 "across the board." Before we could recommend that a school adopt one method or the other, we would first want to know whether the school was rural or urban.

The advice usually given is that whenever there is a significant interaction, one should plot the means for the various combinations. Unfortunately, research reports usually do not present sufficient data to allow the reader to follow this advice.

It should be emphasized that "ordinality" and "disordinality" are properties of graphs. A choice exists between placing factor A or factor B on the abscissa when graphing an interaction. The same cell means can give an ordinal interaction when factor A is on the abscissa and a disordinal interaction when factor B is on the abscissa.

A technical article well worth reading when one has acquired an introduction to analysis of variance is Lubin (1962*a*).

17.5
STATEMENT OF NULL
HYPOTHESES

If in Fig. 17.1 factor B, "sex," was disregarded, the data would be identical to those gathered in a one-factor experiment comparing three teaching methods. Eight observations would have been gathered under each level of factor A, and the one-factor ANOVA model would be appropriate for a statistical inferential test of the hypothesis that the three population means underlying the teaching methods were equal. This null hypothesis, namely that the population means for the three teaching methods are equal, is identical to one null hypothesis of interest in the two-factor ANOVA. Specifically, we are interested in whether the data gathered in a two-factor ANOVA support or run counter to a decision to accept as true the statement H_0 that $\bar{\mu}_{1.} = \bar{\mu}_{2.} = \bar{\mu}_{3.}$.

In any two-factor ANOVA, the null hypothesis for factor A can be stated as follows:

$$H_0: \bar{\mu}_{1.} = \bar{\mu}_{2.} = \ldots = \bar{\mu}_{I.}$$

(Null hypothesis for factor A)

Notice that the equality of the I population means underlying the I levels of factor A has implications that can be used to state H_0 in several equivalent forms.

Because, when $k = 1, 2, \ldots, n$ for every ijth factor-level combination, μ is the average of the IJ population means (one for each cell), equality of the $\bar{\mu}_{i.}$'s implies that *each $\bar{\mu}_{i.}$ equals μ.* If each $\bar{\mu}_{i.} = \mu$, then $\bar{\mu}_{i.} - \mu = 0$ for the I levels of factor A. Since α_i, the main effect for level i of factor A, is equal to $\bar{\mu}_{i.} - \mu$, all α_i's equal zero if the null hypothesis is true. *The following statements are equivalent ways of stating the null hypothesis for factor A:*

1. $H_0: \bar{\mu}_{1.} = \ldots = \bar{\mu}_{I.}$,

2. $H_0: \sum_{i=1}^{I} (\bar{\mu}_{i.} - \mu)^2 = 0$,

3. $H_0: \sum_{i=1}^{I} \alpha_i^2 = 0$,

4. $H_0:$ all $(\bar{\mu}_{i.} - \mu) = 0$, and

5. $H_0:$ all $\alpha_i = 0$.

In the above discussion, it was immaterial that we chose to talk about factor A instead of factor B. The development of the statement of the null hypothesis for factor B is perfectly analogous to the development of H_0 for A. Specifically, as regards factor B, we are interested in rejecting or accepting the null hypothesis that the J population means underlying the levels of factor B are all equal. *The following statements are equivalent ways of stating the null hypothesis for factor B:*

1. $H_0: \bar{\mu}_{.1} = \bar{\mu}_{.2} = \ldots = \bar{\mu}_{.J}$,

2. $H_0: \sum_{j=1}^{J} (\bar{\mu}_{.j} - \mu)^2 = 0$,

3. $H_0: \sum_{j=1}^{J} \beta_j^2 = 0$,

4. $H_0:$ all $(\bar{\mu}_{.j} - \mu) = 0$, and

5. $H_0:$ all $\beta_j = 0$.

There are many ways in which the null hypothesis about a main effect, i.e., about a single factor, can be false. For factor A, $\bar{\mu}_{1.}$ could equal 20.5 and the remaining $\bar{\mu}_{i.}$ could equal 29.1, for example. Or $\bar{\mu}_{1.} = \bar{\mu}_{2.} = 16.65$ and $\bar{\mu}_{3.} = \bar{\mu}_{4.} = 17.80$. In both instances, H_0 is false. All that it takes for H_0 to be false is for at least two population means to be unequal. The decision faced in an ANOVA is whether one should opt for the truth of H_0 or the truth of H_1, the logical converse of H_0, which is true when H_0 is false. H_1, the alternative hypothesis, can be stated in the following equivalent ways for factor A:

1. H_1: $\bar{\mu}_{i.} \neq \bar{\mu}_{i}*$, where i and $i*$ are distinct,

2. H_1: $\sum\limits_{i=1}^{I} (\bar{\mu}_{i.} - \mu)^2 \neq 0$,

3. H_1: $\sum\limits_{i=1}^{I} \alpha_i^2 \neq 0$,

4. H_1: $\bar{\mu}_{i.} - \mu \neq 0$ for *at least* one i, and

5. H_1: $\alpha_i \neq 0$ for *at least* one i.

Each of the above equivalent statements will be true if and only if the null hypothesis for factor A is false. Hence, if we reject H_0, we automatically accept H_1.

The form of the alternative hypothesis for factor B is perfectly analogous to the form of H_1 for factor A. The reader may wish to state H_1 for factor B in at least five equivalent ways.

There remains one hypothesis of interest, and it concerns the collection of interaction terms, $\alpha\beta_{ij}$. In Sec. 17.4 our attention was directed toward two sets of conditions: (1) the graph of the population means produced parallel lines; (2) the graph of the population means produced nonparallel lines. We saw in Sec. 17.4 that if no interaction exists between A and B, i.e., if the graph of the population means shows parallel lines, then μ_{ij} will equal $\mu + (\bar{\mu}_{i.} - \mu) + (\bar{\mu}_{.j} - \mu) = \mu + \alpha_i + \beta_j$. An equivalent condition is that $\mu_{ij} = \bar{\mu}_{i.} + \bar{\mu}_{.j} - \mu$. Now if this condition is satisfied, then

$$\mu_{ij} - \bar{\mu}_{i.} - \bar{\mu}_{.j} + \mu = 0 \quad \text{for all the } \mu_{ij}\text{'s.}$$

Or, in terms of the model in Eq. (17.2),

$$\alpha\beta_{ij} = 0 \quad \text{for all } i \text{ and } j.$$

If the lines in the graph of the cell means are *not* parallel at any single point on A, then at least one $\alpha\beta_{ij}$ is *not* equal to zero. Hence, parallel lines in the graph of the IJ population means correspond to all of the $\alpha\beta_{ij}$'s equaling zero; nonparallel lines correspond to *at least one* of the $\alpha\beta_{ij}$'s *not* equaling zero. These two conditions represent the null hypothesis and the alternative hypothesis, respectively, about the interaction of factors A and B. There are several equivalent ways of stating the null hypothesis H_0 and the alternative hypothesis H_1 about the interaction effects. Some of these follow:

Equivalent statements of H_0 for the interaction of A and B	*Equivalent statements of H_1 for the interaction of A and B*
1. H_0: all $(\mu_{ij} - \bar{\mu}_{i.} - \bar{\mu}_{.j} + \mu) = 0$,	1. H_1: $\mu_{ij} - \bar{\mu}_{i.} - \bar{\mu}_{.j} + \mu \neq 0$ for at least one μ_{ij},
2. H_0: all $\alpha\beta_{ij} = 0$,	2. H_1: $\alpha\beta_{ij} \neq 0$ for at least one $\alpha\beta_{ij}$,
3. H_0: $\sum_{i=1}^{I}\sum_{j=1}^{J}(\mu_{ij} - \bar{\mu}_{i.} - \bar{\mu}_{.j} + \mu)^2 = 0$, and	3. H_1: $\sum_{i=1}^{I}\sum_{j=1}^{J}(\mu_{ij} - \bar{\mu}_{i.} - \bar{\mu}_{.j} + \mu)^2 \neq 0$, and
4. H_0: $\sum_{i=1}^{I}\sum_{j=1}^{J}\alpha\beta_{ij}^2 = 0$.	4. H_1: $\sum_{i=1}^{I}\sum_{j=1}^{J}\alpha\beta_{ij}^2 \neq 0$.

In summary, there are three pairs of hypotheses that are typically of interest in the two-factor ANOVA: (1) H_0 and H_1 for factor A, (2) H_0 and H_1 for factor B, and (3) H_0 and H_1 for the interaction of A and B. In the remaining sections of this chapter we shall see how the data gathered in a two-factor experiment are brought to bear on the decision to accept either H_0 or H_1 for A, for B, and for the interaction of A and B.

17.6
SUMS OF SQUARES IN THE TWO-FACTOR ANOVA

As in the one-factor ANOVA, the route to statistical inferential tests of the three null hypotheses in the two-factor ANOVA is marked by sums of squares, degrees of freedom, mean squares, expected mean squares, and F-ratios. As you travel this route, you may begin to feel that the markers do not point toward your destination in any obvious way. Patience is required because the meaning of the preliminary steps will not become clear until you are on the last leg of the journey.

There are four *sources of variation*, as they are called, in the two-factor ANOVA: (1) factor A, (2) factor B, (3) the interaction of A and B, and (4) "within" cells or combinations of levels of A and B. We shall define sum of squares for each source of variation in turn.

Sum of Squares for Factor A

The sum of squares for factor A, denoted SS_A, is simply nJ times the sum of the squared least-squares estimates of the α_i's.

$$SS_A = nJ\sum_{i=1}^{I}\hat{\alpha}_i^2 = nJ\sum_{i=1}^{I}(\bar{X}_{i..} - \bar{X}_{...})^2. \tag{17.4}$$

Recall that $\alpha_i = \bar{\mu}_{i.} - \mu$ is estimated by $\bar{X}_{i..}$, the mean of the nJ scores in level i of factor A, minus $\bar{X}_{...}$, the mean of all nIJ scores in the layout of data. The sum over all I levels of A of these squared estimates, $(\bar{X}_{i..} - \bar{X}_{...})^2$, is called the *sum of squares for factor A*.

Equation (17.4) for SS_A is definitional and does not make for easy computing. We shall return to the matter of actually calculating SS_A in Sec. 17.9.

Sum of Squares for Factor B

The sum of squares for factor B is nI times the sum of the squared least-squares estimates of the β_j's:

$$SS_B = nI \sum_{j=1}^{J} \hat{\beta}_j^2 = nI \sum_{j=1}^{J} (\bar{X}_{.j.} - \bar{X}_{...})^2. \tag{17.5}$$

Notice that nI is the number of scores averaged to obtain $\bar{X}_{.j.}$. In SS_A, nJ was the number of scores averaged to obtain $\bar{X}_{i..}$. Again, the above formula for SS_B is not convenient for computation. Computational formulas will be presented in Sec. 17.9.

Sum of Squares for the Interaction of A and B

$$SS_{AB} = n \sum_{i=1}^{I} \sum_{j=1}^{J} \widehat{\alpha\beta}_{ij}^2 = n \sum_{i=1}^{I} \sum_{j=1}^{J} (\bar{X}_{ij.} - \bar{X}_{i..} - \bar{X}_{.j.} + \bar{X}_{...})^2. \tag{17.6}$$

Notice as before that n, the factor multiplying the sum, is the number of scores averaged to obtain $\bar{X}_{ij.}$.

Sum of Squares "Within" Cells

There remains one sum of squares, SS_w, the sum of squares within cells.

$$SS_w = \sum_{i=1}^{I} \sum_{j=1}^{J} \sum_{k=1}^{n} (X_{ijk} - \bar{X}_{ij.})^2. \tag{17.7}$$

The meaning of these four sums of squares will begin to emerge when the corresponding mean squares and their expected values are considered in the following sections.

Incidentally, though it is of no great significance in and of itself, the sum of the squared deviations of each of the nIJ scores in a two-factor design around $\bar{X}_{...}$ is exactly equal to $SS_A + SS_B + SS_{AB} + SS_w$, i.e.,

$$\sum_{i=1}^{I} \sum_{j=1}^{J} \sum_{k=1}^{n} (X_{ijk} - \bar{X}_{...})^2 = SS_A + SS_B + SS_{AB} + SS_w. \tag{17.8}$$

The term on the left-hand side of Eq. (17.8) is called the *total sum of squares* and denoted SS_{total} for obvious reasons. The total *variance* of the collection of nIJ scores is *analyzed* into four additive components; hence, we use the expression *analysis of variance*, abbreviated ANOVA or sometimes anova.

17.7
DEGREES OF FREEDOM

Each of the four sums of squares in the two-factor ANOVA is converted into a mean square by dividing it by its degrees of freedom. The degrees of freedom of a sum of squares equals the number of least-squares estimates of effects that comprise the sum of squares less the number of independent linear restrictions placed on these estimates. Admittedly, this is a difficult and abstract notion, and we shall discuss it in some detail here merely for the sake of comprehensiveness of coverage. If you are reading this section for the first time, the day on which you come to "understand" (rather than "work with") the concept of degrees of freedom probably lies far in the future.

SS_A is calculated from the I least-squares estimates $\hat{\alpha}_1, \ldots, \hat{\alpha}_I$. It was natural and unrestrictive to specify in the model in Eq. (17.2) that $\alpha_1 + \ldots + \alpha_I = 0$. Furthermore, although we did not see it happen, it was necessary to assume that $\hat{\alpha}_1 + \ldots + \hat{\alpha}_I = 0$ before the solution to the mathematical criterion of least-squares estimation could be found. Indeed, as they must, the least-squares estimates of the α_i satisfy this restriction, i.e., $\hat{\alpha}_1 + \ldots + \hat{\alpha}_I = 0$. This is easy to demonstrate:

$$\sum_{i=1}^{I} \hat{\alpha}_i = \sum_{i=1}^{I} (\bar{X}_{i..} - \bar{X}_{...}) = 0,$$

because $\bar{X}_{...}$ is the mean of the I column means $\bar{X}_{i..}$.

There are I least-squares estimates in the calculation of SS_A and they must conform to the single linear restriction that their sum be zero. Hence, the degrees of freedom for SS_A are $I - 1$. An exactly analogous line of reasoning would lead to the correct conclusion that SS_B has degrees of freedom equal to $J - 1$.

The calculation of SS_{AB} involves the IJ least-squares estimates of the $\alpha\beta_{ij}$ terms. The restrictions it was necessary to impose on these estimates to solve the least-squares problem were that summing the estimates across rows for any given column yields a sum of zero *and* summing the estimates across the columns for any given row yields a sum of zero, i.e.,

$$\sum_{j=1}^{J} \widehat{\alpha\beta}_{ij} = 0 \quad \text{for each } i \tag{17.9}$$

$$\sum_{i=1}^{I} \widehat{\alpha\beta}_{ij} = 0 \quad \text{for each } j. \tag{17.10}$$

The conditions in Eq. (17.9) are I in number; there are J restrictions represented in Eq. (17.10). Not all $I + J$ of these restrictions are independent, however. Namely, given the restrictions in Eq. (17.9) and knowing that $\sum_{i=1}^{I} \widehat{\alpha\beta}_{ij}$ equals zero for $j = 1, \ldots, J - 1$, it must necessarily follow that $\sum_{i=1}^{I} \widehat{\alpha\beta}_{iJ} = 0$. Hence only $I + J - 1$ of the linear restrictions on the IJ values of $\widehat{\alpha\beta}_{ij}$ are independent. Therefore, the degrees of freedom for SS_{AB} are

$$IJ - (I + J - 1) = IJ - I - J + 1.$$

Notice that this expression "factors" into $(I - 1)(J - 1)$.

The sum of squares within cells, SS_w, is actually the sum of the squares of the nIJ least-squares estimates of the e_{ijk} terms in the model in Eq. (17.2). Any single e_{ijk} is estimated by $\hat{e}_{ijk} = X_{ijk} - \bar{X}_{ij.}$.

Since $\hat{e}_{ijk}$ is the deviation of a score from its cell mean, the sum of the n values of $\hat{e}_{ijk}$ within each cell is zero. Thus, there are IJ independent linear restrictions on the nIJ values of $\hat{e}_{ijk}$. Consequently, the degrees of freedom associated with SS_w are $IJn - IJ = IJ(n - 1)$.

The above results can be summarized as follows:

Sum of squares	Degrees of freedom
SS_A	$I - 1$
SS_B	$J - 1$
SS_{AB}	$(I - 1)(J - 1)$
SS_w	$IJ(n - 1)$

Now look at a very simple example of linear restriction. How many *independent* restraints on the data of the 2×3 table in Fig. 17.11 are there?

Row number	Column number			Row sums
	1	2	3	
1	1			7
2		4		9
Column sums	4	6		

FIG. 17.11

(Try filling in the four missing cell entries, the missing column sum, and the missing grand sum.)

If the number of degrees of freedom is the number of cells (here, $2 \times 3 = 6$) minus the number of independent linear restrictions on the data, how many degrees of freedom are there for a table of this type? That is, how many cell entries are *free* to vary? Is this analogous to the degrees of freedom for the interaction of factor A with factor B in a 2×3 factorial design? [Hint: For that ANOVA, the cell entries are interaction residuals, the six $(\bar{X}_{ij.} - \bar{X}_{i..} - \bar{X}_{.j.} + \bar{X}_{...})$'s, and every row sum and column sum is zero.]

17.8
MEAN SQUARES

For each sum of squares there is a mean square (abbreviated MS) defined by dividing the sum of squares by its degrees of freedom:

$$MS_A = \frac{SS_A}{I - 1}$$

$$MS_B = \frac{SS_B}{J - 1},$$

$$MS_{AB} = \frac{SS_{AB}}{(I - 1)(J - 1)},$$

$$MS_w = \frac{SS_w}{IJ(n - 1)}.$$

As in the one-factor ANOVA, the mean squares are the final stage in calculations leading toward significance tests of the null hypotheses.

17.9
COMPUTATIONAL PROCEDURES

In this section we shall see how computational formulas are applied in finding the sums of squares and mean squares. For a two-factor ANOVA design in which factor A has I levels, factor B has J levels, and each of the IJ cells contains n observations, the four sums of squares can be obtained most conveniently from the formulas in Table 17.2.

From a population of 2500 tenth-grade geometry classes 48 were selected at random for use in an experiment. The researcher wished to determine the efficiency of two different methods and media for geometry instruction and their interactions. Classes were randomly assigned in equal numbers to the four combinations of media and method. After one semester

TABLE 17.2   COMPUTATIONAL FORMULAS FOR SUMS OF SQUARES IN THE TWO-FACTOR ANOVA WITH EQUAL n's

$$SS_A = \sum_{i=1}^{I} \frac{\left(\sum_{j=1}^{J}\sum_{k=1}^{n} X_{ijk}\right)^2}{nJ} - \frac{\left(\sum_{i=1}^{I}\sum_{j=1}^{J}\sum_{k=1}^{n} X_{ijk}\right)^2}{nIJ}$$

$$SS_B = \sum_{j=1}^{J} \frac{\left(\sum_{i=1}^{I}\sum_{k=1}^{n} X_{ijk}\right)^2}{nI} - \frac{\left(\sum_{i=1}^{I}\sum_{j=1}^{J}\sum_{k=1}^{n} X_{ijk}\right)^2}{nIJ}$$

$$SS_{AB} = \sum_{i=1}^{I}\sum_{j=1}^{J} \frac{\left(\sum_{k=1}^{n} X_{ijk}\right)^2}{n} - SS_A - SS_B - \frac{\left(\sum_{i=1}^{I}\sum_{j=1}^{J}\sum_{k=1}^{n} X_{ijk}\right)^2}{nIJ}$$

$$SS_w = \sum_{i=1}^{I}\sum_{j=1}^{J}\sum_{k=1}^{n} X_{ijk}^2 - \sum_{i=1}^{I}\sum_{j=1}^{J} \frac{\left(\sum_{k=1}^{n} X_{ijk}\right)^2}{n}$$

of instruction the researcher administered the same geometry achievement test to each class. Since the sampling unit was "classroom," the unit of analysis is taken to be the class mean (to the nearest whole number) on the criterion achievement test. The results are tabulated in Fig. 17.12.*

In the above example, $i = 1, 2$; $j = 1, 2$; and $k = 1, \ldots, 12$. Certain basic calculations are indicated in Fig. 17.12. In addition, one more quantity is required: the sum of all 48 scores after each has been squared. This quantity is:

$$\sum_{i=1}^{2}\sum_{j=1}^{2}\sum_{k=1}^{12} X_{ijk}^2 = 2^2 + 5^2 + \ldots + 35^2 = 14{,}969.$$

Only those quantities in Fig. 17.12 are required to find the four sums of squares by the formulas in Table 17.2.

The sum of squares for factor A, SS_A, is calculated as follows:

$$SS_A = \frac{(229)^2 + (506)^2}{2 \cdot 12} - \frac{(735)^2}{2 \cdot 2 \cdot 12} = 1598.52.$$

The remaining sums of squares are found as indicated hereafter.

$$SS_B = \frac{(235)^2 + (500)^2}{2 \cdot 12} - \frac{(735)^2}{2 \cdot 2 \cdot 12} = 1463.02.$$

* Twenty-four score points have been subtracted from each class mean to make the calculations less arduous on a desk calculator. Recall that $s_{(x+c)}^2 = s_x^2$, so the sums of squares and the mean squares of an analysis of variance are not affected by adding a constant to each observation. However, the mean of $(X + c)$ is $\bar{X}_. + c$, so every mean in the ANOVA has been reduced 24 points.

Factor *B*, media

	Classroom lecture (1)	Programmed instruction (2)	Row sums

Traditional (1)

2, 5, 6, 7, 4, 6
7, 8, 4, 6, 7, 10

9, 12, 14, 15, 10, 13
14, 16, 10, 13, 14, 17

$$\sum_{k=1}^{12} X_{11k} = 72$$

$$\sum_{k=1}^{12} X_{12k} = 157$$

$$\sum_{j=1}^{2}\sum_{k=1}^{12} X_{1jk} = 229$$

Modern (2)

10, 13, 14, 16, 10, 13
14, 17, 11, 13, 15, 17

21, 25, 31, 33, 22, 26
32, 34, 22, 30, 32, 35

$$\sum_{k=1}^{12} X_{21k} = 163$$

$$\sum_{k=1}^{12} X_{22k} = 343$$

$$\sum_{j=1}^{2}\sum_{k=1}^{12} X_{2jk} = 506$$

Column sums

$$\sum_{i=1}^{2}\sum_{k=1}^{12} X_{i1k} = 235$$

$$\sum_{i=1}^{2}\sum_{k=1}^{12} X_{i2k} = 500$$

$$\sum_{i=1}^{2}\sum_{j=1}^{2}\sum_{k=1}^{12} X_{ijk} = 735$$

Factor *A*, methods

FIG. 17.12   Illustration of basic calculations in a two-way analysis of variance.

$$SS_{AB} = \frac{(72)^2 + (157)^2 + (163)^2 + (343)^2}{12} - SS_A - SS_B - \frac{(735)^2}{2 \cdot 2 \cdot 12}$$

$$= \frac{(72)^2 + (157)^2 + (163)^2 + (343)^2}{12} - 1598.52 - 1463.02 - \frac{(735)^2}{2 \cdot 2 \cdot 12}$$

$$= 188.02.$$

$$SS_w = 14{,}969 - \frac{(72)^2 + (157)^2 + (163)^2 + (343)^2}{12} = 464.75.$$

The sums of squares, degrees of freedom, and mean squares are reported in Table 17.3.

TABLE 17.3   SUMS OF SQUARES, DEGREES OF FREEDOM, AND MEAN SQUARES FOR THE 2 × 2 LAYOUT OF DATA IN FIG. 17.12

Source of variation	df	SS	MS
Factor *A* (method)	$I - 1 = 1$	1598.52	1598.52
Factor *B* (media)	$J - 1 = 1$	1463.02	1463.02
Interaction of *A* and *B*	$(I-1)(J-1) = 1$	188.02	188.02
Within cells	$IJ(n-1) = 44$	464.75	10.56

17.10
EXPECTED VALUES OF MEAN SQUARES

The computational aspects of the two-factor ANOVA are complete. Now it is time to turn our attention once again to the purpose of the computations. We are seeking a statistical inferential test for deciding whether the data support the null hypothesis H_0 or the alternative hypothesis H_1 about the main effects of factors A and B and their interaction effects. As was true in the one-factor ANOVA, the expected values of the mean squares reveal how they bear on the truth or falsity of the three null hypotheses.

The expected value (or "long-run average value") of MS_w is the mean of all the MS_w's that *would* be obtained if the same two-factor ANOVA design were performed an infinite number of times with independent observations. Another way to look at $E(MS_w)$ is that it is the variance of the population from which the observations in any one cell of the two-factor ANOVA design have been sampled. *We shall assume that the variance of the population from which the n observations in any cell have been sampled is equal to σ_e^2.* In other words, the variances of each of the populations underlying each of the IJ cells are equal to the same value, σ_e^2. This is an extension to the two-factor ANOVA of the assumption of homogeneous variances that we saw in the one-factor ANOVA.

If the n observations in the ijth cell are assumed to have been drawn from a population with variance σ_e^2, then $E(s_{ij}^2) = \sigma_e^2$. MS_w has the following form:

$$MS_w = \frac{SS_w}{IJ(n-1)} = \frac{\sum\limits_{i}^{I} \sum\limits_{j}^{J} \sum\limits_{k}^{n} (X_{ijk} - \bar{X}_{ij.})^2}{IJ(n-1)}.$$

We recognize MS_w to be the average of the IJ within cell sample variances, i.e.,

$$MS_w = \frac{\sum\limits_{i}^{I} \sum\limits_{j}^{J} s_{ij}^2}{IJ}.$$

We see, then, that

$$E(MS_w) = E\left[\frac{\sum\limits_{i}^{I} \sum\limits_{j}^{J} s_{ij}^2}{JI}\right] = \sum\limits_{i}^{I} \sum\limits_{j}^{J} \frac{E(s_{ij}^2)}{IJ} = \sum\limits_{i}^{I} \sum\limits_{j}^{J} \frac{\sigma_e^2}{IJ} = \frac{IJ\sigma_e^2}{IJ} = \sigma_e^2.$$

The expected value of MS_A is the average of an infinite number of MS_A's, each one obtained from an independent replication of the same two-factor ANOVA design—I levels of factor A, J levels of factor B, and n cases in each of the IJ cells. In the 2×2 experiment in the preceding section, the value of MS_A was 1598.52. This is just one observation from a hypothetically infinite population of MS_A's that could be generated by replicating the same methods × media experiment with a new set of 48 classrooms randomly drawn from the population. We don't know whether 1598.52 is above or below the population average value of MS_A, i.e., the expected value of MS_A, $E(MS_A)$.

From one replication of the experiment, we can calculate one value of MS_A. However, we cannot calculate the numerical value of $E(MS_A)$; if we could there would be no need for inferential statistics. The algebraic formula for $E(MS_A)$ in terms of the parameters of the model in Eq. (17.2) can be found. We shall not bother with the details of the derivation here; we shall simply state that $E(MS_A)$ has the following form:

$$E(MS_A) = \sigma_e^2 + \frac{nJ \sum_i^I \alpha_i^2}{I - 1}, \qquad (17.11)$$

where σ_e^2 is the variance of the error term in Eq. (17.2) and is estimated by MS_w, and

α_i is the main effect of the ith level of factor A, i.e., $\alpha_i = \bar{\mu}_{i.} - \mu$.

Suppose that, unknown to the researcher, the true value of σ_e^2 (the true "within cell" variance) is 15.0, and that $\bar{\mu}_1 = 12$ and $\bar{\mu}_2 = 22$. Since $\mu = \frac{1}{2}(12 + 22) = 17$, α_1 is $12 - 17 = -5$ and α_2 is $22 - 17 = 5$. Substituting these values and $J = 2$ and $n = 12$ into Eq. (17.11) yields

$$E(MS_A) = 15.0 + 12 \cdot 2 \frac{[(-5)^2 + 5^2]}{2 - 1} = 1215.$$

The above calculations were performed to illustrate the nature of the terms in Eq. (17.11). It must be emphasized that one never actually calculates a value for $E(MS_A)$. What *is* important is to note the relationship between the expression for $E(MS_A)$ and the truth or falsity of the null hypothesis about factor A. Notice that the third of several equivalent statements of H_0 for factor A in Sec. 17.5 is H_0: $\sum_1^I \alpha_i^2 = 0$. The quantity hypothesized to be zero in H_0 for factor A is the same quantity, $\sum \alpha_i^2$, that appears in the numerator of the second term for $E(MS_A)$. Thus, *if H_0 is true*—which means that $\sum \alpha_i^2 = 0$—*then*

$$E(MS_A) = \sigma_e^2 + \frac{nJ(0)}{I - 1} = \sigma_e^2.$$

On the other hand, *if H_0 is false*—which means that $\sum \alpha_i^2$ is positive—*then*

$$E(MS_A) = \sigma_e^2 + \frac{nJ \sum \alpha_i^2}{I - 1} > \sigma_e^2.$$

This is an important relationship to understand: *If H_0 is true, we expect*

MS_A to be the same size as the true within-cell variance, σ_e^2; if H_0 is false, we expect MS_A to be larger than σ_e^2.

The expected value of MS_B has the form

$$E(MS_B) = \sigma_e^2 + \frac{nI \sum\limits_{j}^{J} \beta_j^2}{J - 1}. \qquad (17.12)$$

The null hypothesis H_0 for the main effect of factor B is H_0: $\sum\limits_{j}^{J} \beta_j^2 = 0$. If H_0 for factor B is true, then

$$E(MS_B) = \sigma_e^2 + \frac{nI(0)}{J - 1} = \sigma_e^2.$$

If H_0 for factor B is true, we expect MS_B to be equal to $E(MS_w) = \sigma_e^2$; MS_B can be expected to be larger than σ_e^2 when H_0 for factor B is false.

The expected value of MS_{AB} is

$$E(MS_{AB}) = \sigma_e^2 + \frac{n \sum\limits_{i}^{I} \sum\limits_{j}^{J} \alpha\beta_{ij}^2}{(I - 1)(J - 1)}. \qquad (17.13)$$

The null hypothesis for the interaction of factors A and B can be stated as H_0: $\sum\limits_{i}^{I} \sum\limits_{j}^{J} \alpha\beta_{ij}^2 = 0$. Thus, we see that if H_0 for the interaction of A and B is true, then $E(MS_{AB})$ equals σ_e^2; if H_0 is false, then $E(MS_{AB}) > \sigma_e^2$.

All of these important relationships are summarized in Table 17.4.

TABLE 17.4   RELATIONSHIPS BETWEEN NULL HYPOTHESES AND EXPECTED VALUES OF MEAN SQUARES

Mean square	Expected mean square when H_0 is true for source of variation in question	Expected mean square when H_0 is false
Factor A, MS_A	σ_e^2	$\sigma_e^2 + \dfrac{nJ \sum \alpha_i^2}{I - 1}$
Factor B, MS_B	σ_e^2	$\sigma_e^2 + \dfrac{nI \sum \beta_j^2}{J - 1}$
Interaction of A and B, MS_{AB}	σ_e^2	$\sigma_e^2 + \dfrac{n \sum \sum \alpha\beta_{ij}^2}{(I - 1)(J - 1)}$
Within cells, MS_w	σ_e^2	σ_e^2

As we shall see in greater detail later, the comparison of MS_A with MS_w reflects on the truth of H_0: $\sum \alpha_i^2 = 0$. If H_0 is true, then MS_A and MS_w have the same expected value; if H_0 is false, then MS_A has an expected value larger than σ_e^2 but the expected value of MS_w is still σ_e^2. Naturally, if MS_A proves to be much larger than MS_w in a particular run of the experiment, we are inclined to think that H_0 is false; if MS_A and MS_w are much the same size in a particular replication of the experiment, we are inclined to think that they are both estimating the same quantity, σ_e^2, which is the case when H_0 is true. Comparisons of either MS_B or MS_{AB} with MS_w bear on the truth or falsity of the null hypotheses about the main effects of B and the interaction effects of A and B, respectively, in the same manner that comparing MS_A with MS_w tells us something about the plausibility of $\sum \alpha_i^2 = 0$ being true.

The problem of deciding when MS_A (MS_B or MS_{AB}) is sufficiently larger than MS_w so that we should consider the truth of H_0 implausible is a problem of the variability of the values of mean squares from one replication of the two-factor experiment to the next. This problem will occupy our attention in the next section.

17.11
THE DISTRIBUTIONS OF THE MEAN SQUARES

Before proceeding to the question of the statistical distributions of the four mean squares in a two-factor ANOVA design, it is advisable to clarify the nature of the statistical inference one makes in this situation. In the two-factor design in Sec. 17.9, 12 observations were taken in each of the $2 \times 2 = 4$ cells of the design. These 48 observations can be considered to be randomly drawn from four hypothetical populations (one for each cell) that contain the scores an infinite number of classrooms would obtain under the same experimental conditions. The 48 observations in Fig. 17.12 will be called a *complete replication of the experiment*. This complete replication produced the following mean squares: $MS_A = 1598.52$, $MS_B = 1463.02$, $MS_{AB} = 188.02$, and $MS_w = 10.56$. A second complete replication of the experiment *could* be obtained by performing the same experiment with a different set of 48 classrooms (12 in each cell); this second replication would yield different values for each of the four mean squares. Conceptually at least, third, fourth, fifth, etc. replications of the experiment could be run, and each replication would produce its own set of four mean squares. Now the question is, what will be the distribution of values of MS_A obtained from an infinite number of replications of the experiment? We ask the same question individually about MS_B, MS_{AB}, and MS_w.

Before these questions can be answered, it is necessary to add an assumption to our model in Eq. (17.2). You will recall that the model in Eq. (17.2) is itself an assumption and that in Sec. 17.10 it was necessary to assume that the variances of the hypothetical populations underlying the IJ cells of the experiment all have the same variance, σ_e^2. *To these assumptions we now add the assumption that these populations are normally distributed.*

The Distribution of MS_w

With the addition of the normality assumption, we know that the n observations in any cell—the ijth cell—constitute a random sample from a normal distribution with mean μ_{ij} and variance σ_e^2. Each cell variance s_{ij}^2 is an unbiased estimator of σ_e^2; furthermore, we can conclude that

$$\frac{s_{ij}^2}{\sigma_e^2} \sim \frac{\chi_{n-1}^2}{n-1}$$

that is, s_{ij}^2/σ_e^2 has a distribution equal to the chi-square distribution $(df = n - 1)$ divided by $n - 1$. This statement is true for the IJ independent cell variances s_{ij}^2. From the additive property of chi-square variables, we know that

$$\sum_i^I \sum_j^J \frac{s_{ij}^2}{\sigma_e^2} \sim \frac{\chi_{n-1}^2}{n-1} + \cdots + \frac{\chi_{n-1}^2}{n-1} \sim \frac{\chi_{IJ(n-1)}^2}{n-1}.$$

Dividing the above quantities by IJ yields:

$$\frac{\sum_i^I \sum_j^J s_{ij}^2}{IJ\sigma_e^2} = \frac{MS_w}{\sigma_e^2} \sim \frac{\chi_{IJ(n-1)}^2}{IJ(n-1)}.$$

MS_w/σ_e^2 has a chi-square distribution, $df = IJ(n - 1)$, divided by $IJ(n - 1)$. For example, in the problem in Sec. 17.9, $I = J = 2$ and $n = 12$. Suppose the value of σ_e^2 is 15. Then

$$\frac{MS_w}{15} \sim \frac{\chi_{44}^2}{44}$$

and the single observed value of $MS_w = 10.56$ over 15 is one observation from a chi-square distribution $(df = 44)$ that has been rescaled by division by 44.

The Distribution of MS_A

We must consider two cases in this instance: the distribution of MS_A when $H_0: \sum \alpha_i^2 = 0$ is true and when H_0 is false. If H_0 is true, then

$$\frac{MS_A}{\sigma_e^2} \sim \frac{\chi_{I-1}^2}{I-1},$$

that is, MS_A/σ_e^2 has a distribution over complete replications of the two-factor design that is the chi-square distribution $(df = I - 1)$ divided by $I - 1$.

If H_0 is false, then MS_A/σ_e^2 has what is called a *noncentral chi-square distribution* $(df = I - 1)$ divided by $I - 1$. The noncentral chi-square distribution with $df = I - 1$ is a mathematical curve that has a higher mean

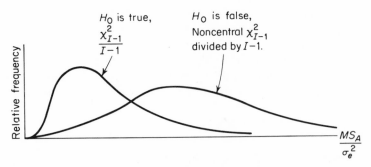

FIG. 17.13   Distribution of MS_A/σ_e^2.

and is generally to the right of the chi-square distribution $(df = I - 1)$. The relationship of the chi-square distribution to the noncentral chi-square distribution is illustrated in Fig. 17.13.

When H_0 is false, the values of MS_A tend to be larger than those of MS_A when H_0 is true. This is reflected in the displacement to the right of the non-central chi-square distribution. The larger the value of $\sum \alpha_i^2$, the further to the right of $\chi_{I-1}^2/(I - 1)$ the values of MS_A/σ_e^2 will be displaced. Thus, the noncentral chi-square distribution in Fig. 17.13 is for one particular value of $\sum \alpha_i^2$ only; there exists a separate noncentral χ^2 distribution for each value of $\sum \alpha_i^2$.

The Distribution of MS_B

The distributional statements that can be made about MS_B are quite analogous to those for MS_A, as you might expect.

If $H_0: \sum \beta_j^2 = 0$ is true, then

$$\frac{MS_B}{\sigma_e^2} \sim \frac{\chi_{J-1}^2}{J - 1}.$$

If H_0 is false, then MS_B/σ_e^2 has a noncentral chi-square distribution $(df = J - 1)$ divided by $J - 1$.

The Distribution of MS_{AB}

If $H_0: \sum\sum \alpha\beta_{ij}^2 = 0$, i.e., if there is no interaction between factors A and B, then

$$\frac{MS_{AB}}{\sigma_e^2} \sim \frac{\chi_{(I-1)(J-1)}^2}{(I - 1)(J - 1)},$$

that is, MS_{AB}/σ_e^2 has a chi-square distribution, $df = (I - 1)(J - 1)$, divided by $(I - 1)(J - 1)$.

Again, if the null hypothesis about the interaction of A and B is false, MS_{AB}/σ_e^2 has a noncentral chi-square distribution, $df = (I-1)(J-1)$, divided by $(I-1)(J-1)$.

We are now prepared to combine the above facts into the major results of this section. Recall that the ratio of two independent chi-square variables, each divided by its own degrees of freedom, has an F-distribution.

Suppose that H_0: $\sum \alpha_i^2 = 0$ is true; then $MS_A/\sigma_e^2 \sim \chi_{I-1}^2/(I-1)$. Regardless of whether H_0 is true or false, MS_w/σ_e^2 has a chi-square distribution divided by $IJ(n-1)$. Now

$$\frac{MS_A/\sigma_e^2}{MS_w/\sigma_e^2} \sim F_{I-1,IJ(n-1)}.$$

But notice that

$$\frac{MS_A/\sigma_e^2}{MS_w/\sigma_e^2} = \frac{MS_A}{MS_w} \sim F_{I-1,IJ(n-1)}.$$

(Luckily we have eliminated σ_e^2 without having to know its actual value.)

What we have shown is that the ratio of MS_A to MS_w has an F-distribution with $I-1$ and $IJ(n-1)$ degrees of freedom *when H_0 is true*. Thus if the value of MS_A/MS_w for a replication of a two-factor experiment looks like a "typical" observation from the distribution $F_{I-1,IJ(n-1)}$—by "typical" we mean that MS_A/MS_w does not exceed the 90th or 95th or 99th percentile, say, of that distribution—we are inclined to think that H_0 is true. On the other hand, if H_0 is false, then we expect the value of MS_A to be larger than the value of MS_w. Hence, if we obtain a very large value of MS_A/MS_w—a value that *seems* not to have been drawn from $F_{I-1,IJ(n-1)}$ since it exceeds the 99th percentile, say, of that distribution—then we think that H_0 is probably false.

When H_0: $\sum \beta_j^2 = 0$ is true,

$$\frac{MS_B/\sigma_e^2}{MS_w/\sigma_e^2} = \frac{MS_B}{MS_w} \sim F_{J-1,IJ(n-1)}.$$

When H_0: $\sum\sum \alpha\beta_{ij}^2 = 0$ is true, then

$$\frac{MS_{AB}/\sigma_e^2}{MS_w/\sigma_e^2} = \frac{MS_{AB}}{MS_w} \sim F_{(I-1)(J-1),IJ(n-1)}.$$

The effect of a false null hypothesis about either the main effects of factor B or the interaction effects of A and B is to increase MS_B or MS_{AB} without systematically increasing MS_w, thus producing a distribution, over complete replications of the design, of ratios of mean squares that is displaced to the right of the F-distribution. These relationships are illustrated for factor B in Fig. 17.14.

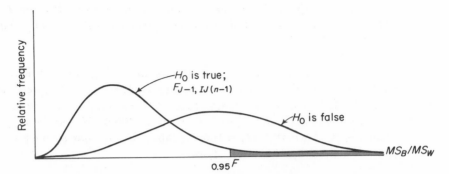

FIG. 17.14   Distribution of MS_B/MS_w over complete replications of the two-factor design when H_0 is true and when it is false. (Shaded portion contains the 5% of the ratios that exceed the 95th percentile in the F-distribution.)

17.12
HYPOTHESIS TESTS OF THE
NULL HYPOTHESES

The discussion to this point has led us to three ratios of mean squares that will be called F-ratios:

$$F_A = \frac{MS_A}{MS_w}, \qquad F_B = \frac{MS_B}{MS_w}, \qquad F_{AB} = \frac{MS_{AB}}{MS_w}.$$

For the data in Table 17.3 these F-ratios have the following values:

$$F_A = \frac{1598.52}{10.56} = 151.38, \qquad F_B = \frac{1463.02}{10.56} = 138.54,$$

$$F_{AB} = \frac{188.02}{10.56} = 17.80.$$

We shall now point out how statistical tests of the three null hypotheses can be made using the F-ratios. These F-tests are similar to the F-test in the one-factor fixed-effects ANOVA. The F-test will be illustrated with the main effects of factor A.

First, one adopts a level of significance α, which is, of course, the probability of rejecting $H_0 : \sum \alpha_i^2 = 0$ when it is in fact true. The α so chosen determines a critical region, i.e., values of the ratio MS_A/MS_w that will lead one to reject as true $H_0 : \sum \alpha_i^2 = 0$. This critical region is all numbers greater than the $100(1 - \alpha)$ percentile in the distribution $F_{I-1, IJ(n-1)}$, i.e., all values larger than $_{1-\alpha}F_{I-1, IJ(n-1)}$. If the calculated value of $F_A = MS_A/MS_w$ exceeds the critical value $_{1-\alpha}F_{I-1, IJ(n-1)}$, then H_0 is rejected. If F_A is less than the critical value, H_0 is not rejected.

Let's go back to the example in Fig. 17.12 to illustrate the hypothesis tests. There we found that $F_A = 151.38$. If $H_0: \sum \alpha_i^2 = 0$ were true, the distribution of F_A over repeated complete replications of the 2×2 design would describe an F-distribution with $I - 1 = 1$ and $IJ(n - 1) = 44$ degrees of freedom. We would not wish to conclude erroneously that H_0 is false when in fact it is true. Indeed, we wish to adopt a decision rule for choosing between H_0 and $H_1: \sum \alpha_i^2 \neq 0$ that will lead us to decide erroneously to reject H_0 in favor of H_1 only one time in 100, say. Hence, we want to adopt a risk of $\alpha = .01$ of committing a type I error, rejecting H_0 when it is true. Since the only evidence in favor of H_1 is a large value of F_A, we shall place the entire critical region of the test in the upper tail of the distribution $F_{1,44}$; hence, the critical value for the test becomes $_{.99}F_{1,44}$. From Table E in Appendix A, we can determine that the 99th percentile in the F-distribution with 1 and 44 degrees of freedom is approximately 7.25.

Any F-ratio F_A exceeding 7.25 will be taken to be evidence that the hypothesis $H_0: \sum \alpha_i^2 = 0$ is false. This statement constitutes the decision rule of the hypothesis test. If in reality H_0 is true, this decision rule will have a probability of $\alpha = .01$ of falsely rejecting H_0. Such is the magnitude of the risk one takes in agreeing to reject H_0 if F_A is greater than 7.25.

For the data in Fig. 17.12 the value of F_A is 151.38. Since this F-ratio exceeds the critical value of 7.25, the hypothesis that $\sum \alpha_i^2 = 0$ is rejected. One concludes that the two sample means $\overline{X}_{1..}$ and $\overline{X}_{2..}$ are significantly different at the .01 level.

The F-test of the hypothesis $H_0: \sum \beta_j^2 = 0$ proceeds along similar lines. Suppose it was decided to test H_0 with an α of .05. From Table E we see that the 95th percentile in the F-distribution with $J - 1 = 1$ and $IJ(n - 1) = 44$ degrees of freedom is 4.06. Hence, if H_0 is true, the chances of obtaining a value of F_B exceeding 4.06 are 1 in 20. The chances of obtaining an F_B of 138.54 or greater when $\sum \beta_j^2 = 0$ are infinitesimally small. Thus, rather than regard F_B as a one-in-a-million occurrence that just so happened to occur even though H_0 was true, we take the more logical course and regard it as evidence that H_0 is false. Our conclusion is stated formally as "$H_0: \sum \beta_j^2 = 0$ is rejected with an α of .05." Of course, this implies that we are deciding in favor of the conclusion that $\beta_1 \neq \beta_2$, i.e., that the means for the two media (classroom lecture vs. programmed instruction) of the populations sampled are different.

The F-test of the null hypothesis about the interaction of factors A and B is carried out in a similar manner. If $H_0: \sum \sum \alpha\beta_{ij}^2 = 0$ is true, then F_{AB} has an F-distribution with $(I - 1)(J - 1) = 1$ and $IJ(n - 1) = 44$ degrees of freedom. Suppose that we wish to run a test of H_0 with a risk of .01 of rejecting H_0 when it is actually true. The critical value that F_{AB} must exceed to be counted as evidence of a false H_0 is 7.25, the 99th percentile in the F-distribution with 1 and 44 degrees of freedom.

The value of F_{AB} is $188.02/10.56 = 17.80$. The position of this obtained

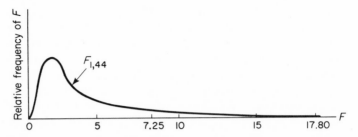

FIG. 17.15   Position of an F-ratio of 17.80 relative to the F-distribution with one and 44 degrees of freedom.

F-ratio relative to the F-distribution with 1 and 44 *df*—the distribution F_{AB} would follow if H_0 were true—is illustrated in Fig. 17.15.

By inspecting Fig. 17.15, it would appear to be foolish to regard 17.80 as having been drawn at random from the distribution $F_{1,44}$, but to argue that the data support the null hypothesis that $\sum \sum \alpha\beta_{ij}^2 = 0$ would be equivalent to doing so.   Thus, the conclusion is to reject H_0, and the probability that this conclusion is erroneous is far less than .01.

Since a significant interaction of A and B has been found, it will be illuminating to graph it.   The four cell means for the data in Fig. 17.12 are 6.00 for traditional method and classroom lecture, 13.08 for traditional method and programmed instruction, 13.58 for modern method and classroom lecture, and 28.58 for modern method and programmed instruction. The four cell means are depicted in Fig. 17.16.

The departure from parallelism of the two lines in Fig. 17.16 reflects the

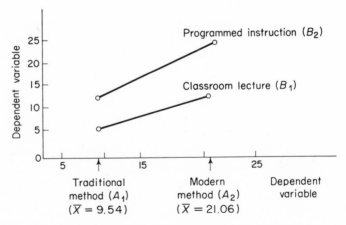

FIG. 17.16   Graph of the interaction of factors A and B for the data in Fig. 17.12.

interaction of method with media.   The departure of the two lines from parallelism was judged by the F-test to be overwhelmingly statistically significant, i.e., there is hardly the slightest chance that graphing the unknown population means would reveal parallel lines.   The interpretation of this interaction is that the modern teaching method emphasized the superiority of programmed instruction over the classroom lecture over what that superiority was for the traditional method.   Programmed instruction is about seven points better than classroom lecture under the traditional method; but it is 15 points better with the modern method.   Perhaps the modern method lent itself to programming better than did the traditional method.

17.13
REVIEW OF THE TWO-FACTOR ANOVA WITH EQUAL NUMBERS OF OBSERVATIONS PER CELL

In outline form, the two-factor fixed-effects model ANOVA with n observations per cell is performed as follows:

1. The following model is postulated for the data: $X_{ijk} = \mu + \alpha_i + \beta_j + \alpha\beta_{ij} + e_{ijk}$.
2. It is assumed that the n observations in any one of the IJ cells come from a normal distribution with variance σ_e^2, which is constant for each cell, and that the IJ samples are independent of one another.
3. A level of significance α is adopted for each of the three F-tests: the tests of the null hypothesis for the main effects of factor A and factor B and of the interaction effect of A and B.
4. The three critical values for the F-tests are determined by reference to Table E in Appendix A.   These critical values are as follows:

$$\text{For } F_A: {}_{1-\alpha}F_{I-1,IJ(n-1)};$$
$$\text{For } F_B: {}_{1-\alpha}F_{J-1,IJ(n-1)};$$
$$\text{For } F_{AB}: {}_{1-\alpha}F_{(I-1)(J-1),IJ(n-1)}.$$

5. The four mean squares, MS_A, MS_B, MS_{AB}, and MS_w, are calculated from the computational formulas for sums of squares in Table 17.2 and the degrees of freedom.
6. The three F-ratios are calculated:

$$F_A = \frac{MS_A}{MS_w} \qquad F_B = \frac{MS_B}{MS_w} \qquad F_{AB} = \frac{MS_{AB}}{MS_w}.$$

7. The F-ratios in step 6 are compared with the corresponding critical values found in step 4.   If an F-ratio exceeds the critical value, the

corresponding null hypothesis is rejected at the α-level of significance. If an F-ratio does not exceed the critical value, the corresponding null hypothesis is not rejected.

8. The results are tabulated as illustrated in Table 17.4.

TABLE 17.4   TABULATION OF RESULTS OF A TWO-FACTOR FIXED-EFFECTS MODEL ANOVA

Source of variation	df	MS	F	p
Factor A (methods)	1	1598.52	151.38*	$p < .001$
Factor B (media)	1	1463.02	138.54*	$p < .001$
$A \times B$	1	188.02	17.80*	$p < .001$
Within cells	44	10.56		

* F-ratio significant at the $\alpha = .01$ level.

Probability values appear in the last column of Table 17.4. It is becoming customary to report with each F-ratio the proportion, p, of the area in the F-distribution that lies to the right of the obtained F-ratio. For example, if F_{AB} had been 3.47, one would have indicated that p was between .10 and .05, i.e., that less than 10% but more than 5% of the area in the distribution $F_{1,44}$ lies above 3.47. One would know immediately that the null hypothesis about interaction could be rejected with an α of .10 but *not* with an α of .05.

17.14
TWO-FACTOR FIXED-EFFECTS ANOVA WITH UNEQUAL *n*'s

You will probably be surprised to learn that the generalization of the two-factor ANOVA from the equal *n*'s case to that of unequal *n*'s is not simple and straightforward as in the case of the one-factor ANOVA. Of the totality of two-factor layouts of data with unequal *n*'s a subclass of them presents no real difficulties in either theory or application. Unfortunately, the other class does present problems. The remainder of this section is divided into two parts corresponding to the two classes of conditions on the unequal *n*'s.

Proportional Cell Frequencies

Now that we are considering the possibility of different cells having different numbers of observations we must adopt a new system of denoting such numbers. To this point, the common number of observations in the *IJ* cells of a two-factor design has been denoted by *n*. Henceforth, the number of

Factor A (i)	Factor B (j)		Row sums
	1	2	
1	$n_{11} = 2$	$n_{12} = 4$	$n_{1.} = 6$
2	$n_{21} = 3$	$n_{22} = 6$	$n_{2.} = 9$
3	$n_{31} = 2$	$n_{32} = 4$	$n_{3.} = 6$
Column sums	$n_{.1} = 7$	$n_{.2} = 14$	$n_{..} = 21$

FIG. 17.17   Notation for factorial designs where the n_{ij}'s are not equal.

observations in the ijth cell of such a design will be denoted by n_{ij}. Consider the 3×2 design ($I = 3, J = 2$) for which the n's are shown in Fig. 17.17.

The number of observations in the cell at the intersection of the first column ($i = 1$) and first row ($j = 1$) is $n_{11} = 2$. There are $n_{32} = 4$ observations in the cell at the intersection of column three ($i = 3$) and row two ($j = 2$)

It will be necessary eventually to make use of the numbers of observations in any one row or column of a two-factor design. Notice in Fig. 17.17 that there are $2 + 3 + 2 = 7$ observations in the first column. This number is found by adding up n_{ij}'s as follows:

$$ n_{.1} = n_{11} + n_{21} + n_{31} = \sum_{i=1}^{3} n_{i1}. $$

The notation $n_{.1}$ for the total frequencies in the first column conforms to our usage of the subscripted dot to denote having summed over an index. In general, the total frequencies in the jth column is denoted by $n_{.j}$. The total number of observations in row 3 is

$$ n_{3.} = n_{31} + n_{32} = \sum_{j=1}^{2} n_{3j} = 2 + 4 = 6. $$

In general, there are $n_{i.}$ observations in the ith row.

The term $n_{..}$ denotes $\sum_{i=1}^{3} \sum_{j=1}^{2} n_{ij}$, which is the total number of observations in the entire layout of data. We shall also use the familiar notation of N for the total number of observations, i.e., by definition $n_{..} = N$. What is the meaning of $n_{.2}$ and $n_{1.}$?

Relatively simple computational procedures may be applied to a two-factor fixed-effects ANOVA with unequal n's provided the cell frequencies are proportional. What does it mean to have proportional cell frequencies? *The cell frequencies are proportional when*

$$n_{ij} = \frac{n_{i.}n_{.j}}{n_{..}} \tag{17.14}$$

for all IJ values of n_{ij}.

In words, the condition of proportionality is satisfied when for each cell the number of observations in that cell equals the product of the numbers of observations in the entire row and entire column in which the cell lies, divided by the total number of observations.* Notice that this condition is satisfied by each of the six values of n_{ij} in Fig. 17.17:

$$n_{11} = \frac{6 \cdot 7}{21} = 2, \qquad n_{21} = \frac{9 \cdot 7}{21} = 3, \qquad n_{31} = \frac{7 \cdot 6}{21} = 2,$$

$$n_{12} = \frac{6 \cdot 14}{21} = 4, \qquad n_{22} = \frac{9 \cdot 14}{21} = 6, \qquad n_{32} = \frac{6 \cdot 14}{21} = 4.$$

Thus the six cell frequencies in Fig. 17.17 are proportional. "Proportional" here means that $2:3:2::4:6:4$, and $2:4::3:6::2:4$. Both of these are true because the first reduces to "2 is to 3 is to 2, as 2 is to 3 is to 2," and the second reduces to "1 is to 2, as 1 is to 2, as 1 is to 2." Thus the two sets of column frequencies are proportional to each other (or to the column of row sums), and the three sets of row frequencies are proportional to each other (or to the row of column sums).†

Having determined that the cell frequencies are proportional, one may proceed with the calculations as outlined below. The calculations will be illustrated on the data (running long-jump distance measured in feet for boys and girls of three races) in Fig. 17.18.

Notice in the summation signs in Fig. 17.18 that n_{ij} replaces n in the symbol for the sum of all of the observations in the ijth cell, i.e., the sum

---

* Where did we get Eq. (17.14)? Recall from Chapter 10 the formula for the probability of the occurrence of both of two *independent* events, $(P_A)(P_B)$, where P_A is the probability of occurrence of event A, and P_B is the probability of occurrence of event B. Similarly, if $n_{ij}/n_{..}$ is "determined" entirely by the proportion of the $n_{..}$ cases that lie in row i and the proportion of the $n_{..}$ cases that lie in column j, then it will equal $(n_{i.}/n_{..})(n_{.j}/n_{..})$. Solve the equation for n_{ij} itself and you have Eq. (17.14).

† Viewed another way, but equivalently, when the n_{ij}'s are proportional one can consider each as being composed of a proportionality constant for the row, r_i, and a proportionality constant for the column, c_j. Then $n_{ij} = r_i c_j$. For the data of Fig. 17.17 the three row constants are $r_1 = 2$, $r_2 = 3$, and $r_3 = 2$. The two column constants are $c_1 = 1$ and $c_2 = 2$. Using these, one finds, for example, that $n_{21} = r_2 c_1 = 3(1) = 3$, which is true.

Factor A (race)	Factor B (sex)		Row sums	Row means
	Girls (1)	Boys (2)		
Negro (1)	11.5, 15.0	18.2, 11.3 14.2, 15.9	$\displaystyle\sum_{j=1}^{2}\sum_{k=1}^{n_{1j}} X_{1jk}$ $=86.1$	14.4
White (2)	13.1, 10.4 11.9	14.3, 15.3 11.8, 11.0 10.9, 10.5	$\displaystyle\sum_{j=1}^{2}\sum_{k=1}^{n_{2j}} X_{2jk}$ $=109.2$	12.1
Oriental (3)	10.1, 6.9	12.8, 8.4 10.6, 10.0	$\displaystyle\sum_{j=1}^{2}\sum_{k=1}^{n_{3j}} X_{3jk}$ $=58.8$	9.8
Column sums	$\displaystyle\sum_{i=1}^{3}\sum_{k=1}^{n_{i1}} X_{i1k}$ $=78.9$	$\displaystyle\sum_{i=1}^{3}\sum_{k=1}^{n_{i2}} X_{i2k}$ $=175.2$	$\displaystyle\sum_{i=1}^{3}\sum_{j=1}^{2}\sum_{k=1}^{n_{ij}} X_{ijk}$ $=254.1$	
Column means	11.3	12.5		Grand mean 12.1

FIG. 17.18   Illustrative data for the proportional-cell-frequency design of Fig. 17.17.

of the n_{ij} observations in the ijth cell is denoted by

$$\sum_{k=1}^{n_{ij}} X_{ijk}.$$

The six cell sums for the data in Fig. 17.18 are shown in Fig. 17.19.

The only remaining quantity required for the calculation of the mean squares in the two-factor ANOVA is the sum of the squares of the 21 observations in Fig. 17.18:

$$\sum_{i=1}^{3}\sum_{j=1}^{2}\sum_{k=1}^{n_{ij}} X_{ijk}^{2} = 11.5^{2} + 15.0^{2} + \ldots + 10.0^{2} = 3216.27.$$

	1	2
1	26.5	59.6
2	35.6	73.8
3	17.0	41.8

FIG. 17.19

The computational formulas for the four sums of squares bear a close resemblance to those for the equal n's case. The four computational formulas appear in Table 17.5.

TABLE 17.5   COMPUTATIONAL FORMULAS FOR SUMS OF SQUARES IN THE TWO-FACTOR ANOVA WITH PROPORTIONAL CELL FREQUENCIES

$$SS_A = \sum_{i=1}^{I} \frac{\left(\sum_{j=1}^{J} \sum_{k=1}^{n_{ij}} X_{ijk}\right)^2}{n_{i.}} - \frac{(\sum \sum \sum X_{ijk})^2}{N}$$

$$SS_B = \sum_{j=1}^{J} \frac{\left(\sum_{i=1}^{I} \sum_{k=1}^{n_{ij}} X_{ijk}\right)^2}{n_{.j}} - \frac{(\sum \sum \sum X_{ijk})^2}{N}$$

$$SS_{AB} = \sum_{i=1}^{I} \sum_{j=1}^{J} \frac{\left(\sum_{k=1}^{n_{ij}} X_{ijk}\right)^2}{n_{ij}} - SS_A - SS_B - \frac{(\sum \sum \sum X_{ijk})^2}{N}$$

$$SS_w = \sum_{i=1}^{I} \sum_{j=1}^{J} \sum_{k=1}^{n_{ij}} X_{ijk}^2 - \sum_{i=1}^{I} \sum_{j=1}^{J} \frac{\left(\sum_{k=1}^{n_{ij}} X_{ijk}\right)^2}{n_{ij}}$$

The use of the formulas in Table 17.5 will now be illustrated with the data in Figure 17.18.

$$SS_A = \frac{(86.1)^2}{6} + \frac{(109.2)^2}{9} + \frac{(58.8)^2}{6} - \frac{(254.1)^2}{21}$$

$$= 3136.735 - 3074.610 = 62.125.$$

$$SS_B = \frac{(78.9)^2}{7} + \frac{(175.2)^2}{14} - \frac{(254.1)^2}{21} = 3081.819 - 3074.610 = 7.209.$$

$$SS_{AB} = \frac{(26.5)^2}{2} + \frac{(59.6)^2}{4} + \frac{(35.4)^2}{3} + \frac{(73.8)^2}{6} + \frac{(17.0)^2}{2}$$

$$+ \frac{(41.8)^2}{4} - 62.125 - 7.209 - \frac{(254.1)^2}{21}$$

$$= 3145.935 - 62.125 - 7.209 - 3074.610 = 1.991.$$

$$SS_w = 3216.270 - \left[\frac{(26.5)^2}{2} + \ldots + \frac{(41.8)^2}{4} \right]$$

$$= 3216.270 - 3145.935 = 70.335.$$

The degrees of freedom and expected values of the four mean squares for the two-factor ANOVA with unequal n's are given in Table 17.6. The

TABLE 17.6   DEGREES OF FREEDOM AND EXPECTED VALUES OF MEAN SQUARES IN THE TWO-FACTOR ANOVA WITH UNEQUAL n's

Source of variation	df	E(MS)
Factor A	$I - 1$	$\sigma_e^2 + \dfrac{\sum\limits_{i=1}^{I} n_{i.}\alpha_i^2}{I - 1}$
Factor B	$J - 1$	$\sigma_e^2 + \dfrac{\sum\limits_{j=1}^{J} n_{.j}\beta_j^2}{J - 1}$
$A \times B$	$(I - 1)(J - 1)$	$\sigma_e^2 + \dfrac{\sum\limits_{i=1}^{I}\sum\limits_{j=1}^{J} n_{ij}\alpha\beta_{ij}^2}{(I - 1)(J - 1)}$
Within cells	$N - IJ$	σ_e^2

obtained values of the four mean squares are as follows:

$$MS_A = \frac{62.125}{2} = 31.062, \qquad MS_B = \frac{7.209}{1} = 7.209,$$

$$MS_{AB} = \frac{1.991}{2} = 0.996, \qquad MS_w = \frac{70.335}{15} = 4.689.$$

The entries in Table 17.6 possess only minor differences from their counterparts in the equal n's ANOVA. With the unequal n's ANOVA, we write the degrees of freedom within cells as $N - IJ$ instead of $IJ(n - 1)$; notice, however, that $IJ(n - 1) = IJn - IJ = N - IJ$.

The $E(MS)$'s differ from those in the equal n's case only in that *each* squared effect—main or interaction—is differentially weighted by the number of observations available to estimate it in the layout of data. n_{ij} is the general case, of which

$$n_{1.} = n_{2.} = \ldots = n_{I.}, \qquad n_{.1} = n_{.2} = \ldots = n_{.J}, \qquad n_{11} = n_{12} = \ldots = n_{IJ}$$

(i.e., equal column frequencies, equal row frequencies, or equal frequencies for each of the IJ factor-level combinations) are special cases that permit the "weights" ($n_{i.}$, $n_{.j}$, or n_{ij}) to be moved to the left of one or both of the summation signs. Note, for example, that in Table 17.6 if the n_i's are all equal, say, to c, the $E(MS)$ for factor A becomes

$$\sigma_e^2 + \frac{c \sum_{i=1}^{I} \alpha_i^2}{I - 1}.$$

Inspection of the $E(MS)$'s in Table 17.6 indicates appropriate F-tests of the three null hypotheses:

$$H_0: \sum_i^I \alpha_i^2 = 0, \qquad H_0: \sum_j^J \beta_j^2 = 0, \qquad H_0: \sum_i^I \sum_j^J \alpha\beta_{ij}^2 = 0.$$

(Notice that if $\sum_i^I \alpha_i^2 = 0$, then $\sum_i^I n_{i.}\alpha_i^2$ is also equal to zero since if the first condition holds then all I α_i's are zero. The same is true for the β_j's and $\alpha\beta_{ij}$'s.)

If $H_0: \sum_i^I \alpha_i^2 = 0$ is true, then $MS_A = SS_A/(I - 1)$ will be an unbiased estimator of σ_e^2. Regardless of whether H_0 is true or false, $MS_w = SS_w/(N - IJ)$ is an unbiased estimator of σ_e^2 and is independent of MS_A. Thus $F_A = MS_A/MS_w$ will follow the F-distribution with $I - 1$ and $N - IJ$ df when H_0 is true. When H_0 is false, i.e., $\sum \alpha_i^2 > 0$, the MS_A/MS_w will have a distribution over complete replications of the two-factor design that lies generally above the F-distribution with $I - 1$ and $N - IJ$ df. Hence, if F_A lies above $_{1-\alpha}F_{I-1,N-IJ}$, H_0 can be rejected at the α-level of significance; otherwise, H_0 cannot be rejected. For example, for the data in Fig. 17.18 $F_A = 31.062/4.689 = 6.62$. If α had been set at .01, the critical value against which F_A would be compared is $_{.99}F_{2,15} = 6.36$. Thus the data constitute evidence for the rejection of $H_0: \sum \alpha_i^2 = 0$.

Leaving α at .01, the following conclusions will be drawn concerning the main effect of factor B and the interaction of A and B:

The critical value for F_B is $_{.99}F_{1,15} = 8.68$. The value of F_B is $7.209/4.689 = 1.54$. Thus the data do not support rejection of $H_0: \sum \beta_j^2 = 0$. There is insufficient evidence to support the conclusion that boys and girls of this age differ in long-jumping ability.

The critical value for F_{AB} is $_{.99}F_{2,15} = 6.36$. The value of F_{AB} is $0.996/4.689 = 0.21$. Thus the data do not support rejection of the hypothesis of no interaction of race and sex.

The results may be tabulated as in Table 17.7.

TABLE 17.7   RESULTS OF THE TWO-FACTOR ANOVA OF THE DATA IN FIGURE 17.12

Source of variation	df	MS	F	p
Race (A)	2	31.062	6.62	$p < 0.01$
Sex (B)	1	7.209	1.54	$p > 0.25$
Race $\times$ sex ($A \times B$)	2	0.996	0.21	$p < 0.50$
Within race-sex groups	15	4.689		

Disproportional Cell Frequencies

The numbers of observations in the cells of the two-factor layout shown in Fig. 17.20 are disproportional. Notice, for example, that n_{11} is *not* equal to $n_{1.}n_{.1}/n_{..}$:

$$5 \neq \frac{12 \cdot 25}{68} = 4.4.$$

Though it is by no means readily apparent, proportional cell frequencies can be achieved in the layout of Fig. 17.20 by the simple expedient of *randomly* discarding one of the five scores in the cell in row 1 and column 1 and one of the five scores in the cell in row 2 and column 3. After so doing, the cell frequencies are proportional (see Fig. 17.21). (You may check the cell frequencies of Fig. 17.21 against Eq. (17.14) to satisfy yourself that they are actually proportional.)

When proportional cell frequencies can be achieved from disproportional frequencies by *randomly* discarding only a few observations from the total layout, then by all means one should do so. Avoiding the computational

Factor B (j)

		1	2	3	
Factor A (i)	1	$n_{11} = 5$	$n_{12} = 5$	$n_{13} = 2$	$n_{1.} = 12$
	2	$n_{21} = 8$	$n_{22} = 10$	$n_{23} = 5$	$n_{2.} = 23$
	3	$n_{31} = 12$	$n_{32} = 15$	$n_{33} = 6$	$n_{3.} = 33$
		$n_{.1} = 25$	$n_{.2} = 30$	$n_{.3} = 13$	$n_{..} = 68$

FIG. 17.20

Factor B (j)

		1	2	3	
Factor A (i)	1	$n_{11} = 4$	$n_{12} = 5$	$n_{13} = 2$	$n_{1.} = 11$
	2	$n_{21} = 8$	$n_{22} = 10$	$n_{23} = 4$	$n_{2.} = 22$
	3	$n_{31} = 12$	$n_{32} = 15$	$n_{33} = 6$	$n_{3.} = 33$
		$n_{.1} = 24$	$n_{.2} = 30$	$n_{.3} = 12$	$n_{..} = 66$

FIG. 17.21

labor necessary for the analysis of disproportional designs is worth the trivial reduction in power resulting from discarding 5%, say, of the data. When proportional cell frequencies cannot be easily or inexpensively achieved (in terms of power of the F-test) by randomly discarding data from various cells, the analysis that will now be presented is recommended.

The *unweighted means analysis* is probably the simplest and one of the most justifiable techniques for analyzing disproportional designs. First we shall outline briefly the rationale for the unweighted means analysis; then this technique will be illustrated.

Suppose that data are gathered in a two-factor design with disproportional cell frequencies. Next, consider replacing the n_{ij} observations in any one cell by a single observation $\bar{X}_{ij.}$, the mean of those n_{ij} scores. Now we have a new layout of data: IJ cells in a two-factor design with one observation per cell, the mean of the original n_{ij} scores in the cell. Surely this new layout of data has proportional cell frequencies; indeed, the n's are all equal to 1. It is possible to calculate MS'_A, MS'_B, and MS'_{AB} on this new layout of data. (The primes indicate that these are not the MS's based on the original individual observations.) However, there exist no degrees of freedom within cells when $n = 1$; hence, we cannot calculate a MS'_w from the two-factor array of cell means.

We can find a useful analogue of MS'_w. Any MS'_w must estimate the variance of the normal populations from which the observation (or observations) in any one of the IJ cells is sampled. Since we assume that the n_{ij} observations in the ijth cell come from a normal population with variance σ_e^2, the variance of $\bar{X}_{ij.}$ is σ_e^2/n_{ij}, by a well-known theorem. We can see from σ_e^2/n_{ij} that the population variances of the IJ cell means are heterogeneous (since n_{ij} differs from cell to cell). However, when n's are equal (as they are in the case of the layout of IJ cell means—$n = 1$), it has been shown that the F-tests operate as they would if all of the variances were equal and equalled the average of the IJ cell variances (see Scheffé, 1959, chap. 10). Hence, if we can find an estimate of the average variance of the IJ cell means, we can use it as the denominator of any F-ratio.

Now,

$$\text{average variance of } \bar{X}_{ij.} = \frac{\displaystyle\sum_{i}^{I}\sum_{j}^{J}\frac{\sigma_e^2}{n_{ij}}}{IJ},$$

which equals

$$\sigma_e^2\,\frac{\displaystyle\sum_{i}^{I}\sum_{j}^{J}\frac{1}{n_{ij}}}{IJ}.$$

We can estimate σ_e^2, the variance of the populations of the original n_{ij} observations. It is estimated by MS_w, *the mean square within for the original layout of N individual observations.* Hence, we take

$$MS'_w = MS_w \frac{\displaystyle\sum_i^I \sum_j^J \frac{1}{n_{ij}}}{IJ}. \tag{17.15}$$

Denote the multiplier of MS_w in Eq. (17.15) by c; c is the average of the reciprocals of the numbers of observations in the IJ cells. MS'_w is appropriate as a denominator for testing MS'_A, MS'_B, and MS'_{AB}.

The unweighted means analysis is illustrated on data in Fig. 17.22. These hypothetical data can be thought of as having been gathered in an experiment to test the effects on intelligence of a chemical that enhances the ability of brain tissue to absorb oxygen; interest centers both on the overall effectiveness of the drug and its possible interaction with diagnosis of the child (normal vs. brain damaged). Intelligence is measured with the Stanford-Binet Intelligence Test.

The data in the top half of Fig. 17.22 are transformed into the layout of cell means in the bottom half of the figure. [Note that $(92 + 114 + 107)/3 = 104.33$.] The layout of data in the bottom half of Fig. 17.22 is now regarded

1. Original Data Evidencing Disproportional Cell Frequencies.

Factor *B* – Glutamic acid dosage

	1 No Dosage	2 Half Dosage	3 Full Dosage
1 Normal	92, 114, 107 $n_{11} = 3$	101, 118, 98, 96, 105 $n_{12} = 5$	89, 120, 110, 115 $n_{13} = 4$
2 Brain damaged	91, 74, 65, 90 $n_{21} = 4$	101, 68, 59 $n_{22} = 3$	79, 88, 55, 67, 93 $n_{23} = 5$

Factor *A* – Diagnosis

2. Layout of Cell Means.

Factor *B*

	1	2	3	Row totals	Row means
Factor *A* 1	104.33	103.60	108.50	316.43	105.48
Factor *A* 2	80.00	76.00	76.40	232.40	77.47
Column totals	184.33	179.60	184.90	548.83	
Column means	92.17	89.80	92.45		

FIG. 17.22   Layout of data for the unweighted means analysis.

as a two-factor ANOVA with $n = 1$ observation per cell. The sums of squares are calculated as follows:

$$SS'_A = \sum_{j=1}^{2} \frac{\left(\sum_{i=1}^{3} X_{ij}\right)^2}{3} - \frac{\left(\sum_{i=1}^{3}\sum_{j=1}^{2} X_{ij}\right)^2}{6} = \frac{(316.43)^2 + (232.40)^2}{3} - \frac{(548.83)^2}{6}$$

$$= 51,379.235 - 50,202.395 = 1176.840.$$

$$SS'_B = \sum_{i=1}^{3} \frac{\left(\sum_{j=1}^{2} X_{ij}\right)^2}{2} - \frac{\left(\sum_{i=1}^{3}\sum_{j=1}^{2} X_{ij}\right)^2}{6}$$

$$= \frac{(184.33)^2 + (179.60)^2 + (184.90)^2}{2} - \frac{(548.83)^2}{6}$$

$$= 50,210.860 - 50,202.395 = 8.465.$$

$$SS'_{AB} = \sum_{i=1}^{3}\sum_{j=1}^{2} X_{ij}^2 - SS'_A - SS'_B - \frac{\left(\sum_{i=1}^{3}\sum_{j=1}^{2} X_{ij}\right)^2}{6}$$

$$= (104.33)^2 + (103.60)^2 + \ldots + (76.40)^2$$

$$- 1176.840 - 8.465 - \frac{(548.83)^2}{6}$$

$$= 51,402.919 - 1176.840 - 8.465 - 50,202.395 = 15.219.$$

MS'_w is obtained by calculating MS_w from the 24 scores in the top half of Fig. 17.22 and multiplying by c. SS_w is given by

$$SS_w = \sum_{i}^{I}\sum_{j}^{J}\sum_{k}^{n_{ij}} X_{ijk}^2 - \sum_{i}^{I}\sum_{j}^{J} \frac{\left(\sum_{k}^{n_{ij}} X_{ijk}\right)^2}{n_{ij}}$$

$$= 92^2 + 114^2 + 107^2 + \ldots + 93^2 - \left[\frac{313^2}{3} + \ldots + \frac{382^2}{5}\right]$$

$$= 209,061 - 205,522.933 = 3538.067.$$

The value of c is given by

$$c = \frac{\sum_{i}^{I}\sum_{j}^{J} \frac{1}{n_{ij}}}{IJ} = \frac{\frac{1}{3} + \frac{1}{4} + \frac{1}{5} + \frac{1}{3} + \frac{1}{4} + \frac{1}{5}}{6} = 0.2611.$$

Now we are prepared to calculate mean squares and F-ratios:

$$MS'_A = \frac{SS'_A}{1} = \frac{1176.840}{1} = 1176.840.$$

$$MS'_B = \frac{SS'_B}{2} = \frac{8.465}{2} = 4.233.$$

$$MS'_{AB} = \frac{SS'_{AB}}{2} = \frac{15.219}{2} = 7.610.$$

$$MS'_w = c\frac{SS_w}{18} = 0.2611\frac{3538.067}{18} = 0.2611(196.559) = 51.322$$

The F-ratios for testing the three null hypotheses are:

$$F_A = \frac{MS'_A}{MS'_w} = \frac{1176.840}{51.322} = 22.93. \qquad F_B = \frac{MS'_B}{MS'_w} = \frac{4.233}{51.322} = 0.08.$$

$$F_{AB} = \frac{MS'_{AB}}{MS'_w} = \frac{7.610}{51.322} = 0.15.$$

Quite obviously there exists no evidence to conclude a significant main effect for factor B—glutamic acid dosage or interaction effect of A and B. The F-ratio for factor A is 22.93, which exceeds $_{.99}F_{1,18} = 8.28$. The probability p of obtaining an F_A as large as 22.93 or larger if the null hypothesis for factor A is true is less than .01. Hence, $H_0: \sum_i^2 \alpha_i^2 = 0$ is rejected.

The results of the unweighted means analysis can be presented as is usual for a two-factor ANOVA:

Source of variation	df	MS	F	p
Diagnosis (A)	1	1176.840	22.93	$p < .01$
Glutamic acid dosage (B)	2	4.233	0.08	$p > .50$
$A \times B$	2	7.610	0.15	$p > .50$
Within cells	18	51.322		

17.15
MULTIPLE COMPARISONS IN THE TWO-FACTOR ANOVA

The rejection of a null hypothesis about the main effect of factor A implies only that at least two of the I population means differ. All I population means may differ, only two may differ, or any number in between may differ; the F-test does not distinguish among these possibilities. As was true with the one-factor ANOVA, multiple-comparisons procedures are required to determine which of the pairs of I sample means show differences large enough to permit the conclusion that the underlying population means differ. The above remarks apply to factor B as well. The Tukey and Scheffé methods of multiple comparisons were presented in Chapter 16. In this section, we shall indicate how each method would typically be employed in the two-factor case.

When the number of observations upon which each of the I sample means for factor A is based is equal for all I means and when one is interested only in the $I(I - 1)/2$ differences between I population means, the Tukey method should be used. The set of $I(I - 1)/2$ simultaneous confidence intervals on the $\bar{\mu}_{i.} - \bar{\mu}_{i.}^*$ with confidence coefficient $1 - \alpha$ is constructed as follows:

$$(\bar{X}_{i..} - \bar{X}_{i..}^*) \pm {}_{1-\alpha}q_{I,N-IJ} \sqrt{\frac{MS_w}{N/I}}, \qquad (17.16)$$

where ${}_{1-\alpha}q_{I,N-IJ}$ is the $100(1 - \alpha)$ percentile point in the Studentized range distribution with I and $N - IJ$ degrees of freedom (see Table F in Appendix A),

MS_w is the mean square within from the two-factor ANOVA, and

N/I is the common number of observations on which each of the I sample means is based. (Recall that this number of observations must be equal for each group to use the Tukey method.) When the n's in the IJ cells are equal, $N/I = nJ$.

Construction of a set of simultaneous confidence intervals by the Tukey method will be illustrated on the data in Fig. 17.23 for which the ratio F_B proved to be significant at the $\alpha = .01$ level.

Notice that $N = 27$, $I = 2$, and $J = 3$; furthermore, the number of observations upon which each column mean is based equals $N/J = 27/3 = 9$.

	Factor B			
	1	2	3	
Factor A 1	$\bar{X}_{11.} = 24.00$ $n_{11} = 3$	$\bar{X}_{12.} = 17.33$ $n_{12} = 3$	$\bar{X}_{13.} = 16.33$ $n_{13} = 3$	
Factor A 2	$\bar{X}_{21.} = 26.17$ $n_{21} = 6$	$\bar{X}_{22.} = 15.34$ $n_{22} = 6$	$\bar{X}_{23.} = 18.00$ $n_{23} = 6$	$MS_w = 24.62$
Column means	$\bar{X}_{.1.} = 25.44$	$\bar{X}_{.2.} = 16.00$	$\bar{X}_{.3.} = 17.44$	

FIG. 17.23

The value of MS_B is 232.78; hence, $F_B = 232.78/24.62 = 9.45$, which is significant at the .01 level with 2 and 21 degrees of freedom. The questions remain whether group 1 differs significantly from *both* groups 2 and 3 or whether groups 2 and 3 are significantly different.

A set of simultaneous confidence intervals may be constructed around the three differences between pairs of means by the method outlined in Table 17.7.

TABLE 17.7   CONSTRUCTION OF A SET OF SIMULTANEOUS CONFIDENCE INTERVALS AROUND THE DIFFERENCES BETWEEN PAIRS OF MEANS BY THE TUKEY METHOD ($J = 3$, $\alpha = .01$)

Differences between means	$_{.99}q_{3, 21}\sqrt{\dfrac{MS_w}{N/J}}$	Confidence interval [Eq. (17.16)]
$\bar{X}_{.1.} - \bar{X}_{.2.} = 9.44$	$(4.61)\sqrt{\dfrac{24.62}{9}} = 7.62$	$(1.82, 17.06)$
$\bar{X}_{.1.} - \bar{X}_{.3.} = 8.00$	7.62	$(0.38, 15.62)$
$\bar{X}_{.2.} - \bar{X}_{.3.} = -1.44$	7.62	$(-9.06, 6.18)$

The confidence intervals on $\bar{\mu}_{.1} - \bar{\mu}_{.2}$ and $\bar{\mu}_{.1} - \bar{\mu}_{.3}$ do *not* include zero; hence, we conclude a significant difference between $\bar{X}_{.1.}$ and $\bar{X}_{.2.}$ and between $\bar{X}_{.1.}$ and $\bar{X}_{.3.}$. The confidence interval on $\bar{\mu}_{.2}$ and $\bar{\mu}_{.3}$ includes zero; there exists no evidence that $\bar{\mu}_{.2}$ and $\bar{\mu}_{.3}$ differ. The confidence afforded by the Tukey method is 99% that all three of these conclusions are simultaneously correct.

The above techniques apply to factor A as well, of course, the only alterations being in the use of $_{1-\alpha}q_{I, N-IJ}$ and N/I as a divisor of MS_w.

When one desires to perform multiple comparisons on the means of one factor in a two-factor design in which these row or column means are based on differing numbers of observations, the Scheffé method should be employed. The Scheffé method was discussed at length in Chapter 16. The only alterations to Eq. (16.5) occasioned by the fact that a two-factor ANOVA is being analyzed are that MS_w now stands for "within cells mean square" and $n_1, \ldots, n_J$ now become $n_{1.}, \ldots, N_{I.}$, i.e., the n's are the total numbers of observations upon which the column (or row) means are based. The formula for constructing a set of simultaneous confidence intervals around contrasts of the row means by the Scheffé method is as follows:

$$(c_1\bar{X}_{1..} + \ldots + c_I\bar{X}_{I..}) \pm \sqrt{MS_w\left(\frac{c_1^2}{n_{1.}} + \ldots + \frac{c_I^2}{n_{I.}}\right)}\sqrt{(I-1)_{1-\alpha}F_{I-1, N-IJ}}.$$

$$(17.17)$$

PROBLEMS AND EXERCISES

1. Complete the ANOVA table and make F-tests of the null hypotheses for factors A and B and the interaction of A and B at the $\alpha = .01$ level of significance.

Source of variation	df	SS	MS
Factor A	4	64.26	
Factor B	5	46.85	
$A \times B$			
Within	120	1136.53	
Total	149	2411.69	

2. The figure below represents cell, row, and column population means in a two-factor ANOVA design.

Factor B

	1	2	3	
Factor A 1	$\mu_{11} = 15$	$\mu_{12} = 10$	$\mu_{13} = 5$	$\bar{\mu}_{1.} = 10$
2	$\mu_{21} = 5$	$\mu_{22} = 10$	$\mu_{23} = 15$	$\bar{\mu}_{2.} = 10$
	$\bar{\mu}_{.1} = 10$	$\bar{\mu}_{.2} = 10$	$\bar{\mu}_{.3} = 10$	$\mu = 10$

a. Is $H_0: \sum_{i=1}^{I} \alpha_i^2 = 0$ true or false?

b. Is $H_0: \sum_{j=1}^{J} \beta_j^2 = 0$ true or false?

c. Is $H_0: \sum_{i=1}^{I} \sum_{j=1}^{J} \alpha\beta_{ij}^2 = 0$ true or false?

3. You have been told that research shows no interaction between "sex" and "method of foreign language instruction." The main effect of the aural-oral method of instruction is $+6$ points on a French language mastery test; the main effect for females is $+2$ points on the same mastery test. In what direction and by how many points should the mean of females studying French by the aural-oral method deviate from the grand mean (the mean for both sexes studying under each method)?

4. Graph the interaction of factor B, traditional orthography vs. Initial Teaching Alphabet, and factor A, sex, from the following cell means on the dependent variable, reading performance measured in grade-placement units:

	T.O.	I.T.A.
Boys	$\bar{X}_{11.} = 4.61$	$\bar{X}_{12.} = 4.48$
Girls	$\bar{X}_{21.} = 5.12$	$\bar{X}_{22.} = 4.96$

5. For each of the following arrangements of data, graph the interaction of factor B, sex, with factor A, "treatments." Place factor B on the abscissa so that each treatment level yields one line in the graph. Which cases show ordinal interaction (all questions of statistical significance aside)? Which show disordinal interaction?

(a)

	Male	Female
Treatments 1	$\bar{X}_{11.} = 18.65$	$\bar{X}_{12.} = 21.68$
2	$\bar{X}_{21.} = 25.20$	$\bar{X}_{22.} = 14.17$
3	$\bar{X}_{31.} = 16.44$	$\bar{X}_{32.} = 17.89$

(b)

	Male	Female
Treatments 1	$\bar{X}_{11.} = 19.63$	$\bar{X}_{12.} = 14.81$
2	$\bar{X}_{21.} = 10.21$	$\bar{X}_{22.} = 13.55$

(c)

	Male	Female
Treatments 1	$\bar{X}_{11.} = 9.43$	$\bar{X}_{12.} = 13.95$
2	$\bar{X}_{21.} = 11.06$	$\bar{X}_{22.} = 15.58$

6. Graph the interaction of "sex" and "treatments" for the data under (b) of Prob. 5. Place "treatments" on the abscissa. Is the interaction ordinal or disordinal? Was the interaction ordinal or disordinal when "sex" was placed on the abscissa of the graph?

7. A researcher is studying the effects on learning of inserting questions into instructional materials. There is some doubt whether these questions would be more effective preceding or following the passage about which the question is posed. In addition, the researcher wonders if the effect of the position of the questions is the same for factual questions and for questions that require the learner to compose a thoughtful and original response. A group of 24 students is split at random into four groups of six students each. One group is assigned to each of the four combinations of factor B, "position of question (before vs. after the passage)" and factor A "type of question (factual vs. thought-provoking)." After 10 hours of studying under these conditions, the 24 students are given a 50-item test over the content of the instructional materials. The following test scores are obtained:

Position of question

		Before		After	
		19	23	31	28
	Fact	29	26	26	27
		30	17	35	32
		27	21	36	29
	Thought	20	26	39	31
		15	24	41	35

(Types of question)

Perform a two-factor ANOVA on the above data. Test the null hypotheses for both main effects and the interaction effects at the .10 level of significance.

8. Analyze the following scores on a 50-item vocabulary test administered to 24 students of high and average intelligence (factor A) after one year of studying a foreign language under one of three methods (factor B):

Factor B

		Aural–oral method	Translation method	Combined methods
		36	26	19
	High	29	23	30
	(115 and above)	25	21	28
		31	18	20
		33	20	17
	Average	19	22	13
	(115 and below)	37	14	23
		28	15	18

Factor A (Intelligence)

a. Perform *F*-tests of the null hypotheses for rows, columns, and interaction at the .05 level.

b. These same data were analyzed under Prob. 8 at the end of Chapter 15. However, there the data were regarded as a one-factor ANOVA, "method of instruction" being the only factor. Verify that SS_B and MS_B are the same whether the data are considered in a one-factor or two-factor design. Also verify that SS_w for the one-factor ANOVA of the data in Prob. 8 of Chapter 15 equals $SS_A + SS_{AB} + SS_w$ for the two-factor ANOVA of the same data.

9. D. L. Williams (1968) experimented with rewriting sixth-grade science materials so that the reading difficulty was appropriate for the third grade. (The following data are based on his study.) A group of 240 sixth-grade pupils were randomly assigned to one or the other of two levels of reading difficulty: "Grade 6 reading difficulty" or "Grade 3 reading difficulty." For three days, pupils read "Resources of the Sea," a chapter in a science text, at either the third-grade or sixth-grade reading difficulty level. A 129-item multiple-choice test was administered at the end of the experiment to assess comprehension. Within both levels of reading difficulty, pupils were classified as either high, average, or low scorers on the reading section of the Stanford Achievement Test. The following data were obtained for the two levels of reading difficulty and three levels of reading achievement:

	Reading difficulty	
	Grade 6	Grade 3
High	$n = 40$ $\bar{X}_{11.} = 89.93$ $s_{11} = 12.02$	$n = 40$ $\bar{X}_{12.} = 93.89$ $s_{12} = 13.02$
Average	$n = 40$ $\bar{X}_{21.} = 70.79$ $s_{21} = 14.76$	$n = 40$ $\bar{X}_{22.} = 72.55$ $s_{22} = 15.90$
Low	$n = 40$ $\bar{X}_{31.} = 52.09$ $s_{31} = 11.30$	$n = 40$ $\bar{X}_{32.} = 56.84$ $s_{32} = 12.21$

(Reading achievement, vertical label on left)

Perform a two-factor ANOVA on these data. Test all three null hypotheses at the .05 level of significance. (Hint: MS_w is the average of the six within-cell *variances*.)

10. All of the first-grade pupils in a school were given a reading readiness test in September. According to the test manual, a total of 12 girls and 18 boys had scores so low that "formal reading instruction should be postponed and 'reading readiness activities' should be substituted." A reading researcher randomly assigned the 12 girls and 18 boys in equal numbers to one of the following three conditions: (1) give 18 weeks of reading readiness activities before beginning instruction; (2) give 9 weeks of readiness activities; (3) commence reading

instruction immediately (0 weeks of readiness activities). A reading achievement test was administered to all 30 pupils at the end of the third grade. The following grade-placement scores were obtained:

Reading readiness activities

		18 weeks		9 weeks		None	
		3.4	4.0	3.7	4.3	4.1	4.4
	Boys	4.1	3.8	4.2	3.3	3.7	3.2
Sex		3.9	4.4	3.8	3.1	3.4	4.0
	Girls	4.0	3.8	4.6	4.2	4.4	4.3
		4.3	4.7	3.9	3.6	4.0	4.6

Perform F-tests at the .05 level of the null hypotheses of no difference among amounts of readiness activities, no differences between the sexes, and no interaction between the two factors.

11. In which of the following designs are the cell frequencies proportional, i.e., in which instances are $n_{ij} = (n_{i.}n_{.j})/n_{..}$?

(a)

	1	2	3
1	$n_{11} = 4$	$n_{12} = 8$	$n_{13} = 2$
2	$n_{21} = 6$	$n_{22} = 12$	$n_{23} = 3$

(b)

	1	2
1	$n_{11} = 5$	$n_{12} = 6$
2	$n_{21} = 10$	$n_{22} = 14$

(c)

	1	2	3
1	$n_{11} = 5$	$n_{12} = 10$	$n_{13} = 15$
2	$n_{21} = 4$	$n_{22} = 8$	$n_{23} = 12$
3	$n_{31} = 2$	$n_{32} = 4$	$n_{33} = 6$

(d)

	1	2
1	$n_{11} = 6$	$n_{12} = 10$
2	$n_{21} = 3$	$n_{22} = 8$
3	$n_{31} = 4$	$n_{32} = 8$

12. From which one cell could two observations be discarded to achieve proportional cell frequencies:

$n_{11} = 10$	$n_{12} = 15$	$n_{13} = 10$
$n_{21} = 6$	$n_{22} = 9$	$n_{23} = 6$
$n_{31} = 2$	$n_{32} = 3$	$n_{33} = 4$

13. A sample of 40 tenth-grade pupils drawn randomly from either public or parochial schools (factor B) can be classified as of either high, middle, or low socio-economic status (factor A). The pupils earned the following grade-placement scores on a mathematics achievement test:

Type of school

		Public		Parochial	
		9.5	10.1	10.4	8.5
	High	8.7	10.4	11.6	10.3
				9.3	10.2
Socioeconomic status		8.4	11.4	10.4	11.1
		10.5	10.6	9.4	10.3
	Middle	9.8	10.4	10.6	10.6
		10.6		11.0	10.7
		8.6	8.9	10.0	9.9
		7.3	9.7	9.5	10.6
	Low	10.2	10.0	8.9	10.4
		9.5	7.1		
		9.8			

Because the cell frequencies are disproportional, perform an unweighted-means analysis of variance to test the null hypotheses for rows, columns, and interaction.

18

ONE-FACTOR AND MULTI-FACTOR ANALYSIS OF VARIANCE: RANDOM, MIXED, AND FIXED EFFECTS

18.1
INTRODUCTION

This chapter has three objectives: (1) to introduce an alternative to the analysis of variance model that underlies Chapters 15 through 17; (2) to show a combination of this new model and the previous ANOVA model that is of great importance in experimental research; (3) to present rules for generating the fundamental elements (sums of squares, degrees of freedom, expected values of mean squares, etc.) of most analyses of variance one is apt to meet in practice. These three topics will be dealt with in the order indicated.

18.2
THE RANDOM-EFFECTS
ANOVA MODEL

In this section we shall introduce an analysis of variance model and applications of the model that are fundamentally different from those of the fixed-effects ANOVA model of Chapter 15. Fortunately, many similarities between

452

the techniques of Chapter 15 and those to be presented here should sub-stantially facilitate learning the material in this chapter. The model which we shall now develop is called the *random-effects* analysis of variance model.

The reasons for having spoken of a "fixed-effects" ANOVA model in Chapter 15 were never made clear. It is simpler to comprehend the meaning of "fixed effects" when they can be contrasted with "random effects." In the ANOVA model of Chapter 15, we were primarily interested in making statistical inferences about the set of main effects $\alpha_1, \ldots, \alpha_J$. The inference to be made was from a set of sample data (J groups of n persons) to J populations. We conceived of an infinite sequence of replications of the experiment in each of which there were n persons under each of J levels. Our interest in the J population means—or equivalently the J main effects—led us to consider only replications of the experiment in which the same J treatment levels appeared. In a sense, then, we "fixed" (as opposed to allowing to vary) the J populations so that each one—and only these ones—yielded one sample of size n in each replication of the experiment.

Now we wish to allow the populations that give rise to the samples in each replication of the experiment to vary across replications; this time we shall sample populations A, B, and C, and next time populations D, E, and F will be sampled. This procedure would be adopted if our interest were in the variance of the means of a large collection of populations only a few of which could be observed in one experiment. We might, then, randomly select for a given experiment both a sample of J populations from a large collection of populations and then samples of size n observations from each population. If we ran the experiment again, we would not "fix" the factor levels so that the same J populations were again represented; rather we would randomly sample a different set of J populations. As there were "effects" of the form $\alpha_j = \mu_j - \mu$ in the fixed-effects model, so there are effects of the form $a_j = \mu_j - \mu$ for this new model. However, whereas formerly the complete set of α_j's was present in every replication of the fixed-effects analysis, now we want to consider the case of having only a *random* sample of the a_j *effects* present in a replication of the experiment. Hence, the name *random-effects* ANOVA model. Figure 18.1 is an attempt to capture graphically this distinction between the fixed-effects and random-effects models.

As part of its testing program, a school system administers the Metro-politan Achievement Tests to the 7th, 8th, and 9th grades of all junior high schools in the system each May. Often these data are used to make com-parisons. Is school A showing higher performance than school B? Has school C improved since last May? The administrators realize that not all aspects of the testing are standardized. In particular, the tests are given at different times of the day in different schools. If there is some substantial variability in test performance associated with the time of day at administra-tion of the test, then a comparison of schools A and B might be telling more

Fixed–effects model $(J=3)$ $x = \mu + a_j + e$		Random–effects model $(J=3)$ $x = \mu + a_j + e$	
Main effects: $\alpha_1, \alpha_2, \alpha_3$.		Main effects: $a_1, a_2, \ldots, a_\infty$	
Replication of experiment	Main effects present in replication	Replication of experiment	Main effects present in replication
1	$\alpha_1, \alpha_2, \alpha_3$	1	a_5, a_{31}, a_8
2	$\alpha_1, \alpha_2, \alpha_3$	2	a_{16}, a_3, a_9
3	$\alpha_1, \alpha_2, \alpha_3$	3	a_{21}, a_{11}, a_{50}

FIG. 18.1   Representation of fixed-effects and random-effects ANOVA models.

about *when* schools A and B gave their tests than which school has reached a higher level of performance. For example, if school A gave the test at 9 a.m. when the students were fresh and school B gave the test at 2 p.m. near the end of a hard day, A might outscore B even though B would outscore A if the tests were given at the same time.

The school system is preparing to do a study to determine whether "time of day" is an important source of variance in test scores.

We shall take the administrator's concerns and attempt to embody them in a statistical model. First, conceive of a population of 50-minute periods with starting times at any minute between 9 a.m. and 3 p.m. There are 360 such periods, a large number, but by no means "infinite." Nonetheless, 360 potential testing periods qualifies as a "huge" number, and it will not concern us at all that the methods to be developed rest on the assumption of an infinite number of levels of a factor.

Suppose that all of the junior-high-school students in the school system were given the advanced form of the Metropolitan Reading Test (an objective test comprising 44 multiple-choice items) starting at 9:35 a.m. The period from 9:35–10:25 a.m. is the 36th period in the population of 360 periods during the day. We shall denote the average score in the population of students for this period by μ_{36}. In general, μ_j is the mean test score in the population of students for the jth testing period, $j = 1, \ldots, 360$.

The administrator of the testing program is concerned about the collection of μ_j's. Do the μ_j's differ? They very likely do; so, how much do they differ? How variable are the μ_j's? Now if every school either gave the test at 10:45 a.m., 1:30 p.m., or 2:15 p.m. we would merely run an experiment comparing these three periods and test the hypothesis $\mu_1 = \mu_2 = \mu_3$ with the fixed-effects ANOVA model of Chapter 15. But individual schools may choose any 50-minute period to administer the test; so we need to find out something about all the μ_j's. The variance of the μ_j's tells us what sort of differences to expect in the μ_j's, the mean test scores for the population of students across all 360 testing periods.

We shall now formalize the random-effects model. Suppose we have a virtually infinite population of μ_j's. (Again, we are not worried, because in our example we have only 360 μ_j's.) Denote the average of all these μ_j's by μ. The ith student earns a score of X_{ij} during the jth testing period. The difference between the ith student's score at period j and the mean of all students' scores in that period is denoted by e_{ij}; hence,

$$X_{ij} = \mu_j + e_{ij}, \tag{18.1}$$

where X_{ij} is the score for student i in level j of the factor "time of day,"

$\quad\quad \mu_j$ is the mean of all students' scores for the jth level of the factor, and

$\quad\quad e_{ij}$ is the deviation of the ith student's score from the mean of all students' scores at the jth level of the factor.

The model in Eq. (18.1) will be altered in form slightly by deviating the μ_j's around μ, the mean of all the μ_j's, as follows:

$$X_{ij} = \mu + (\mu_j - \mu) + e_{ij}. \tag{18.2}$$

The model in Eq. (18.2) follows by adding in and subtracting out μ from Eq. (18.1). A notation simplification of Eq. (18.2) will put the random-effects ANOVA model into its customary form:

$$X_{ij} = \mu + a_j + e_{ij}, \tag{18.3}$$

where

$$a_j = \mu_j - \mu \quad \text{and} \quad e_{ij} = X_{ij} - \mu_j.$$

Suppose that μ, the mean test score of all students over all 360 testing periods, is 30; and suppose that all students average 4 points *above* 30 when they take the test during the 36th testing period (9:35–10:25 a.m.); and finally suppose that the fourth student scores 8 points *below* the average of all students tested at this period. If the model in Eq. (18.3) holds, what test score will the fourth student obtain during the 36th testing period?

$$X_{4.36} = \mu + a_j + e_{ij} = 30 + 4 - 8 = 26.$$

Initially, we were interested in the variance of the μ_j's. How has this concern changed now that the μ_j's have been "eliminated" from the model? Since a_j is simply μ_j minus a constant, μ, the variance of the μ_j's is the same as the variance of the a_j's. Thus, differences in test scores due to the time of day of administration of the test will be reflected in the variance of the a_j's, i.e., in σ_a^2.

Before we can proceed to estimate σ_a^2 and make statistical inferential statements about it, it will be necessary to make some assumptions about the model in Eq. (18.3):

1. The random-effects a_j are *normally* distributed with a mean of zero and a variance of σ_a^2, i.e., $a \sim N(0, \sigma_a^2)$.

2. The error component e_{ij} is *normally* distributed with mean zero and variance σ^2, i.e., $e \sim N(0, \sigma^2)$.

3. The random-effects a_j and the error components e_{ij} are independent, from which it follows that $\rho_{ae} = 0$. Furthermore, the e_{ij} are all independent of one another.

These assumptions have several implications for the testing study. If the random-effects model is an adequate description of the data in the testing study, then:

1. The means (μ_j's) of populations of students' scores for all possible testing times during the day should appear to be normally distributed around μ and have a variance of σ_a^2. Since $a_j = \mu_j - \mu$, the a_j should have a normal distribution around zero with a variance of σ_a^2.

2. The test scores X_{ij} for all students for a single time period (the jth time period) should be normally distributed around a mean of μ_j with variance σ^2. Since $e_{ij} = X_{ij} - \mu_j$, e_{ij} will be normally distributed around zero with variance σ^2. This is assumed to be true for all values of j. This assumption is the counterpart of the homogeneous variances assumption in the fixed-effects model.

3. If samples of n test scores were taken from the populations of scores for a randomly designated J time periods, the value of a_j would give no information about whether $\bar{e}_{.j}$ was above or below zero and similarly, the value of $\bar{e}_{.j}$ would give no information about whether a different $\bar{e}_{.j*}$ was above or below zero.

After these preliminaries, we come at last to the techniques for actually estimating both σ_a^2 and σ^2 from data. The problem to be solved is one of estimating the variability in test scores due to the time of administering the test, σ_a^2, and the variance in test scores due to differences among students taking the test at the same time, σ^2.

Data are gathered in a two-phased sampling plan. First, J levels of the random-effects factor are drawn at random. For example, $J = 5$ time periods from the population of 360 periods are *randomly chosen*. Just as random sampling of persons from populations permits generalizations to the population of persons, randomly sampling levels of a factor allows generalization to a population of levels. Second, a random sample of n observations is drawn from the populations in each of the J levels. In our example, this procedure is simulated by administering the Metropolitan Reading Test at each of the five time periods to $n = 7$ students randomly drawn from the population of all students. *Restricting the n's to be equal is not a matter of convenience here; the methods of this section have never been fully developed for the unequal n's case.*

In our study, we have sampled $J = 5$ a's and $Jn = 35$ e's. The scores on the 44-item reading test may be arranged as in Table 18.1.

TABLE 18.1   DATA FROM A STUDY OF THE EFFECTS OF TESTING TIME ON TEST SCORES

		Testing time period		
1 (11:09–11:59 a.m.)	2 (10:14–11:04 a.m.)	3 (1:31–2:21 p.m.)	4 (9:50–10:40 a.m.)	5 (1:53–2:43 p.m.)
$X_{11} = 35$	$X_{12} = 36$	$X_{13} = 28$	$X_{14} = 27$	$X_{15} = 32$
$X_{21} = 32$	$X_{22} = 32$	$X_{23} = 27$	$X_{24} = 16$	$X_{25} = 34$
$X_{31} = 41$	$X_{32} = 34$	$X_{33} = 23$	$X_{34} = 40$	$X_{35} = 26$
$X_{41} = 42$	$X_{42} = 40$	$X_{43} = 15$	$X_{44} = 32$	$X_{45} = 28$
$X_{51} = 31$	$X_{52} = 37$	$X_{53} = 29$	$X_{54} = 36$	$X_{55} = 23$
$X_{61} = 36$	$X_{62} = 44$	$X_{63} = 28$	$X_{64} = 38$	$X_{65} = 36$
$X_{71} = 35$	$X_{72} = 42$	$X_{73} = 33$	$X_{74} = 22$	$X_{75} = 28$
$\bar{X}_{.1} = 36.00$	$\bar{X}_{.2} = 37.86$	$\bar{X}_{.3} = 26.14$	$\bar{X}_{.4} = 30.14$	$\bar{X}_{.5} = 29.59$
$s_1^2 = 17.33$	$s_2^2 = 18.81$	$s_3^2 = 32.81$	$s_4^2 = 78.81$	$s_5^2 = 21.29$

It should come as no great surprise that the variance of the J sample means, $\bar{X}_{.1}, \ldots, \bar{X}_{.J}$, bears on the question of how large the variance of the μ_j's is. Nor should it be unexpected that the variance of the X_{ij}'s within each sample yields an estimate of σ^2.

As in the fixed-effects ANOVA model, each of the J groups of scores produces a sample variance s_j^2 that is an estimator of σ^2, the variance of the population of scores for the jth factor level. The average of these J sample variances is the best estimator available for σ^2. For the fixed-effects model, the average within-sample variance was called MS_w, the mean-square within:

$$MS_w = \frac{s_1^2 + \ldots + s_J^2}{J} = \frac{\sum\limits_{j=1}^{J} \sum\limits_{i=1}^{n} (X_{ij} - \bar{X}_{.j})^2}{J(n-1)}. \qquad (18.4)$$

MS_w is an estimator of σ^2 in the following senses:

1. The expected value of MS_w is equal to σ^2, i.e., $E(MS_w) = \sigma^2$. Thus, MS_w is an unbiased estimator of σ^2, the variance of scores within each factor level.

2. Over replications of the study with J factor levels and n observations within each level, the sampling distribution of MS_w is given by:

$$MS_w \sim \sigma^2 \frac{\chi^2_{J(n-1)}}{J(n-1)},$$

i.e., the sampling distribution of MS_w is σ^2 times a chi-square distribution with $J(n-1)$ degrees of freedom divided by $J(n-1)$.

It is simple to prove that the expected value of MS_w is σ^2 if one remembers that the expected value of χ_n^2 is simply n:

$$E(MS_w) = E\left[\frac{\sigma^2 \chi_{J(n-1)}^2}{J(n-1)}\right] = \frac{\sigma^2}{J(n-1)}[J(n-1)] = \sigma^2.$$

As in Chapter 15, the definitional formula for MS_w in Eq. (18.4) is not convenient for computations. In its place, one should use the following formula to compute MS_w:

$$MS_w = \frac{\displaystyle\sum_{j=1}^{J}\sum_{i=1}^{n} X_{ij}^2 - \sum_{j=1}^{J}\frac{\left(\displaystyle\sum_{i=1}^{n} X_{ij}\right)^2}{n}}{J(n-1)}. \tag{18.5}$$

The application of Eq. (18.5) to the data in Table 18.1 will be illustrated in Table 18.2.

TABLE 18.2   ILLUSTRATION OF CALCULATION OF MS_b AND MS_w ON THE DATA IN TABLE 18.1

		Testing time period		
1	2	3	4	5
$\displaystyle\sum_{i=1}^{7} X_{i1} = 252$	$\displaystyle\sum_{i=1}^{7} X_{i2} = 265$	$\displaystyle\sum_{i=1}^{7} X_{i3} = 183$	$\displaystyle\sum_{i=1}^{7} X_{i4} = 211$	$\displaystyle\sum_{i=1}^{7} X_{i5} = 207$
$\displaystyle\sum_{i=1}^{7} X_{i1}^2 = 9176$	$\displaystyle\sum_{i=1}^{7} X_{i2}^2 = 10{,}145$	$\displaystyle\sum_{i=1}^{7} X_{i3}^2 = 4981$	$\displaystyle\sum_{i=1}^{7} X_{i4}^2 = 6833$	$\displaystyle\sum_{i=1}^{7} X_{i5}^2 = 6249$

$$\sum_{j=1}^{5}\sum_{i=1}^{7} X_{ij} = 1118 \qquad \sum_{j=1}^{5}\sum_{i=1}^{7} X_{ij}^2 = 37{,}384$$

$$SS_b = \frac{(252)^2 + (265)^2 + (183)^2 + (211)^2 + (207)^2}{7} - \frac{(1118)^2}{35} = \frac{254{,}588}{7} - \frac{1{,}249{,}924}{35}$$

$$= 36{,}369.71 - 35{,}712.11 = 657.60$$

$$MS_b = \frac{SS_b}{J-1} = \frac{657.60}{4} = 164.40$$

$$SS_w = 37{,}384 - \frac{(252)^2 + (265)^2 + (183)^2 + (211)^2 + (207)^2}{7} = 37{,}384 - 36{,}369.71$$

$$= 1014.29$$

$$MS_w = \frac{SS_w}{J(n-1)} = \frac{1014.29}{30} = 33.81$$

The function MS_b, mean-square between groups, with which you became familiar in Chapter 15 was there seen to be closely related to the variance of J sample means. Having defined MS_b before, we can use it now in estimating σ_a^2, the variance of the population of a's or, what is equivalent, the variance of the population of μ_j's. You will recall that

$$MS_b = \frac{n \sum_{j=1}^{J} (\bar{X}_{.j} - \bar{X}_{..})^2}{J - 1}, \tag{18.6}$$

i.e., MS_b is n times the sample variance of the J sample means, $\bar{X}_{.1}, \ldots, \bar{X}_{.J}$.

Again, the definitional formula for a mean square makes for clumsy calculation. A more efficient computational formula for MS_b is:

$$MS_b = \frac{\sum_{j=1}^{J} \dfrac{\left(\sum_{i=1}^{n} X_{ij}\right)^2}{n} - \dfrac{\left(\sum_{j=1}^{J} \sum_{i=1}^{n} X_{ij}\right)^2}{Jn}}{J - 1}. \tag{18.7}$$

It can be shown—though we shall not do so here—that the expected value of MS_b has the following form:

$$E(MS_b) = \sigma^2 + n\sigma_a^2, \tag{18.8}$$

i.e., on the average—the average across an infinite collection of independent replications of the same study with J randomly chosen levels with n randomly chosen observations at each level—MS_b will equal σ^2, the same variance that is estimated by MS_w, plus n times the variance of the population of a_j's (which is the same as the variance of the population of μ_j's).

Thus we see that MS_b estimates all that MS_w estimates and more. The something "more" is n times the quantity of interest, σ_a^2.

It happens that the sampling distribution of MS_b is given by the following:

$$MS_b \sim (\sigma^2 + n\sigma_a^2) \frac{\chi_{J-1}^2}{J - 1}, \tag{18.9}$$

i.e., over repeated samplings of $J \times n$ layouts of data in which both factor levels and observations within levels are randomly sampled, the sampling distribution of MS_b is that of chi-square with $J - 1$ degrees of freedom multiplied by the constant $\sigma^2 + n\sigma_a^2$ over $J - 1$. Unlike the fixed-effects model, MS_b has a sampling distribution that is a constant times the chi-square distribution even when there are differences among the μ_j's.

In Table 18.2 the calculation of MS_b and MS_w is illustrated using the data in Table 18.1. We see in Table 18.2 that the best estimate we have of σ^2, the variance of Metropolitan Reading Test scores in the population of junior-high-school students, is MS_w, which equals 33.81. We shall denote this estimate by $\hat{\sigma}^2$, the "$\hat{\ }$" indicating an estimate of the parameter below it.

The mean of all five groups is approximately 32; we would then expect that Metropolitan Reading Test scores for junior-high-school students would be normally distributed around a mean of 32 with a standard deviation of approximately $\sqrt{33.81} = 5.82$.

The value of MS_b is an estimate of $\sigma^2 + n\sigma_a^2$. We can obtain an estimate of σ_a^2 alone from MS_b and MS_w in the following manner:

$$E\left[\frac{MS_b - MS_w}{n}\right] = \frac{E(MS_b) - E(MS_w)}{n} = \frac{\sigma^2 + n\sigma_a^2 - \sigma^2}{n} = \frac{n\sigma_a^2}{n} = \sigma_a^2.$$

$$(18.10)$$

The best estimate we can attain of σ_a^2 is given by $(MS_b - MS_w)/n$. This function estimates σ_a^2 unbiasedly. If MS_w were larger than MS_b—which could happen—the estimate $\hat{\sigma}_a^2$ of σ_a^2 would be negative. We know, of course, that σ_a^2 is positive, or at the very least, zero. Thus, if ever a negative estimate of σ_a^2 were obtained, it would automatically be set equal to zero instead. For the data in Table 18.1, we have

$$\hat{\sigma}_a^2 = \frac{MS_b - MS_w}{n} = \frac{164.40 - 33.81}{7} = 18.66.$$

Thus the best estimate, $\hat{\sigma}_a^2$, of the variance of the means of populations of test scores obtained at each of the 360 possible testing periods during the day is 18.66. The standard deviation of these population means is approximately 4.32.

This estimate of σ_a has some meaning in and of itself. For example, if schools A and B chose to administer the Metropolitan Reading Test at times 1 and 2, respectively, and if $a_1 = +4$ and $a_2 = -4$ (*not an unusual occurrence since each time-period effect lies only one standard deviation from zero, the mean of all a_j's*), then the two schools would be expected to differ by 8 points on the test even if they were achieving at the same level. An obtained difference between them of 8 points might easily be due to the fact that they administered the test at different times of the day. Note that this would be highly improbable if σ_a were .25, for example; it would be highly unlikely that an 8 point difference between school means could be attributed to "time of day" effects if σ_a were .25. An estimated variance component of 18.66 in our example indicates that for test scores to be comparable from school to school in the system, an effort must be made by the administration to see that the tests are administered at the same time of day in each school.

While this "absolute" interpretation of σ_a^2 is occasionally possible, more often σ_a^2 only takes on meaning when compared with σ^2. For example, we might find it more informative to know that the ratio of $\hat{\sigma}_a^2$ to $\hat{\sigma}^2$ is $\frac{1}{2}$ or 3 or .005. In our example, $\hat{\sigma}_a^2/\hat{\sigma}^2$ is 0.55. In the parlance popular among statisticians, it is said that "the variance due to 'time of day' is about half as great as the variance among students' test scores."

One can identify at least three inferential questions in the one-way random-effects model: (1) How can a confidence interval on σ_a^2 be established around $\hat{\sigma}_a^2$? (2) How can a confidence interval on σ_a^2/σ^2 be established around $\hat{\sigma}_a^2/\hat{\sigma}^2$? (3) How can the hypothesis that $\sigma_a^2 = 0$ be tested?

Unfortunately, the techniques for setting a confidence interval around $\hat{\sigma}_a^2$ on σ_a^2 cannot be derived in a straightforward manner from the original model. Approximate techniques are available; however, they are quite complex (see Scheffé, 1959, pp. 231–35).

It is a relatively simple matter to establish a confidence interval on σ_a^2/σ^2 around $\hat{\sigma}_a^2/\hat{\sigma}^2$. The $1 - \alpha$ confidence interval on σ_a^2/σ^2 is given in Eq. (18.11):

$$\text{prob} \left\{ \frac{1}{n} \left[\frac{MS_b}{MS_w} \left(\frac{1}{{}_{1-(\alpha/2)}F_{J-1, J(n-1)}} \right) - 1 \right] \leqslant \frac{\sigma_a^2}{\sigma^2} \right.$$

$$\left. \leqslant \frac{1}{n} \left[\frac{MS_b}{MS_w} \left(\frac{1}{{}_{\alpha/2}F_{J-1, J(n-1)}} \right) - 1 \right] \right\} = 1 - \alpha. \quad (18.11)$$

Both the $100[1 - (\alpha/2)]$ and the $100(\alpha/2)$ percentile points in $F_{J-1, J(n-1)}$ are required in Eq. (18.11). Recall that

$$_{\alpha/2}F_{J-1, J(n-1)} = \frac{1}{{}_{1-(\alpha/2)}F_{J(n-1), J-1}}.$$

Suppose we wish to construct the 95% confidence interval on σ_a^2/σ^2 for the data in Table 18.1. From Table E in Appendix A we first find the value of $_{.975}F_{4, 30} = 3.25$. Next the value of $_{.975}F_{30, 4}$ is found from which the other required percentile is calculated as follows:

$$_{.025}F_{4, 30} = \frac{1}{{}_{.975}F_{30, 4}} = \frac{1}{8.46} = 0.12.$$

Substituting the two percentiles along with the values of MS_b, MS_w, and n into Eq. (18.11) yields the 95% confidence interval on σ_a^2/σ^2:

$$\frac{1}{7} \left(\frac{164.40}{33.81} \frac{1}{3.25} - 1 \right); \quad \frac{1}{7} \left(\frac{164.40}{33.81} \frac{1}{0.12} - 1 \right) = (.07, 5.64).$$

The 95% confidence interval on σ_a^2/σ^2 extends from .07 to 5.64. This interval tells how very uninformative our study has been. According to our data, we have little reason not to believe that σ_a^2 could be anywhere from one-tenth as large as σ^2 to about $5\frac{1}{2}$ times larger than σ^2. A study that produces stable estimates of σ_a^2 and σ^2, i.e., short confidence intervals on σ_a^2/σ^2, cannot be done cheaply; both J and n must be fairly large.

Testing the null hypothesis H_0: $\sigma_a^2 = 0$ is not of as much interest as was the test of H_0: $\sum_1^J \alpha_j^2 = 0$ in the fixed model. We can often become sufficiently skeptical to entertain the possibility that a small set of means are equal—as in the fixed-effects model ANOVA—in which case we wish to test the hypothesis of no differences. Certainly far less frequently does it strike us as even remotely possible that an infinite number of levels of a factor all have the same population mean, as must be true if H_0: $\sigma_a^2 = 0$ is true. Hence, when the random-effects ANOVA model is applied, interest will center on the estimation of σ_a^2 more often than on testing whether $\sigma_a^2 = 0$.

However, if compelling reasons exist for testing H_0: $\sigma_a^2 = 0$, it can be tested readily as follows: *If $F = MS_b/MS_w$ exceeds the $100(1 - \alpha)$ percentile point of the F-distribution with $J - 1$ and $J(n - 1)$ degrees of freedom, H_0: $\sigma_a^2 = 0$ can be rejected at the α-level of significance.* For example, with the data in Table 18.1, $F = MS_b/MS_w = 164.40/33.81 = 4.86$, which exceeds 4.02, the 99th percentile in $F_{4,30}$. Thus, H_0: $\sigma_a^2 = 0$ can be rejected with $\alpha = .01$.

For all values of σ_a^2, the sampling distribution of $F = MS_b/MS_w$ is given by:

$$F = \frac{MS_b}{MS_w} \sim \left(1 + \frac{n\sigma_a^2}{\sigma^2}\right) F_{J-1,\,J(n-1)}. \qquad (18.12)$$

Several major points developed in this section about the one-factor random-effects ANOVA model are summarized in Table 18.3.

TABLE 18.3   SUMMARY OF THE ONE-FACTOR RANDOM-EFFECTS ANOVA

Source of variation	df	SS	E(MS)	Estimated variances
Between levels	$J - 1$	$\displaystyle\sum_{j=1}^{J} \frac{\left(\sum_{i=1}^{n} X_{ij}\right)^2}{n} - \frac{\left(\sum_{j=1}^{J}\sum_{i=1}^{n} X_{ij}\right)^2}{Jn}$	$\sigma^2 + n\sigma_a^2$	$\hat\sigma_a^2 = \dfrac{MS_b - MS_w}{n}$
Within levels	$J(n - 1)$	$\displaystyle\sum_{j=1}^{J}\sum_{i=1}^{n} X_{ij}^2 - \sum_{j=1}^{J} \frac{\left(\sum_{i=1}^{n} X_{ij}\right)^2}{n}$	σ^2	$\hat\sigma^2 = MS_w$

A final word is in order on the question of the consequences of violating the assumptions of the random-effects ANOVA model. In Chapter 15 we saw that the consequences for the validity of the fixed-effects ANOVA of violation of the normality assumption were negligible; in addition, hetero-geneous variances are immaterial in the fixed-effects model if all n's are equal. However, the situation is different for the random-effects ANOVA model. In particular, *if the kurtosis of the random-effects $a_j = \mu_j - \mu$ deviates from the kurtosis of the normal distribution, the validity of confidence intervals on σ_a^2/σ^2 or of the test of H_0: $\sigma_a^2 = 0$ may be open to serious question. Non-normality of the observations within the factor levels of the random-effects factor is of little consequence.*

18.3 THE MIXED-EFFECTS ANOVA MODEL

The third and final distinctly different analysis of variance model that will be dealt with is a coalition of the fixed-effects and the random-effects models. This union of the two models into a *mixed-effects* model is particularly useful in experimental research.

As the name "mixed-effects model" might suggest, the mixed model involves two sets of effects: one fixed and the other random. Naturally, then, the model describes data gathered in a two-factor design, similar in appearance only to the two-factor fixed model of Chapter 17. One factor, e.g., the row factor, comprises a set of I fixed effects; the column factor is a random sample of J random effects from a supposedly infinite population of normally distributed effects. Consider a hypothetical experiment in which evaluators are comparing three elementary science curricula: (1) the American Association for the Advancement of Science curriculum (AAAS); (2) the Elementary Science Study curriculum (ESS); (3) the Science Curriculum Improvement Study (SCIS) curriculum. The dependent variable of the experiment is "knowledge of the processes of scientific inquiry," which is measured by a 75-item objective test. The experiment is designed as follows: 10 elementary schools are chosen to participate; six experimental classrooms are available within each school; *by random methods*, two classrooms are assigned to each curriculum within each school. Observations of the dependent variable are taken by administering the "processes of science" test to all 60 experimental classrooms and averaging the scores of the students within each class; thus, the 60 observations in the experiment are *classroom means*. The data from the experiment may be laid out as in Table 18.4.

TABLE 18.4 LAYOUT OF DATA FROM AN EXPERIMENT IN WHICH THREE ELEMENTARY SCIENCE CURRICULA ARE COMPARED (SCORES ARE CLASS MEANS TO THE NEAREST WHOLE NUMBER ON A 75-ITEM TEST)

		School (j)											
		A	B	C	D	E	F	G	H	I	J	Row sums	Row means
Curriculum (i)	AAAS	31, 27	21, 26	41, 40	24, 29	35, 28	36, 33	21, 21	31, 34	35, 40	24, 26	603	30.15
	ESS	39, 46	32, 30	46, 50	34, 32	42, 47	39, 43	26, 30	32, 35	44, 43	30, 27	747	37.35
	SCIS	35, 28	31, 25	42, 39	36, 38	41, 37	38, 38	27, 25	29, 31	45, 41	31, 26	683	34.15
Column sums		206	165	258	193	230	227	150	192	248	164	2033	

The general observation in Table 18.4 is denoted by X_{ijk}, where i ranges over rows (curricula) from 1 to 3, j ranges over columns (schools) from 1 to 10, and k ranges over observations within cells (classrooms) from 1 to 2. In general, $i = 1, \ldots, I$; $j = 1, \ldots, J$; and $k = 1, \ldots, n$. The notation is equivalent to that for the two-factor fixed-effects ANOVA of Chapter 17.

The two-factor design in Table 18.4 presents two sets of main effects plus one set of interaction effects. The two main effects are "curricula," which will be called factor A, and "schools," factor B. Clearly the three science curricula were not sampled from a large population of such curricula, nor are the evaluators interested in generalizing to a hypothetical population of other curricula from which they could have conceivably been sampled. Interest focuses on the question of which one of these curricula is superior to the other two. Hence, the three main effects of factor A are considered "fixed." On the other hand, the 10 schools represented in the experiment can be considered to have been sampled from a population of schools; or more importantly, the evaluators do not want the results of their study to be limited to the 10 schools of the experiment. Their conclusion about the relative superiority of the curricula must be generalized beyond the 10 experimental schools to have any utility. Hence, the 10 schools are regarded as randomly sampled levels of the random-effects factor B. We have, then, a fixed-effects and a random-effects factor crossed in the same design. The structural model postulated for the observations in this design is aptly named the mixed-effects model:

$$X_{ijk} = \mu + \alpha_i + b_j + \alpha b_{ij} + e_{ijk}, \qquad (18.13)$$

where X_{ijk} is the kth observation in the ijth cell,

μ is the grand population mean of all observations,

α_i is the main effect $(\mu_i - \mu)$ of the ith level of the fixed factor,

b_j is the main effect $(\mu_j - \mu)$ of the jth level of the random factor,

αb_{ij} is the interaction effect $(\mu_{ij} - \mu_i - \mu_j + \mu)$ of the ijth combination of the fixed and random factor, and

e_{ijk} is the error, or "residual," component that accounts for variation of observations within the ijth cell.

The following restrictions (not assumptions) are placed on the terms of the mixed-effects model in Eq. (18.13):

1. $\alpha_1 + \ldots + \alpha_I = 0$.
2. The population mean of the infinite number of b_j's—only 10 of which are present in the science curriculum experiment—is zero.
3. $\alpha b_{1j} + \alpha b_{2j} + \ldots + \alpha b_{Ij} = 0$ for all j.
4. The population of the infinite set of αb_{ij}'s for a single i (row) has a mean of zero.

The above restrictions imply that if we sum across the rows of the data layout in Table 18.4 the fixed-effects and interaction effects will "add out," i.e., sum to zero; however, summing across the columns of the design to obtain a particular row mean, for example, will not cause the J values of b_j or the J values of αb_{ij} to sum to zero.

Suppose we wish to compare $\bar{X}_{1..}$ and $\bar{X}_{2..}$, i.e., the means of the classrooms under the AAAS and ESS curricula. These two means have the following structure in terms of the model in Eq. (18.13):

$$\bar{X}_{1..} = \frac{1}{JK}\left[\sum_1^J \sum_1^K (\mu + \alpha_1 + b_j + \alpha b_{1j} + e_{1jk})\right]$$

$$= \mu + \alpha_1 + \bar{b}_. + \overline{\alpha b}_{1.} + \bar{e}_{1..}.$$

$$\bar{X}_{2..} = \mu + \alpha_2 + \bar{b}_. + \overline{\alpha b}_{2.} + \bar{e}_{2..}.$$

The difference between $\bar{X}_{1..}$ and $\bar{X}_{2..}$ is

$$\bar{X}_{1..} - \bar{X}_{2..} = (\alpha_1 - \alpha_2) + (\overline{\alpha b}_{1.} - \overline{\alpha b}_{2.}) + (\bar{e}_{1..} - \bar{e}_{2..}).$$

Because the αb's do not sum to zero across the J columns and because a replication of the experiment with a different set of J random effects would produce different values of $\overline{\alpha b}_{1.}$ and $\overline{\alpha b}_{2.}$, the sampling variance of the difference between $\bar{X}_{1..} - \bar{X}_{2..}$ will contain a component for the interaction effects, αb. This fact will be fully appreciated when we discuss the expected values of mean squares for the mixed model. But before entering upon that subject, we must state the assumptions which must be made about the mixed model of Eq. (18.13).

The following assumptions are made about the terms of the model

$$X_{ijk} = \mu + \alpha_i + b_j + \alpha b_{ij} + e_{ijk}.$$

1. The random effects, $b_j = \mu_j - \mu$, are normally distributed with a mean of zero and a variance of σ_b^2.

2. The interaction effects αb_{ij} are normally distributed over j for each i with a mean of zero and a variance of $\sigma_{\alpha b}^2$.

3. The error components e_{ijk} are distributed normally and independently of the b's and αb's with mean zero and variance σ^2.

A fourth very important assumption is necessary to insure the validity of the hypothesis test of the fixed main effects:

4. For all pairs of levels of the fixed factor, the correlation (across the *population* of random effects) of the scores under one level with the scores under the other level of the pair must be the same. For example, if in the population of all schools the correlation of classroom mean test scores for the AAAS and ESS curricula is .50, then the population correlation for AAAS and SCIS and for ESS and SCIS must be .50 as well.

We shall indicate later how the methods of this section should be modified when assumption 4, *homogeneous correlations*, is suspected to be seriously violated.

With the model and its assumptions stated, we can proceed to develop the methods by which null hypotheses about the fixed and random main effects and the interaction effects may be tested. Our objective, then, is to test the following three pairs of hypotheses:

1. $H_0: \sum_1^I \alpha_i^2 = 0$ vs. $H_1: \sum \alpha_i^2 \neq 0$.

2. $H_0: \sigma_b^2 = 0$ vs. $H_1: \sigma_b^2 \neq 0$.

3. $H_0: \sigma_{\alpha b}^2 = 0$ vs. $H_1: \sigma_{\alpha b}^2 \neq 0$.

Not surprisingly, perhaps, the road to the hypothesis tests leads through the familiar sums of squares, degrees of freedom, mean squares, and expected values of mean squares. In fact, the computations of SS, df, and MS in the mixed model are identical to the calculations in the two-factor fixed model. The two models do not part company until the expected values of the mean squares are reached. The computations in the two-factor mixed model are presented in Table 18.5 and are illustrated on the data of Table 18.4 in Table 18.6.

TABLE 18.5   COMPUTATIONAL FORMULAS FOR SUMS OF SQUARES, DEGREES OF FREEDOM, AND MEAN SQUARES IN THE TWO-FACTOR MIXED MODEL

Source of variation	df	SS	MS
Among rows (fixed factor A)	$I - 1$	$SS_A = \sum_i^I \dfrac{\left(\sum_j^J \sum_k^n X_{ijk}\right)^2}{Jn} - \dfrac{\left(\sum_i^I \sum_j^J \sum_k^n X_{ijk}\right)^2}{IJn}$	$\dfrac{SS_A}{I - 1}$
Among columns (random factor B)	$J - 1$	$SS_B = \sum_j^J \dfrac{\left(\sum_i^I \sum_k^n X_{ijk}\right)^2}{In} - \dfrac{\left(\sum_i^I \sum_j^J \sum_k^n X_{ijk}\right)^2}{IJn}$	$\dfrac{SS_B}{J - 1}$
Interaction of A and B	$(I - 1)(J - 1)$	$SS_{AB} = \sum_i^I \sum_j^J \dfrac{\left(\sum_k^n X_{ijk}\right)^2}{n} - SS_A - SS_B - \dfrac{\left(\sum_i^I \sum_j^J \sum_k^n X_{ijk}\right)^2}{IJn}$	$\dfrac{SS_{AB}}{(I - 1)(J - 1)}$
Within cells	$IJ(n - 1)$	$SS_w = \sum_i^I \sum_j^J \sum_k^n X_{ijk}^2 - \sum_i^I \sum_j^J \dfrac{\left(\sum_k^n X_{ijk}\right)^2}{n}$	$\dfrac{SS_w}{IJ(n - 1)}$

TABLE 18.6   ILLUSTRATION OF CALCULATION OF SUMS OF SQUARES AND MEAN SQUARES ON THE DATA IN TABLE 18.4

1. $SS_A = \dfrac{(603)^2 + (747)^2 + (683)^2}{20} - \dfrac{(2033)^2}{60} = 520.53$

$MS_A = \dfrac{SS_A}{I-1} = \dfrac{520.53}{2} = 260.27$

2. $SS_B = \dfrac{(206)^2 + (165)^2 + \ldots + (164)^2}{6} - \dfrac{(2033)^2}{60} = 2059.68$

$MS_B = \dfrac{SS_B}{J-1} = \dfrac{2059.68}{9} = 228.85$

3. $SS_{AB} = \dfrac{(58)^2 + (47)^2 + \ldots + (57)^2}{2} - 520.53 - 2059.68 - \dfrac{(2033)^2}{60} = 268.47$

$MS_{AB} = \dfrac{SS_{AB}}{(I-1)(J-1)} = \dfrac{268.47}{18} = 14.92$

4. $SS_w = (31)^2 + (27)^2 + \ldots + (26)^2 - \dfrac{(58)^2 + (47)^2 + \ldots + (57)^2}{2} = 71{,}971$

$\qquad - 71{,}733.50 = 237.50$

$MS_w = \dfrac{SS_w}{IJ(n-1)} = \dfrac{237.50}{30} = 7.92$

Once again it is by way of the expected values of mean squares that we can see how various ratios of mean squares bear on the question of whether or not a null hypothesis is true. The expected values—long-run average values over replications of the experiment in Table 18.4 with different schools and classrooms each time, for example—of the mean squares in Table 18.5 are given in Table 18.7.

TABLE 18.7   EXPECTED VALUES OF MEAN SQUARES IN THE TWO-FACTOR MIXED-EFFECTS MODEL

Mean square	E(MS)
MS_A (fixed factor)	$\sigma^2 + n\sigma_{\alpha b}^2 + \dfrac{nJ \sum_{i=1}^{I} \alpha_i^2}{I-1}$
MS_B (random factor)	$\sigma^2 + nI\sigma_b^2$
MS_{AB} (mixed interaction)	$\sigma^2 + n\sigma_{\alpha b}^2$
MS_w	σ^2

The expected mean squares in Table 18.7 present a far different picture from the $E(MS)$'s for the two-factor fixed-effects model. Particularly, the variance of the interaction effects, $\sigma_{\alpha b}^2$, that appears in $E(MS_A)$ looks unusual at first. The presence of $\sigma_{\alpha b}^2$ in $E(MS_A)$ was anticipated in our discussion of comparing $\bar{X}_{1..}$ and $\bar{X}_{2..}$, the difference between which contained $\bar{e}_{1..} - \bar{e}_{2..}$ [from which we obtain σ^2 in $E(MS_A)$] and $\overline{\alpha b_{1.}} - \overline{\alpha b_{2.}}$ [from which we obtain $\sigma_{\alpha b}^2$ in $E(MS_A)$]. No comparable situation existed in the two-factor fixed model; there it was seen that summing across any one row would "add out" the J interaction effects since

$$\sum_{j=1}^{J} \alpha\beta_{ij} = 0.$$

Consider first the problem of testing the null hypothesis that all the α_i's are zero, i.e.,

$$H_0: \sum_{i=1}^{I} \alpha_i^2 = 0.$$

You must repress what is perhaps your first inclination to divide MS_A by MS_w and refer the ratio to the F-distribution. Notice that MS_A/MS_w does not bear directly on the question of whether

$$\sum_{i=1}^{I} \alpha_i^2$$

is zero or not. The quantity $\sum \alpha_i^2$ could be zero and yet MS_A/MS_w might be large because $\sigma_{\alpha b}^2$ is not zero. The difference between MS_A and MS_w estimates $n\sigma_{\alpha b}^2 + nJ \sum \alpha_i^2/(I-1)$ instead of just $nJ \sum \alpha_i^2/(I-1)$, as it did in the two-factor fixed model. It can be seen by inspecting the above expected mean squares that $E(MS_A)$ differs from $E(MS_{AB})$ only in that term, $\sum \alpha_i^2$, which is being tested. Thus, the size of the discrepancy between MS_A and MS_{AB}, or the ratio of MS_A to MS_{AB}, bears on the size of $\sum \alpha_i^2$. More specifically, *given the assumptions of the mixed-effects model (particularly assumption 4), $F = MS_A/MS_{AB}$ will have the F-distribution with degrees of freedom $I - 1$ and $(I - 1)(J - 1)$ if*

$$H_0: \sum \alpha_i^2 = 0$$

is true. A positive value of $\sum \alpha_i^2$ will tend to inflate MS_A above MS_{AB} and give values of $F = MS_A/MS_{AB}$ that are larger than the typical values in the $F_{I-1,(I-1)(J-1)}$ distribution.

Though the null hypothesis $H_0: \sigma_b^2 = 0$ is of less interest than the hypothesis about the fixed main effects, it can be tested by referring the ratio $F = MS_B/MS_w$ to the table of the F-distribution with $J - 1$ and $IJ(n - 1)$ degrees of freedom. Moreover, σ_b^2 can be estimated by $(MS_B - MS_w)/(nI)$, which is unbiased. The $1 - \alpha$ confidence interval on σ_b^2/σ^2 can be constructed by using Eq. (18.11) of Sec. 18.2; MS_B, nI, and $F_{J-1,IJ(n-1)}$ are substituted for MS_b, n, and $F_{J-1,J(n-1)}$ in that equation.

The null hypothesis $H_0: \sigma_{\alpha b}^2 = 0$ may be tested by referring $F =$

MS_{AB}/MS_w to the F-distribution with $(I-1)(J-1)$ and $IJ(n-1)$ degrees of freedom.

For the data in Table 18.4, the three null hypotheses mentioned above have been tested at the .05 level of significance. The results appear in Table 18.8.

TABLE 18.8   NULL HYPOTHESIS TESTS FOR THE DATA IN TABLE 18.4

Null hypothesis	F-ratio	Critical F ($\alpha = .05$)	Decision
$H_0: \sum_{i=1}^{I} \alpha_i^2 = 0$	$F = \dfrac{MS_A}{MS_{AB}} = \dfrac{260.27}{14.92} = 17.44$	$_{.95}F_{2,18} = 3.55$	Reject H_0
$H_0: \sigma_b^2 = 0$	$F = \dfrac{MS_B}{MS_w} = \dfrac{228.85}{7.92} = 28.90$	$_{.95}F_{9,30} = 2.21$	Reject H_0
$H_0: \sigma_{\alpha b}^2 = 0$	$F = \dfrac{MS_{AB}}{MS_w} = \dfrac{14.92}{7.92} = 1.88$	$_{.95}F_{18,30} = 1.95$	Do not reject H_0

We see in Table 18.8 that the main effects for both the fixed and random factors are quite statistically significant. The test for interaction is significant with an α of .10 but not at the .05 level. It would now be legitimate to apply the Tukey method of multiple comparisons, which was discussed in Chapter 16, to factor A ("science curricula") to determine which pairs of means differ significantly. In place of MS_w with $J(n-1)$ degrees of freedom that are used in the Tukey method in the one-factor ANOVA, one uses MS_{AB} with $(I-1)(J-1)$ degrees of freedom (Scheffé, 1959, p. 270).

The two-factor mixed-effects ANOVA model with $n = 1$, i.e., one observation per cell, is frequently encountered. For example, six persons (random factor B) may each be observed under four treatment conditions (fixed factor A), as shown in Fig. 18.2. This design is commonly referred to as a *reqeated measures design*, because observations of persons are made several times instead of once. In general, an observation in the repeated measures design is denoted by X_{ij}, i indicating the row in which an observation lies and j indicating its column. The mean squares between rows (the fixed

Persons
(j)

		1	2	3	4	5	6
	1	X_{11}	X_{12}	X_{13}	X_{14}	X_{15}	X_{16}
Treatments	2	X_{21}	X_{22}	X_{23}	X_{24}	X_{25}	X_{26}
(i)	3	X_{31}	X_{32}	X_{33}	X_{34}	X_{35}	X_{36}
	4	X_{41}	X_{42}	X_{43}	X_{44}	X_{45}	X_{46}

FIG. 18.2

factor), between columns (the random factor), and for the interaction of rows and columns can all be calculated by means of the computational formulas in Table 18.5 by letting $n = 1$ and dropping out the index k and all summations over it. Since $n = 1$, there are $IJ(n - 1) = 0$ degrees of freedom for variation within cells; thus, the variance of scores around the mean of the ijth cell cannot be estimated. The analysis of variance table for the sources of variation that do exist appears as Table 18.9.

TABLE 18.9   ANOVA TABLE FOR THE TWO-WAY MIXED-EFFECTS ANOVA WITH $n = 1$

Source of variation	df	E(MS)
Factor A (fixed factor)	$I - 1$	$\sigma^2 + \sigma_{\alpha b}^2 + \dfrac{J \sum\limits_{i}^{I} \alpha_i^2}{I - 1}$
Factor B (random factor)	$J - 1$	$\sigma^2 + \sigma_b^2$
Interaction of A and B	$(I - 1)(J - 1)$	$\sigma^2 + \sigma_{\alpha b}^2$

If we assume that the I levels of the fixed factor would all correlate equally in the population of persons (the random factor), then $F = MS_A/MS_{AB}$ will have an F-distribution with $I - 1$ and $(I - 1)(J - 1)$ degrees of freedom when H_0: $\sum \alpha_i^2 = 0$ is true. Hence, $F = MS_A/MS_{AB}$ can be compared with $_{1-\alpha}F_{I-1,(I-1)(J-1)}$ to test H_0 at the α-level of significance.

No tests of the null hypotheses H_0: σ_b^2 and H_0: $\sigma_{\alpha b}^2 = 0$ are possible in the mixed-effects model when $n = 1$.

An important assumption for the test of H_0: $\sum \alpha_i^2 = 0$ to be valid in the mixed model is that the correlations of all pairs of levels of the fixed factor across the population of random factor levels must be the same. Violations of this assumption work to increase the actual probability of a type I error above the value believed to hold, the "nominal" value. When heterogeneous correlations among the pairs of levels of the fixed factor are suspected, special measures must be taken to insure the validity of the F-test of the null hypothesis about the fixed main effects. Box (1954b) showed that the effect of heterogeneous correlations of the fixed factor levels was to produce a sampling distribution of $F = MS_A/MS_{AB}$ that has degrees of freedom *less than* $I - 1$ and $(I - 1)(J - 1)$ when H_0 is true. Greenhouse and Geisser (1959) showed that, at worst, the degrees of freedom could only be reduced to 1 and $J - 1$ for the sampling distribution of $F = MS_A/MS_{AB}$ under a true null hypothesis. (Also see Lana and Lubin, 1963.) These findings suggested a contingent hypothesis testing procedure that should be used if heterogeneous correlations are suspected:

1. If $F = MS_A/MS_{AB}$ exceeds the $1 - \alpha$ percentile point in the F-

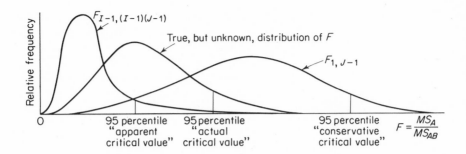

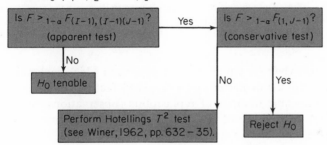

To test H_0: $\mu_1 = \mu_2 = \ldots = \mu_I$:

FIG. 18.3   Schematic diagrams of the analysis of the repeated measures design.

distribution with 1 and $J - 1$ degrees of freedom, reject H_0: $\sum \alpha_i^2 = 0$ at the α-level of significance.   (The *conservative test*.)

2. If $F = MS_A/MS_{AB}$ falls below the $1 - \alpha$ percentile point in the F-distribution with $I - 1$ and $(I - 1)(J - 1)$ degrees of freedom, do not reject H_0: $\sum \alpha_i^2 = 0$ at the α-level of significance.   (The *apparent test*.)

3. If $F = MS_A/MS_{AB}$ falls between $_{1-\alpha}F_{1,J-1}$ and $_{1-\alpha}F_{I-1,(I-1)(J-1)}$, one must resort to a multivariate technique known as *Hotelling's T^2 test* (see Scheffé, 1959, or Winer, 1962).

The strategy for analyzing a repeated measures design is depicted in Fig. 18.3.

18.4
RULES OF THUMB FOR
WRITING THE ANOVA TABLE

The following sections of this chapter consist of a collection of "rules of thumb" for finding all entries in an analysis of variance (ANOVA) table for a

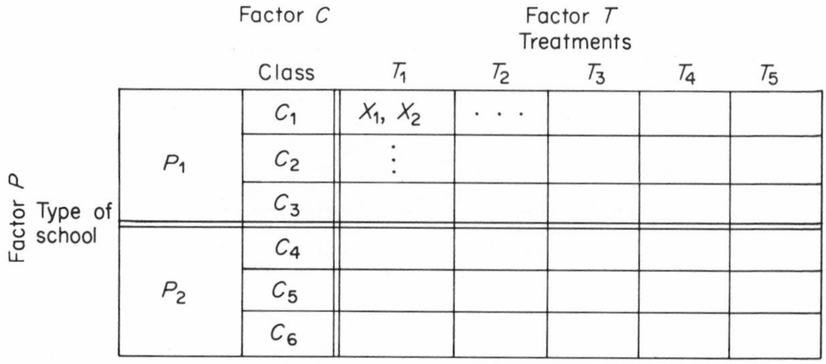

| Factor C | | Factor T Treatments | | | | |
	Class	T_1	T_2	T_3	T_4	T_5
P_1	C_1	X_1, X_2	$\cdots$			
	C_2	$\vdots$				
	C_3					
P_2	C_4					
	C_5					
	C_6					

Factor P Type of school

FIG. 18.4   Data layout of the example used to illustrate the application of the ANOVA rules of thumb.

large class of ANOVA models.* For designs in which each pair of factors is completely crossed or nested, in which each factor is random or fixed, and in which the same number of replications (observations) are taken within the smallest subdivision of the design (cell), rules are provided that specify the possible sources of variation, the associated degrees of freedom, computational formulas for sums of squares, and expectations of mean squares. If you master these simple rules you will hopefully come to regard complex analyses of variance as less inconvenient and be encouraged to attempt them when they are appropriate.

Many sources exist that provide rules of thumb for finding some of the entries in an ANOVA table from some of the designs considered here (e.g., see Bennett and Franklin, 1954; Cornfield and Tukey, 1956; Guenther, 1964; Henderson, 1959; Scheffé, 1959; Schultz, 1955; Winer, 1962). None of them, however, duplicates the coverage of this section, although the somewhat inaccessible Henderson (1959) paper is the most similar to the presentation to follow.

The following experiment involving six classrooms will be used to illustrate the application of the rules presented. Three of six classrooms included in an experiment are from public schools (P_1) and three from private schools (P_2). Each classroom was administered five treatments. Suppose that each class was split into 10 subgroups at random and that two subgroups responded independently under each of the five treatments. Thus, two observations, X_1 and X_2, on the single dependent variable X exist for each classroom. This design is illustrated in Fig. 18.4.

---

* These sections are revised from Millman and Glass (1967).

18.5
DEFINITIONS OF TERMS

I-A. Crossed and Nested Factors

Two factors are *crossed* if every level (the different categories of a factor are called *levels*) of one of the factors appears with every level of the other factor. That is, there must be at least one observation for every possible combination of levels of factors that are completely crossed. Thus "type of school" and "treatments" (having two and five levels, respectively) crossed since there are observations taken at each of the 10 school-treatment combinations.

A factor is said to be *nested* in a second factor if each level of the first (the nested factor) appears in exactly one level of the second. In our experiment, "classroom" is nested. No classroom appears in both a public (P_1) and a private (P_2) school. If, however, the same three classrooms were involved in both P_1 and P_2, then C would not be nested in P. Nesting exists when one level of a variable does not appear with all levels of another variable. Since C_1 under P_1 is not the same class as C_4 under P_2, C_1 does not appear in both levels of P. Note that C_1 is combined with all levels of T ("treatments"); the factor "classroom" is *not* nested in T. For the purposes of this discussion, *any nested factor must have the same number of levels in each level of the factor in which it is nested.* In our illustration, there are three levels of "classroom" nested under both levels of "type of school."

II-B. Random and Fixed Factors

A factor may be considered *random* if the levels of that factor used in the study are a simple random sample from a population of levels with normally distributed effects. "Students" and "classrooms" are two factors frequently considered random. Results of an ANOVA may be generalized to the population of levels of a random factor. When all levels of a factor are in the study (e.g., male-female or high-average-low), when only the levels of interest to the investigator are in the study (e.g., method A and method B where the other methods are not of interest), or when a systematic selection of levels is used, the factor is considered *fixed*. Results of an ANOVA may be generalized only to the population of replications of the experiment in which the specific levels of the fixed factor included in the study are present. For example, a study that systematically selected grades three, six, nine, and 12 can generalize its results only to those four grades.

Actually, the status (fixed or random) of a factor depends as much upon the population of replications of a study to which one wishes to generalize as it does upon the way in which the levels were chosen. Five levels of a factor could be randomly sampled from a virtually infinite population of levels, but the factor would be "fixed" if one made inferences to replications of the study in which only those five levels chosen appear. This is an abstruse point about which we will have no more to say.

In our example, "classrooms" is considered a random factor, and "type of school" and "treatments" are fixed. We shall also call "replication" within the smallest cell of a design a nested factor that is always random and is nested within *all* the other factors of the design. *This point is important and allows us to specify rules of thumb that are simpler than many others proposed.*

18.6
DETERMINING THE POSSIBLE LINES (SOURCES OF VARIATION) OF THE ANOVA TABLE

II-A. Notation

1. The source of variation for a factor that is not nested within any other factors is denoted by a capital letter, e.g., $A, B, C, \ldots$.

2. The source of variation for a nested factor is denoted by a capital letter followed by a colon and then the letter or letters denoting the factors within which it is nested, e.g., $A:B$ for factor A nested within factor B.

3. The source of variation for an interaction is denoted by a combination of letters identifying the interacting factors followed by a colon and the letter or letters of the factors within which the interaction is nested, e.g., AB or $AB:C$.

II-B. Rules

1. The ANOVA table has one line for each factor both crossed and nested (this includes the factor "replications").

2. The ANOVA table has one line for all possible (two factor, three factor, etc.) interactions among factors. To determine which interactions can exist, all possible pairs, trios, etc. of factors are formed by the following rules (if there is no nesting other than "replications," there will be $2^k - k - 1$ such interactions, where k is the number of crossed factors):
   a. In the symbol denoting the interaction, write to the left of the colon the letters to the left of the colons in the factors being combined. (If no colon appears in the notation for a factor, it is understood to be at the right of all letters.)
   b. Write following the colon, but with no repetition of a letter,

those letters to the right of the colons in the factors being combined.

  c. Delete any combination having a letter to the left of the colon that is repeated to the right of the colon.

II-C. Illustration of the Rules Under II-B (for the example in Sec. 18.3)

1. P (types of school), T (treatments), $C:P$ (classrooms nested within P), and $R:PCT$ (replications nested within P, C, T combinations) represent the crossed and nested factors and are lines in the table by rule II-B.1.

2. The possible interactions among the factors above include:
PT which is retained and may be written TP.
$PC:P$ which is deleted because P appears both before and after the colon (rule II-B.2c).
$TC:P$ which is retained and may be written $CT:P$.
$PTC:P$ which is also deleted because P appears both before and after the colon.
All the interactions involving $R:PCT$ are deleted because of rule II-B.2c.

3. Thus, the lines of the ANOVA table in our example consist of P, $C:P$, T, PT, $CT:P$, and $R:PCT$.

18.7
DETERMINING THE DEGREES OF FREEDOM FOR SOURCES OF VARIATION

III-A. Notation

1. The number of levels of a factor not nested within any other factor is denoted by the lower case of the letter identifying the factor. In our example, $p = 2$ and $t = 5$.

2. The number of levels of a nested factor within *each* level or combination of levels of the factors in which it is nested is denoted by the lower case of the letter to the left of the colon identifying the nested factor. For example, in the nested classification $C:P$, the number of levels of C in each level of P is denoted by c, which is 3 in our example. In the nested classification $R:PCT$, r denotes the number of replications within a cell, which equals 2 in our example.

3. The total number of observations N equals the product of all the lower case letters for the crossed and nested classifications. In our example, this number is $p \times c \times t \times r = 2 \times 3 \times 5 \times 2 = 60$.

III-B. Rules

1. Let a lower case letter correspond to each capital letter. The degrees of freedom for any line in the ANOVA table are found by subtracting one from each lower case letter to the left of the colon and multiplying the grand product of these differences by the grand product of the lower case letters to the right of the colon.

2. As a check, the computed degrees of freedom should add to $N - 1$.

III-C. Illustration of the Rules Under III-B (for the example in Sec. 18.3)

1. The degrees of freedom for $P = p - 1 = (2 - 1) = 1$.
   The degrees of freedom for $C:P = (c - 1)p = (3 - 1)2 = 4$.
   The degrees of freedom for $T = (t - 1) = (5 - 1) = 4$.
   The degrees of freedom for

$$PT = (p - 1)(t - 1) = (2 - 1)(5 - 1) = 4.$$

   The degrees of freedom for

$$CT:P = (c - 1)(t - 1)p = (3 - 1)(5 - 1)2 = 16.$$

   The degrees of freedom for

$$R:PCT = (r - 1)pct = (2 - 1)(2)(3)(5) = 30.$$

2. As a check, $1 + 4 + 4 + 4 + 16 + 30 = N - 1 = 59$.

18.8 COMPUTING SUMS OF SQUARES

IV-A. Notation

1. Capital letter X will be used to denote an observation on the dependent variable and will have as subscripts all the different lower case letters used in expressing degrees of freedom. For example, X_{pctr} is used to denote a general observation in our example.

2. Lower case letters will also be used to denote the upper limits of subscripts. For example, $t = 1, 2, \ldots, t$, which means that the levels of variable t are 1, 2, up to the tth level, which is five in our example.

IV-B. Rules

1. For each line in the ANOVA table write down the degrees of

freedom (df) in their symbolic form (i.e., using lower case letters) and expand algebraically. For example, the line PT has degrees of freedom $(p-1)(t-1)$ which equals $+pt-p-t+1$. The computational formula for the sum of squares of a source of variation will consist of as many terms as there are terms in the expanded symbolic expression for the degrees of freedom (four terms in the case of the PT interaction), and these terms will have the same algebraic signs as their corresponding terms in the symbolic expression for the df [$+$, $-$, $-$, and $+$ in the case of the expansion of $(p-1)(t-1)$ shown above].

2. For each term in the expanded algebraic representation for the df write a multiple summation corresponding to each subscript of the general observation. Precede the summation with the algebraic sign of the term to which it corresponds. For example, for the term $+pt$ in the algebraic expansion of $(p-1)(t-1)$ one would write

$$+ \sum_{1}^{p} \sum_{1}^{t} \sum_{1}^{c} \sum_{1}^{r} X_{ptcr}.$$

3. For each multiple summation expression, place within parentheses X and those summation signs whose upper limits do *not* appear in the corresponding term in the expanded expression for the df. For example, for the term $+pt$ one would place the parentheses as follows:

$$+ \sum_{1}^{p} \sum_{1}^{t} \left(\sum_{1}^{c} \sum_{1}^{r} X_{ptcr} \right).$$

4. Square the expression inside the parentheses and divide by the total number of observations summed over to get the quantity inside the parentheses. This number will be the product of the upper limits of the summation signs inside the parentheses. If no summation sign appears inside the parentheses, one "sums" over 1 value, so the term is divided by 1. The part of the computational formula for the PT interaction that corresponds to the $+pt$ term is then

$$+ \frac{\sum_{1}^{p} \sum_{1}^{t} \left(\sum_{1}^{c} \sum_{1}^{r} X_{ptcr} \right)^{2}}{cr}.$$

IV-C. Illustration of the Rules Under IV-B (for the example in Sec. 18.3)

In Sec. 18.7 above, six sources of variation were identified for the example problem. Thus, six sums of squares must be calculated in the analysis of the design. Only the formulas for the sums of squares PT and $R{:}PCT$ will be demonstrated. Attempt to write the remaining formulas by following rules IV-B.1 through IV-B.4. Four subscripts are needed to denote a general observation: X_{pctr}.

1. Sum of squares for PT.

Rule 1. df for $(PT) = (p-1)(t-1) = pt - p - t + 1$.

Rule 2. $pt - p - t + 1$:

$$\sum_1^p \sum_1^c \sum_1^t \sum_1^r X_{pctr} - \sum_1^p \sum_1^c \sum_1^t \sum_1^r X_{pctr} - \sum_1^p \sum_1^c \sum_1^t \sum_1^r X_{pctr}$$
$$+ \sum_1^p \sum_1^c \sum_1^t \sum_1^r X_{pctr}.$$

Rule 3. $pt - p - t + 1$:

$$\sum_1^p \sum_1^t \left(\sum_1^c \sum_1^r X_{pctr} \right) - \sum_1^p \left(\sum_1^c \sum_1^t \sum_1^r X_{pctr} \right) - \sum_1^t \left(\sum_1^p \sum_1^c \sum_1^r X_{pctr} \right)$$
$$+ \left(\sum_1^p \sum_1^t \sum_1^c \sum_1^r X_{pctr} \right).$$

Rule 4. $pt - p - t + 1$:

$$\frac{\sum_1^p \sum_1^t \left(\sum_1^c \sum_1^r X_{pctr} \right)^2}{cr} - \frac{\sum_1^p \left(\sum_1^c \sum_1^t \sum_1^r X_{pctr} \right)^2}{ctr}$$
$$- \frac{\sum_1^t \left(\sum_1^p \sum_1^c \sum_1^r X_{pctr} \right)^2}{pcr} + \frac{\left(\sum_1^p \sum_1^c \sum_1^t \sum_1^r X_{pctr} \right)^2}{pctr}.$$

The result of the application of rule 4 above is the computational formula for the sum of squares for the interaction of factors P and T.

2. Sum of squares for $R:PCT$.

Rule 1. df for $(R:PCT) = (r-1)pct = pctr - pct$.

Rule 2. $pctr - pct$:

$$\sum_1^p \sum_1^c \sum_1^t \sum_1^r X_{pctr} - \sum_1^p \sum_1^c \sum_1^t X_{pctr}.$$

Rule 3. $pctr - pct$:

$$\sum_1^p \sum_1^c \sum_1^t \sum_1^r (X_{pctr}) - \sum_1^p \sum_1^c \sum_1^t \left(\sum_1^r X_{pctr} \right).$$

Rule 4. $pctr - pct$:

$$\frac{\sum_1^p \sum_1^c \sum_1^t \sum_1^r (X_{pctr})^2}{1} - \frac{\sum_1^p \sum_1^c \sum_1^t \left(\sum_1^r X_{pctr} \right)^2}{r}.$$

The preceding formula yields the sum of squares for replications (or "within").

18.9
DETERMINING THE
EXPECTATIONS OF MEAN
SQUARES

V-A. Notation

1. The symbol σ^2, having to the left of the colon in its subscript *only* lower case letters corresponding to random or finite factors, denotes the variance of a random variable underlying those random and finite factors. For example, $\sigma^2_{c:p}$ denotes the variance of the effects associated with all the classrooms (C) included in the population of classrooms found in a particular type of school (P).

2. The symbol σ^2, having included to the left of the colon in its subscript lower case letters corresponding to fixed factors, denotes a function of the sum of the squared effects of the variables represented to the left of the colon.* For·example, σ^2_t denotes a function of squared fixed effects associated with treatments, e.g., $\sigma^2_t = \sum \alpha_i^2 / (I - 1)$.

V-B. Rules

1. Unless deleted by rule V-B.2 below, the expectation of a mean square of any factor contains a σ^2 for each line in the ANOVA table that has in its denotation all the letters denoting the mean square under consideration.

2. Certain of the σ^2 components of an expectation for a mean square given in V-B.1 above vanish according to the following rule: any σ^2 having to the left of the colon a letter denoting a fixed classification disappears except when the source of variation of the mean square includes this letter. Remember, if there is no colon in the subscript, the colon is by definition at the right of all letters.

3. The coefficient of a particular σ^2 in a particular mean square includes the product of all the lower case letters not found in the subscript of σ^2.

* Although it has become customary to adopt the σ^2 notation, the reader should keep in mind that for factors or combinations of factors involving fixed factors, the σ^2 is *not* a variance of a random variable; it is related to a sum of squared constants (the fixed effects).

V-C. Illustrations of the Rules Under V-B (for the example in Sec. 18.3)

One way of determining the expected values of mean squares is first to list all possible σ^2, then to eliminate selected σ^2 by rule V-B.1, then eliminate more σ^2 by rule V-B.2, and finally to attach coefficients to the remaining components by rule V-B.3. This procedure will be followed here.

1. The expected mean square for any line *could* contain σ_p^2, σ_t^2, $\sigma_{c:p}^2$ σ_{pt}^2, and $\sigma_{ct:p}^2$ as well as $\sigma_{r:pct}^2$.* In the $E(MS)$ for P, delete σ_t^2 because σ_t^2 does not have a p among its subscripts (rule V-B.1).
   In the $E(MS)$ for $C:P$, eliminate σ_p^2, σ_t^2, and σ_{pt}^2 because none of these has *both* a c and a p among its subscripts (rule V-B.1).
   In the $E(MS)$ for T, eliminate σ_p^2 and $\sigma_{c:p}^2$ (rule V-B.1).
   In the $E(MS)$ for PT, eliminate σ_p^2, $\sigma_{c:p}^2$, and σ_t^2 (rule V-B.1).
   In the $E(MS)$ for $CT:P$ eliminate all σ^2 except $\sigma_{ct:p}^2$ and σ^2 since none contains all the letters c, t, and p in its subscripts (rule V-B.1).
   In the $E(MS)$ for $R:CTP$, eliminate all σ^2 except σ^2, since none contains all the letters c, t, p, and r (rule V-B.1).

2. Recall that C and R are considered random, P and T fixed. In addition to σ^2, the $E(MS)$ for P so far contains σ_p^2, $\sigma_{c:p}^2$, σ_{pt}^2, and $\sigma_{ct:p}^2$. Now σ_p^2 contains fixed factor P to the left of the colon, but the mean square under consideration (P) contains (is) this letter, so σ_p^2 stays. $\sigma_{c:p}^2$ contains only random factor C to the left of the colon, so $\sigma_{c:p}^2$ also stays. σ_{pt}^2 contains *fixed* factor t to the left of the colon *and* t is not part of the mean square under consideration (P), so σ_{pt}^2 is eliminated. For the same reason $\sigma_{ct:p}^2$ is eliminated. σ^2 (that is, $\sigma_{r:ptc}^2$) always remains since only the random factor R is to the left of the colon.
   In addition to σ^2, the $E(MS)$ for $C:P$ contains so far only $\sigma_{c:p}^2$ and $\sigma_{ct:p}^2$. $\sigma_{c:p}^2$ is retained because C is random, and it is also retained since c is part of $C:P$. However, $\sigma_{ct:p}^2$ contains t to the left of the colon and T is *both fixed and* t is not part of the mean square under consideration $(C:P)$. Thus $\sigma_{ct:p}^2$ is eliminated.
   In addition to σ^2, the $E(MS)$ for T contains so far σ_t^2, σ_{pt}^2, and $\sigma_{ct:p}^2$. σ_t^2 is retained because t is part of T. σ_{pt}^2 is eliminated because P is *fixed and* p is not part of T, the mean square under consideration. $\sigma_{ct:p}^2$ survives because C is random. Note that p is to the *right* of the colon, and thus not affected by rule V-B.2.

---

* The expected mean square $E(MS)$ for the random factor replications within the smallest cell is usually denoted simply as σ^2 or σ_e^2 (*e* for "error"). This practice has been followed here. σ^2 always appears as a source of variation even if $r = 1$, in which case there are no degrees of freedom for this source.

Similarly, it can be shown that the $E(MS)$ for PT is σ^2, σ^2_{pt}, and $\sigma^2_{ct:p}$; and the $E(MS)$ for $CT:P$ is σ^2 and $\sigma^2_{ct:p}$.

3. The coefficients of the surviving components are found by a straightforward application of rule V-B.3. For example, the coefficient of $\sigma^2_{c:p}$ is $(t \times r) = (5)(2) = 10$. See Table 18.10 for the final results.

TABLE 18.10   SUMMARY ANOVA TABLE (FOR THE EXAMPLE IN SEC. 18.3)

Source of variation	df		$E(MS)$
P	$(p-1)$	$= 1$	$\sigma^2 + 10\sigma^2_{c:p} \qquad\qquad + 30\sigma^2_p$
$C:P$	$p(c-1)$	$= 4$	$\sigma^2 + 10\sigma^2_{c:p}$
T	$(t-1) =$	4	$\sigma^2 \qquad\qquad + 2\sigma^2_{ct:p} + 12\sigma^2_t$
PT	$(p-1)(t-1) =$	4	$\sigma^2 \qquad\qquad + 2\sigma^2_{ct:p} + 6\sigma^2_{pt}$
$CT:P$	$p(c-1)(t-1) =$	16	$\sigma^2 \qquad\qquad + 2\sigma^2_{ct:p}$
$R:PCT$	$pct(r-1)$	$= 30$	σ^2
Total	$pctr - 1 = N - 1 =$	$\overline{59}$	

18.10
SIGNIFICANCE TESTING

It is usually the researcher's purpose to test one or more null hypotheses, i.e., that particular variance components, fixed effects, or mixed effects are zero. To test any one such hypothesis, one first identifies the source of variation corresponding to the variance component, fixed effect, or mixed effect in question. The mean square for this source of variation becomes the numerator of the F-ratio, the test statistic used in testing the null hypothesis. One then determines what the expected value of this mean square is *when the variance component, fixed effect, or mixed effect in question is zero*. Call this new expected value, $E(MS \mid H_0 \text{ true})$. The denominator of the F-ratio is the mean square that has the expected value $E(MS \mid H_0 \text{ true})$. In other words, the null hypothesis is tested with the ratio of two mean squares such that both would have the same expected value if the null hypothesis in question were true. (The mean square in the numerator corresponds to the source of variation being tested.)

Suppose in our example we were interested in the hypothesis that $\sigma^2_p = 0$. Since the expected value of the mean square for P contains σ^2_p and since the expected value of P equals the expected value of $C:P$ when $\sigma^2_p = 0$, the ratio of the mean square for P to the mean square for $C:P$ is appropriate for testing the hypothesis that $\sigma^2_p = 0$.

If no appropriate F-ratio exists for testing an effect, approximate methods are sometimes applicable. (See, e.g., Winer, 1962, pp. 199–202.)

In spite of the fact that the above significance testing procedures are common practice, a somewhat more enlightened skepticism concerning the distribution properties of F-ratios in mixed designs (i.e., having both fixed and random factors) would seem to be called for by the considerations raised in Sec. 18.2 concerning mixed model assumptions and in Scheffé (1959, chap. 8) for example.

PROBLEMS AND EXERCISES

1. A random sample of $J = 10$ judges was drawn from a population of judges. Each judge rated an independent random sample of $n = 20$ children on a 7 point scale of "emotional adjustment." The analysis of variance yielded the following results:

Source of variance	df	MS	E(MS)
Between judges	9	10.48	$\sigma^2 + 20\sigma_a^2$
Within judges	190	9.64	σ^2

   a. Estimate the variance of judges, σ_a^2, from the above data.
   b. Compare the sizes of $\hat{\sigma}_a^2$ and $\hat{\sigma}^2$. Who differs more, children being rated by the same judge or judges on the average across all children?
   c. Establish the 95% confidence interval on σ_a^2/σ^2.

2. A population of 30,000 spelling words is identified. A measurement researcher is interested in the variability to be expected among 50-item spelling tests that could be formed from the pool of 30,000 words. The total number of possible 50-item tests is equal to the combinations of 30,000 items taken 50 at a time, i.e., $C_{50}^{30,000}$, which is a staggeringly large number. The researcher constructs six 50-item spelling tests by randomly sampling items from the item pool. Thus, the six tests can be considered to be randomly sampled from the population of all possible 50-item tests. Each test is given to an independent random sample of $n = 12$ pupils. The following test scores (total number of correct spellings out of 50) are obtained:

			Test		
1	*2*	*3*	*4*	*5*	*6*
21	34	44	12	30	27
14	19	31	26	18	32
11	26	36	22	14	26
27	31	24	30	29	29
19	39	40	35	36	34
32	42	38	14	27	20
21	27	42	19	30	15
23	14	35	24	25	25
18	25	27	23	25	31
25	29	29	31	20	39
24	33	30	27	32	23
23	36	33	25	19	29

   a. Using the one-factor random-effects ANOVA, calculate the estimate of the variance among all possible spelling means, $\hat{\sigma}_a^2$, and the estimate of the variance of pupils' scores within any spelling test, $\hat{\sigma}^2$. That is, calculate

$$\hat{\sigma}_a^2 = \frac{MS_A - MS_w}{12} \quad \text{and} \quad \hat{\sigma}^2 = MS_w.$$

b. Calculate the 95% confidence interval around $\hat{\sigma}_a^2/\hat{\sigma}^2$ on σ_a^2/σ^2.

3. In a two-factor random-effects ANOVA with I levels of factor A, J levels of factor B, and n observations per cell, the expected values of the mean squares are as follows:

$$E(MS_A) = \sigma^2 + n\sigma_{ab}^2 + nJ\sigma_a^2,$$
$$E(MS_B) = \sigma^2 + n\sigma_{ab}^2 + nI\sigma_b^2,$$
$$E(MS_{AB}) = \sigma^2 + n\sigma_{ab}^2,$$
$$E(MS_w) = \sigma^2.$$

Find a linear combination of the mean squares that provides an unbiased estimator of σ_a^2. [Hint: Notice how σ_b^2 can be estimated:

$$E\frac{MS_B - MS_{AB}}{nI} = \frac{E(MS_B) - E(MS_{AB})}{nI}$$
$$= \frac{\sigma^2 + n\sigma_{ab}^2 + nI\sigma_b^2 - \sigma^2 - n\sigma_{ab}^2}{nI} = \frac{nI\sigma_b^2}{nI} = \sigma_b^2.]$$

4. It has often been maintained that neurologically handicapped children evidence a lower Performance IQ than Verbal IQ on the Wechsler Intelligence Scale for Children (WISC). Hopkins (1964) compared the Verbal and Performance IQ's for a group of about 30 children ranging in age from six years to 12 years who were diagnosed as neurologically handicapped independently of the intelligence testing. The following data were obtained:

Person	Verbal IQ	Performance IQ	Person	Verbal IQ	Performance IQ
1	87	83	16	83	85
2	80	89	17	83	77
3	95	100	18	92	84
4	116	117	19	95	85
5	77	86	20	100	95
6	81	97	21	85	99
7	106	114	22	89	90
8	97	90	23	86	93
9	103	89	24	86	100
10	109	80	25	103	94
11	79	106	26	80	100
12	103	96	27	99	107
13	126	121	28	101	82
14	101	93	29	72	106
15	113	82	30	96	108

Consider the "Persons" to be a random factor and the "Verbal IQ vs. Performance IQ" to be a fixed factor. Using the mixed-effects ANOVA model, test the null hypothesis at the .05 level that populations of Verbal and Performance IQ's have the same mean for neurologically handicapped children. (The F-test will lead to the same decision that would be arrived at if a dependent-groups t-test of the hypothesis $\mu_1 = \mu_2$ were made.)

5. Scores on the Information, Vocabulary, Digit Span, and Block Design subtests of the Wechsler Intelligence Scale for Children are tabulated below for a group of 12 neurologically handicapped children (Hopkins, 1964):

| | | Test | | |
Person	Infor.	Voc.	Dig. S.	Bl. Des.
1	7	8	7	7
2	5	10	8	12
3	9	11	9	11
4	17	18	9	13
5	4	7	7	9
6	6	9	8	11
7	11	11	7	7
8	10	14	12	7
9	8	11	7	13
10	12	11	5	9
11	13	16	6	18
12	11	10	11	5

WISC subtest scores are scaled to a mean of 10 and standard deviation of 3 for the general population. It has often been asserted that patterns of subtest scores on the WISC can be used to diagnose neurological handicaps. Test the null hypothesis that the twelve test scores above were randomly sampled from four normal distributions with the same mean.

The design should be regarded as a repeated measures design; hence, in performing the F-test use the flow chart in Fig. 18.3.

6. Twenty raters are drawn at random from a population of 10,000 raters. Thirty-two ratees are drawn at random from a population of 20,000 ratees. Eight traits are "drawn at random" from a population of eight traits (i.e., *all* traits of interest to the investigator for this particular study are used). Each of the 20 raters rated each of the 32 ratees once on each of the eight traits in a well-conducted study.

a. How many ratings does this yield?
b. Which factors are "random" and which "fixed"? Are any factors "nested" within any other factors? Which?
c. How many sources of variation are there in these ratings? List them.
d. Using the rules of thumb given in the chapter, work out all the expected mean squares for this design, indicate the appropriate ratio of mean squares and the degrees of freedom for each F, and provide the formulas for estimating all estimable components of variance.

For another way to analyze data from this particular design, see Stanley (1961*b*).

7. Two raters who were Democrats and two raters who were Republicans each rated three ratees who were prominent Democrats and three ratees who were prominent Republicans on each of four different traits. This yielded a total of $2 \times 2 \times 2 \times 3 \times 4 = 96$ ratings. The design is shown below. There are five factors, two of which are "nested."

Party of ratee	Ratee number	Trait rated, Party of rater, Rater number															
		Intelligence				Honesty				Friendliness				Generosity			
		D		R		D		R		D		R		D		R	
		1	2	3	4	1	2	3	4	1	2	3	4	1	2	3	4
R	1	7	6	8	7	8	2	8	7	5	1	8	2	5	0	10	5
	2	7	7.	6	7	7	6	6	6	6	6	9	1	5	6	8	2
	3	6	6	4	5	8	9	8	6	10	5	9	8	9	5	10	6
D	4	8	8	6	6	9	10	3	1	8	8	7	6	9	7	4	4
	5	8	5	6	7	9	5	4	4	5	1	4	1	9	1	3	1
	6	5	4	3	3	7	8	1	0	7	7	8	4	7	8	0	0

a. Identify the two nested factors. Within what is each such factor nested?
b. Do the nested factors "cross" any other factors? Which ones?
c. Which factors does the "political party of rater" factor cross?
d. Which of the factors were probably considered as each having had its levels drawn randomly from an infinite (hypothetical) population of levels?
e. $\hat{\sigma}^2_{(\text{party of rater} \times \text{party of ratee})}$ contributed most to variation of the ratings. Would you have expected this result in advance of the rating procedure? What does this interaction probably mean?
f. The second largest estimated component of variance was that for party of rater $\times$ party of ratee $\times$ trait. What does this three-factor interaction mean? (One sometimes sees a three-factor interaction referred to as a "second-order" interaction, because a zero-order "interaction" would be a main effect, not interacting with anything. Thus a two-factor interaction such as that in (e), above, may be called a "first-order" interaction.)
    For further results, see Stanley (1961a).

19

FUNDAMENTALS
OF
EXPERIMENTAL DESIGN*

19.1
INTRODUCTION

The word "experimentation" has come to have many meanings for behavioral scientists. The most common meaning might be termed "experi*en*tation," trying new approaches and subjectively evaluating their effectiveness. In this chapter we are concerned with a more structured inquiry, akin to that carried out in many of the sciences. It involves control by the experimenter of at least one variable, such as method of teaching arithmetic, that he can *manipulate*. Thus, experimentation of this kind differs from observation of naturally occurring events in that the stage has been set by the experimenter so that the possibly differential effects of at least two "treatments" can be observed in a situation where assignment of *experimental units* (often, pupils or classes) to the several treatments has been made without bias. "Nature" almost always makes biased assignments to its treatments; even before a natural experiment, the experimental units to be subjected to one treatment are usually not comparable to those to be subjected to another treatment.

---

* For a simple, general approach to this topic see Stanley (1967*b*).

For example, as a group, smokers differ in many ways from nonsmokers, any one of which ways might be the cause of a greater incidence of lung cancer among smokers.

In brief, nature rarely assigns experimental units to treatments randomly, whereas the careful experimenter almost always does. One can define a controlled, variable-manipulating, comparative experiment as a study in which the available experimental units are assigned *at random* (either simply or restrictively) to the various treatments. More generally, if we consider each *factor* to be manipulated (e.g., several ways to teach arithmetic; sex; overt versus covert response in programmed instruction; or 100% reinforcement versus 50% reinforcement) as having two or more *levels* or categories (e.g., SMSG* curriculum versus two other ways to teach mathematics would constitute three levels of the teaching-of-mathematics factor), we can then talk about *factor-level combinations*, such as the six generated by three ways to teach mathematics *crossed* with two levels of sex (male-female). This is a 3 × 2 factorial design—one factor at three levels crossed with a second factor at two levels.

The basic experimental design involves one or more factors that are either manipulated by the experimenter, as illustrated above, or not manipulated by him (e.g., male or female sex, day of the week, height above average or below average). The levels of one factor may be crossed with those of another, or the levels of one or more factors may be *nested* within the levels of another factor. For instance, when three male raters and three female raters rate each of 10 ratees on each of seven traits, raters are nested within sex, because no male rater is also a female rater (i.e., the rater levels do not cross the sex levels, though they do cross the ratee and the trait levels). You have already seen examples of nesting in Chapter 18, including Prob. 7 at the end of that chapter.

Another example would be an experiment in which the manipulated factors were immediate reinforcement versus delayed reinforcement and 50% reinforcement versus 100% reinforcement, all levels of one factor crossing all levels of the other, with the experimental subjects (i.e., persons) classified as male versus female, blond versus brunette versus redhead, and volunteers versus nonvolunteers. The subjects would be nested within the 12 "nests" created by the intersection of sex with hair color with volunteering. One-fourth of the subjects in each nest would be assigned randomly to a given factor-level combination of the manipulated factors.

Hierarchical nesting occurs when some factors are subclasses of others; e.g., cities could be nested within counties, counties within states, and states within regions. An experimenter might assign cities at random to experimental treatments. He would then have a partly nested and partly crossed

---

* SMSG means "School Mathematics Study Group," a group composed of mathematics educators who pioneered in bringing modern mathematics to secondary-school courses in the United States.

design, with the geographical units not crossing each other but crossing the levels of the treatment factor. One then has no basis for concluding that a certain city would have done relatively better in the experiment had it been in another state.

Nesting and crossing can occur only when there are at least two factors. In a given study there may be no nesting, no crossing, all of one or the other, or a mixture of nesting and crossing, as in the above examples. Note, though, that nesting rarely occurs when all the factors are manipulated.

The term "factorial design" is taken by some statisticians to mean a fully crossed set of two or more factors, with an equal or unequal number of experimental units assigned completely randomly to each of the factor-level combinations. (See Kendall and Buckland, 1957, p. 106.) For one factor, with random assignment of n_j experimental units to each of the J levels of the factor, there would be no crossing, of course. Other definitions of factorial design include cases where only restricted assignment of the experimental units is possible, as when the N available experimental units must be considered as having been drawn from two or more different populations (e.g., men versus women); each such population defines a level of a nonmanipulated factor.

(See Stanley, 1967, pp. 204–205, for an argument about whether "randomized-block designs" are factorial designs. We shall see subsequently in this chapter that they involve full crossing of factor levels, but with the restricted randomization that necessarily results when a given experimental unit already has "tied" to it a level of a factor such as sex or school attended. No harm will be done if one refers to any design created by the crossing and/or nesting of factor levels as a factorial design, provided that distinctions among such designs that are important for interpreting the results of the experiment or status study are not overlooked.)

19.2
AN EXAMPLE

For concreteness, let us consider a controlled experiment involving four styles of printing type crossed with three sizes of printing type, a 4×3 factorial design yielding 12 factor-level combinations: each style is tried with every size, and each size is tried with every style. This is a *complete* design. If we take 12 pupils and assign one at random to each of the 12 combinations, we produce one *replicate*. Usually, as a minimum, we shall assign 24 pupils, two at random to each of the 12 combinations, and thereby create two replicates. In order to have a powerful enough experiment, we may need to assign more than two pupils to each combination. Some number of replicates, n, will yield the power we require. Methods for determining n exist.

How do we conduct this *factorial-design* experiment involving four styles crossed with these sizes? Of course, we must decide which styles and sizes to use. Probably we have firmly in mind four styles that are candidates for use in the textbook or test we plan to prepare. We also know which three sizes to try for our purposes—perhaps 8 point, 12 point, and 16 point. These four styles and three sizes produce 12 factor-level combinations that are the only ones of interest to us in this experiment. In the jargon of experimental design, we have two *fixed*-effects factors and therefore employ a *fixed-effects model*, because we have "drawn" the four styles from a target population of just four styles and the three sizes from a target population of just three sizes.

Where do we get the experimental units with which to do the experiment? We might secure a "grab-group" consisting of the first $12n$ individuals who happen our way, or we might define a population of individuals, such as all fourth graders in a large school system, and draw $12n$ individuals at random from that population. Using a grab-group limits rigorous statistical generalization from the outcome of the experiment to just those $12n$ persons, whereas drawing the experimental units randomly from a population permits statistical generalization to that population, thereby increasing *external validity*, i.e., generalizability. (We may, however, be able to generalize nonstatistically from the members of the grab-group to other persons "like them" if we know enough about the adventitiously chosen individuals to be reasonably sure that none of their characteristics determining the outcome of the experiment differ enough from those of the target population to change the results there. This is difficult to ascertain, and in any event we have no *probabilistic* warrant for generalizing from the grab-group to anyone else whatsoever.)

After we secure the $12n$ experimental units by one of the above methods, we randomly assign n of them to each of the factor-level combinations, which have common content but different combinations of style and size. We wish to vary only style and size. All other variables should be held constant (as for example, by using just males in the experiment, thereby keeping the sex factor at one level) or randomized over all 12 factor-level combinations. This is where experimental control becomes crucial. It might be practicable, for instance, to seat all $12n$ pupils randomly in the room. (That could be done by passing out random seat assignments at the door as the pupils arrived.) If a nonrandom room arrangement were used, this would have to be considered as part of the design, making it more complex than a 4×3 factorial. Control of extraneous variables calls for great care and ingenuity so that the experiment will be *internally* valid, i.e., produce comparisons that are free from bias.

After the $12n$ pupils have read the same passage with the same time limit under the same conditions except for style and size of printing type, they will be given a common test to determine how much each learned from the particular combination of style and size of type to which he was exposed. The total score of each pupil on this outcome test will constitute the observations on the *dependent variable* to be analyzed.

19.3
ADVANTAGES AND
DISADVANTAGES OF THE
FACTORIAL DESIGN

Complete, *balanced* factorial designs (designs where each of the possible factor-level combinations occurs and has $n \geq 1$ experimental units assigned to it) permit testing more than one hypothesis about *main effects* (e.g., the influence of type size or the influence of style) efficiently in the same experiment. They also make it possible, where two or more factors are used, to study how the factors interact. Perhaps the least effective of the three sizes when combined with the least effective of the four styles does not produce the least effective of the twelve factor-level combinations. If the effects are *additive*, so that knowing the effectiveness of a certain size factor level and a certain style factor level one can predict the effectiveness of that factor-level combination as well as "chance" permits, then we say that the two factors do not interact. One cannot study interaction statistically in one-factor studies, and yet appreciable interaction may greatly limit generalization of the results of one-factor experiments.

The factorial design is relatively simple. It does not require any pre-measurements or "matching" of the experimental units, because bias is avoided (in the probabilistic sense) by the random assignment of the experimental units to the factor-level combinations. On the other hand, it permits the within-factor-level-combination variability to be as great as true-score variation among individuals treated alike plus errors of measurement dictate. Thus the *signals* (the genuine effects) may be drowned out by the *noise* (the within-combination variability) if the signal-to-noise ratio is low This noise (or *error*, as it is usually called) lowers the *power* of the significance tests used and increases the width of the confidence intervals computed. True-score error can be lessened by various techniques such as *blocking*, *stratifying*, *leveling*, and *covarying*, all of which depend on classification or pre-measurement of the experimental units and are used to reduce the within-combination variability of true scores. Measurement error can be reduced somewhat by using a more reliable outcome measure.

But more important, *sampling error* in the estimation of main and interaction effects can be reduced (and thus power of significance tests increased) simply by making n larger, provided that the larger experiment can be conducted as efficiently (i.e., no greater error per observation) as the smaller one.

19.4
BLOCKING

Of course, one can often lower within-factor-level variability of the outcome measures by drawing the experimental units from a homogeneous sub-population—e.g., persons all the same age, sex, IQ, and socio-economic level. This may reduce "error" considerably, but it does so at the expense of limiting the generalizability of the findings to other persons of the same age, sex, IQ, and socio-economic level as the ones used in the experiment. It will usually be better to set up explicitly as factors in the experiment those characteristics thought likely to be most closely related to the outcome measure(s) of the study—i.e., to the dependent variable(s). This factorialization will reduce error almost as well as would the subpopulation method. One can then test the interactions of the status variables with the manipulated variable(s) to determine whether or not the findings can be generalized over age groups, sexes, etc. Indeed, the thoughtful experiment designer often has his cake and eats it, too, as Ronald Fisher showed convincingly long ago.

One of the earliest crossed classifications developed by Fisher for agricultural research was the *randomized-block design*. (See Fisher, 1925, pp. 226–29.) If V different varieties of wheat were to be planted in a field, he suggested that the field first be divided into B blocks of ground, the fertility within a given block being as homogeneous as possible. Then each block was divided into V plots, one for each variety of wheat. One variety was assigned at random to each plot within a given block, so that on each block all V varieties were planted once each. This, then, produced $B \times V$ factor-level combinations and BV observations when the wheat matured. See Table 19.1 for the layout of the observations.

Note that varieties were assigned randomly to plots within blocks. Fisher showed that this randomization was crucial. Also, the B blocks in the experiment might be considered a random sample drawn from a hypothetical population of blocks "like these," whereas the V varieties were probably the "target population" of varieties of wheat, i.e., all the varieties in which the experimenter was interested. This is a mixed model: random block effects and fixed variety effects. The $E(MS)$'s shown in Table 19.1 are such that

$$MS_{varieties} / MS_{(blocks \times varieties)}$$

is distributed as

$$F_{V-1, (B-1)(V-1)}$$

under the null hypothesis that the V varieties produce equal quantities of wheat.

By choosing homogeneous parts of the field (the blocks) rather than merely assigning the varieties wholly at random throughout the field, Fisher removed the between-block variance from the mean square for error and

TABLE 19.1   OUTLINE OF DATA FROM A RANDOMIZED-BLOCK-DESIGN EXPERIMENT; X_{bv} NOTATION, WHERE $b = 1, 2, \ldots$, B BLOCKS AND $v = 1, 2, \ldots$, V VARIETIES OF WHEAT; RANDOM BLOCKS, FIXED VARIETIES

Block of ground	Variety of wheat			
	1	2	...	V
1	X_{11}	X_{12}	...	X_{1V}
2	X_{21}	X_{22}	...	X_{2V}
.	.	.		.
.	.	.		.
.	.	.		.
B	X_{B1}	X_{B2}	...	X_{BV}

Source of variation	df	E(MS)
Between blocks (a)	$B - 1$	$\sigma^2 \qquad\quad + V\sigma_a^2$
Between varieties (β)	$V - 1$	$\sigma^2 + \sigma_{a\beta}^2 + B\sigma_\beta^2$
Blocks $\times$ varieties $(a\beta)$	$(B-1)(V-1)$	$\sigma^2 + \sigma_{a\beta}^2$

increased the power of the significance test for varieties. He was not much interested in MS_{blocks}, except that it should be as large as possible under the conditions of a particular experiment. The general principle of homogeneous subsorting of experimental material can be extended beyond agriculture to a number of situations of great interest to behavioral scientists. In some of these, blocks cannot reasonably be considered a random-effects factor. Also, in many of them there will be more than one observation per factor-level combination. (Fisher allowed for that in some situations, but the more plots there were per block, the less the within-block homogeneity was in many agricultural situations.)

Our discussion below is based on three scales of measurement: nominal-scale factor, which we call a *blocking* variable; ordinal, which we call *stratifying*; and interval or ratio, which we call *leveling*. These three terms are our own coinage for this situation. We believe that they serve behavioral science more usefully than does the single, ancestral expression "randomized-block design." Blocking, stratifying, and leveling variables are classificatory, rather than manipulated. They are antecedent to the beginning of the experiment itself, as for example when the field was divided into blocks before the varieties were planted on plots within these blocks. Let us now consider each of these three types of factorialization that are useful for reducing error and improving generalizationability.

Blocking on a Nominal-Scale Variable

A familiar example of blocking is the classification of each pupil as being either male or female and the introduction of this two-level factor explicitly into the experimental design. Physiological sex is not a manipulated variable, but in the experimental design it is treated statistically like the manipulated factors. With two levels of sex, three levels of type size, and four levels of type style one has $2 \times 3 \times 4 = 24$ factor-level combinations and needs $24n$ experimental units.

Main effects of sex, size, and style can be estimated. Also, one can study the interaction of sex with size, sex with style, and size with style, and the three-factor interaction of sex, size, and style. If the main effect of sex is significant, then by having a sex factor one has reduced the error variance significantly. If sex interacts with either or both of the manipulated factors, then by having sex as an explicit factor one has learned how to limit his generalizations appropriately. For example, it *might* be discovered that women find Style 3 easiest to read, whereas men find Style 1 easiest. When pursued further, this might have practical consequences for the design of textual materials.

Another example of blocking is the use of identical twins in an experiment where one factor is manipulated at two levels. Twin A of each pair is assigned at random to a level of the manipulated factor, and twin B of that same pair then receives the other level. With P pairs of twins, one has $2P$ experimental units. The three sources of variation are between twin pairs, between the two treatments, and interaction of pairs with treatments. Note that this is just one replicate, so no direct statistical test of the interaction is afforded. If the variation among the twin pairs is significant, one has reduced the error term significantly, but because one sacrifices half his degrees of freedom for error in so doing, the power of the statistical test of the two-level treatment effect may not be improved or may even be lessened. In this design, the factor "twin pairs" would almost surely be regarded as random, since one would probably want the comparison of A and B to be generalized to a population of twins. Incidentally, this is a social- or biological-science version of Fisher's randomized-block design. The twin pairs are unordered, having been "measured" on a nominal scale.

Stratifying on Ordinal-Scale Variables

We call an ordinal-scale variable used as an explicit factor in the experimental design, such as socio-economic status of each experimental unit, a *stratifying variable*. There might be five levels, such as high, upper-middle,

middle-middle, lower-middle, and low socio-economic status, creating a five-level *classificatory* (i.e., not manipulated) factor.

Leveling on Interval- or Ratio-Scale Variables

An interval or nearly interval scale or a ratio scale can be used to yield what is called a *leveling variable*. To reduce within-factor-level-combination variability one may group the experimental units before the experiment begins

TABLE 19.2 SCHEMA OF DATA FOR THE LEVELING DESIGN, WITH REPLICATION; X_{lti} NOTATION, $l = 1, 2, \ldots, L$ LEVELS, $t = 1, 2, \ldots, T$ TREATMENTS, AND $i = \ldots, n$ INDIVIDUALS FOR EACH TREATMENT WITHIN EACH LEVEL*

Levels	*Treatments*			
	1	2	. . .	T
1	X_{111} X_{112} . . . X_{11n}	X_{121} X_{122} . . . X_{12n}	. . . .	X_{1T1} X_{1T2} . . . X_{1Tn}
2	X_{211} X_{212} . . . X_{21n}	X_{221} X_{222} . . . X_{22n}	. . . .	X_{2T1} X_{2T2} . . . X_{2Tn}
. . .	. . .	. . .	. . .	. . .
L	X_{L11} X_{L12} . . . X_{L1n}	X_{L21} X_{L22} . . . X_{L2n}	. . . .	X_{LT1} X_{LT2} . . . X_{LTn}

* One can let $i = 1, 2, \ldots, n_{lt}$, instead of constant n, especially when levels and treatments are both fixed-effects factors, as they usually will be. This may be preferable when the number of individuals available at certain levels of a natural or desired classification differs from that available at others. Recall or consult again the discussion of proportional-cell-frequencies analyses. Here the proportionality condition would be that $n_{lt} = (n_{l.})(n_{.t})/n_{..}$.

on something, such as measured reading comprehension or height, that is expected to correlate well within treatments with the outcome measure of the experiment. If there are T levels of a treatment factor and LT experimental units, one would arrange the experimental units from highest to lowest on the pre-measured factor into L levels. Within each such level, one experimental unit would be assigned at random to each of the T treatments (i.e., the T levels of the manipulated variable), creating one replicate of an $L \times T$ design. If the measures of the leveling factor do correlate significantly greater than zero with the outcome measures, then (as in the twin design outlined above) the within-treatment variability will be reduced significantly.

Alternatively, one might choose to use $N = nLT$ experimental units, where n is greater than 1. (In the above paragraph, $n = 1$.) Then one would group the N experimental units, from highest to lowest, into $L = N/nT$ sets, and would assign at random n experimental units to each treatment within each level. This would permit testing the interaction of levels with treatments, which the $n = 1$ design does not allow directly. See Table 19.2 for an outline of this design.

19.5
ORDERED LEVELS OF FACTORS

If one has three equally spaced sizes of printing type, such as 8, 12, and 16 point, he has three equally spaced levels of an *ordered* factor. A significant *trend* for size of type might be linear, representing an equal increment (or decrement) as one goes from 8 point type to 12 point type and from 12 point type to 16 point type. The trend might be quadratic (i.e., second-order), as when 8 and 16 are equally effective but 12 is much better, or it might combine both linear and quadratic components.

Style of printing type, you note, is a nominal-scale factor, not ordered. It is quite possible to have two or more ordered factors in the same study, however, as for example if one introduced five equally spaced weights of paper into the print study; the various trends that result could then be evaluated. (E.g., see Winer, 1962, and Edwards, 1968.)

19.6
RANDOM SELECTION OF
FACTOR LEVELS

Earlier in this chapter it was hinted that the four styles of printing type might have been drawn at random from a larger target population of printing styles to which one wished to generalize. If that population contained, say, 40 styles, then the four drawn would be 10% of the entire population, a small but hardly negligible percentage. If, on the other hand, one drew four schools out of a target population of 4000 schools, the one-tenth of 1% that the schools in the experiment constitute of the population would be tiny, so one might choose to consider that essentially the four schools had been drawn from an infinite population of schools, in which case one would (using the jargon of the field) say that the schools are a *random-effects factor*.

If one has both fixed-effects and random-effects factors in an experiment, we say that he should use a *mixed-model* analysis of his results. (See Chapter 18 for the mixed-effects ANOVA model.) Genuine random-effects factors seem rare in educational and psychological research, but often we choose to act as if the levels of a factor such as teachers, schools, classes, ratees, or twin pairs had been drawn randomly from a virtually infinite population of such levels. We do this by arguing that the particular levels used are plausibly a random sample from a hypothetical population to which we wish to generalize: teachers "like these," schools "like these," etc. This logic has the endorsement of several top-level mathematical statisticians who have debated it rather hotly with each other. (E.g., see Cornfield and Tukey, 1956.) If we are going to generalize to other teachers, other schools, and the like anyway, then we should use the analytical model that fits such generalization, rather than using the model that applies just to the particular levels in the experiment itself.

19.7
NATURAL AND CONTROLLED
EXPERIMENTS

Sampling factor levels from a population of factor levels larger than the number to be used in the experiment brings controlled experimentation closer to the methodology of sample surveys than it was until the early 1950's. A difference that persists is the manipulation by the experimenter of the levels of one or more factors, along with the random assignment of the experimental units to the factor-level combinations. Sampling of occupations might occur in a survey of salaries, where respondents are classified by occupation, sex, and marital status, as when the occupations to be studied are drawn at random from a large list of occupations. The analysis of the results of such a study might proceed formally in much the same way as that for an experiment involving styles of printing type, sex, and marital status, but in the status study nothing was manipulated, whereas in the experiment style of type was. Of course, one can *conceive* of an experiment in which experimental units representing the crossing of the two sexes and three marital statuses are assigned at random to occupations, thereby distributing ability, interests, education, age, and the like randomly across the occupations and in this way removing the confounding of occupation with those personal characteristics. Generally, interpretation of the results of a controlled experiment will be easier than that of the analogous "natural experiment." A more familiar example than the occupational one is investigation of the effects on general English vocabulary of studying Latin in high school. If students elect (i.e., volunteer) to take Latin or not to take it, the inputs for the two conditions will almost always be substantially different, the students taking Latin being better *initially* on English vocabulary, IQ, and a host of other cognitive and affective variables. If, however, half the prospective enrollees in Latin could be assigned at random to Latin in the ninth and tenth grades and the other half in, say, the eleventh and twelfth grades, nonreactively so that disappointment and frustration did not upset the operation of the school, it should be possible to compare both groups unbiasedly at the end of the tenth grade, after half had completed two years of Latin and the other half had taken none. Because of the random assignment, there would be no systematic confounding of any antecedent variables with the experimental variable (i.e., took Latin versus did not take it). Results should be much more readily interpretable than in the natural experiment.

One has only to recall the great difficulties encountered by statisticians when analyzing the results of the vast natural-smoking experiment that has been going on for many years. Is cigarette smoking one of the potent "causes" of lung cancer? Of other ills? After much comparison of human subgroups and animal experimentation in order to discredit plausible alternative hypotheses, most researchers in this area have concluded that smoking cigarettes does increase the probability that a person will develop lung cancer and have certain other ailments, but because the work with humans was not controlled experimentation, no proof *overwhelmingly* convincing to *all* intelligent persons has yet been provided. Indeed, associational analyses cannot eliminate all plausible alternative hypotheses, whereas controlled experiments *if conducted impeccably* can rule out all systematic ones, leaving only chance fluctuations (usually of quite low probability and largely under the experimenter's control) as the alternative explanation. This is not to say that a single experiment can be definitive or perfect; none ever is. Often an experiment will raise more new questions than it answers old ones, but at least the process of *randomized* assignment of experimental units to factor-level combinations removes the chief source of systematic bias that afflicts most natural experiments.

Control may exact a high price in terms of lowered external validity (i.e., generalizability), however. For example, one probably cannot assign persons at random to unidentified-flying-object (UFO) versus non-UFO clubs and preserve the sense of the distinction as it occurs naturally. One might try paying some persons to smoke and others to refrain from smoking, but very likely this would not simulate well enough the natural situation where persons of certain temperaments and backgrounds cannot resist smoking several packages of cigarettes daily, whereas other types of individuals are not tempted. One cannot very well assign occupations randomly in a meaningful way. Even assigning Latin versus no Latin to eligible high-school students by deferring this subject for half of them has never been done, so far as we are aware. However, this technique of delaying treatment for a randomly selected group of control subjects has been employed frequently in evaluating the effects of psychotherapy.

But in general, researchers in the behavioral and social sciences and education have not made use of the simple and powerful expedient of random assignment to comparison groups even when to do so would be uncomplicated. There do not even seem to be any controlled experiments involving cursive handwriting versus manuscript handwriting in the primary grades, despite the fact that all school children throughout the country are taught to write by some combination of such methods.

In this chapter we have dealt only with attempts to make causal inferences from comparative data. Questions such as "What is the distribution of the ages of female first-grade teachers in California?" and "Are there more male than female elementary-school principals in the United States?" are examples of perfectly reputable inquiries not directly concerned with causal influences. Without a great store of such information, one is hardly ready to design controlled experiments. We can get answers to important questions by the use of questionnaires, interviews, and case studies. Survey researchers have developed powerful analytical techniques for inferring causation from status data, too. For examples, see Blalock (1964).

19.8
OTHER EXPERIMENTAL DESIGNS

Because this is meant to be a systematic textbook, rather than a handbook, we have not attempted to explain or even mention previously a number of experimental designs that are sometimes of value to behavioral scientists, including educational researchers. Among these are Latin and Greco-Latin squares, balanced and partially balanced incomplete-block designs, and fractional-factorial designs. The interested reader is at this point equipped to consult specialized books for these. The most comprehensive manual is probably Cochran and Cox (1957). A simpler treatment, less statistical but still rather comprehensive, is by Cox (1958). Winer (1962) deals with many of the statistical issues. For a simple approach to Latin and Greco-Latin squares, fractional replication, and randomized-block designs, see Edwards (1968). Snedecor and Cochran (1967) provide the sixth edition of a classic applied-statistics textbook that covers some of these special topics. Also see Brownlee (1965) and McLean (1966, 1967).

19.9
THE ANALYSIS OF COVARIANCE

Fisher developed the analysis of variance *and covariance* as a procedure for analyzing the results from factorial designs of many types. Most reluctantly, we have not discussed the analysis of covariance (ANCOVA) in this textbook because to have done so systematically and thoroughly would have required many pages and made an already-long book appreciably longer. For experimentation, the basic principle of ANCOVA is that there are measures of one or more antecedent variables, i.e., measures secured *before* the random assignment of experimental units to treatments is made. These are chosen with the hope that the regression of the outcome measures on these antecedent measures will be considerable (i.e., that the linear association of the X's, the premeasures, with the Y's, the postmeasures, will be appreciable).

In effect, an analysis of variance is performed on the $(Y - \hat{Y})$'s, where the $\hat{Y}$'s are predicted from the X's in the usual $b_1 X + b_0$ way described earlier in this book. Some complexity arises because, even with only a single antecedent measure, one has at least two levels of the treatment factor, and hence at least two columns of Y's. With two or more antecedent measures multiple-regression methods must be used, because one is securing the best-weighted composite of the several antecedent variables for predicting the Y's.

A hypothetical illustration of use of the analysis of covariance may make its purpose clearer. Suppose that one is studying four different ways to teach computation of one-way ANOVAs. As his antecedent variables the experimenter has, for each person later to be used in the experiment, a verbal-aptitude score (V), a quantitative-aptitude score (Q), and previous grade-point average (G) in quantitative courses. He assigns n_j (preferably $n = N/4$) of the persons randomly to each of the four teaching methods, without any reference to their test scores or GPAs. Then he carries out the experiment and at its end administers to all persons a test of computing one-way ANOVAs; this yields the outcome measures, Y's. Finally, he performs an analysis of covariance on the data to determine whether, after he has used the antecedent information statistically, the adjusted means of the four methods differ significantly. If the regression of the final-test scores on the three predictors is significant, his adjusted *within*-method mean square will be smaller than if he had not used this antecedent information, thus giving him a more powerful significance test and permitting smaller confidence limits to be constructed around differences between method means. The data layout is sketched in Table 19.3.

For details of such analyses (especially of the case where there is just one predictor variable) see Edwards (1968), Brownlee (1965, pp. 376–96), Winer (1962), McNemar (1962), Lindquist (1953), and Scheffé (1959). Also, for a

TABLE 19.3 OUTLINE OF DATA FOR ANALYSIS OF COVARIANCE OF THREE PREDICTORS AND FOUR LEVELS OF A SINGLE FACTOR; V_{ij}, Q_{ij}, G_{ij}, AND Y_{ij} NOTATION, WHERE $i = 1, 2, \ldots, n_j$ AND $j = 1, 2, 3, 4$

Method						
1		2		3	4
Scores on predictors	*Scores on criterion*	*Scores on predictors*	*Scores on criterion*		
V_{11} Q_{11} G_{11}	Y_{11}	V_{12} Q_{12} G_{12}	Y_{12}	Etc.	Etc.
V_{21} Q_{21} G_{21}	Y_{21}	V_{22} Q_{22} G_{22}	Y_{22}		
. . .	.	. . .	.		
. . .	.	. . .	.		
. . .	.	. . .	.		
V_{n_11} Q_{n_11} G_{n_11}	Y_{n_11}	V_{n_22} Q_{n_22} G_{n_22}	Y_{n_22}		

distinctive point of view about designing large-scale research projects see Baker (1967). For statistical aspects of mental-test theory see Lord and Novick (1968).

In the above example, the experimenter might, instead, have "leveled" on one of the three predictor variables—e.g., have used 5 levels of GPA as an explicit factor in his design—and then applied the analysis of covariance, now with two predictors (verbal- and quantitative-aptitude scores), to the out- come scores from the two-factor (5 levels × 4 methods) design. Now, ever, he would have one classificatory factor (GPA) and one mani- factor (method), the former of which is probably not uncorrelated of the two predictors, whereas the latter, by randomized assi- experimental units to methods, is. (Note that GPA is not an- the aptitude variables, whereas it and they are antecedent to me- analyzer can compute adjusted means for the five GPA levels a- four methods levels, as well as adjusted means for the GPA- and he can test the significance of both the unadjusted means an- means. He must be careful, though, about interpretations of- MS_{GPA} and $MS_{(GPA \times methods)}$, because GPA is not a manipul- For a discussion of interpreting ANCOVA of experiments versus- of status studies or experiments in which some factors are classificat- than manipulated, see Stanley (1967c, 1966a).

Where there is just one interval- or ratio-scale antecedent variable- experiment, it may be preferable to set up levels of that variable as an exp- factor in the design, rather than to use it in an ANCOVA. Cox (1957) di- cusses this point. We would add the caution that if leveling reduces the degrees of freedom for the error term drastically, as when there are just two levels of the treatment factor, and the number of experimental units for the experiment is small, more statistical power may be lost than was gained by the superiority of leveling otherwise.   This is a rather complicated topic, concerning which most experimenters will need help from professional statisticians.

19.10
QUASI-EXPERIMENTATION

Although randomization is the method of choice in experimentation,

> There are many natural social settings in which the research person can introduce something like experimental design into his scheduling of data collection procedures (e.g., the *when* and *to whom* of measurement), even though he lacks the full control over the scheduling of experimental stimuli (the *when* and *to whom* of exposure and the ability to randomize exposures) which makes a true experiment possible.   Collectively, such situations can be regarded as quasi-experimental designs.   One purpose of this [book] is to encourage the utilization of such quasi-experiments and to increase the awareness of the kinds of settings in which opportunities to employ them occur. But just because full experimental control *is* lacking, it becomes imperative that the researcher be thoroughly aware of which specific variables his particular design fails to control.   It is for this need in evaluating quasi-experiments, more than for understanding true experiments, that the check lists of sources of invalidity in [this book] were developed.   (Campbell and Stanley, 1966, p. 34.)

Quasi-experimentation, as devised by Campbell (1957) and developed further by Campbell and Stanley (1963 or 1966), seems to offer a middle ground between the controlled experiment of the laboratory and the uncontrolled experiment of nature.   If not used carelessly and faddishly, it may helpfully augment the armament of the experimenter.

19.11
THE EXPERIMENTAL UNIT
AND THE UNIT OF
STATISTICAL ANALYSIS:
COMPARATIVE EXPERIMENTS
WITH INTACT GROUPS

If the statistical analysis of an experiment is to yield a valid probability statement about the chances of drawing false conclusions from the data, there must exist an agreement between the purely mathematical assumptions about the data from which probabilities are calculated and the dynamics of the experimental situation.   For example, the probability—calculated assuming fair dice and independent tosses—of 15 straight "passes" in craps is irrelevant in a crap game with loaded dice. Similarly, the probability of a type I error may be substantially incorrect if the data of the experiment do not conform to the statistical-mathematical model from which that probability was derived. We are here concerned primarily with the assumption of independence of the replications of a comparative experiment.

Illustration of the Invalidating Effect of Nonindependence of Replications of an Experiment

Imagine that methods A and B of teaching students how to balance chemical equations are being compared. The design for comparing the two methods involves the pairing of 120 pupils into 60 pairs of similar ability and the random assignment of the members of each pair to either method A or method B. All 120 pupils are taught by the same teacher, but they must be divided into four groups of 30 each for instruction. The design can be depicted as shown in Fig. 19.1. Each of the four squares in Fig. 19.1 encloses 30 pupils who study together in a single class.

Suppose that methods A and B will be compared by observing which member of each matched pair (the A pupil or the B pupil) scores higher on a test of proficiency in balancing chemical equations. This is a legitimate, though not very powerful, method of comparing A and B and making a hypothesis test; you may recognize it as the method used in the nonparametric "sign test."

Now let us imagine that a researcher has carried out the above experiment and that in each of the 60 pairs of pupils, the pupil studying under method B scored higher on the proficiency test than his matched partner who studied under method A. (Of course this is an improbable set of results even if method B was far superior to method A. We use this exaggerated example because it portrays more clearly the point we wish to make.) The researcher reasons as follows:

"Suppose that the null hypothesis that methods A and B were equally effective is, in fact, true. What, then, is the probability that pupil B will score higher than pupil A in each of the 60 pairs? If in fact method A and method B are no different, then the probability is 1/2 in any single pair that pupil B will score higher than pupil A. (Random assignment of pupils in a pair to methods A and B assures us of this.) The probability that chance alone conspired to make pupil B better than pupil A in all 60 pairs is equal to $(1/2)^{60}$, which is an incredibly small number. Hence, we can safely reject the hypothesis that method A and method B are equally effective."

Implicit in the researcher's calculations which caused him to reject the null hypothesis because of its lack of plausibility in view of the obtained data was the hypothesis that *under a true null hypothesis each matched pair*

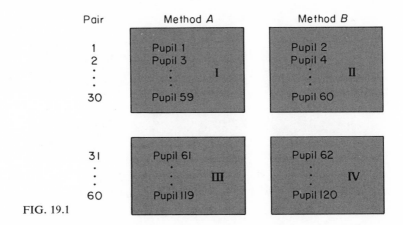

FIG. 19.1

represents an independent opportunity for the occurrence of an event (namely, that pupil B exceeds pupil A) that has probability 1/2. Actually, each matched pair is an experiment: one pupil is taught by method A; the other, by method B. One pair of pupils is an *unreplicated experiment*. Observation of the relative superiority of methods A and B on several pairs of pupils constitutes replication of the experiment. There are as many replications of the experiment as there are matched pairs whose performance is observed. Our researcher made the assumption—gratuitous, perhaps—that the replications of his experiment were independent.

Let us examine this assumption by digging beneath the outward appearances of the experiment—the obtained data—down to the dynamics of the experiment that produced the data. Is it plausible that if pupil B scored higher than pupil A in pair 1 that this does not affect the chances of pupil B scoring higher than pupil A in pair 2? As most classrooms are now constituted, it does not seem plausible. Recall that the 120 pupils were placed into four separate and intact classrooms. Anyone who knows anything about instruction knows that the members of an intact class interact during instruction in a way that enhances or interferes with the learning in the group.

Again, let us exaggerate so as to make the point more clearly. In one sense we will exaggerate by describing a sort of nonindependence of replications that is far stronger than any that would be met in practice. In another sense, we will exaggerate, or "fantasize" might be a better word, by assuming that the researcher knows how the nonindependence operates, which he seldom will know. Suppose that in the group of 120 pupils there are two troublemakers who are so obnoxious and disruptive that they will successfully inhibit the instruction in any class of which they are a part. These two bait their teachers, annoy their classmates, and generally cause a ruckus. If a method A classroom has one of these troublemakers and the matched method B classroom does not, he will so depress the scores on the final proficiency test that each of his classmates in method A will perform more

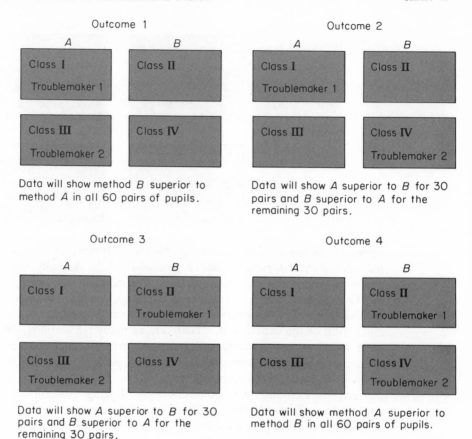

FIG. 19.2

poorly than their matched pair in method *B*. (Of course, if this troublemaker was assigned to method *B* instead, he would cause a similar appearance of superiority for method *A*.)

To guard against the possibility that both of these troublemakers should happen to be assigned to the same classroom (Heaven forbid!), our experimenter made certain that one of them would be assigned at random to either classroom I or II and the other to either classroom III or IV. In any event, the assignment of the pupils in each pair to either method *A* or *B* was made at random so that the comparison was not intentionally biased.

In light of what we now know about the activities in the classrooms that produced the data, let us calculate the probability of the obtained results—60 "points" for method *B* and none for method *A*—*assuming that the null hypothesis of no difference is true*. In the random assignment of the single troublemaker to either method *A* or method *B* for classrooms I and II, there is probability 1/2 that he will be assigned to classroom I (and cause its 30 pupils to do more poorly than their 30 matched pairs in classroom II) and a probability of 1/2 that he will be assigned to classroom II.   The same considerations apply to the assignment of the second troublemaker to either classroom III or classroom IV.   The random assignments of the two troublemakers to classrooms are independent.   Hence there are four possible outcomes of the experiment (see Fig. 19.2).   (Recall that the presence of a troublemaker in a class will cause the 30 members of that class to do more poorly than their matched partners in the class receiving the other treatment.)

Each of the four outcomes is equally likely.   The probability of any one of them is 1/4.   In particular, outcome 1 will occur one-fourth of the time this same experiment is executed.   Consequently, given that methods A and B are equally effective, the probability is *not* $(1/2)^{60}$ that the B pupil will perform better than the A pupil in all 60 matched pairs (as our researcher originally calculated); *the probability of this overwhelming apparent superiority of method B is* 1/4 *when, in fact, A and B are equally effective.*   The probability of falsely concluding that method B was superior to method A was 1/4 instead of $(1/2)^{60}$.   In fact, the experiment was no more sensitive to the discovery of superiority of one method than an experiment in which only two independent matched pairs of pupils were used.

The researcher was so completely in error in his first analysis of the probability of a false conclusion because he failed to recognize that conducting his experiment with intact classrooms did not produce 60 *independent* replications of his experiment.

Experimental Unit Versus Unit of Statistical Analysis

In the analysis of experiments a distinction must be made between the *unit of statistical analysis* and the *experimental unit*.   Before valid probability statements can be made about types of errors, these two units must coincide, i.e., the statistical analysis must be carried out on the legitimate experimental units.

Definition: The *units of statistical analysis* are the data (the actual numbers) that we consider to be the outcomes of independent replications of our experiment.   If you will, the units of statistical analysis are the numbers that we count when we count up degrees of freedom "within" or "for replications."

Imagine that 10 pupils study method I and ten pupils study method II. A *t*-test is performed on the 20 scores on the dependent variable; hence, the "pupil" is the unit of statistical analysis. *For the sake of analysis*, each pupil is considered to be a replication of the experiment; method I is replicated 10 times, and method II is replicated 10 times.

By looking at a researcher's statistical analysis, we can easily determine which unit he chose as the unit of statistical analysis.

It is somewhat more difficult to state an adequate definition of the experimental unit.

Definition: The *experimental units* are the smallest divisions of the collection of experimental subjects that have been randomly assigned to the different conditions in the experiment *and* that have responded independently of each other for the duration of the experiment.

(This definition clearly reflects the fact that it was proposed with experimentation on living organisms in mind—note the word "respond.")

Independence is the crux of the matter; the following remarks are an attempt to illustrate the notion of independent replications. Suppose that the effects of methods A and B are equal when measured on a particular dependent variable. The probability that subject 1 under method A will score higher on the dependent variable than subject 1 under method B is $1/2$ when subjects are randomly assigned to methods. Now consider subject 2 under A and subject 2 under B, i.e., the second replication of the experiment. If the probability that subject 2 under method A will score higher than subject 2 under method B is $1/2$ regardless of the outcome of the experiment on the first replication (with subjects 1), then the two replications are independent.

Judging the validity of the assumption that the replications of an experiment are independent is no easy matter. The assumption of homogeneous variances is easily tested with Bartlett's test (if we are confident the normality assumption is met) or Levene's test. The assumption of normality is easily tested with a chi-square or Kolmogorov-Smirnov test if n is reasonably large. However, the researcher will usually be faced with the task of making a considered judgment of the degree of independence of the replications rather than the task of applying a particular statistical test. His judgment must be based on an intimate knowledge of the dynamics of the experimental setting. In some instances, blatant nonindependence of the replications will be impossible to overlook, as in our example. In other experiments, nonindependence of replications will be subtle and can go unrecognized.

In the example at the beginning of this section, the experimental subjects were the 120 pupils. The smallest division of this group of subjects that was randomly assigned to methods A and B was an individual pupil. *However*, the individual pupils did not respond to instruction independently. In two classrooms, a troublemaker caused the remaining pupils to learn nothing about balancing chemical equations.

Each classroom did respond independently of the other three classrooms, we might assume; *and* the classrooms were randomly assigned to methods *A* and *B*. Therefore, the "classroom" is the smallest division of the 120 pupils that satisfies the conditions of random assignment and independent responding. Therefore, the "classroom" is the experimental unit in our example.

A valid analysis of the illustrative experiment would be carried out on four observations: the *average* proficiency test scores of the four classrooms. In other words, *a valid analysis would use the four classroom means as the units of statistical analysis.* The experiment comparing methods *A* and *B* was only replicated twice (once for each classroom) for each method. "Classroom" is the experimental unit; hence, the classroom means must be the unit of statistical analysis. A valid statistical inferential analysis is possible, but it is hardly worth the bother. The results of the two replications of the experiment give us no more evidence to conclude that method *B* is better than method *A*, than we have evidence to conclude that a coin is biased in favor of "heads" because the first two times we flipped it we got "heads." (However, means based on 30 pupils each should be more stable than means based on one pupil each, i.e., the experimental results should be better for the 120 pupils than they would have been for just four, one in each class.)

Educational researchers are especially prone to making the error of analyzing data in terms of units other than the legitimate experimental unit. Almost all of the comparative experiments carried out under actual school conditions face the same dilemma. At most, no more than five or six intact classrooms have been involved in the experiment. Perhaps pupils have been assigned to classrooms at random, perhaps not. At least, the classrooms have been assigned at random to the experimental conditions being compared. The researcher has two alternatives, though he is seldom aware of the second one: (1) he can run a potentially illegitimate analysis of the experiment by using the "pupil" as the unit of statistical analysis, or (2) he can run a legitimate analysis on the means of the five or six classrooms, "classroom" being the actual experimental unit, in which case he is almost certain to obtain statistically nonsignificant results (with only five or six replications, the power of his significance test is low).

If the researcher chooses the first alternative and is led into error, he can find solace in the knowledge that methodologists themselves have long sanctioned his actions either explicitly or by example.

As early as 1940, Lindquist presented a *legitimate* analysis of variance of data gathered from an experiment involving intact groups (see Lindquist, 1940, pp. 107ff.). Lindquist's thinking was far ahead of that of his colleagues, if McNemar was representative of the latter.   In a review of Lindquist's text McNemar (1940) wrote as follows:

> We next raise a puzzling question for which we have no definite answer. Beginning on page 107, the analysis of variance technique is applied to an educational-methods experiment involving five schools and three methods, with twenty pupils in each of fifteen classes. The analysis is carried through on the basis of the fifteen class means in such a way that neither the number of pupils nor the pupil variation enters into the analysis. This at first struck the reviewer as being indefensible, but a few pages later (p. 117) one finds that the pupils have their inning *via* the 'within classes' variation, but this latter variation is not utilized because the 'interaction variance' is larger than the 'within classes' variance. The reviewer suspects that something is wrong with a test of significance which does not involve the variation of the individuals upon which the means are based. We are unable to locate the fallacy here, if there be such, but we have in mind a worked-out example in sex differences which shows no significant difference in length at birth when analyzed by the variance technique using means, but which yields highly significant differences when analyzed by the ordinary critical ratio procedure. We are not arguing that the author is wrong in arguing that intact groups are the proper sampling units, but rather that the case is not convincingly stated.

Notice that McNemar's worked-out example, which he considered to be contrary to Lindquist's example, is quite unlike a classroom experiment of the sort Lindquist discussed. What if McNemar's example involved 20 boys (four from each of five families) and 20 girls (four from each of five families)?

Further Reading

Fortunately, there now exist about a half-dozen discussions of the problem of determining the appropriate experimental unit and unit of statistical analysis:

1. Campbell, D. T. and J. C. Stanley. "Experimental and quasi-experimental designs in research on teaching." Chapter 5 in *Handbook of Research on Teaching*, ed. N. L. Gage. Chicago: Rand-McNally, 1963. Relevant pages: 192, *passim.*

2. Cox, David R. *Planning of Experiments*. New York: Wiley, 1958. Relevant pages: 2–3, 155, 171–73, 191, 196. The designated pages deal with the problem of experimenting with intact groups. The context is agricultural experimentation and the discussion is at a high level. Save this one to read after you have mastered some preliminary material.

3. Hovland, C. I., A. A. Lumsdaine, and F. D. Sheffield. *Experiments on Mass Communication*. Princeton, N.J.: Princeton University Press, 1949.

4. Lindquist, E. F. *Design and Analysis of Experiments in Psychology and Education.* Boston: Houghton Mifflin, 1953. Relevant pages: 192–93. A short discussion of experimenting with intact classrooms. Lindquist discusses the problem in an educational context. An important reference. *However, it must be read carefully and critically.* When Lindquist prepared this textbook, the procedures we presented for finding $E(MS)$'s had not yet been worked out fully.

5. Lumsdaine, A. A. "Instruments and media of instruction." Chapter 12 in *Handbook of Research on Teaching*, ed. N. L. Gage. Chicago: Rand-McNally, 1963. See especially pages 656–59. Pages 656–59 are probably the best readily available discussion of this crucial problem of running comparative experiments with intact groups of persons instead of individual persons.

6. Peckham, Perc D., Gene V. Glass, and Kenneth D. Hopkins. "The experimental unit in statistical analysis: comparative experiments with intact groups." *Journal of Special Education*, 3 (1969).

TABLES

TABLE A 5000 RANDOM DIGITS

03	99	11	04	61	93	71	61	68	94	66	08	32	46	53	84	60	95	82	32	88	61	81	91	61
38	55	59	55	54	32	88	65	97	80	08	35	56	08	60	29	73	54	77	62	71	29	92	38	53
17	54	67	37	04	92	05	24	62	15	55	12	12	92	81	59	07	60	79	36	27	95	45	89	09
32	64	35	28	61	95	81	90	68	31	00	91	19	89	36	76	35	59	37	79	80	86	30	05	14
69	57	26	87	77	39	51	03	59	05	14	06	04	06	19	29	54	96	96	16	33	56	46	07	80
24	12	26	65	91	27	69	90	64	94	14	84	54	66	72	61	95	87	71	00	90	89	97	57	54
61	19	63	02	31	92	96	26	17	73	41	83	95	53	82	17	26	77	09	43	78	03	87	02	67
30	53	22	17	04	10	27	41	22	02	39	68	52	33	09	10	06	16	88	29	55	98	66	64	85
03	78	89	75	99	75	86	72	07	17	74	41	65	31	66	35	20	83	33	74	87	53	90	88	23
48	22	86	33	79	85	78	34	76	19	53	15	26	74	33	35	66	35	29	72	16	81	86	03	11

Reprinted from *A Million Random Digits With 100,000 Normal Deviates* (New York: The Free Press, 1955), by permission of the RAND Corporation and the publisher.

```
60  36  59  46  53     35  07  53  39  49     42  61  42  92  97     01  91  82  83  16     98  95  37  32  31
83  79  94  24  02     56  62  33  44  42     34  99  44  13  74     70  07  11  47  36     09  95  81  80  65
32  96  00  74  05     36  40  98  32  32     99  38  54  16  00     11  13  30  75  86     15  91  70  62  53
19  32  25  38  45     57  62  05  26  06     66  49  76  86  46     78  13  86  65  59     19  64  09  94  13
11  22  09  47  47     07  39  93  74  08     48  50  92  39  29     27  48  24  54  76     85  24  43  51  59

31  75  15  72  60     68  98  00  53  39     15  47  04  83  55     88  65  12  25  96     03  15  21  91  21
88  49  29  93  82     14  45  40  45  04     20  09  49  89  77     74  84  39  34  13     22  10  97  85  08
30  93  44  77  44     07  48  18  38  28     73  78  80  65  33     28  59  72  04  05     94  20  52  03  80
22  88  84  88  93     27  49  99  87  48     60  53  04  51  28     74  02  28  46  17     82  03  71  02  68
78  21  21  69  93     35  90  29  13  86     44  37  21  54  86     65  74  11  40  14     87  48  13  72  20

41  84  98  45  47     46  85  05  23  26     34  67  75  83  00     74  91  06  43  45     19  32  58  15  49
46  35  23  30  49     69  24  89  34  60     45  30  50  75  21     61  31  83  18  55     14  41  37  09  51
11  08  79  62  94     14  01  33  17  92     59  74  76  72  77     76  50  33  45  13     39  66  37  75  44
52  70  10  83  37     56  30  38  73  15     16  52  06  96  76     11  65  49  98  93     02  18  16  81  61
57  27  53  68  98     81  30  44  85  85     68  65  22  73  76     92  85  25  58  66     88  44  80  35  84

20  85  77  31  56     70  28  42  43  26     79  37  59  52  20     01  15  96  32  67     10  62  24  83  91
15  63  38  49  24     90  41  59  36  14     33  52  12  66  65     55  82  34  76  41     86  22  53  17  04
92  69  44  82  97     39  90  40  21  15     59  58  94  90  67     66  82  14  15  75     49  76  70  40  37
77  61  31  90  19     88  15  20  00  80     20  55  49  14  09     96  27  74  82  57     50  81  69  76  16
38  68  83  24  86     45  13  46  35  45     59  40  47  20  59     43  94  75  16  80     43  85  25  96  93

25  16  30  18  89     70  01  41  50  21     41  29  06  73  12     71  85  71  59  57     68  97  11  14  30
65  25  10  76  29     37  23  93  32  95     05  87  00  11  19     92  78  42  63  40     18  47  76  56  22
36  81  54  36  25     18  63  73  75  09     82  44  49  90  05     04  92  17  37  01     14  70  79  39  97
64  39  71  16  92     05  32  78  21  62     20  24  78  17  59     45  19  72  53  32     83  74  52  25  67
04  51  52  56  24     95  09  66  79  46     48  46  08  55  58     15  19  11  87  82     16  93  03  33  61

83  76  16  08  73     43  25  38  41  45     60  83  32  59  83     01  29  14  13  49     20  36  80  71  26
14  38  70  63  45     80  85  40  92  79     43  52  90  63  18     38  38  47  47  61     41  19  63  74  80
51  32  19  22  46     80  08  87  70  74     88  72  25  67  36     66  16  44  94  31     66  91  93  16  78
72  47  20  00  08     80  89  01  80  02     94  81  33  19  00     54  15  58  34  36     35  35  25  41  31
05  46  65  53  06     93  12  81  84  64     74  45  79  05  61     72  84  81  18  34     79  98  26  84  16

39  52  87  24  84     82  47  42  55  93     48  54  53  52  47     18  61  91  36  74     18  61  11  92  41
81  61  61  87  11     53  34  24  42  76     75  12  21  17  24     74  62  77  37  07     58  31  91  59  97
07  58  61  61  20     82  64  12  28  20     92  90  41  31  41     32  39  21  97  63     61  19  96  79  40
90  76  70  42  35     13  57  41  72  00     69  90  26  37  42     78  46  42  25  01     18  62  79  08  72
40  18  82  81  93     29  59  38  86  27     94  97  21  15  98     62  09  53  67  87     00  44  15  89  97

34  41  48  21  57     86  88  75  50  87     19  15  20  00  23     12  30  28  07  83     32  62  46  86  91
63  43  97  53  63     44  98  91  68  22     36  02  40  08  67     76  37  84  16  05     65  96  17  34  88
67  04  90  90  70     93  39  94  55  47     94  45  87  42  84     05  04  14  98  07     20  28  83  40  60
79  49  50  41  46     52  16  29  02  86     54  15  83  42  43     46  97  83  54  82     59  36  29  59  38
91  70  43  05  52     04  73  72  10  31     75  05  19  30  29     47  66  56  43  82     99  78  29  34  78

09  18  82  00  97     32  82  53  95  27     04  22  08  63  04     83  38  98  73  74     64  27  85  80  44
90  04  58  54  97     51  98  15  06  54     94  93  88  19  97     91  87  07  61  50     68  47  66  46  59
73  18  95  02  07     47  67  72  62  69     62  29  06  44  64     27  12  46  70  18     41  36  18  27  60
75  76  87  64  90     20  97  18  17  49     90  42  91  22  72     95  37  50  58  71     93  82  34  31  78
54  01  64  40  56     66  28  13  10  03     00  68  22  73  98     20  71  45  32  95     07  70  61  78  13
```

```
08 35 86 99 10   78 54 24 27 85   13 66 15 88 73   04 61 89 75 53   31 22 30 84 20
28 30 60 32 64   81 33 31 05 91   40 51 00 78 93   32 60 46 04 75   94 11 90 18 40
53 84 08 62 33   81 59 41 36 28   51 21 59 02 90   28 46 66 87 95   77 76 22 07 91
91 75 75 37 41   61 61 36 22 69   50 26 39 02 12   55 78 17 65 14   83 48 34 70 55
89 41 59 26 94   00 39 75 83 91   12 60 71 76 46   48 94 97 23 06   94 54 13 74 08

77 51 30 38 20   86 83 42 99 01   68 41 48 27 74   51 90 81 39 80   72 89 35 55 07
19 50 23 71 74   69 97 92 02 88   55 21 02 97 73   74 28 77 52 51   65 34 46 74 15
21 81 85 93 13   93 27 88 17 57   05 68 67 31 56   07 08 28 50 46   31 85 33 84 52
51 47 46 64 99   68 10 72 36 21   94 04 99 13 45   42 83 60 91 91   08 00 74 54 49
99 55 96 83 31   62 53 52 41 70   69 77 71 28 30   74 81 97 81 42   43 86 07 28 34

33 71 34 80 07   93 58 47 28 69   51 92 66 47 21   58 30 32 98 22   93 17 49 39 72
85 27 48 68 93   11 30 32 92 70   28 83 43 41 37   73 51 59 04 00   71 14 84 36 43
84 13 38 96 40   44 03 55 21 66   73 85 27 00 91   61 22 26 05 61   62 32 71 84 23
56 73 21 62 34   17 39 59 61 31   10 12 39 16 22   85 49 65 75 60   81 60 41 88 80
65 13 85 68 06   87 64 88 52 61   34 31 36 58 61   45 87 52 10 69   85 64 44 72 77

38 00 10 21 76   81 71 91 17 11   71 60 29 29 37   74 21 96 40 49   65 58 44 96 98
37 40 29 63 97   01 30 47 75 86   56 27 11 00 86   47 32 46 26 05   40 03 03 74 38
97 12 54 03 48   87 08 33 14 17   21 81 53 92 50   75 23 76 20 47   15 50 12 95 78
21 82 64 11 34   47 14 33 40 72   64 63 88 59 02   49 13 90 64 41   03 85 65 45 52
73 13 54 27 42   95 71 90 90 35   85 79 47 42 96   08 78 98 81 56   64 69 11 92 02

07 63 87 79 29   03 06 11 80 72   96 20 74 41 56   23 82 19 95 38   04 71 36 69 94
60 52 88 34 41   07 95 41 98 14   59 17 52 06 95   05 53 35 21 39   61 21 20 64 55
83 59 63 56 55   06 95 89 29 83   05 12 80 97 19   77 43 35 37 83   92 30 15 04 98
10 85 06 27 46   99 59 91 05 07   13 49 90 63 19   53 07 57 18 39   06 41 01 93 62
39 82 09 89 52   43 62 26 31 47   64 42 18 08 14   43 80 00 93 51   31 02 47 31 67

59 58 00 64 78   75 56 97 88 00   88 83 55 44 86   23 76 80 61 56   04 11 10 84 08
38 50 80 73 41   23 79 34 87 63   90 82 29 70 22   17 71 90 42 07   95 95 44 99 53
30 69 27 06 68   94 68 81 61 27   56 19 68 00 91   82 06 76 34 00   05 46 26 92 00
65 44 39 56 59   18 28 82 74 37   49 63 22 40 41   08 33 76 56 76   96 29 99 08 36
27 26 75 02 64   13 19 27 22 94   07 47 74 46 06   17 98 54 89 11   97 34 13 03 58

91 30 70 69 91   19 07 22 42 10   36 69 95 37 28   28 82 53 57 93   28 97 66 62 52
68 43 49 46 88   84 47 31 36 22   62 12 69 84 08   12 84 38 25 90   09 81 59 31 46
48 90 81 58 77   54 74 52 45 91   35 70 00 47 54   83 82 45 26 92   54 13 05 51 60
06 91 34 51 97   42 67 27 86 01   11 88 30 95 28   63 01 19 89 01   14 97 44 03 44
10 45 51 60 19   14 21 03 37 12   91 34 23 78 21   88 32 58 08 51   43 66 77 08 83

12 88 39 73 43   65 02 76 11 84   04 28 50 13 92   17 97 41 50 77   90 71 22 67 69
21 77 83 09 76   38 80 73 69 61   31 64 94 20 96   63 28 10 20 23   08 81 64 74 49
19 52 35 95 15   65 12 25 96 59   86 28 36 82 58   69 57 21 37 98   16 43 59 15 29
67 24 55 26 70   35 58 31 65 63   79 24 68 66 86   76 46 33 42 22   26 65 59 08 02
60 58 44 73 77   07 50 03 79 92   45 13 42 65 29   26 76 08 36 37   41 32 64 43 44

53 85 34 13 77   36 06 69 48 50   58 83 87 38 59   49 36 47 33 31   96 24 04 36 42
24 63 73 87 36   74 38 48 93 42   52 62 30 79 92   12 36 91 86 01   03 74 28 38 73
83 08 01 24 51   38 99 22 28 15   07 75 95 17 77   97 37 72 75 85   51 97 23 78 67
16 44 42 43 34   36 15 19 90 73   27 49 37 09 39   85 13 03 25 52   54 84 65 47 59
60 79 01 81 57   57 17 86 57 62   11 16 17 85 76   45 81 95 29 79   65 13 00 48 60
```

TABLE B   AREAS AND ORDINATES OF THE UNIT NORMAL DISTRIBUTION

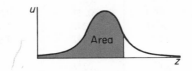

z	Area	u Ordinate	z	Area	u Ordinate
−3.00	.0013	.0044			
−2.99	.0014	.0046	−2.69	.0036	.0107
−2.98	.0014	.0047	−2.68	.0037	.0110
−2.97	.0015	.0048	−2.67	.0038	.0113
−2.96	.0015	.0050	−2.66	.0039	.0116
−2.95	.0016	.0051	−2.65	.0040	.0119
−2.94	.0016	.0053	−2.64	.0041	.0122
−2.93	.0017	.0055	−2.63	.0043	.0126
−2.92	.0018	.0056	−2.62	.0044	.0129
−2.91	.0018	.0058	−2.61	.0045	.0132
−2.90	.0019	.0060	−2.60	.0047	.0136
−2.89	.0019	.0061	−2.59	.0048	.0139
−2.88	.0020	.0063	−2.58	.0049	.0143
−2.87	.0021	.0065	−2.57	.0051	.0147
−2.86	.0021	.0067	−2.56	.0052	.0151
−2.85	.0022	.0069	−2.55	.0054	.0154
−2.84	.0023	.0071	−2.54	.0055	.0158
−2.83	.0023	.0073	−2.53	.0057	.0163
−2.82	.0024	.0075	−2.52	.0059	.0167
−2.81	.0025	.0077	−2.51	.0060	.0171
−2.80	.0026	.0079	−2.50	.0062	.0175
−2.79	.0026	.0081	−2.49	.0064	.0180
−2.78	.0027	.0084	−2.48	.0066	.0184
−2.77	.0028	.0086	−2.47	.0068	.0189
−2.76	.0029	.0088	−2.46	.0069	.0194
−2.75	.0030	.0091	−2.45	.0071	.0198
−2.74	.0031	.0093	−2.44	.0073	.0203
−2.73	.0032	.0096	−2.43	.0075	.0208
−2.72	.0033	.0099	−2.42	.0078	.0213
−2.71	.0034	.0101	−2.41	.0080	.0219
−2.70	.0035	.0104	−2.40	.0082	.0224

z	Area	u Ordinate	z	Area	u Ordinate
−2.39	.0084	.0229	−1.94	.0262	.0608
−2.38	.0087	.0235	−1.93	.0268	.0620
−2.37	.0089	.0241	−1.92	.0274	.0632
−2.36	.0091	.0246	−1.91	.0281	.0644
−2.35	.0094	.0252	−1.90	.0287	.0656
−2.34	.0096	.0258	−1.89	.0294	.0669
−2.33	.0099	.0264	−1.88	.0301	.0681
−2.32	.0102	.0270	−1.87	.0307	.0694
−2.31	.0104	.0277	−1.86	.0314	.0707
−2.30	.0107	.0283	−1.85	.0322	.0721
−2.29	.0110	.0290	−1.84	.0329	.0734
−2.28	.0113	.0297	−1.83	.0336	.0748
−2.27	.0116	.0303	−1.82	.0344	.0761
−2.26	.0119	.0310	−1.81	.0351	.0775
−2.25	.0122	.0317	−1.80	.0359	.0790
−2.24	.0125	.0325	−1.79	.0367	.0804
−2.23	.0129	.0332	−1.78	.0375	.0818
−2.22	.0132	.0339	−1.77	.0384	.0833
−2.21	.0136	.0347	−1.76	.0392	.0848
−2.20	.0139	.0355	−1.75	.0401	.0863
−2.19	.0143	.0363	−1.74	.0409	.0878
−2.18	.0146	.0371	−1.73	.0418	.0893
−2.17	.0150	.0379	−1.72	.0427	.0909
−2.16	.0154	.0387	−1.71	.0436	.0925
−2.15	.0158	.0396	−1.70	.0446	.0940
−2.14	.0162	.0404	−1.69	.0455	.0957
−2.13	.0166	.0413	−1.68	.0465	.0973
−2.12	.0170	.0422	−1.67	.0475	.0989
−2.11	.0174	.0431	−1.66	.0485	.1006
−2.10	.0179	.0440	−1.65	.0495	.1023
−2.09	.0183	.0449	−1.64	.0505	.1040
−2.08	.0188	.0459	−1.63	.0516	.1057
−2.07	.0192	.0468	−1.62	.0526	.1074
−2.06	.0197	.0478	−1.61	.0537	.1092
−2.05	.0202	.0488	−1.60	.0548	.1109
−2.04	.0207	.0498	−1.59	.0559	.1127
−2.03	.0212	.0508	−1.58	.0571	.1145
−2.02	.0217	.0519	−1.57	.0582	.1163
−2.01	.0222	.0529	−1.56	.0594	.1182
−2.00	.0228	.0540	−1.55	.0606	.1200
−1.99	.0233	.0551	−1.54	.0618	.1219
−1.98	.0239	.0562	−1.53	.0630	.1238
−1.97	.0244	.0573	−1.52	.0643	.1257
−1.96	.0250	.0584	−1.51	.0655	.1276
−1.95	.0256	.0596	−1.50	.0668	.1295

z	Area	u Ordinate	z	Area	u Ordinate
−1.49	.0681	.1315	−1.04	.1492	.2323
−1.48	.0694	.1334	−1.03	.1515	.2347
−1.47	.0708	.1354	−1.02	.1539	.2371
−1.46	.0721	.1374	−1.01	.1562	.2396
−1.45	.0735	.1394	−1.00	.1587	.2420
−1.44	.0749	.1415	−0.99	.1611	.2444
−1.43	.0764	.1435	−0.98	.1635	.2468
−1.42	.0778	.1456	−0.97	.1660	.2492
−1.41	.0793	.1476	−0.96	.1685	.2516
−1.40	.0808	.1497	−0.95	.1711	.2541
−1.39	.0823	.1518	−0.94	.1736	.2565
−1.38	.0838	.1539	−0.93	.1762	.2589
−1.37	.0853	.1561	−0.92	.1788	.2613
−1.36	.0869	.1582	−0.91	.1814	.2637
−1.35	.0885	.1604	−0.90	.1841	.2661
−1.34	.0901	.1626	−0.89	.1867	.2685
−1.33	.0918	.1647	−0.88	.1894	.2709
−1.32	.0934	.1669	−0.87	.1922	.2732
−1.31	.0951	.1691	−0.86	.1949	.2756
−1.30	.0968	.1714	−0.85	.1977	.2780
−1.29	.0985	.1736	−0.84	.2005	.2803
−1.28	.1003	.1758	−0.83	.2033	.2827
−1.27	.1020	.1781	−0.82	.2061	.2850
−1.26	.1038	.1804	−0.81	.2090	.2874
−1.25	.1056	.1826	−0.80	.2119	.2897
−1.24	.1075	.1849	−0.79	.2148	.2920
−1.23	.1093	.1872	−0.78	.2177	.2943
−1.22	.1112	.1895	−0.77	.2206	.2966
−1.21	.1131	.1919	−0.76	.2236	.2989
−1.20	.1151	.1942	−0.75	.2266	.3011
−1.19	.1170	.1965	−0.74	.2296	.3034
−1.18	.1190	.1989	−0.73	.2327	.3056
−1.17	.1210	.2012	−0.72	.2358	.3079
−1.16	.1230	.2036	−0.71	.2389	.3101
−1.15	.1251	.2059	−0.70	.2420	.3123
−1.14	.1271	.2083	−0.69	.2451	.3144
−1.13	.1292	.2107	−0.68	.2483	.3166
−1.12	.1314	.2131	−0.67	.2514	.3187
−1.11	.1335	.2155	−0.66	.2546	.3209
−1.10	.1357	.2179	−0.65	.2578	.3230
−1.09	.1379	.2203	−0.64	.2611	.3251
−1.08	.1401	.2227	−0.63	.2643	.3271
−1.07	.1423	.2251	−0.62	.2676	.3292
−1.06	.1446	.2275	−0.61	.2709	.3312
−1.05	.1469	.2299	−0.60	.2743	.3332

z	Area	u Ordinate	z	Area	u Ordinate
−0.59	.2776	.3352	−0.14	.4443	.3951
−0.58	.2810	.3372	−0.13	.4483	.3956
−0.57	.2843	.3391	−0.12	.4522	.3961
−0.56	.2877	.3410	−0.11	.4562	.3965
−0.55	.2912	.3429	−0.10	.4602	.3970
−0.54	.2946	.3448	−0.09	.4641	.3973
−0.53	.2981	.3467	−0.08	.4681	.3977
−0.52	.3015	.3485	−0.07	.4721	.3980
−0.51	.3050	.3503	−0.06	.4761	.3982
−0.50	.3085	.3521	−0.05	.4801	.3984
−0.49	.3121	.3538	−0.04	.4840	.3986
−0.48	.3156	.3555	−0.03	.4880	.3988
−0.47	.3192	.3572	−0.02	.4920	.3989
−0.46	.3228	.3589	−0.01	.4960	.3989
−0.45	.3264	.3605	0.00	.5000	.3989
−0.44	.3300	.3621	0.01	.5040	.3989
−0.43	.3336	.3637	0.02	.5080	.3989
−0.42	.3372	.3653	0.03	.5120	.3988
−0.41	.3409	.3668	0.04	.5160	.3986
−0.40	.3446	.3683	0.05	.5199	.3984
−0.39	.3483	.3697	0.06	.5239	.3982
−0.38	.3520	.3712	0.07	.5279	.3980
−0.37	.3557	.3725	0.08	.5319	.3977
−0.36	.3594	.3739	0.09	.5359	.3973
−0.35	.3632	.3752	0.10	.5398	.3970
−0.34	.3669	.3765	0.11	.5438	.3965
−0.33	.3707	.3778	0.12	.5478	.3961
−0.32	.3745	.3790	0.13	.5517	.3956
−0.31	.3783	.3802	0.14	.5557	.3951
−0.30	.3821	.3814	0.15	.5596	.3945
−0.29	.3859	.3825	0.16	.5636	.3939
−0.28	.3897	.3836	0.17	.5675	.3932
−0.27	.3936	.3847	0.18	.5714	.3925
−0.26	.3974	.3857	0.19	.5753	.3918
−0.25	.4013	.3867	0.20	.5793	.3910
−0.24	.4052	.3876	0.21	.5832	.3902
−0.23	.4090	.3885	0.22	.5871	.3894
−0.22	.4129	.3894	0.23	.5910	.3885
−0.21	.4168	.3902	0.24	.5948	.3876
−0.20	.4207	.3910	0.25	.5987	.3867
−0.19	.4247	.3918	0.26	.6026	.3857
−0.18	.4286	.3925	0.27	.6064	.3847
−0.17	.4325	.3932	0.28	.6103	.3836
−0.16	.4364	.3939	0.29	.6141	.3825
−0.15	.4404	.3945	0.30	.6179	.3814

z	Area	u Ordinate	z	Area	u Ordinate
0.31	.6217	.3802	0.76	.7764	.2989
0.32	.6255	.3790	0.77	.7794	.2966
0.33	.6293	.3778	0.78	.7823	.2943
0.34	.6331	.3765	0.79	.7852	.2920
0.35	.6368	.3752	0.80	.7881	.2897
0.36	.6406	.3739	0.81	.7910	.2874
0.37	.6443	.3725	0.82	.7939	.2850
0.38	.6480	.3712	0.83	.7967	.2827
0.39	.6517	.3697	0.84	.7995	.2803
0.40	.6554	.3683	0.85	.8023	.2780
0.41	.6591	.3668	0.86	.8051	.2756
0.42	.6628	.3653	0.87	.8078	.2732
0.43	.6664	.3637	0.88	.8106	.2709
0.44	.6700	.3621	0.89	.8133	.2685
0.45	.6736	.3605	0.90	.8159	.2661
0.46	.6772	.3589	0.91	.8186	.2637
0.47	.6808	.3572	0.92	.8212	.2613
0.48	.6844	.3555	0.93	.8238	.2589
0.49	.6879	.3538	0.94	.8264	.2565
0.50	.6915	.3521	0.95	.8289	.2541
0.51	.6950	.3503	0.96	.8315	.2516
0.52	.6985	.3485	0.97	.8340	.2492
0.53	.7019	.3467	0.98	.8365	.2468
0.54	.7054	.3448	0.99	.8389	.2444
0.55	.7088	.3429	1.00	.8413	.2420
0.56	.7123	.3410	1.01	.8438	.2396
0.57	.7157	.3391	1.02	.8461	.2371
0.58	.7190	.3372	1.03	.8485	.2347
0.59	.7224	.3352	1.04	.8508	.2323
0.60	.7257	.3332	1.05	.8531	.2299
0.61	.7291	.3312	1.06	.8554	.2275
0.62	.7324	.3292	1.07	.8577	.2251
0.63	.7357	.3271	1.08	.8599	.2227
0.64	.7389	.3251	1.09	.8621	.2203
0.65	.7422	.3230	1.10	.8643	.2179
0.66	.7454	.3209	1.11	.8665	.2155
0.67	.7486	.3187	1.12	.8686	.2131
0.68	.7517	.3166	1.13	.8708	.2107
0.69	.7549	.3144	1.14	.8729	.2083
0.70	.7580	.3123	1.15	.8749	.2059
0.71	.7611	.3101	1.16	.8770	.2036
0.72	.7642	.3079	1.17	.8790	.2012
0.73	.7673	.3056	1.18	.8810	.1989
0.74	.7704	.3034	1.19	.8830	.1965
0.75	.7734	.3011	1.20	.8849	.1942

TABLE B (*cont.*)

z	Area	u Ordinate	z	Area	u Ordinate
1.21	.8869	.1919	1.66	.9515	.1006
1.22	.8888	.1895	1.67	.9525	.0989
1.23	.8907	.1872	1.68	.9535	.0973
1.24	.8925	.1849	1.69	.9545	.0957
1.25	.8944	.1826	1.70	.9554	.0940
1.26	.8962	.1804	1.71	.9564	.0925
1.27	.8980	.1781	1.72	.9573	.0909
1.28	.8997	.1758	1.73	.9582	.0893
1.29	.9015	.1736	1.74	.9591	.0878
1.30	.9032	.1714	1.75	.9599	.0863
1.31	.9049	.1691	1.76	.9608	.0848
1.32	.9066	.1669	1.77	.9616	.0833
1.33	.9082	.1647	1.78	.9625	.0818
1.34	.9099	.1626	1.79	.9633	.0804
1.35	.9115	.1604	1.80	.9641	.0790
1.36	.9131	.1582	1.81	.9649	.0775
1.37	.9147	.1561	1.82	.9656	.0761
1.38	.9162	.1539	1.83	.9664	.0748
1.39	.9177	.1518	1.84	.9671	.0734
1.40	.9192	.1497	1.85	.9678	.0721
1.41	.9207	.1476	1.86	.9686	.0707
1.42	.9222	.1456	1.87	.9693	.0694
1.43	.9236	.1435	1.88	.9699	.0681
1.44	.9251	.1415	1.89	.9706	.0669
1.45	.9265	.1394	1.90	.9713	.0656
1.46	.9279	.1374	1.91	.9719	.0644
1.47	.9292	.1354	1.92	.9726	.0632
1.48	.9306	.1334	1.93	.9732	.0620
1.49	.9319	.1315	1.94	.9738	.0608
1.50	.9332	.1295	1.95	.9744	.0596
1.51	.9345	.1276	1.96	.9750	.0584
1.52	.9357	.1257	1.97	.9756	.0573
1.53	.9370	.1238	1.98	.9761	.0562
1.54	.9382	.1219	1.99	.9767	.0551
1.55	.9394	.1200	2.00	.9772	.0540
1.56	.9406	.1182	2.01	.9778	.0529
1.57	.9418	.1163	2.02	.9783	.0519
1.58	.9429	.1145	2.03	.9788	.0508
1.59	.9441	.1127	2.04	.9793	.0498
1.60	.9452	.1109	2.05	.9798	.0488
1.61	.9463	.1092	2.06	.9803	.0478
1.62	.9474	.1074	2.07	.9808	.0468
1.63	.9484	.1057	2.08	.9812	.0459
1.64	.9495	.1040	2.09	.9817	.0449
1.65	.9505	.1023	2.10	.9821	.0440

z	Area	u Ordinate	z	Area	u Ordinate
2.11	.9826	.0431	2.56	.9948	.0151
2.12	.9830	.0422	2.57	.9949	.0147
2.13	.9834	.0413	2.58	.9951	.0143
2.14	.9838	.0404	2.59	.9952	.0139
2.15	.9842	.0396	2.60	.9953	.0136
2.16	.9846	.0387	2.61	.9955	.0132
2.17	.9850	.0379	2.62	.9956	.0129
2.18	.9854	.0371	2.63	.9957	.0126
2.19	.9857	.0363	2.64	.9959	.0122
2.20	.9861	.0355	2.65	.9960	.0119
2.21	.9864	.0347	2.66	.9961	.0116
2.22	.9868	.0339	2.67	.9962	.0113
2.23	.9871	.0332	2.68	.9963	.0110
2.24	.9875	.0325	2.69	.9964	.0107
2.25	.9878	.0317	2.70	.9965	.0104
2.26	.9881	.0310	2.71	.9966	.0101
2.27	.9884	.0303	2.72	.9967	.0099
2.28	.9887	.0297	2.73	.9968	.0096
2.29	.9890	.0290	2.74	.9969	.0093
2.30	.9893	.0283	2.75	.9970	.0091
2.31	.9896	.0277	2.76	.9971	.0088
2.32	.9898	.0270	2.77	.9972	.0086
2.33	.9901	.0264	2.78	.9973	.0084
2.34	.9904	.0258	2.79	.9974	.0081
2.35	.9906	.0252	2.80	.9974	.0079
2.36	.9909	.0246	2.81	.9975	.0077
2.37	.9911	.0241	2.82	.9976	.0075
2.38	.9913	.0235	2.83	.9977	.0073
2.39	.9916	.0229	2.84	.9977	.0071
2.40	.9918	.0224	2.85	.9978	.0069
2.41	.9920	.0219	2.86	.9979	.0067
2.42	.9922	.0213	2.87	.9979	.0065
2.43	.9925	.0208	2.88	.9980	.0063
2.44	.9927	.0203	2.89	.9981	.0061
2.45	.9929	.0198	2.90	.9981	.0060
2.46	.9931	.0194	2.91	.9982	.0058
2.47	.9932	.0189	2.92	.9982	.0056
2.48	.9934	.0184	2.93	.9983	.0055
2.49	.9936	.0180	2.94	.9984	.0053
2.50	.9938	.0175	2.95	.9984	.0051
2.51	.9940	.0171	2.96	.9985	.0050
2.52	.9941	.0167	2.97	.9985	.0048
2.53	.9943	.0163	2.98	.9986	.0047
2.54	.9945	.0158	2.99	.9986	.0046
2.55	.9946	.0154	3.00	.9987	.0044

TABLE C PERCENTILE POINTS OF CHI-SQUARE DISTRIBUTIONS*

Percentile

df	1	2	5	10	20	30	50	70	80	90	95	98	99	99.9
1	.0002	.0006	.00393	.0158	.0642	.148	.455	1.074	1.642	2.706	3.841	5.412	6.635	10.827
2	.0201	.0404	.103	.211	.446	.713	1.386	2.408	3.219	4.605	5.991	7.824	9.210	13.815
3	.115	.185	.352	.584	1.005	1.424	2.366	3.665	4.642	6.251	7.815	9.837	11.341	16.268
4	.297	.429	.711	1.064	1.649	2.195	3.357	4.878	5.989	7.779	9.488	11.668	13.277	18.465
5	.554	.752	1.145	1.610	2.343	3.000	4.351	6.064	7.289	9.236	11.070	13.388	15.086	20.517
6	.872	1.134	1.635	2.204	3.070	3.828	5.348	7.231	8.558	10.645	12.592	15.033	16.812	22.457
7	1.239	1.564	2.167	2.833	3.822	4.671	6.346	8.383	9.803	12.017	14.067	16.622	18.475	24.322
8	1.646	2.032	2.733	3.490	4.594	5.527	7.344	9.524	11.030	13.362	15.507	18.168	20.090	26.125
9	2.088	2.532	3.325	4.168	5.380	6.393	8.343	10.656	12.242	14.684	16.919	19.679	21.666	27.877
10	2.558	3.059	3.940	4.865	6.179	7.267	9.342	11.781	13.442	15.987	18.307	21.161	23.209	29.588
11	3.053	3.609	4.575	5.578	6.989	8.148	10.341	12.899	14.631	17.275	19.675	22.618	24.725	31.264
12	3.571	4.178	5.226	6.304	7.807	9.034	11.340	14.011	15.812	18.549	21.026	24.054	26.217	32.909
13	4.107	4.765	5.892	7.042	8.634	9.926	12.340	15.119	16.985	19.812	22.362	25.472	27.688	34.528
14	4.660	5.368	6.571	7.790	9.467	10.821	13.339	16.222	18.151	21.064	23.685	26.873	29.141	36.123
15	5.229	5.985	7.261	8.547	10.307	11.721	14.339	17.322	19.311	22.307	24.996	28.259	30.578	37.697
16	5.812	6.614	7.962	9.312	11.152	12.624	15.338	18.418	20.465	23.542	26.296	29.633	32.000	39.252
17	6.408	7.255	8.672	10.085	12.002	13.531	16.338	19.511	21.615	24.769	27.587	30.995	33.409	40.790
18	7.015	7.906	9.390	10.865	12.857	14.440	17.338	20.601	22.760	25.989	28.869	32.346	34.805	42.312
19	7.633	8.567	10.117	11.651	13.716	15.352	18.338	21.689	23.900	27.204	30.144	33.687	36.191	43.820
20	8.260	9.237	10.851	12.443	14.578	16.266	19.337	22.775	25.038	28.412	31.410	35.020	37.566	45.315
21	8.897	9.915	11.591	13.240	15.445	17.182	20.337	23.858	26.171	29.615	32.671	36.343	38.932	46.797
22	9.542	10.600	12.338	14.041	16.314	18.101	21.337	24.939	27.301	30.813	33.924	37.659	40.289	48.268
23	10.196	11.293	13.091	14.848	17.187	19.021	22.337	26.018	28.429	32.007	35.172	38.968	41.638	49.728
24	10.856	11.992	13.848	15.659	18.062	19.943	23.337	27.096	29.553	33.196	36.415	40.270	42.980	51.179
25	11.524	12.697	14.611	16.473	18.940	20.867	24.337	28.172	30.675	34.382	37.652	41.566	44.314	52.620
26	12.198	13.409	15.379	17.292	19.820	21.792	25.336	29.246	31.795	35.563	38.885	42.856	45.642	54.052
27	12.879	14.125	16.151	18.114	20.703	22.719	26.336	30.319	32.912	36.741	40.113	44.140	46.963	55.476
28	13.565	14.847	16.928	18.939	21.588	23.647	27.336	31.391	34.027	37.916	41.337	45.419	48.278	56.893
29	14.256	15.574	17.708	19.768	22.475	24.577	28.336	32.461	35.139	39.087	42.557	46.693	49.588	58.302
30	14.953	16.306	18.493	20.599	23.364	25.508	29.336	33.530	36.250	40.256	43.773	47.962	50.892	59.703

Table C is adapted from Table IV of Fisher & Yates: *Statistical Tables for Biological, Agricultural and Medical Research*, published by Oliver & Boyd Ltd., Edinburgh, and by permission of the authors and publishers.

* If χ^2 is a chi-square variable with df greater than 30, then

$$z = \sqrt{2\chi^2} - \sqrt{2df - 1}$$

is very nearly normally distributed with mean 0 and standard deviation 1.

TABLE D PERCENTILE POINTS OF t-DISTRIBUTIONS

*Percentile**

df	55	60	65	70	75	80	85	90	95	97.5	99	99.5	99.95
1	.158	.325	.510	.727	1.000	1.376	1.963	3.078	6.314	12.706	31.821	63.657	636.619
2	.142	.289	.445	.617	.816	1.061	1.386	1.886	2.920	4.303	6.965	9.925	31.598
3	.137	.277	.424	.584	.765	.978	1.250	1.638	2.353	3.182	4.541	5.841	12.941
4	.134	.271	.414	.569	.741	.941	1.190	1.533	2.132	2.776	3.747	4.604	8.610
5	.132	.267	.408	.559	.727	.920	1.156	1.476	2.015	2.571	3.365	4.032	6.859
6	.131	.265	.404	.553	.718	.906	1.134	1.440	1.943	2.447	3.143	3.707	5.959
7	.130	.263	.402	.549	.711	.896	1.119	1.415	1.895	2.365	2.998	3.499	5.405
8	.130	.262	.399	.546	.706	.889	1.108	1.397	1.860	2.306	2.896	3.355	5.041
9	.129	.261	.398	.543	.703	.883	1.100	1.383	1.833	2.262	2.821	3.250	4.781
10	.129	.260	.397	.542	.700	.879	1.093	1.372	1.812	2.228	2.764	3.169	4.587
11	.129	.260	.396	.540	.697	.876	1.088	1.363	1.796	2.201	2.718	3.106	4.437
12	.128	.259	.395	.539	.695	.873	1.083	1.356	1.782	2.179	2.681	3.055	4.318
13	.128	.259	.394	.538	.694	.870	1.079	1.350	1.771	2.160	2.650	3.012	4.221
14	.128	.258	.393	.537	.692	.868	1.076	1.345	1.761	2.145	2.624	2.977	4.140
15	.128	.258	.393	.536	.691	.866	1.074	1.341	1.753	2.131	2.602	2.947	4.073
16	.128	.258	.392	.535	.690	.865	1.071	1.337	1.746	2.120	2.583	2.921	4.015
17	.128	.257	.392	.534	.689	.863	1.069	1.333	1.740	2.110	2.567	2.898	3.965
18	.127	.257	.392	.534	.688	.862	1.067	1.330	1.734	2.101	2.552	2.878	3.922
19	.127	.257	.391	.533	.688	.861	1.066	1.328	1.729	2.093	2.539	2.861	3.883
20	.127	.257	.391	.533	.687	.860	1.064	1.325	1.725	2.086	2.528	2.845	3.850
21	.127	.257	.391	.532	.686	.859	1.063	1.323	1.721	2.080	2.518	2.831	3.819
22	.127	.256	.390	.532	.686	.858	1.061	1.321	1.717	2.074	2.508	2.819	3.792
23	.127	.256	.390	.532	.685	.858	1.060	1.319	1.714	2.069	2.500	2.807	3.767
24	.127	.256	.390	.531	.685	.857	1.059	1.318	1.711	2.064	2.492	2.797	3.745
25	.127	.256	.390	.531	.684	.856	1.058	1.316	1.708	2.060	2.485	2.787	3.725
26	.127	.256	.390	.531	.684	.856	1.058	1.315	1.706	2.056	2.479	2.779	3.707
27	.127	.256	.389	.531	.684	.855	1.057	1.314	1.703	2.052	2.473	2.771	3.690
28	.127	.256	.389	.530	.683	.855	1.056	1.313	1.701	2.048	2.467	2.763	3.674
29	.127	.256	.389	.530	.683	.854	1.055	1.311	1.699	2.045	2.462	2.756	3.659
30	.127	.256	.389	.530	.683	.854	1.055	1.310	1.697	2.042	2.457	2.750	3.646
40	.126	.255	.388	.529	.681	.851	1.050	1.303	1.684	2.021	2.423	2.704	3.551
60	.126	.254	.387	.527	.679	.848	1.046	1.296	1.671	2.000	2.390	2.660	3.460
120	.126	.254	.386	.526	.677	.845	1.041	1.289	1.658	1.980	2.358	2.617	3.373
∞	.126	.253	.385	.524	.674	.842	1.036	1.282	1.645	1.960	2.326	2.576	3.291

Table D is adapted from Table III of Fisher & Yates: *Statistical Tables for Biological, Agricultural and Medical Research*, published by Oliver & Boyd Ltd., Edinburgh, and by permission of the authors and publishers.
* The lower percentiles are related to the upper percentiles which are tabulated above by the equation $_p t_n = -_{1-p} t_n$. Thus, the 10th percentile in the t-distribution with $15 df$ equals the negative of the 90th percentile in the same distribution, i.e., $_{10} t_{15} = -1.341$.

TABLE E   PERCENTILE POINTS OF F-DISTRIBUTIONS

75th percentiles

n_2 \ n_1	1	2	3	4	5	6	7	8	9	10	12	15	20	24	30	40	60	120	∞
1	5.83	7.50	8.20	8.58	8.82	8.98	9.10	9.19	9.26	9.32	9.41	9.49	9.58	9.63	9.67	9.71	9.76	9.80	9.85
2	2.57	3.00	3.15	3.23	3.28	3.31	3.34	3.35	3.37	3.38	3.39	3.41	3.43	3.43	3.44	3.45	3.46	3.47	3.48
3	2.02	2.28	2.36	2.39	2.41	2.42	2.43	2.44	2.44	2.44	2.45	2.46	2.46	2.46	2.47	2.47	2.47	2.47	2.47
4	1.81	2.00	2.05	2.06	2.07	2.08	2.08	2.08	2.08	2.08	2.08	2.08	2.08	2.08	2.08	2.08	2.08	2.08	2.08
5	1.69	1.85	1.88	1.89	1.89	1.89	1.89	1.89	1.89	1.89	1.89	1.89	1.88	1.88	1.88	1.88	1.87	1.87	1.87
6	1.62	1.76	1.78	1.79	1.79	1.78	1.78	1.78	1.77	1.77	1.77	1.76	1.76	1.75	1.75	1.75	1.74	1.74	1.74
7	1.57	1.70	1.72	1.72	1.71	1.71	1.70	1.70	1.69	1.69	1.68	1.68	1.67	1.67	1.66	1.66	1.65	1.65	1.65
8	1.54	1.66	1.67	1.66	1.66	1.65	1.64	1.64	1.63	1.63	1.62	1.62	1.61	1.60	1.60	1.59	1.59	1.58	1.58
9	1.51	1.62	1.63	1.63	1.62	1.61	1.60	1.60	1.59	1.59	1.58	1.57	1.56	1.56	1.55	1.54	1.54	1.53	1.53
10	1.49	1.60	1.60	1.59	1.59	1.58	1.57	1.56	1.56	1.55	1.54	1.53	1.52	1.52	1.51	1.51	1.50	1.49	1.48
11	1.47	1.58	1.58	1.57	1.56	1.55	1.54	1.53	1.53	1.52	1.51	1.50	1.49	1.49	1.48	1.47	1.47	1.46	1.45
12	1.46	1.56	1.56	1.55	1.54	1.53	1.52	1.51	1.51	1.50	1.49	1.48	1.47	1.46	1.45	1.45	1.44	1.43	1.42
13	1.45	1.55	1.55	1.53	1.52	1.51	1.50	1.49	1.49	1.48	1.47	1.46	1.45	1.44	1.43	1.42	1.42	1.41	1.40
14	1.44	1.53	1.53	1.52	1.51	1.50	1.49	1.48	1.47	1.46	1.45	1.44	1.43	1.42	1.41	1.41	1.40	1.39	1.38
15	1.43	1.52	1.52	1.51	1.49	1.48	1.47	1.46	1.46	1.45	1.44	1.43	1.41	1.41	1.40	1.39	1.38	1.37	1.36
16	1.42	1.51	1.51	1.50	1.48	1.47	1.46	1.45	1.44	1.44	1.43	1.41	1.40	1.39	1.38	1.37	1.36	1.35	1.34
17	1.42	1.51	1.50	1.49	1.47	1.46	1.45	1.44	1.43	1.43	1.41	1.40	1.39	1.38	1.37	1.36	1.35	1.34	1.33
18	1.41	1.50	1.49	1.48	1.46	1.45	1.44	1.43	1.42	1.42	1.40	1.39	1.38	1.37	1.36	1.35	1.34	1.33	1.32
19	1.41	1.49	1.49	1.47	1.46	1.44	1.43	1.42	1.41	1.41	1.40	1.38	1.37	1.36	1.35	1.34	1.33	1.32	1.30
20	1.40	1.49	1.48	1.47	1.45	1.44	1.43	1.42	1.41	1.40	1.39	1.37	1.36	1.35	1.34	1.33	1.32	1.31	1.29
21	1.40	1.48	1.48	1.46	1.44	1.43	1.42	1.41	1.40	1.39	1.38	1.37	1.35	1.34	1.33	1.32	1.31	1.30	1.28
22	1.40	1.48	1.47	1.45	1.44	1.42	1.41	1.40	1.39	1.39	1.37	1.36	1.34	1.33	1.32	1.31	1.30	1.29	1.28
23	1.39	1.47	1.47	1.45	1.43	1.42	1.41	1.40	1.39	1.38	1.37	1.35	1.34	1.33	1.32	1.31	1.30	1.28	1.27
24	1.39	1.47	1.46	1.44	1.43	1.41	1.40	1.39	1.38	1.38	1.36	1.35	1.33	1.32	1.31	1.30	1.29	1.28	1.26
25	1.39	1.47	1.46	1.44	1.42	1.41	1.40	1.39	1.38	1.37	1.36	1.34	1.33	1.32	1.31	1.29	1.28	1.27	1.25
26	1.38	1.46	1.45	1.44	1.42	1.41	1.39	1.38	1.37	1.37	1.35	1.34	1.32	1.31	1.30	1.29	1.28	1.26	1.25
27	1.38	1.46	1.45	1.43	1.42	1.40	1.39	1.38	1.37	1.36	1.35	1.33	1.32	1.31	1.30	1.28	1.27	1.26	1.24
28	1.38	1.46	1.45	1.43	1.41	1.40	1.39	1.38	1.37	1.36	1.34	1.33	1.31	1.30	1.29	1.28	1.27	1.25	1.24
29	1.38	1.45	1.45	1.43	1.41	1.40	1.38	1.37	1.36	1.35	1.34	1.32	1.31	1.30	1.29	1.27	1.26	1.25	1.23
30	1.38	1.45	1.44	1.42	1.41	1.39	1.38	1.37	1.36	1.35	1.34	1.32	1.30	1.29	1.28	1.27	1.26	1.24	1.23
40	1.36	1.44	1.42	1.40	1.39	1.37	1.36	1.35	1.34	1.33	1.31	1.30	1.28	1.26	1.25	1.24	1.22	1.21	1.19
60	1.35	1.42	1.41	1.38	1.37	1.35	1.33	1.32	1.31	1.30	1.29	1.27	1.25	1.24	1.22	1.21	1.19	1.17	1.15
120	1.34	1.40	1.39	1.37	1.35	1.33	1.31	1.30	1.29	1.28	1.26	1.24	1.22	1.21	1.19	1.18	1.16	1.13	1.10
∞	1.32	1.39	1.37	1.35	1.33	1.31	1.29	1.28	1.27	1.25	1.24	1.22	1.19	1.18	1.16	1.14	1.12	1.08	1.00

90th percentiles

n_2 \ n_1	1	2	3	4	5	6	7	8	9	10	12	15	20	24	30	40	60	120	∞
1	39.86	49.50	53.59	55.83	57.24	58.20	58.91	59.44	59.86	60.19	60.71	61.22	61.74	62.00	62.26	62.53	62.79	63.06	63.33
2	8.53	9.00	9.16	9.24	9.29	9.33	9.35	9.37	9.38	9.39	9.41	9.42	9.44	9.45	9.46	9.47	9.47	9.48	9.49
3	5.54	5.46	5.39	5.34	5.31	5.28	5.27	5.25	5.24	5.23	5.22	5.20	5.18	5.18	5.17	5.16	5.15	5.14	5.13
4	4.54	4.32	4.19	4.11	4.05	4.01	3.98	3.95	3.94	3.92	3.90	3.87	3.84	3.83	3.82	3.80	3.79	3.78	3.76
5	4.06	3.78	3.62	3.52	3.45	3.40	3.37	3.34	3.32	3.30	3.27	3.24	3.21	3.19	3.17	3.16	3.14	3.12	3.10
6	3.78	3.46	3.29	3.18	3.11	3.05	3.01	2.98	2.96	2.94	2.90	2.87	2.84	2.82	2.80	2.78	2.76	2.74	2.72
7	3.59	3.26	3.07	2.96	2.88	2.83	2.78	2.75	2.72	2.70	2.67	2.63	2.59	2.58	2.56	2.54	2.51	2.49	2.47
8	3.46	3.11	2.92	2.81	2.73	2.67	2.62	2.59	2.56	2.54	2.50	2.46	2.42	2.40	2.38	2.36	2.34	2.32	2.29
9	3.36	3.01	2.81	2.69	2.61	2.55	2.51	2.47	2.44	2.42	2.38	2.34	2.30	2.28	2.25	2.23	2.21	2.18	2.16
10	3.29	2.92	2.73	2.61	2.52	2.46	2.41	2.38	2.35	2.32	2.28	2.24	2.20	2.18	2.16	2.13	2.11	2.08	2.06
11	3.23	2.86	2.66	2.54	2.45	2.39	2.34	2.30	2.27	2.25	2.21	2.17	2.12	2.10	2.08	2.05	2.03	2.00	1.97
12	3.18	2.81	2.61	2.48	2.39	2.33	2.28	2.24	2.21	2.19	2.15	2.10	2.06	2.04	2.01	1.99	1.96	1.93	1.90
13	3.14	2.76	2.56	2.43	2.35	2.28	2.23	2.20	2.16	2.14	2.10	2.05	2.01	1.98	1.96	1.93	1.90	1.88	1.85
14	3.10	2.73	2.52	2.39	2.31	2.24	2.19	2.15	2.12	2.10	2.05	2.01	1.96	1.94	1.91	1.89	1.86	1.83	1.80
15	3.07	2.70	2.49	2.36	2.27	2.21	2.16	2.12	2.09	2.06	2.02	1.97	1.92	1.90	1.87	1.85	1.82	1.79	1.76
16	3.05	2.67	2.46	2.33	2.24	2.18	2.13	2.09	2.06	2.03	1.99	1.94	1.89	1.87	1.84	1.81	1.78	1.75	1.72
17	3.03	2.64	2.44	2.31	2.22	2.15	2.10	2.06	2.03	2.00	1.96	1.91	1.86	1.84	1.81	1.78	1.75	1.72	1.69
18	3.01	2.62	2.42	2.29	2.20	2.13	2.08	2.04	2.00	1.98	1.93	1.89	1.84	1.81	1.78	1.75	1.72	1.69	1.66
19	2.99	2.61	2.40	2.27	2.18	2.11	2.06	2.02	1.98	1.96	1.91	1.86	1.81	1.79	1.76	1.73	1.70	1.67	1.63
20	2.97	2.59	2.38	2.25	2.16	2.09	2.04	2.00	1.96	1.94	1.89	1.84	1.79	1.77	1.74	1.71	1.68	1.64	1.61
21	2.96	2.57	2.36	2.23	2.14	2.08	2.02	1.98	1.95	1.92	1.87	1.83	1.78	1.75	1.72	1.69	1.66	1.62	1.59
22	2.95	2.56	2.35	2.22	2.13	2.06	2.01	1.97	1.93	1.90	1.86	1.81	1.76	1.73	1.70	1.67	1.64	1.60	1.57
23	2.94	2.55	2.34	2.21	2.11	2.05	1.99	1.95	1.92	1.89	1.84	1.80	1.74	1.72	1.69	1.66	1.62	1.59	1.55
24	2.93	2.54	2.33	2.19	2.10	2.04	1.98	1.94	1.91	1.88	1.83	1.78	1.73	1.70	1.67	1.64	1.61	1.57	1.53
25	2.92	2.53	2.32	2.18	2.09	2.02	1.97	1.93	1.89	1.87	1.82	1.77	1.72	1.69	1.66	1.63	1.59	1.56	1.52
26	2.91	2.52	2.31	2.17	2.08	2.01	1.96	1.92	1.88	1.86	1.81	1.76	1.71	1.68	1.65	1.61	1.58	1.54	1.50
27	2.90	2.51	2.30	2.17	2.07	2.00	1.95	1.91	1.87	1.85	1.80	1.75	1.70	1.67	1.64	1.60	1.57	1.53	1.49
28	2.89	2.50	2.29	2.16	2.06	2.00	1.94	1.90	1.87	1.84	1.79	1.74	1.69	1.66	1.63	1.59	1.56	1.52	1.48
29	2.89	2.50	2.28	2.15	2.06	1.99	1.93	1.89	1.86	1.83	1.78	1.73	1.68	1.65	1.62	1.58	1.55	1.51	1.47
30	2.88	2.49	2.28	2.14	2.05	1.98	1.93	1.88	1.85	1.82	1.77	1.72	1.67	1.64	1.61	1.57	1.54	1.50	1.46
40	2.84	2.44	2.23	2.09	2.00	1.93	1.87	1.83	1.79	1.76	1.71	1.66	1.61	1.57	1.54	1.51	1.47	1.42	1.38
60	2.79	2.39	2.18	2.04	1.95	1.87	1.82	1.77	1.74	1.71	1.66	1.60	1.54	1.51	1.48	1.44	1.40	1.35	1.29
120	2.75	2.35	2.13	1.99	1.90	1.82	1.77	1.72	1.68	1.65	1.60	1.55	1.48	1.45	1.41	1.37	1.32	1.26	1.19
∞	2.71	2.30	2.08	1.94	1.85	1.77	1.72	1.67	1.63	1.60	1.55	1.49	1.42	1.38	1.34	1.30	1.24	1.17	1.00

TABLE E (cont.)

95th percentiles

n_2 \ n_1	1	2	3	4	5	6	7	8	9	10	12	15	20	24	30	40	60	120	∞
1	161.4	199.5	215.7	224.6	230.2	234.0	236.8	238.9	240.5	241.9	243.9	245.9	248.0	249.1	250.1	251.1	252.2	253.3	254.3
2	18.51	19.00	19.16	19.25	19.30	19.33	19.35	19.37	19.38	19.40	19.41	19.43	19.45	19.45	19.46	19.47	19.48	19.49	19.50
3	10.13	9.55	9.28	9.12	9.01	8.94	8.89	8.85	8.81	8.79	8.74	8.70	8.66	8.64	8.62	8.59	8.57	8.55	8.53
4	7.71	6.94	6.59	6.39	6.26	6.16	6.09	6.04	6.00	5.96	5.91	5.86	5.80	5.77	5.75	5.72	5.69	5.66	5.63
5	6.61	5.79	5.41	5.19	5.05	4.95	4.88	4.82	4.77	4.74	4.68	4.62	4.56	4.53	4.50	4.46	4.43	4.40	4.36
6	5.99	5.14	4.76	4.53	4.39	4.28	4.21	4.15	4.10	4.06	4.00	3.94	3.87	3.84	3.81	3.77	3.74	3.70	3.67
7	5.59	4.74	4.35	4.12	3.97	3.87	3.79	3.73	3.68	3.64	3.57	3.51	3.44	3.41	3.38	3.34	3.30	3.27	3.23
8	5.32	4.46	4.07	3.84	3.69	3.58	3.50	3.44	3.39	3.35	3.28	3.22	3.15	3.12	3.08	3.04	3.01	2.97	2.93
9	5.12	4.26	3.86	3.63	3.48	3.37	3.29	3.23	3.18	3.14	3.07	3.01	2.94	2.90	2.86	2.83	2.79	2.75	2.71
10	4.96	4.10	3.71	3.48	3.33	3.22	3.14	3.07	3.02	2.98	2.91	2.85	2.77	2.74	2.70	2.66	2.62	2.58	2.54
11	4.84	3.98	3.59	3.36	3.20	3.09	3.01	2.95	2.90	2.85	2.79	2.72	2.65	2.61	2.57	2.53	2.49	2.45	2.40
12	4.75	3.89	3.49	3.26	3.11	3.00	2.91	2.85	2.80	2.75	2.69	2.62	2.54	2.51	2.47	2.43	2.38	2.34	2.30
13	4.67	3.81	3.41	3.18	3.03	2.92	2.83	2.77	2.71	2.67	2.60	2.53	2.46	2.42	2.38	2.34	2.30	2.25	2.21
14	4.60	3.74	3.34	3.11	2.96	2.85	2.76	2.70	2.65	2.60	2.53	2.46	2.39	2.35	2.31	2.27	2.22	2.18	2.13
15	4.54	3.68	3.29	3.06	2.90	2.79	2.71	2.64	2.59	2.54	2.48	2.40	2.33	2.29	2.25	2.20	2.16	2.11	2.07
16	4.49	3.63	3.24	3.01	2.85	2.74	2.66	2.59	2.54	2.49	2.42	2.35	2.28	2.24	2.19	2.15	2.11	2.06	2.01
17	4.45	3.59	3.20	2.96	2.81	2.70	2.61	2.55	2.49	2.45	2.38	2.31	2.23	2.19	2.15	2.10	2.06	2.01	1.96
18	4.41	3.55	3.16	2.93	2.77	2.66	2.58	2.51	2.46	2.41	2.34	2.27	2.19	2.15	2.11	2.06	2.02	1.97	1.92
19	4.38	3.52	3.13	2.90	2.74	2.63	2.54	2.48	2.42	2.38	2.31	2.23	2.16	2.11	2.07	2.03	1.98	1.93	1.88
20	4.35	3.49	3.10	2.87	2.71	2.60	2.51	2.45	2.39	2.35	2.28	2.20	2.12	2.08	2.04	1.99	1.95	1.90	1.84
21	4.32	3.47	3.07	2.84	2.68	2.57	2.49	2.42	2.37	2.32	2.25	2.18	2.10	2.05	2.01	1.96	1.92	1.87	1.81
22	4.30	3.44	3.05	2.82	2.66	2.55	2.46	2.40	2.34	2.30	2.23	2.15	2.07	2.03	1.98	1.94	1.89	1.84	1.78
23	4.28	3.42	3.03	2.80	2.64	2.53	2.44	2.37	2.32	2.27	2.20	2.13	2.05	2.01	1.96	1.91	1.86	1.81	1.76
24	4.26	3.40	3.01	2.78	2.62	2.51	2.42	2.36	2.30	2.25	2.18	2.11	2.03	1.98	1.94	1.89	1.84	1.79	1.73
25	4.24	3.39	2.99	2.76	2.60	2.49	2.40	2.34	2.28	2.24	2.16	2.09	2.01	1.96	1.92	1.87	1.82	1.77	1.71
26	4.23	3.37	2.98	2.74	2.59	2.47	2.39	2.32	2.27	2.22	2.15	2.07	1.99	1.95	1.90	1.85	1.80	1.75	1.69
27	4.21	3.35	2.96	2.73	2.57	2.46	2.37	2.31	2.25	2.20	2.13	2.06	1.97	1.93	1.88	1.84	1.79	1.73	1.67
28	4.20	3.34	2.95	2.71	2.56	2.45	2.36	2.29	2.24	2.19	2.12	2.04	1.96	1.91	1.87	1.82	1.77	1.71	1.65
29	4.18	3.33	2.93	2.70	2.55	2.43	2.35	2.28	2.22	2.18	2.10	2.03	1.94	1.90	1.85	1.81	1.75	1.70	1.64
30	4.17	3.32	2.92	2.69	2.53	2.42	2.33	2.27	2.21	2.16	2.09	2.01	1.93	1.89	1.84	1.79	1.74	1.68	1.62
40	4.08	3.23	2.84	2.61	2.45	2.34	2.25	2.18	2.12	2.08	2.00	1.92	1.84	1.79	1.74	1.69	1.64	1.58	1.51
60	4.00	3.15	2.76	2.53	2.37	2.25	2.17	2.10	2.04	1.99	1.92	1.84	1.75	1.70	1.65	1.59	1.53	1.47	1.39
120	3.92	3.07	2.68	2.45	2.29	2.17	2.09	2.02	1.96	1.91	1.83	1.75	1.66	1.61	1.55	1.50	1.43	1.35	1.25
∞	3.84	3.00	2.60	2.37	2.21	2.10	2.01	1.94	1.88	1.83	1.75	1.67	1.57	1.52	1.46	1.39	1.32	1.22	1.00

97.5th percentiles

n_2 \ n_1	1	2	3	4	5	6	7	8	9	10	12	15	20	24	30	40	60	120	∞
1	647.8	799.5	864.2	899.6	921.8	937.1	948.2	956.7	963.3	968.6	976.7	984.9	993.1	997.2	1001	1006	1010	1014	1018
2	38.51	39.00	39.17	39.25	39.30	39.33	39.36	39.37	39.39	39.40	39.41	39.43	39.45	39.46	39.46	39.47	39.48	39.49	39.50
3	17.44	16.04	15.44	15.10	14.88	14.73	14.62	14.54	14.47	14.42	14.34	14.25	14.17	14.12	14.08	14.04	13.99	13.95	13.90
4	12.22	10.65	9.98	9.60	9.36	9.20	9.07	8.98	8.90	8.84	8.75	8.66	8.56	8.51	8.46	8.41	8.36	8.31	8.26
5	10.01	8.43	7.76	7.39	7.15	6.98	6.85	6.76	6.68	6.62	6.52	6.43	6.33	6.28	6.23	6.18	6.12	6.07	6.02
6	8.81	7.26	6.60	6.23	5.99	5.82	5.70	5.60	5.52	5.46	5.37	5.27	5.17	5.12	5.07	5.01	4.96	4.90	4.85
7	8.07	6.54	5.89	5.52	5.29	5.12	4.99	4.90	4.82	4.76	4.67	4.57	4.47	4.42	4.36	4.31	4.25	4.20	4.14
8	7.57	6.06	5.42	5.05	4.82	4.65	4.53	4.43	4.36	4.30	4.20	4.10	4.00	3.95	3.89	3.84	3.78	3.73	3.67
9	7.21	5.71	5.08	4.72	4.48	4.32	4.20	4.10	4.03	3.96	3.87	3.77	3.67	3.61	3.56	3.51	3.45	3.39	3.33
10	6.94	5.46	4.83	4.47	4.24	4.07	3.95	3.85	3.78	3.72	3.62	3.52	3.42	3.37	3.31	3.26	3.20	3.14	3.08
11	6.72	5.26	4.63	4.28	4.04	3.88	3.76	3.66	3.59	3.53	3.43	3.33	3.23	3.17	3.12	3.06	3.00	2.94	2.88
12	6.55	5.10	4.47	4.12	3.89	3.73	3.61	3.51	3.44	3.37	3.28	3.18	3.07	3.02	2.96	2.91	2.85	2.79	2.72
13	6.41	4.97	4.35	4.00	3.77	3.60	3.48	3.39	3.31	3.25	3.15	3.05	2.95	2.89	2.84	2.78	2.72	2.66	2.60
14	6.30	4.86	4.24	3.89	3.66	3.50	3.38	3.29	3.21	3.15	3.05	2.95	2.84	2.79	2.73	2.67	2.61	2.55	2.49
15	6.20	4.77	4.15	3.80	3.58	3.41	3.29	3.20	3.12	3.06	2.96	2.86	2.76	2.70	2.64	2.59	2.52	2.46	2.40
16	6.12	4.69	4.08	3.73	3.50	3.34	3.22	3.12	3.05	2.99	2.89	2.79	2.68	2.63	2.57	2.51	2.45	2.38	2.32
17	6.04	4.62	4.01	3.66	3.44	3.28	3.16	3.06	2.98	2.92	2.82	2.72	2.62	2.56	2.50	2.44	2.38	2.32	2.25
18	5.98	4.56	3.95	3.61	3.38	3.22	3.10	3.01	2.93	2.87	2.77	2.67	2.56	2.50	2.44	2.38	2.32	2.26	2.19
19	5.92	4.51	3.90	3.56	3.33	3.17	3.05	2.96	2.88	2.82	2.72	2.62	2.51	2.45	2.39	2.33	2.27	2.20	2.13
20	5.87	4.46	3.86	3.51	3.29	3.13	3.01	2.91	2.84	2.77	2.68	2.57	2.46	2.41	2.35	2.29	2.22	2.16	2.09
21	5.83	4.42	3.82	3.48	3.25	3.09	2.97	2.87	2.80	2.73	2.64	2.53	2.42	2.37	2.31	2.25	2.18	2.11	2.04
22	5.79	4.38	3.78	3.44	3.22	3.05	2.93	2.84	2.76	2.70	2.60	2.50	2.39	2.33	2.27	2.21	2.14	2.08	2.00
23	5.75	4.35	3.75	3.41	3.18	3.02	2.90	2.81	2.73	2.67	2.57	2.47	2.36	2.30	2.24	2.18	2.11	2.04	1.97
24	5.72	4.32	3.72	3.38	3.15	2.99	2.87	2.78	2.70	2.64	2.54	2.44	2.33	2.27	2.21	2.15	2.08	2.01	1.94
25	5.69	4.29	3.69	3.35	3.13	2.97	2.85	2.75	2.68	2.61	2.51	2.41	2.30	2.24	2.18	2.12	2.05	1.98	1.91
26	5.66	4.27	3.67	3.33	3.10	2.94	2.82	2.73	2.65	2.59	2.49	2.39	2.28	2.22	2.16	2.09	2.03	1.95	1.88
27	5.63	4.24	3.65	3.31	3.08	2.92	2.80	2.71	2.63	2.57	2.47	2.36	2.25	2.19	2.13	2.07	2.00	1.93	1.85
28	5.61	4.22	3.63	3.29	3.06	2.90	2.78	2.69	2.61	2.55	2.45	2.34	2.23	2.17	2.11	2.05	1.98	1.91	1.83
29	5.59	4.20	3.61	3.27	3.04	2.88	2.76	2.67	2.59	2.53	2.43	2.32	2.21	2.15	2.09	2.03	1.96	1.89	1.81
30	5.57	4.18	3.59	3.25	3.03	2.87	2.75	2.65	2.57	2.51	2.41	2.31	2.20	2.14	2.07	2.01	1.94	1.87	1.79
40	5.42	4.05	3.46	3.13	2.90	2.74	2.62	2.53	2.45	2.39	2.29	2.18	2.07	2.01	1.94	1.88	1.80	1.72	1.64
60	5.29	3.93	3.34	3.01	2.79	2.63	2.51	2.41	2.33	2.27	2.17	2.06	1.94	1.88	1.82	1.74	1.67	1.58	1.48
120	5.15	3.80	3.23	2.89	2.67	2.52	2.39	2.30	2.22	2.16	2.05	1.94	1.82	1.76	1.69	1.61	1.53	1.43	1.31
∞	5.02	3.69	3.12	2.79	2.57	2.41	2.29	2.19	2.11	2.05	1.94	1.83	1.71	1.64	1.57	1.48	1.39	1.27	1.00

TABLE E (cont.)

99th percentiles

n_2 \ n_1	1	2	3	4	5	6	7	8	9	10	12	15	20	24	30	40	60	120	∞
1	4052	4999.5	5403	5625	5764	5859	5928	5982	6022	6056	6106	6157	6209	6235	6261	6287	6313	6339	6366
2	98.50	99.00	99.17	99.25	99.30	99.33	99.36	99.37	99.39	99.40	99.42	99.43	99.45	99.46	99.47	99.47	99.48	99.49	99.50
3	34.12	30.82	29.46	28.71	28.24	27.91	27.67	27.49	27.35	27.23	27.05	26.87	26.69	26.60	26.50	26.41	26.32	26.22	26.13
4	21.20	18.00	16.69	15.98	15.52	15.21	14.98	14.80	14.66	14.55	14.37	14.20	14.02	13.93	13.84	13.75	13.65	13.56	13.46
5	16.26	13.27	12.06	11.39	10.97	10.67	10.46	10.29	10.16	10.05	9.89	9.72	9.55	9.47	9.38	9.29	9.20	9.11	9.02
6	13.75	10.92	9.78	9.15	8.75	8.47	8.26	8.10	7.98	7.87	7.72	7.56	7.40	7.31	7.23	7.14	7.06	6.97	6.88
7	12.25	9.55	8.45	7.85	7.46	7.19	6.99	6.84	6.72	6.62	6.47	6.31	6.16	6.07	5.99	5.91	5.82	5.74	5.65
8	11.26	8.65	7.59	7.01	6.63	6.37	6.18	6.03	5.91	5.81	5.67	5.52	5.36	5.28	5.20	5.12	5.03	4.95	4.86
9	10.56	8.02	6.99	6.42	6.06	5.80	5.61	5.47	5.35	5.26	5.11	4.96	4.81	4.73	4.65	4.57	4.48	4.40	4.31
10	10.04	7.56	6.55	5.99	5.64	5.39	5.20	5.06	4.94	4.85	4.71	4.56	4.41	4.33	4.25	4.17	4.08	4.00	3.91
11	9.65	7.21	6.22	5.67	5.32	5.07	4.89	4.74	4.63	4.54	4.40	4.25	4.10	4.02	3.94	3.86	3.78	3.69	3.60
12	9.33	6.93	5.95	5.41	5.06	4.82	4.64	4.50	4.39	4.30	4.16	4.01	3.86	3.78	3.70	3.62	3.54	3.45	3.36
13	9.07	6.70	5.74	5.21	4.86	4.62	4.44	4.30	4.19	4.10	3.96	3.82	3.66	3.59	3.51	3.43	3.34	3.25	3.17
14	8.86	6.51	5.56	5.04	4.69	4.46	4.28	4.14	4.03	3.94	3.80	3.66	3.51	3.43	3.35	3.27	3.18	3.09	3.00
15	8.68	6.36	5.42	4.89	4.56	4.32	4.14	4.00	3.89	3.80	3.67	3.52	3.37	3.29	3.21	3.13	3.05	2.96	2.87
16	8.53	6.23	5.29	4.77	4.44	4.20	4.03	3.89	3.78	3.69	3.55	3.41	3.26	3.18	3.10	3.02	2.93	2.84	2.75
17	8.40	6.11	5.18	4.67	4.34	4.10	3.93	3.79	3.68	3.59	3.46	3.31	3.16	3.08	3.00	2.92	2.83	2.75	2.65
18	8.29	6.01	5.09	4.58	4.25	4.01	3.84	3.71	3.60	3.51	3.37	3.23	3.08	3.00	2.92	2.84	2.75	2.66	2.57
19	8.18	5.93	5.01	4.50	4.17	3.94	3.77	3.63	3.52	3.43	3.30	3.15	3.00	2.92	2.84	2.76	2.67	2.58	2.49
20	8.10	5.85	4.94	4.43	4.10	3.87	3.70	3.56	3.46	3.37	3.23	3.09	2.94	2.86	2.78	2.69	2.61	2.52	2.42
21	8.02	5.78	4.87	4.37	4.04	3.81	3.64	3.51	3.40	3.31	3.17	3.03	2.88	2.80	2.72	2.64	2.55	2.46	2.36
22	7.95	5.72	4.82	4.31	3.99	3.76	3.59	3.45	3.35	3.26	3.12	2.98	2.83	2.75	2.67	2.58	2.50	2.40	2.31
23	7.88	5.66	4.76	4.26	3.94	3.71	3.54	3.41	3.30	3.21	3.07	2.93	2.78	2.70	2.62	2.54	2.45	2.35	2.26
24	7.82	5.61	4.72	4.22	3.90	3.67	3.50	3.36	3.26	3.17	3.03	2.89	2.74	2.66	2.58	2.49	2.40	2.31	2.21
25	7.77	5.57	4.68	4.18	3.85	3.63	3.46	3.32	3.22	3.13	2.99	2.85	2.70	2.62	2.54	2.45	2.36	2.27	2.17
26	7.72	5.53	4.64	4.14	3.82	3.59	3.42	3.29	3.18	3.09	2.96	2.81	2.66	2.58	2.50	2.42	2.33	2.23	2.13
27	7.68	5.49	4.60	4.11	3.78	3.56	3.39	3.26	3.15	3.06	2.93	2.78	2.63	2.55	2.47	2.38	2.29	2.20	2.10
28	7.64	5.45	4.57	4.07	3.75	3.53	3.36	3.23	3.12	3.03	2.90	2.75	2.60	2.52	2.44	2.35	2.26	2.17	2.06
29	7.60	5.42	4.54	4.04	3.73	3.50	3.33	3.20	3.09	3.00	2.87	2.73	2.57	2.49	2.41	2.33	2.23	2.14	2.03
30	7.56	5.39	4.51	4.02	3.70	3.47	3.30	3.17	3.07	2.98	2.84	2.70	2.55	2.47	2.39	2.30	2.21	2.11	2.01
40	7.31	5.18	4.31	3.83	3.51	3.29	3.12	2.99	2.89	2.80	2.66	2.52	2.37	2.29	2.20	2.11	2.02	1.92	1.80
60	7.08	4.98	4.13	3.65	3.34	3.12	2.95	2.82	2.72	2.63	2.50	2.35	2.20	2.12	2.03	1.94	1.84	1.73	1.60
120	6.85	4.79	3.95	3.48	3.17	2.96	2.79	2.66	2.56	2.47	2.34	2.19	2.03	1.95	1.86	1.76	1.66	1.53	1.38
∞	6.63	4.61	3.78	3.32	3.02	2.80	2.64	2.51	2.41	2.32	2.18	2.04	1.88	1.79	1.70	1.59	1.47	1.32	1.00

99.5th percentiles

n_1 \ n_2	1	2	3	4	5	6	7	8	9	10	12	15	20	24	30	40	60	120	∞
1	16211	20000	21615	22500	23056	23437	23715	23925	24091	24224	24426	24630	24836	24940	25044	25148	25253	25359	25465
2	198.5	199.0	199.2	199.2	199.3	199.3	199.4	199.4	199.4	199.4	199.4	199.4	199.4	199.5	199.5	199.5	199.5	199.5	199.5
3	55.55	49.80	47.47	46.19	45.39	44.84	44.43	44.13	43.88	43.69	43.39	43.08	42.78	42.62	42.47	42.31	42.15	41.99	41.83
4	31.33	26.28	24.26	23.15	22.46	21.97	21.62	21.35	21.14	20.97	20.70	20.44	20.17	20.03	19.89	19.75	19.61	19.47	19.32
5	22.78	18.31	16.53	15.56	14.94	14.51	14.20	13.96	13.77	13.62	13.38	13.15	12.90	12.78	12.66	12.53	12.40	12.27	12.14
6	18.63	14.54	12.92	12.03	11.46	11.07	10.79	10.57	10.39	10.25	10.03	9.81	9.59	9.47	9.36	9.24	9.12	9.00	8.88
7	16.24	12.40	10.88	10.05	9.52	9.16	8.89	8.68	8.51	8.38	8.18	7.97	7.75	7.65	7.53	7.42	7.31	7.19	7.08
8	14.69	11.04	9.60	8.81	8.30	7.95	7.69	7.50	7.34	7.21	7.01	6.81	6.61	6.50	6.40	6.29	6.18	6.06	5.95
9	13.61	10.11	8.72	7.96	7.47	7.13	6.88	6.69	6.54	6.42	6.23	6.03	5.83	5.73	5.62	5.52	5.41	5.30	5.19
10	12.83	9.43	8.08	7.34	6.87	6.54	6.30	6.12	5.97	5.85	5.66	5.47	5.27	5.17	5.07	4.97	4.86	4.75	4.64
11	12.23	8.91	7.60	6.88	6.42	6.10	5.86	5.68	5.54	5.42	5.24	5.05	4.86	4.76	4.65	4.55	4.44	4.34	4.23
12	11.75	8.51	7.23	6.52	6.07	5.76	5.52	5.35	5.20	5.09	4.91	4.72	4.53	4.43	4.33	4.23	4.12	4.01	3.90
13	11.37	8.19	6.93	6.23	5.79	5.48	5.25	5.08	4.94	4.82	4.64	4.46	4.27	4.17	4.07	3.97	3.87	3.76	3.65
14	11.06	7.92	6.68	6.00	5.56	5.26	5.03	4.86	4.72	4.60	4.43	4.25	4.06	3.96	3.86	3.76	3.66	3.55	3.44
15	10.80	7.70	6.48	5.80	5.37	5.07	4.85	4.67	4.54	4.42	4.25	4.07	3.88	3.79	3.69	3.58	3.48	3.37	3.26
16	10.58	7.51	6.30	5.64	5.21	4.91	4.69	4.52	4.38	4.27	4.10	3.92	3.73	3.64	3.54	3.44	3.33	3.22	3.11
17	10.38	7.35	6.16	5.50	5.07	4.78	4.56	4.39	4.25	4.14	3.97	3.79	3.61	3.51	3.41	3.31	3.21	3.10	2.98
18	10.22	7.21	6.03	5.37	4.96	4.66	4.44	4.28	4.14	4.03	3.86	3.68	3.50	3.40	3.30	3.20	3.10	2.99	2.87
19	10.07	7.09	5.92	5.27	4.85	4.56	4.34	4.18	4.04	3.93	3.76	3.59	3.40	3.31	3.21	3.11	3.00	2.89	2.78
20	9.94	6.99	5.82	5.17	4.76	4.47	4.26	4.09	3.96	3.85	3.68	3.50	3.32	3.22	3.12	3.02	2.92	2.81	2.69
21	9.83	6.89	5.73	5.09	4.68	4.39	4.18	4.01	3.88	3.77	3.60	3.43	3.24	3.15	3.05	2.95	2.84	2.73	2.61
22	9.73	6.81	5.65	5.02	4.61	4.32	4.11	3.94	3.81	3.70	3.54	3.36	3.18	3.08	2.98	2.88	2.77	2.66	2.55
23	9.63	6.73	5.58	4.95	4.54	4.26	4.05	3.88	3.75	3.64	3.47	3.30	3.12	3.02	2.92	2.82	2.71	2.60	2.48
24	9.55	6.66	5.52	4.89	4.49	4.20	3.99	3.83	3.69	3.59	3.42	3.25	3.06	2.97	2.87	2.77	2.66	2.55	2.43
25	9.48	6.60	5.46	4.84	4.43	4.15	3.94	3.78	3.64	3.54	3.37	3.20	3.01	2.92	2.82	2.72	2.61	2.50	2.38
26	9.41	6.54	5.41	4.79	4.38	4.10	3.89	3.73	3.60	3.49	3.33	3.15	2.97	2.87	2.77	2.67	2.56	2.45	2.33
27	9.34	6.49	5.36	4.74	4.34	4.06	3.85	3.69	3.56	3.45	3.28	3.11	2.93	2.83	2.73	2.63	2.52	2.41	2.29
28	9.28	6.44	5.32	4.70	4.30	4.02	3.81	3.65	3.52	3.41	3.25	3.07	2.89	2.79	2.69	2.59	2.48	2.37	2.25
29	9.23	6.40	5.28	4.66	4.26	3.98	3.77	3.61	3.48	3.38	3.21	3.04	2.86	2.76	2.66	2.56	2.45	2.33	2.21
30	9.18	6.35	5.24	4.62	4.23	3.95	3.74	3.58	3.45	3.34	3.18	3.01	2.82	2.73	2.63	2.52	2.42	2.30	2.18
40	8.83	6.07	4.98	4.37	3.99	3.71	3.51	3.35	3.22	3.12	2.95	2.78	2.60	2.50	2.40	2.30	2.18	2.06	1.93
60	8.49	5.79	4.73	4.14	3.76	3.49	3.29	3.13	3.01	2.90	2.74	2.57	2.39	2.29	2.19	2.08	1.96	1.83	1.69
120	8.18	5.54	4.50	3.92	3.55	3.28	3.09	2.93	2.81	2.71	2.54	2.37	2.19	2.09	1.98	1.87	1.75	1.61	1.43
∞	7.88	5.30	4.28	3.72	3.35	3.09	2.90	2.74	2.62	2.52	2.36	2.19	2.00	1.90	1.79	1.67	1.53	1.36	1.00

TABLE E (cont.)

99.9th percentiles

n_2 \ n_1	1	2	3	4	5	6	7	8	9	10	12	15	20	24	30	40	60	120	∞
1	4053*	5000*	5404*	5625*	5764*	5859*	5929*	5981*	6023*	6056*	6107*	6158*	6209*	6235*	6261*	6287*	6313*	6340*	6366*
2	998.5	999.0	999.2	999.2	999.3	999.3	999.4	999.4	999.4	999.4	999.4	999.4	999.5	999.5	999.5	999.5	999.5	999.5	999.5
3	167.0	148.5	141.1	137.1	134.6	132.8	131.6	130.6	129.9	129.2	128.3	127.4	126.4	125.9	125.4	125.0	124.5	124.0	123.5
4	74.14	61.25	56.18	53.44	51.71	50.53	49.66	49.00	48.47	48.05	47.41	46.76	46.10	45.77	45.43	45.09	44.75	44.40	44.05
5	47.18	37.12	33.20	31.09	29.75	28.84	28.16	27.64	27.24	26.92	26.42	25.91	25.39	25.14	24.87	24.60	24.33	24.06	23.79
6	35.51	27.00	23.70	21.92	20.81	20.03	19.46	19.03	18.69	18.41	17.99	17.56	17.12	16.89	16.67	16.44	16.21	15.99	15.75
7	29.25	21.69	18.77	17.19	16.21	15.52	15.02	14.63	14.33	14.08	13.71	13.32	12.93	12.73	12.53	12.33	12.12	11.91	11.70
8	25.42	18.49	15.83	14.39	13.49	12.86	12.40	12.04	11.77	11.54	11.19	10.84	10.48	10.30	10.11	9.92	9.73	9.53	9.33
9	22.86	16.39	13.90	12.56	11.71	11.13	10.70	10.37	10.11	9.89	9.57	9.24	8.90	8.72	8.55	8.37	8.19	8.00	7.81
10	21.04	14.91	12.55	11.28	10.48	9.92	9.52	9.20	8.96	8.75	8.45	8.13	7.80	7.64	7.47	7.30	7.12	6.94	6.76
11	19.69	13.81	11.56	10.35	9.58	9.05	8.66	8.35	8.12	7.92	7.63	7.32	7.01	6.85	6.68	6.52	6.35	6.17	6.00
12	18.64	12.97	10.80	9.63	8.89	8.38	8.00	7.71	7.48	7.29	7.00	6.71	6.40	6.25	6.09	5.93	5.76	5.59	5.42
13	17.81	12.31	10.21	9.07	8.35	7.86	7.49	7.21	6.98	6.80	6.52	6.23	5.93	5.78	5.63	5.47	5.30	5.14	4.97
14	17.14	11.78	9.73	8.62	7.92	7.43	7.08	6.80	6.58	6.40	6.13	5.85	5.56	5.41	5.25	5.10	4.94	4.77	4.60
15	16.59	11.34	9.34	8.25	7.57	7.09	6.74	6.47	6.26	6.08	5.81	5.54	5.25	5.10	4.95	4.80	4.64	4.47	4.31
16	16.12	10.97	9.00	7.94	7.27	6.81	6.46	6.19	5.98	5.81	5.55	5.27	4.99	4.85	4.70	4.54	4.39	4.23	4.06
17	15.72	10.66	8.73	7.68	7.02	6.56	6.22	5.96	5.75	5.58	5.32	5.05	4.78	4.63	4.48	4.33	4.18	4.02	3.85
18	15.38	10.39	8.49	7.46	6.81	6.35	6.02	5.76	5.56	5.39	5.13	4.87	4.59	4.45	4.30	4.15	4.00	3.84	3.67
19	15.08	10.16	8.28	7.26	6.62	6.18	5.85	5.59	5.39	5.22	4.97	4.70	4.43	4.29	4.14	3.99	3.84	3.68	3.51
20	14.82	9.95	8.10	7.10	6.46	6.02	5.69	5.44	5.24	5.08	4.82	4.56	4.29	4.15	4.00	3.86	3.70	3.54	3.38
21	14.59	9.77	7.94	6.95	6.32	5.88	5.56	5.31	5.11	4.95	4.70	4.44	4.17	4.03	3.88	3.74	3.58	3.42	3.26
22	14.38	9.61	7.80	6.81	6.19	5.76	5.44	5.19	4.99	4.83	4.58	4.33	4.06	3.92	3.78	3.63	3.48	3.32	3.15
23	14.19	9.47	7.67	6.69	6.08	5.65	5.33	5.09	4.89	4.73	4.48	4.23	3.96	3.82	3.68	3.53	3.38	3.22	3.05
24	14.03	9.34	7.55	6.59	5.98	5.55	5.23	4.99	4.80	4.64	4.39	4.14	3.87	3.74	3.59	3.45	3.29	3.14	2.97
25	13.88	9.22	7.45	6.49	5.88	5.46	5.15	4.91	4.71	4.56	4.31	4.06	3.79	3.66	3.52	3.37	3.22	3.06	2.89
26	13.74	9.12	7.36	6.41	5.80	5.38	5.07	4.83	4.64	4.48	4.24	3.99	3.72	3.59	3.44	3.30	3.15	2.99	2.82
27	13.61	9.02	7.27	6.33	5.73	5.31	5.00	4.76	4.57	4.41	4.17	3.92	3.66	3.52	3.38	3.23	3.08	2.92	2.75
28	13.50	8.93	7.19	6.25	5.66	5.24	4.93	4.69	4.50	4.35	4.11	3.86	3.60	3.46	3.32	3.18	3.02	2.86	2.69
29	13.39	8.85	7.12	6.19	5.59	5.18	4.87	4.64	4.45	4.29	4.05	3.80	3.54	3.41	3.27	3.12	2.97	2.81	2.64
30	13.29	8.77	7.05	6.12	5.53	5.12	4.82	4.58	4.39	4.24	4.00	3.75	3.49	3.36	3.22	3.07	2.92	2.76	2.59
40	12.61	8.25	6.60	5.70	5.13	4.73	4.44	4.21	4.02	3.87	3.64	3.40	3.15	3.01	2.87	2.73	2.57	2.41	2.23
60	11.97	7.76	6.17	5.31	4.76	4.37	4.09	3.87	3.69	3.54	3.31	3.08	2.83	2.69	2.55	2.41	2.25	2.08	1.89
120	11.38	7.32	5.79	4.95	4.42	4.04	3.77	3.55	3.38	3.24	3.02	2.78	2.53	2.40	2.26	2.11	1.95	1.76	1.54
∞	10.83	6.91	5.42	4.62	4.10	3.74	3.47	3.27	3.10	2.96	2.74	2.51	2.27	2.13	1.99	1.84	1.66	1.45	1.00

* Multiply these entries by 100.

TABLE F PERCENTILE POINTS OF STUDENTIZED RANGE, q, DISTRIBUTIONS
FOR J AND ν DEGREES OF FREEDOM*

90th Percentiles

ν \\ J	2	3	4	5	6	7	8	9	10
1	8.929	13.44	16.36	18.49	20.15	21.51	22.64	23.62	24.48
2	4.130	5.733	6.773	7.538	8.139	8.633	9.049	9.409	9.725
3	3.328	4.467	5.199	5.738	6.162	6.511	6.806	7.062	7.287
4	3.015	3.976	4.586	5.035	5.388	5.679	5.926	6.139	6.327
5	2.850	3.717	4.264	4.664	4.979	5.238	5.458	5.648	5.816
6	2.748	3.559	4.065	4.435	4.726	4.966	5.168	5.344	5.499
7	2.680	3.451	3.931	4.280	4.555	4.780	4.972	5.137	5.283
8	2.630	3.374	3.834	4.169	4.431	4.646	4.829	4.987	5.126
9	2.592	3.316	3.761	4.084	4.337	4.545	4.721	4.873	5.007
10	2.563	3.270	3.704	4.018	4.264	4.465	4.636	4.783	4.913
11	2.540	3.234	3.658	3.965	4.205	4.401	4.568	4.711	4.838
12	2.521	3.204	3.621	3.922	4.156	4.349	4.511	4.652	4.776
13	2.505	3.179	3.589	3.885	4.116	4.305	4.464	4.602	4.724
14	2.491	3.158	3.563	3.854	4.081	4.267	4.424	4.560	4.680
15	2.479	3.140	3.540	3.828	4.052	4.235	4.390	4.524	4.641
16	2.469	3.124	3.520	3.804	4.026	4.207	4.360	4.492	4.608
17	2.460	3.110	3.503	3.784	4.004	4.183	4.334	4.464	4.579
18	2.452	3.098	3.488	3.767	3.984	4.161	4.311	4.440	4.554
19	2.445	3.087	3.474	3.751	3.966	4.142	4.290	4.418	4.531
20	2.439	3.078	3.462	3.736	3.950	4.124	4.271	4.398	4.510
24	2.420	3.047	3.423	3.692	3.900	4.070	4.213	4.336	4.445
30	2.400	3.017	3.386	3.648	3.851	4.016	4.155	4.275	4.381
40	2.381	2.988	3.349	3.605	3.803	3.963	4.099	4.215	4.317
60	2.363	2.959	3.312	3.562	3.755	3.911	4.042	4.155	4.254
120	2.344	2.930	3.276	3.520	3.707	3.859	3.987	4.096	4.191
∞	2.326	2.902	3.240	3.478	3.661	3.808	3.931	4.037	4.129

ν \\ J	11	12	13	14	15	16	17	18	19
1	25.24	25.92	26.54	27.10	27.62	28.10	28.54	28.96	29.35
2	10.01	10.26	10.49	10.70	10.89	11.07	11.24	11.39	11.54
3	7.487	7.667	7.832	7.982	8.120	8.249	8.368	8.479	8.584
4	6.495	6.645	6.783	6.909	7.025	7.133	7.233	7.327	7.414
5	5.966	6.101	6.223	6.336	6.440	6.536	6.626	6.710	6.789
6	5.637	5.762	5.875	5.979	6.075	6.164	6.247	6.325	6.398
7	5.413	5.530	5.637	5.735	5.826	5.910	5.988	6.061	6.130
8	5.250	5.362	5.464	5.558	5.644	5.724	5.799	5.869	5.935
9	5.127	5.234	5.333	5.423	5.506	5.583	5.655	5.723	5.786
10	5.029	5.134	5.229	5.317	5.397	5.472	5.542	5.607	5.668
11	4.951	5.053	5.146	5.231	5.309	5.382	5.450	5.514	5.573
12	4.886	4.986	5.077	5.160	5.236	5.308	5.374	5.436	5.495
13	4.832	4.930	5.019	5.100	5.176	5.245	5.311	5.372	5.429
14	4.786	4.882	4.970	5.050	5.124	5.192	5.256	5.316	5.373
15	4.746	4.841	4.927	5.006	5.079	5.147	5.209	5.269	5.324
16	4.712	4.805	4.890	4.968	5.040	5.107	5.169	5.227	5.282
17	4.682	4.774	4.858	4.935	5.005	5.071	5.133	5.190	5.244
18	4.655	4.746	4.829	4.905	4.975	5.040	5.101	5.158	5.211
19	4.631	4.721	4.803	4.879	4.948	5.012	5.073	5.129	5.182
20	4.609	4.699	4.780	4.855	4.924	4.987	5.047	5.103	5.155
24	4.541	4.628	4.708	4.780	4.847	4.909	4.966	5.021	5.071
30	4.474	4.559	4.635	4.706	4.770	4.830	4.886	4.939	4.988
40	4.408	4.490	4.564	4.632	4.695	4.752	4.807	4.857	4.905
60	4.342	4.421	4.493	4.558	4.619	4.675	4.727	4.775	4.821
120	4.276	4.353	4.422	4.485	4.543	4.597	4.647	4.694	4.738
∞	4.211	4.285	4.351	4.412	4.468	4.519	4.568	4.612	4.654

Reproduced from H. Leon Harter, "Tables of range and studentized range," *Annals of Mathematical Statistics*, 31 (1960), 1122–47, by permission of the author and editor.
  * In the one-factor ANOVA with n observations in each of J groups, $\nu = J(n-1)$. In general, ν is the number of degrees of freedom for the mean-square "within" in an analysis of variance.

TABLE F (cont.)

95th Percentiles

ν \ J	2	3	4	5	6	7	8	9	10
1	17.97	26.98	32.82	37.08	40.41	43.12	45.40	47.36	49.07
2	6.085	8.331	9.798	10.88	11.74	12.44	13.03	13.54	13.99
3	4.501	5.910	6.825	7.502	8.037	8.478	8.853	9.177	9.462
4	3.927	5.040	5.757	6.287	6.707	7.053	7.347	7.602	7.826
5	3.635	4.602	5.218	5.673	6.033	6.330	6.582	6.802	6.995
6	3.461	4.339	4.896	5.305	5.628	5.895	6.122	6.319	6.493
7	3.344	4.165	4.681	5.060	5.359	5.606	5.815	5.998	6.158
8	3.261	4.041	4.529	4.886	5.167	5.399	5.597	5.767	5.918
9	3.199	3.949	4.415	4.756	5.024	5.244	5.432	5.595	5.739
10	3.151	3.877	4.327	4.654	4.912	5.124	5.305	5.461	5.599
11	3.113	3.820	4.256	4.574	4.823	5.028	5.202	5.353	5.487
12	3.082	3.773	4.199	4.508	4.751	4.950	5.119	5.265	5.395
13	3.055	3.735	4.151	4.453	4.690	4.885	5.049	5.192	5.318
14	3.033	3.702	4.111	4.407	4.639	4.829	4.990	5.131	5.254
15	3.014	3.674	4.076	4.367	4.595	4.782	4.940	5.077	5.198
16	2.998	3.649	4.046	4.333	4.557	4.741	4.897	5.031	5.150
17	2.984	3.628	4.020	4.303	4.524	4.705	4.858	4.991	5.108
18	2.971	3.609	3.997	4.277	4.495	4.673	4.824	4.956	5.071
19	2.960	3.593	3.977	4.253	4.469	4.645	4.794	4.924	5.038
20	2.950	3.578	3.958	4.232	4.445	4.620	4.768	4.896	5.008
24	2.919	3.532	3.901	4.166	4.373	4.541	4.684	4.807	4.915
30	2.888	3.486	3.845	4.102	4.302	4.464	4.602	4.720	4.824
40	2.858	3.442	3.791	4.039	4.232	4.389	4.521	4.635	4.735
60	2.829	3.399	3.737	3.977	4.163	4.314	4.441	4.550	4.646
120	2.800	3.356	3.685	3.917	4.096	4.241	4.363	4.468	4.560
∞	2.772	3.314	3.633	3.858	4.030	4.170	4.286	4.387	4.474

ν \ J	11	12	13	14	15	16	17	18	19
1	50.59	51.96	53.20	54.33	55.36	56.32	57.22	58.04	58.83
2	14.39	14.75	15.08	15.38	15.65	15.91	16.14	16.37	16.57
3	9.717	9.946	10.15	10.35	10.53	10.69	10.84	10.98	11.11
4	8.027	8.208	8.373	8.525	8.664	8.794	8.914	9.028	9.134
5	7.168	7.324	7.466	7.596	7.717	7.828	7.932	8.030	8.122
6	6.649	6.789	6.917	7.034	7.143	7.244	7.338	7.426	7.508
7	6.302	6.431	6.550	6.658	6.759	6.852	6.939	7.020	7.097
8	6.054	6.175	6.287	6.389	6.483	6.571	6.653	6.729	6.802
9	5.867	5.983	6.089	6.186	6.276	6.359	6.437	6.510	6.579
10	5.722	5.833	5.935	6.028	6.114	6.194	6.269	6.339	6.405
11	5.605	5.713	5.811	5.901	5.984	6.062	6.134	6.202	6.265
12	5.511	5.615	5.710	5.798	5.878	5.953	6.023	6.089	6.151
13	5.431	5.533	5.625	5.711	5.789	5.862	5.931	5.995	6.055
14	5.364	5.463	5.554	5.637	5.714	5.786	5.852	5.915	5.974
15	5.306	5.404	5.493	5.574	5.649	5.720	5.785	5.846	5.904
16	5.256	5.352	5.439	5.520	5.593	5.662	5.727	5.786	5.843
17	5.212	5.307	5.392	5.471	5.544	5.612	5.675	5.734	5.790
18	5.174	5.267	5.352	5.429	5.501	5.568	5.630	5.688	5.743
19	5.140	5.231	5.315	5.391	5.462	5.528	5.589	5.647	5.701
20	5.108	5.199	5.282	5.357	5.427	5.493	5.553	5.610	5.663
24	5.012	5.099	5.179	5.251	5.319	5.381	5.439	5.494	5.545
30	4.917	5.001	5.077	5.147	5.211	5.271	5.327	5.379	5.429
40	4.824	4.904	4.977	5.044	5.106	5.163	5.216	5.266	5.313
60	4.732	4.808	4.878	4.942	5.001	5.056	5.107	5.154	5.199
120	4.641	4.714	4.781	4.842	4.898	4.950	4.998	5.044	5.086
∞	4.552	4.622	4.685	4.743	4.796	4.845	4.891	4.934	4.974

ν \ J	2	3	4	5	6	7	8	9	10
1	35.99	54.00	65.69	74.22	80.87	86.29	90.85	94.77	98.20
2	8.776	11.94	14.01	15.54	16.75	17.74	18.58	19.31	19.95
3	5.907	7.661	8.808	9.660	10.34	10.89	11.37	11.78	12.14
4	4.943	6.244	7.088	7.716	8.213	8.625	8.976	9.279	9.548
5	4.474	5.558	6.257	6.775	7.186	7.527	7.816	8.068	8.291
6	4.199	5.158	5.772	6.226	6.586	6.884	7.138	7.359	7.554
7	4.018	4.897	5.455	5.868	6.194	6.464	6.695	6.895	7.072
8	3.892	4.714	5.233	5.616	5.919	6.169	6.382	6.568	6.732
9	3.797	4.578	5.069	5.430	5.715	5.950	6.151	6.325	6.479
10	3.725	4.474	4.943	5.287	5.558	5.782	5.972	6.138	6.285
11	3.667	4.391	4.843	5.173	5.433	5.648	5.831	5.989	6.130
12	3.620	4.325	4.762	5.081	5.332	5.540	5.716	5.869	6.004
13	3.582	4.269	4.694	5.004	5.248	5.449	5.620	5.769	5.900
14	3.550	4.222	4.638	4.940	5.178	5.374	5.540	5.684	5.811
15	3.522	4.182	4.589	4.885	5.118	5.309	5.471	5.612	5.737
16	3.498	4.148	4.548	4.838	5.066	5.253	5.412	5.550	5.672
17	3.477	4.118	4.512	4.797	5.020	5.204	5.361	5.496	5.615
18	3.458	4.092	4.480	4.761	4.981	5.162	5.315	5.448	5.565
19	3.442	4.068	4.451	4.728	4.945	5.123	5.275	5.405	5.521
20	3.427	4.047	4.426	4.700	4.914	5.089	5.238	5.368	5.481
24	3.381	3.983	4.347	4.610	4.816	4.984	5.126	5.250	5.358
30	3.337	3.919	4.271	4.523	4.720	4.881	5.017	5.134	5.238
40	3.294	3.858	4.197	4.439	4.627	4.780	4.910	5.022	5.120
60	3.251	3.798	4.124	4.356	4.536	4.682	4.806	4.912	5.006
120	3.210	3.739	4.053	4.276	4.447	4.587	4.704	4.805	4.894
∞	3.170	3.682	3.984	4.197	4.361	4.494	4.605	4.700	4.784

ν \ J	11	12	13	14	15	16	17	18	19
1	101.3	104.0	106.5	108.8	110.8	112.7	114.5	116.2	117.7
2	20.52	21.03	21.49	21.91	22.30	22.67	23.01	23.32	23.62
3	12.46	12.75	13.01	13.26	13.48	13.69	13.88	14.06	14.23
4	9.788	10.01	10.20	10.39	10.55	10.71	10.85	10.99	11.11
5	8.490	8.670	8.834	8.984	9.124	9.253	9.374	9.486	9.593
6	7.729	7.887	8.031	8.163	8.286	8.399	8.506	8.605	8.698
7	7.230	7.373	7.504	7.624	7.735	7.839	7.935	8.025	8.111
8	6.879	7.011	7.132	7.244	7.347	7.443	7.532	7.616	7.695
9	6.617	6.742	6.856	6.961	7.058	7.148	7.232	7.311	7.385
10	6.416	6.534	6.643	6.742	6.834	6.920	7.000	7.075	7.146
11	6.256	6.369	6.473	6.568	6.657	6.739	6.815	6.887	6.955
12	6.125	6.235	6.335	6.427	6.512	6.591	6.665	6.734	6.799
13	6.017	6.123	6.220	6.309	6.392	6.468	6.539	6.607	6.670
14	5.926	6.029	6.123	6.210	6.290	6.364	6.434	6.499	6.560
15	5.848	5.949	6.041	6.125	6.203	6.276	6.344	6.407	6.467
16	5.781	5.879	5.969	6.052	6.128	6.199	6.265	6.328	6.386
17	5.722	5.818	5.907	5.987	6.062	6.132	6.197	6.258	6.315
18	5.670	5.765	5.852	5.931	6.004	6.073	6.137	6.197	6.253
19	5.624	5.718	5.803	5.881	5.954	6.020	6.083	6.142	6.198
20	5.583	5.675	5.759	5.836	5.907	5.974	6.036	6.093	6.148
24	5.455	5.543	5.623	5.697	5.764	5.827	5.886	5.941	5.994
30	5.330	5.414	5.490	5.560	5.624	5.684	5.740	5.792	5.841
40	5.208	5.288	5.360	5.426	5.487	5.544	5.597	5.646	5.693
60	5.089	5.164	5.232	5.295	5.352	5.406	5.456	5.503	5.546
120	4.972	5.043	5.107	5.166	5.221	5.271	5.318	5.362	5.403
∞	4.858	4.925	4.985	5.041	5.092	5.139	5.183	5.224	5.262

99th Percentiles

v \ J	2	3	4	5	6	7	8	9	10
1	90.03	135.0	164.3	185.6	202.2	215.8	227.2	237.0	245.6
2	14.04	19.02	22.29	24.72	26.63	28.20	29.53	30.68	31.69
3	8.261	10.62	12.17	13.33	14.24	15.00	15.64	16.20	16.69
4	6.512	8.120	9.173	9.958	10.58	11.10	11.55	11.93	12.27
5	5.702	6.976	7.804	8.421	8.913	9.321	9.669	9.972	10.24
6	5.243	6.331	7.033	7.556	7.973	8.318	8.613	8.869	9.097
7	4.949	5.919	6.543	7.005	7.373	7.679	7.939	8.166	8.368
8	4.746	5.635	6.204	6.625	6.960	7.237	7.474	7.681	7.863
9	4.596	5.428	5.957	6.348	6.658	6.915	7.134	7.325	7.495
10	4.482	5.270	5.769	6.136	6.428	6.669	6.875	7.055	7.213
11	4.392	5.146	5.621	5.970	6.247	6.476	6.672	6.842	6.992
12	4.320	5.046	5.502	5.836	6.101	6.321	6.507	6.670	6.814
13	4.260	4.964	5.404	5.727	5.981	6.192	6.372	6.528	6.667
14	4.210	4.895	5.322	5.634	5.881	6.085	6.258	6.409	6.543
15	4.168	4.836	5.252	5.556	5.796	5.994	6.162	6.309	6.439
16	4.131	4.786	5.192	5.489	5.722	5.915	6.079	6.222	6.349
17	4.099	4.742	5.140	5.430	5.659	5.847	6.007	6.147	6.270
18	4.071	4.703	5.094	5.379	5.603	5.788	5.944	6.081	6.201
19	4.046	4.670	5.054	5.334	5.554	5.735	5.889	6.022	6.141
20	4.024	4.639	5.018	5.294	5.510	5.688	5.839	5.970	6.087
24	3.956	4.546	4.907	5.168	5.374	5.542	5.685	5.809	5.919
30	3.889	4.455	4.799	5.048	5.242	5.401	5.536	5.653	5.756
40	3.825	4.367	4.696	4.931	5.114	5.265	5.392	5.502	5.599
60	3.762	4.282	4.595	4.818	4.991	5.133	5.253	5.356	5.447
120	3.702	4.200	4.497	4.709	4.872	5.005	5.118	5.214	5.299
∞	3.643	4.120	4.403	4.603	4.757	4.882	4.987	5.078	5.157

v \ J	11	12	13	14	15	16	17	18	19
1	253.2	260.0	266.2	271.8	277.0	281.8	286.3	290.4	294.3
2	32.59	33.40	34.13	34.81	35.43	36.00	36.53	37.03	37.50
3	17.13	17.53	17.89	18.22	18.52	18.81	19.07	19.32	19.55
4	12.57	12.84	13.09	13.32	13.53	13.73	13.91	14.08	14.24
5	10.48	10.70	10.89	11.08	11.24	11.40	11.55	11.68	11.81
6	9.301	9.485	9.653	9.808	9.951	10.08	10.21	10.32	10.43
7	8.548	8.711	8.860	8.997	9.124	9.242	9.353	9.456	9.554
8	8.027	8.176	8.312	8.436	8.552	8.659	8.760	8.854	8.943
9	7.647	7.784	7.910	8.025	8.132	8.232	8.325	8.412	8.495
10	7.356	7.485	7.603	7.712	7.812	7.906	7.993	8.076	8.153
11	7.128	7.250	7.362	7.465	7.560	7.649	7.732	7.809	7.883
12	6.943	7.060	7.167	7.265	7.356	7.441	7.520	7.594	7.665
13	6.791	6.903	7.006	7.101	7.188	7.269	7.345	7.417	7.485
14	6.664	6.772	6.871	6.962	7.047	7.126	7.199	7.268	7.333
15	6.555	6.660	6.757	6.845	6.927	7.003	7.074	7.142	7.204
16	6.462	6.564	6.658	6.744	6.823	6.898	6.967	7.032	7.093
17	6.381	6.480	6.572	6.656	6.734	6.806	6.873	6.937	6.997
18	6.310	6.407	6.497	6.579	6.655	6.725	6.792	6.854	6.912
19	6.247	6.342	6.430	6.510	6.585	6.654	6.719	6.780	6.837
20	6.191	6.285	6.371	6.450	6.523	6.591	6.654	6.714	6.771
24	6.017	6.106	6.186	6.261	6.330	6.394	6.453	6.510	6.563
30	5.849	5.932	6.008	6.078	6.143	6.203	6.259	6.311	6.361
40	5.686	5.764	5.835	5.900	5.961	6.017	6.069	6.119	6.165
60	5.528	5.601	5.667	5.728	5.785	5.837	5.886	5.931	5.974
120	5.375	5.443	5.505	5.562	5.614	5.662	5.708	5.750	5.790
∞	5.227	5.290	5.348	5.400	5.448	5.493	5.535	5.574	5.611

99.5th Percentiles

ν \ J	2	3	4	5	6	7	8	9	10
1	180.1	270.1	328.5	371.2	404.4	431.6	454.4	474.0	491.1
2	19.93	26.97	31.60	35.02	37.73	39.95	41.83	43.46	44.89
3	10.55	13.50	15.45	16.91	18.06	19.01	19.83	20.53	21.15
4	7.916	9.814	11.06	11.99	12.74	13.35	13.88	14.33	14.74
5	6.751	8.196	9.141	9.847	10.41	10.88	11.28	11.63	11.93
6	6.105	7.306	8.088	8.670	9.135	9.522	9.852	10.14	10.40
7	5.699	6.750	7.429	7.935	8.339	8.674	8.961	9.211	9.433
8	5.420	6.370	6.981	7.435	7.797	8.097	8.354	8.578	8.777
9	5.218	6.096	6.657	7.074	7.405	7.680	7.915	8.120	8.303
10	5.065	5.888	6.412	6.800	7.109	7.365	7.584	7.775	7.944
11	4.945	5.727	6.222	6.588	6.878	7.119	7.325	7.505	7.664
12	4.849	5.597	6.068	6.416	6.693	6.922	7.118	7.288	7.439
13	4.770	5.490	5.943	6.277	6.541	6.760	6.947	7.111	7.255
14	4.704	5.401	5.838	6.160	6.414	6.626	6.805	6.962	7.101
15	4.647	5.325	5.750	6.061	6.308	6.511	6.685	6.837	6.971
16	4.599	5.261	5.674	5.977	6.216	6.413	6.582	6.729	6.859
17	4.557	5.205	5.608	5.903	6.136	6.329	6.493	6.636	6.763
18	4.521	5.156	5.550	5.839	6.067	6.255	6.415	6.554	6.678
19	4.488	5.113	5.500	5.783	6.005	6.189	6.346	4.482	6.603
20	4.460	5.074	5.455	5.732	5.951	6.131	6.285	6.418	6.537
24	4.371	4.955	5.315	5.577	5.783	5.952	6.096	6.221	6.332
30	4.285	4.841	5.181	5.428	5.621	5.780	5.914	6.031	6.135
40	4.202	4.731	5.053	5.284	5.465	5.614	5.739	5.848	5.944
60	4.122	4.625	4.928	5.146	5.316	5.454	5.571	5.673	5.762
120	4.045	4.523	4.809	5.013	5.172	5.301	5.410	5.504	5.586
∞	3.970	4.424	4.694	4.886	5.033	5.154	5.255	5.341	5.418

ν \ J	11	12	13	14	15	16	17	18	19
1	506.3	520.0	532.4	543.6	554.0	563.6	572.5	580.9	588.7
2	46.16	47.31	48.35	49.30	50.17	50.99	51.74	52.45	53.12
3	21.70	22.20	22.66	23.08	23.46	23.82	24.15	24.46	24.76
4	15.10	15.42	15.72	15.99	16.24	16.48	16.70	16.90	17.09
5	12.21	12.46	12.69	12.90	13.09	13.27	13.44	13.60	13.75
6	10.63	10.83	11.02	11.20	11.36	11.51	11.65	11.78	11.90
7	9.632	9.812	9.977	10.13	10.27	10.40	10.52	10.64	10.75
8	8.955	9.117	9.265	9.401	9.527	9.644	9.754	9.857	9.953
9	8.466	8.614	8.749	8.874	8.990	9.097	9.198	9.292	9.381
10	8.096	8.234	8.360	8.476	8.583	8.683	8.777	8.865	8.947
11	7.807	7.937	8.055	8.164	8.265	8.359	8.447	8.530	8.608
12	7.575	7.697	7.810	7.914	8.009	8.099	8.183	8.261	8.335
13	7.384	7.502	7.609	7.708	7.800	7.886	7.965	8.040	8.111
14	7.225	7.338	7.442	7.537	7.625	7.707	7.784	7.856	7.924
15	7.091	7.200	7.300	7.392	7.477	7.556	7.630	7.699	7.765
16	6.976	7.081	7.178	7.267	7.349	7.426	7.498	7.566	7.629
17	6.876	6.979	7.072	7.159	7.239	7.314	7.384	7.449	7.511
18	6.788	6.888	6.980	7.064	7.142	7.215	7.283	7.347	7.407
19	6.711	6.809	6.898	6.981	7.057	7.128	7.195	7.257	7.316
20	6.642	6.738	6.826	6.907	6.981	7.051	7.116	7.177	7.235
24	6.431	6.520	6.602	6.677	6.747	6.812	6.872	6.930	6.983
30	6.227	6.310	6.387	6.456	6.521	6.581	6.638	6.691	6.741
40	6.030	6.108	6.179	6.244	6.304	6.360	6.412	6.461	6.507
60	5.841	5.913	5.979	6.039	6.094	6.146	6.194	6.239	6.281
120	5.660	5.726	5.786	5.842	5.893	5.940	5.984	6.025	6.064
∞	5.485	5.546	5.602	5.652	5.699	5.742	5.783	5.820	5.856

r	z_r	r	z_r	r	z_r	r	z_r	r	z_r
.000	.000	.200	.203	.400	.424	.600	.693	.800	1.099
.005	.005	.205	.208	.405	.430	.605	.701	.805	1.113
.010	.010	.210	.213	.410	.436	.610	.709	.810	1.127
.015	.015	.215	.218	.415	.442	.615	.717	.815	1.142
.020	.020	.220	.224	.420	.448	.620	.725	.820	1.157
.025	.025	.225	.229	.425	.454	.625	.733	.825	1.172
.030	.030	.230	.234	.430	.460	.630	.741	.830	1.188
.035	.035	.235	.239	.435	.466	.635	.750	.835	1.204
.040	.040	.240	.245	.440	.472	.640	.758	.840	1.221
.045	.045	.245	.250	.445	.478	.645	.767	.845	1.238
.050	.050	.250	.255	.450	.485	.650	.775	.850	1.256
.055	.055	.255	.261	.455	.491	.655	.784	.855	1.274
.060	.060	.260	.266	.460	.497	.660	.793	.860	1.293
.065	.065	.265	.271	.465	.504	.665	.802	.865	1.313
.070	.070	.270	.277	.470	.510	.670	.811	.870	1.333
.075	.075	.275	.282	.475	.517	.675	.820	.875	1.354
.080	.080	.280	.288	.480	.523	.680	.829	.880	1.376
.085	.085	.285	.293	.485	.530	.685	.838	.885	1.398
.090	.090	.290	.299	.490	.536	.690	.848	.890	1.422
.095	.095	.295	.304	.495	.543	.695	.858	.895	1.447
.100	.100	.300	.310	.500	.549	.700	.867	.900	1.472
.105	.105	.305	.315	.505	.556	.705	.877	.905	1.499
.110	.110	.310	.321	.510	.563	.710	.887	.910	1.528
.115	.116	.315	.326	.515	.570	.715	.897	.915	1.557
.120	.121	.320	.332	.520	.576	.720	.908	.920	1.589
.125	.126	.325	.337	.525	.583	.725	.918	.925	1.623
.130	.131	.330	.343	.530	.590	.730	.929	.930	1.658
.135	.136	.335	.348	.535	.597	.735	.940	.935	1.697
.140	.141	.340	.354	.540	.604	.740	.950	.940	1.738
.145	.146	.345	.360	.545	.611	.745	.962	.945	1.783
.150	.151	.350	.365	.550	.618	.750	.973	.950	1.832
.155	.156	.355	.371	.555	.626	.755	.984	.955	1.886
.160	.161	.360	.377	.560	.633	.760	.996	.960	1.946
.165	.167	.365	.383	.565	.640	.765	1.008	.965	2.014
.170	.172	.370	.388	.570	.648	.770	1.020	.970	2.092
.175	.177	.375	.394	.575	.655	.775	1.033	.975	2.185
.180	.182	.380	.400	.580	.662	.780	1.045	.980	2.298
.185	.187	.385	.406	.585	.670	.785	1.058	.985	2.443
.190	.192	.390	.412	.590	.678	.790	1.071	.990	2.647
.195	.198	.395	.418	.595	.685	.795	1.085	.995	2.994

* Values reported in this table were calculated by Thomas O. Maguire and are reproduced with his kind permission.

DETERMINATION OF r_{tet} FOR VARIOUS VALUES OF *bc/ad* OR *ad/bc* FROM A FOUR-FOLD CONTINGENCY TABLE†

r_{tet}	$\dfrac{bc}{ad}$ or $\dfrac{ad}{bc}$	r_{tet}	$\dfrac{bc}{ad}$ or $\dfrac{ad}{bc}$	r_{tet}	$\dfrac{bc}{ad}$ or $\dfrac{ad}{bc}$	r_{tet}	$\dfrac{bc}{ad}$ or $\dfrac{ad}{bc}$
0	1.000	.26	1.941–1.993	.51	4.068–4.205	.76	11.513–12.177
.010	1.013–1.039	.27	1.994–2.048	.52	4.206–4.351	.77	12.178–12.905
.02	1.040–1.066	.28	2.049–2.105	.53	4.352–4.503	.78	12.906–13.707
.03	1.067–1.093	.29	2.106–2.164	.54	4.504–4.662	.79	13.708–14.592
.04	1.094–1.122	.30	2.165–2.225	.55	4.663–4.830	.80	14.593–15.574
.05	1.123–1.151	.31	2.226–2.288	.56	4.831–5.007	.81	15.575–16.670
.06	1.152–1.180	.32	2.289–2.353	.57	5.008–5.192	.82	16.671–17.899
.07	1.181–1.211	.33	2.354–2.421	.58	5.193–5.388	.83	17.900–19.287
.08	1.212–1.242	.34	2.422–2.491	.59	5.389–5.595	.84	19.288–20.865
.09	1.243–1.275	.35	2.492–2.563	.60	5.596–5.813	.85	20.866–22.674
.10	1.276–1.308	.36	2.564–2.638	.61	5.814–6.043	.86	22.675–24.766
.11	1.309–1.342	.37	2.639–2.716	.62	6.044–6.288	.87	24.767–27.212
.12	1.343–1.377	.38	2.717–2.797	.63	6.289–6.547	.88	27.213–30.105
.13	1.378–1.413	.39	2.798–2.881	.64	6.548–6.822	.89	30.106–33.577
.14	1.414–1.450	.40	2.882–2.968	.65	6.823–7.115	.90	33.578–37.815
.15	1.451–1.488	.41	2.969–3.059	.66	7.116–7.428	.91	37.816–43.096
.16	1.489–1.528	.42	3.060–3.153	.67	7.429–7.761	.92	43.097–49.846
.17	1.529–1.568	.43	3.154–3.251	.68	7.762–8.117	.93	49.847–58.758
.18	1.569–1.610	.44	3.252–3.353	.69	8.118–8.499	.94	58.759–71.035
.19	1.611–1.653	.45	3.354–3.460	.70	8.500–8.910	.95	71.036–88.964
.20	1.654–1.697	.46	3.461–3.571	.71	8.911–9.351	.96	88.965–117.479
.21	1.698–1.743	.47	3.572–3.687	.72	9.352–9.828	.97	117.480–169.503
.22	1.744–1.790	.48	3.688–3.808	.73	9.829–10.344	.98	169.504–292.864
.23	1.791–1.838	.49	3.809–3.935	.74	10.345–10.903	.99	292.865–923.687
.24	1.839–1.888	.50	3.936–4.067	.75	10.904–11.512	1.00	923.688– ∞
.25	1.889–1.940						

* Values in this table were calculated by Thomas O. Maguire.
† If *bc/ad* is greater than 1, the value of r_{tet} is read directly from this table. If *ad/bc* is greater than 1, the table is entered with *ad/bc* and the value of r_{tet} is *negative*.

TABLE I   CRITICAL VALUES OF THE CORRELATION COEFFICIENT*

$df = n - 2$	$\alpha = .10$	.05	.02	.01
1	.988	.997	.9995	.9999
2	.900	.950	.980	.990
3	.805	.878	.934	.959
4	.729	.811	.882	.917
5	.669	.754	.833	.874
6	.622	.707	.789	.834
7	.582	.666	.750	.798
8	.549	.632	.716	.765
9	.521	.602	.685	.735
10	.497	.576	.658	.708
11	.476	.553	.634	.684
12	.458	.532	.612	.661
13	.441	.514	.592	.641
14	.426	.497	.574	.623
15	.412	.482	.558	.606
16	.400	.468	.542	.590
17	.389	.456	.528	.575
18	.378	.444	.516	.561
19	.369	.433	.503	.549
20	.360	.423	.492	.537
21	.352	.413	.482	.526
22	.344	.404	.472	.515
23	.337	.396	.462	.505
24	.330	.388	.453	.496
25	.323	.381	.445	.487
26	.317	.374	.437	.479
27	.311	.367	.430	.471
28	.306	.361	.423	.463
29	.301	.355	.416	.456
30	.296	.349	.409	.449
35	.275	.325	.381	.418
40	.257	.304	.358	.393
45	.243	.288	.338	.372
50	.231	.273	.322	.354
60	.211	.250	.295	.325
70	.195	.232	.274	.302
80	.183	.217	.256	.283
90	.173	.205	.242	.267
100	.164	.195	.230	.254

Table I is reprinted from Table V.A. of Fisher & Yates, *Statistical Methods for Research Workers*, published by Oliver and Boyd Ltd., Edinburgh, and by permission of the author and publishers.

   * If the *absolute value* of an r from a sample of size n exceeds the tabled value for α and $n - 2$, the null hypothesis that $\rho = 0$ may be rejected at the α-level of significance; the alternative hypothesis is that $\rho \neq 0$. For example, a sample r of .59 with $n = 20$ leads to rejection of the hypothesis $\rho = 0$ at the .01 level of significance.

TABLE J   CONFIDENCE INTERVALS AROUND r ON ρ FOR $n = 3, 4, \ldots, 400$
(FIND UPPER-LIMIT VALUE ABOVE THE PRINCIPAL DIAGONAL,
AND LOWER-LIMIT VALUE BELOW IT)

Confidence coefficient 0.95

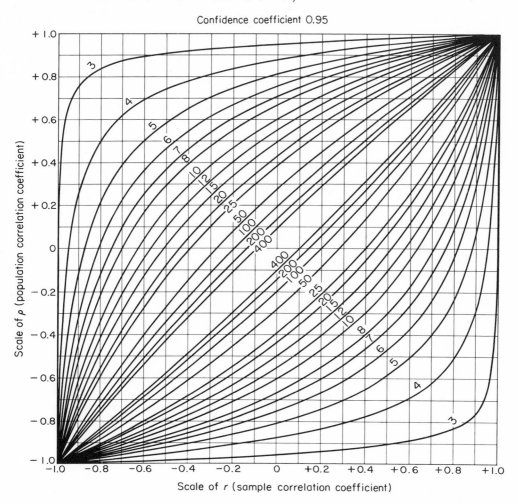

Scale of r (sample correlation coefficient)

Scale of ρ (population correlation coefficient)

Confidence coefficient 0.99

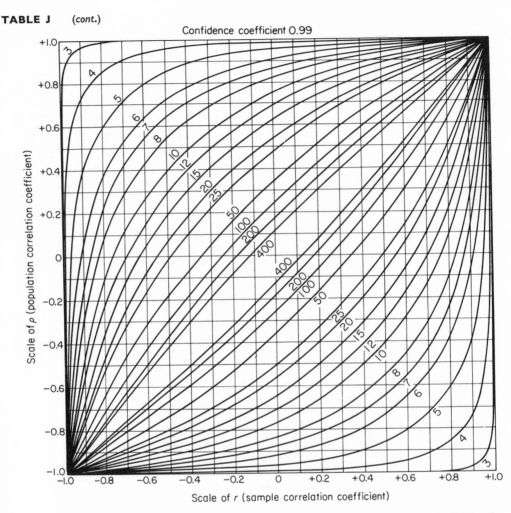

Scale of ρ (population correlation coefficient)

Scale of r (sample correlation coefficient)

ABSOLUTE VALUES OF THE CRITICAL VALUES OF SPEARMAN'S RANK CORRELATION COEFFICIENT, r_s, FOR TESTING THE NULL HYPOTHESIS OF NO CORRELATION WITH A TWO-TAILED TEST*

n	$\alpha = .10$	$\alpha = .05$	$\alpha = .02$	$\alpha = .01$
5	0.900	—	—	—
6	0.829	0.886	0.943	—
7	0.714	0.786	0.893	—
8	0.643	0.738	0.833	0.881
9	0.600	0.683	0.783	0.833
10	0.564	0.648	0.745	0.818
11	0.523	0.623	0.736	0.794
12	0.497	0.591	0.703	0.780
13	0.475	0.566	0.673	0.745
14	0.457	0.545	0.646	0.716
15	0.441	0.525	0.623	0.689
16	0.425	0.507	0.601	0.666
17	0.412	0.490	0.582	0.645
18	0.399	0.476	0.564	0.625
19	0.388	0.462	0.549	0.608
20	0.377	0.450	0.534	0.591
21	0.368	0.438	0.521	0.576
22	0.359	0.428	0.508	0.562
23	0.351	0.418	0.496	0.549
24	0.343	0.409	0.485	0.537
25	0.336	0.400	0.475	0.526
26	0.329	0.392	0.465	0.515
27	0.323	0.385	0.456	0.505
28	0.317	0.377	0.448	0.496
29	0.311	0.370	0.440	0.487
30	0.305	0.364	0.432	0.478

Adapted from E. G. Olds, "Distributions of sums of squares of rank differences for small numbers of individuals," *Annals of Mathematical Statistics*, 9 (1938), 133–48, and "The 5% significance levels for sums of squares of rank differences and a correction," *Annals of Mathematical Statistics*, 20 (1949), 117–18, by permission of The Institute of Mathematical Statistics.

* The tabled values are *absolute values* of the critical values for *two-tailed tests*. For example, the critical values of r_s for $n = 10$ and $\alpha = .10$ are $+0.564$ and -0.564.

TABLE L PROBABILITIES ASSOCIATED WITH VALUES AS LARGE AS OBSERVED VALUES OF S IN KENDALL'S τ WHEN THE NULL HYPOTHESIS OF NO CORRELATION IS TRUE

S	Values of N				S	Values of N		
	4	5	8	9		6	7	10
0	.625	.592	.548	.540	1	.500	.500	.500
2	.375	.408	.452	.460	3	.360	.386	.431
4	.167	.242	.360	.381	5	.235	.281	.364
6	.042	.117	.274	.306	7	.136	.191	.300
8		.042	.199	.238	9	.068	.119	.242
10		.0083	.138	.179	11	.028	.068	.190
12			.089	.130	13	.0083	.035	.146
14			.054	.090	15	.0014	.015	.108
16			.031	.060	17		.0054	.078
18			.016	.038	19		.0014	.054
20			.0071	.022	21		.00020	.036
22			.0028	.012	23			.023
24			.00087	.0063	25			.014
26			.00019	.0029	27			.0083
28			.000025	.0012	29			.0046
30				.00043	31			.0023
32				.00012	33			.0011
34				.000025	35			.00047
36				.0000028	37			.00018
					39			.000058
					41			.000015
					43			.0000028
					45			.00000028

Adapted from M. G. Kendall, *Rank Correlation Methods*, 3rd ed. (London: Charles Griffin & Company Limited, 1962), Appendix Table 1, by permission of the publisher.

TABLE M SQUARES AND SQUARE ROOTS OF THE INTEGERS FROM 1 TO 1000

N	N^2	$\sqrt{N}$	N	N^2	$\sqrt{N}$	N	N^2	$\sqrt{N}$
1	1	1.0000	71	5041	8.4261	106	11236	10.2956
2	4	1.4142	72	5184	8.4853	107	11449	10.3441
3	9	1.7321	73	5329	8.5440	108	11664	10.3923
4	16	2.0000	74	5476	8.6023	109	11881	10.4403
5	25	2.2361	75	5625	8.6603	110	12100	10.4881
6	36	2.4495	76	5776	8.7178	111	12321	10.5357
7	49	2.6458	77	5929	8.7750	112	12544	10.5830
8	64	2.8284	78	6084	8.8318	113	12769	10.6301
9	81	3.0000	79	6241	8.8882	114	12996	10.6771
10	100	3.1623	80	6400	8.9443	115	13225	10.7238
11	121	3.3166	81	6561	9.0000	116	13456	10.7703
12	144	3.4641	82	6724	9.0554	117	13689	10.8167
13	169	3.6056	83	6889	9.1104	118	13924	10.8628
14	196	3.7417	84	7056	9.1652	119	14161	10.9087
15	225	3.8730	85	7225	9.2195	120	14400	10.9545
16	256	4.0000	86	7396	9.2736	121	14641	11.0000
17	289	4.1231	87	7569	9.3274	122	14884	11.0454
18	324	4.2426	88	7744	9.3808	123	15129	11.0905
19	361	4.3589	89	7921	9.4340	124	15376	11.1355
20	400	4.4721	90	8100	9.4868	125	15625	11.1803
21	441	4.5826	91	8281	9.5394	126	15876	11.2250
22	484	4.6904	92	8464	9.5917	127	16129	11.2694
23	529	4.7958	93	8649	9.6437	128	16384	11.3137
24	576	4.8990	94	8836	9.6954	129	16641	11.3578
25	625	5.0000	95	9025	9.7468	130	16900	11.4018
26	676	5.0990	96	9216	9.7980	131	17161	11.4455
27	729	5.1962	97	9409	9.8489	132	17424	11.4891
28	784	5.2915	98	9604	9.8995	133	17689	11.5326
29	841	5.3852	99	9801	9.9499	134	17956	11.5758
30	900	5.4772	100	10000	10.0000	135	18225	11.6190
31	961	5.5678	101	10201	10.0499	136	18496	11.6619
32	1024	5.6569	102	10404	10.0995	137	18769	11.7047
33	1089	5.7446	103	10609	10.1489	138	19044	11.7473
34	1156	5.8310	104	10816	10.1980	139	19321	11.7898
35	1225	5.9161	105	11025	10.2470	140	19600	11.8322
36	1296	6.0000						
37	1369	6.0828						
38	1444	6.1644						
39	1521	6.2450						
40	1600	6.3246						
41	1681	6.4031						
42	1764	6.4807						
43	1849	6.5574						
44	1936	6.6332						
45	2025	6.7082						
46	2116	6.7823						
47	2209	6.8557						
48	2304	6.9282						
49	2401	7.0000						
50	2500	7.0711						
51	2601	7.1414						
52	2704	7.2111						
53	2809	7.2801						
54	2916	7.3485						
55	3025	7.4162						
56	3136	7.4833						
57	3249	7.5498						
58	3364	7.6158						
59	3481	7.6811						
60	3600	7.7460						
61	3721	7.8102						
62	3844	7.8740						
63	3969	7.9373						
64	4096	8.0000						
65	4225	8.0623						
66	4356	8.1240						
67	4489	8.1854						
68	4624	8.2462						
69	4761	8.3066						
70	4900	8.3666						

TABLE M (cont.)

N	N²	√N	N	N²	√N	N	N²	√N	N	N²	√N
141	19881	11.8743	176	30976	13.2665	211	44521	14.5258	246	60516	15.6844
142	20164	11.9164	177	31329	13.3041	212	44944	14.5602	247	61009	15.7162
143	20449	11.9583	178	31684	13.3417	213	45369	14.5945	248	61504	15.7480
144	20736	12.0000	179	32041	13.3791	214	45796	14.6287	249	62001	15.7797
145	21025	12.0416	180	32400	13.4164	215	46225	14.6629	250	62500	15.8114
146	21316	12.0830	181	32761	13.4536	216	46656	14.6969	251	63001	15.8430
147	21609	12.1244	182	33124	13.4907	217	47089	14.7309	252	63504	15.8745
148	21904	12.1655	183	33489	13.5277	218	47524	14.7648	253	64009	15.9060
149	22201	12.2066	184	33856	13.5647	219	47961	14.7986	254	64516	15.9374
150	22500	12.2474	185	34225	13.6015	220	48400	14.8324	255	65025	15.9687
151	22801	12.2882	186	34596	13.6382	221	48841	14.8661	256	65536	16.0000
152	23104	12.3288	187	34969	13.6748	222	49284	14.8997	257	66049	16.0312
153	23409	12.3693	188	35344	13.7113	223	49729	14.9332	258	66564	16.0624
154	23716	12.4097	189	35721	13.7477	224	50176	14.9666	259	67081	16.0935
155	24025	12.4499	190	36100	13.7840	225	50625	15.0000	260	67600	16.1245
156	24336	12.4900	191	36481	13.8203	226	51076	15.0333	261	68121	16.1555
157	24649	12.5300	192	36864	13.8564	227	51529	15.0665	262	68644	16.1864
158	24964	12.5698	193	37249	13.8924	228	51984	15.0997	263	69169	16.2173
159	25281	12.6095	194	37636	13.9284	229	52441	15.1327	264	69696	16.2481
160	25600	12.6491	195	38025	13.9642	230	52900	15.1658	265	70225	16.2788
161	25921	12.6886	196	38416	14.0000	231	53361	15.1987	266	70756	16.3095
162	26244	12.7279	197	38809	14.0357	232	53824	15.2315	267	71289	16.3401
163	26569	12.7671	198	39204	14.0712	233	54289	15.2643	268	71824	16.3707
164	26896	12.8062	199	39601	14.1067	234	54756	15.2971	269	72361	16.4012
165	27225	12.8452	200	40000	14.1421	235	55225	15.3297	270	72900	16.4317
166	27556	12.8841	201	40401	14.1774	236	55696	15.3623	271	73441	16.4621
167	27889	12.9228	202	40804	14.2127	237	56169	15.3948	272	73984	16.4924
168	28224	12.9615	203	41209	14.2478	238	56644	15.4272	273	74529	16.5227
169	28561	13.0000	204	41616	14.2829	239	57121	15.4596	274	75076	16.5529
170	28900	13.0384	205	42025	14.3178	240	57600	15.4919	275	75625	16.5831
171	29241	13.0767	206	42436	14.3527	241	58081	15.5242	276	76176	16.6132
172	29584	13.1149	207	42849	14.3875	242	58564	15.5563	277	76729	16.6433
173	29929	13.1529	208	43264	14.4222	243	59049	15.5885	278	77284	16.6733
174	30276	13.1909	209	43681	14.4568	244	59536	15.6205	279	77841	16.7033
175	30625	13.2288	210	44100	14.4914	245	60025	15.6525	280	78400	16.7332

N	N^2	$\sqrt{N}$
281	78961	16.7631
282	79524	16.7929
283	80089	16.8226
284	80656	16.8523
285	81225	16.8819
286	81796	16.9115
287	82369	16.9411
288	82944	16.9706
289	83521	17.0000
290	84100	17.0294
291	84681	17.0587
292	85264	17.0880
293	85849	17.1172
294	86436	17.1464
295	87025	17.1756
296	87616	17.2047
297	88209	17.2337
298	88804	17.2627
299	89401	17.2916
300	90000	17.3205
301	90601	17.3494
302	91204	17.3781
303	91809	17.4069
304	92416	17.4356
305	93025	17.4642
306	93636	17.4929
307	94249	17.5214
308	94864	17.5499
309	95481	17.5784
310	96100	17.6068
311	96721	17.6352
312	97344	17.6635
313	97969	17.6918
314	98596	17.7200
315	99225	17.7482
316	99856	17.7764
317	100489	17.8045
318	101124	17.8326
319	101761	17.8606
320	102400	17.8885
321	103041	17.9165
322	103684	17.9444
323	104329	17.9722
324	104976	18.0000
325	105625	18.0278
326	106276	18.0555
327	106929	18.0831
328	107584	18.1108
329	108241	18.1384
330	108900	18.1659
331	109561	18.1934
332	110224	18.2209
333	110889	18.2483
334	111556	18.2757
335	112225	18.3030
336	112896	18.3303
337	113569	18.3576
338	114244	18.3848
339	114921	18.4120
340	115600	18.4391
341	116281	18.4662
342	116964	18.4932
343	117649	18.5203
344	118336	18.5472
345	119025	18.5742
346	119716	18.6011
347	120409	18.6279
348	121104	18.6548
349	121801	18.6815
350	122500	18.7083
351	123201	18.7350
352	123904	18.7617
353	124609	18.7883
354	125316	18.8149
355	126025	18.8414
356	126736	18.8680
357	127449	18.8944
358	128164	18.9209
359	128881	18.9473
360	129600	18.9737
361	130321	19.0000
362	131044	19.0263
363	131769	19.0526
364	132496	19.0788
365	133225	19.1050
366	133956	19.1311
367	134689	19.1572
368	135424	19.1833
369	136161	19.2094
370	136900	19.2354
371	137641	19.2614
372	138384	19.2873
373	139129	19.3132
374	139876	19.3391
375	140625	19.3649
376	141376	19.3907
377	142129	19.4165
378	142884	19.4422
379	143641	19.4679
380	144400	19.4936
381	145161	19.5192
382	145924	19.5448
383	146689	19.5704
384	147456	19.5959
385	148225	19.6214
386	148996	19.6469
387	149769	19.6723
388	150544	19.6977
389	151321	19.7231
390	152100	19.7484
391	152881	19.7737
392	153664	19.7990
393	154449	19.8242
394	155236	19.8494
395	156025	19.8746
396	156816	19.8997
397	157609	19.9249
398	158404	19.9499
399	159201	19.9750
400	160000	20.0000
401	160801	20.0250
402	161604	20.0499
403	162409	20.0749
404	163216	20.0998
405	164025	20.1246
406	164836	20.1494
407	165649	20.1742
408	166464	20.1990
409	167281	20.2237
410	168100	20.2485
411	168921	20.2731
412	169744	20.2978
413	170569	20.3224
414	171396	20.3470
415	172225	20.3715
416	173056	20.3961
417	173889	20.4206
418	174724	20.4450
419	175561	20.4695
420	176400	20.4939

N	N²	√N
421	177241	20.5183
422	178084	20.5426
423	178929	20.5670
424	179776	20.5913
425	180625	20.6155
426	181476	20.6398
427	182329	20.6640
428	183184	20.6882
429	184041	20.7123
430	184900	20.7364
431	185761	20.7605
432	186624	20.7846
433	187489	20.8087
434	188356	20.8327
435	189225	20.8567
436	190096	20.8806
437	190969	20.9045
438	191844	20.9284
439	192721	20.9523
440	193600	20.9762
441	194481	21.0000
442	195364	21.0238
443	196249	21.0476
444	197136	21.0713
445	198025	21.0950
446	198916	21.1187
447	199809	21.1424
448	200704	21.1660
449	201601	21.1896
450	202500	21.2132
451	203401	21.2368
452	204304	21.2603
453	205209	21.2838
454	206116	21.3073
455	207025	21.3307
456	207936	21.3542
457	208849	21.3776
458	209764	21.4009
459	210681	21.4243
460	211600	21.4476
461	212521	21.4709
462	213444	21.4942
463	214369	21.5174
464	215296	21.5407
465	216225	21.5639
466	217156	21.5870
467	218089	21.6102
468	219024	21.6333
469	219961	21.6564
470	220900	21.6795
471	221841	21.7025
472	222784	21.7256
473	223729	21.7486
474	224676	21.7715
475	225625	21.7945
476	226576	21.8174
477	227529	21.8403
478	228484	21.8632
479	229441	21.8861
480	230400	21.9089
481	231361	21.9317
482	232324	21.9545
483	233289	21.9773
484	234256	22.0000
485	235225	22.0227
486	236196	22.0454
487	237169	22.0681
488	238144	22.0907
489	239121	22.1133
490	240100	22.1359
491	241081	22.1585
492	242064	22.1811
493	243049	22.2036
494	244036	22.2261
495	245025	22.2486
496	246016	22.2711
497	247009	22.2935
498	248004	22.3159
499	249001	22.3383
500	250000	22.3607
501	251001	22.3830
502	252004	22.4054
503	253009	22.4277
504	254016	22.4499
505	255025	22.4722
506	256036	22.4944
507	257049	22.5167
508	258064	22.5389
509	259081	22.5610
510	260100	22.5832
511	261121	22.6053
512	262144	22.6274
513	263169	22.6495
514	264196	22.6716
515	265225	22.6936
516	266256	22.7156
517	267289	22.7376
518	268324	22.7596
519	269361	22.7816
520	270400	22.8035
521	271441	22.8254
522	272484	22.8473
523	273529	22.8692
524	274576	22.8910
525	275625	22.9129
526	276676	22.9347
527	277729	22.9565
528	278784	22.9783
529	279841	23.0000
530	280900	23.0217
531	281961	23.0434
532	283024	23.0651
533	284089	23.0868
534	285156	23.1084
535	286225	23.1301
536	287296	23.1517
537	288369	23.1733
538	289444	23.1948
539	290521	23.2164
540	291600	23.2379
541	292681	23.2594
542	293764	23.2809
543	294849	23.3024
544	295936	23.3238
545	297025	23.3452
546	298116	23.3666
547	299209	23.3880
548	300304	23.4094
549	301401	23.4307
550	302500	23.4521
551	303601	23.4734
552	304704	23.4947
553	305809	23.5160
554	306916	23.5372
555	308025	23.5584
556	309136	23.5797
557	310249	23.6008
558	311364	23.6220
559	312481	23.6432
560	313600	23.6643

N	N²	√N
561	314721	23.6854
562	315844	23.7065
563	316969	23.7276
564	318096	23.7487
565	319225	23.7697
566	320356	23.7908
567	321489	23.8118
568	322624	23.8328
569	323761	23.8537
570	324900	23.8747
571	326041	23.8956
572	327184	23.9165
573	328329	23.9374
574	329476	23.9583
575	330625	23.9792
576	331776	24.0000
577	332929	24.0208
578	334084	24.0416
579	335241	24.0624
580	336400	24.0832
581	337561	24.1039
582	338724	24.1247
583	339889	24.1454
584	341056	24.1661
585	342225	24.1868
586	343396	24.2074
587	344569	24.2281
588	345744	24.2487
589	346921	24.2693
590	348100	24.2899
591	349281	24.3105
592	350464	24.3311
593	351649	24.3516
594	352836	24.3721
595	354025	24.3926
596	355216	24.4131
597	356409	24.4336
598	357604	24.4540
599	358801	24.4745
600	360000	24.4949
601	361201	24.5153
602	362404	24.5357
603	363609	24.5561
604	364816	24.5764
605	366025	24.5967
606	367236	24.6171
607	368449	24.6374
608	369664	24.6577
609	370881	24.6779
610	372100	24.6982
611	373321	24.7184
612	374544	24.7386
613	375769	24.7588
614	376996	24.7790
615	378225	24.7992
616	379456	24.8193
617	380689	24.8395
618	381924	24.8596
619	383161	24.8797
620	384400	24.8998
621	385641	24.9199
622	386884	24.9399
623	388129	24.9600
624	389376	24.9800
625	390625	25.0000
626	391876	25.0200
627	393129	25.0400
628	394384	25.0599
629	395641	25.0799
630	396900	25.0998
631	398161	25.1197
632	399424	25.1396
633	400689	25.1595
634	401956	25.1794
635	403225	25.1992
636	404496	25.2190
637	405769	25.2389
638	407044	25.2587
639	408321	25.2784
640	409600	25.2982
641	410881	25.3180
642	412164	25.3377
643	413449	25.3574
644	414736	25.3772
645	416025	25.3969
646	417316	25.4165
647	418609	25.4362
648	419904	25.4558
649	421201	25.4755
650	422500	25.4951
651	423801	25.5147
652	425104	25.5343
653	426409	25.5539
654	427716	25.5734
655	429025	25.5930
656	430336	25.6125
657	431649	25.6320
658	432964	25.6515
659	434281	25.6710
660	435600	25.6905
661	436921	25.7099
662	438244	25.7294
663	439569	25.7488
664	440896	25.7682
665	442225	25.7876
666	443556	25.8070
667	444889	25.8263
668	446224	25.8457
669	447561	25.8650
670	448900	25.8844
671	450241	25.9037
672	451584	25.9230
673	452929	25.9422
674	454276	25.9615
675	455625	25.9808
676	456976	26.0000
677	458329	26.0192
678	459684	26.0384
679	461041	26.0576
680	462400	26.0768
681	463761	26.0960
682	465124	26.1151
683	466489	26.1343
684	467856	26.1534
685	469225	26.1725
686	470596	26.1916
687	471969	26.2107
688	473344	26.2298
689	474721	26.2488
690	476100	26.2679
691	477481	26.2869
692	478864	26.3059
693	480249	26.3249
694	481636	26.3439
695	483025	26.3629
696	484416	26.3818
697	485809	26.4008
698	487204	26.4197
699	488601	26.4386
700	490000	26.4575

TABLE M (cont.)

N	N²	√N
701	491401	26.4764
702	492804	26.4953
703	494209	26.5141
704	495616	26.5330
705	497025	26.5518
706	498436	26.5707
707	499849	26.5895
708	501264	26.6083
709	502681	26.6271
710	504100	26.6458
711	505521	26.6646
712	506944	26.6833
713	508369	26.7021
714	509796	26.7208
715	511225	26.7395
716	512656	26.7582
717	514089	26.7769
718	515524	26.7955
719	516961	26.8142
720	518400	26.8328
721	519841	26.8514
722	521284	26.8701
723	522729	26.8887
724	524176	26.9072
725	525625	26.9258
726	527076	26.9444
727	528529	26.9629
728	529984	26.9815
729	531441	27.0000
730	532900	27.0185
731	534361	27.0370
732	535824	27.0555
733	537289	27.0740
734	538756	27.0924
735	540225	27.1109
736	541696	27.1293
737	543169	27.1477
738	544644	27.1662
739	546121	27.1846
740	547600	27.2029
741	549081	27.2213
742	550564	27.2397
743	552049	27.2580
744	553536	27.2764
745	555025	27.2947
746	556516	27.3130
747	558009	27.3313
748	559504	27.3496
749	561001	27.3679
750	562500	27.3861
751	564001	27.4044
752	565504	27.4226
753	567009	27.4408
754	568516	27.4591
755	570025	27.4773
756	571536	27.4955
757	573049	27.5136
758	574564	27.5318
759	576081	27.5500
760	577600	27.5681
761	579121	27.5862
762	580644	27.6043
763	582169	27.6225
764	583696	27.6405
765	585225	27.6586
766	586756	27.6767
767	588289	27.6948
768	589824	27.7128
769	591361	27.7308
770	592900	27.7489
771	594441	27.7669
772	595984	27.7849
773	597529	27.8029
774	599076	27.8209
775	600625	27.8388
776	602176	27.8568
777	603729	27.8747
778	605284	27.8927
779	606841	27.9106
780	608400	27.9285
781	609961	27.9464
782	611524	27.9643
783	613089	27.9821
784	614656	28.0000
785	616225	28.0179
786	617796	28.0357
787	619369	28.0535
788	620944	28.0713
789	622521	28.0891
790	624100	28.1069
791	625681	28.1247
792	627264	28.1425
793	628849	28.1603
794	630436	28.1780
795	632025	28.1957
796	633616	28.2135
797	635209	28.2312
798	636804	28.2489
799	638401	28.2666
800	640000	28.2843
801	641601	28.3019
802	643204	28.3196
803	644809	28.3373
804	646416	28.3549
805	648025	28.3725
806	649636	28.3901
807	651249	28.4077
808	652864	28.4253
809	654481	28.4429
810	656100	28.4605
811	657721	28.4781
812	659344	28.4956
813	660969	28.5132
814	662596	28.5307
815	664225	28.5482
816	665856	28.5657
817	667489	28.5832
818	669124	28.6007
819	670761	28.6182
820	672400	28.6356
821	674041	28.6531
822	675684	28.6705
823	677329	28.6880
824	678976	28.7054
825	680625	28.7228
826	682276	28.7402
827	683929	28.7576
828	685584	28.7750
829	687241	28.7924
830	688900	28.8097
831	690561	28.8271
832	692224	28.8444
833	693889	28.8617
834	695556	28.8791
835	697225	28.8964
836	698896	28.9137
837	700569	28.9310
838	702244	28.9482
839	703921	28.9655
840	705600	28.9828

N	N^2	$\sqrt{N}$	N	N^2	$\sqrt{N}$	N	N^2	$\sqrt{N}$
841	707281	29.0000	881	776161	29.6816	961	923521	31.0000
842	708964	29.0172	882	777924	29.6985	962	925444	31.0161
843	710649	29.0345	883	779689	29.7153	963	927369	31.0322
844	712336	29.0517	884	781456	29.7321	964	929296	31.0483
845	714025	29.0689	885	783225	29.7489	965	931225	31.0644
846	715716	29.0861	886	784996	29.7658	966	933156	31.0805
847	717409	29.1033	887	786769	29.7825	967	935089	31.0966
848	719104	29.1204	888	788544	29.7993	968	937024	31.1127
849	720801	29.1376	889	790321	29.8161	969	938961	31.1288
850	722500	29.1548	890	792100	29.8329	970	940900	31.1448
851	724201	29.1719	891	793881	29.8496	971	942841	31.1609
852	725904	29.1890	892	795664	29.8664	972	944784	31.1769
853	727609	29.2062	893	797449	29.8831	973	946729	31.1929
854	729316	29.2233	894	799236	29.8998	974	948676	31.2090
855	731025	29.2404	895	801025	29.9166	975	950625	31.2250
856	732736	29.2575	896	802816	29.9333	976	952576	31.2410
857	734449	29.2746	897	804609	29.9500	977	954529	31.2570
858	736164	29.2916	898	806404	29.9666	978	956484	31.2730
859	737881	29.3087	899	808201	29.9833	979	958441	31.2890
860	739600	29.3258	900	810000	30.0000	980	960400	31.3050
861	741321	29.3428	901	811801	30.0167	981	962361	31.3209
862	743044	29.3598	902	813604	30.0333	982	964324	31.3369
863	744769	29.3769	903	815409	30.0500	983	966289	31.3528
864	746496	29.3939	904	817216	30.0666	984	968256	31.3688
865	748225	29.4109	905	819025	30.0832	985	970225	31.3847
866	749956	29.4279	906	820836	30.0998	986	972196	31.4006
867	751689	29.4449	907	822649	30.1164	987	974169	31.4166
868	753424	29.4618	908	824464	30.1330	988	976144	31.4325
869	755161	29.4788	909	826281	30.1496	989	978121	31.4484
870	756900	29.4958	910	828100	30.1662	990	980100	31.4643
871	758641	29.5127	911	829921	30.1828	991	982081	31.4802
872	760384	29.5296	912	831744	30.1993	992	984064	31.4960
873	762129	29.5466	913	833569	30.2159	993	986049	31.5119
874	763876	29.5635	914	835396	30.2324	994	988036	31.5278
875	765625	29.5804	915	837225	30.2490	995	990025	31.5436
876	767376	29.5973	916	839056	30.2655	996	992016	31.5595
877	769129	29.6142	917	840889	30.2820	997	994009	31.5753
878	770884	29.6311	918	842724	30.2985	998	996004	31.5911
879	772641	29.6479	919	844561	30.3150	999	998001	31.6070
880	774400	29.6648	920	846400	30.3315	1000	1000000	31.6228

From E. S. Pearson and H. O. Hartley, *Biometrika* 38 (1951), pp. 115–22. Reproduced by permission of the *Biometrika* Trustees.

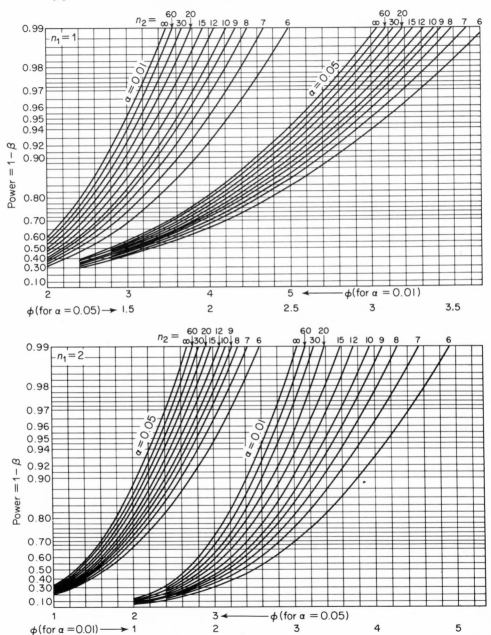

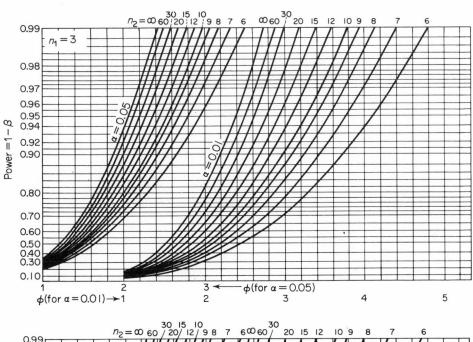

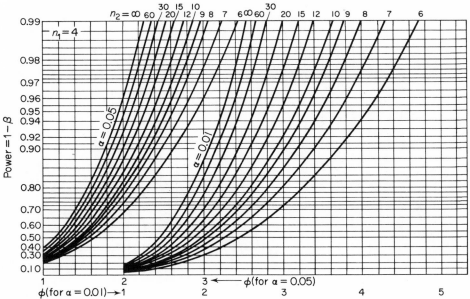

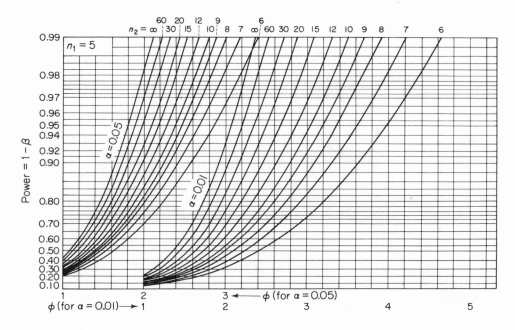

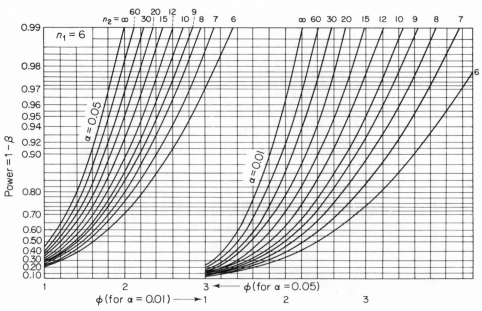

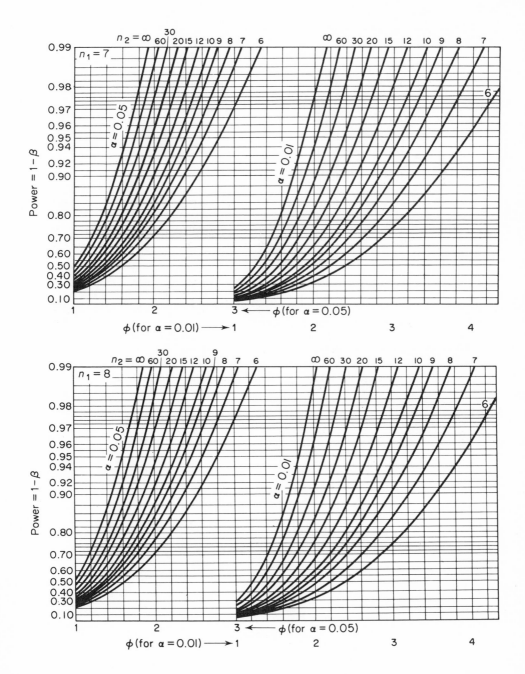

TABLE O z-SCORE EQUIVALENTS OF SELECTED PERCENTILES IN THE UNIT NORMAL DISTRIBUTION*

Percentile	z	Percentile	z	Percentile	z
0.01	−3.719	28	−0.583	74	0.643
0.05	−3.291	30	−0.524	75	0.675
0.1	−3.090	32	−0.468	76	0.706
0.5	−2.576	34	−0.412	78	0.772
1	−2.326	36	−0.358	80	0.842
2	−2.054	38	−0.305	82	0.915
3	−1.881	40	−0.253	84	0.994
4	−1.751	42	−0.202	86	1.080
5	−1.645	44	−0.151	88	1.175
6	−1.555	46	−0.100	90	1.282
7	−1.476	48	−0.050	91	1.341
8	−1.405	50	0.000	92	1.405
9	−1.341	52	0.050	93	1.476
10	−1.282	54	0.100	94	1.555
12	−1.175	56	0.151	95	1.645
14	−1.080	58	0.202	96	1.751
16	−0.994	60	0.253	97	1.881
18	−0.915	62	0.305	98	2.054
20	−0.842	64	0.358	99	2.326
22	−0.772	66	0.412	99.5	2.576
24	−0.706	68	0.468	99.9	3.090
25	−0.675	70	0.524	99.95	3.291
26	−0.643	72	0.583	99.99	3.719

* Values in this table were found by interpolating in Table B.

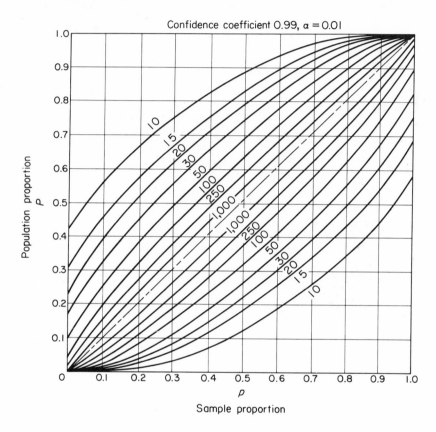

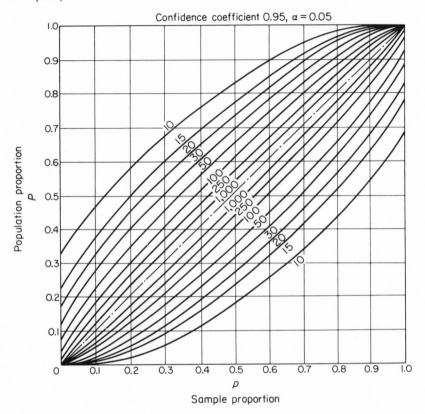

Confidence coefficient 0.95, $\alpha = 0.05$

Population proportion P

Sample proportion p

ANSWERS
TO PROBLEMS
AND EXERCISES

CHAPTER 2

1. a. nominal   b. ordinal   c. ratio   d. nominal

2. a. nominal   b. ordinal

3. a. 6 yr 4.5 mos. – 6 yr 5.5 mos.
   b. 2 lb 12.75 oz–2 lb 13.25 oz
   c. \$342.50–\$343.50

4. a. X_{12} b. X_{41} c. X_{2j}

5. a. 19   b. 10   c. 11   d. 13

6. a. 60   b. 30.5   c. 5   d. $15^2 = 225$

7. a. 26   b. 15   c. 7   d. $9 + 4 + 1 + 25 = 39$

8. a. $X_1^2 + X_2^2 + X_3^2 + X_4^2$ b. $X_4 + X_5 + X_6$ c. $(X_1 + X_2 + X_3)^2$

9. a. $3 \sum_{i=1}^{3} X_i$ b. $\left(\sum_{i=1}^{10} X_i \right)^2$ c. $\sum_{i=1}^{n} (X_i + 7)$

   d. $\sum_{i=1}^{5} X_i(X_i + 1) = \sum_{i=1}^{5} (X_i^2 + X_i)$

CHAPTER 3

2. $P_{50} = 108.41$

CHAPTER 4

1. Mean $= 2.56$; median $= 2.8$; mode $= 3.05$.

2. Mean $= 3.06$; median $= 3.3$.

3. Mean $= 14.34$; median $= 14.45$.

4. Mean $= 3(14.34) = 43.02$; median $= 43.35$.

5. Mean $= 8.86$; median $= 9.65$.

6. Mean $= 13.3$; combined median can't be determined from a knowledge of individual medians and n's only.

7. At point D.

CHAPTER 5

1. Inclusive range $= 21$; variance, $s^2 = 32.24$; standard deviation, $s = 5.68$; mean deviation $= 4.22$.

2. $Q = \dfrac{126.17 - 96.17}{2} = 15$.

3. $s_x^2 = 0.039$. $s_x = 0.198$.

4. a. positively skewed   b. positively skewed
    c. positively skewed   d. negatively skewed

5. "greater than"; variance of combined groups is 66.9.

6. b. 0.73   c. 2.60   d. -2.60

7. a. Student B.   b. Test 1: $z_A = -.64$, $z_B = +.41$.
                       Test 2: $z_A = 2.49$, $z_B = -.07$.

    c. Student A.

8. $\displaystyle\sum_1^n z_i^2 = \sum_1^n \frac{(X_i - \bar{X})^2}{s_x^2} = \frac{1}{s_x^2}\sum_1^n (X_i - \bar{X})^2 = \frac{1}{s_x^2}(n-1)s_x^2 = n - 1$.

CHAPTER 6

1. a. .1587   b. .9772   c. .0505   d. .0250   e. .4987   f. .6915
    g. .8664

2. a. .2420   b. .2420   c. .0317   d. .3945

3. a. 0.00   b. $+1.00$ c. -1.00 d. $+1.645$ e. $+2.58$ f. -2.58
    g. $+1.28$

4. a. 50   b. 89   c. 6   d. 38   e. 99

5. Variance of Y for $X = 1.50$ is also 0.50.

CHAPTER 7

1. If $z_x = z_y$, then $r_{xy} = (\sum z_x z_y)/(n-1) = (\sum z_x^2)/(n-1)$.   In Prob. 8 in Chapter 5, it was shown that $\sum z_x^2 = n - 1$.   Hence

$$r_{xy} = \frac{\sum z_x^2}{n-1} = \frac{n-1}{n-1} = 1, \quad \text{when } z_x = z_y.$$

2. Brown and Smith will obtain the same value for the correlation coefficient, since height in inches is 12 times height in feet.   A linear transformation of X and/or Y will not change the value of the correlation coefficient.

3. a. positive   b. negative   c. positive   d. positive   e. negative

4. Since r_{xy} can't exceed $+1$, $r_{xy} = (s_{xy})/(s_x s_y) \leqslant 1$.   We know that $s_x = 5$ and $s_y = 4$; hence $(s_{xy})/(5 \cdot 4) \leqslant 1$, which implies that $s_{xy} \leqslant 20$.

5. X is more closely linearly related to Z than to Y.

6. The researcher is inferring a causal relationship solely from correlational evidence.   He has no justification for doing so.   It may well be the case—and probably is so—that teachers' salaries and the "drop-out rate" are *both* a function of the social and economic status of the community and that increasing teachers' salaries in a given school would not bring about a decrease in the "drop-out rate."

7. a. $r = -.04$.
   c. X and Y are curvilinearly related.   There is almost no linear relationship between them as indicated by the Pearson product-moment correlation coefficient of $-.04$.

8. a. $r_{xy} = .92$.   b. $r_{xy} = .33$.

CHAPTER 8

1. c. $Y = 2 + X$

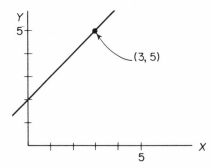

2. As the line moves from $X = 2$ to $X = 3$, it *drops* one unit, from $Y = 2$ to $Y = 1$.   Hence the slope, b_1, of the line is -1.   If the line *falls* one unit on the Y axis for each unit it moves to the *right* on the X axis, then the line must rise one unit for each unit it moves to the left on the X axis.   Thus, as X moves from 2 to 0, the line *rises* 2 units on the Y axis from 2 to 4.   Hence, $b_0 = 4$.

3. a. 2.93   b. 1.80   c. 2.06   d. 3.24

4. $b_0 = 46.76$, $b_1 = .194$. Thus $\hat{Y} = .194X + 46.76$. $\hat{Y}$ for an X of 36 is 53.16.

5. $s_e = 7.16$.

7. $Y_1 = 99.37$, $Y_2 = 93.63$.

8. No.

9. Smith's regression line will have the equation $\hat{Y} = 5X + 250$.

10. Transforming X into $cX + d$ divides b_1 by c, i.e., for the transformed X's, the slope of the regression line is b_1/c. Since $b_0 = \bar{Y}_. - b_1\bar{X}_.$, the Y intercept for the transformed data, denoted by b_0^*, is

$$b_0^* = \bar{Y}_. - \frac{b_1}{c}(c\bar{X}_. + d) = \bar{Y}_. - b_1\bar{X}_. - b_1\frac{d}{c} = b_0 - b_1\frac{d}{c}.$$

CHAPTER 9

1. a. point biserial   b. Spearman's rho   c. rank biserial
   d. Pearson's r e. Phi coefficient   f. rank biserial

2. a. $\phi = 0.08$.   b. $\phi = 0.35$.

3. $r_{pb} = 0.25$.

4. $r_{bis} = 0.66$.

5. $r_{bis} = -0.75$.

6. $\tau = 0.60$.

7. $r_{tet} = 0.50$.

8. a. $r_s = 0.87$.   b. $\tau = 0.76$.

9. $r_{rb} = -0.36$.

10. a. Partial r equals 0.32.   b. $R_{x\cdot y, z} = 0.38$.

11. $b_0 = 0$, $b_1 = .32$, $b_2 = .12$. $R_{y\cdot 1,2} = 0.41$.

12. No.

CHAPTER 10

1. a. $P(A) = 13/52 = 1/4$.   b. $P(A) = 1/52$.   c. $P(A \cap B) = 0/52 = 0$.
   d. $P(A \cup B) = P(A) + P(B) - P(A \cap B) = (13/52) + (4/52) - (1/52) =$
   $16/52 = 4/13$.

2. A: a child has perceptual problems.
   B: a child has emotional problems.
   $A \cap B$: a child has both perceptual and emotional problems.
   $P(A) = .03$, $P(B) = .06$, $P(A \cap B) = .015$.
   $P(A \cup B) = .03 + .06 - .015 = .075$.

3. a. 24   b. 210   c. 20
   d. If $n = 19$, then $(n + 1)! = 20! = 20(19!)$.

4. No.

5. a. 20   b. 1   c. 1

6. $\binom{13}{5} = 1287.$

7. $1 + 4 + 6 + 4 + 1 = 16; 2^4 = 16.$

8. $\frac{1}{2}\binom{10}{5} = \frac{1}{2}(252) = 126.$

9. $P(X = 0) = \binom{10}{0}(1/2)^0(1/2)^{10} = (1/2)^{10}.$

$P(X = 1) = \binom{10}{1}(1/2)^1(1/2)^9 = 10(1/2)^{10}.$

$P(X = 2) = \binom{10}{2}(1/2)^2(1/2)^8 = 45(1/2)^{10}.$

$P(X = 3) = \binom{10}{3}(1/2)^3(1/2)^7 = 120(1/2)^{10}.$

$P(X = 0 \text{ or } 1 \text{ or } 2 \text{ or } 3) = (1 + 10 + 45 + 120)(1/2)^{10} = 176(1/2)^{10}.$

$P(X = 4 \text{ or more}) = 1 - 176(1/2)^{10} = 1 - 176/1024 = 1 - .17 = .83.$

10.

X	Expected frequency
0	81
1	108
2	54
3	12
4	1
	$\overline{256}$

12. $(1/2)^5 = 1/32.$

13. a. .79   b. .006   c. $(.6915)^3 = .331.$

14. $E(X) = 2\frac{1}{5}.$

15. a. $E(X) = 2$ b. $\sigma_x^2 = 1.$

CHAPTER II

1. a. 0.10   b. 2.09   c. 1.28   d. 1.29   e. 0.87   f. 3.65   g. 37.70

2. $_{.95}F_{8,\infty} = 1.94; \dfrac{_{.95}\chi_8^2}{8} = \dfrac{15.507}{8} = 1.94.$

3. Probability equals .02.

4. $_{.05}F_{4,8} = 1/_{.95}F_{8,4} = 1/6.04 = 0.166.$

5. Positively skewed.

6. Median is below n.

7. $_{.95}\chi^2_{20} = 31.41$. Setting $(X - 20)/6.32$ equal to 1.64, the 95th percentile of the unit normal distribution, gives a value of X equal to 30.36.

8. $\sigma^2_t = E(t^2_n) = E(F_{1,n}) = n/(n - 2)$.

CHAPTER 12

2. a. same   b. different   c. same   d. same   e. different

3. The probability that s^2_x exceeds σ^2_x is *less* than .50.

4. a.

$\sigma^2_{\bar{x}.}$	$\sigma_{\bar{x}.}$
25.0	5.00

 b. 12.5 3.54

 c. 6.25 2.50

 d. 3.13 1.77

 e. 1.56 1.25

 f. 0.781 0.883

 g. 0.050 0.224

 h. 0.025 0.158

5. A sample of size 40 would have to be taken.

6. a. .68   b. .90   c. .99   d. .50   e. .997

7. The 95% confidence interval is 105.97 to 107.53.

8.

	95%	99%
a.	$(-.01, .65)$	$(-.14, .71)$
b.	$(-.89, -.12)$	$(-.93, .09)$
c.	$(.03, .25)$	$(-.01, .28)$

9. The statistic in b has the smaller variance error; however, as an estimator of the population mean, it is biased.

CHAPTER 13

1. a. The null hypothesis H_0 is a hypothesis about a parameter or parameters of a distribution that may or may not be "nullified" (rejected) on the basis of evidence provided by a sample from the distribution.

 b. The alternative hypothesis H_1 is a hypothesis about a parameter of a distribution that specifies values of the parameter other than that specified in H_0. If H_0 is rejected H_1 is accepted, and *vice versa*.

 c. A type I error is the rejection of H_0 when it is true.

 d. A type II error is the acceptance of H_0 when it is false.

 e. The level of significance, α, is the probability of committing a type I error.

 f. The power of a test, $1 - \beta$, is the probability of rejecting H_0 when it is false.

 g. The critical region is all of those values of a sample statistic for which the investigator will reject H_0 if his sample yields one such value.

2. In none of the cases can it be concluded with *certainty* that H_0: $\rho = 0$ is false.

3. a. type I error   **b.** no error   **c.** no error   **d.** type II error

4. A type II error cannot be committed if H_0 was rejected since the definition of a type II error is that it is the *acceptance* of a false H_0.

5. Probability of a type I error is approximately .16.

6. a. Critical region is split between both tails.
b. upper tail   **c.** lower tail

7. a. The probability of a type I error is the same for both researchers; $\alpha = .05$.
b. Rowe has a larger probability of committing a type II error when $\rho = .10$.
c. Null

8. a. .10   **b.** .95   **c.** .95   **d.** above .99

9. Probability of a type II error when $\rho = .10$ is greater than .99; hence, the power of the test of H_0: $\rho = 0$ against the alternative H_1: $\rho = .10$ is less than .01. If there is believed to be a high probability that ρ surely deviates no more from 0 than $+.10$ or $-.10$ if at all, then the investigator is wasting his time; he is almost certain to end up accepting H_0. He should either increase α, which would have the effect of moving the critical values of r closer to zero, or he should increase n.

CHAPTER 14

1. $t = \dfrac{-3.54}{10.47} = -.34$, which is *not* significant at the .01 level since $_{.995}t_{40} = 2.704$.

2. $t = (7.90/3.10) = 2.55$. Since $_{.975}t_{18} = 2.101$, the value of t is significant at the .05 level.

3. $Z_r \pm 2.58/\sqrt{n-3} = (-.221, .605)$, which equals $(-.217, .540)$ when converted back to the scale of r_{xy}.

4. a. $t = r\sqrt{(n-2)/(1-r^2)} = 1.033$. Since $_{.975}t_{73}$ is approximately equal to 2.00, the value of r of .12 is nonsignificantly different from zero at the .05 level. (Corroborate this result by use of Table I in Appendix A.)
b. $z = \dfrac{.12 - (-.01)}{\sqrt{1/72 + 1/81}} = 0.81$. Since $_{.975}z = 1.96$, the difference between the two r's is not significant at the .05 level. (Note that the numerator of z is in terms of Z_r's and not r's. It just happens that in this instance the two Z_r's and r's are identical to two decimal places.)

5. $z = (3.178/1.128) = 2.82$. Since 2.82 exceeds $_{.975}z = 1.96$, r_{xy} and r_{xz} are significantly different. The results indicate that the Miller Analogies Test (X) is more highly related to a vocabulary test (Y) than to a nonverbal reasoning test (Z).

6. $z = -4.72$, which is significant far beyond the .01 level.

7. $z = \sqrt{n}\,\phi = \sqrt{69}\,(.24) = \sqrt{3.97} = 1.99$. Since $_{.95}z = 1.64$ and $_{.05}z = -1.64$, reject the null hypothesis at the .10 level.

8. $z = \dfrac{.28 - .27}{\sqrt{(.28)(.72)[(1/873) + (1/837)]}} = 0.47$, which is nonsignificant at the .01 level.

9. The obtained value of χ^2 is 24.69. The 95th percentile in the χ^2 distribution with 6 degrees of freedom is 12.59. Hence, reject the null hypothesis of "no association" between the two factors of classification at the .05 level.

10. The obtained value of χ^2 is approximately 2.50. The 90th and 95th percentiles in the χ^2 distribution with 1 degree of freedom are 2.71 and 3.84 respectively; hence the obtained χ^2 is nonsignificant at both the .10 and .05 levels.

11. The obtained value of χ^2 is 13.27. The 99th percentile in the χ^2 distribution with 4 degrees of freedom is 13.28. While the obtained value of χ^2 is strictly *nonsignificant* at the .01 level, one should have few compunctions about announcing *significance* at the .02 level.

12. Since zero lies between the limits of the confidence interval, it is true that

$$(\bar{X}_{.1} - \bar{X}_{.2}) - {}_{.975}t_{18}s_{\bar{X}_{.1} - \bar{X}_{.2}} < 0 < (\bar{X}_{.1} - \bar{X}_{.2}) + {}_{.975}t_{18}s_{\bar{X}_{.1} - \bar{X}_{.2}}.$$

By subtracting $(\bar{X}_{.1} - \bar{X}_{.2})$ from all three sides of the above inequality and then dividing all sides of the inequality by $-s_{\bar{X}_{.1} - \bar{X}_{.2}}$ (which reverses the direction of the inequality), one obtains

$$+ {}_{.975}t_{18} > \dfrac{(\bar{X}_{.1} - \bar{X}_{.2})}{s_{\bar{X}_{.1} - \bar{X}_{.2}}} > - {}_{.975}t_{18},$$

which shows that the t-statistic for testing H_0: $\mu_1 = \mu_2$ lies between the critical values for testing the null hypothesis at the .05 level.

CHAPTER 15

1. a. $df_b = 1$, $df_w = 6$.   **b.** $df_b = 4$, $df_w = 5$.
   c. $df_b = 2$, $df_w = 10$.   **d.** $df_b = 2$, $df_w = 7$.

2. a. ${}_{.99}F_{1.10} = 10.04$.   **b.** ${}_{.90}F_{4.30} = 2.14$.   **c.** ${}_{.95}F_{2.15} = 3.68$.

3. a. Yes, this statement is equivalent to the statement of the alternative hypothesis, H_1.
   b. No.   **c.** Yes.   **d.** No.

4. $MS_B = 20.31$; $MS_w = 6.61$; $F = 3.07$.

5. $MS_B = 190.68$; $MS_w = 221.56$; $F = 0.86$. Since ${}_{.99}F_{2.27} = 5.49$, F is not significant at the .01 level.

6. $MS_B = 312.05$; $MS_w = 48.20$; $F = 6.5$; $(2.55)^2 = 6.50$.

7. ANOVA table:

Source of var.	df	MS	F
Between groups	3	35.735	6.51
Within groups	68	5.49	

Since ${}_{.95}F_{3.68} = 2.74$, H_0 is rejected at the .05 level.

8. ANOVA table:

Source of var.	df	MS	F
Between groups	2	233.79	8.34
Within groups	21	28.02	

Since $_{.95}F_{2,21} = 3.47$, H_0 is rejected at the .05 level.

9. ANOVA table:

Source of var.	df	MS	F
Between groups	2	9.733	4.38
Within groups	27	2.222	

An F-ratio of 4.38 exceeds the 95th percentile in $F_{2,27}$, but fails to exceed the 99th percentile in that distribution.

10. ANOVA table:

Source of var.	df	MS	F
Between groups	3	145.61	35.43
Within groups	13	4.11	

Reject H_0 at the .01 level.

11. The value of ϕ is $\sqrt{2} = 1.414$; $n_1 = J - 1 = 4$; $n_2 = N - J = 20$; and $\alpha = .05$. From Table N in Appendix A (the power of the F-test) we see that the power, $1 - \beta$, is approximately .60.

12. Since $s_{\bar{X}.}^2$ estimates σ^2/n, $ns_{\bar{X}.}^2$ estimates σ^2. Hence, the estimate of σ^2 is $20(2.40) = 48.0$.

13. $E(MS_b) = \sigma^2 + \dfrac{n \sum\limits_{1}^{J} (\mu_j - \bar{\mu}.)^2}{J - 1} = 20 + 250 = 270.$

CHAPTER 16

1. a. $_{.95}q_{4,30} = 3.845$.   b. $_{.95}q_{6,120} = 4.872$.   c. $_{.90}q_{10,10} = 4.913$.
   d. $_{.99}q_{12,6} = 9.485$.   e. $_{.95}q_{2,60} = 2.829$.

2. a. Probability equals .05; note the value of $_{.95}q_{5,30}$.
   b. One percent would exceed 5.048; note the value of $_{.99}q_{5,30}$.

3. Any pair of means must differ by at least $_{.95}q_{6,60}\sqrt{MS_w/n} = 8.32$ to be judged significantly different at the .05 level. By this criterion, the following differences between means are statistically significant:

$$\bar{X}_{.3} - \bar{X}_{.1} = 9.32 \qquad \bar{X}_{.5} - \bar{X}_{.2} = 16.94$$
$$\bar{X}_{.4} - \bar{X}_{.1} = 12.17 \qquad \bar{X}_{.6} - \bar{X}_{.2} = 17.45$$
$$\bar{X}_{.5} - \bar{X}_{.1} = 20.41 \qquad \bar{X}_{.5} - \bar{X}_{.3} = 11.09$$
$$\bar{X}_{.6} - \bar{X}_{.1} = 20.92 \qquad \bar{X}_{.6} - \bar{X}_{.3} = 11.60$$
$$\bar{X}_{.4} - \bar{X}_{.2} = 8.70 \qquad \bar{X}_{.6} - \bar{X}_{.4} = 8.75$$

4. $MS_w = 5.49$, $n = 18$, $J = 4$, $_{.95}q_{4.68} \doteq 3.72$. The value of $_{.95}q_{4.68}\sqrt{MS_w/n} = 2.05$. If any two means differ by more than 2.05 units, then they will be judged significantly different at the .05 level by the T-method. By this criterion, the following pairs of means are significantly different:

$$\bar{X}_{.1} - \bar{X}_{.4} = 3.33, \qquad \bar{X}_{.2} - \bar{X}_{.4} = 2.21, \qquad \bar{X}_{.3} - \bar{X}_{.4} = 2.38.$$

We see that the "control group," group 4, differs from the three experimental groups that cannot be judged to differ among themselves.

5. $MS_w = 102.05$, $n = 20$, $J = 3$, $_{.99}q_{3.57} \doteq 4.282$. The value of $_{.99}q_{3.57}\sqrt{MS_w/n}$ is 9.68. Any pairs of means differing by at least 9.68 units will be judged significantly different at the .01 level. The following pairs of means are significantly different:

$$\bar{X}_{.1} - \bar{X}_{.2} = -13.70 \qquad \bar{X}_{.1} - \bar{X}_{.3} = -15.75.$$

6. a. ANOVA table:

Source of var.	df	MS	F
Between groups	3	276.731	15.94
Within groups	24	17.365	

Since the obtained F-ratio exceeds $_{.95}F_{3.24} = 3.01$, the null hypothesis of no differences among the four population means is rejected at the .05 level.

b. $MS_w = 17.37$, $J = 4$, $n = 7$. $_{.95}F_{3.24} = 3.01$, $_{.95}q_{4.24} = 3.901$. For the two means to differ significantly by the T-method, the absolute value of the difference between them must exceed $_{.95}q_{4.24}\sqrt{MS_w/n} = 6.14$.

For two means to differ significantly by the S-method, the absolute value of the difference between them must exceed $\sqrt{(J-1)_{.95}F_{3.24}}$ $\times \sqrt{MS_w(2/n)} = 6.69$. The results of the multiple comparisons appear below:

Comparison	Is difference significant by T-method?	Is difference significant by S-method?
$\bar{X}_{.1} - \bar{X}_{.2} = -2.57$	No	No
$\bar{X}_{.1} - \bar{X}_{.3} = -9.16$	Yes	Yes
$\bar{X}_{.1} - \bar{X}_{.4} = -13.84$	Yes	Yes
$\bar{X}_{.2} - \bar{X}_{.3} = -6.59$	Yes	No
$\bar{X}_{.2} - \bar{X}_{.4} = -11.27$	Yes	Yes
$\bar{X}_{.3} - \bar{X}_{.4} = -4.68$	No	No

c. In the contrast $(\mu_2 + \mu_3)/2 - (\mu_1 + \mu_4)/2$, the coefficients are

$$c_1 = -\tfrac{1}{2}, \qquad c_2 = \tfrac{1}{2}, \qquad c_3 = \tfrac{1}{2}, \qquad c_4 = -\tfrac{1}{2}.$$

Thus the value of $\hat{\sigma}_{\hat{\psi}}$ is

$$\hat{\sigma}_{\hat{\psi}} = \sqrt{MS_w(\tfrac{1}{4} + \tfrac{1}{4} + \tfrac{1}{4} + \tfrac{1}{4})/7} = 1.575.$$

The value of $\hat{\psi}$ is

$$\hat{\psi} = (21.25 + 27.84)/2 - (18.68 + 32.52)/2 = -1.05.$$

The 95% confidence interval is

$$\hat{\psi} \pm \sqrt{(J-1)}_{.95}F_{3.24}\,\hat{\sigma}_{\hat{\psi}} = -1.05 \pm 4.73 = (-5.78, 3.68).$$

7. a. ANOVA table:

Source of var.	df	MS	F
Between groups	4	695.06	10.57
Within groups	95	65.75	

The obtained value of F is significant at the .05 level.

b. $MS_w = 65.75$, $J = 5$, $n = 20$, $_{.95}q_{5.95} \doteq 3.94$. Any difference between two means which is larger in absolute value than $_{.95}q_{5.95}\sqrt{MS_w/n} = 7.13$ is significant at the .05 level by the T-method. The significant differences are identified by an asterisk in the following table of differences:

Differences between means

	Acc	SY	SO	AY
SY	−1.25			
SO	−8.40*	−7.15*		
AY	8.00*	9.25*	16.40*	
AO	1.70	2.95	10.10*	−6.30

* Difference is significant at the .05 level.

c. The 95% confidence interval on $\mu_1 - (\mu_2 + \ldots + \mu_5)/4$ is $(-6.35, 6.37)$.

CHAPTER 17

1. ANOVA table:

Source of var.	df	SS	MS	F
Factor A	4	64.26	16.07	1.70
Factor B	5	46.85	9.37	0.99
$A \times B$	20	1164.05	58.20	6.15
Within	120	1136.53	9.47	
Total	149	2411.69		

	Critical value	Obtained value	Decision
Factor A	$_{.99}F_{4.120} = 3.48$	1.70	Do not reject H_0
Factor B	$_{.99}F_{5.120} = 3.17$	0.99	Do not reject H_0
$A \times B$	$_{.99}F_{20.120} = 2.03$	6.15	Reject H_0

2. a. True   b. True   c. False

3. Females studying French by the aural-oral method should score 8 points above the general mean on the language mastery test:

$$\mu_{11} = \mu + \alpha_1 + \beta_1 + \alpha\beta_{11} = \mu + 6 + 2 + 0 = \mu + 8.$$

5. Case a shows a disordinal interaction. Case b shows an ordinal interaction. In case c there is no interaction since the two lines of the graph are parallel.

6. When "treatments" is placed on the abscissa, the ordinal interaction graphed in case b of 5 becomes disordinal.

7. ANOVA table:

Source of var.	df	MS	F
Type of question	1	18.38	0.91
Position of question	1	532.04	26.43
Interaction	1	77.04	3.83
Within cells	20	20.13	

The critical values against which each of the three F-ratios is compared are all the same: $_{.90}F_{1,20} = 2.97$. Hence, we see that the F-tests for "Position of Question" and "Interaction" result in rejection of the null hypothesis.

8. ANOVA table:

Source of var.	df	MS	F
Intelligence	1	92.04	3.56
Method of instruction	2	233.79	9.03
Interaction	2	15.29	0.59
Within cells	18	25.88	

Hypothesis tested	Critical value	Obtained F	Decision
$H_0: \sum \alpha_i^2 = 0$	$_{.95}F_{1.18} = 4.41$	3.56	Do not reject H_0
$H_0: \sum \beta_j^2 = 0$	$_{.95}F_{2.18} = 3.55$	9.03	Reject H_0
$H_0: \sum \sum \alpha\beta_{ij}^2 = 0$	$_{.95}F_{2.18} = 3.55$	0.59	Do not reject H_0

9. ANOVA table:

Source of var.	df	MS	F
Reading achievement	2	28,103.97	158.86*
Reading difficulty	1	730.81	4.13*
Interaction	2	48.02	0.27
Within cells	234	176.91	

* Significant at the .05 level.

10. ANOVA table:

Source of var.	df	MS	F
Sex	1	1.028	6.31*
Reading readiness activity	2	0.083	0.45
Interaction	2	0.042	0.26
Within cells	24	0.163	

* Significant at the .05 level.

11. a. proportional   b. disproportional
c. proportional   d. disproportional

12. If two observations are randomly discarded from the cell at the intersection of the third row and third column, the cell frequencies would be proportional.

13. The layout of cell means is as follows:

Factor B

	9.675	10.050
Factor A	10.242	10.512
	9.011	9.883

From these data, the following sums of squares are found:

$$SS'_A = 0.868, \qquad SS'_B = 0.384, \qquad SS'_{AB} = 0.104.$$

From the original layout of 40 observations, MS_w is found to be equal to 0.7830.

The value of c in Eq. (17.15) is 0.1604. Hence, $MS'_w = 0.126$. The remainder of the analysis is reported in the ANOVA table below:

Source of var.	df	MS'	F
Socio-economic status (A)	2	0.434	3.44
Type of school (B)	1	0.384	3.05
$A \times B$	2	0.052	0.41
Within cells	34	0.126	

The critical value of F for testing the null hypothesis for factor B at the .05 level is about $_{.95}F_{1.34} = 4.12$. Hence, the hypothesis of no difference between types of school cannot be rejected.

For testing factor A and the interaction of factors A and B at the .05 level, a critical value of $_{.95}F_{2.34} = 3.27$ is used. The null hypothesis for factor A can be rejected, but no evidence exists for rejecting the hypothesis of no interaction.

CHAPTER 18

1. a. $\hat{\sigma}_a^2 = .042$.
b. Based upon our estimates, the variance of ratings for children being rated by the same judge is about 250 times as large as the variance of judges.
c. The 95 % confidence interval on σ_a^2/σ^2 is $(-.03, .13)$. Since it is impossible for σ_a^2/σ^2 to be negative we could set the interval from 0 to .13.

2. a. $MS_A = 237.25$; $MS_w = 43.92$.
$\hat{\sigma}_a^2 = (MS_A - MS_w)/12 = 16.11$.
$\hat{\sigma}^2 = 43.92$.
b. The 95 % confidence interval on σ_a^2/σ^2 is $(.16, 2.66)$.

3. $\hat{\sigma}_a^2 = (MS_A - MS_{AB})/(nJ)$

4. ANOVA table:

Source of var.	df	MS	F
V IQ vs. *P* IQ	1	10.42	0.10
Persons	29	183.84	
Interaction	29	108.52	

The critical value for the *F*-test is $_{.95}F_{1.29} = 4.18$. Obviously the obtained *F*-ratio is far below this critical value. Hence, the hypothesis of no difference between Verbal and Performance IQ can *not* be rejected.

5. ANOVA table:

Source of var.	df	MS	F
Between subtests	3	23.41	3.22
Persons	11	19.07	
Interaction	33	7.26	

Set $\alpha = .01$. Apparent test: The critical value for the *F*-ratio with the "apparent test" is $_{.99}F_{3.33} = 4.40$. Since the *F*-ratio of 3.22 does not exceed the critical value, the null hypothesis of no differences among population means on the four types of test is *not* rejected at the .01 level.

6. a. $20 \times 32 \times 8 = 5120$.

b. "Raters" and "ratees" are essentially random-effects factors, because 20/10,000 and 32/20,000 are negligibly different from 0. "Traits" is a fixed-effects factor, because 8/8 = 1. This is a fully crossed design; there is no nesting.

c. There are seven sources of variation in these data: three main effects, three two-factor interactions, and one three-factor interaction (untestable residual, here). The sources of variation are as follows: between raters, between ratees, between traits, raters × ratees, raters × traits, ratees × traits, and raters × ratees × traits.

d. Let raters be factor 1, ratees factor 2, and traits factor 3. Then

$$E(MS_1) = \sigma^2 \qquad + 8\sigma_{12}^2 \qquad\qquad + 256\sigma_1^2$$
$$E(MS_2) = \sigma^2 \qquad + 8\sigma_{12}^2 \qquad\qquad + 160\sigma_2^2$$
$$E(MS_3) = \sigma^2 + \sigma_{123}^2 \qquad + 32\sigma_{13}^2 + 20\sigma_{23}^2 + 640\sigma_3^2$$
$$E(MS_{12}) = \sigma^2 \qquad + 8\sigma_{12}^2$$
$$E(MS_{13}) = \sigma^2 + \sigma_{123}^2 \qquad + 32\sigma_{13}^2$$
$$E(MS_{23}) = \sigma^2 + \sigma_{123}^2 \qquad\qquad + 20\sigma_{23}^2$$
$$E(MS_{123}) = \sigma^2 + \sigma_{123}^2$$

$$F_{19,589} = \frac{MS_1}{MS_{12}}. \qquad F_{31,589} = \frac{MS_2}{MS_{12}}.$$

$$F_{7,f_2} = \frac{MS_3}{MS_{13} + MS_{23} - MS_{123}},$$

where f_2 is approximately

$$\frac{(MS_{13} + MS_{23} - MS_{123})^2}{\dfrac{MS_{13}^2}{133} + \dfrac{MS_{23}^2}{217} + \dfrac{MS_{123}^2}{4123}}$$

(see Brownlee, 1965, p. 301).

$$F_{589.4123} \geq \frac{MS_{12}}{MS_{123}},$$

there being no exactly appropriate F for testing the interaction of raters with ratees.

$$F_{133.4123} = \frac{MS_{13}}{MS_{123}}. \qquad F_{217.4123} = \frac{MS_{23}}{MS_{123}}.$$

$\hat{\sigma}_1^2 = (MS_1 - MS_{12})/256.$

$\hat{\sigma}_2^2 = (MS_2 - MS_{12})/160.$

$\hat{\sigma}_3^2 = (MS_3 - MS_{13} - MS_{23} + MS_{123})/640.$

$\hat{\sigma}_{12}^2 \geq (MS_{12} - MS_{123})/8.$

$\hat{\sigma}_{13}^2 = (MS_{13} - MS_{123})/32.$

$\hat{\sigma}_{23}^2 = (MS_{23} - MS_{123})/20.$

$\hat{\sigma}_{123}^2$ is not estimable from these data, because there is no MS_e whose $E(MS_e) = \sigma^2$.

7. a. The two nested factors are raters (nested within political party of rater) and ratees (nested within political party of ratee). It happens here that the political parties are the same for raters and ratees. This is a doubly nested design.
   b. Yes. Raters cannot cross political party of rater, and ratees cannot cross political party of ratee, but they can cross everything else. See Stanley (1961a) for further details.
   c. "Political party of rater" crosses everything except "rater."
   d. Rater and ratee are likely to be considered random-effects factors.
   e. As you probably surmised, Democrat raters tended to rate Democrat ratees much higher than they rated Republican ratees, and Republican raters tended to rate Republican ratees much higher than they rated Democrat ratees. Thus raters tended to prefer the ratees who were prominent in their own party.
   f. The interaction of party of rater with party of ratee with trait rated suggests that raters' bias in favor of their own party was not uniform across traits Raters tended to rate ratees of their own party relatively higher on some traits than on others, and similarly for ratees of the other party.

APPENDIX C

VERIFICATION OF STANDARD SOLUTION TO LEAST-SQUARES CRITERION

See page 149 first. We begin here with

$$\hat{Y}_i = b_1 X_i + b_0 = b_1 X_i + (\overline{Y}_. - b_1 \overline{X}_.) = b_1(X_i - \overline{X}_.) + \overline{Y}_..$$

Then consider adding the constant c to b_1 and the constant d to b_0, where c and d may be any real numbers, negative, zero, or positive:

$$\hat{Y}_i' = (b_1 + c)X_i + [(\overline{Y}_. - b_1\overline{X}_.) + d] = [b_1(X_i - \overline{X}_.) + \overline{Y}_.] + (cX_i + d).$$

We need to show that $\sum_{i=1}^{n} (Y_i - \hat{Y}_i)^2 \leq \sum_{i=1}^{n} (Y_i - \hat{Y}_i')^2$. By substituting for $\hat{Y}_i$ and $\hat{Y}_i'$ their values shown above, we secure the following inequality to be proved:

$$\sum_{=1}^{n} [Y_i - b_1(X_i - \overline{X}_.) - \overline{Y}_.]^2 \leq \sum_{i=1}^{n} \{[Y_i - b_1(X_i - \overline{X}_.) - \overline{Y}_.] - (cX_i + d)\}^2.$$

After squaring and summing, we have

$$\sum_{i=1}^{n} [Y_i - b_1(X_i - \overline{X}_.) - \overline{Y}_.]^2 \leq \sum_{i=1}^{n} [Y_i - b_1(X_i - \overline{X}_.) - \overline{Y}_.]^2$$

$$+ \sum_{i=1}^{n} (cX_i + d)^2 - 2 \sum_{i=1}^{n} [(Y_i - \overline{Y}_.) - b_1(X_i - \overline{X}_.)](cX_i + d).$$

570

Subtract $\sum\limits_{i=1}^{n} [Y_i - b_1(X_i - \bar{X}) - \bar{Y}]^2$ from both sides and obtain

$$0 \leq \sum_{i=1}^{n} (cX_i + d)^2 - 2 \sum_{i=1}^{n} [(Y_i - \bar{Y}) - b_1(X_i - \bar{X})](cX_i + d).$$

$\sum\limits_{i=1}^{n} (cX_i + d)^2$ cannot be negative. To complete the proof we shall show in a straightforward manner that, when $b_1 = s_{xy}/s_x^2$,

$$\sum_{i=1}^{n} [(Y_i - \bar{Y}) - b_1(X_i - \bar{X})](cX_i + d) = 0.$$

First, express $cX_i + d$ as $(cX_i + d - c\bar{X}) + c\bar{X}$, which is equivalent to $c(X_i - \bar{X}) + (c\bar{X} + d)$. Then

$$\sum_{i=1}^{n} [(Y_i - \bar{Y}) - b_1(X_i - \bar{X})][c(X_i - \bar{X}) + (c\bar{X} + d)]$$

$$= c \sum_{i=1}^{n} (X_i - \bar{X})(Y_i - \bar{Y}) + (c\bar{X} + d) \sum_{i=1}^{n} (Y_i - \bar{Y}) - b_1 c \sum_{i=1}^{n} (X_i - \bar{X})^2$$

$$- b_1(c\bar{X} + d) \sum_{i=1}^{n} (X_i - \bar{X})$$

$$= c(n-1)s_{xy} + (c\bar{X} + d)0 - \frac{s_{xy}}{s_x^2} c(n-1)s_x^2 - b_1(c\bar{X} + d)0$$

$$= c(n-1)s_{xy} + 0 - c(n-1)s_{xy} - 0 = 0.$$

Note that this is equivalent to saying, as in Sec. 9.4, that the covariance of the X_i's—or of the linear transformation of the X_i's, which is $cX_i + d$ here—with the discrepancies between the actual Y_i's and the Y_i's predicted from the X_i's via b_1 and b_0 is always exactly zero. Thus the correlation between initial status, X_i or $cX_i + d$, and the $Y_i - \hat{Y}_i$ is zero.

Therefore,

$$0 \leq \sum_{i=1}^{n} (cX_i + d)^2,$$

which is a correct statement. This completes the proof.

Thus, if one were to use as his regression-slope coefficient $b_1 + c$ rather than $b_1 = s_{xy}/s_x^2$, and as his intercept $b_0 + d$ rather than $b_0 = \bar{Y} - b_1\bar{X}$, he would increase the sum of the squared errors of estimate by the nonnegative amount $\sum\limits_{i=1}^{n} (cX_i + d)^2$.

This proves the contention, but it does not show how b_1 and b_0 were derived (via the differential calculus) in the first place. That derivation appears in most textbooks of basic mathematical statistics.

BIBLIOGRAPHY

Acton, F. S. *Analysis of Straight-line Data*. New York: John Wiley, 1959.

Adkins, Dorothy. *Statistics*. Columbus, Ohio: Charles E. Merrill, 1964.

Arkin, H. and R. R. Colton. *Graphs: How to Make and Use Them*. New York: Harper, 1936.

Asher, John W. and Marian N. Schusler. "Students' grades and access to cars." *Journal of Educational Research*, 60 (1967), 435–37.

Baker, Frank B. "An investigation of the sampling distributions of item discrimination indices." *Psychometrika*, 30 (1965), 165–78.

———. "Experimental design considerations associated with large-scale research projects." *Improving Experimental Design and Statistical Analysis*, ed. Julian C. Stanley. Chicago: Rand McNally, 1967.

Bartlett, M. S. "The effect of non-normality on the *t* distribution." *Proceedings of the Cambridge Philosophical Society*, 31 (1935), 223–31.

———. "Properties of sufficiency and statistical tests." *Proceedings of the Royal Society of London*, Series A, 160 (1937), 268–82.

Bennett, Carl A. and Norman Franklin. *Statistical Analysis in Chemistry and the Chemical Industry*. New York: John Wiley, 1954.

Bereiter, Carl E. "Some persisting dilemmas in the measurement of change." *Problems in Measuring Change*, ed. Chester W. Harris. Madison, Wisconsin: University of Wisconsin Press, 1963.

Binder, Arnold. "The choice of an error term in analysis of variance design." *Psychometrika*, 20 (1955), 29–50.

———. "Considerations of the place of assumptions in correlational analysis." *American Psychologist*, 14 (1959), 504–10.

———. "Further considerations on testing the null hypothesis and the strategy and tactics of investigating theoretical models." *Psychological Review*, 70 (1963), 107–15.

Blalock, Hubert M., Jr. *Social Statistics.* New York: McGraw-Hill, 1960.

———. *Causal Inferences in Nonexperimental Research.* Chapel Hill: University of North Carolina Press, 1964.

Bock, R. Darrell, "Multivariate analysis of variance of repeated measurements." *Problems in Measuring Change*, ed. Chester W. Harris. Madison, Wisconsin: University of Wisconsin Press, 1963.

———. "Contributions of multivariate experimental designs to educational research." *Handbook of Multivariate Experimental Psychology*, ed. Raymond B. Cattell. Chicago: Rand McNally, 1967.

——— and Ernest A. Haggard. "The use of multivariate analysis of variance in behavioral research." *Handbook of Measurement and Assessment in Behavioral Sciences*, ed. Dean K. Whitla. Reading, Massachusetts: Addison-Wesley, 1968.

Bolch, B. W. "More on unbiased estimation of the standard deviation." *American Statistician*, 20 (June, 1968), 27.

Boneau, C. A. "The effects of violations of assumptions underlying the *t*-test." *Psychological Bulletin*, 57 (1960), 49–64.

Boring, Edwin G. "The logic of the normal law of error in mental measurement." *American Journal of Psychology*, 31 (1920), 1–33.

Bouvier, E. A., Norman C. Perry, William B. Michael, and A. F. Hertzka. "A study of the error in the cosine-pi approximation to the tetrachoric coefficient of correlation." *Educational and Psychological Measurement*, 14 (1954), 690–99.

Box, George E. P. "Non-normality and tests on variances." *Biometrika*, 40 (1953), 318–35.

———. "Some theorems on quadratic forms applied in the study of analysis of variance problems. I, Effect of inequality of variance in the one-way classification." *Annals of Mathematical Statistics*, 25 (1954a), 290–302.

———. "Some theorems on quadratics forms applied in the study of analysis of variance problems. II, Effects of inequality of variance and of correlation between errors in the two-way classification." *Annals of Mathematical Statistics*, 25 (1954b), 484–98.

Box, G. E. P. and Anderson, S. L. "Permutation theory in the derivation of robust criteria and the study of departures from assumption." *Journal of the Royal Statistical Society, Series B*, 17 (1955), 1–26.

Bracht, Glenn H. and Gene V. Glass. "The external validity of experiments." *American Educational Research Journal*, 5 (1968), 437–74.

Braithwaite, Richard B. *Scientific Explanation.* Cambridge, England: Cambridge University Press, 1953.

Bravais, A. "Analyse mathématique sur les probabilités des erreurs de situation d'un point." *Mémoires Présentés par Divers Savants à L'Académie des Sciences de L'Institut de France*, 9 (1846), 255–332.

Brown, George I. "The relationship between barometric pressure and relative humidity and classroom behavior." *Journal of Educational Research*, 57 (1964), 368–70.

Brownlee, K. A. *Statistical Theory and Methodology*, 2nd Ed. New York: John Wiley, 1965.

Burke, Cletus J. "Letter to the editor on Peters' reply to Lewis and Burke." *Psychological Bulletin*, 48 (1951), 81–82.

———. "A brief note on one-tailed tests." *Psychological Bulletin*, 50 (1953), 384–87.

———. "Further remarks on one-tailed tests." *Psychological Bulletin*, 51 (1954), 587–90.

Campbell, Donald T. "Factors relevant to the validity of experiments in social settings." *Psychological Bulletin*, 54 (1957), 297–312.

——— and Julian C. Stanley. "Experimental and quasi-experimental designs for research on teaching." *Handbook of Research on Teaching*, ed. N. L. Gage. Chicago: Rand McNally, 1963, pp. 171–246. Also appears as *Experimental and Quasi-experimental Designs for Research*. Chicago: Rand McNally, 1966.

Carroll, John B. "The nature of the data, or how to choose a correlation coefficient." *Psychometrika*, 26 (1961), 347–72.

Clark, Cherry A. "Hypothesis testing in relation to statistical methodology." *Review of Educational Research*, 33 (1963), 455–73.

Cochran, William G. "Some consequences when the assumptions for the analysis of variance are not satisfied." *Biometrics*, 3 (1947), 22–38.

———. "The comparison of percentages in matched samples." *Biometrika*, 37 (1950), 256–66.

———. "Testing a linear relation among variances." *Biometrics*, 7 (1951), 17–32.

———. *Sampling Techniques*. New York: John Wiley, 1963.

——— and Gertrude M. Cox. *Experimental Designs*, 2nd ed. New York: John Wiley, 1957.

Coleman, James S. *et al.* "Equality of Educational Opportunity." Washington, D.C.: U.S. Government Printing Office, 1966.

Cornfield, Jerome and John W. Tukey. "Average values of mean squares in factorials." *Annals of Mathematical Statistics*, 27 (1956), 907–49.

Cox, David R. "The use of a concomitant variable in selecting an experimental design." *Biometrika*, 44 (1957), 150–58.

———. *Planning of Experiments*. New York: Wiley, 1958.

———. "A remark on multiple comparison methods." *Technometrics*, 7 (1965), 223–24.

Cronbach, Lee J. "The two disciplines of scientific psychology." *American Psychologist*, 12 (1957), 671–84.

Cureton, Edward E. "Rank-biserial correlation." *Psychometrika*, 21 (1956), 287–90.

Cureton, Edward E. "Note on ϕ/ϕ max." *Psychometrika*, 24 (1959), 89–91.

————. "Rank-biserial correlation when ties are present." *Educational and Psychological Measurement*, 28 (1968a), 77–79.

————. "Unbiased estimation of the standard deviation." *American Statistician*, 22 (February, 1968b), 22.

————. "Priority correction to 'Unbiased estimation of the standard deviation.'" *American Statistician*, 22 (June, 1968c), 27.

David, Florence N. and N. L. Johnson. "The effect of non-normality on the power function of the *F*-test in the analysis of variance." *Biometrika*, 38 (1951), 43–57.

Davidoff, M. D. and Howard W. Goheen. "A table for the rapid determination of the tetrachoric correlation coefficient." *Psychometrika*, 18 (1953), 115–21.

Delacato, C. H. *Neurological Organization and Reading*. Springfield, Illinois: Thomas, 1966.

Diamond, Solomon. *Information and Error*. New York: Basic Books, 1960.

————. *The World of Probability*. New York: Basic Books, 1965.

Dispensa, J. "Relationship of the thyroid with intelligence and personality." *Journal of Psychology*, 6 (1938), 181–86.

Dixon, Wilfred J. and Frank J. Massey. *Introduction to Statistical Analysis*, 2nd ed. New York: McGraw-Hill, 1957. (3rd edition, 1969)

Dizney, Henry F. and Lauren Gromen. "Predictive validity and differential achievement on three MLA Comparative Foreign Language Tests." *Educational and Psychological Measurement*, 27 (1967), 1127–30.

Draper, Norman R. and H. Smith. *Applied Regression Analysis*. New York: John Wiley, 1966.

DuBois, Philip H. *Multivariate Correlational Analysis*. New York: Harper, 1957.

Duncan, David B. "Multiple range and multiple *F* tests." *Biometrics*, 11 (1955), 1–42.

————. "A Bayesian approach to multiple comparisons." *Technometrics*, 7 (1965), 171–222.

Dunn, Olive J. "Multiple comparisons among means." *Journal of the American Statistical Association*, 56 (1961), 52–64.

Dunnett, C. W. "A multiple comparison procedure for comparing several treatments with a control." *Journal of the American Statistical Association*, 50 (1955), 1096–1121.

Durbin, J. and Alan Stuart. "Inversions and rank correlation coefficients." *Journal of the Royal Statistical Society, Series B*, 13 (1951), 303–9.

Dyson, Ernest. "A study of ability grouping and the self-concept." *Journal of Educational Research*, 60 (1967), 403–5.

Edwards, Allen L. "On 'the use and misuse of the chi-square test'—the case of the 2×2 contingency table." *Psychological Bulletin*, 47 (1950), 341–46.

————. *Expected Values of Discrete Random Variables and Elementary Statistics*. New York: John Wiley, 1964.

Edwards, Allen L. *Experimental Design in Psychological Research*, 3rd ed. New York: Holt, Rinehart and Winston, 1968.

Edwards, Ward, Harold Lindman, and Leonard J. Savage. "Bayesian statistical inference for psychological research." *Psychological Review*, 70 (1963), 193–242.

Erlenmeyer-Kimling, L. and L. F. Jarvik. "Genetics and intelligence: a review." *Science*, 142 (1963), 1477–79.

Ezekiel, M. and Karl A. Fox. *Methods of Correlation and Regression Analysis*, 3rd ed. New York: John Wiley, 1959. (4th edition, 1963)

Feller, William. *An Introduction to Probability Theory and Its Application*, *Volume I*, 2nd ed. New York: John Wiley, 1957.

Ferguson, George A. *Statistical Analysis in Psychology and Education*, 2nd ed. New York: McGraw-Hill, 1966. (First edition, 1959)

Fisher, Ronald A. "On the 'probable error' of a coefficient of correlation deduced from a small sample." *Metron*, 1, Part 4 (1921), 3–32.

———. *Statistical methods for research workers*, eds. 1–13. Edinburgh: Oliver and Boyd, 1925–58.

———. *The Design of Experiments*, eds. 1–8. Edinburgh: Oliver and Boyd, 1935–66.

———. *Statistical Methods and Scientific Inference*, 2nd ed. New York: Hafner, 1959.

——— and Frank Yates. *Statistical Tables for Biological, Agricultural, and Medical Research*, 2nd ed. Edinburgh: Oliver and Boyd, 1943.

Forehand, G. A. and W. L. Libby, Jr. "Effects of educational programs and perceived organizational climate upon changes in innovative administrative behavior." 'In *Innovative Behavior*. Chicago: University of Chicago Center for Programs in Government Administration, 1962.

Fryer, H. C. *Concepts and Methods of Experimental Statistics*. Boston: Allyn and Bacon, 1966.

Furfey, Paul H. "Comment on 'the needless assumption of normality in Pearson's *r*.'" *American Psychologist*, 13 (1958), 545–46.

Gayen, A. K. "The distribution of 'Student's' *t* in random samples of any size drawn from non-normal universes." *Biometrika*, 36 (1949), 353–69.

———. "The distribution of the variance ratio in random samples of any size drawn from non-normal universes." *Biometrika*, 37 (1950*a*), 236–55.

———. "Significance of difference between the means of two non-normal samples." *Biometrika*, 37 (1950*b*), 399–408.

Geary, R. C. "The distribution of 'student's' ratio for non-normal samples." *Journal of the Royal Statistical Society*, Series B, Supplement (1936), 178–84.

Glass, Gene V. "Testing homogeneity of variances." *American Educational Research Journal*, 3 (1966*a*), 187–90.

———. "Note on rank-biserial correlation." *Educational and Psychological Measurement*, 26 (1966*b*), 623–31.

——— and James R. Collins. "Geometric proof of the restriction on the possible values of r_{xy} when r_{xz} and r_{yz} are fixed." *Educational and Psychological Measurement*, 29 (1969).

Glass, Gene V and A. Ralph Hakstian. "Measures of association in comparative experiments: their development and interpretation." *American Educational Research Journal*, 6 (1969), 403–14.

Godard, R. H. and E. F. Lindquist. "An empirical study of the effect of heterogeneous within-groups variance upon certain F-tests of significance in analysis of variance." *Psychometrika*, 5 (1940), 263–74.

Goldfried, M. A. "One-tailed tests and 'unexpected' results." *Psychological Review*, 66 (1959), 79–80.

Goodman, Leo A. "Simultaneous confidence intervals for contrasts among multinomial populations." *Annals of Mathematical Statistics*, 35 (1964) 716–25.

Goolsby, T. M. "Comparability and validity of three forms of SCAT." *Educational and Psychological Measurement*, 27 (1967), 1041–45.

Grant, David A. "Testing the null hypothesis and the strategy and tactics of investigating theoretical models." *Psychological Review*, 69 (1962), 54–61.

Graybill, Franklin A. *An Introduction to Linear Statistical Models, Volume 1*. New York: McGraw-Hill, 1961.

Green, Bert F. and John W. Tukey. "Complex analysis of variance: general problems." *Psychometrika*, 25 (1960), 127–52.

Greenhouse, S. W. and S. Geisser. "On methods in the analysis of profile data." *Psychometrika*, 24 (1959), 95–112.

Gronow, D. G. C. "Test for the significance of difference between means in two normal populations having unequal variances." *Biometrika*, 38 (1951), 252–56.

Guenther, W. C. *Analysis of Variance*. Englewood Cliffs, N.J.: Prentice-Hall, 1964.

———. *Concepts of Statistical Inference*. New York: McGraw-Hill, 1965.

Guthrie, John T. "Expository instruction versus a discovery method." *Journal of Educational Psychology*, 58 (1967), 45–49.

Haggard, Ernest A. *Intra-class Correlation and the Analysis of Variance*. New York: Dryden Press, 1958.

Harrington, Scott A. "Sequencing organizers in meaningful verbal learning." *Research Paper No. 10*. Boulder: University of Colorado, Laboratory of Educational Research, 1968.

Harris, Chester W. *Problems in Measuring Change*. Madison, Wisconsin: University of Wisconsin Press, 1963.

Harter, H. Leon. "Tables of range and studentized range." *Annals of Mathematical Statistics*, 31 (1960), 1122–47.

Hays, William L. *Statistics for Psychologists*. New York: Holt, Rinehart and Winston, 1963.

Henderson, C. R. "Design and analysis of animal husbandry experiments." In *Techniques and Procedures of Animal Production Research*. American Society of Animal Production, Beltsville, Maryland, 1959.

Herman, William L. "Teaching attitude as related to academic grades and athletic ability of prospective physical education teachers." *Journal of Educational Research*, 61 (1967), 40–42.

Hick, W. E. "A note on one-tailed and two-tailed tests." *Psychological Review*, 59 (1952), 316–18.

Hinton, R. T., Jr. "A further study on the role of the basal metabolic rate in the intelligence of children." *Journal of Educational Psychology*, 30 (1939), 309–14.

Hopkins, Kenneth D. "An empirical analysis of the efficacy of the WISC in the diagnosis of organicity in children of normal intelligence." *Journal of Genetic Psychology*, 105 (1964), 163–72.

—— and Russel A. Chadbourn. "A scheme for proper utilization of multiple comparisons in research and a case study." *American Educational Research Journal*, 4 (1967), 407–12.

Horsnell, G. "The effect of unequal group variances on the F-test for the homogeneity of group means." *Biometrika*, 40 (1953), 128–36.

Horst, Paul. "A proof that the point from which the sum of the absolute deviations is a minimum is the median." *Journal of Educational Psychology*, 22 (1931), 463–64.

——. *Matrix Algebra for Social Scientists*. New York: Holt, Rinehart and Winston, 1963.

Huff, Darrell. *How to Lie With Statistics*. New York: Norton, 1954.

Jarrett, Rheem F. "A minor exercise in history." *American Statistician*, 22 (June, 1968), No. 3, 25–26.

Jaspen, Nathan. "Serial correlation." *Psychometrika*, 11 (1946), 23–30.

Jeffrey, W. E. and S. Jay Samuels. "Effect of method of reading training on initial learning and transfer." *Journal of Verbal Learning and Verbal Behavior*, 6 (1967), 354–58.

Jenkins, William L. "An improved method for tetrachoric r." *Psychometrika*, 20 (1955), 253–58.

Jensen, Arthur R. "Social class, race, and genetics: implications for education." *American Educational Research Journal*, 5 (1968), 1–42.

Johnson, Palmer O. *Statistical Methods in Research*. Englewood Cliffs, N.J.: Prentice-Hall, 1949.

Jones, Lyle V. "Tests of hypotheses: one-sided vs. two-sided alternatives." *Psychological Bulletin*, 49 (1952), 43–46.

——. "A rejoinder on one-tailed tests." *Psychological Bulletin*, 51 (1954), 585–86.

Kaiser, Henry F. "Directional statistical decisions." *Psychological Review*, 67 (1960), 160–67.

Kaplan, Abraham. *The Conduct of Inquiry*. San Francisco: Chandler, 1964.

Keeping, E. S. *Introduction to Statistical Inference*. Princeton, N.J.: Van Nostrand, 1962.

Kelley, Truman L. "A new measure of dispersion." *Publications of the American Statistical Association*, 17 (1921), 743–49.

Kelley, Truman L. "The principles and techniques of mental measurement." *American Journal of Psychology*, 34 (1923), 408–32.

———. *Fundamentals of Statistics*. Cambridge, Massachusetts: Harvard University Press, 1947.

Kendall, Maurice G. *Rank Correlation Methods*, 3rd ed. London: Griffin, 1962.

——— and William Buckland. *A Dictionary of Statistical Terms*. Edinburgh: Oliver and Boyd, 1957.

——— and Alan Stuart. *The Advanced Theory of Statistics, Volumes 1–3*. London: Griffin, 1961–66.

Kennedy, W. A., V. Van de Riet, and J. White. "A normative sample of intelligence and achievement of Negro elementary school children in the Southeastern United States." *Monographs of the Society for Research in Child Development*, 28 (1963), No. 6.

Kenyon, Gerald S. "Multiple comparisons and the analysis of variance: an empirical illustration." *Research Quarterly of the American Association for Health, Physical Education, and Recreation*, 36 (1965), 413–19.

Kerlinger, Fred N. *Foundations of Behavioral Research*. New York: Holt, Rinehart and Winston, 1964.

Keuls, M. "The use of the 'studentized range' in connection with an analysis of variance." *Euphytica*, 1 (1952), 112–22.

Kimmel, Herbert D. "Three criteria for the use of one-tailed tests." *Psychological Bulletin*, 54 (1957), 531–33.

Klausmeier, Herbert J. "Effects of accelerating bright older elementary pupils." *Journal of Educational Psychology*, 54 (1963), 165–71.

Kruskal, William H. "Ordinal measures of association." *Journal of the American Statistical Association*, 53 (1958), 814–61.

———. "Tests of significance." *International Encyclopedia of the Social Sciences*, Vol. 14, ed. David L. Sills. New York: Macmillan and Free Press, 1968.

LaForge, R. "Comment on 'the needless assumption of normality in Pearson's *r*.'" *American Psychologist*, 13 (1958), 546.

Lana, Robert D. and A. Lubin. "The effect of correlation on the repeated measures design." *Educational and Psychological Measurement*, 23 (1963), 729–39.

Lancaster, H. O. and M. A. Hamden. "Estimate of the correlation coefficient in contingency tables with possibly nonmetrical characters." *Psychometrika*, 29 (1964), 383–91.

Lerner, Daniel (ed.) *Cause and Effect*. New York: Free Press, 1965.

Levene, H. "Robust tests for equality of variances." *Contributions to Probability and Statistics,* ed. I. Olkin. Stanford, California: Stanford University Press, 1960, pp. 278–92.

Lewis, Donald and Cletus J. Burke. "The use and misuse of the chi-square test." *Psychological Bulletin*, 46 (1949), 433–89.

———. "Further discussion on the use and misuse of the chi-square test." *Psychological Bulletin*, 47 (1950), 347–55.

Leyman, Laretha. "Prediction of freshman and sophomore grade-point averages of women physical education major students." *Educational and Psychological Measurement*, 27 (1967), 1139–41.

Lindquist, E. F. *Statistical Analysis in Educational Research.* New York: Houghton Mifflin, 1940.

———. *Design and Analysis of Experiments in Psychology and Education.* Boston: Houghton Mifflin, 1953.

Lord, Frederic M. "Biserial estimates of correlation." *Psychometrika,* 28 (1963a), 81–85.

———. "Elementary models for measuring change." *Problems in Measuring Change*, ed. C. W. Harris. Madison, Wisconsin: University of Wisconsin Press, 1963b, 21–38.

——— and Melvin R. Novick. *Statistical Theories of Mental Test Scores.* Reading, Massachusetts: Addison-Wesley, 1968.

Lubin, Ardie. "The interpretation of significant interaction." *Educational and Psychological Measurement*, 21 (1962a), 807–17.

———. "Statistics." *Annual Review of Psychology* (1962b), 345–70.

Marascuilo, Leonard A. "Large sample multiple comparisons." *Psychological Bulletin*, 65 (1966), 280–90.

Marks, Melvin R. "Two kinds of experiment distinguished in terms of statistical operations." *Psychological Review*, 58 (1951), 179–84.

———. "One- and two-tailed tests." *Psychological Review*, 60 (1953), 207–8.

McHugh, Richard B. and D. S. Ellis. "The 'post-mortem' testing of experimental comparisons." *Psychological Bulletin*, 52 (1955), 425–28.

McLean, Leslie D. "Phantom classrooms." *School Review*, 74 (1966), 139–49.

———. "Some important principles for the use of incomplete designs in behavioral research." *Improving Experimental Design and Statistical Analysis*, ed. Julian C. Stanley. Chicago: Rand McNally, 1967.

McNamara, Walter J. and J. W. Dunlap. "A graphical method for computing the standard error of biserial *r*." *Journal of Experimental Education*, 2 (1934), 274–77.

McNemar, Quinn. "Note on the sampling error of the difference between correlated proportions or percentages." *Psychometrika*, 12 (1947), 153–57.

———. *Psychological Bulletin*, 37 (1940), 747.

———. *Psychological Statistics*, 3rd ed. New York: John Wiley, 1962.

Michael, William B., Henry F. Kaiser, and Cherry Ann Clark. "Research tools: statistical methods." *Review of Educational Research*, 27 (1957), 498–527.

Milholland, John E. "Comment on 'the needless assumption of normality in Pearson's *r*.'" *American Psychologist*, 13 (1958), 544–45.

Miller, Rupert G. *Simultaneous Statistical Inference.* New York: McGraw-Hill, 1966.

Millman, Jason and Gene V. Glass. "Rules of thumb for writing the ANOVA table." *Journal of Educational Measurement*, 4 (1967), 41–51.

Mises, Richard von. *Probability, Statistics, and Truth*, 2nd ed. New York: Macmillan, 1957.

Mood, Alexander and Franklin A. Graybill. *Introduction to the Theory of Statistics*, 2nd ed. New York: McGraw-Hill, 1963.

Moses, Lincoln E. "Statistical theory and research design." *Annual Review of Psychology*, 7 (1956), 233–58.

Nefzger, M. D. and James Drasgow. "The needless assumption of normality in Pearson's *r*." *American Psychologist*, 12 (1957), 623–25.

Newman, D. "The distribution of range in samples from a normal population, expressed in terms of an independent estimate of standard deviation." *Biometrika*, 31 (1939), 20–30.

Norris, Raymond C. and Howard F. Hjelm. "Non-normality and product moment correlation." *Journal of Experimental Education*, 29 (1961), 261–70.

North, George E. and O. Lee Buchanan. "Teacher views of poverty area children." *Journal of Educational Research*, 61 (1967), 53–55.

Nunnally, J. C. "The place of statistics in psychology." *Educational and Psychological Measurement*, 20 (1960), 641–50.

Ohnmacht, Fred W. "Achievement, anxiety, and creative thinking." *American Educational Research Journal*, 3 (1966), 131–38.

Olds, E. G. "Distributions of sums of squares of rank differences for small numbers of individuals." *Annals of Mathematical Statistics*, 9 (1938), 133–48.

————. "The 5% significance levels for sums of squares of rank differences and a correction." *Annals of Mathematical Statistics*, 20 (1949), 117–18.

Olkin, Ingram. "Correlations revisited." *Improving Experimental Design and Statistical Analysis*, ed. Julian C. Stanley. Chicago: Rand McNally, 1967.

———— and John W. Pratt. "Unbiased estimation of certain correlation coefficients." *Annals of Mathematical Statistics*, 29 (1958), 201–11.

———— and M. Siotani. "Asymptotic distribution functions of a correlation matrix." Stanford, California: Stanford University Laboratory for Quantitative Research in Education, Report No. 6, 1964.

Pastore, Nicholas. "Some comments on the use and misuse of the chi-square test." *Psychological Bulletin*, 47 (1950), 338–40.

Pearson, Egon S. "The analysis of variance in cases of non-normal variation." *Biometrika*, 23 (1931), 114–33.

———— and C. J. Clopper. "The use of confidence intervals or fiducial limits illustrated in the case of the binomial." *Biometrika*, 26 (1934), 404–13.

———— and H. O. Hartley. *Biometrika Tables for Statisticians*, 3rd ed. Cambridge, England: Cambridge University Press, 1966.

————. "Charts of the power function for analysis of variance tests, derived from the non-central *F*-distribution." *Biometrika*, 38 (1951), 112–30.

Pearson, Karl. "On further methods of determining correlation." *Drapers' Company Memoirs, Biometric Series*, IV (1907).

Peckham, Perc D., Gene V Glass, and Kenneth D. Hopkins. "The experimental unit in statistical analysis: comparative experiments with intact groups." *Journal of Special Education*, 3 (1969).

Peizer, David B. "A note on directional inference." *Psychological Bulletin*, 68 (1967), 448.

Peters, C. C. "The misuse of chi-square—a reply to Lewis and Burke." *Psychological Bulletin*, 47 (1950), 331–37.

Pitman, E. J. G. "Significance tests which may be applied to samples from any populations. III: The analysis of variance test." *Biometrika*, 29 (1937), 322–35.

Platt, John R. "Strong inference." *Science*, 146 (1964), 347–53.

Pugh, R. C. "The partitioning of criterion-score variance accounted for in multiple correlation." *American Educational Research Journal*, 5 (1968), 639–46.

RAND Corporation. *A Million Random Digits with 100,000 Normal Deviates.* New York: Free Press, 1955.

Rozeboom, W. W. "The fallacy of the null-hypothesis significance test." *Psychological Bulletin*, 57 (1960), 416–28.

———. *Foundations of the Theory of Prediction.* Homewood, Illinois: Dorsey Press, 1966.

Rugg, H. O. *Statistical Methods Applied to Education.* Boston: Houghton Mifflin, 1917.

Ryan, Thomas A. "Multiple comparisons in psychological research." *Psychological Bulletin*, 56 (1959), 26–47.

———. "The experiment as the unit for computing rates of error." *Psychological Bulletin*, 59 (1962), 301–5.

Samuels, S. Jay. "Attentional process in reading: the effect of pictures on the acquisition of reading responses." *Journal of Educational Psychology*, 58 (1967), 337–42.

Sawrey, W. L. "A distinction between exact and approximate nonparametric methods." *Psychometrika*, 23 (1958), 171–77.

Scandura, Joseph M. and Jay N. Wells. "Advance organizers in learning abstract mathematics." *American Educational Research Journal*, 4 (1967), No. 3, 295–301.

Scannell, D. P. and J. C. Marshall. "The effect of selected composition errors on grades assigned to essay examinations." *American Educational Research Journal*, 3 (1966), 125–30.

Scates, Douglas E. "Reporting, summarizing, and implementing educational research." *Review of Educational Research*, 12 (1942), 558–74.

Scheffé, Henry. *The Analysis of Variance.* New York: John Wiley, 1959.

Schultz, E. F., Jr. "Rules of thumb for determining expectations of mean squares in analysis of variance." *Biometrics*, 11 (1955), 123–35.

Sears, Pauline S. "Levels of aspiration in academically successful and unsuccessful children." *Journal of Abnormal and Social Psychology*, 35 (1940), 498–536.

Senders, Virginia L. *Measurement and Statistics.* London: Oxford University Press, 1958.

Sigel, Sidney. *Nonparametric Statistics for the Behavioral Sciences.* New York: McGraw-Hill, 1956.

Snedecor, George W. and William G. Cochran. *Statistical Methods*, 6th ed. Ames, Iowa: Iowa State University Press, 1967.

Soper, H. E. "On the probable error of the bi-serial expression for the correlation coefficient." *Biometrika*, 10 (1914), 384–90.

Sparks, Jack N. "Expository notes on the problem of making multiple comparisons on a completely randomized design." *Journal of Experimental Education*, 31 (1963), 343–49.

Spear, Mary E. *Charting Statistics*. New York: McGraw-Hill, 1952.

Srivastava, A. B. L. "Effect of non-normality on the power of the analysis of variance test." *Biometrika*, 46 (1959), 114–22.

Staff, Harvard University Computational Laboratory. *Harvard Tables of the Cumulative Binomial Distribution*. Cambridge, Massachusetts: Harvard University Press, 1956.

Stanley, Julian C. "Additional 'post-mortem' tests of experimental comparisons." *Psychological Bulletin*, 54 (1957*a*), 128–30.

——. "Index of means vs. mean of indices." *American Journal of Psychology*, 70 (1957*b*), 467–68.

——. "Analysis of a double nested design." *Educational and Psychological Measurement*, 21 (1961*a*), 831–37. Errata, 22 (1962), ii.

——. "Analysis of unreplicated three-way classifications, with applications to rater bias and trait independence." *Psychometrika*, 26 (1961*b*), 205–19.

——. *Measurement in Today's Schools*, 4th ed. Englewood Cliffs, N.J.: Prentice-Hall, 1964.

——. "Quasi-experimentation." *School Review*, 73 (1965), 197–205.

——. "A common class of pseudo-experiments." *American Educational Research Journal*, 3 (1966*a*), 79–87.

——. "The influence of Fisher's *The Design of Experiments* on educational research thirty years later." *American Educational Research Journal*, 3 (1966*b*), 223–29.

——. "On improving certain aspects of educational experimentation." *Improving Experimental Design and Statistical Analysis*, ed. Julian C. Stanley. Chicago: Rand McNally, 1967*a*.

——. "Elementary experimental design—an expository treatment." *Psychology in the Schools*, 4 (1967*b*), 195–203.

——. "Problems in equating groups in mental retardation research." *Journal of Special Education*, 1 (1967*c*), 241–56.

——. "Linear hypotheses. II. Analysis of variance." *International Encyclopedia of the Social Sciences*, Vol. 9, ed. David L. Sills. New York: Macmillan and Free Press, 1968*a*, pp. 324–36.

——. "An important similarity between biserial *r* and the Brogden-Cureton-Glass biserial *r* for ranks." *Educational and Psychological Measurement*, 28 (1968*b*), 249–53.

——. "Plotting anova interactions for ease of visual interpretation." *Educational and Psychological Measurement,* 29 (1969*a*), 793–97.

Stanley, Julian C. and Marilyn D. Wang. "Restrictions on the possible values of r_{12}, given r_{13} and r_{23}." *Educational and Psychological Measurement,* 29 (1969*b*), 579–81.

Steel, R. G. and J. H. Torrie. *Principles and Procedures of Statistics.* New York: McGraw-Hill, 1960.

Stennett, R. G. "Absence from school: norms by sex and grade." *Journal of Educational Research,* 60 (1967), 351–54.

Stevens, S. S. (ed). *Handbook of Experimental Psychology.* New York: John Wiley, 1951.

"Student." "The probable error of a mean." *Biometrika,* 6 (1908), 1–25.

Tables of the cumulative binomial probabilities. *Ordnance Corps Pamphlet ORDP* 20-1. Washington, D.C.: U.S. Government Printing Office, 1953.

Tate, Merle W. and R. C. Clelland. *Nonparametric and Shortcut Statistics in the Social, Biological, and Medical Sciences.* Danville, Illinois: Interstate Printers, 1957.

Terman, Lewis M. and Maud A. Merrill. *Stanford-Binet Intelligence Scale: Manual for the Third Revision, Form L-M.* Boston: Houghton Mifflin, 1960.

Thalberg, Stanton P. "Reading rate and immediate versus delayed retention." *Journal of Educational Psychology,* 58 (1967), 373–78.

Townsend, John C. *Introduction to Experimental Method.* New York: McGraw-Hill, 1953.

Travers, Robert M. W., R. K. Van Wagenen, D. H. Haygood, and Mary McCormick. "Learning as a consequence of the learner's task involvement under different conditions of feedback." *Journal of Educational Psychology,* 55 (1964), 167–73.

Tucker, L. R., Fred Damarin, and Samuel Messick. "A base-free measure of change." *Psychometrika,* 31 (1966), 457–73.

Varberg, D. E. "The development of modern statistics." *The Mathematics Teacher,* 56 (1963), 252–57, 344–48.

Walker, Helen M. *Studies in the History of Statistical Method.* Baltimore: Williams and Wilkins, 1929.

——. "Degrees of freedom." *Journal of Educational Psychology,* 31 (1940), 253–69.

——. *Mathematics Essential for Elementary Statistics,* revised ed. New York: Holt, Rinehart and Winston, 1951.

—— and Walter N. Durost. *Statistical Tables: Their Structure and Use.* New York: Teachers College, Columbia University, 1936.

—— and Joseph Lev. *Statistical Inference.* New York: Holt, Rinehart and Winston, 1953.

Wallen, Norman E. and Mary Lou A. Campbell. "Vocabulary and non-verbal reasoning components of verbal analogies tests (Miller Analogies Test and Concept Mastery Test)." *Journal of Educational Research,* 61 (1967), 87–89.

Wallis, W. Allen and Harry V. Roberts. *Statistics: A New Approach.* Glencoe, Illinois: Free Press, 1956.

——. *The Nature of Statistics.* New York: Free Press, 1965.

Webb, Eugene J., Donald T. Campbell, Richard D. Schwartz, and Lee Sechrest. *Unobtrusive Measures: Nonreactive Research in the Social Sciences.* Chicago: Rand McNally, 1966.

Webster, Harold A. and Carl E. Bereiter. "The reliability of changes measured by mental test scores." *Problems in Measuring Change,* ed. Chester W. Harris. Madison, Wisconsin: University of Wisconsin Press, 1963.

Welch, B. L. "The significance of the difference between two means when the population variances are unequal." *Biometrika,* 29 (1937), 350–62.

Wert, J. E., Charles O. Neidt, and J. Stanley Ahmann. *Statistical Methods in Educational and Psychological Research.* New York: Appleton-Century-Crofts, 1954.

Werts, Charles E. "The partitioning of variance in school effects studies." *American Educational Research Journal,* 5 (1968), 311–18.

Whitfield, J. W. "Rank correlation between two variables, one of which is ranked, the other dichotomous." *Biometrika,* 34 (1947), 292–96.

Wilks, S. S. *Mathematical Statistics.* New York: John Wiley, 1962.

Williams, D. L. "Rewritten science materials and reading comprehension." *Journal of Educational Research,* 61 (1968), 204–6.

Williams, E. J. "Linear hypotheses. I. Regression." *International Encyclopedia of the Social Sciences, Vol. 9,* ed. David L. Sills. New York: Macmillan and Free Press, 1968, pp. 310–24.

Wilson, W. R. "A note on the inconsistency inherent in the necessity to perform multiple comparisons." *Psychological Bulletin,* 59 (1962), 296–300.

——— and H. Miller. "A note on the inconclusiveness of accepting the null hypothesis." *Psychological Review,* 71 (1964), 238–42.

Wine, R. Lowell. *Statistics for Scientists and Engineers.* Englewood Cliffs, N.J.: Prentice-Hall, 1964.

Winer, Ben J. *Statistical Principles in Experimental Design.* New York: McGraw-Hill, 1962.

Yamamoto, Kaoru. "Creativity and unpredictability in school achievement." *Journal of Educational Research,* 60 (1967), 321–25.

Yates, Frank. "Contingency tables involving small numbers and the χ^2 test." *Journal of the Royal Statistical Society,* Supplement, 1 (1934), 217–35.

AUTHOR INDEX

SUBJECT INDEX